The Black Middle

The Black Middle

Africans, Mayas, and Spaniards in Colonial Yucatan

Matthew Restall

STANFORD UNIVERSITY PRESS

STANFORD, CALIFORNIA

Stanford University Press
Stanford, California
© 2009 by the Board of Trustees of the Leland Stanford
Junior University. All rights reserved.

Published with the assistance of the College of Liberal
Arts at Penn State University.

Printed in the United States of America on acid-free,
archival-quality paper

Library of Congress Cataloging-in-Publication Data

Restall, Matthew, 1964–
The Black middle : Africans, Mayas, and Spaniards in colonial
Yucatan / Matthew Restall.
p. cm.
Includes bibliographical references and index.
ISBN 978-0-8047-4983-1 (cloth : alk. paper)
ISBN 978-0-8047-9208-0 (pbk. : alk. paper)
1. Africans—Yucatán Peninsula—History.
2. Blacks—Yucatán Peninsula—History.
3. Yucatán Peninsula—Race relations.
4. Mexico—History—Spanish colony, 1540–1810. I. Title.
F1376.r47 2009
972'.600496—dc22
2008036651

Typeset by Westchester Book Group in 10/12 Sabon

Contents

Figures, Maps, and Tables, vii

Preface and Acknowledgments, xi

A Note on Sources, xv

Abbreviations of Archival Sources, xvii

Introduction: Making the Boatloads Visible, 1

1. Involuntary Colonists, 6
The Story of Sebastián Toral, 6   Involuntary Colonists, 9
The Structure of the Slave Trade, 15   A Brief Demography, 26

2. People as Property, 34
The Story of María Dolores Molina, 34   Attached Subordination, 36
Naming Property, 43   The Slave Owners, 49   Abolition, 67

3. Race and Rank, 75
The Story of Francisco de Aguilar, 75   Pride and Prejudice, 77
Caste of Characters, 87

4. Ways of Work, 112
The Story of Joaquín Chasarretta, 112   Managers in the Middle:
Town and Country, 114   Afro-Yucatecan Artisans and
Other Independents, 131   As Rustic as Indians, 142

5. Ways Up and Ways Out, 153
The Story of Captain Lázaro del Canto and Augustina Bergara, 153
A Way Up: The Pardo Militia, 155
Ways Out: Escape and Manumission, 178   Mobilities, 190

6. Communities, 200
The Story of Isabel Toquero, 200   Afro-Campeche, 204
Afro-Merida, 215   Pardos in the Pueblos, 220

Community Bases: Christians of African Descent, 227
Community Bases: The Nexus of Work, Family, and Home, 238

7. Magical Meetings, 247
The Story of Joseph Zavala, 247   The Slave and the Postman:
Between Mayas and Spaniards, 249   Afro-Maya Marriage, 257
Love-Magic and Other Meetings, 265

Conclusion: The Afro-Yucatecan Middle, 278

Appendices

A: *Selection of Documents Written or Dictated by Afro-Yucatecans*, 286

B: *Afro-Yucatecans and the Population of Colonial Yucatan
(1781–1815)*, 296

C: *Afro-Yucatecans Traveling Under License from Spain to Yucatan
(1579–1779)*, 309

D: *Sales and Values of Slaves in Yucatan*, 312

E: *Spanish Slave Owners in Merida (1710–89)*, 321

F: *Afro-Yucatecans Accused of Witchcraft and Love-Magic*, 335

G: *Afro-Yucatecan Baptism Records, Merida (1710–97)*, 341

Reference Matter

Notes, 357

Glossary, 405

References, 409

Index, 427

Figures, Maps, and Tables

FIGURES

Figure 1.1   View of colonial Campeche from the sea.   18

Figure 3.1   A Spaniard with the black mother of his
              mulatto son.   93

Figure 4.1   A black slave or domestic servant preparing chocolate in
              the kitchen of a Spanish household.   117

Figure 4.2   Signature of José Antonio, 16-year-old black slave
              coachman of assassinated governor don José de
              Gálvez, 1793.   118

Figure 4.3   Casta Painting depicting two black men working mules
              on a sugar estancia and a third offering food to his
              native wife.   126

Figure 5.1   "Infantry Regiment of Pardo Militias of Merida,
              Yucatan."   161

Figure 5.2   "Companies of Pardo Fusiliers of the 1st Division of
              Merida, Yucatan."   162

Figure 5.3   "The Watchtower," Campeche.   171

Figure 5.4   Annual tribute paid by free Afro-Yucatecans,
              1581–1618.   174

Figure 6.1   Signature of Isabel Toquero, 1711.   204

Figure 6.2   Tooth chipping of the upper and lower incisors belonging
              to an African man buried in Campeche's plaza in the early
              colonial period.   209

Figure 6.3   Racial distribution of the Campeche district population of
              23,479 in 1779.   214

Figure 6.4   Merida in 1610.   216

Figure 6.5   Church of Santa Lucía, Merida.   218

Figure 6.6 Racial distribution of the Merida district population of 15,821 in 1779. 220

Figure 7.1 An Afro-Mesoamerican family. 262

Figure 7.2 Love–magic accusations and Afro-Yucatecans accused of witchcraft by the Inquisition; Merida and Campeche, seventeenth century. 274

MAPS

All maps are by the author, unless otherwise indicated.

Map 1.1 Early colonial Yucatan. 8

Map 1.2 The structure of the slave trade. 19

Map 1.3 Distribution of the Afro-Yucatecan population, 1779. 30

Map 4.1 Afro-Yucatecans in the late colonial countryside. 116

Map 4.2 Northern late colonial Yucatan, showing rural communities with an Afro-Yucatecan majority and other settlements. 148

Map 5.1 Afro-Yucatecans and Yucatan's late colonial defenses. 159

Map 6.1 The world of Isabel Toquero. 201

Map 6.2 Early colonial Campeche. 205

Map 6.3 The church and graveyard of early colonial Campeche, based on archaeological evidence. 208

Map 6.4 Colonial Merida. 217

Map 6.5 San Francisco de Paula. 225

TABLES

Table 1.1 Examples of the various ways African slaves came to Yucatan. 10

Table 1.2 Afro-Yucatecan population estimates, 1570–1805. 28

Table 1.3 The Afro-Yucatecan population in comparative context: Afro-Yucatecans in relation to the population of colonial Yucatan. 28

Table 1.4 Distribution of the Afro-Yucatecan population, 1779. 31

Table 1.5 The Afro-Yucatecan population in comparative context: Afro-American populations in eighteenth-century colonies. 32

Table 2.1   Peso values of Afro-Yucatecan slaves, 1661–1829.   38

Table 2.2   A comparison of slave prices in some Spanish
              American colonies.   40

Table 2.3   Slave mortgages in Campeche, 1768–1823.   42

Table 2.4   Comparative naming patterns among slave owners,
              slaves, children of slaves, and free Afro-Yucatecans
              in Merida, 1710–89.   45

Table 2.5   Governors and Bishops of Yucatan as slave owners,
              1546–1792.   51

Table 2.6   Some members of the cathedral chapter whose slaves
              were baptized in Merida, 1711–27 and 1762–78.   56

Table 2.7   Incidence of titles among slave owners in Merida,
              1710–89.   58

Table 2.8   Merida's principal slave-owning families,
              1710–89.   60

Table 2.9   The value of an Afro-Yucatecan slave in the context
              of other types of property in late colonial Yucatan.   64

Table 3.1   Comparison of self-descriptions with language used to
              refer to Afro-Yucatecans.   99

Table 3.2   Population and use of casta categories by parish priests
              in 53 Yucatec pueblos, 1700.   103

Table 3.3   Use of Afro-Yucatecan casta categories by parish priests
              in 35 Yucatec pueblos, 1700.   106

Table 3.4   Use of Afro-Yucatecan casta categories in baptisms
              of infants by priests of Merida's Jesús parish,
              1710–95.   107

Table 4.1   Afro-Yucatecan incomes: Some examples,
              1660–1787.   115

Table 4.2   Afro-Yucatecan occupations: Some examples,
              1660–1787.   121

Table 4.3   Making a living in the countryside in 1700:
              Afro-Yucatecan men's occupations.   123

Table 4.4   Making a living in the countryside in 1700:
              Afro-Yucatecan men's occupations in comparative
              context.   134

Table 4.5   Making a living in the countryside in 1700:
              Afro-Yucatecan women's occupations in comparative
              context.   146

Table 5.1   Attacks on Campeche, 1556–1685.   157

Table 5.2   Yucatan's militia forces, 1778.   163

Table 5.3   Yucatan's militia forces, 1794.   164

Table 5.4   Occupations of pardo militiamen, 1789–90.   167

Table 5.5   Gender and slave-free balance of black adults baptized in eighteenth-century Merida.   187

Table 5.6   Patterns of mobility of some Africans who were sometimes resident in the Yucatan, c.1540–1832.   191

Table 5.7   Racial classifications of students graduating from Yucatan's colleges of San Ildefonso, San Pedro, and San Miguel de Estrada, 1722–1860.   196

Table 6.1   Origins of African adults in eighteenth-century Merida.   230

Table 6.2   Isabel Toquero's personal community of family, friends, and acquaintances.   239

Table 6.3   Incidence of familial relations among slaves in the same household, Merida, 1710–89.   245

Table 7.1   Crime and casta in Merida, 1811–21.   253

Table 7.2   Marriage choices by Afro-Yucatecan men in Merida, 1567–1797.   260

Table 7.3   The surnames of Afro-Yucatecan men's "Indian" wives in mid-eighteenth-century Merida.   261

Table 7.4   Marriage choices by non-Spaniards in Campeche, 1688–1700.   263

Table 7.5   Marriage choices in the Yucatec countryside, 1700.   264

Table 7.6   The materials of magic: Objects used by Afro-Yucatecan curers and love–magic professionals.   271

Preface and Acknowledgments

This book is a social, cultural, and economic history of Africans and people of African descent in the peninsula of Yucatan. My temporal focus is the colonial period, technically 1541–1821, although my discussion ranges from the 1530s to the 1830s, and the sources I have found are concentrated on the mid-to-late-colonial period (roughly 1640–1820). This book's purpose is to tell a story that has never before been told; Africans in colonial Latin America as a whole are understudied and in Yucatan almost completely unstudied. This story not only transforms our understanding of Yucatan's history, but opens a new window onto Spanish America and African America. *The Black Middle* is thus intended as a contribution to the history of the African diaspora,[1] as well as to the histories of Mexico and of colonial Latin America.

I hope that this book's thesis will thus be of interest to, and provoke debate among, all those who study the African diaspora and colonial societies in the Americas. I have taken hundreds of pages to explore the thesis—its dimensions, implications, and limitations. But in its simplest form it is encapsulated in this book's title. It might also be crammed into a single (albeit bloated) sentence: Although the presence of people of African descent in Yucatan was rooted in slavery, Yucatan was not a slave society; Afro-Yucatecans primarily played interstitial roles in the colony, filling a middle position between Spaniards and Mayas, thereby impacting colonial society, from Spanish city to Maya village, in profound ways that have hitherto been unrecognized.

This book's purpose is also to contribute more specifically to the history of Yucatan, as the second monograph in a trilogy on this southeastern province of New Spain. The first volume in the trilogy was *The Maya World*, a social and cultural history of Yucatan's indigenous people during the colonial centuries.[2] The projected third volume, titled *The Colonial Crucible*, will focus mostly on Spanish society while also pulling together many of the threads of *The Maya World* and *The Black Middle*.

A word on terminology: The archival sources that underpin this book often do not make clear each individual's socioracial category, nor are such categories as precise as they are often assumed to be. I have therefore invented a term—"Afro-Yucatecan"—to denote anyone of African descent living in colonial Yucatan. Wherever possible, I am more specific, using the term "African" to refer specifically to the African-born and generally to those of African racial heritage whom Spaniards termed *negro* or "black"— terms that I also use (with the Spanish *negro* always italicized, to avoid confusion with the English "negro"). Where an archival source indicates that a person was of mixed-race, I use "mulatto" or *pardo*; Spaniards in Yucatan tended to use *negro* or *bozal* to refer to black Africans and *pardo* or *mulato* to refer to mixed-race Afro-Yucatecans (that is, people of African-Maya as well as African–Spanish descent), but colonial usage was inconsistent for various reasons (see Chapter Three in particular).

The research, writing, and publication of this book were made possible by funding and support from the John Simon Guggenheim Memorial Foundation, the National Endowment for the Humanities, the John Carter Brown Library, the Pennsylvania State University (including a subvention from the College of Liberal Arts), and Boston College; and with the generous assistance of the directors and staff of the Archivo General del Estado de Yucatán, Merida (AGEY) (especially Piedad Peniche Rivero); the Archivo General del Estado de Campeche, Campeche (AGEC) (especially Sergio Bautista Vázquez and Gaspar Cauich); the Archivo General y Notaria Eclesiastica de la Arquidiocesis de Yucatán, Merida (AGAY) (especially Sonia Guadalupe López Heredia); the Centro de Apoyo a la Investigación Historica de Yucatán, Merida (CAIHY) (especially Yolanda López Moguel); the Archivo General de Indias, Seville (AGI) (especially Pilar Lázaro de la Escosura and Estrella Solís Giráldez); the Archivo General Militar de Madrid (AGMM); the Archivo General de la Nación, Mexico City (AGN); the Archivo Histórico Nacional, Madrid (AHN); the Archivo Notarial del Estado de Yucatán, Merida (ANEY); the Biblioteca Nacional, Mexico City (BN); the British Library, London (BL); the John Carter Brown Library, Providence (JCBL); the Real Academia de la Historia, Madrid; and the Tozzer Library, Harvard University (TLH) (especially Greg Finnegan).

Invaluable comments were made on earlier drafts of portions of the work by the following colleagues, to whom I am most grateful—Herman Bennett, Tony Kaye, Susan Kellogg, John Kicza, Jane Landers, Colin Palmer, Robert Schwaller, and Ben Vinson. Important contributions to this project's development were also made by Mark Christensen, John Chuchiak, Spencer Delbridge, Michael Francis, Jake Frederick, Rick Goulet, Susan Kepecs, Kris Lane, Mark Lentz, Michel Oudijk, Robin Restall, Dr. Lydia Sada de González, Amara Solari, Paul Sullivan, and Vera Tiesler. I am especially grateful to Eric Van Young for taking the trouble to write a careful, insightful, and encouraging reader's report for the press. I am likewise indebted to the fifteen Penn State students who unflinchingly identified and debated the weaknesses of the manuscript in my Fall 2005 graduate seminar.

M.B.R.
STATE COLLEGE, PA
JUNE 2007

A Note on Sources

Archival sources on the history of almost any topic in colonial Yucatec history are widely scattered due to several reasons, not least of which was the province's location in an imperial administrative structure that allowed some written records to travel to Spain, some to make it to Mexico City, some to end up in Merida or Campeche, and others to remain in the small towns and villages where they were composed. Sources on Africans in colonial Yucatan are no exception. I was initially misled by the paucity of secondary sources on the topic into thinking that Afro-Yucatecans were few in number and their existence not well documented. Early archival forays in 1994–95 seemed to confirm this impression, as none of the archives in Spain or Mexico store records in sections specifically devoted to Africans, blacks, or slaves, and using such keywords to search catalogues—analog or digital—produced relatively few documents.

However, these early finds turned out to be the tip of the iceberg. Beginning in 1996, and through my final archival forays in Spain in 2006, I discovered that Afro-Yucatecans could be found in significant numbers in many categories of written record; it was simply a question of knowing where and how to look. For example, because slaves arrived in ships and they were traded, I found them in the *Marina* section of Mexico City's AGN and in the *Contratación* and *Indiferente* sections of Seville's AGI. Black conquistadors played a role in Yucatan's early colonial history, and are thus mentioned in the probanzas of the first settlers, an immensely rich historical source preserved in the *Patronato* and *Justicia* sections of the AGI and barely touched on in this book. Because Spaniards who applied for licenses in Seville to travel to the colonies listed their black slaves or mulatto servants, the AGI's (now digitized) passenger records turned up relevant details. Because Spaniards were quick to classify the folk beliefs and practices of Afro-Yucatecans as superstitions, if not outright witchcraft, dozens of cases in the AGN's Inquisition files proved fruitful. For similar reasons, blacks and mulattoes appeared in the *Criminal* sections of the AGN and of Merida's AGEY. I had been collecting bigamy files for years as part of a separate project, finding them both in the AGN and AGEY; several of these bigamists turned out to be black or mulatto, thereby revealing entire Afro-Yucatecan biographies. Bequeathed slaves were found buried in the wills and testaments of élite Spaniards; documents that themselves were sometimes buried in probate proceedings or property disputes. Matters of defense were a high priority to imperial administrators, and therefore militia-related documents ended up in numerous archives, most notably in Spain (in the AGI, AGS, AHN, and the recently created AGMM). Merida's Afro-Yucatecan parish of Jesús no longer exists—even its church has been torn down—but its parish records have been preserved in a sideroom of the Cathedral (in the AGAY, which is not the main church archive). By chance, the organizing of a similar archive in Campeche (the AHDC) was completed the very month I arrived at the Cathedral in search of hitherto uncatalogued colonial Campechanos of African descent.

If sources on Afro-Yucatecans seemed elusive at first, their discovery did not guarantee their ongoing availability. Having made a preliminary survey of Merida's Jesús parish records in 1999, I returned in 2003 to discover that the previous autumn a hurricane had destroyed the roof of the AGAY. The documents had been removed in the middle of the storm, suffering some damage, and remained indefinitely inaccessible. Shortly before this disaster, the entire colonial section of the ANEY, scheduled to be transferred to the AGEY, was stolen. The leather-bound volumes—which, I had realized not long before, contained records of scores of slave sales, employment contracts, and other matters relevant to my project—were recovered by the police in Mexico City, where they remained for years before being deposited at last in the AGEY. Fortunately, both the AGAY parish records and the ANEY books were microfilmed decades ago, the former by the Church of Jesus Christ of Latter-Day Saints, the latter by the University of Texas at Arlington. In the end, one way or another, I was able to access everything I needed (although I have no doubt that much more remains to be discovered). Fortunate too is the fact that in the dozens of archives relevant to this project in Yucatan and Campeche, in Mexico and Spain, even in London and in university collections in the United States, there are professionals dedicated to the preservation and availability of these sources. If it seems miraculous that so much historical material on colonial Yucatan has survived at all, it is in no small measure due to the heroic intervention of the archivists thanked in the Preface that began this book.

Abbreviations of Archival Sources

The following abbreviations are used in the endnotes, figures, maps, and tables. All citations are from the Colonial sections of each archive unless otherwise stated. I use the following system of archival citation: AGI-*Escribanía* 316b, 75: f. 2v means the cited information is in the Archivo General de Indias (Seville), the *Escribanía de Camara* section, *legajo* number 316b (all such numbers and letters being the archive's designations, not mine), *expediente* or *pieza* number 75: the verso side of folio 2. All archives were visited by me and documents accessed on site, unless otherwise stated.

AGAY	Archivo General y Notaria Eclesiastica de la Arquidiócesis de Yucatán, Merida (accessed both on site and via LDS Church microfilm)
AGEC	Archivo General del Estado de Campeche, Campeche
AGEY	Archivo General del Estado de Yucatán, Merida
AGI	Archivo General de Indias, Seville
AGMM	Archivo General Militar de Madrid, Madrid
AGN	Archivo General de la Nación, Mexico City
AGS	Archivo General de Simancas, Simancas (accessed online and via Paso y Troncoso 1940)
AHAY	Archivo Histórico de la Arquidiócesis de Yucatán, Merida
AHDC	Archivo Histórico de la Diócesis de Campeche, Campeche
AHN	Archivo Histórico Nacional, Madrid
AME	Archivo de la Mitra Emeritense, Merida (accessed via Arrigunaga y Peón 1975, and Dumond and Dumond 1982)
ANEY	Archivo Notarial del Estado de Yucatán, Merida (accessed both on site and via UTA microfilm, copies of which were acquired in 2006 by the Pennsylvania State University)
BL	British Library (Rare Manuscript Room), London
BN	Biblioteca Nacional, Mexico City

CAIHY — Centro de Apoyo a la Investigación Historica de Yucatán, Merida

CCA — Colección Carrillo y Ancona, in CAIHY

CDH — *Colección de Documentos para la Historia de la Formación Social de Hispanoamérica, 1493–1810* (see Konetzke 1953)

CI — *Cartas de Indias* (Madrid, 1877)

DCP — *Discurso Sobre la Constitución de las Provincias de Yucatán y Campeche* (1766) in BN (Archivo Franciscano 55/1150) and in DHY

DHY — *Documentos para la Historia de Yucatán* (Merida, 1936–38)

JCBL — John Carter Brown Library, Providence

LLIU — Lilly Library, Indiana University (accessed on site by Jason Frederick)

PRO — -CO (Colonial Office), -A (Admiralty), (formerly) Public Record Office, (now called) National Archives, Kew (UK) (see Burdon 1931)

RAH — Real Academia de la Historia, Madrid

TULAL — Tulane University (New Orleans), Latin American Library Manuscript Collection

UTA — University of Texas, Arlington (references to roll numbers are to microfilms of the ANEY)

The Black Middle

Introduction

Making the Boatloads Visible

I am invisible, understand, simply because people refuse to see me."
—Ralph Ellison[1]

I felt intimidated by what had befallen them, their suffering, which was beyond my grasp. My discomfort annoyed them—'Stop that! Stop!'— and they insisted I see that life in that place had kept all its diversity, with comedy as well as sorrow, tenderness as well as horror. Out of their love for life, they refused to be transformed into legend, into a monument to misfortune.   —Milan Kundera[2]

1547 años lai hab ca paxi u chem ex boxe ecabe ca bini españolesob Baksahticob u ahob katun yok box te ecabe uak ek boxil lae [1547 was the year when a boatload of black people was shipwrecked at Ecab and the Spaniards went to capture them; they waged war upon the blacks at Ecab and brought out those black people tied together].
—The Titles of the Pech[3]

"A boatload of black people"—thus did a Maya notary economically evoke the transatlantic slave trade. The epigraph is an annals entry from a Maya-language account of the Spanish conquest of Yucatan. It is the sole mention in Maya conquest narratives of the presence of Africans in the peninsula in the sixteenth century. Likewise, in the historical literature on colonial Yucatan, those of African descent are given but scant and passing attention; to borrow Ellison's famous use of the word, they are the invisible men and women of the Yucatec past. The best single-volume history of the peninsula to date, Sergio Quezada's recent *Breve historia de Yucatán*, contains ninety-seven sections in thirteen chapters, none of whose titles and headings make any reference to Africans.

But Quezada can hardly be blamed. Despite the fact that both at the start and the end of colonial times there were almost as many people of African descent as there were Spaniards, Afro-Yucatecans wrote virtually nothing in the colonial period (in contrast to Mayas as well as Spaniards), and very little has been written about them since; in other words, Quezada had very little secondary material on Afro-Yucatecans to draw upon.[4]

Africans wrote little in colonial Yucatan because they had limited access both to literacy and to the legal system, yet even European sources tend to be peculiarly blind to the black presence in the colony, or dismissive of it. Spaniards sometimes give us fleeting glimpses of the black men and women who lived among them, tantalizing moments of visibility for those mostly unmentioned and unseen on the page. Fray Cristóbal Asensio wrote that in 1570 he "hired a horse and a black man" in Valladolid for his journey to Cozumel to evangelize the island's Mayas; but while the friar's report is detailed in many ways, the black man never appears again.[5] In his "description of the Indies" of 1620, fray Antonio Vásquez de Espinosa included over a dozen pages on Yucatan, permitting such details as descriptions of native dress, the precise locations of towns, the nature of local fruits, and a comprehensive list of all convents, curacies, and the number of Maya parishioners. But there is only one passing reference in Espinosa's account to the existence of "blacks and mulattoes" in the colony, despite the fact that there were thousands of Afro-Yucatecans by this time.[6] Similarly, don Joachin Fernando Prieto penned a report on Yucatan in 1757 whose thirty pages informed the reader of the various types of wood found in the peninsula, the revenue from port taxes, and the number of Maya parishes—but nary a mention of enslaved African or free-colored contributions to Yucatan's economy.[7]

One might argue that this is to be expected from Spaniards, who took the black presence in their colonies—in their own homes, even—for granted, but we encounter the same myopia in an outsider such as Lieutenant James Cook. Cook traveled through the colonial Yucatec town of Bacalar in 1769 and described it as "a small, poor, straggling village, of ill-built huts, of stakes of the Palmeta-tree drove in the ground, plaistered with earth, and thatched with the leaves; in number not more than a hundred Spaniards and Indians, of the former they are most of the soldiers militia of the province."[8] Yet we know from a census of 10 years later that there were at least 263 people of African descent living in Bacalar and its environs. This was out of a population of some four thousand, almost all of whom seem to have been working outside the town walls when Cook visited. Similarly, more than one in eight of the sixteen thousand residents of the provincial capital of Merida were black or mulatto, but Cook failed to make any mention of them either.[9]

The very existence of Africans in colonial Yucatan is reason enough to study them; but the fact that they were demographically, economically, and socially significant while being almost entirely ignored by all those who have written about Yucatan over the past five centuries renders the telling of their story even more urgent and fascinating. At the heart of this study, therefore, is a conundrum: if Africans were so significant to the history of colonial Yucatan, how and why did they become so invisible? The solution—the sum of various factors, most of them rooted in the nature of the Afro-Yucatecan experience—is discussed in the Conclusion. The concluding chapter also summarizes several other key, intertwined questions that I explore during the course of this book. For example, was colonial Yucatan a slave society or a society with slaves? Why did Spaniards in Yucatan own slaves? How did the rise of the free-colored population impact the "black middle"?

While the study of the indigenous and settler histories of colonial Yucatan is greatly facilitated by extensive archival sources in Spanish and Yucatec Maya, the evidence relating to Africans is fragmented and relatively scattered. This study is therefore based on a wide variety of source genres and individual documents, collected from a dozen archives and libraries in Europe, Mexico, and the United States; only parish records and census records come close to offering quantifiable evidence, although even those can sometimes be patchy and unreliable. In recognition of the anecdotal nature of many of the sources, I have tabulated sources not usually presented as tables, and tried to be as transparent as possible in analyzing archival sources in the text and notes. I have selected a sample case or source to begin each chapter; other sources are then analyzed partly with a view to determine the accuracy of the impressions given by the opening sample stories.

This Introduction's sample source—the brief passage from the Titles of the Pech quoted earlier—has been chosen because, despite its brevity, it raises so many of the issues around which this study is structured. The first set of issues stems from the implication of this quote that Africans came to Yucatan through the accident of shipwreck, an ironic image in view of the fact that the first Europeans to set foot on the peninsula were themselves the survivors of a shipwreck.[10] Certainly, Africans were involuntary colonists,[11] but they did not come to Yucatan by accident. The questions prompted here (and tackled in Chapters One through Four) are thus demographic and socioeconomic: When did Africans come to Yucatan? How many came? Where in the peninsula did they go? What roles did they play in the formation of the Spanish colony? The answers center initially on slavery (the focus of Chapters One and Two), and on relations between Spaniards and Afro-Yucatecans (the broad focus of the first three chapters). But when we look at the full array of Afro-Yucatecan work experiences (Chapter Four), slavery does not feature as the defining institution of labor arrangements and patterns.

The second set of issues suggested by the epigraph in Maya is to do with identities. In the earlier quote the Maya authors of the annals refer to the African slaves as *ek box*, or "black people."[12] Presumably these shipwreck survivors had only recently been removed from their African homeland and thus were culturally and racially distinct from both Mayas and Spaniards. To what extent, however, did Africans and their descendants remain culturally distinct from the other inhabitants of Yucatan? How meaningful were distinctions of "race"? Did Africans in Yucatan develop a sense of community based on race and/or affiliation to the province or any part of it? How differently viewed were the enslaved and the free, the full-blooded and the mixed-blooded? How did they view themselves? Can we talk of "Afro-Yucatecans"? Answers to these questions are proposed throughout this book, but most directly in Chapters Three through Seven.

The third set of issues raised by the Maya annals excerpt and closely related to the previous two is that of interracial relations. Through their focus on demographic issues, economic roles, and questions of identity, all the chapters address aspects of Spanish–African relations; African–Maya relations are also discussed to some extent in all the chapters, but I turn increasingly to the topic from Chapters Three to Six, devoting Chapter Seven entirely to the complexities of interaction between Mayas and Afro-Yucatecans. The Pech quote suggests that relations between Spaniards and Africans were delineated by the antagonisms inherent to slavery, whereas the Mayas remained dispassionate bystanders. To what extent was this the case; that is, were people of African descent really tied involuntarily to the Spanish community while being utterly distanced from the Maya world? How did Mayas perceive Africans? What were the means and loci of African–Maya interaction? To what extent were Afro-Yucatecans caught in the middle, between the prejudices of Spaniards on the one hand and of Mayas on the other?

The answer to the latter question is of course anticipated by the book's title, which reflects the underlying thesis of this book—that those of African descent in Yucatan were positioned and caught in various ways in a middle ground between Spanish colonists and the peninsula's native people, the Yucatec Mayas. The title is also of course intended as an echo of the phrase "the Middle Passage," the transatlantic voyage that brought Africans to the Americas.[13] In addition to the African slaves that Spaniards held as prestige property and personal servants, the substantial free-colored population was also tied to the colonists in a relationship of attached subordination. However, I try to demonstrate that despite being victimized by slavery, subordination, and the prejudices of both Spaniards and Mayas, Afro-Yucatecans still found ample space in this middle ground to build complex and varied lives—to pursue careers, seek opportunities, raise families, and often push against and even transcend the social and economic restrictions that they inherited.

Within this framework, then, the black middle became multidimensional. Afro-Yucatecans were heterogeneous; they lived in "the space in-between, among, and through" various socioracial arenas (to borrow Ben Vinson's words).[14] Many of these arenas comprised a dynamic social space created by free-colored families seeking to attain some mobility and access to the political and economic center. This they achieved in part by distancing themselves from the enslaved and engaging the Spanish and native communities that they bridged. If native Americans have historically been seen as the "other, as essentially different" from Europeans, with "the descendents of black Africans" positioned "more ambiguously as both inside and outside the society of their masters and observers" (in the words of anthropologist Peter Wade), then my argument is that Afro-Yucatecans were indeed ambiguously located, but were both inside and outside the societies of Spaniards *and* Mayas.[15]

Consequently, Afro-Yucatecans forever altered the Maya communities in which they settled, in both town and countryside. Indeed, perhaps the most surprising result of my research into Afro-Yucatan was the realization that by late colonial times, the Mayas of Yucatan had in a sense become Afro-Mayas. This fact not only alters our view of colonial Yucatan, but has profound implications for the study of modern Yucatan.

Thus the history being presented here is far more than a tale of tragedy. It is a story of human endeavor; one of suffering, most certainly, but also one of survival, and in many cases, triumph. The reader may or may not be familiar with the historical and geographical setting of this book, but the patterns of human behavior that are illustrated should be all too familiar.

My efforts to demonstrate that people of African descent were able in various ways to transcend the horrors of slavery and racial subordination should in no way be taken as an apologia for the slave trade; on the contrary, it is in riposte both to the dehumanizing nature of the slave trade, and to the concomitant scarcity of Africans in the human historical record, that I have sought to make visible in all its human richness the African experience in colonial Yucatan.

CHAPTER ONE

Involuntary Colonists

More than forty years ago he entered this province and since then he
has served us with his weapons on the occasions that have arisen,
especially in helping to place that province under our command and
afterwards, in things relating to our service, according to the orders of
our governors.   —King Philip II, 1578[1]

Is there anybody who wishes to make a bid on two black English slaves
of the king's who hereby appear, with the highest bid made to be
accepted at noon on this day?
—Isidoro, bilingual Maya town crier, Merida, 1792[2]

THE STORY OF SEBASTIÁN TORAL

In 1578 the king of Spain, sitting in Madrid, signed a royal edict and dispatched it to the governor of the province of Yucatan. The edict stated that the
provincial administration was to cease demanding tribute payments from one
Sebastián Toral, a resident of Merida, the colony's capital. Toral's wife was
also to be spared the burden of tribute, as were their children when they
reached taxable age. The edict was a response to petitions sent to the king
from Toral, whose pleas were based on his citation of service to the crown during the Spanish conquest of Yucatan. In particular, stated the edict, Toral had
"helped place that province under our command and afterwards served us according to the orders of our governors, acting as a guard in various places as
necessity required, without drawing any salary or receiving any reward."[3]

As described thus far, neither the edict nor the petitions to which it responded were unusual. Spanish conquistadors were never salaried, holding
at best a license to conquer and promises of future royal favors. Thus, Spanish kings in the sixteenth century were besieged by—and often responded
favorably to—requests for privileges and rewards from those who had carved
out Spain's empire in the Americas. Indeed, for centuries after the Conquest
the royal treasury and its American branches were paying annual pensions of

hundreds of *pesos* to descendents of conquistadors and even to native nobles such as the descendents of the Mexica royal family of the Moctezumas.[4] However—and this is what makes the edict unusual—Sebastián Toral was neither a native nobleman nor a Spaniard. He was a black African.

Toral was born in the second decade of the sixteenth century either in West Africa or in Portugal; one record states that his parents were black slaves in the Portuguese town of Mora. How he was sold to Spaniards is not known, but by his early teens Toral experienced the crossing of the Atlantic and the invasion of unconquered Native American territory. He first entered Yucatan as a slave owned by one of the conquistadors on the failed campaign into the peninsula of the early 1530s. His service on that expedition probably earned him his freedom. Thus, when he returned to Yucatan in 1540, he went as a free conquistador along with the Spaniards who came to try and subdue the Mayas for the third time.

Once a colony was founded in the early 1540s, Toral lived among Yucatan's new settlers as a Christian Spanish-speaker with, eventually, a family; in the words of the royal edict, "he is married and has his own house, wife, and children in that city [Merida]." His occupation was that of guard [*guardia y çentinela*], one commonly associated with blacks and mulattoes in the Spanish colonies.[5] Yet he remained, in the Spanish parlance of the time (and in the terms used by the edict), a black man, dark in color [*negro; de color moreno*]. That identity placed Toral in a separate and subordinate category within colonial society, despite the fact that long before 1578 he had become a free man. It also meant that, when in 1574 the crown "ordered that the [black] slaves and free mulattoes of these parts [the colonies] pay us tribute . . . twelve *reales* each year, and for his wife and children, twelve more reales," Toral was liable for what amounted to three *pesos* a year, equivalent to a laborer's monthly salary.[6]

Presumably Toral wrote to Madrid from Merida protesting the tax, but in vain, for in the late 1570s he took the extraordinary step of traveling to Spain—extraordinary because the voyage involved several weeks of expense, risk, and discomfort and Toral was almost sixty (an old man for the sixteenth century). He must have been thinking not of himself and his own pocket, but of his children and of the principle of the thing—paying tribute put him in the same category as the Mayas he had fought against in his youth; being exempt categorized him with the Spaniards he had fought beside. It must have gratified the Afro-Yucatecan veteran, therefore, to read that the king deemed that in being asked to pay this tribute, Toral "had been wronged, because he is worthy of receiving much favor for the service he has done us in the manner that is all made very clear in certain documents which have been presented to us in our Council of the Indies."[7]

In January 1579, four months after the king signed the edict in Madrid, Toral appeared before customs officials in Seville. Described by those who certified his travel documents as "black" or "dark in color," and "sixty years old,

Map 1.1 Early colonial Yucatan. The dotted areas represent frontier zones where the colonial border fluctuated from the mid-sixteenth to late seventeenth centuries.

more or less, and dark-bearded," Toral received a permit "to travel and return to the province of Yucatan . . . with the New Spain fleet." Furthermore, in another royal order dictated a week later, Toral was given the right to take back to Yucatan, "in order to guard and defend person and home, four swords, four daggers, and an harquebus"—of which, once back home, he could carry one sword and one dagger, which in Yucatan and New Spain "is what the Spaniards carry."[8]

The next (and last) we hear of Toral is a year later, in January of 1580, when he appeared in the viceroy's office in Mexico City to request a license to carry arms. He had with him the royal edict granting him that right, but claimed that "some officials and others" in the city had accused him of not being the man named in that license. Toral wanted—and was granted—a local license to carry his sword and dagger. After this, he presumably returned to Yucatan, dying in the 1580s in Merida, surrounded by his family. Toral died a veteran of three transatlantic voyages and two Conquest expeditions, a man who had successfully petitioned the great Spanish king, walked the streets of Lisbon, Seville, and Mexico City, and helped found a capital city in the Americas.[9]

Two centuries later, the city Toral had helped to establish was the capital of a colony that in many ways had changed dramatically; but in other ways, little had changed. Before placing the tale of Sebastián Toral in the larger context of African slavery and settlement in Yucatan, I would like to detour very briefly through another case study. This story takes us south, to the Belize River (see Map 1.1). In 1759, that river was crossed by a Capt. don Juan de Sosa, who was accompanied by fourteen other armed Spaniards and a patent from the crown to halt British commercial expansion in northern Belize. Sosa and his men soon came across a small riverside ranch, which they raided, capturing an Englishman and his two African slaves. The captured Englishman, in return for his release, led Sosa and company to another ranch where an English couple were robbed of their movable goods, including three more black slaves.

The slaves were taken by Sosa up to Merida and four of them put up for sale; the fate of the fifth, who was blind and declared to be of no value, was not recorded. Canon Mendicuti of Merida cathedral estimated their combined value to be five hundred pesos, but his offer of that sum was bettered by Capt. don Lorenzo Villaelriego, to whom the slaves were sold for six hundred pesos. Within two years, one of those Africans, an elderly woman, was dead; there is no record of the fate of the others.[10]

INVOLUNTARY COLONISTS

Thus, in various ways over several centuries, usually against their will and by the hand of Europeans, Africans came to the Yucatan peninsula. The two stories above—that of Toral and that of the black slaves made Belizean booty—are hardly enough to convey the full variety and complexity of how Africans became a part of the Spanish colonization of Yucatan (Table 1.1 is a preview of the complex picture that will emerge during the course of this book). But Toral and the Afro-Belizeans suffice to introduce four points on the demographic and mechanical essentials of the African presence in this province of the Spanish Empire.

The first point is the obvious but important fact that the presence of Africans in Yucatan was a product of the Spanish Conquest. Spaniards had

TABLE 1.1 Examples of the various ways African slaves came to Yucatan

Slave's name	Arrived in Yucatan from where and when	Details
Sebastián Toral	Mexico, 1529	Arrived as a slave and fought with the second Montejo-led invasion (1529–34) and the third invasion of 1540; settled in Merida in 1540s as a free black guard; visited Spain in the late 1570s; sailed from Spain to Mexico 1579; in Mexico City 1580; probably died in Yucatan 1580s
Marcos	Honduras, 1540	Brought by his owner, don Francisco de Montejo; used in 1540s as an interpreter and procurer of Maya servants
Juan	Seville, 1602	Born in Africa; purchased in Yucatan by Joseph Franquez de Ortega in 1590s; taken on a round-trip to Spain 1600–1602
Francisco Antonio	Seville, 1643	Born in Africa c.1603; a slave by the 1630s of Venezuela's governor, don Francisco Núñez Melián, who took him to Spain and then to Yucatan when Núñez Melián became governor there
Juana María	Mina, 1715	Brought from Africa by English slave traders, part of shipment of about 16 slaves arriving in Yucatan that summer; sold to the governor, don Alonso Meneses Bravo; baptized in Merida on September 9, 1715
Agustín de Leira	Seville, 1718	Born 1704 in Africa or Spain; brought to Yucatan by his owner, don Diego de Santesteban, lessor of the income from salt sales and taxes in Yucatan
Santiago Antonio	Congo, 1751	Route from Africa to Yucatan not known; purchased by Capt. don Pedro García de la

TABLE 1.1 (*continued*)

Slave's name	Arrived in Yucatan from where and when	Details
Matias	Havana, 1785	Piedra, probably from slave traders in Campeche; baptized in Merida July 18, 1751 Mortgaged for 92 pesos by his Havana owners, don Francisco Josef Bazquez and don Francisco Camacho, and sent to creditor don Antonio Arolas in Campeche
Juana	Xalapa, 1787	A mulatta; at age 18, given to doña Maria Josefa del Castillo in Merida, by her son in Xalapa; resold in 1794 in Merida and still a slave there in 1816
Plato	Belize, 1792	Together with "Coiys" [Gaius?], taken from British owners in northern Belize by Spaniards, sold at auction for 400 pesos (for the pair) in Merida to Bishop Piña y Mazo via his nephew–agent don Toribio del Mazo; renamed at baptism
Francisco Aznar	Havana, 1817	Sold by don Francisco Bengoechea in Havana to don Tomás Aznar y Peón in Sisal, transported by don Francisco Quintana, a merchant with whom Aznar did regular business, paid for part in cash and part in candle tallow

Sources (in order): AGI-*México* 2999, 2, 1: ff. 187r–88r (with additional evidence in AGI-*Contratación* 5227, 2, 25 and *Indiferente* 1969, 22, 1: f. 404; and AGN-*General de Parte* 2, 489: f. 97); AGI-*Justicia* 300, 3: ff. 388–442; AGI-*Contratación* 5272, 2, 71; AGI-*Contratación* 5425, 1, 1; AGAY-*Bautismos*, Jesús María Vol. 1: f. 65r; AGI-*Contratación* 5470, 1, 23; AGAY-*Bautismos*, Jesús María Vol. 2: f. 239r; AGEC-*Registro Público de la Propriedad* [*Fondo Gobernación*], 2, 1: f. 81; AGEY-*Varios*, 1, 29; AHAY-*Asuntos Terminados* 1792 (transcribed in Ruz Menéndez 1970: 22–25); AGEY-*Justicia* [*Poder Ejecutivo*] 2, 20: f. 4 (Ruz Menéndez [1970: 13] identifies don Tomás Aznar as Subteniente de Milicias, b. 1786 in Merida, d. 1849).

begun to colonize the Caribbean in the 1490s, exploring the Yucatec coast in the 1510s. Spanish Conquest campaigns in Mesoamerica (a native civilizational area that ran from northern Mexico into Central America) began in 1519, with the Cortés-led expedition against the Mexica (or Aztec) Empire. However, a permanent Spanish settlement in the Yucatan peninsula was not established until the 1540s, for several reasons. The discoveries of impressive and wealthy empires in central Mexico and the Andes drew Spanish attention and resources. The Yucatan peninsula proved to contain no precious metals or other obvious source of wealth, making it difficult to finance a sustained campaign. The local Maya population was divided into more than a dozen minor polities, or kingdoms, but relations between these polities were not so hostile that invaders could easily forge solid alliances with one group against another.

Having secured a formal invader's or *adelantado* license in 1526, don Francisco de Montejo and his son and nephew of the same name made two failed attempts to conquer the Mayas in 1527–28 and 1530–34. The legacy of these campaigns was epidemic disease and increased hostilities between Maya polities. Thus when the younger Montejos returned in 1540, this time accompanied by thousands of native allies from elsewhere in Mesoamerica, they were able to settle the northwest corner of the peninsula (see Map 1.1). Campeche was founded in 1540, and in 1542 Spaniards established a colonial capital at Tiho. Renamed Merida, the city was within the polity ruled by the Pech, the Maya dynasty that proved most willing to ally with the foreign settlers. This small colony was reasonably secure by 1547, but the peninsula as a whole was never fully conquered, and there were military campaigns against uncolonized Mayas into the eighteenth century. Africans in Yucatan were thus residents of a colony that had been established with considerable difficulty, one that was built upon its subject Maya population but always bordered to the south with unconquered Maya polities, and that remained a relatively poor and peripheral province of the Spanish Empire.[11]

The second essential point here is the very fact of African slavery. Many of the individuals discussed in this book were free for part or all of their lives. Yet in the beginning, Africans were brought to Yucatan as slaves, and for two and a half centuries continued to be brought against their will to work in the colony. Even though there came to be many Sebastián Torals in the colony, well-settled, socially integrated blacks and mulattoes whom we might justifiably call Afro-Yucatecans, and even though free mulattoes would come to far outnumber enslaved *negros*, it is important to note that involuntariness was at the heart of the African genesis in Yucatan—as much as it was elsewhere in the Americas.

The third essential point on Africans in Yucatan is one of numbers—not the larger demographic picture (presented later in this chapter), but the scale of importation and sale. The question of scale is important because it reflects the broad typology of slavery in Yucatan. Most of the millions who suffered through the Middle Passage to work out their lives in the Americas were sold in large groups (meaning dozens, sometimes hundreds) to work on sugar plantations or other enterprises, mostly in Brazil or the Caribbean. Of the minority (some 15%) who ended up in Spanish America, most did not become plantation slaves, working instead as domestic servants or auxiliaries to Spaniards in relatively small-scale enterprises.[12] African slaves in Yucatan were part of this latter category; they were auxiliary slaves rather than mass slaves (that is, slaves purchased and put to work in large numbers on plantations or other large-scale enterprises).[13] Put a different way, Yucatan was a society with slaves, not a slave society—meaning that African slaves were not central to economic production, they were not the laboring majority, let alone the population majority (Mayas were both), and the master–slave relationship was not the foundation of the entire colonial social order.[14]

Enslaved Africans were thus brought to Yucatan in relatively small groups, and were purchased in even smaller numbers, often individually; those who migrated from other colonies, Spanish or British, also came as individuals or in very small groups. As shall be detailed below, the *negro* population in the colony thus remained relatively small throughout the colonial period and by its end had almost disappeared; while mulattoes, often called *pardos* in Yucatan (see Chapter Three for a full explanation of terminological trends), grew steadily in number and over the centuries spread through the colony.

What do I mean by relatively small groups? The annual arrival rate of Africans to the colony probably ranged from a handful to about a hundred. A cargo of forty-seven slaves, sold illegally in Campeche in the summer of 1599, was unusually large for one shipment.[15] Juan Ortuño de Olano regularly plied the trade route between Veracruz, Campeche, and Havana in the 1610s, and was occasionally entrusted with thousands of pesos in tribute money to be shipped to Spain. I found only one instance, however, of Ortuño trading in slaves; his *Espiritu Santo* brought a handful of Africans from Veracruz to Campeche in 1618. Ortuño probably did a little illicit slave trading, as did a local merchant, Juan de Nogal—who was caught when he got greedy, trying to smuggle 106 black slaves into Merida in 1618.[16]

The sporadic importation of slaves into early colonial Yucatan gave way to a late colonial pattern that was almost as uneven. In 1674, the crown licensed seven hundred slaves a year to be shared between the ports of Havana, Veracruz, Campeche, and Honduras, but as that put Yucatan in competition with Cuba, central Mexico, and greater Guatemala, it is very unlikely that Campeche subsequently received even close to a quarter of that annual legal allotment.[17] Two British traders, Blackwood and Cathcart, were given a license to bring 199 slaves into Campeche in 1730–33, although Spanish records show that the total legal importation of enslaved Africans into the port in 1731–33 was 167—an average rate of three ships a year and just over 18 slaves per ship.[18] In 1738, a British ship sold one hundred slaves in Campeche, and another did the same the following year, but these were unusually large shipments for the colony.[19] A more typical human cargo was the seventeen slaves that British traders brought to Campeche in 1737, or the fourteen *negros* who entered the port in 1791.[20] The flow of black slaves into the colony fluctuated considerably. For example (and for reasons explained shortly), the number of newly arrived black slaves baptized in Merida held at fifty-five for the 1710s (these are decade, not annual, totals), sixty-six for the 1720s, and sixty for the 1730s, but plummeted to just twenty-one for the 1740s. These numbers recovered to 69 in the 1750s, peaked at 150 in the 1760s, fell again to 29 in the 1770s before rising to 112 in the 1780s, and trailing off after that.[21] In 1805, twenty-seven African men and women were recorded as arrivals in Tabasco on a United States ship out of Charleston; they were purchased in Villahermosa by Spaniards from Yucatan and then shipped up the coast to Campeche.[22]

By 1805 there were no longer *encomenderos* buying slaves (encomenderos were elite Spaniards like Capt. Villalriego, who held grants of Maya tribute and labor). But the encomendero class outlived the institution and there were plenty of Spaniards—*hacendados*, priests, merchants, military officers, and those able to support well-staffed households—who purchased Africans. Slaves were bought in small numbers. In the larger port and slave market of Veracruz, Spaniards bought between one and twelve slaves each, albeit typically fewer than six; in Campeche, Africans were sold to Spanish owners in ones and twos.[23] The smallness of the Yucatec slave market probably helps explain why a Spanish frigate made an illegal attempt in 1735 to offload in Veracruz 100 Africans from a shipment of 150 delivered to Campeche by English traders earlier in the year; the frigate was sent back to Campeche, so its unfortunate cargo may have ended up in Yucatan after all.[24] Spaniards making business trips from Yucatan back to Spain typically spent two years doing so and traveled with one or two black or mulatto slaves or servants (see Appendix C). Slave baptism records from eighteenth-century Merida show Spaniards owning an average of between one and two slaves, although the real average was probably between two and three (see Appendix E). Certainly it was not unusual for well-to-do Spaniards to own three slaves. But for a Spaniard to own more than four African slaves, as Capt. Diego de Acevedo did in the 1690s, was less common. In any one decade of the eighteenth century, among the several hundred elite Spaniards who owned slaves, there were no more than a handful of men and just a few women who owned six or more slaves at once. Don Rodrigo Chacon, for example, one of the top few slave owners of the century, had twenty-four adult and infant slaves baptized in Merida, but this was over a twenty-four-year period (1711–35); similarly, doña Petrona Alpuche, perhaps the top female slave owner in Merida, had a dozen slaves baptized, but over thirty years (1726–56). Incoming governors of the colony tended to buy slaves within months of taking office, as did bishops shortly before their episcopate ended, but mostly in numbers of one to four; only two governors bought more, roughly a dozen each, and they were the exceptions.[25] As Table 1.1 illustrates, the pattern of small-scale arrival persisted from the first to final decades of the colonial period.

As was the case in many other regions of Spanish America, the local native population met most colonial labor demands. But African slaves from the onset comprised a permanent labor force that was more directly and closely tied to the colonists.[26] As represented by Sebastián Toral's tale, the African role was often a military one in the decades of conquest and early colonization, a role that placed Africans firmly within the Spanish world at a time when Spanish and Maya worlds were colliding.[27] Before long, Africans were participating in all areas of colony-building as auxiliaries to Spaniards and often as overseers of Maya workers. With the possible exception of slave laborers on the few sugar plantations that were set up later in the colonial period, African slaves in Yucatan, like the free blacks and pardos of the province, were not anonymous members of a mass labor force; they were individuals.[28]

THE STRUCTURE OF THE SLAVE TRADE

The first three basic points, then, raised by the anecdotal cases that began this chapter, amount to this: (1) as a result of Spanish conquest and colonization in Yucatan, beginning in the 1540s, (2) Africans came to the peninsula as slaves, and (3) while the scale of the trade was relatively small, it was persistent and lasted throughout the colonial period. A fourth essential point involves the structure of the slave trade and the role played by Spaniards, Englishmen, and other Europeans—as individuals and as representatives of institutions—in developing the mechanisms of the slave trade as it directly affected Yucatan. Whether slaves came from Belize, Spain, or through the Caribbean from Africa, they almost always entered Yucatan through the efforts of private entrepreneurs—be they Spanish, Portuguese, or English; be they agents of merchant companies holding royal *asientos* or slave-trade licenses; or be they piratical companies of armed, licensed investors such as that led by Capt. don Juan de Sosa. The usual role of the crown and colonial government was a parasitic fiscal one: to sell or grant licenses to import or raid for slaves; and to collect taxes on the importation and sale of slaves. The six hundred pesos that don Lorenzo Villaelriego paid for the four slaves captured by Sosa was deposited in the royal treasury pending an investigation into the capture of the Africans and an evaluation of taxes due. Three years after the Sosa expedition, a treasury official in Madrid declared the capture valid and set tax at thirty-three pesos plus a third of the slaves' value; the funds were then released to be paid as shares to Sosa's men.[29]

Indeed, it was a license much like Sosa's of 1758 that first brought Africans to the shores of Yucatan in the sixteenth century. In 1533, don Francisco de

Montejo acquired a license to bring up to one hundred slaves to the mines that the Spaniards hoped they would find.[30] Montejo already had a license from the crown to conquer the peninsula, and during the course of a series of conquest campaigns from 1527 to 1547, he, his son, and his nephew (both of them his namesakes) brought an indeterminate number of black slaves to Yucatan (among them the African who was, or who became, Sebastián Toral). The imagined mines never materialized and the Montejos themselves seemed not to have used their license to its full allotment.

Still, Toral was clearly not the only black conquistador in Yucatan. The Italian chronicler Girolamo Benzoni, who traveled through Merida within a decade of its founding, recounted a tale that must have been circulating among the conquistadors themselves in the city:

Some [Maya] chiefs came to visit him [the adelantado Francisco de Montejo] under pretence of wishing for his friendship, and remained a good while in his company, until seeing an opportunity, one of them attempted to kill him with a scimitar which he had seized from a Moor [i.e., an African]; but the governor [Montejo] perceiving it, immediately drew his sword and defended himself, so they ran away without doing any harm.[31]

Benzoni must have seen the surviving Africans who had fought with "scimitars" alongside Spaniards against Mayas, but he makes no mention of them (the same myopia shared by Lieutenant James Cook, mentioned in the Introduction above). He may also have heard stories about such slaves as the squad of twenty Africans who were brought in to assist in the Conquest (and may have fought in it) but who fled into the Yucatec countryside sometime in the late 1540s. Alonso Rosado, a veteran of all three Spanish invasions of Yucatan and the loyalist who had captured the Spanish rebels that had fled Peru and allegedly tried to seize Yucatan, was appointed to round up the escaped slaves. Using Maya warriors assigned to the Spaniards who also accompanied him, Rosado captured the "black rebels" in the hills south of Merida, thus "preventing the damage they could have done to the natives of this province." The slave squad was delivered to Licenciado Herrera, the senior royal judge in Merida, where the Africans were put to work "for His Majesty"—probably on construction projects.[32]

Benzoni may also have heard stories about one African in Yucatan in particular, the invaluable (to some) and infamous (to others) Marcos. Marcos (or Marcos Negro) was one of the Africans brought by don Francisco de Montejo from Honduras in or shortly after 1540. Marcos may not have fought against Mayas, but he was reputed to be greatly feared by them, "more than they feared the adelantado, his master."[33] Marcos (referred to variously as a slave of Montejo's or of his wife, doña Beatriz de Herrera), appears regularly in the thousand pages of Montejo's 1544–53 *residencia* [official inquiry into a governor's term in office]. The Spaniards who testified as to Marcos's activities and reputation may have had good reason to resent him, so their statements must be read carefully. But if there is some truth to them, they reveal why Marcos was so useful to the Montejos.

Allegedly, in the 1530s, Marcos had been "the captain" of a group of rebel or maroon slaves in central Mexico, from where he had fled to Honduras. There he was acquired somehow by Montejo and in the 1540s put to use in Yucatan taking Mayas from their villages to work as domestic servants in Spanish households in Merida. According to residencia testimony, the dominant familial faction among the conquistador-settlers (including Montejo himself, his wife doña Beatriz, her brother Alonso López, and her son Juan de Esquivel) staffed their houses on Merida's plaza with Mayas brought there "against their will." In the city and on a Montejo *estancia* [ranch], Maya women "cooked and worked" in houses built by Maya men, most of them allegedly procured by Marcos. Worse still, the Montejo faction shipped "*naborías* and other Indian men and women" out of the province to be sold as slaves. Some of these naborías [native dependents or servants] were allegedly taken by Marcos from the households of other Spaniards. Witnesses referred to Marcos as a *nahuatlato* [literally meaning "Nahuatl speaker" but used throughout New Spain to refer to a bilingual speaker of Spanish and a native language]. Marcos had apparently become "a great linguist [*grande lengua*]," speaking both Nahuatl and Maya. Some claimed that "it is publicly said that he fakes [*contrahace*] what the Indians say, and does not tell the truth," and that the Franciscans had received complaints from natives and Spaniards alike regarding Marcos's deliberate mistranslations and general abuse of Mayas. Others accused Marcos of having his own house in Merida, staffed with Maya women.[34]

It is significant that the most powerful Spaniards in the fledgling colony solved two basic needs—for labor and cash—by exploiting the Maya population with black-slave assistance; they did not attempt to create a large-scale African labor force. Such a labor force was neither necessary nor affordable; instead, black individuals such as Marcos functioned as skilled auxiliaries, so effective as to be feared by Mayas and resented by the settlers who were not in their master's faction. Resentment of Marcos by some Spaniards was clearly an extension of resentment against the Montejo faction, not a reflection of any disapproval of the use of black auxiliaries in positions of power.

The fact is, all the conquistadors and settlers who could afford to brought slaves with them to Merida; indeed, in the early decades of the colony, there were almost as many Africans as Spaniards. Don Guillen de las Casas, as incoming governor in 1579, was granted the right "to bring to that land three slaves, *negros*, for his service, free of taxes," a practice that was probably typical for the fifteen Spaniards who governed Yucatan in the colony's first fifty years, while other members of the tiny Spanish elite acquired their own small staff of enslaved Africans.[35] Most of the first generations of slaves in the colony were probably men, but a significant minority were women; there were black slave women in the households of the Montejos and the other founding encomenderos of the colony.[36]

The colony of Yucatan was connected to the outside world primarily through the port town of Campeche. Sisal (north of Merida) was an additional entry point for goods from the end of the sixteenth century on, but it was through Campeche that most African slaves arrived during the first two centuries of colonial rule (see Figure 1.1). Originating in West Africa and West Central Africa, slaves destined for Yucatan did not come directly across the Atlantic to Campeche; they first had to survive the grueling Middle Passage from West Africa to a primary slave port in the Caribbean, such as Veracruz or Jamaica, from where they were transported for sale in Campeche or Merida (see Map 1.2).[37]

In the first few decades of colonial rule in Yucatan, it was primarily Spanish ships that brought slaves across the Atlantic to New Spain. However, the unification of the Portuguese and Spanish crowns between 1580

Figure 1.1 View of colonial Campeche from the sea. For most enslaved Africans born outside Yucatan, this would have been their first view of the colony. Source: Arnoldus Montanus, *Beschryving van America* (Amsterdam, 1671), pp. 258–59 inter; reproduced courtesy of the John Carter Brown Library, Brown University.[38]

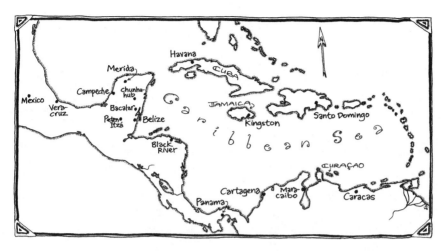

Map 1.2 The structure of the slave trade, showing places mentioned in this chapter.

and 1640 allowed the Portuguese to become the primary suppliers of slaves to Spanish American markets. For forty-five years up to 1640 Portuguese traders held a series of monopolistic asientos, paying the Spanish crown for the rights to import 3,500 to 4,250 Africans a year into the American colonies, primarily through Veracruz and Cartagena.[39] By 1650, these markets had acquired over 300,000 African slaves, of which something in the vicinity of 1% made it to Yucatan. Most of these slaves would have come directly from West Africa, through Veracruz, to Campeche. A minority would have arrived illegally into Campeche, either from Africa or another Spanish American port, like the above-mentioned forty-seven Africans sold in Campeche in 1599 to avoid paying royal taxes in Veracruz. Some slaves came under license from Spain with their owners (as did free-colored servants with patrons) and others arrived through trade (often illegal) between Yucatan and other Spanish centers such as Havana and Mexico City (see Map 1.2).

In the centuries after 1640, increased demand in Brazil and the non-Spanish Caribbean primarily fueled the slave trade. Meanwhile, during the second half of the seventeenth century, the structure of the slave trade changed significantly. The Caribbean went from being Spanish to international, and violently so. The Portuguese lost their monopoly and the Casa de Contratación (the empire's department of trade and customs, based in Seville) lost its control over the slave trade. Jamaica and Curaçao became major slave-trade centers. Faced with the proliferation of contraband trade and competition from other European powers, beginning in the 1660s, the Spanish crown adopted a compromise approach to try and control the trade; from 1663 to 1674 the royal asiento was held by two Genoese merchants,

Grillo and Lomelín, who purchased slaves not in Africa but in the Caribbean from English and Dutch traders, reselling them in designated Spanish American ports.[40]

This pattern persisted, and in subsequent decades Spaniards purchased Africans either through intermediaries or directly from northern European merchants. The French held the slave asiento in 1702–13, but continued to sell Africans to Spanish colonists illegally for decades after this.[41] The Dutch also held various licenses between the 1680s and 1780s. One such license, drawn up and printed in 1682, provided for the purchase of two thousand slaves a year (from 1683 to 1690) at Cumaná, where Dutch ships brought them from West Africa. Spanish ships could then transport specified numbers to Caracas, Maracaibo, Cartagena, Panama, Havana, and Veracruz—the last of these to receive just 250 slaves a year, a handful of which probably made it to Campeche.[42]

Thus, through the seventeenth century Yucatan's slaves continued to make the Middle Passage on Portuguese ships, joined in the late seventeenth and eighteenth centuries by ships flying northern European flags. The most significant of these European powers was England, both in the larger terms of the trade to Spanish America and in the narrower terms of Afro-Yucatec history. Asiento contracts between the Spanish crown and English companies began in 1663 and started being filled in 1672. For eighty years after this date, the Royal African Company, its sister organization the South Sea Company, and numerous private English (later British) traders supplied the Spanish colonies with slaves from Africa. After its seizure in 1655, Jamaica became the hub of British slave trading to Spanish colonists. Slave-trade historian Colin Palmer has estimated that during the thirty-year period of the South Sea Company's asiento (1713–43), British ships introduced some seventy-five thousand Africans into Spanish America. Campeche was included in this trade, and in the years 1725 to 1739 licensed British ships legally sold a total of 805 slaves in the Yucatec port, an average of 54 per year and 36 per ship. Adding illegal importation to this figure would put the total at more like nine hundred, or sixty per year. Figures like this cannot be extrapolated across the decades, as war, politics, and natural disasters frequently interrupted the trade. Yet seldom were official figures real totals, as unlicensed British merchants did a brisk business in trading slaves for logwood in and south of Campeche—before, during, and after the period of the South Sea Company's asiento. When Spanish officials intercepted such illegal business they sold the slaves at auction in town; in 1725, British agents in Jamaica filed a formal complaint against Campeche officials for failing to turn over the proceeds of such sales, as they were (unrealistically) obliged to do under the asiento contract.[43]

The British never classified Campeche as a major market, always treating it as a secondary-level *factoria* ["factory," or permanent trading office]. But the Spanish crown officially recognized the port as one where British agents could sell slaves, and from the late seventeenth to early nineteenth centuries there were British merchants in Campeche—as well as in Merida and later in Bacalar—trading in slaves both inside and outside the formal system.[44] In the seventeenth century a London-born merchant named Diego Joseph Bear sold slaves in the capital. Likewise, Peter Williams (aka don Pedro de los Guillermos) was in the slave trade with a Thomas Book. Book brought slaves in from Belize and up through Bacalar-at-Chunhuhub, where he was partly based (see Map 1.2), and they were sold in twos and threes in Merida, where Williams lived (he had previously traded slaves in Havana, and was married to a Spanish woman).[45] In the 1730s, the British slave-trade agents in Campeche were David Campbell and William Orem (known to locals as don Guillermo Orem).[46] At the turn of the nineteenth century a Joseph William Bates (aka don José Guillermo Bates) and a Robert Thompson (aka don Roberto Tonsom, with various spelling variants of his surname) worked with the colonial authorities in Merida interrogating African slaves seized or escaped from English settlements in Belize.[47] Thompson was listed in the 1796 census of foreigners as don Roberto Thomson and described as a thirty-three-year-old Irish merchant who had come to Yucatan from Jamaica fifteen years earlier. Bates was not listed in this census as he was not considered a foreigner, having been born in Yucatan; in 1766 his father Joseph (aka Doctor don José Bates) had come from Jamaica to Yucatan, where the doctor's three surviving sons became integrated into the local elite and made their mark on Yucatec history. Thompson and at least one of the Bates sons also sold slaves in Yucatan, and were thus considered useful by local Spanish officials for their knowledge of the slave trade and their familiarity with British-traded Africans, as well as their bilingualism.[48]

Campeche was the most common point of entry into Yucatan for Africans throughout the colonial period. Even after the British asiento ended (effectively by 1740), and the monopoly system was dissolved by the crown, Spanish and other trading companies brought small numbers of slaves into Campeche.[49] But, as the activities of Book, Bates, and Thompson illustrate, even prior to its resettlement in its original location in 1729, there was also significant traffic through the small and relatively isolated Spanish town of Bacalar, located in the southeast corner of the peninsula close to the border with the British territory of Belize. Indicative of its role as a slave-trading border town was the fact that by 1779 Bacalar and its district had the third highest number of *negros* in the colony, after Campeche and Merida—although these only numbered 55, along with 208 pardos or free-coloreds, out of a town and district population of just over 4,000.[50]

Some of Bacalar's pardos were like Manuel Bolio, an African-born free *negro* who moved to Bacalar from Merida in the 1760s to find work, after a few years moving briefly to Havana and then further down the Caribbean basin to Cartagena.[51] But other Africans, free and enslaved, came up from Belize. The intensification of British logging activity in Belize during the course of the eighteenth century increased the number of British settlers and their African slaves in the region, inspired the Spanish resettlement of Bacalar in 1729 and its subsequent fortification, and fostered both Maya–British and Spanish–British hostilities. The first phase of the history of the Yucatan–Belize frontier (1655–1722) had been characterized by the growing informal settlement of English loggers and their African slaves. During these decades the English (later British) government was unwilling to extend official recognition and support to what Governor Modyford of Jamaica called (in 1670, when there were some seven hundred settlers in Belize) these "new sucking [sic] colonies." At the same time, Spain was unable to assert its claim on the region; the original site of Bacalar was abandoned between about 1648 and 1729, and the Yucatec government was distracted by Maya revolt in the southwest in the 1660s, by the war against the Itza Maya kingdom in the 1690s, and by subsequent attempts to establish a colony in the Petén. A 1695 attack on the main English settlement in Belize, on Cayo Cocina, was claimed as a success by its leader (Capt. Francisco de Hariza, the senior official in Bacalar), but there is no evidence that Hariza actually engaged the loggers.[52]

The second phase (1722–1812) was marked by a steady series of violent attempts by Spaniards in Yucatan to destroy British Belize once and for all. The history of the Yucatan–Belize frontier has been little studied and poorly understood; Spaniards and Britons threatened each other's settlements to a degree that was taken very seriously at the time, and for a century beginning in the 1720s there was more violence and—in spite of such hostilities—more trade and movement across the border than has been recognized.[53] Afro-Yucatecans and Africans in Belize were closely caught up in the border's drama and conflict—as refugees, as combatants, and as the spoils of war. As the Sosa case illustrates, under royal license, Spanish bands raided British settlements along the Belize River, taking African slaves as war booty and selling them in Yucatan. If these resales were conducted legally, they took place publicly in Merida; if illegal, they occurred privately where there was demand, which was primarily Merida and Campeche. In 1722, viceregal officials in Mexico City warned that captured foreign loggers would be condemned to work as slaves in the Mexican mines. In 1727, British "pirates" from Belize, accompanied by Mosquito natives, attacked Maya villages as far as Chunhuhub, resulting in a formal demand issued by the Spanish crown the following year for full British evacuation. Spanish threats were backed up in 1733 and 1737 in the form of attacks on Belize initiated by Yucatec governors Figueroa and Salcedo. British settlements were sacked in 1745, and a major assault on Belize in 1747 forced the British to retreat to the colony of Black River at Cape Honduras; when they returned in 1749, Belize was formally placed under the Black River superintendency. Formal war between Britain and Spain, begun in 1739 following the Jenkins' Ear incident, had ended in 1748, but that did not stop Spaniards from making major descents into Belize in 1752 and 1754 (when Spaniards suffered a rare outright defeat), and minor raids (like Sosa's in 1759).

In 1761 Spain joined the Seven Years War, losing Cuba to the British the following year; in the 1763 Treaty of Paris, in which Cuba was returned in exchange for Florida, Spanish sovereignty over Belize was recognized but—more importantly—British loggers were granted the right to live and work in Belize. Despite this, on December 29, 1763, Governor Estenoz ordered British loggers to retreat from the Hondo River back to the Belize River, dispatching militia forces (including pardo companies) south to back up the demand. But no hostilities ensued; five or six hundred loggers relocated farther south and initiated diplomatic proceedings, which resulted by September 1764 in Madrid commanding Governor Estenoz to rescind his order and permit the loggers to move back up to the Hondo River. This they did, while British ships sat off the Belizean coast, and in 1765 a British naval lieutenant named James Cook (not his famous namesake) was received by Estenoz's successor in Merida with assurances of peace.[54]

Sporadic minor raids continued until 1779, when Spain and Britain again went to war. When the Yucatec governor was ordered to attack British settlements south of the Hondo River, he organized a series of autumn raids carried out from Bacalar. These caused considerable damage as far south as the Sibun River—and reaped a booty that included dozens of African slaves. During Christmas week of that year fifteen Africans were branded "YR" (for Yucatán and Rey, the king), and then auctioned off in the courtyard of the *Palacio de Gobierno* in the heart of Merida. The governor ordered that the new owners rename the slaves, as they were recorded at auction with their English and African names. There was another auction in February (1780) and further sales in April. Whole families, seized from logging settlements and ranches along the Sibun river, were sold to new owners in Merida.[55] From December 28, 1779, through the end of June 1780, these owners brought a total of forty-one slaves to be baptized in Merida's Jesús parish church, almost all stating Cayo Cocina as the place of origin (Cay Kitchen or Key Kitchen, apparently pronounced by the Afro-Belizeans as "Kikichin," lay just off the Belizean coast; officially named St. George's Cay, it was the main British settlement until the 1779 attack). Cay Kitchen slaves continued to appear in the city's baptism records to 1784, creating the last spike in slave imports into the colony and one of the biggest spikes in its history.[56]

The Yucatec invasion of Belize in 1779 forced the British to abandon all their settlements there until 1784. The Anglo–Spanish treaties of 1783 and 1786, which confirmed British logging rights between the Hondo and Belize rivers, and extended those rights to the Sibun River, might appear to have sacrificed the efforts of the Yucatecans on the altar of larger strategic concerns (just as the Treaty of Paris had done in 1763). The Belize of the late 1780s and 1790s was closer than ever to a formal British colony, and now had its own superintendent and a small garrison of troops. Yet the ongoing marginalization of Belize in British strategic policy in the area meant that the logging settlements continued to represent less a threat than an opportunity for pillage and plunder. Plundered British property primarily took the form of black slaves; by 1760 the majority of the Belizean population was black—three-quarters was by 1800—and most of these Afro-Belizeans were slaves.[57]

The final Spanish attempt to oust the British from Belize ended in failure with the defeat of Spanish forces at St. George's Cay (Cayo Cocina) in 1798. This defeat was a turning point, proving to be the last major Spanish assault on Belize. After 1798, there was ongoing frontier violence, but it was sporadic, and the planned major attacks never materialized. In 1801 the British managed to build a battery on Isla Mujeres, but a surprise night attack by militiamen from Merida and Tizimin put the British to flight in their frigate, leaving the Yucatec soldiers in possession of a flag and "five pieces of very good artillery."[58] The Governor of Yucatan devised a major attack on Belize in 1803, and over the next two years worked to fine-tune the plan and acquire thousands of rifles, cannonballs, and sabres for "the projected expedition against Wallix"; in the end, the weapons were used against insurgents in Mexico, not against the British in Belize.[59]

As they had done for much of the previous century, in the first decade of the nineteenth century officials in Bacalar continued to grant *pasaportes* to junior officers to take captured Belizean slaves up to Merida, where the soldiers received a percentage of their appraised value, effectively selling the Africans to Yucatan's colonial administration. For example, on April 4, 1801, such a passport was written out for Corporal Pantaleon Silva to take to the city "two *negros* and a mulatto, English who have come up from the settlements in Belize [Walix]"; a week later Corporal Juan Gómez was given a similar license to transport "four *negros* from the English settlements and a fugitive slave of a Campeche resident, don Pedro Arguelles." All six of the *negros* had voluntarily fled owners in Belize and subsequently been arrested near or in the town of Bacalar.[60]

The century-long use of African slaves as pawns and booty in this frontier war would not last long into the nineteenth century; the British outlawed the slave trade in 1807 (Mexico abolished slavery in 1829). When in 1812 three British ships under John Coatguelwin (as he appears in the Spanish records) sailed into the mouth of the Hondo River and announced that the Belizean border had shifted a tad northward, the Yucatecans merely protested.[61] In the third stage of the frontier's history (1812–62), there would be none of the Spanish assaults on British settlements and slave raids by Yucatecans that had characterized the border in the previous century.

The British role in the slave trade into and within Yucatan is therefore significant for several reasons. First, British logging settlements helped create a Yucatan–Belize border south of Bacalar, opening up an entry point for

African slaves that served as an alternative to Campeche. Second, the British connection made Yucatan unique among mainland Spanish colonies, placing it in some respects as much within a British–Spanish Caribbean orbit as within the Mexico-centered orbit of New Spain. Finally, and consequently, Afro-Yucatecan identities and experiences were profoundly altered during the course of the eighteenth century. Striking evidence of this impact can be found in the baptism records of adult African slaves in Merida. A full presentation of this evidence is in Chapter Six, but suffice to note here that beginning in the 1750s roughly half of these adults arriving annually in Merida had come not from Africa but from the British Empire—meaning they were either born in the empire (mostly in Jamaica or Belize, but also the North American colonies and even England itself) or they were born in Africa but spent sufficient years in a British colony to consider it their native place of origin.[62]

The cases mentioned above of Afro-Yucatecans originating in Belize do not illustrate the sole means whereby Africans entered the Spanish colony, but they do reflect an important dimension to the demographic and historical structure of the slave trade in the peninsula. The fact that the captured slaves ended up being sold in Merida reflects the centrality of the city to the Spanish community—and thus by extension the subordinate African community—in the province. Likewise the roles of Bacalar and Campeche as gateways to the colony help explain the African presence there; the other Spanish town in Yucatan, Valladolid, which was neither a gateway nor a provincial capital, had a negligible African population.[63]

Although Bacalar and Campeche were the gateways through which enslaved Africans entered the colony, the Spanish population of Bacalar was too small to sustain a regular slave market. Rather it was in Campeche and Merida, the two major Spanish settlements in the peninsula, where slaves were sold. Local transactions of slaves between Spanish owners took place in Campeche or Merida at an average rate of one every few weeks (in the 1660s, tax receipts from local slave sales came to 8% of all sales tax revenue in the colony; see Appendix D). All auctions of "king's slaves" (that is, slaves seized under license from the British) were held in the capital city of Merida. A very late example of such an auction is one held on the morning of December 1, 1792. Present at the event were two black slaves, seized from English owners in Belize, where they were known as "Pleto" and "Coiys" (presumably Plato and Gaius), five Spanish officials (the adviser to the governor-intendant; the administration's treasurer; accountant; and fiscal; and the notary), and a town crier (a bilingual Maya man named Isidoro). Isidoro repeatedly demanded whether there was "anybody who wishes to make a bid on two black English slaves of the king's who hereby appear, with the highest bid made to be accepted at noon on this day?" After a while Lieutenant don Toribio del Mazo, acting as agent for his uncle, Bishop Piña y Mazo, bid four hundred pesos for the pair (don Toribio was at the time under investigation as prime suspect in the assassination of the intendant governor six months earlier, a scandal that must have been in the back of the minds of everyone save the Afro-Belizeans). At noon, Isidoro asked, "Four hundred pesos is given for these two *negros*; will anyone pay more, will anyone say more?" As there was "nobody who will pay, nor say, more, at one, at two, at the third, *buena*, buena, buena"—the auction was closed. Nine days later, as no higher bidder had come forth and as don Toribio's uncle had produced the four hundred pesos, the governor's office completed the paperwork, certifying that the bishop had taken possession of the two African men, and the royal treasury had received the funds. From the four hundred pesos was taken six reales in notarial fees, and unspecified sums for the local sales tax and for "the expenses incurred in the maintenance" of the slaves.[64]

This example evokes well the late colonial ritual of arrival and transfer for Africans in Yucatan, omitting two details. One was the branding of "YR" on each slave's shoulder, and would have occurred before the auction, had it taken place at all (as mentioned earlier, the burning of the king's brand was noted in the records of the great slave auction of Christmas 1779, but there is no mention of branding at the two-slave sale of thirteen years later). The other ritual was that of baptism; probably sometime during 1793, the bishop would have had Plato and Gaius baptized as Catholics and given Spanish Christian names in the Jesús María church in central Merida, a formal admission into Spanish society (discussed further in the next chapter).

This brings us to the final questions of this chapter. We have seen how Africans came as slaves to Yucatan, and where they were sold; where in the province did these involuntary colonists settle? How did these settlement patterns change as the Afro-Yucatecan population itself changed?

A BRIEF DEMOGRAPHY

As mentioned above, the early colony of Yucatan covered but a portion of the peninsula, centered in the northwest around the provincial capital of Merida, established in 1542. Not long after Merida's founding, a report prepared for the archbishop in Mexico City described the Yucatec capital as a city primarily inhabited by domesticated animals and "Indians" and featuring "100 houses and 190 Spaniards, 150 [African] slaves, 100 horses, 20 *mestizos*, and a very few mulattoes, not even 10."[65] By 1570 the Spanish population of the entire colony may still only have been four hundred, while there were perhaps three hundred Africans and a couple of dozen pardos and mulattoes. By contrast the Maya population, despite a demographic disaster that may have reduced its numbers by 90% during the sixteenth century, stood at over 200,000 in that year.[66]

The Spanish conquest of Yucatan had thus brought three races together in an approximate Spanish–African–Maya ratio of 1:1:500. If only "pure-blooded" residents of the colony are counted, the changes in this ratio during the seventeenth and eighteenth centuries are not very dramatic, reflecting a gradual growth in the small Spanish population, virtually no relative growth in the number of *negros*, and the failure of the Maya population to recover from demographic disaster until the late colonial period. However, when the mixed-race population is taken into account, a dramatic demographic shift emerges, beginning in the early seventeenth century. By mid-century, while some estimates put *negro* numbers at five hundred (and Spanish numbers at little more), the mulatto and pardo population had exploded to over fifteen thousand (see Tables 1.2 and 1.3), the majority of whom were free. As the indigenous population had continued to fall, there was now one free-colored Afro-Yucatecan for every ten Mayas.

The increasing outnumbering of African slaves by free coloreds happened in the city and, even more so, in the countryside. For example, marriage and death records for Afro-Yucatecans in late seventeenth-century Merida list ten times as many free residents as enslaved ones; the 1700 census of rural *pueblos* [small towns and villages governed by Maya town councils] details 325 Afro-Yucatecans, of which only 3 men were classified as free *negros* and 2 women as slaves.[67] There were no doubt more black rural residents, free and enslaved, than this in 1700, but the point is clear; by the turn of the eighteenth century, the Spanish–African–Maya ratio (with mestizos included under "Spanish" and free coloreds included under "African") was more like 1:1:8, as much due to the growth in the mixed-race population as due to the slowness of Maya demographic recovery.

Furthermore, Maya demographic recovery took place partially through increased miscegenation, to some extent with Spaniards but more with Afro-Yucatecans; as we shall see in subsequent chapters, late colonial Maya villages were, in demographic and biological terms, Afro-Maya communities. So while census records indicate that 13% of the colony's population was Afro-Yucatecan in the eighteenth century, there were actually many more inhabitants with some African ancestry. I suspect that by 1821, most people in Yucatan had an African ancestor.

The trend toward miscegenation or *mestizaje* thus continued in the eighteenth century. The Spanish population grew but remained a definite minority, while the numbers of African slaves actually fell according to some estimates, picking up somewhat with the local sugar boom after 1770 and with the liberalization of the slave trade in New Spain in 1784.[68] Meanwhile, by the mid-eighteenth century, there were tens of thousands of pardos and mulattoes and Spanish–Maya mestizos. The final decades of colonial rule saw a population boom in all ethnic sectors, but again this was most pronounced among pardos and mestizos. Afro-Yucatecans of all kinds grew from constituting 8.8% of the province's population in 1779 to 12.4%

TABLE 1.2 Afro-Yucatecan population estimates, 1570–1805

Year	Negros	Pardos/ Mulattoes	All	Source
1570	265	20		[A]
1574			500	[G]
1600	500			[G]
1605		350		[C]
1618			2,000	[G]
1646	497	15,770		[A]
1742	274	35,712		[A]
1779	1,490	17,605		[P]
1790	2,800	43,426		[F]
1791			45,201	DHY/[R]
1805			28,100	[C]

Sources: [A] Aguirre Beltrán (1989: 197–222); [G] García Bernal (1978: 154–58); [C] Cook and Borah (1974: 79, 95); [P] Patch (1993: 234); [F] Farriss (1984: 65); DHY, I: 99; [R] Rubio Mañé (1942, I: 250).

TABLE 1.3 The Afro-Yucatecan population in comparative context: Afro-Yucatecans in relation to the population of colonial Yucatan

Year	Mayas	Spaniards and Mestizos	Negros, Pardos, and Mulattoes (%)	Source
c.1580	170,000	500	500 (0.3)	[C]/[G]
c.1645	200,000	16,000	16,000 (6.9)	[A]/[G]
c.1725	190,000	37,000	36,000 (13.7)	[A]
c.1790	270,000	55,000	45,000 (12.2)	DHY/[R]

Sources: [C] Cook and Borah (1974: 77); [G] García Bernal (1978: 151, 155–56, 160); [A] Aguirre Beltrán (1989: 212–22); DHY, I: 99; [R] Rubio Mañé (1942, I: 250).

by 1791, when by some estimates they therefore outnumbered Spaniards. The population boom was least pronounced among *negros*, who by this time constituted less than 1% of the total population in the colony.[69] Most incoming Africans ended up in Campeche or Merida, but even there they were a small minority; in eighteenth-century Merida, black adults were on average only 5.3% of Afro-Yucatecans baptized each year.[70] By the time the church authorized a series of censuses in the final two decades of colonial rule, *negros* had effectively disappeared; individuals who may once have been categorized as black were now viewed as part of the pardo/mulatto population (see Appendix B). At the same time, free coloreds had become a presence throughout the colony; in the 1700 census, 55% (29/53) of rural pueblos contained Afro-Yucatecans (Table B.1), but by the census at the beginning of the nineteenth century, that figure had risen to 96% (49/51) (Table B.2).

Reflecting on the paucity of black residents in rural communities in the 1700 census, Cristina García Bernal (the prominent Spanish historian of colonial Yucatan) remarked thirty years ago that "the role of the *negro* was of very little importance in Yucatan."[71] Demographic estimates would seem to support such a generalization (taking it at face value as a reference to blacks, not mulattoes). Nevertheless, as we have seen, Africans continued to be imported into the peninsula as slaves right through the colonial period. Indeed, Gonzalo Aguirre Beltrán (the pioneering historian of Afro-Mexico) singled out the marginalized regions of Tabasco, Campeche, and northwest Yucatan as being the only part of New Spain after the mid-eighteenth century where there was there still a demand for newly imported African slaves.[72] In my view, Aguirre Beltrán's analysis is misleading; as I shall argue in the next chapter, slavery declined as an institution in the final decades of colonial rule in Yucatan as it did throughout New Spain. Yet the role played by Belize as a source of African labor in the late eighteenth century meant that black men and women continued to enter Yucatan in steady numbers, even if many were subsequently classified as servants rather than slaves. This apparent paradox—Yucatan as an exception to the decline in the African slave trade in New Spain and yet a colony where African slaves were "of very little importance"—may be resolved by emphasizing three points.

The first point is that Africans, especially slaves and free *negros*, were not evenly distributed throughout the colony; thus their role and social significance varied greatly between town and countryside and from district to district. As Map 1.3 / Table 1.4 demonstrate with respect to the late colonial period, the Spanish town and surrounding district of Campeche contained the vast majority of the colony's black residents and more of its pardos and mulattoes than any other region. As the peninsula had no reliable road connecting it to the outside world, the colony was effectively an island, making the port of Campeche Yucatan's gateway; this fact helps explain why Campeche played such a central role in Afro-Yucatecan history. As the provincial capital, Merida was also a logical place for Africans to be concentrated. Indeed, the districts of Merida and Campeche, combined with the three districts that more or less lay between them (Camino Real, Hunucma, and Sierra), contained 62.8% of the colony's free coloreds in 1779 and 90.7% of its black residents. The vast majority of the late colonial Afro-Yucatecan population lived within a sweep of settlements, running from Campeche to Merida to Tizimin, that might be called the *colored crescent* (also see Map 4.1 in Chapter Four; Afro-Yucatecan Campeche and Merida are discussed primarily in Chapter Six).

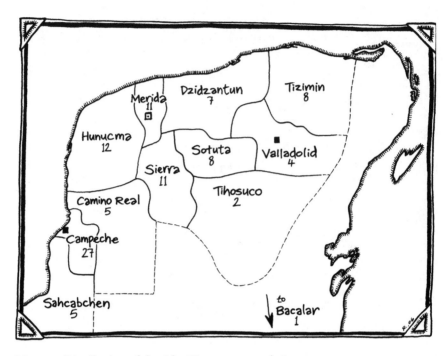

Map 1.3 Distribution of the Afro-Yucatecan population, 1779

TABLE 1.4 Distribution of the Afro-Yucatecan population, 1779

Political district	Negros (%)	Pardos/Mulattoes (%)	Both (%)
Sahcabchen	0.7	5.0	4.6
Campeche	73.9	22.9	26.9
Camino Real	0.8	5.4	5.0
Hunucma	0.2	12.4	11.5
Merida	15.4	10.1	10.5
Sierra	0.4	12.0	11.1
Dzidzantun	2.1	7.7	7.3
Sotuta	0.4	8.7	8.0
Tihosuco	0.4	2.0	1.8
Valladolid	0.9	3.9	3.7
Tizimin	0.9	8.7	8.1
Bacalar	3.7	1.2	1.4
Total	100	100	100

Source: Data presented in Patch (1993: 235) from the census in AGI-México 3061.

Note: The numbers in the map are rounded off from the percentages in the far right column of the table (representing the total Afro-Yucatecan population).

As mentioned above, free coloreds did not just settle and have children in Merida and Campeche, but were omnipresent in the colony by the end of the eighteenth century (when free blacks, pardos, and mulattoes tended to be lumped together in the pardo category). To be sure, numbers remained small compared to the Maya majority (for example, Afro-Yucatecans averaged 5.9% in rural parishes in 1806 compared to 80.1% for Mayas). But there were pardos in the head-community [*cabecera*] of almost every parish as well as in most subject communities. Whereas mestizos had significantly outnumbered Afro-Yucatecans in the 1700 census, a century later there were almost as many pardos as mestizos in most parishes—and often more pardos than Spaniards. How these demographic trends affected the way that Afro-Yucatecans lived and worked is explored in Chapters Four and Five; how it affected the development of Afro-Yucatecan communities is the subject of Chapter Six.

The distribution, both geographic and diachronic, of Afro-Yucatecans is thus the first of three points that helps explain why free and enslaved blacks remained important throughout the colonial period, despite being increasingly outnumbered by pardos and mulattoes. The second point involves Afro-Yucatecan labor roles. As mentioned above, and as subsequent chapters show in detail, there was not a large population of plantation slaves in Yucatan that was distinct from the urban black community; in terms of work, Afro-Yucatecans, black and mulatto, free and enslaved, tended to share similar or comparable occupations and experiences.

The third point relates to Spanish concepts of race and racial categories. So far I have used racial terminology with little explanation; indeed, Spanish terms like *pardo* are often treated as though they were concrete racial categories in a caste system, and historians have tended to translate the term *casta* as "caste" and to take too literally Spanish notions of how colonial society was racially divided. However, as I shall discuss in Chapter Three, a casta label was a socioracial category that was too elastic and vague to justify the terms *caste* and *system*. There was a fundamental and permanent disjuncture between Spanish ideas on race and rank, and the realities of colonial society; more than that, such a disjuncture was at the heart of how Spaniards (and, to some degree, Afro-Yucatecans themselves) viewed and used casta categories. In other words, Spaniards appeared to attach casta labels to all the middle people between Spaniards and Mayas as though Yucatan's inhabitants all shared a common understanding of those labels—when in reality their meaning shifted from year to year, between communities, among individuals, and even according to the moment. This had myriad implications, but I shall just make one point here: the distinction between *negro* and colored became increasingly blurred as the nineteenth century approached; thus while *negro* numbers seem insignificant compared to those of pardos and mulattoes, the increasing inclusion of all Afro-Yucatecans in the pardo category makes it hard for us to discount any sector of the Afro-Yucatecan population. Inclusionism, indeed, is at the heart of this study.

In sum, an African population that began in Yucatan as a few hundred *negro* slaves in the mid-sixteenth century ended in the early nineteenth as tens of thousands of Afro-Yucatecans, almost all of them free pardos or mulattoes. Afro-Yucatecans, like all non-Mayas, remained greatly outnumbered by the indigenous population. Africans arrived mostly on Portuguese ships in the early colonial period, and mostly on English ones in mid-to-late-colonial times. Some were brought as personal slaves or servants by Spaniards trav-

TABLE 1.5 The Afro-Yucatecan population in comparative context: Afro-American populations in eighteenth-century colonies

Region or colony	Population that was of African descent (%)	Source
Yucatan	12 (0.5 slaves)	Tables 1.2 and 1.3
OTHER SOCIETIES WITH SLAVES		
British American Northeast	7 (4 slaves)	Berlin
New Spain	9.7 (0.1 slaves)	Aguirre Beltrán
Central Mexico	11	Aguirre Beltrán
Papantla (Veracruz)	12	Frederick
Mendoza (Chile)	23	Lacoste
Rio de la Plata	28	Bernand
Buenos Aires/Córdoba	30 (24 slaves in B.A.)	Mallo
SLAVE SOCIETIES		
Chesapeake/Upper South	32 (30 slaves)	Berlin
Lowcountry/Lower South	51 (50 slaves)	Berlin
Louisiana	50 (50 slaves)	Berlin
Iguape (Brazil)	92 (54 slaves)	Barickman

Sources: Berlin (1998: 369–75; 2003: 272–79); Aguirre Beltrán (1989: 222, 230; New Spain estimates for 1793, Central Mexico for 1742); Frederick (2005: chap. 6; based on 1770s burial records); Lacoste (2003: 118, 145; based on a rough "one quarter" for 1739 and a 21% estimate for 1770); Bernand (2000: 95; figure for the viceroyalty, averaging estimates of 1778 and 1810); Mallo (2001: 312–13; I averaged similar estimates for Córdoba and Buenos Aires, all for 1778); Barickman (2003: 294; Iguape figures taken from an 1835 census, but I include them here as they contribute to the general contrast between plantation-based slave societies and societies with slaves). In some slave societies, slaves rose to as much as 75% of the total population (as in the Natchez district of Mississippi in the 1840s; Kaye 2007: 3).
Note: The "slaves" percentages are, like the other figures, percentages of the total population in each colony (not percentages just of the black/mulatto population).

eling to Yucatan from Spain. In the mid-to-late-eighteenth century, it was increasingly common for newly arrived free and enslaved blacks to have come from Belize, Jamaica, or other British possessions.

Between the founding of the colony in 1542 and the abolition of slavery in Mexico in 1829, it is probable that between ten thousand and twenty thousand African slaves were brought into Yucatan. Thus throughout its history, the colony was a society with slaves (like other Spanish American colonies), but it never became a slave society (as some European colonies did; see Table 1.5). In the larger context of the whole transatlantic slave trade, fifteen thousand is a tiny number, a mere 0.1% of the trade's total—and only 5% of the trade into colonial Mexico.[73]

But the number was significant enough in Yucatan, especially considering the degree to which incoming Africans contributed to mestizaje, or the race-mixing dynamic, in the colony.[74] We have already seen how population numbers suggest high levels of miscegenation; subsequent chapters will detail how rapidly Afro-Yucatecans contributed to the creation of multiracial communities in the colony. People of African descent were comparable in number to Spaniards throughout the colonial period and never far behind the Spanish-Maya mestizo population (which would continue to gradually absorb much of the Afro-Yucatecan population). Sebastián Toral arrived as an enslaved African in the involuntary service of the first Spanish settlers; he died as a free member of that settler community, an Afro-Yucatecan whose descendents became part of the permanent demographic fabric of the peninsula.

CHAPTER TWO

People as Property

I have suffered much poverty and privation [and] had many expenses
and losses, having another just the other day, when a black man that I
left in my benefice died on me.
　　　—Yucatec clergyman Andrés de Mexía, 1590[1]

I have known the governor for a long time, him as well as the blacks
Francisco Antonio and Juan Criollo; and I know that they are slaves of
the governor's, his own property, which he brought from the Indies when
he came from there, and they are included in the Royal License [to travel]
because I knew them in the province of Venezuela and other parts of the
Indies, and in these kingdoms I have always seen him treat them as his
slaves, and they are reputed and known to be had and held as such.
　　　—witness in Spain on the relationship between Yucatec Governor
　　　　　Nuñez de Melián and his two slaves, 1643[2]

We have all the necessary rights to a property from which we have been
illegally dispossessed.
　　　—Slave owners protesting abolition, Villa del Carmen, 1831[3]

THE STORY OF MARÍA DOLORES MOLINA

In 1818 doña María Joaquina Molina, of the elite Spanish Yucatecan dynasty of the Molinas, passed away. The inventory of her impressive estate,
worth almost ten thousand pesos, took nearly two hundred pages to detail.
Buried within the inventory was a category titled *Piezas de Esclavo*. The term
pieza, literally meaning "piece" or (as a hunting term) "catch," was used
throughout the empire. A pieza was a standard able-bodied slave, such as a
healthy young man; others, depending on sex, age, health, and degree of
Hispanization and skill, were classified as fractions of a pieza.[4] In the
Molina inventory these fractions were implied by peso values: "a *negra*
named María Dolores" was valued at 356 pesos; "a little mulatta of about
3 years old, daughter of the above" was valued at 100 pesos; and "a little

African boy [*un negrito Bosal*] named José Joaquin of about 9 years old—200 pesos."[5]

That two of Molina's Africans, María Dolores and the small boy José Joaquin, were named after their owner reflects the paradox inherent to the notion of people as personal property—the names simultaneously humanized and objectified the slaves. Scholars of slavery in the Americas have tended to view the naming of slaves as dehumanizing and contemptuous. We shall see below that while naming patterns certainly functioned as a system of marking, the assigning of an owner's name to a slave was an extension of a similar custom for naming one's own children—a proprietary but not necessarily dehumanizing tradition. In Yucatan such names also identified their recipients as Christian or soon-to-be-Christian members of the Spanish-speaking world—a world of gross inequity where people could be property, but a human world nonetheless.

The peso values of slaves were also an integral part of their assigned identities. María Dolores' age meant that she could be given, in effect, a performance evaluation, her work record converted to a specific peso value. Children, on the other hand, such as María Dolores's own three-year-old daughter, were given round-number values based on their sex and their place of birth; *bozal* or *bosal* meant African-born, and implied an inferior degree of Hispanization, although José Joaquin's early abduction to the New World meant his bozal status did not offset the potential advantage of his sex.

Spain's most prominent scholar of Yucatan has observed that people of African descent were seen by Spaniards as a group apart, "suffering an obvious segregation [*una evidente segregación*] within Yucatec society."[6] Unlike the Spanish *segregación*, the English term "segregation," evoking as it does the history of governmental policies toward blacks in the United States, may be too strong a word to apply to colonial Yucatan. Certainly the crown issued edicts that were broadly segregationist, forbidding Africans to live among or marry non-Africans, and Spanish settlers condoned such laws. But, as we shall see in the next chapter, the state had difficulties defining the various populations of the colonies, let alone keeping them apart. Social reality, as much as state weakness, made segregation an imperial pipe dream. Slaves and others of African descent were subordinated to Spanish owners and masters, and thus Afro-Yucatecans as a roughly defined group were subordinated to Spaniards within Yucatec society; but Afro-Yucatecans were attached to that society and thus an inseparable part of it. With respect to slaves, this status of attached subordination is most obviously expressed in Spanish records through the language of proprietorship.

This chapter, then, examines the master-slave dynamic through a series of four closely related topics: (1) the categorization and evaluation of slaves as items of property; (2) slave-naming patterns and their implications; (3) the identity of the slave owners (who they were and why they owned slaves);

and (4) the abolition of slavery a decade after the death of doña María Joaquina Molina. Her will raises questions related to all these topics—how typical were the values and names given to her slaves, for example? To what extent can she be taken as representative of slave owners in the colony? Does her possession of slaves at the end of the colonial period indicate that slave-owning culture was as central to Spanish colonial society as it had been three centuries earlier?

ATTACHED SUBORDINATION

Let us return briefly to a story first introduced near the start of the previous chapter—that of the Sosa raid. The reader will recall that in 1759 five African slaves were brought to Merida from Belize, where they had been taken from their English owners by Capt. Sosa and his Spanish company raiding settlements on the Belize River. Shortly after arriving in the Yucatec capital, the Africans were assigned peso values. Their age, the sex of the two women, and the fact that all five spoke English, not Spanish, no doubt explains why the *negras* were determined to be worth a mere 100 pesos each and the *negros* only 150 pesos each; the blind man was deemed to have no value at all (see Table D.3 in Appendix D). That the slaves were soon sold for one hundred pesos more than their combined estimated worth may suggest that they had been undervalued; however, within a couple of years the price paid was called into question by the owner.

    In early 1761 it became apparent that the two old women were both seriously ill—one with a fistulous ulcer on her right thigh, "which she had been secretly hiding for at least three months," the other with "an abscess on her private parts." When the physician attending to them, a Franciscan friar named fray Juan Miguel de Quiñones, admitted to their owner that the women's recovery was not imminent and that the elder one was in mortal danger, the owner, don Lorenzo Villaelriego, petitioned the authorities for the return of part of the purchase price (at the time the royal treasury still held the money from the sale pending a tax evaluation and an investigation into the slaves' capture in Belize). Villaelriego had paid six hundred pesos for the four slaves, outbidding the canon of the cathedral, who had offered five hundred. Villaelriego now requested a refund of the additional hundred pesos; he was refused. In fray Juan Quiñones' testimony there are signs of a genuine regret that his medical efforts were in vain, that a human life could not be saved. For Villaelriego, however, the records reveal only that the tragedy was for him a financial one.[7] It is difficult to sympathize with the encomendero; after all, slaves were an investment, complete with the potential for financial return and the risk of a loss of capital. In his petition for a refund, Villaleriego does not mention that the other black woman, whom he had renamed María de la Luz, had given birth to a son the year after he had purchased her. The infant was baptized Joseph Dario, father unknown, in Merida's cathedral two days after Christmas, 1759; María de la Luz herself was baptized three weeks later "by oils," having earlier received an interim baptism "by water." Perhaps her pregnancy, or her owner's lack of attention to the matter, had delayed her formal appearance at the cathedral font.[8]

The proprietorial perspective behind Villaelriego's sense of loss over the death of a slave is commonly found in the historical record. One Spanish priest in late sixteenth-century Yucatan, lamenting the downward turn in his fortunes since being called before the Inquisition in Mexico City, pleaded for the sympathy of the inquisitors with the words: "After the year that has passed since I left home, I have had many expenses and losses, having another just the other day, when a *negro* that I left in my benefice died on me."[9] The priest, like Villaelriego and thousands of other Spaniards, highly valued African slaves. This value tended to be expressed more in economic terms than sentimental ones; slaves were possessions first, human beings second.

Yet the small-scale auxiliary nature of slavery in Yucatan meant that a slave's humanity was not necessarily eclipsed by his or her identity as a "piece" of property. When the time came to declare the value or ownership of slaves—for example, during the settling of an estate, during the drawing up of a ship's inventory in Campeche, or when refugee Belizean slaves were recategorized as slaves of the Spanish crown—their value to Spaniards was expressed in individualized terms. Africans were identified by name and often some physical description, in addition to monetary value. Spaniards sailing between Spain and Yucatan with black manservants or slaves usually named and described them in their travel documents, but never gave them monetary values.[10] This was in contrast to slaves inventoried as an anonymous number for the Middle Passage across the Atlantic; once in Yucatan, the numbered African was given a semblance of a mostly new personal identity. Africans in Yucatan retained some prior identity, and acquired some new aspects of identity, yet from the Spanish perspective their assigned status as property remained central to who slaves were.

For example, ships entering the port of Campeche listed any Africans on board not with the passengers, but with the cargo. In 1791 the *Nuestra Señora del Pilar* listed fourteen *negros* and negras along with 75 barrels of coffee and 103 pounds of cacao as its most valuable goods, all of which (and whom) were impounded by local officials pending an evaluation of taxes and fines because the captain could not produce "the necessary documents"; the Africans were not listed with the three passengers who were en route on the *Pilar* from Trinidad (Cuba) to Veracruz—a Spaniard, an Italian, and a German.[11]

The values assigned to doña María Joaquina Molina's slaves were fairly typical for the time, both in terms of range (100-400 pesos) and average (just over 200 pesos; see Table 2.1). My impression from working with

TABLE 2.1 Peso values of Afro-Yucatecan slaves, 1661–1829

	1661–64	1667–72	1678–1829	[1661–1829]
Average value of slave men	211	240	208	[215]
Average value of slave women	258	238	204	[223]
Average value of both	222	239	206	[216]

Source: Tables in Appendix D, which present detailed data and list the wide array of archival sources behind these numbers.

Note: The 1661–64 numbers are estimates based on tax amounts from 74 sales; 1667–72 numbers are calculated from 54 actual sales; 1678–1829 numbers are based on a variety of 64 sales, wills, and other records (representing a larger database of 168, which likewise produces an average of 206 pesos).

slave records is that women tended to be worth a tad more than men (this was true in Mexico City and Guanajuato, and thus probably across the viceroyalty of New Spain); Table 2.1 would seem to confirm this, although the better-evidenced late colonial portion of my database suggest that men and women were worth the same.[12] In the end, gender was but one of many evaluatory factors. When Spanish officials priced six Belizean slaves, arrested as escapees in Bacalar and acquired as state property by the Crown in 1801, their ages and health were placed against the importance of their professed trades or skills. One was given the solid value of 200 pesos "for his age and experience as a storekeeper, although he is lame in one foot," another rated at 215 pesos for being "a healthy 30-year-old and a cook by trade," and another valued at only 180 pesos because although he was a carpenter, he was 30 years old and "defective" in one finger and one toe. A young man offered for sale at the end of the colonial period for a very high price was billed as able to cook, make shoes, and lay bricks.[13]

Thus, slave values at a particular place and time tended to be governed by the type of labor for which slaves were sought. Because slaves were employed in Yucatan more as individuals in households and estates than as mass laborers on plantations, and their return as an investment was therefore gauged more in terms of service than fiscal profit, their market values were relatively low and stable for most of the colonial period. If the examples presented in Table 2.1 were charted by date, they would exhibit a bumpy flat line right through the last century and a half of colonial rule. Simply put, African slaves were never going to sell for high prices without a significant source of wealth and profit (such as the silver mines of northern Mexico and Bolivia) or a boom in some local commodity (such a boom would occur in Yucatan, in henequen, but not until long after African slavery had faded and been abolished). Indeed, Campechanos purchased slaves from English traders in the early eighteenth century not with pesos but with logwood—just 5 of 151 Africans sold in the port in 1730–33 were exchanged for cash—and logwood was hardly in the same profit league as silver and sugar.[14] English traders could buy an able-bodied slave in Jamaica and transport him or her for resale in Campeche for about 180 pesos; furthermore, they preferred to sell slaves for commodities (logwood in Campeche, cacao in Caracas, and so on), as they made additional profit on reselling those commodities.[15] These combined facts meant that traders were still motivated to bring Africans to Campeche even if the Yucatec market could only support prices as low as two hundred pesos for a healthy young slave.[16]

The many variables that determined slaves prices make it hard to systematically compare valuations in Yucatan with those made elsewhere in Spanish America. Table 2.2, however, helps make the point that the late colonial Yucatec economy supported slave prices that were generally lower than in more lucrative colonies, such as seventeenth-century Peru and Mexico.

A specific comparison with slave prices in the Jalapa and Orizaba regions of colonial Veracruz is also instructive. There a boom in the sugar industry in the late sixteenth and seventeenth centuries placed a premium on young African men, skilled or unskilled. In the final decades of the sixteenth century such *negros* were worth 400 pesos; values fluctuated in the seventeenth century, but around 1700 slaves still typically sold for 350 pesos if skilled, 325 if unskilled (see Table 2.2.). However, as sugar in Veracruz declined and the regional labor system continued to shift in late colonial times from *negro* slaves to mixed-race free-wage laborers, the value of enslaved Africans fell to levels comparable to those in Yucatan—with skilled and unskilled black men selling for 250 pesos or less. Also as in Yucatan, in late colonial Veracruz women were worth as much as men, if not more. Again, these patterns reflected changes in labor use, as Africans in Veracruz became increasingly likely to end up working as personal servants in circumstances characteristic of the African experience in Yucatan (although sugar was always more important to the Veracruz economy than it was to the Yucatec one, where late colonial sugar planters relied on Maya wage laborers, not African slaves).[17]

In fact, Yucatan saw something of a reverse trend relative to Veracruz. Yucatec slave prices became erratic in the final decades of colonial rule, with skilled domestic slaves in Merida selling for as much as four hundred pesos at the time of Independence in 1821; in the same year, an able-bodied young man was advertised at six hundred pesos.[18] However, there is no evidence that any slave was sold for more than four hundred pesos throughout the three centuries of black slavery in Yucatan. The appearance of higher prices in the 1820s was probably due to the scarcity of *negros* relative to the late colonial pardo population, although prices were not consistently high. Either way, as we shall see below, slavery as an institution had begun to wither in the colony some time before its official abolition in 1829, and inconsistent prices after 1800 probably reflected the erratic fluctuation of supply and demand that accompanied slavery's decline.

TABLE 2.2 A comparison of slave prices in some Spanish American colonies

Place	Time period	Price range (pesos)	Average price (pesos)
Yucatan	1661–1829	40–450	216
Mexico City	1520s	100–200	
Mexico City	1530s	100	
Mexico City	1550s	over 200	
Mexico City	1625–75		367
Mexico City and Guanajuato	1700–1750		268
Jalapa	1580s–1590s		403
Jalapa	1600s–1610s		359
Jalapa and Orizaba	1700	325–350	
Jalapa and Orizaba	1800		250
Nuevo León	1600		400
Nuevo León	1750		300
Nuevo León	1790		160
Havana and Santiago	1716–18		230
Caracas	1735	230–300	250
Cartagena	1715–19		180
Quito	1640s	330–350	
Central Peru	Late 1530s	100–250	
Central Peru	Late 1540s	150–300	
Central Peru	Late 1550s	250–500	
Pisco, Peru	1620	500–600	
Cuzco, Peru	1646–58	250–950	
Buenos Aires	1715–19		190

Sources: Yucatan: Table 2.1; Mexico City: Altman (1991: 437); Proctor (2003a: 49); Jalapa and Orizaba: Carroll (1991: 34, 75–76); Nuevo León: Gómez Danés (1996: 34–35) (details or verifiable data not provided); Havana and Santiago de Cuba, Cartagena, Buenos Aires: Palmer (1981: 123); Caracas: AGI-*Indiferente General* 2817 (average value of 199 slaves delivered by English traders; almost all were valued in the 230–300 peso range); Quito: Gauderman (2003: 86); central Peru: Lockhart (1994: 202) (these are typical prices that do not include the exceptionally skilled—master artisans, for example, sold for 700–1,000 pesos; p. 207); Pisco: Espinosa (1942 [1620]: 479); Cuzco: Tardieu (1998: 91–92) (based on a database of 30 slaves; one entry of 1,000, not included above, is for a woman and her daughter).

Slave sales are the most obvious way of illustrating the status of Africans as property. Specific sales were recorded for posterity, albeit consistently, in two ways: (1) the sale itself was notarized in Campeche or Merida (where the record remained); and (2) within a year or two of the transaction a 4% sales tax [an *alcabala*] was collected and noted in the Royal Treasury accounts, which were sent to Seville (where they remain to this day). Alcabala records in particular illustrate how on one level slaves were one among various categories of property; the tax on slave sales was listed among levies on the sale of houses in town, plots of land in the country, boats and shares of ships, and a range of imported merchandise—from all the wine sold in a year in a certain Merida tavern to a shipment of Maracaibo cacao unloaded in Campeche.[19]

Less obvious, and thus perhaps more revealing, ways are the giving of slaves as dowries and the mortgaging of slaves by their Spanish owners. Dowries were not recorded in the colonial period as a genre of document, but dowry details can sometimes be found in the testaments of the Spanish elite. For example, when don Iñigo de Mendoza y Magaña's son married the daughter of don Iñigo's business partner, the encomendero don Pedro de Cepeda y Lira, don Pedro provided a dowry that included a fourteen-year-old mulatta slave girl to be the bride's maidservant. Similarly, in 1720 Capt. don Felipe de Ayora y Argaiz gave a fifteen-year-old "mulatilla" named Salomé Ayora in dowry to his daughter doña Petrona, on the occasion of her marriage to don Nicolas Bermejo. Salomé had grown up in the Ayora household with doña Petrona, and one might reasonably speculate that the young bride and her slave-maid were related.[20] The significance of these dowries was not just economic (fungible items of property) but social (slaves acted as important status markers, as we shall see).

Surviving mortgage records from Merida are too scattered to reveal much in the way of patterns, beyond the simple fact that slaves were mortgaged in the capital from at least 1725 and as late as 1802. Those dates mark Merida's earliest and latest extant mortgage notes, the former recording an Angolan woman put up as collateral by a nun in the convent of Nuestra Señora de la Consolación, the latter notarizing a 150-peso mortgage on José Antonio Solano, owned by the cathedral archdeacon.[21]

Mortgage records from Campeche, on the other hand, have survived apparently in their entirety from the last half-century of the colonial period. Between 1768 and 1823 Campechanos had 1,336 mortgage contracts [*hipotecas*] notarized. The vast majority of these were for houses, either of stone or in the Maya style of wattle and daub [*cal y canto*], and for other landed properties (such as a cattle ranch or a cacao *hacienda* or estate). After 1799 other types of property increasingly feature in the records, mostly related to the economic activites of Campeche's port, such as warehouses [*bodegas*] and various kinds of boats (from *fragatas* to *goletas* to *bongos*, all named; one bongo, [a large canoe or barge], was named *True Love*, for example).

Interestingly, it is also after 1799 that slave mortgages cease to appear in the records. As Table 2.3 details, just nine Africans were mortgaged in six contracts in late colonial Campeche, all between 1773 and 1799 (representing 1.5% of mortgages up to 1799, or 0.7% of the full run of surviving mortgages of 1768–1823). Two of the six contracts were between family members (father and daughter; a woman and her uncle-in-law), and two

TABLE 2.3 Slave mortgages in Campeche, 1768–1823

Slave	Details	Year	Peso	Mortgage debtor (m); value and creditor (c)
Mariano, *negro*	Criollo, 20 years old (1st item), with a stone house on Calle de Guadalupe in Campeche (2nd item); settled 1780	1773	1,000	Don Josef Quintero and his wife, doña Rosa Lenteno (m); don Vicente Sarricolea (c)
María Dolores, negra		1781	400 and 4½ reales	Don José Quintero (m); his daughter doña Joaquina Quintero and her husband don José Roldara (c)
Matias, *negro*	Mortgagers and slave resident in Havana; creditor resident in Campeche	1785	92	Don Francisco Josef Bazquez and don Francisco Camacho (m); don Antonio Arolas (c)
Barbara Mazo, negra	A 2-month contract; to restructure a prior debt of 685 pesos 6 reales	1787	300	Don Agustín Mazo (m); don Tomás Riuz y Sanz (c)
Rafaela and Rita Gertrúdiz, negras	Together with household furniture and store merchandise	1796	477 and 4 reales	Doña Rudecinda Ponce de León (m); don Buenaventura Gualva, her husband's uncle (c)
Three unnamed negras, a mother and her two daughters	A 2-year contract	1799	500	Doña María Saragosa Barberis (m); Capt. don Manuel Anselmo López Carta (c)

Source: AGEC-*Registro Público de la Propriedad* (*Fondo Gobernación*), 2, 1: ff. 4v, 36, 81, 106; 2, 2: ff. 66v, 87v-88.

bundled slaves in with nonhuman collateral (in one case, the house where the slave was presumably a domestic servant; in the other, the furniture and merchandise of the home and shop where the slaves worked). One contract related to a prior loan, with the implication that the slave, Barbara Mazo, was being put up as collateral in lieu of a payment that was due or overdue; the creditor took the slave for three-hundred pesos, a high but not implausible market value for an enslaved African woman in late eighteenth-century Campeche, so perhaps he anticipated having to keep her when the contract expired. The impact on mortgaged slaves is not made clear in these contracts, but no doubt some were forced to relocate as if they had been sold. An African named Matias, for example, was mortgaged to a creditor in Campeche by his owners in Havana; if the Cubans defaulted, Matias might have been brought to Campeche.[22]

The existence of slave mortgages confirms that owned Africans were viewed both at individual and institutional levels as items of property. But the small numbers of such mortgages, and their disappearance after 1799, suggest that slaves were either considered poor-risk properties or viewed as a different type of property—which, as human beings, they obviously were. I suspect that both explanations are applicable, but mostly the latter. Certainly slaves were poor-risk fungible goods because they could escape, but by the same token, they were portable; for this reason, Matias may have been more attractive to a Campeche creditor than, say, a house in Havana. Economic rationales alone do not explain why slaves were not a prefered form of collateral in the late colonial period; an equally (if not more) important factor was the culture of slave holding. As property, slaves appeared in a wide variety of economic transactions, business affairs, and legal documentation—sales, wills, dowries, mortgages, powers of attorney, debt settlement, punitive property seizures by the state, and so on. But as human individuals connected through personal relationships with owners, slaves contributed to the complexity and particular characteristics of such business.[23] This was, after all, not a slave society but a society with slaves—not mass or plantation slaves, but personal auxiliaries.

NAMING PROPERTY

One revealing aspect of the culture of slave owning was that of naming patterns. Giving a name to a piece of property does not humanize it (Campechanos named their boats, after all),[24] but name choices do reflect a society's conceptions of property categories. I noted above that doña María Joaquina Molina had named her slaves María Dolores and José Joaquin after herself, an act that simultaneously humanized and objectified the black woman and her son. Although Molina's will does not identify the slaves with her surname, it was probably taken for granted that their full names included "Molina"; it was common practice in Yucatan for slaves to be given their owner's surname, particularly when they were working or living away from the owner (on a cattle ranch, for example, or doing business in Maya villages, as opposed to domestic duties in the owner's urban home). As was the case elsewhere in New Spain (but unlike Peru), African-born slaves did not retain their African names in Yucatan, at least not in any formal way reflected in written records.[25] Often, albeit not always, slaves changed surnames when sold by one owner to another; Manuel de Lara, for example, became Felis Manuel Bolio upon changing hands.[26]

Slave naming was consequently part of a larger pattern in colonial Yucatan whereby name conveyed status, within both Hispanic and Maya societies.[27] Patronyms served to tie individual black slaves to particular owners. To some extent, such patronyms subsequently helped identify free blacks and pardos as descendents of slaves. The ironic result of naming slaves after owners meant that both the highest-ranked Spaniards and the lowest-ranked Afro-Yucatecans often bore the same names, although nobody at the time would have confused the two, and the inflexible and highly significant use of the "don" and "doña" prefixes clearly marked the difference between don Manuel Bolio and Manuel Bolio, and between (the) doña Isabel Cavallero and (the two or more) Isabel Cavalleros. Furthermore, the steady process of miscegenation and the growth of the free-colored population meant that, in terms of names, black slaves were increasingly indistinguishable from everyone else in that middle sector between elite Spaniards (with their "doña," "Captain," and "Bachiller" prefixes) and Mayas (who retained their native surnames).

Scholars of African American slaves have argued that the imposition of European names onto Africans was designed "to negate and annihilate the human being inside the slave," that the names given to slaves "reflected the contempt in which their owners held them."[28] This may have been true in the English colonies, where slaves were typically denied surnames and given diminutive Christian names like Jack and Sukey, or names usually given farm animals like Jumper and Postilion, or classical names like Hercules or Claudius "as a kind of cosmic jest."[29] Perhaps such a naming pattern was reflective of a slave society (but not a society with slaves). No doubt many Afro-Yucatecan slaves were called diminutive names by their owners (José, rather than Joseph Antonio, for example), but so too were Spaniards, especially children. Indeed, the pattern here is not one of contempt, but of familiarity and subordination. The records of the hundreds of slaves baptized in Merida in the eighteenth century show no Africans being given diminutive, animal, or mock-classical names; rather they are named after owners or godparents, or simply given the most common Christian name in the Spanish world of the day—Joseph or María.

Table 2.4 makes this point more systematically. The table compares naming patterns between the following four groups: (1) Merida's slave-owning

TABLE 2.4 Comparative naming patterns among slave owners, slaves, children of slaves, and free Afro-Yucatecans in Merida, 1710–89

Men	Slave owners (%)	Slaves baptized as adults (%)	Sons of slaves (%)	Sons of free coloreds (%)
Most common Christian names in order of popularity	Juan (23) Joseph (13) Pedro Francisco Antonio	Joseph (27) Juan (16) Francisco Antonio Manuel/Miguel	Joseph (25) Juan (16) Pedro Francisco Manuel	Joseph (11) Juan (9) Manuel Francisco Antonio/Felipe
Variation 1	27	10	38	34
Variation 1 and 2	40	64	88	83

Women	Slave owners (%)	Slaves baptized as adults (%)	Daughters of slaves (%)	Daughters of free coloreds (%)
Most common Christian names in order of popularity	María (28) Josepha (9) Juana Isabel Antonia	María (61) Juana (7) Ana Josepha Antonia/Isabel	María (47) Juana (8) Antonia Francisca Manuela	María (55) Juana (7) Manuela Josepha Augustina/Felipa
Variation 1	36	14	32	33
Variation 1 and 2	52	95	80	67

Source: AGAY-*Jesús*, Libros de Bautismos Vols. 1–6.

Notes: Variation 1 is the variation rate of first names only; Variation 1 and 2 takes second names into account as well. A zero variation rate means everyone had the same name; 100% variation means no two persons had the same name. The percentages of Juans, Marías, and so on are based on first names only.

The complete data for slave owners is in Appendix E (E.1 lists full names; E.4 tabulates Christian names). As slave owners were not being named at the moment of their own baptisms (unlike all the Afro-Yucatecans), some surely had their second names omitted, making the Variation 1 and 2 percentages for slave owners lower than they really were. More detailed data for slaves is in Appendix G (G.7 for men; G.8 for women).

The data is drawn from the following total numbers of individuals and time periods:

Men: 155 slave owners, 1710–89; 355 adult slaves, 1710–89; 101 sons of slaves, 1710–89; 375 sons of free coloreds, 1710–89.

Women: 67 slave owners, 1710–89; 200 adult slaves, 1710–89; 85 daughters of slaves, 1710–89; 341 daughters of free coloreds, 1710–89.

I attempted to note every individual in the first three categories (owners, slaves, and slaves' children), so those are close to comprehensive; the fourth category (free-coloreds' children) is merely a sampling of the 2,996 free-colored children baptized in Merida in 1710–95, concentrated mostly in the 1756–74 period due to the vagaries of casta labeling (see Table 3.4 in Chapter Three for details).

Spanish elite (named by their parents) (see Appendix E); (2) African slaves purchased, baptized, and re-named as adults imported into Yucatan (see Appendix G); (3) the children of slaves (named by parents, possibly influenced by slave owners); and (4) the children of free Afro-Yucatecans (named by their parents). The initial impression given by the table is also its most significant finding—that there was an enormous similarity of Christian names among all four groups. The most common names across the board were Joseph and María, the second most popular were Juan and Juana. About one in five men were called Joseph in eighteenth-century Merida, with a third carrying Joseph or Juan as their first name—both enslaved and free, owners and owned, whether of Spanish or African descent. The predominance of María as a first name was even greater; roughly one in two women in the city of all categories were thus named. The next most popular names were also similar across all four categories. However, the fact that so many people carried the same first names was not confusing, as most people had second Christian names (almost all Juans, Josephs, and Marías had second names, and some had third names). Again, this was true across the board, from Spanish slave owners to free mulatto children.

A closer look at Table 2.4, however, reveals several minor but clear differences between groups. First, the predominance of Joseph and María among Afro-Yucatecans was modified among Spanish slave owners; for Spanish men, Juan was more popular than Joseph, and only a quarter of Spanish women were called María, as opposed to a half to two-thirds of Afro-Yucatecan women. Second, naming patterns were most conservative among the slave-owning elite; Spanish slave owners were more likely to be named one of the five most popular names, and less likely to have varied or multiple second or third Christian names. The only pattern (not reflected in the table) that changed notably over time was the increased number of Christian names from which people chose in the second half of the century; but, significantly, this was manifested primarily at the level of second and third Christian names, and overwhelmingly among Afro-Yucatecans, not among the Spanish elite.

This conservatism carried over into the names given to slaves baptized in Merida as adults, no doubt a result of slave owners' influence. Giving imported adults Christian names was not just a custom among the elite; it was official imperial policy—one formally reiterated by Governor Hugo O'Conor Cunco y Fally at a slave auction in Merida in 1779, for example.[30] A look at such names alone might give the impression that the high percentage of Josephs and Juans, Marías and Juanas, reflected a lack of imagination by slave owners, as though such names were simply gender markers. The comparison with slave owners' names is important, then, because it shows that slave owners gave slaves their own names, and the names of their own parents and children. Such a tradition was conservative, perhaps paternalistic and proprietary, but hardly dehumanizing.

The low variation rate of adult slave first names necessitated a higher variation rate of second names. In rare cases, this may have resulted from owners wishing to differentiate among their slaves—as in the winter of 1779–80, when don Juan Esteban Quijano brought to the font over several months some two dozen black slaves purchased at the auctions held in the wake of the recent attack on Belize, and gave them an unusual variety of baptismal names. However, because most slaves were owned in small numbers, and baptized individually, the cause of second-name variation may not have been out of necessity, but (and this is pure speculation) the input of slaves themselves; months typically passed between an adult slave's arrival in Yucatan and his or her baptism, sufficient time to develop opinions about Spanish Christian names.

Such opinions might have formed within Afro-Yucatecan circles, where name choice was less conservative among black-slave and free-colored parents than it was among Spaniards. Spanish owners may have influenced the naming of their slaves' children to some extent, but owners were not always present at such baptisms. Thus, when black slaves and free coloreds brought their own children to be baptized, they still favored Joseph and María but chose a wide variety of second (sometimes third, and even fourth) Christian names—a variation so high that there are few children of Afro-Yucatecan parents in the baptismal record with exactly the same set of Christian names. Slaves and free coloreds may have been more imaginative in naming their own children partly as an expression of freedom from the ignominy of having an owner assign a name to an adult who already had a name. After all, for those African-born adults who came to Yucatan in the eighteenth century after toiling in a British colony, the ritual of baptism in a Spanish church was the second colonialist imposition of a new identity that such a slave experienced.[31]

The example of slaves whose Spanish Christian names overlay an English slave name and an African birth name brings us to a final point about naming patterns. Slaves were not just assigned first names by owners, they were given Christian names through the ritual of formal baptism in the Jesús parish church in downtown Merida or Campeche. The similarity of naming patterns shown in Table 2.4 reflects the fact that everyone received names through the same baptismal ritual. Certainly this was a further way of marking slaves with a new identity, but the act was one of inclusion, not contempt; a slave's new identity included being a Christian member of the Spanish-speaking community—an unjust and unequal community where some people were property, but undeniably a human community. From the Spanish viewpoint, baptized slaves not only became members of local, Spanish-speaking Christian society, but they became Catholics—as opposed to the heretics they were forced to be by the English (if they had been English-owned, as many had been in late colonial times). In Spanish eyes, this placed enslaved Afro-Yucatecans on the right side of a cosmic line that divided the king's Catholic subjects from the heretics and enemies of God and crown.[32]

Illustrative of how naming patterns symbolized this contrast is the example of "Pleto" and "Coiys"—no doubt Plato and Gaius, respectively,—two black slaves taken from their British owners in Belize and sold at auction in Merida in 1792. We have no comment by their new owner, the colony's prelate, don fray Luis de Piña y Mazo, on how he viewed the two black men for whom he paid four hundred pesos. But we can well imagine that the bishop must have seen their sale as a kind of spiritual liberation; rescued from heretical owners who did not even give them Christian names, the *negros* were baptized as Catholics with Spanish Christian names, symbolizing their salvation—both on earth, in the bishop's hands, and in the afterlife.[33]

Thus, the naming of slaves in Yucatan was situated within both a ritual of religious inclusion and a pattern of naming conservatism that stretched from owners to the children of free coloreds—all a far cry from the dehumanizing contempt that historians have detected among slave-naming patterns in the British colonies and the United States. There is, however, a coda to this conclusion, one that underscores the relative benevolence of baptism and slave naming in Yucatan while also helping us to see, from the slave's perspective, how important such relativism was. That coda is branding.

Branding—that unambiguously dehumanizing ritual of imposed identity—does not seem to have been very commonly done in Yucatan, mostly because the colony lacked a full-fledged factoria (as discussed in the previous chapter). Branding tended to be carried out about a month after arrival in the Americas (to avoid taxes on slaves who died in port before being sold) in major slave factorias, such as Jamaica, Curaçao, and Cartegena, with slaves given both the markings of the crown and the asiento or license holder. Thus for most Afro-Yucatecan slaves, baptism did not immediately follow branding, although the memory of the iron lingered long and the scar, by design, never faded. In exceptional circumstances, slaves were rebranded in Yucatan. One such case was the Yucatec attack on Belize in 1779, in the wake of which the dozens of black slaves captured in the war as booty were branded "YR" (Yucatan and Rey) before being sold in Merida.[34] Those Belizean slaves born in Africa (as opposed to Belize or Jamaica) would have suffered a prior branding by British slave traders. Indeed, by the time most enslaved Africans reached Yucatan, they already had initials burned into their chest or shoulder; not even children were spared a painful and humiliating experience that intentionally left a scar. For example, Agustín de Leira, an enslaved black teenager, was brought from Spain to Yucatan by his Spanish owner in 1718 "with branding marks on his right arm and on the middle of his ear."[35]

The rationale behind branding was that, in the event of an escape or an inspection by royal tax officials, the marking showed under which asiento a slave had been imported and often into which port. But there was an obvious deeper symbolism to branding; it marked the crossing into the Americas as a journey into a bondage from which there could be no turning back (a very few became free again, but none returned to freedom in Africa). The contrast between the branding ritual and the baptismal ritual was thus a dramatic one. The rituals were only similar in that they both involved the imposing of new identity markers by owners, the erasing of free African identities with New World slave identities. But one ritual was an unceremonial (and no doubt to many, especially children, terrifying and incomprehensible) act of violence whose mark was permanent and whose message signaled without qualification that a person had been reduced to a piece of property. The other ritual was intended as a welcoming message, signaling that the slave had left behind a world of barbarism and heresy for one of civilization and salvation. Although this ethnocentric perspective denied the slave any say in the matter, baptism was nonetheless a nonviolent and solemn act conducted peacefully in a church and leaving no permanent mark; a slave's new Christian and Spanish name could in the future be changed, not just through resale but also through the acquisition of freedom.

THE SLAVE OWNERS

African slaves may have willingly embraced Catholicism, or aspects of it, for various reasons (treated in Chapter Six), but they do not appear to have come to baptism alone; they were brought to the font by their new masters. Although a variety of legal records reveal to us the identity of slaves and masters (from wills like doña María Joaquina Molina's to sales such as those resulting from the 1759 Sosa raid), it is baptismal records that provide the greatest body of information on who slave owners were in Yucatan. The most striking pattern that emerges from these records is that of the prominence of governors and bishops; in other words, slave owning began at the top.

For example, don Francisco Núñez Melián sailed to Yucatan from Cádiz in 1643 with an entourage of eight, consisting of four Spaniards, the wives of two who were married, and two black slaves. His travel documents included statements that don Francisco "always had with him" these two *negros*, that they had been with him in Caracas when he was governor of Venezuela, and had traveled to Panama with him, then to Spain, and now to Yucatan. Such testimony was solicited to show that he was not trafficking illegally in slaves, that he was traveling with his paperwork in order. But such testimony also reflected the fact that a man of Núñez Melián's standing went nowhere without his slaves.[36]

Although evidence is patchy before the eighteenth century, it suggests that early and mid-colonial governors both traveled with one or two black or mulatto slaves and purchased slaves in office. This was certainly true in the eighteenth century, as illustrated by Table 2.5; the table compiles all available data on slave ownership among governors and bishops, primarily eighteenth-century data culled from baptism records. I have not, therefore, found every slave owned by every governor and bishop. But governors and bishops missing from the table did not necessarily refrain from slaveholding; on the contrary, I suspect that all governors and prelates of Yucatan owned at least one black slave and also had at least one free-colored servant.[37]

Slaveholders were obliged to bring newly purchased and arrived black slaves into the Jesús church for baptism—that is, assuming they had come from Africa or the British colonies or even another Spanish colony if the slave could convince neither owner nor priest that he or she was already a baptized Catholic. Governors could not easily shirk this obligation, and so we can be fairly certain that almost all governor-bought slaves made it into the parish books, making the 1710s–90s entries in Table 2.5 close to comprehensive. These show a remarkably consistent pattern, not only of governors owning slaves, but of governors buying slaves not long after taking up office, as though it were a ritual expression of gubernatorial authority—which, indeed, I believe it was.

For example, six consecutive governors who held office between 1708 and 1743 purchased between one and fourteen black slaves and had them baptized in Merida within a few years—if not months—of taking power. The biggest of these slave owners, don Alonso de Meneses y Bravo de Sarabia, purchased newly arrived black slaves regularly, fourteen in total, throughout his three years in office. The 1745–52 gap in the pattern (the terms of don Antonio Benavides and the Marquis of Izcar) can be explained by the dramatic drop in general slave imports into the colony at this time (only twenty-one free and enslaved black adults are baptized in Merida in the whole decade of the 1740s).[38] The pattern resumed with don Melchor de Navarrete, who owned at least ten slaves while governor in 1753–60. Of the nineteen Spaniards who served as governor between 1708 and 1792, at least eleven purchased slaves while in office—a total of fifty-seven slaves, or an average of five per governor (way above the colony's slave-owning average of between one and two slaves per Spanish owner). The slow and irregular trickle of slaves into the colony meant that the market (when new slaves arrived) was probably more of a factor than capital; in other words, the office was sufficiently lucrative that governors could secure capital or credit before the next shipment of slaves arrived in Campeche or (in the second half of the century) were brought up from Belize.

The pattern for slave ownership by bishops is very similar, but with a small twist. The four bishops who held office in 1715–33 and 1753–72 all purchased newly imported black slaves, likewise between one and four in number, with the 1733–53 gap partially explained by the temporary decline in slave imports. Bishop Piña y Mazo, who was prelate in 1779–95, also bought at least two Africans. However, bishops bought new slaves at the *end*, rather than the start or middle, of their terms of office—Gómez de Parada

TABLE 2.5 Governors and Bishops of Yucatan as slave owners, 1546–1792

Governor	Slaves owned[a]		
Don Francisco de Montejo (Governor 1546–50)	2+	1540s	Marcos, *negro* slave, and Sebastian Toral, freed *negro*, brought in 1540; possibly dozens more *negros* and negras imported in 1540s
Don Guillen de las Casas (Governor 1579–82)	3	1579	3 *negros* brought into Yucatan "for his service"
Don Francisco Núñez Melián (Governor 1643–44)	2	1643	2 *negros* brought with him from Venezuela to Yucatan, via Panama and Spain
Don Martín de Ursúa y Arizmendi (Governor 1694–1708)	4	1695	4 *negro* musicians, either acquired in Yucatan or brought from Mexico City in 1694
Don Fernando de Meneses y Bravo de Sarabia (Governor 1708–12)	4	1711	4 *negros* from Papá, Mandinga, Nanga, and Angola baptized in Merida
Don Alonso de Meneses y Bravo de Sarabia (Governor 1712–15)	14	1713–15	2 *negros* baptized 1713; 2 *negros* from Calemanti and Jamaica baptized 1714; *negro* from Yola baptized May 1715; 6 *negros* from Mina, Canca, and Mandinga baptized 1715; 3 negras from Danguira, Mina, and Guavere baptized 1715; all in Merida
Don Juan Joseph de Vertiz y Ontañón (Governor 1715–20)	3	1710–17	Free *negro* brought from Cádiz to Yucatan 1710; 3 *negros* from Caboverde, Guinea, and Holland baptized 1717; in Merida
Don Antonio de Cortaire y Terreros (Governor 1720–25)	1	1724	*Negro* from Guinea baptized in Merida
Don Antonio de Figueroa y Silva Lasso de la Vega (Governor 1725–33)	3	1727–32	2 *negros* from Mina baptized 1727; negra criada (free?) baptized 1732; all in Merida
Don Manuel Salcedo (Governor 1736–43)	3	1736–39	Negra from Ibo baptized 1736; negra from Mandinga baptized 1738; *negro* baptized 1739; all in Merida

TABLE 2.5 (*continued*)

Governor	Slaves owned[a]		
Don Melchor de Navarrete (Governor 1753–60)	11[b]	1753–58	Infant son of a negra slave of his baptized 1753; *Negro* from Congo baptized 1754; free negra from Belize baptized 1756; infant son of a pair of married slaves of his baptized 1756; 2 *negros* from Belize and England and 2 negras from Jamaica and Guinea baptized 1758; all in Merida
Don Alonso Fernández de Heredía (Governor 1761)	3	1761	2 *negros* and a negra from Belize and Guinea baptized in Merida
Don Cristóbal de Zayas Guzmán Moscoso (Governor 1765–71)	4	1768–69	Negra from Jamaica baptized 1768; 3 *negros* from Jamaica and Havana baptized 1769; all in Merida
Don Roberto de Rivas Betancourt (Governor 1779–83)	8	1779–83	Infant son of a married black slave couple of his baptized in Merida; a *negro* from Guinea baptized 1780; a negra from Caye Kitchen (Belize) and a *negro* from Jamaica baptized 1781; infant daughter of another slave of his baptized 1783; all in Merida
Don Lúcas de Gálvez (Governor 1789–92)	2	1790–92	*Negro* from Congo baptized in Merida in 1790; *negro* coachman and governor's slave witnesses owner's assassination in 1792

Bishop	Slaves owned[a]		
Dr. don Juan Gómez de Parada (Bishop 1715–28)	4	1725	2 *negros* and 2 negras, all bosal, baptized in Merida
Don Juan Ignacio de Castorena y Urzúa (Bishop 1729–33)	2	1733	Nine-year-old negra baptized in Merida; mulatto slave given freedom papers
Dr. Don fray Ignacio de Padilla y Estrada (Archbishop 1753–60)	3	1760	3 *negros* from Congo baptized in Merida

TABLE 2.5 *(continued)*

Bishop	Slaves owned[a]		
Don fray Antonio Alcalde (Bishop 1761–72)	2	1763	2 free *negros*, his criados, one from Cartagena, brought with him from Seville to Yucatan
Don fray Luis de Piña y Mazo (Bishop 1779–95)	2	1792	2 *negros* from Belize purchased at auction in Merida

Sources on Montejo's slaves: AGI-*Justicia* 300, 3; *México* 2999, 2: ff. 187–88r; Herrera (1601, VIII: 10, 23); Benzoni (1857 [1565]: 142–43). Also see discussion in Chapter One.

Sources on other governors, in order: AGI-*México* 2999, 2: f. 193r; AGI-*Contratación* 5425, 1; Jones (1998: 113, 119, 185); AGAY-*Jesús*, Libros de Bautismos Vol. 1: f. 16v; f. 43v; f. 61v; f. 64v–65r; AGI-*Contratación* 5465, 2, 77; AGAY-*Jesús*, Libros de Bautismos Vol. 1: f. 86v; f. 163; f. 208v; 269v; Vol. 2: f. 53v–54r; f. 78v; f. 88v; Vol. 3: f. 19v; f. 38v; f. 59r; f. 67r; f. 96v; f. 103v; f. 105v; ff. 173r–74v; Vol. 4: f. 128r; f. 150r; f. 154v; Vol. 5: f. 138r; f. 159v; 170v; 206r; Vol. 6: 158v; AGN-*Criminal* 301, 1: ff. 5v–6v.

Sources on bishops, in order: AGAY-*Jesús*, Libros de Bautismos Vol. 1: ff. 182v–83r; Vol. 2: f. 1r; ANEY, Montero, 1729–35 (UTA roll 3): ff. 332v–33; AGAY-*Jesús*, Libros de Bautismos Vol. 3: ff. 147v–48r; AGI-*Contratación* 5506, 2, 7; AHAY-*Asuntos Terminados* 1792 (transcribed in Rúz Menéndez 1970: 22–25).

Sources on full names and dates of governors and bishops: Carrillo y Ancona (1880: 77–88); Pérez Galaz (1942: 3–4); Victoria Ojeda (1995: 187–206); above sources and others in AGN and AGI (such as *residencia* reports in *Escribanía*).

[a] Including a small number of free black dependents, identified as such below. Numbers of slaves listed and years of ownership are not comprehensive, but reflect the information in the sources cited here.

[b] This includes infants and their slave parents, as well as the free negra from Belize.

after a decade in office, Castorena and Padilla both in their final year as bishop, Piña y Mazo after thirteen years in office. The exception (at least within the data presented in Table 2.5) proves the pattern; the two black men brought to baptism by Bishop Alcalde near the start of his decade in office were not slaves purchased in Yucatan but free-colored servants brought by the bishop from Seville.

Why this difference in slave-buying habits between governors and bishops? My theory is that governors needed slaves and servants not only to staff their households and coaches in Merida with appropriate pomp and display, but also in order to amass wealth within the two or three years of a single term. This was primarily achieved through the illegal but customary mechanism of *repartimientos* or forced sales and purchases of goods in Maya villages.[39] As we shall see in the next chapter, Afro-Yucatecan slaves and servants played major roles as rural and itinerant agents for the Spanish elite. Furthermore, the experience and connections gained by a governor's slave would have made his resale profitable at the end of that governor's term (although I have not yet found sale records to prove that this was common).

Bishops, by contrast, did not set out to systematically exploit their parishioners as quickly as possible. Their terms were longer (there were sixty-four governors between 1546 and 1821, but only twenty-five bishops between 1561 and 1827),[40] and they were able to accrue wealth gradually through the steady income of church fees and tithes, and through investment in local property. Seen in this context, bishops must have bought slaves at the end of their terms not for resale or to serve them in office, but as a way of making acquired wealth more fungible—converting landed property, for example, into a type of property that they could take with them when returning to Spain or moving on to their next appointment.

The bishops listed in Table 2.5 only tell part of the tale of elite ecclesiastical slaveholding in Yucatan. Sale records and other notarial documents give the anecdotal impression that priests appear as slave owners as frequently as do other Spaniards—that the clergy were, in fact, disproportionately involved in slaveholding. This evidence is too substantial to present in full, but four clusters of examples will suffice to make the point. The first example cluster is that of sales from the 1690s. Capt. don Nicolás de Sugasti, for example, captain of Sotuta (but resident in Merida), bought from the priest Bachiller Mateo de Evia for 150 pesos a 20-year-old slave named Manuel Salvador; Capt. don Pedro de Aguilar y Santoyo of Campeche paid the same sum for a mulatto named Antonio; Alférez Pedro Rodríguez de la Paz bought a slave named Juan Rosado from Br. Diego de Burgos (Rosado had run the priest's estancia).[41]

The second example cluster is from the records of Atlantic crossings (see Appendix C). Only the highest-ranking Spaniards could afford to cross between Spain and Yucatan with their black slaves or free-colored servants. Most of those who traveled with such an entourage came to take up high administrative posts—such as the above-mentioned don Francisco Núñez Melián, who sailed with eight dependents from Cádiz in 1643 to take up the governorship of Yucatan, or Governor don Juan Joseph de Vertiz y Ortañón, who crossed to Yucatan from Spain in 1710 with three unmarried Spanish dependents and a free black servant. Elite Spaniards who journeyed more modestly, without Spanish dependents or servants, still went with the minimum of a servant of African descent. This was true of high-ranking clergy, not only bishops, but also members of the cathedral chapter such as deans and schoolmasters. Dr. don Pedro Sánchez de Aguilar, dean and former Vicar General of the province, took a teenage mulatto servant named Francisco de Aguilar with him to Spain in 1619, but the boy was so homesick that the dean let him sail back to Yucatan; Br. don Manuel Núñez de Matos sailed to Yucatan in 1623 as Merida's cathedral *maestre escuela* [master of divinity] with two Spanish dependents, a free mulatto servant, and a black slave; fray don Antonio Alcalde sailed to Yucatan as its new bishop in 1763 with an entourage of eight (four priests, a nephew, and three servants—two of them black); and Dr. don Rafael de Castillo y Sucre, also a cathedral schoolmaster, crossed the ocean to Yucatan in 1779 with an entourage of three, including a free black servant boy.[42]

The third example cluster is that of monastery and convent records: For example, there were enslaved Africans working as domestic servants in the first and for a while only nunnery in Merida, the convent of Nuestra Señora de la Consolación. Founded in 1596, the convent flourished as a school for girls, supported in part by one of the taxes levied on Mayas (the *holpatán*), until its slow decline in the late eighteenth and nineteenth centuries; like the pupils, the nuns were from elite Spanish families, so the convent's black slaves were not easily confused with its *esclavas*, as the first-year novices were called.[43] There were also slaves working in the other convent of nuns in Merida, that of Nuestra Señora de la Concepción; the convent mother, Isidora Pérez, owned a black slave whom she had named María Pérez, and María had at least one child who grew up as a slave in the convent (Joseph María de la Luz, born in 1743).[44]

The fourth and final example cluster takes us back to the eighteenth-century records from Merida's Jesús María parish, which show that slave owning extended down from the bishop's office throughout the cathedral chapter (see Table 2.6). Not all cathedral chapter members took their slaves to be baptized in the Jesús church, and when they did the parish priest did not always note their rank (which would have been taken for granted). Still, Table 2.6 illustrates the fact that from the bishop and vicar general through the archdeacon and precentor to the canons, high-ranking priests tended to be slave owners (even the lay members of the chapter, the alms collectors, were members of the slave-owning elite). Priests were thus a group of slave owners in parallel with nonclerical owners—with the bishop corresponding to the governor, and the senior clergy (from the cathedral chapter to the better-off priests of the more lucrative parishes) being parallel in rank and slave owning to the encomenderos and captains. The point, in other words, is not so much that priests disproportionately owned slaves, but that higher-ranking priests owned slaves because they were members of the Spanish elite.

Indeed, slave owning emerges in the archival record as a key marker of elite status, almost as much so as having a title—be that title an indicator of office (civil or ecclesiastical) or the simple but highly significant don and doña. Not all Spaniards were members of the Spanish elite; just as there was an increasingly complex multiracial social pyramid in the colony, so was there an increasingly diverse social pyramid among Spaniards in the province. The top of that pyramid—the colony's aristocracy—was occupied by the encomenderos and other elite Spaniards closely tied to them by marriage and business arrangements. About 150 *encomiendas* [grants of labor and tribute from Maya villages] were allotted during the Conquest; there were still 115 in the early eighteenth century and 77 when the institution finally died in Yucatan in the 1780s. About six in ten of the conquistador–settlers of the 1540s were encomenderos, but by the eighteenth century less than 5% of Spaniards enjoyed

TABLE 2.6 Some members of the cathedral chapter whose slaves were baptized in Merida, 1711–27 and 1762–78

Rank	Member	Slave or slave's child	Year of baptism
Alms collector	Don Juan Tomás Caballero	Negro	1726
Canon	Dr. don Sancho del Puerto	Newborn daughter of slave couple	1711
Canon	Dr. don Sancho del Puerto	Newborn son of same slave couple	1713
Canon	Dr. don Sancho del Puerto	Newborn son of another slave couple	1715
Precentor	Don Joseph de Aranda y Aguaio	Canca negra, baptized Juana de Aguaio	1715
Archdean	Don Joseph de Aranda y Aguaio	Newborn daughter of same Juana	1721
Archdean	Don Juan de la Cueva Caldera	Congo negro	1725
Archdean	Don Juan de la Cueva Caldera	Negro	1727
Canon	Dr. Mendicuti	Carabeo negro	1762
Canon	Dr. don Agustín Pimentel	Newborn son of his negro slave	1764
Canon	Dr. don Agustín Pimentel	Newborn daughter of his negro slave	1771
[not stated]	Dr. don Juan Agustín de Lousel	Newborn daughter of his negro slave	1762
Vicar Gen.	Dr. don Juan Agustín de Lousel	Newborn daughter of his negra slave	1778

Source: AGAY-Jesús, Libros de Bautismos Vols. 1, 4–5.

Notes: These slave owners also are included in Appendix E. For slave-owning bishops, see Table 2.5.

Lousel was vicar general 1776–80 (Chuchiak 2000: 108); the vicar general (who in Yucatan also was the judge provisor [juez provisor y vicario general]), was technically ranked above the cathedral chapter [cabildo eclesiástico], although a chapter member sometimes filled the vicar general's post; the upper tier of members of the chapter were the dignitaries [dignidades], consisting of dean [dean], archdean [arcediano], precentor [chantre], master of divinity [maestrescuela], and treasurer [tesorero]; canons [canonigos], of which there were two in Yucatan, comprised the second tier; a third tier consisted of two bacineros or racioneros (written bacinero in the AGAY records), charged with collecting alms in the cathedral and often a layman (as in the case above). There were a couple of tesoreros who appeared in these baptism records, but both were treasurers of the provincial government and not the cathedral chapter.

the profit and prestige of these grants. There was still an encomendero aristocracy in the colony after the 1780s as the crown paid pensions to holders of encomendero titles into the early nineteenth century; besides, it was these same families who dominated the haciendas or large landed estates that were the primary source of serious wealth in late colonial times. Indeed, as far back as the early seventeenth century the encomendero class had ceased to be dependent on encomienda income and begun diversifying its assets and sources of income by investing in urban property and rural estates or *estancias*.[45]

All encomenderos owned slaves, not only because they could afford to, but because slaves were an elemental part of the *casa poblada*, the fully staffed urban household that was a requisite part of being an encomendero. In other words, slaves were part of the full package of property and personal dependents that made a man an honorable and respected member of the local colonial elite. The linking of honor and social worth to these material and human accoutrements goes back to the sixteenth century, to the language used in the *probanzas* or merit reports of the first conquistador–settlers. Witnesses to the 1570 probanza of conquistador–settler Alonso Rosado, for example, confirmed that what gave substance to his reputation as "an upright person [*persona honrrada*]" who lived "very honorably [*muy honrrosamente*]" was his city household (his *casa poblada*) of legitimate family members, "weapons, horses, servants, and slaves."[46]

Early in the colonial period a new category of Spanish elite developed—Spanish men with military titles, most notably that of captain [*capitán*]. This elite group overlapped with that of the encomenderos, about half of whom in the seventeenth and eighteenth centuries also had military titles. Following the first pirate attacks on Campeche, the governor of the province was named *capitán general*, the latter a military post accountable directly to Spain, not to Mexico City (the first to hold the double post was don Luis de Céspedes, appointed in 1564 and in office 1565–71).[47] As the defense needs of the colony multiplied (detailed in Chapter Five), so did the captain general receive approval to increase the number of captaincies. By the mid-seventeenth century, there were a hundred or so Spaniards with the "captain" title, and dozens with other military titles, men with militia appointments but who spent little or no time engaged in military activities. The encomenderos were a privileged subset of the *capitanes a guerra*, along with other "dons" descended from conquistadors. The other captains were merchants or men of property closely associated with merchants. This was also broadly true of those few who held the title of *maestre de campo* [field marshal, a title given if one led an expedition of some kind, and kept for life]. Other less prestigious, but still respectable, titles were *sargento*, *teniente* [first lieutenant] and *alférez* [ensign or second lieutenant; like sargento, this was with or without a *mayor*], *castellano* [warden of a fort] and his teniente, and *ayudante* [adjutant].

The existence of the pardo militia meant that there were also Afro-Yucatecans who held some of these titles (as we shall see in Chapter Five).

However, unlike Afro-Yucatecans, Spaniards with military titles tended to carry the "don" prefix before their name. Indeed, almost all captains (perhaps all), like all encomenderos (with the exception of some members of the first generation of conquistador–encomenderos) were dons. The remaining Spanish dons were high-ranking priests and other members of families whose senior patriarch or promient members were encomenderos or captains. Elite Spanish women could not hold military titles, but they were sometimes *encomenderas* [women holding encomienda grants], and are easily identifiable by their "doña" prefixes.[48]

This elite—the encomenderos, captains, dons with other military titles or positions in the church, and the doñas to whom they were related—were the slave-owning class in Yucatan (as Appendix E makes clear). There were other slave owners—lesser-privileged Spaniards and even higher-ranking free Afro-Yucatecans, such as militia captains—but they were very much the minority. In fact, the correlation between the titled elite and slave owning was such that to own slaves was part of what marked a Spaniard as a member of that elite. Of the 155 Spanish men who brought adult and infant slaves to be baptized in Merida's Jesús parish church in the eighteenth century (1710-89), 88% were dons (and I suspect the real figure was higher, as priests tended to scribble the entries and abbreviate names). Of the sixty-seven women who had slaves baptized during this period, 94% were doñas (see Table 2.7).

TABLE 2.7 Incidence of titles among slave owners in Merida, 1710–89

	Number	Percentage
TITLE (155 MEN)		
Don	137	88
Clergy	22	14
TITLE (133 MEN, NON-CLERGY)		
Captain	40	30
Government (city cabildo)	34	26
Government (province)	17	13
Other military titles	17	13
TITLE (67 WOMEN)		
Doñas	63	94

Source: AGAY-*Jesús*, Libros de Bautismos Vols. 1–6.

Notes: The percentages do not add to 100 because of the overlap between "don" and other titles.

The positions under "Government (province)" were governor (10), treasurer and accountant (6), and defender of the Indians (1).

"Government (city)" refers to Merida cabildo positions; the figure was created by cross-referencing the 133 nonclerical slave owners in the baptism records with cabildo listings for the century (in Martínez Ortega 1993: 249–64).

Not only were the vast majority of these slave-owning men dons, but two-thirds of them also carried titles that were either military, governmental, or clerical. To be more specific, 14% were priests, while among nonclerical slave owners, almost a third were captains—a total of forty, which was almost half the captains in the whole colony. Another 13% had other military titles, still another 13% had high-ranking positions in provincial government (almost all the governor himself or the treasury posts of *contador* and *tesorero*).

The data in Tables 2.5 to 2.7 (and in Appendix E) allow us to do more than simply demonstrate the correlation between slave owners and the Spanish elite; they also confirm the eighteenth-century shift of power within the elite, as indicated by the holding of regidor posts on the Merida cabildo. The Spanish historian Ana Isabel Martínez Ortega showed in her doctoral analysis of cabildo lists that the old conquistador-descended families still dominated the cabildo at the turn of the eighteenth century. But after that their control over cabildo offices declined; their hold on regidor positions, for example, fell from 55% in 1705 to a quarter at mid-century to none by 1800.[49] If slave owning was as much a litmus test of elite status as cabildo positions were, we should find two things: Merida's cabildo officers well represented among the city's slave owners; and an eighteenth-century shift within the slave-owning elite from deep-rooted families to more recent immigrants. We find both.

First of all, over a quarter of all nonclerical slave owners in eighteenth-century Merida served on the cabildo. This figure is based on slave-baptism data, a net which does not catch all slave owners, so the real correlation was probably higher. Indeed, viewed from a different angle, we find that of the eleven regidors of Merida in 1725, eight appear as slave owners in the baptism records—raising the figure from a quarter to three-quarters. Cross-referencing the same data base for 1748 and 1776 produces a slave owners/regidors correlation of 40%. The actual correlation for the eighteenth century was probably such that, on average, two in three cabildo officers in Merida owned slaves. The overwhelming majority of those slave-owning regidors in 1725, 1748, and 1776 were Spanish-born or from families that had migrated into Yucatan in mid-to-late-colonial times; very few were descended from the conquistadors.

Indeed (the second point), we can even detect a shift *during* the century. Table 2.8 isolates the principal slave-owning families in eighteenth-century Merida and organizes them into three categories: (1) older elite families, descended from conquistadors or pre-1700 immigrants; (2) newer elite families, comprising the Spanish-born [*peninsulares*] and those who had arrived in the eighteenth century, either in socioeconomic terms or literally as immigrants; and (3) others whose origins are not clear or who contained members from both the other categories. A startlingly clear pattern emerges: slave owning followed—indeed marked—the shift from the old elite to the new

TABLE 2.8 Merida's principal slave-owning families, 1710–89

Surname of slave-owning families	Number and sex of slave owners (male/ female)	Number of black slaves owned, by duodecades				
		1710–29	1730–49	1750–69	1770–89	Total
OLDER ELITE FAMILIES						
Alpuche	1 f	2	9	1		12
Ávila	1 f		11			11
Caballero	5 m/f	3	6	5		14
Castillo	8 m/f	7	11	2		20
Castro	4 m	4	3		3	10
Chacón	4 m/f	21	8	2		31
del Campo	3 m/f	7	5			12
Fernández	5 m	4		5		9
García	4 m/f		3	2		5
Helguera	4 m	3	8	1	1	13
Maldonado	2 m	1		5		6
Pérez	7 m/f	5	7	1		13
Rendón	2 m	4	7			11
Roela	1 m	3	3			6
Solís	4 m/f	3	9	1		13
NEWER ELITE FAMILIES						
Bermejo	2 m/f		2		9	11
Calderón	4 m/f		8	1	6	15
Cano	1 m			6	8	14
Lanz	2 m			3	3	6
Navarrete	1 m			10		10
Pordio	1 m			2	8	10
Quijano	2 m/f		2	16	39	57
Sanpedro	1 m				6	6
Zubiaur	2 m/f			10		10
OTHER ELITE FAMILIES						
Aguirre	4 m/f	1	3	2	3	9
Figueroa	3 m	2	1		2	5
González	4 m/f	5	1		5	11
Martínez	3 m/f	3	3		1	7
Meneses	4 m	18			7	25
Mugartegui	2 m		8			8
Noguera	1 m		11			11
Pino	3 m		2	1	4	7

TABLE 2.8 (*continued*)

Surname of slave-owning families	Number and sex of slave owners (male/ female)	Number of black slaves owned, by duodecades				
		1710–29	1730–49	1750–69	1770–89	Total
Priego	2	m	2	4			6
Rivas	3	m	4	6		8	18
Rodríguez	3	m/f				9	9
Vásquez	4	m/f		4	1		5

Source: Slave-owning data from AGAY-*Jesús*, Libros de Bautismos Vols. 1–6.
Notes: Families selected are those whose members owned at least 5 slaves throughout this period, as recorded by slave baptisms in Merida.
   A comprehensive list of slaves owned by each family (including, for example, slave sale records and data from Campeche slave baptisms) would produce higher total numbers.
   My categorization of families is based on biographical information in Martínez Ortega (1993) ("other elite families" are those whose origins are unclear or whose members come from both the other categories).

elite. Earlier in the century, slave owning in the city was the preserve of elite families with deep roots in Yucatan, like Caballero, Chacón, Castillo, Pérez, and Solís. Later in the century the big slave owners came from families that a century before had modest or no presence in the colony, like Cano, Lanz, Pordio, Quijano, and Zubiaur.

Of course, the interconnectedness of all these families—the multiple marital links between the families of what was after all a small elite group— makes the exercise of categorizing families somewhat contrived. For example, I have listed doña Isabel María de Ávila Carranza under "Ávila" as old elite (she was an encomendera, widow of Governor don Antonio de Figueroa, and a major slave owner in the second quarter of the century), while I have categorized Capt. don Juan Esteban de Quijano under "Quijano" as new elite (he was on the Merida cabildo nine times, including regidor in 1792, an encomendero, owner of four or five estates, and probably the single largest slave owner in Yucatec history). Yet doña Isabel was don Juan Esteban's paternal grandmother. Did that not make them part of the same small elite? Not entirely. Figueroa had only come to Yucatan from Spain in 1725 (to take up the governorship). Furthermore, don Juan Esteban was illegitimate—actually the bastard son of Figueroa and another Ávila woman.

As for the Quijano name, as recently as the 1690s it was a surname that in Yucatan was most likely to be carried by a mestizo or Afro-Yucatecan. The wealthy Quijano family of the late colony had been founded by a Spanish merchant who had based himself in Merida early in the eighteenth century; he had adopted Juan Esteban (the boy's mother was a cousin of

Quijano's wife's), who went on to run the family store in Merida, acquire haciendas around Merida, along with formal legitimacy and "don" status. By 1780 the Quijanos were one of the top three landowning clans in Yucatan (along with the Peón and Count of Miraflores families), representing the *gremio de estancieros* [estancia owners cabal] before the Merida cabildo. In that same year, the single largest auction of booty slaves in Yucatan's history was held in Merida; close to fifty Africans seized from British owners in Belize were sold off over a six month period. Don Juan Esteban Quijano purchased almost half of them. Not coincidentally, the family that economic historian Robert Patch calls "clearly at the top of the ranching elite" dominated slave owning in the 1770s and 1780s. Don Juan Esteban, his brother and sons, and other family members are found all over the records of slave baptisms as owners and godparents; don Juan Esteban himself appears as owner of fifty-six black slaves. No other Spaniard in the baptism records of the eighteenth century appears as owning even half this many slaves. The closest owned twenty-four; this was don Rodrigo Chacón, which symbolically underscores my point about the shift from older to new elite, as Chacón was from an old elite family in Yucatan and his slaves were baptized between 1714 and 1734. This was before the old elite had been subsumed into the new commercial elite headed by the likes of don Juan Esteban Quijano.[50]

This is not the place to further detail the changes that took place within the Yucatec Spanish elite in the eighteenth century; suffice to reiterate that such changes are visible in the slave-owning record, largely because slave owning was a perennial marker of elite status. This prompts the final question to be tackled in this section: If slave owning was one of the determinants of elite status among Spaniards, does this explain why there were black and mulatto slaves in the colony? Or do we need to dig further to explain the existence of Afro-Yucatecan slavery?

In fact, slavery in Spanish America was too complex a phenomenon to be so easily explained; there were other factors that shall emerge in subsequent chapters and be summarized in the Conclusion. Nevertheless, viewing slave owning as a status marker goes most of the way to answering the question, especially when placed in the context of a set of interrelated explanatory factors that all tend to lead back to issues of elite status. For example, slaves were obviously a source of labor and, as we saw above, valued according to economic criteria of utility and investment. But two important points offset the notion that slaves were simply a source of labor.

First, although they were less expensive than slaves in wealthier colonies, Yucatan's relative poverty prevented slave owning from spreading significantly from the elite down to less-privileged Spaniards, the rural Spanish elite, or members of the non-Spanish elite. There were exceptions to this general pattern—the archives contain occasional examples of wealthy mestizos or mulattoes who owned a slave, such as ex-slave, pardo militia captain, and mule-train owner Eugenio de Acosta, who owned a *negro* named Juan Durán in the 1690s.[51] But I have found not a single case of a Maya nobleman owning an Afro-Yucatecan slave.[52]

Furthermore, my survey of dozens of wills and probates of Spaniards living in late colonial rural towns like Izamal, Tekanto, and Motul produced not a single slave—not surprising when one considers that a Spaniard dying in one of these communities in the 1790s was typically worth 260 pesos, which was not much more than the average price of a slave (see Table 2.9). Even higher up the socioeconomic ladder, slaves were effectively out of reach. For example, the Spaniard Marcos Gómez died in Cacalchen in 1794 with an estate worth 1,318 pesos; this was a considerable sum and Gómez may have been the richest man in Cacalchen, but he owned no slaves, probably because a single, skilled, young black man would have cost him a third of the value of his principal asset, his cattle hacienda.[53]

During the same period, a little to the south, Spaniards invested the profits from their sugar haciendas not in slaves but in house plots in Tekax.[54] Not only were slaves costly and the colony poor, but Mayas provided cheap labor—both in male-associated occupations, such as construction and agriculture (including the sugar farms around late colonial Tekax), and in domestic work (Spaniards did not want Spanish women doing certain types of work, but that cultural objection did not extend to Maya women).[55]

Table 2.9 helps to place the cost of an African slave in the context of the cost of living and sources of wealth in the colony. For the highest-ranking Spaniards, especially those with wealth acquired outside Yucatan, slaves were easily acquired. But for the vast majority of Yucatan's inhabitants outside the Spanish elite in Merida and Campeche, slaves were not even an affordable luxury. In short, because only the wealthiest could afford the economic cost of a slave, slaves were more than just economic assets and slave owning was more than just an economic issue.[56]

The second point to offset the notion that slaves were simply a labor source is the fact that slaves in Yucatan tended to be used in skilled or specialized roles, and often to be attached to owners in personal ways. Those personal attachments were certainly labor-based—we have seen above how elite slave owners were also encomenderos and estate owners, the kind of men always in need of Afro-Yucatecan majordomos and managers—but they were also social in various ways. Afro-Yucatecan occupations are the subject of Chapter Four, so for now we shall return to the data on slave owning in eighteenth-century Merida that is presented in Appendix E.

In Merida, slaves were owned under personalized, domestic circumstances. For example, all elite Spanish families owned slaves, but they owned them in small numbers. Only 5% of both male and female owners had ten or more slaves. Men owned an average of 1.42 male slaves and 1.34 female slaves, while women were more likely to own female slaves—an average of 1.46, compared to an average of 0.60 male slaves. Thus, while fewer Spanish

TABLE 2.9 The value of an Afro-Yucatecan slave in the context of other types of property in late colonial Yucatan

Property type	Peso value	Date/source	Archival source
Weekly salary for a Maya working for a priest	2 reales (a quarter peso)	1737 bishop's letter to king	AGN-*Justicia Eclesiástica* 23: f. 278
Cotton shirt; silk shirt	3–8; 12–13	1690s wills	ANEY, Baeza (UTA roll 1); Hunt (1974: 68)
Gold rosary	25	1738 will	ANEY, Montero (UTA roll 5): nf
Transatlantic passage (Cádiz to Yucatan)	22	1710 travel documents	AGI-*Contratación* 5465, 2, 77: f. 2r
Horse	12–30	court cases of 1670 and 1816	AGI-*Escribanía* 316b, 47: f. 2–3; AGEY-*Criminal* 1, 9
Slave	216	1661–1829	(see Table 2.1)
Average value of Spaniards' estates in Tekanto, Izamal, and Motul	260	1790s wills	AGEY-*Sucesiones Testamentarias* 1, 1–12
Annual salary of *castellano* (Spanish warden, San Benito fort, Merida)	400	late 17th to early 18th centuries	ANEY, Baeza (UTA roll 1); Hunt (1974: 38)
Mulchechem (large livestock estancia near Merida)	1,645	1740 sale	ANEY, Montero (UTA roll 5): nf
Typical dowry of an encomendero's daughter	1,500–2,000	late 17th century	ANEY, Baeza (UTA roll 1); Hunt (1974: 75)

women owned slaves than did Spanish men (a third of slave owners were women, and the total slaveholdings of women were smaller), women were actually more likely to own female slaves than men were likely to own male or female slaves. In other words, owning a female Afro-Yucatecan domestic servant (or two) was as much a part of being an elite Spanish woman in Yucatan as the "doña" title was.[57]

Furthermore, where Spaniards owned more than one slave, these Afro-Yucatecans tended to be linked to each other through family relations—in addition to sharing owners and often work experiences. Thirty-eight percent of slave-owning Spaniards owned two or more Afro-Yucatecans related as parent and child (the parent was usually the mother, as the children of enslaved women, but not men, were born as slaves). Among Spanish women, this figure rose to 48% (probably because women were more likely to own women). Ten percent of all slave owners in Merida owned entire slave families consisting of two married parents (with one or usually both enslaved) and anywhere from one to six children (usually slaves too). It is true that owners benefited economically by encouraging female slaves to have children; but such children had to be fed and clothed for years before their labor became a return on the owner's investment. More important was the contribution of these children to the elite household and its public image— to the casa poblada. Slave-trade historian David Eltis has said that "the profit-maximizing model of human behavior makes little sense unless it is placed within a cultural framework,"[58] and I would argue that this is especially true in Yucatan, where the culture of slave owning was as important— perhaps more so—than its economic rationale. In other words, while there was an undeniable benefit to slaves working and reproducing, their relatively high cost in a poor colony made them luxury commodities, and their peso value was greatly exceeded by their social value as household members and status markers.

There was also a twist to the tale of slave families in elite Spanish households. In some of these households, Spanish masters fathered illegitimate children by the black slaves and mulatta servants working for them. The phenomenon of sexual relationships between master and slave is hardly unique to Yucatan; arguably it is a defining characteristic of slavery in the early modern world. Gilberto Freyre extended his own initiation "into physical love" by a young mulatta into the experience of "every Brazilian," making "sexual and family life" the core of his study of African slavery in Brazil. More recent scholars have argued that colonial rule and exploitation inevitably become gendered and then sexualized, what Zine Magubane (an Africanist writing about British South Africa) has called "the transformation of commodification into sexuality." Historian of African American slavery Edward Baptist has argued that "white-on-black rape" was an inextricable part of the slave trade and "an old story" in the United States by the early nineteenth century; in Anthony Kaye's words, "the ravages of the planters were too numerous to catalogue." Megan Vaughan, writing about African slavery in eighteenth-century Mauritius, concluded that the lack of direct evidence on master–slave rape was "a deafening silence" reflecting the ubiquity of incestuous sex "within the fantasy family of slavery."[59]

There is little direct evidence to prove that Spanish men impregnated, or even sexually exploited, their Afro-Yucatecan slaves or servants.[60] But the morsels of evidence thus far uncovered are clear enough. For example, one of don Francisco de Anguas's slaves, named Diego Anguas, was also his son—a fact revealed when Diego's daughter [a *parda*] was baptized in 1788. Diego's mother must also have been a black slave owned by don Francisco and a servant in his household in Merida. Similarly, María Bartola, a parda baptized in Merida in 1794, was a granddaughter of an elite Spaniard, don Lucas Villamil; María's mother's official parents were don Lucas and his Spanish wife, but María's biological grandmother must have been an Afro-Yucatecan slave or servant in the Villamil household. In both these cases, it is significant that the sexual relationship between elite Spaniard and Afro-Yucatecan slave or servant is only exposed at the more distant moment of a grandchild's baptism.[61]

Furthermore, the indirect evidence also seems persuasive. For example, the household context of master–slave power relations and the common occurrence of a sexual component in such relations elsewhere, from the Atlantic world to the Indian Ocean, suggests that this was likely to be the case in Yucatan too. And the absence of Spanish–negra or Spanish–mulatta marriages means that the growth of a mulatto population (at least an Afro-Spanish one) could only have come about through illicit relations and illegitimate births.

Specifically, the baptism records for eighteenth-century Merida reveal an interesting pattern of illegitimacy. Unfortunately only the records of 1760–74 give consistent details, but they show that of the 1,663 Afro-Yucatecan children baptized in Jesús parish during this decade and a half, 253 (or 15%) were illegitimate (see Appendix G). In every case, these were "natural" children of an identified mother and "*padre no conosido* [father unknown]"; the vast majority of these mothers were free mulattas (238 of them, with just 11 enslaved negras, 2 free negras, 1 mestiza, and 1 Maya woman). Why did a mulatta choose not to identify the father of her child? Perhaps in some cases because she was not married to him, but surely not in most cases, as there are many other "natural" children in the parish records with two named, unmarried parents. More likely, then, the father was a Spanish employer who wished not to be identified, a wish that the Spanish priest would have respected (even if the mulatta mother did not).[62] My suggestion, therefore, is that this is indirect evidence of illicit sexual relations between Spanish employers and their mulatta servants.

What, then, of master–slave sexual relations? Why did so few negra slaves bring babies with "unknown fathers" to be baptized? There are several possible explanations. Negra slaves may have had few illegitimate children (unlikely). Or their illegitimate children were fathered by Afro-Yucatecan men, not Spanish masters; a third of negra slaves were owned by Spanish women and thus protected from Spanish seducers or predators in the household (possible, but surely not applicable to most slave women). Or the true identity of the father (ranging from a Spanish owner who raped his slave to an illicit Afro-Yucatecan lover) may have been masked by marriage; that is, the mother's husband appears in the record as the father, although in reality he was not (this was possible, but probably not common). Or the Spanish owner adopted the child as legitimately his and his wife's, taking the child to be baptized in the cathedral as a legitimate Spanish baby (again, possible, but probably not common). Or negra mothers impregnated by Spanish masters were discouraged from taking their children to be baptized; the stigma of conception was such that the birth was not made fully public, even if secrets were hard to keep in the small world that was colonial Merida (more likely).[63]

Whatever the explanation—and whatever the actual incidence of sexual relations and sexual exploitation of slave women by Spanish masters—the likelihood of such relations contributes to the social rationale behind slavery in the colony. Spaniards in Yucatan owned slaves for three reasons: (1) as skilled workers who ran or assisted in Spanish enterprises; (2) as domestic servants; and (3) as symbols of social prestige—as luxury commodities to be displayed and in a sense (economic and sexual exploitation) consumed.[64] Far from being mutually exclusive, these three factors often functioned in unison. The slave owners were the Spanish elite, partly because only the elite could afford them, but also because slave ownership was a defining social and cultural marker of elite status.

As important as that status marker was, it declined and disappeared in the early nineteenth century with relative speed and minimal controversy; it is to that topic—the end of slavery—that we now turn.

ABOLITION

On the day that slavery was abolished "only a keen observer could have marked the day as anything special, for there was no exodus, no angry revolts, no flooding of freedom lawsuits into the courts . . . thousands of slaves greeted the official, legal end of slavery by staying right where they were."[65] These words are a historian's account of abolition in the West African city–states of Fante in 1874, although they could just as well apply to much of the young Mexican republic, Yucatan included, in 1829.[66] Why was there not more of a negative reaction by the slave-holding elite—or a publicly positive one by emancipated slaves? Conversely, if abolition was not an explosive issue, why did it not take place in 1821, at the moment of Independence?

The roots of abolition in Mexico go back to the turn of the century. After the defeat of Napoleon in 1805, the abolitionist movement in Britain gained a series of political victories that culminated in 1807 in the complete suppression of slavery and the slave trade throughout the British Empire— followed by decades of pressure on other nations to follow suit. The British position did not mean that abolition would inevitably follow in the Americas; after all, slavery persisted in Brazil, Cuba, and the United States into the late nineteenth century. But it certainly influenced the thinking of Independence leaders, especially the exiles who spent time in England.[67] Abolitionist rhetoric was thus present in the earliest manifestations of the Independence

movement throughout Spanish America; the Venezuelan revolutionary constitution of 1811, for example, included the prohibition of "the vile traffic
in slaves."[68] In Mexico, rebel leaders Miguel Hidalgo and José María Morelos both proclaimed the end of slavery in 1810 and 1813, respectively. Indeed the October 19, 1810, decree written by Hidalgo's aide, José María
Ansorena, while saying nothing at all about Independence from Spain, did
declare that all owners in New Spain were to free their slaves immediately
"under penalty of death and confiscation of all property." Morelos sought
not only the end of slavery but also the abolition of casta classifications and
distinctions, turning everyone into "Americans."[69]

Such rhetoric implied social revolution even more than it did nationalist
independence, and was therefore precisely the kind of thinking that was opposed first by royalists in the 1810s and then by early Independence leaders
in the 1820s—often one and the same, including the first president and emperor, Agustín de Iturbide. The Spanish constitution of 1812 was "liberal"
in most regards, but the liberalism of the time did not preclude the attitudes
that underlay Article 22, which specifically denied citizenship and all its
rights to "those with some known trace of African lineage."[70] There was
nothing this explicit in the laws passed by the conservative governments of
the 1820s, but symbolic of Iturbide's position was his granting not of freedom but of new imperial livery to the slave coachmen who adorned the carriages of the imperial regime of 1822. Arguably, the issue of slavery in the
1820s was not really one of slavery, but of social equality. The elite feared
not abolition per se, but its potential, larger social ramifications. The same
was true elsewhere in Spanish America; in Venezuela, for example, abolition
had been declared in 1821, and then rescinded. Such fears underpinned the
compromise legislation of 1824 in Mexico, which banned the slave trade
without abolishing slavery (and while permitting Texas an exemption). Even
when slavery was finally abolished—by a presidential edict from Vicente
Guerrero, written on September 15, 1829, for the following day's Independence celebration—the new law provided for owners to be indemnified, albeit "when the circumstances of the treasury permit." There was an outcry
in Texas, and in December that year, under pressure from congress, Guerrero gave Texas slave owners another exemption from the law. Within days
of the Texas exemption, Guerrero's vice president, Anastasio Bustamante,
took up arms in Jalapa and declared himself in revolt against the president.
The Campeche elite, many of them slave owners, allegedly joined the revolt.
Congress backed Bustamante and impeached Guerrero, who was forced to
flee Mexico City; he was assassinated just over a year later by the Bustamante government.[71]

It is tempting to see abolition, and the reaction to it in Texas and perhaps
even in Campeche, as a causal factor in the timing of Guerrero's fall. However, the revolt by Bustamante was part of a larger pattern of pendulum
swings between factions, of frequent and violent transitions between gov-

ernments for decades after 1821; Bustamante was a former royalist general whose close associates in 1829 were mostly former royalist officers as well, including old enemies of Guerrero's from the wars of independence. Furthermore, the relationship between Texas and Mexico City was far more complex and troubled than a difference of opinion over slavery—as subsequent Texan history shows. Likewise, the so-called Campeche revolt was both more and less than an anti-abolition reaction—as we shall see in a moment. Finally, Bustamante's government nullified most of Guerrero's legislation, but not the abolition of slavery, even overturning the Texas exemption. Viewed from Mexico City, the principle of central authority was more important than the question of slavery.

Abolition, therefore, was a secondary issue in the 1820s, to be sanctioned or contested according to the political circumstances and opportunities that surrounded more vital power issues. Why was this the case, considering that there were still slaves in the new republic of Mexico, and slave owners among its ruling elite? Six factors are relevant. First, in all the mainland Spanish colonies that became independent in the 1820s, slavery was not a major part of the system of labor exploitation and economic production (unlike, for example, Brazil). Second, nor did slaves comprise more than 10% of the population (again, unlike Brazil), partly due to the decline in slave imports but also due to extensive miscegenation during the colonial centuries. Third, the new regimes guaranteed all other property rights, including those, most importantly, over land. When, eventually, slave owning was made an exception to this guarantee, it was precisely that—an exception, not the start of the revolution in property holding that the elite feared. Fourth, nor was abolition to be a social revolution; it was intended more as a gesture than an instrument for changing the working and living conditions of blacks and mulattoes. Fifth, in most Spanish American republics manumission was conceived as a gradual, judicial process, complete with indemnities paid by the state to slave owners.[72] Sixth, slavery as an institution had already declined considerably; in many colonies by the turn of the nineteenth century it was not as viable or important to economic and social life as it had been earlier.[73]

These factors applied to most of Spanish America, and certainly to Mexico; to what extent were they relevant to the Yucatan peninsula? In the eight years between Independence and the abolition decree, one might at first have the impression that the business of slavery continued in what was now the Mexican state of Yucatan. For example, in the early 1820s, fledgling newspapers in Merida were advertising slaves for sale. One notice, which ran in *El Constitucionalista* on April 7, 1821, and again in the *Periodico Constitutional* two days later, offered "Hipólito Ramírez, 18-to-20 years old, healthy and without defects, [knowing] the essentials of shoemaking, cooking, and the masonry trade, for 600 pesos, in the house of doña Lorenza Lara on Avocado St., next to the San Juan plaza; reason [for the sale] will be given."[74] This was an unusually high price for a slave in Yucatan (as Tables 2.1 and D.3 in Appendix D show). Did these mean that the demand for slaves in Yucatan persisted, even as the trade came under attack, thus pushing up prices? Most likely this was not the case. There is no record of doña Lorenza Lara actually selling Hipólito Ramírez, and if she did, she would have been lucky to receive as much as six hundred pesos. Values of two to three hundred pesos were more common in the 1820s, as illustrated by the values recorded for the slaves registered as freed in 1829. In other words, as the trade declined, so did sales, while prices remained stable—if not a tad below the averages of the previous decades. Slaves were still bought and sold, but they were no longer mortgaged, the days of regular public auctions were over, and state governors and bishops did not buy groups of slaves when they first took office as their colonial predecessors had done. By the 1790s, black adult slaves had fallen to less than 3% of all baptisms in Merida's Afro-Yucatecan parish of Jesús; in the following decade, the tiny minority of *negros* disappeared as a category, folded into that of mulattoes, who were then folded into that of mestizos after 1821.[75] The elision of blacks into mulattoes was paralleled by an elision of slaves into servants—in particular ex-slaves, who continued to be viewed and treated as the property of their former owners, "in whose power they existed," as one judicial official put it in 1832.[76] After all, for centuries the word for "freeman," *horro*, had also meant "servant."[77] In other words, the persistence of a category of free-colored servants, who lived and worked in an attached subordination to employers that was similar in some ways to the domestic master–slave relationship, helped ease slavery into decline.

Small numbers of slaves still appear in the archival records after 1800, and the occasional slave can still be found in the 1820s—an 1821 newspaper advertisement is one example; another is from 1825, when one summer night a slave named Manuel was stabbed by a "moreno libre," who was jailed for the assault.[78] There were maybe two hundres slaves in the whole peninsula in 1821, and surely less than that by the time of abolition in 1829; during that decade, slave business gradually faded from the notarial records. In large part due to the six mitigating factors listed above, the Yucatec elite neither rallied to the defense of slavery nor did they embrace its abolition with much conviction or enthusiasm. The state's Congreso Constituyente passed a decree banning any future importation of slaves on September 13, 1823—ten months before a similar federal law was passed in Mexico City.[79] Congress then reiterated this law in the constitution of 1825, adding that Yucatec citizenship was to be extended to "the slaves now existing in the state, upon acquisition within it of their freedom"—but no provision was made for the granting of said freedom.[80] One member of an elite Yucatec family, Lorenzo de Zavala, was finance minister in the 1829 Guerrero administration and became one of the most outspoken abolitionists of his day, although one historian has accused him of having "an abundance of racial prejudice."[81] Whether such a judgment is fair or not, Zavala, like the political newspapers that ran the 1821 "Slave for Sale" advertisement, spoke a great deal about *libertad* without any reference to Afro-Yucatecan slaves.[82]

This is not to say that all Hispanic Yucatecans were ambivalent over the issue, or that slave owners in Yucatan did not protest either partial abolition in 1823 or the full law of 1829. But, as elsewhere in the Mexican republic, the issue was subsumed into larger ones of regionalism and political power. A friendly rivalry between Campeche and Merida in the colonial period developed in the postindependence decades into a feud that was to help push the peninsula into a bloody civil war in the 1840s.[83] In the 1820s, as during the colonial period, both slaves and slave owners made up a greater percentage of the population in Campeche than they did in Merida. But as Merida was the state capital (Campeche would not achieve its own statehood for another three decades), it was in that city that the state congress passed the 1823 law. Consequently it was the Campeche elite who protested in 1824 that the constitution deprived them of property without restitution.[84] Likewise, Yucatan's most vocal complaints against the 1829 law came from Campeche (from the city itself and from Villa del Carmen). A historian of Vicente Guerrero has argued that abolition provoked Yucatan into revolt against the Mexican president in December that year, a revolt organized by plantation owners in Campeche.[85] In fact, Yucatan's military coup d'état of 1829 occurred on November 6, when General don José Segundo Carvajal effectively declared the state's secession from the Mexican republic. In the early nineteenth century, Yucatec elite rivalry pitted centralists against federalists, whose ideological differences were harder to distinguish than were their regional affiliations to Campeche and Merida, respectively.[86] Carvajal's coup was a pro-centralist one and thus favorable to Campeche interests (which included opponents of abolition) and hostile to Mexico City (where Guerrero was president). But the coup had far more to do with the major issues of Campeche–Merida relations and Yucatan–Mexico relations than it did with the relatively minor issue of slavery—as illustrated by a letter from Carvajal to anti-abolitionists (to which we shall turn shortly).

Indeed, considerable insight into this dynamic can be garnered from the few extant archival materials relating to abolition in Yucatan. The decree of September 15, 1829, required slave owners to report to the *cabeceras* or head-towns of each jurisdiction and make a notarized statement recording each slave's release. Yucatan's state government acknowledged and ratified the decree on October 12 and within a matter of days slave owners came forward to register and free their slaves. It may be archival accident, but it may also be symbolic of regional reactions to the decree that all extant records of such registrations are from the northwest (Merida and Hunucmá). The rapid response to the decree may also be explained by the apparent willingness of the state treasury to pay indemnities—in effect, to purchase and then manumit slaves. This was in contrast to the failure of the Mexican government to pay indemnities,[87] although a similar failure may explain the lack of records on slave registration from in and around Campeche. Furthermore, although the genre of record, the *Registro de Esclavos Libertos*, seems full-fledged, it is not clear whether the examples from the northwest represent a small or large percentage of all the registrations that took place.

The first of these examples comes from Hunucmá. There, during four days from the 16th to the 19th of October, four slave owners appeared, most of them from the port of Sisal, a short distance to the north, to show their compliance with the law. Each had a single slave. Showing proof of purchase, the average value of these liberated Afro-Yucatecans was 285 pesos. Two of the owners were men, registering male slaves; don Tomás Aznar y Peón, for example, claimed a value of three hundred pesos for Francisco, whom he had purchased from a Spaniard in Havana in 1817 (fortunately for Francisco, who, had he remained in Cuba, would not have lived long enough to see abolition there). The other two owners were women, both with female slaves; Cecilia Rivas Cacho, for example, had inherited in 1822 from her father José a black girl named María Salomé, whom she now registered as free, for a three-hundred-peso indemnity.[88] The following week, doña María Josefa Lanzos de Morales appeared before officials in Merida with three slaves. Named María Valmina Morales, José Morales, and Juana María Morales, each was registered for an indemnity of four hundred pesos. Doña María Josefa's husband was don Antonio Morales, a Madrid-born prominent local and one-time treasury minister, which may explain why his wife received solid indemnities for all three slaves. It may likewise be significant that the Cecilia Rivas Cacho's husband was the *contador* or government accountant, Antonio Herrera.[89]

Not all slave owners were so well connected, however, nor were they willing to comply with the law, especially in the district of Campeche. In 1831, thirteen of the leading slave-owning citizens of Villa del Carmen (twelve men and one woman) drew up a petition to the governor of Yucatan (the town was in the jurisdiction of Campeche, still part of the state of Yucatan). The petition disingenuously requested clarification of the laws and decrees on slavery "that don Vicente Guerrero issued during his presidency, abusing the extraordinary powers with which he was invested." The petitioners condemned the decree of September 15, 1829, and asked for their former slaves to be returned to them, "considering that we have all the necessary rights to a property from which we have been illegally dispossessed." The petitioners went on to suggest that in their post-emancipacion idleness, these *negros* would represent a loss to the state economy (the "Hacienda Pública") and a threat to national security—as they might "secretly meet up with the foreign ships that frequent this port, some making small embarkations at all hours in the interior, up river and at small ranches," with the ex-slaves "penetrating the settlements of Guatemala, from where it will be difficult to extract them."[90]

The governor's reply is telling, both of the attitude of much of the Merida elite toward abolition and of the simple reality that by 1831 African slavery in Yucatan was a dead issue. The governor—the above-mentioned Carvajal— began by tacitly agreeing that Guerrero had overstepped the bounds of just action. The governor then firmly denied the petitioners' request. Carvajal's position was a predictably regionalist one, tempered by practical considerations. In theory, he suggested, the Mexican federal government should not tell Yucatecans what to do. But in practice:

Suppose that the Government of Yucatan ordered that the slaves be restored to their old servitude, and that the chambers [of Congress], considering in the revision and inspection of these arrangements [i.e., Guerrero's decrees] the grave inconveniences that would result from the appeal of the decree that freed them, declared it [abolition] still in force? What side should be taken in this case? Should our government perhaps go back on its forethought [*providencia*] in order to conform to the national will, or would you have those unfortunates [*desgraciados*] continue in their slavery? The commission [i.e., Carvajal's administration] understands that both extremes would be too indecorous, and that it would be impossible to decide for one better than for the other, but suggests waiting for the chambers to conclude their work of revising and inspecting Article 9 of the sovereign decree that prompted the petition of these citizens, thus to resolve with a wise decision this important business that concerns not only offense against justice but also outrage against humanity.

A week later, the governor's council approved his letter, but added a weak stinger to its tail, agreeing:

. . . that in order to avoid the flight that the petitioners fear, the government dictate the means it believes necessary to prevent their [the ex-slaves'] departure from this province, at least with all due precaution.[91]

Those "means" were not detailed in the addendum to Carvajal's letter, but in essence the council had undermined his diplomatic condemnation of slavery by giving former owners permission to use coercive measure to retain former slaves as employees. Thus, with a wimper, did the enslavement of Afro-Yucatecans come to an end.

National security arguments by anti-abolitionists were a weak coda to the crux of their position, which was a simple claim to property rights. This claim had underpinned African slavery in Yucatan for three centuries. Yet slavery was as much—if not more—a social issue as an economic one. Abolition could not have a major impact on the peninsula's economy, as African slaves had never comprised a large-scale labor force. Certainly, individual Spaniards had paid hundreds of pesos for each human being they owned, and thus abolition financially impacted slave owners. Just as slaves were traded and worked as individuals in Yucatan, so was it individual owners who protested their long overdue emancipation. But the financial impact was mitigated for those who were able to claim indemnities. More importantly, slaves had functioned for centuries as prestigious commodities. As the social value of that prestige declined, so did the significance of slavery; and vice versa. Provincial governors had once bought and given Christian names to Africans almost as a rite of office; by 1831, their heir, the state governor, was calling slavery "an outrage against humanity." Not that this indicated that prejudicial attitudes toward black slaves and free coloreds in colonial Yucatan had faded into tolerance by the early nineteenth century. But the casta structure that had supported those attitudes had shifted into a socioracial system that elided Afro-Yucatecans into a larger category of mestizos, a system that had no place for *negros*, let alone African slaves. This was not tolerance, but a different form of discrimination, one that served to render Afro-Yucatecans invisible. It is to that topic—prejudicial attitudes and the casta structure—that we now turn.

CHAPTER THREE

Race and Rank

Because I have the coloring of a mulatto, the officials molest me and arrest me, believing that I am a captive [slave], [despite] being free, from which I have received well-known abuse.
—Francisco de Aguilar, free Afro-Yucatecan, in Seville, 1619[1]

Having asked for the consent of doña María de Luz Herrera, mother of my betrothed, I encountered in her strong opposition, due to the inequality of status [calidad] between her and me.
—Francisco Medina, free Afro-Yucatecan, Izamal, 1791[2]

There is no more reason [for different skin tones] than God wishing to display his marvels through the variety of colors, as in the flowers of the countryside.   —Juan de Torquemada, 1615[3]

Notwithstanding the bad qualities of the Mulatto, some of them have been found, who from their extraordinary virtues and qualifications have deserved great marks of approbation and distinction from the viceroys, bishops, and other persons of eminence, [which] examples we conceive to be sufficient to shew how little influence the colour of a man has over the endowments of his soul.
—from the "Mulatto" entry in Antonio de Alcedo's 1786–89 *Dictionary*[4]

This important business concerns not only offense against justice but also outrage against humanity.
—Yucatan's governor responding to an anti-abolition petition, 1831[5]

THE STORY OF FRANCISCO DE AGUILAR

On June 14, 1619, an eighteen-year-old named Francisco de Aguilar appeared in the offices of the customs house in Seville. The notary on duty that day, Benito Ruiz Davila, dipped his quill in the inkpot and noted on a fresh sheet of paper Aguilar's request "that I be given license to return to the province of Yucatan, from where I came." Born in Valladolid, Aguilar

had never left that small Yucatec town until his employer, Dr. don Pedro
Sánchez de Aguilar, brought him to Spain earlier in the year. Don Pedro
was cathedral dean and one of the most important clergymen in Yucatan;
when Francisco was a child, don Pedro had conducted campaigns against
Maya "idolatry" in the villages east of Valladolid, and had found a number of pictorial and hieroglyphic codices, which he now brought back to
Spain with him. Francisco was probably charged with helping to keep an
eye on these documents—not because of their monetary value, but because they were evidence of the kind of dangerous recidivism among the
Mayas about which don Pedro had written to the king at length. Francisco could not have known that among these codices was likely the manuscript that survives today as the famous, immensely valuable Madrid
Codex.[6]

While don Pedro sought and gained at least two audiences with the king,
Francisco remained in Seville. One imagines that he might have been fasci-
nated by what was one of the largest and busiest cities in the world. But instead, he hated it. Francisco's short life as a servant had been a great deal
more modest and sheltered than that of his employer, don Pedro; his whole
world had been the boondocks of Valladolid.[7] He now found himself miser-
ably homesick. The chief source of his unhappiness was his treatment at the
hands of local officials in Seville, who harassed and even arrested him on
the mistaken grounds that he was a slave, simply because he had "the coloring of a mulatto."[8]

Francisco's claim that he was a victim of assumptions and attitudes that we
would classify as racist raises crucial questions about race and rank in the
Spanish world; Francisco prompts one to imagine officials in Seville engaging
in a kind of racial profiling. But is such a phrase applicable here, and would
any teenager of "the coloring of a mulatto" have been so readily and negatively labeled in 1619? Were things different by 1719 or 1819? Did a coherent ideology of race circulate among Spaniards, and was theirs thus a "racist"
world? Why was Francisco's public treatment in Seville apparently so different from that of Valladolid, Yucatan?

A closer look at Francisco's request for a travel license only raises further
questions. In the heading at the top of the opening page the notary labels
Francisco "free mulatto [*mulato libre*]," but calls him "creole mulatto [*mulato criollo*]" in the first paragraph. "Criollo" meant American-born and,
unlike "creole," did not carry the additional meaning of African-descended;
before the mid-sixteenth century, "criollo" *did* refer only to a black person
born outside Africa (be it in Europe or the Americas), but it subsequently
came to be used more widely to include Spaniards born in the Americas.[9] By
1619, therefore, the term no longer indicated that someone was necessarily
of African descent, although it was often used in that context (and as a surname would only be used by a black or mulatto); nor was it synonymous
with "free," although it sometimes implied that.

This was certainly how Francisco himself saw the term; he called himself "creole of the Indies and native of the town of Valladolid [*criollo de la yndias natural de la villa de Balladolid*]," and asserted that "I am free and not a slave [*cautibo*], I am a creole and a free person" (see Appendix A).[10] Francisco avoided the term *esclavo* and did not call himself *mulato* (only admitting to "having the coloring of a mulatto [*la color de mulato*]"). He insisted his parents were free, naming his mother as Inés Chica, an "Indian" (Chica was not a Maya patronym, suggesting Inés may have been of mixed race or of Nahua descent). More revealingly, he could not name his father; a space was left blank in his statement, with the word *negro* after it, but then, presumably at Francisco's prompting, the notary went back and squeezed "his father unknown" into the blank space and crossed out *negro*. Although the witnesses, including Sánchez de Aguilar himself, stated that they did not know who Francisco's father was, the dean would not necessarily have had detailed knowledge of all the relationships in his household, especially as he had traveled extensively in northeast Yucatan during Francisco's childhood and must have maintained residences in both Valladolid and Merida. It is thus tempting to imagine Inés Chica as a native servant in the Sanchéz de Aguilar household (*chica*, meaning "girl," was commonly used by Spaniards to mean "domestic servant, maid") and the boy's father as one of the black servants in the same household. But if Francisco was of indigenous-African descent, why was he called a mulatto, not a *pardo* (technically the correct term for such a mixture)? Why was the notary in Seville inconsistent in applying adjectives to the "mulatto" label? What of Francisco's own use and avoidance of racial labels; did Afro-Yucatecans and Spaniards view this terminology differently?

This chapter offers some answers to these questions. The first section examines the nature of Spanish prejudice against black Africans, asking whether such attitudes amounted to an ideology of racism. The second section looks further at Spanish concepts of race and rank, specifically the so-called *casta* system. Each section begins by discussing evidence from the larger Spanish world, before turning to detailed evidence and case studies from colonial Yucatan. Hitherto the book's focus has been primarily on slaves; from here on, our discussion is as much about free coloreds, or free people of African descent, as it is about slaves.

PRIDE AND PREJUDICE

In the previous chapter, we saw how Spanish slave owners in Yucatan saw Africans both as property and as human beings. One might expect that the treatment of slaves as economic units as much as human ones would have been supported by an ideology of race in Spanish America. Indeed, in theory, the Spaniards held to an ideological justification of slavery that clearly relegated Africans to a separate level below Europeans. But in practice, justifications for slavery and the expressions of prejudice that accompanied them amounted to an ideology of race that was more incipient than coherent, and more about rank than race. The details of such justifications varied, depending on who was articulating them and when, and there was never a high-level debate on African slavery of the kind that made the status of "Indians" so controversial in the sixteenth century; as is often pointed out, the most famous defender of indigenous rights, fray Bartolomé de las Casas, condoned slavery and himself owned Africans.[11]

Certainly, expressions of Spanish attitudes toward Africans could be viscerally direct. Two examples, two centuries apart, representing both sides of the transatlantic flow of official correspondence, illustrate the point: A royal cedula of 1578 commented on "the bad customs and viciousness" of mestizos, mulattoes, and blacks, who were "universally so wickedly inclined"; and in 1778, the provincial governor of Santa Marta (Colombia) wrote to the king that to trade local cattle for slaves from Jamaica amounted to "an exchange of meat for meat."[12]

It is not hard to find such expressions of prejudice against Africans or the use of sweeping stereotypes by the administrators of Spanish imperial rule. James Sweet, a historian of colonial Afro-Brazil, has argued that Iberian prejudice against black Africans was already so widespread and virulent in the fifteenth century as to constitute "racism without race."[13] One account of Lima, written in the 1770s, exaggerated the Afro-Peruvian population at more than half the city's residents and complained that "it is impossible that there is another country in the world where these people are as licentious as here"—a comment that might have come from any Spanish American city of the day. The seventeenth-century Spanish jurist and colonial administrator, Juan de Solórzano Pereira, claimed that mulattoes were thus termed because such a mix was that much "more ugly and strange" and they had "the nature of the mule."[14] Early in the colonial period a dichotomy of stereotypes emerged; "the Indians" were a *gente debil* [weak people] or *miserable* [wretched], while Africans were strong, threatening, and inclined to *mal* [wickedness]. Thus the king was advised by senior officials in Mexico City in 1584 that the "weak Indians" be left to their own occupations while the hard work—"the labor of mines, construction, mills," and so on—be reserved for blacks, mulattoes, and mestizos.[15] Modern scholars have viewed this dichotomy in gendered terms; Spaniards feminized natives and masculinized blacks and mulattoes.[16]

Yet it would be misleading to put too much stock in the expressions of such a dichotomy. Most obviously, it did not reflect a consistent, parallel division of labor between black and native men (natives worked the mines, free coloreds farmed corn fields, and so on). Even the apparent parallel dichotomy of attitudes toward (and laws on) slavery was fuzzy around the edges. The enslaving of natives had been banned in 1542, a ban that was regularly reiterated; yet loopholes permitting the enslavement of native rebels in "just" wars remained in place and were widely used (especially in the borderlands of the Mexican far north and the southern Andes).[17] At the same time, Spanish law ensured that the child of an enslaved *negro* (although not of a *negra*) was born free, and that all black slaves had the right to purchase their freedom and go to court to pursue that right.[18] In contrast to slave law in the British colonies, Spanish laws protected slaves from abuse by Spanish masters (even if such laws were not always effective or enforced); in 1693 the king of Spain ordered the authorities in Cuba to oppose the abuse of slaves on the grounds that "their slavery is a sufficient sorrow without at the same time suffering the distempered rigour of their masters."[19] Finally, patterns of manumission and mestizaje meant that for much of the colonial period most people of African descent in Spanish America were free. Therefore, just because in most Spanish colonies (Yucatan included) the slaves were black and the indigenous workers were free, did not mean that Spaniards assumed that the natural order of the world was for all Africans to be enslaved and all natives not.

The ambiguity of Spanish attitudes neither subsided during the colonial centuries nor evolved into something more coherent. But while the set of prejudices and stereotypes regarding non-Spanish inhabitants of the empire remained vague and contradictory throughout the colonial centuries, they were deeply rooted and often virulent by the eighteenth century. This is well illustrated by the entry under *Mulato* in Antonio de Alcedo's dictionary of the history and geography of the Americas, first published in the late 1780s. "America abounds with Mulattoes," stated Alcedo, who are

the offspring of a libidinous intercourse between Europeans and female slaves, which the authority of the one and the sensuality of the other tend to make very general. The colour of the children thus produced participate of both white and black, or are rather of a dingy brown colour. Their hair is less crisp than that of the *Negro* and of a clear chestnut tint. The Mulatto is regularly well made, of fine stature, vigorous, strong, industrious, intrepid, ferocious, but given to pleasure, deceitful, and capable of committing the greatest crimes without compunction. It is a certain fact, that throughout the vast dominions of the king of Spain in America there are no better soldiers than the Mulattoes, nor more infamous men.

Alcedo crowns this summary of positive and negative stereotypes with the remark that many mulattoes have served the state with virtue and distinction, proving that "the colour of a man" has little influence "over the endowments of his soul."[20]

Alcedo's admittance—his celebration, even—of mulatto exceptions to the rule is a parallel to the paradox of slaves as both property and people. Both are part of a larger phenomenon that is central to the colonial Spanish ideology of race and rank: the disjuncture between ideal and reality. This was manifest in numerous ways, from the specific usage in Yucatan of casta terminology (detailed in the next section) to the empire-wide ambiguity of Church attitudes toward African slavery. The position of the Church is worth looking at briefly. For most of the colonial period, the Roman Catholic Church, in step with the Spanish crown, condemned the enslavement of native Americans. But with respect to other slaves, especially black Africans, the Church avoided directly justifying or opposing the institution, waiting to embrace an abolitionist stance until the 1830s—hardly ahead of the political curve.[21]

The contrast between the Church's response to the European discovery of native Americans and its response to the boom in the transatlantic slave trade is a stark one. In 1537 Pope Paul III stated unequivocally to the Archbishop of Toledo, and in a bill of the same year, that "the Indians . . . should not be reduced to slavery," repeating to Charles V in 1542 an insistence on the native right to liberty and evangelization. Influenced in part by the pope, and by the arguments of advocates for native non-slavery (most prominently Bartolomé de Las Casas and Francisco de Vitoria), the emperor promulgated the New Laws of 1542–43, codifying the crown's ban on the enslavement of "the Indians."[22] Although the vigorous sixteenth-century debate over the nature of native Americans was not paralleled by a similar debate over African slavery, there was not total silence on the matter. In 1539 Vitoria denounced the Portuguese role in the Atlantic slave trade (which was then still almost entirely in Portuguese hands). Two Dominicans, Mercado and Albornoz, the latter a law professor in Mexico City, both published condemnations of the slave trade in the 1570s. Over the next century, at least half a dozen theologians, most of them Jesuits, published denunciations of the trade as illegal and immoral. However, the Church either ignored or banned these opinions. Albornoz's book, for example, was placed on the Inquisition index shortly after its first printing; the Jesuit Alonso de Sandoval's grim portrayal of African slavery in Spanish America was published in Latin in 1627 as *De instaurauda Aethiopium salute*, but was not available in Spanish until 1956.[23]

While stopping short of formally justifying the institution, senior clergymen tended to argue that black slavery was a regrettable necessity, an opinion they backed up by owning slaves themselves. Thus not only did Church doctrines fail to provide a theological or moral framework for the condemnation or undermining of the slave trade, they effectively promoted the trade through their relative silence on the subject and their example as slave owners.

The Church's ambiguous yet tacit approval of slavery must also be seen in a larger context still. Any attempt to understand either a slave society (which colonial Yucatan was not) or a society with slaves (which it was) must recognize the contrast between modern and early modern attitudes toward the institution. As Gordon Wood, prominent historian of North American slavery, has observed, "Slavery is virtually inconceivable to us. We can scarcely imagine one person owning another."[24] Yet it is fair to generalize that for the entire span of human history up to the dawn of the abolition movement in the late eighteenth century, slavery was an accepted dimension of human society. Spaniards in the colonial period were heirs to that long legacy.

We may surmise, then, that Spaniards made a pair of related assumptions: that slavery was a part of civilized life; and that people were neither the same nor equal. But assuming difference and inequality is not the same as assuming inferiority in an essentialist racial sense. To be sure, Spaniards were prejudiced against Africans and mulattoes, but they were also prejudiced against "Indians," Italians, and Jews. Furthermore, Castilians were prejudiced against Basques. There is also abundant evidence of English prejudices against black Africans in the sixteenth and seventeenth centuries, but the English were likewise prejudiced against Spaniards—and the Scots, Italians, Jews, "sodomites," and so on.[25] In other words, the ethnocentrism of the early modern world was a kind of racism without race and a precursor to the development of modern racism; but it was not an expression of modern racism and the two should not be conflated.

The modern "discovery" that race is socially constructed obscures three simple facts relevant to how socioracial identity was viewed in Spanish America. First, race, like class, is a particular type of social construction—a historical construction (as slave-trade historian Ira Berlin has pointed out);[26] its development was rooted in a particular time and place, primarily outside and later than mainland colonial Spanish America. Although modern ideas about race were forming toward the end of the colonial period, and Spanish American thinkers may have contributed to that formation, the full-fledged ideologies of race and racism that came to underpin imperialism and slavery in the nineteenth century cannot be projected back onto Spanish America in the sixteenth through eighteenth centuries.

Second, race is in varying ways an articulation of visibly obvious phenotypical differences between individuals. The fact that this is an inexact or controversial science, that it may be driven by prejudice, and that race is thus not "real" in a genetic sense, does not detract from the concrete consequences of individuals in Spanish America perceiving such differences. Biologists tell us that modern racial groups "differ from one another in about 6% of their genes," with the remaining 94% of genetic variation occurring "*within* so-called racial groups" (in the words, emphasis included, of the American Anthropological Association's (AAA) official statement on the subject).[27] Such a fact undermines the notion that race is what primarily differentiates us from each other, but that 6% of difference is enough of a foundation for a society to build an *idea* of race that, combined with other differentiating factors, might amount to a working social structure. This, in fact, as we shall see in detail, is precisely what Spanish Americans did. The AAA statement on "race" juxtaposes "the idea of race" with "mere physical differences," rightly observing that historically the former has tended to carry more meaning than the latter; however, to understand Spanish America, perceptions of physical differences must neither be ignored nor overstated, but rather placed within the context of multiple perceptions of difference, all of which combined to create an idea of rank.

Third, therefore, is that awareness of the socially constructed element to race is nothing new; it has been known for centuries to those who have sought (and declined) to assign racial labels to individuals within racially complex populations. In 1900 census workers in Dallas were asked to classify the city's multiracial residents; "their answers reflect local opinion," reported the census director, "and that opinion probably is based more upon social position and manner of life than upon the relative amounts of blood."[28] As we shall see, he might have been talking about the Yucatan of a century and more earlier.

Indeed, to turn to specific evidence from Yucatan, we find that Spaniards in the colony shared the views of Spaniards elsewhere—hardly surprising as Spanish Yucatan was always linked to the rest of the empire by colonial bureaucracies, commerce, and a small but steady immigration of new settlers. Priests in Yucatan, for example, were no different from priests elsewhere in the Spanish Empire. The Church failed to unambiguously condemn African slavery and so, as we saw in the previous chapter, the colony's priests were highly prominent among its slave owners. For some Spaniards and Mayas in Yucatan, the simple fact that priests owned black slaves must in effect have provided moral support to the institution—and to the notion that Afro-Yucatecans alone, unlike Spaniards, Mayas, and mestizos, fell into the category of the enslaveable.

Indeed, Dr. don Juan Gómez de Parada, the bishop who was arguably the most progressive-minded in the province's history—at least in the sense that he made the greatest effort to reform the system of forced labor that underpinned Spanish exploitation of Mayas—was himself a slave owner. In 1725, when he had been bishop for a decade, he purchased four newly arrived African-born slaves, two men and two women.[29] He sought to free Mayas from their "wretched condition of slavery [*miserable condición de esclavitud*]," but he used the term "slavery" as a metaphor for obligatory, under-paid labor, without questioning whether those who were really enslaved in Yucatan should be freed.[30]

The ideal society that Gómez de Parada envisioned in his reformist mission statements was a semi-segregated one in which interaction between castas, Spaniards, and Mayas was not banned but regulated. The bishop was more realistic than those who over the centuries wrote royal and viceregal edicts banning black and free-colored men from marrying native women or living in native villages; for example, he mandated that mulattoes be separated from Mayas during the teaching of the doctrine, so that colored children could be taught in Spanish and native children in Yucatec Maya. The bishop viewed "Indians" in stereotypical terms as *rudos* ["crude, simple"] and *miserables* ["wretched"], the latter a common adjective to describe natives in New Spain, one that at best made them victims and at worse judged them lazy, rustic, and ignorant.[31] Interestingly, the bishop does not slip into corresponding stereotypes about blacks and mulattoes; indeed he tends to juxtapose "the wretched Indians" with "Spaniards and people of color [*gente de color*]," often placing free coloreds in the same category as Spaniards. In matters such as catechism and the registration of parishioners, mulattoes were to be treated together with mestizos and Spaniards and separate from "Indians." Afro-Yucatecans were certainly not viewed by the bishop as equals to Spaniards, but one looks in vain in his 570-page "Synodal Constitution" of 1722, for example, for coherent racial concepts about non-Mayas or statements of prejudice against people of color.[32]

It is reasonable to imagine that a Spanish bishop's attitude had roots in Spanish religious history, and thus tempting to see in Gómez de Parada's dichotomy between Mayas and non-Mayas an echo of the medieval Iberian dividing line between Christians and non-Christians. The important difference is that medieval Iberians like Alfonso X categorized all Africans as Muslims, putting them on the wrong side of the line, justifying their enslavement.[33] In colonial Yucatan, however, black and colored subjects of the crown were not only Christian but firmly located in the Spanish Christian world—unlike Mayas, whose nature made them superficial converts prone to recidivism. In other words, colonial circumstances meant that the religion factor hindered, rather than helped, the evolution of old prejudices into modern anti-black racism.

Throughout colonial Yucatan's history, bishop and governor, priests and settlers, fought over their access to the labor and production of the Maya majority; Afro-Yucatecans did not constitute a comparable battleground, and therefore one does not find much commentary on blacks and mulattoes in the documentation generated by local church–state conflict. However, there were periodic attempts to find ways of making the colony more prosperous, and the reports surrounding such attempts tended to argue that African slavery was elemental to colonial prosperity.

For example, in the 1766 report on Yucatan's economy prepared for the Visitor General of New Spain, don José de Gálvez, African slavery was justified on three relativist grounds. The first, based on a hyperbolic cultural relativism, argued that Africans had always enslaved each other and tended furthermore to kill their slaves; thus by purchasing them, Europeans saved their lives. The second, drawing upon a combined cultural and economic relativism, argued that African slaves in Spanish America lived "happier lives" than they would "in their own country," being given opportunities to cultivate the land and work in mines and on sugar plantations. The third argument was a somewhat mercantilist one—that the Spanish Empire would fall further behind its European rivals by not engaging in the slave trade with equal vigor.[34]

The argument in the Gálvez report was based on an assumption of historical and cultural difference between Africa and the Spanish world, and by the eighteenth century Spaniards in Yucatan no doubt shared the assumption of Europeans in general that Africans were different in mind and body than they were. For example, a pamphlet on smallpox vaccinations published in Campeche in 1816 noted that "In blacks, one must make incisions a little deeper than in whites, and on the inside of the arm," without explaining why, as though readers shared an assumption of black difference and needed only to be told of its practical implications.[35]

But, as argued above, assumptions of difference did not amount to a coherent ideology of race, let alone assumptions that Afro-Yucatecans, by virtue of their skin color, would or should always be slaves. Evidence of manumissions in Yucatan suggests that it is unlikely that most Spaniards in the colony believed that Africans were always better off as slaves; they no doubt believed (like the 1766 Gálvez report) that Africans were better off in Yucatan than in Africa, but not necessarily as slaves. Some Spaniards—like the Campeche hacendados hoping to expand their sugar farms in the 1780s—wished there were more black slaves in the colony.[36] But the economic booms of the colonial period (like that of sugar in the colony's final decades) were too small to justify major capital investment in imported slave labor; by the time the big boom came, in henequen not sugar, African slavery had long been abolished.[37]

Spaniards in Yucatan probably viewed the institution of slavery as simply the mechanism that brought Africans to a better place, an opportunity for slave and master alike, but not one that by definition condemned slaves to a miserable life or to perpetual bondage. More likely Spaniards shared the view of the king of Spain, that slavery was itself "sufficient sorrow." Not that all Spaniards in the province would have shared the same views. There are sufficient examples of Spaniards in the colony choosing not to own slaves, or to own but not abuse slaves—opting to refrain from imposing the punishments of whipping and mutilation that law permitted, giving slaves considerable flexibility of movement, and granting slaves their freedom—to suggest that Spaniards did not share a monolithic attitude toward the institution. Admittedly, the colony did not depend on African labor, and thus Spaniards there could afford the luxury, as it were, of an ambiguous attitude toward African slavery. Yet slavery could exist in this society, and be associated with one race in particular, without all Spaniards sharing the same racist (or viscerally prejudicial) attitudes. Recent scholarship on the history of slavery in the earliest decades of the United States has highlighted the contrast between the views of George Washington and Thomas Jefferson. Washington, for years an unflinching slave owner, had a profound change of heart in the 1780s and came to see the insititution as morally reprehensible. Jefferson believed that blacks were probably inherently inferior to whites, with whom they could never live in peace; he was, in Gordon Wood's words, "a slave-holding aristocrat with what we today would consider racist views."[38] During these same years, and for the two preceding centuries, Yucatan surely had Washingtons as well as Jeffersons.

One potential way to access the Jeffersons of colonial Yucatan is to look at the treatment of slaves. For example, in the 1690s Juan Martín de Herrera, a Campeche resident, was convicted of murdering his black slave. Can this crime be seen as symbolic of the violent exercise of authority by masters over slaves? Unfortunately, the symbolism of this particular case lies in its silences, not its details. Juan Martín was simultaneously convicted of killing his wife, suggesting a circumstance beyond master–slave relations, the details of which are lost or still buried in the archives.[39] Nor have other, more complete cases emerged from the archives. Sometimes it is the attitudes and habits most taken for granted that are absent from the historical record, and this may include the assumption that slave owners could—and often did—abuse their human property. In such cases, prevalent attitudes can only be gleaned in passing; for example, in one of the many documents stemming from fray Diego de Landa's vicious anti-idolatry campaign of 1562, the Mayas tortured by the Franciscans are described as being "suspended and beaten until a great amount of blood flowed from their backs and legs onto the floor; and they basted them with wax like black slaves."[40] I have found no direct evidence that black slaves in Yucatan were disciplined with hot wax, but in the late sixteenth-century Spanish mind such a torture was clearly associated with the punishment of Africans. We can reasonably assume that slaves in the province were subject to arbitrary acts of violence, especially in the early colonial decades—after all, brutality and the Atlantic slave trade were synonymous, and Yucatan was as violent a place as anywhere in the sixteenth-century Atlantic world.

However, I suspect that blatant maltreatment of slaves in Yucatan became less common and less accepted as the seventeenth and eighteenth centuries wore on, as conquest violence shifted to the peninsula's south and black slaves became increasingly outnumbered by free coloreds. As this was a society with slaves, not a slave society, there were not even slave-worked textile mills (as there were in central Mexico), let alone large-scale sugar plantations, and thus little of the systematic violence that came with such enterprises.[41]

At the start of this project I set out (and expected) to find evidence of sanctioned violence against slaves. But I only found one case of a black slave tortured during questioning—Juan Patricio suffered such an interrogation in 1690, following his arrest for beating a Spanish priest—and the interrogators' motive was not vengeance or arbitrary cruelty, but rather to get the slave to admit that his owner had forced him to commit the crime.[42] The only late colonial torture case I found was downright surprising: When Francisco de Castro fled his master in Campeche in 1793, he was caught and questioned, and accused his owner of various abuses; but it was the owner, don Sebastián Betancourt—not the slave—who ended up jailed, fined, and eventually tortured for refusing to acknowledge the court's authority.[43]

If overseers on plantations in the American South were motivated to punish insolent or uncooperative slaves "tactically and with moderation,"[44] then owners in Yucatan, where slaves were luxury goods rather than the primary source of labor, had strong reason to find nonviolent solutions to master–slave discord. Put in terms of medieval Iberian distinctions between white *mamluk* and black *'abd* slaves, slaves in colonial Yucatan were more like mamluks—investments to be protected rather than a means of production to be expended.[45] This does not mean that slaves were not beaten, sexually assaulted, or otherwise abused—in Yucatan as elsewhere in the Americas—but I have yet to find signs that black slaves in Yucatan were regularly tortured or killed as they were in most slave societies.[46] The defense of a Virginia minister, who beat a slave to death in 1692, that "such accidents will happen now and then," may have reflected Spanish attitudes in the sixteenth century, but for most of the colonial period slave owners in Yucatan were surely more like those in the late eighteenth-century Chesapeake and Lowcountry, who sought to cultivate reputations as indulgent masters.[47]

Colonial Yucatan, therefore, offers supportive evidence for all the Spanish views found elsewhere in the empire: ambiguous attitudes toward slavery by the institutions of church and state, and by the individuals who constituted those institutions; prejudicial attitudes toward people of African descent, prejudices that promoted stereotypes and emphasized difference but that did not yet amount to a coherent ideology of race; and a framework of socioracial rank that assigned casta labels, incorporated stereotypes about Africans and native peoples, and supported Spanish social ideals, but that never amounted to an effective system of control and never closed the gap between ideal and reality.

Yucatan was thus like other Spanish colonies, but not identical to them. The nature of the Afro-Yucatecan experience, and the fact that the colony was never a slave society, meant that Spanish attitudes were probably more ambiguous and prejudices less likely to approximate modern racism than in slave-heavy regions of the empire (such as early Mexico City, mid-colonial Popayán, and Cartagena).[48]

There was another feature of this "system" to which our discussion now turns—the construction and use of casta labels. Were casta terms concrete or plastic? Were they commonly understood in Spanish America, or even in Yucatan, or did they shift in meaning over time and according to circumstances?

CASTE OF CHARACTERS

At dawn on April 10, 1815, don Francisco Ontiveros stormed out of his house in downtown Merida. He had awoken to find his eighteen-year-old daughter missing, and he knew exactly who the culprit was—a young man named José María Correa, who lived in the nearby neighborhood of Santiago. For a year, Correa had been wooing Ontiveros's daughter, doña María Josepha, despite his vociferous disapproval. Ontiveros immediately had Correa thrown in jail under accusation of abducting María Josepha, although she returned to the house that morning, insistent that she was distressed not by anything Correa had done but by her father's rage.[49]

The case appears at first to be no more than the universal and timeless tale of a father opposing a daughter's choice of husband, with the grounds for such opposition simply being that the boy is not good enough. But something more specific about late colonial Yucatan is revealed by a closer look at the specific objections raised by Ontiveros in the lawsuit that he filed to keep Correa in jail and prevent him from marrying doña María Josepha. Correa's crime was, in the words of Ontiveros, that he had "insulted my house with injury to my honor and good reputation." This insult took three forms.

First, Correa had violated the domestic space that was a refuge for women, a place where status and honor were secured. Put another way, the household was where men could better control their wives and daughters, especially in elite Spanish families whose women did not leave the home to work.[50] Correa had begun by "speaking with the girl through the windows," but had gone on to "have the effrontery [*atrebimiento*] to enter my house at inappropriate hours of the night when the family has unwittingly all gone to bed." Even worse—the final straw for Ontiveros—Correa conspired to take doña María Josepha out of the house at night, into the streets and neighborhoods of the city where she risked harm and dishonor. For Ontiveros, symbolic of Correa's intention to socially compromise his daughter was the fact that Correa brought her an *ipil* to wear during her nocturnal escape from the house. Ipil or *ypil* is the Maya word, also used by Spaniards in Yucatan, for the dress worn by indigenous women in Yucatan and elsewhere in New Spain (called *huipil* in central Mexico). Made of light cotton and typically worn over a petticoat, the ipil was appropriate to Yucatan's hot and humid climate, and it was commonly worn by women of all ranks in the colony—with the caveat that elite Spanish women would only wear an ipil at home, never in public. The themes of window-wooing, inappropriate clothing, and the street at night, all combined to make the case scandalous and shocking to Ontiveros—and, he feared, to other Spaniards in the city.

The second crime committed by Correa was that he had "seduced a daughter of mine, a minor," declared Ontiveros, "with the object of marrying her against my will." In colonial central Mexico, a common strategy used by couples seeking to evade parental will was that of "abduction" by the man, making the woman's seduction public; this helped to win the support of the local priest and forced parents to consent to the marriage in order to restore their daughter's honor. Although canon law favored a couple's right to choose to marry, during the eighteenth century parents increasingly asserted the right to veto that choice.[51] Ontiveros effectively accused Correa and his daughter of plotting such a strategy by having Correa arrested for *rapto* [abduction or kidnapping]. Doña María Josepha's willingness to be "abducted" was less relevant than Ontiveros's will that the marriage not occur; family honor and parental will were explicitly connected, with Ontiveros as the infallible guardian of that honor.

Correa's third offense was his calidad or status; as the reader may have guessed, he was a pardo—or a mulatto. That he was variously called both during the investigation is typical of the ambiguity of casta terminology in Yucatan, and also reflected the fact that neither Ontiveros nor the witnesses questioned by the lawyers knew much about Correa's specific parentage; Ontiveros initially refers only to "his inferior status [*su inferior calidad*]." Witnesses reveal that Correa had changed his name from Pérez, for unknown reasons, and confirm that he lived with family members in Santiago, which was one of the original Maya neighborhoods of the city (what I have called a *cah-barrio*), with a mixed-race minority population that grew steadily in late colonial decades.[52] Despite the ambiguity of Correa's identity, what was unambiguous to Ontiveros was Correa's inferiority; it was, indeed, the buttress to his opposition to the marriage and his argument supporting Correa's arrest.

How reasonable was Ontiveros's position, within the context of Merida society at the end of the colonial period? Was his attitude shared by other Spaniards in the city and colony? Did it represent a larger societal and, in view of Correa's imprisonment, institutional prejudice toward Afro-Yucatecans? How does this case help us to relate the Yucatec evidence to the Spanish American evidence briefly discussed above?

The Ontiveros case is in fact one of a dozen similar cases preserved in Yucatan's state archives; the cases are all lawsuits stemming from prenuptial or marital conflicts in Merida or Izamal between 1792 and 1821. I suspect that dozens more cases from these decades, including other towns with small late colonial Spanish populations, have been lost or are still buried in the archives.

I am reluctant thus to place great stock in the patterns revealed by the surviving cases, but those patterns are certainly worth mentioning.

Three of the cases come from Izamal, all generated during a period of less than a year, and all centered on the same type of legal strategy. In October 1791, María de Luz Herrera filed suit to prevent her daughter from marrying Francisco Medina on the grounds that he was a pardo. Medina went to the bishop and asked if it was really possible for a civil suit to render him "free of the obligation" of his betrothal. The bishop sent Medina back to the civil courts (Medina's subsequent petition is presented in full in Appendix A). There, witnesses corroborated the accusation regarding Medina's "calidad," and the betrothal was invalidated.

Statements made during the dispute by Herrera, the putative mother-in-law, reveal what sparked her indignation. It was one thing for an illiterate young man of modest means living on a nearby hacienda to come into town and woo her daughter, but it was quite another for him "to refuse to ask for my consent to enter into marriage with my daughter Manuela Tolosa, without considering that his calidad was inferior to that of my daughter, the difference being repugnant [*repugnante la diferencia*]." To add insult to injury, when Herrera voiced her objection to the betrothal to Medina, he replied that her daughter was a mestiza; this "was a lie," said Herrera, "for it is public knowledge that my daughter is a regular Spaniard [*española ordinaria*]."[53]

Was Herrera prejudiced? Of course; but she was also motivated by a sense of wounded pride, and by her desire, as a widow, to see her daughter marry comfortably and perhaps to a husband who lived in town. Colonial law simply provided Herrera with a legal weapon—specifically a two-decade-old edict known as the Royal Pragmatic, which restricted marriages between coloreds and non-coloreds (explained further below). Even the question of her daughter's calidad was rendered moot; witnesses supported Medina's claim that she was a mestiza, but the local judge [the *subdelegado*] ruled that the Royal Pragmatic determined a pardo–mestiza marriage to be "an inequality of calidad."[54] Furthermore, Herrera's insistence that her daughter was a "regular Spaniard" must be placed in the context of the plasticity of casta labels, not just in the colony as a whole but specifically in late colonial Izamal; as we shall see shortly, most of the town's mestizo population would be reclassified as Spaniards between 1802 and 1806.[55]

No doubt the case was the subject of much discussion and gossip in Izamal that October, especially as lawyers were taking testimony around town that same month on a similar case. This was a dispute between don Domingo Martín y Canto and his son, don Joseph María Martín, over the latter's choice of spouse. In his suit, don Domingo explicitly cited "the Pragmatic" as requiring his son to acquire parental "permission [*lisencia*]" to marry someone of "unequal calidad." Don Joseph had gone ahead and married doña Nicolasa del Canto anyway, and in response don Domingo had "thrown

me out of his house" (in the son's words). Faced with his son's demand that
he approve the marriage, and unable to prove his accusation against his new
daughter-in-law, don Domingo relented and consented to the match. But
the case confirms that inequality of calidad was the default accusation to
make in personal disputes over marriage choices.[56]

Although doña Manuela Estrada lived in Yobaín, she would have heard
about the Herrera and Martín cases in nearby Izamal; the stories may even
have inspired her the following summer to file suit to prevent her sister Narcisa from being married off by their grandfather to Bernardo Aldequa in Izamal. Again, the case appears at first to be primarily about Spanish personal
and institutional prejudice against Afro-Yucatecans. The crux of doña
Manuela's objection is that her sister's betrothed "is known as a mulatto";
he is thus irredeemably inferior ("of lasting inequality [*de constante desigualdad*]"), making the marriage an offense against the honor of both sisters. However, behind the accusation lay a more complex dispute over an
inheritance that Manuela, Narcisa, and a third sister had received from their
father but which was being withheld by their grandfather. The grandfather
had placed some of the property in the hands of a business partner, Antonio
Aldequa (Bernardo's father), prompting legal action by doña Manuela, who
called the elder Aldequa geriatric [*de edad abanzada*], a poor gold-digger,
and *vicioso* (in this case, probably meaning "licentious"). From the viewpoint of the sisters' grandfather and of the Aldequas, the plan to marry
Bernardo to Narcisa was a normal, even conventional, way of cementing a
business relationship between the two families. From doña Manuela's perspective, the plan was a nefarious plot to consolidate the Aldequas hold on
the sisters' inheritance. The fact that Bernardo had African ancestry through
his mother was hardly the point; but, again, the Royal Pragmatic gave doña
Manuela a legal weapon to use in her battle over an inheritance.[57]

The three Izamal cases, like the Ontiveros case, reveal how issues of "race"
were really issues of calidad, with all its complex and ambiguous determinants of social status. It is tempting to take on face value comments by the
plaintiffs in these cases, and assume that race was *the* issue in late colonial
Yucatan, because the likes of Ontiveros, Herrera, and Estrada were able to
use their prejudices as a legal strategy. But that would be to ignore the two
crucial, interrelated factors of parental control and the economic implications of marriage. In other words, *the* issue was not an immutable concept
such as race, but rank and status as determined by things that were mutable
and easily lost—such as honor, respect, and property.

Before further examining the Yucatec context of these cases, we must
once again step back to look at Spanish America as a whole. To begin with,
several terms already used—"race," "casta," and "calidad"—require further
definition and explanation. Race, as it is used in English today, is rooted in
a gradual shift in the eighteenth and nineteenth centuries in how Europeans
classified human groups; race replaced "nation" and took on a biological

meaning. The term therefore cannot easily be applied to colonial Spanish American thinking and, in the historical context of the early modern period, is a false cognate for the Spanish term *raza*. Raza was used from at least the early fifteenth century to mean lineage or ancestry in the specific context of campaigns to exclude Jews and Muslim Moors from Christian kingdoms. Thus *buena raza* was descent from Christians, *mala raza* from Jews or Moors; by the 1610s, the latter use predominated, giving raza a negative connotation. A related term was *limpieza de sangre* [purity of blood], which despite its biological implications was likewise a reference to lineage, rooted in religious identity and specific Iberian historical circumstances. *Casta*, another medieval term, also meant lineage and was sometimes used as a synonym for raza, but without the same kind of negative connotations. The English term "caste" is misleading, as it tends to imply the strict definitions and divisions between caste groups in Hindu India—an inflexibility not found in the Spanish world.[58]

Raza was seldom used in Spanish America (at least, not in the mundane archival documentation that historians use to reconstruct daily life in the colonies); I did not find a single use of it in the archival sources of this book. Casta, on the other hand, was widely used in the colonies, and although it never acquired a negative connotation per se, by the eighteenth century it tended to refer to mixed-race people (sometimes extending to blacks; that is, all non-natives and non-Spaniards). Mixed-race people were not, in theory, supposed to exist, because politics and society were supposed to be divided in the colonies into two unequal spheres, the *república de españoles* and the *república de indígenas* (another example of the disconnect between ideal and reality); blacks were left in the middle of the two "republics," denied access to either, but in theory and largely in practice they existed in what in the previous chapter I called "attached subordination to Spaniards."[59]

There was thus from the onset of the colonial period a taint of illegitimacy about mestizos, soon applied to castas in general, as well as a specific association of castas with illegitimate birth—a status that was not only socially damaging, but by law a barrier to inheritance and the holding of various offices. Tied up with issues of legitimacy was the complex quality of honor. For example, Solórzano wrote that "few Spaniards of honor marry *indias* or negras." His implication was that "the stain of motley coloring [*la mancha de color vario*]"—that is, being of mixed-race descent—was rooted as much in the behavior of the Spanish father as it was in the casta of the mother.[60]

Thus, in origin and in practice for most of the colonial period, several attributes or qualities were attached to questions of casta or socioracial rank: religion; legitimacy of birth; and honor. What is significant about these is that none are definitions of race in the modern biological sense; all can be altered during a person's lifetime (through conversion, through the legal acquisition of legitimacy papers or public exposure of illegitimacy, and through public knowledge of lifestyle or certain deeds). Likewise, attempts by Spanish intellectuals to explain why sub-Saharan Africans had black skin tended not to settle on immutable causes or physical differences. For example, the old Iberian notion of limpieza de sangre was not extended to explain black coloring as being blood-related; the idea did circulate in late colonial times but it was never the dominant explanation. Instead, Juan de Torquemada concluded in 1615 that differences in skin tone were simply God's way of "wishing to display his marvels through the variety of colors." Pedro Cubero Sebastián proposed in 1697 that the cause was environmental (thus Africans would become white if they settled in England). The Spanish Jesuit José Gumilla was unconvinced by the environmental argument, popular in his day, and in 1741 published his theory that the power of the maternal imagination was responsible for babies being born black. Gumilla's treatise was widely read through the end of the century, while various versions of the environmental theory persisted; the Spanish Benedictine Benito Jerónimo Feijoo, for example, maintained that black babies were born white, that their blackness spread from birth spots, and that a person's coloring could change during their lifetime if they were to move to milder climes.[61] To reiterate my point here, not only did such ideas fail to build on each other to create a coherent ideology of race during the colonial period, but they all embodied the idea of mutability; like religion, legitimacy, and honor, skin color was changeable.

The sum of all these factors was something that Spaniards referred to as *calidad*, literally "quality" but better glossed as "status" or "rank." Historians of Spanish America have offered various lists of factors that determined a person's calidad. It was "age, sex, place of residence, race, legitimacy or illegitimacy, civic status (i.e., whether a landowner or not), occupation"; or "color, occupation, and wealth . . . purity of blood, honor, integrity, and even place of origin . . . one's reputation as a whole."[62] In other words, rank was determined by calidad, which was determined by everything that a person was, including a vaguely defined and conceived "racial" category that itself cannot be understood separate from all the other factors constituting calidad.

Of course when an individual's calidad was mentioned by a contemporary, all the determinant factors were not detailed; the shorthand terminology of reference was that of casta categories. Some, but not all, casta terms were in use in the sixteenth century. Those that remained the most common—*negro*, mulato, pardo, mestizo—were in use from the start; others—such as *castizo* [a pale mestizo, or the offspring of a Spaniard and mestizo] and *morisco* [a pale mulatto, or someone with Moorish ancestry]—came into use by the turn of the seventeenth century.[63]

A century later, there had developed over a dozen more. Thus in the second half of the colonial period, Spanish conceptions of rank and miscegenation seemingly became more systematic. Discussions of mestizaje in the colonies (including Gumilla's) began to be accompanied by terminological

Figure 3.1 A Spaniard with the black mother of his mulatto son; the woman is preparing chocolate, an activity that stereotypically represented domestic service in colonial Mexico and Yucatan. Source: José de Alcíbar, *6. De español y negra, mulato*, ca. 1760–70, oil on canvas, 78.8×97.2 cm. Denver Art Museum, Collection of Jan and Frederick Mayer.

charts, typically showing up to sixteen socioracial combinations—"De español y negra, sale mulato" and so on. These same phrases also began to appear as captions to the so-called Casta Paintings, which became popular in Mexico in the first two decades of the eighteenth century and remained so until the turn of the nineteenth. These typically featured illustrations of twelve to sixteen casta triads or father–mother–child combinations (see Figure 3.1).

However, the textual and painted descriptions of casta categories are misleadingly systematic, for several reasons. First, the purpose of charts listing casta combinations was to indicate how miscegenation was a flexible enough process that it could "whiten" individuals from mixed-race families, leading a population back to "pure" categories. For example, someone with seven Spanish great-grandparents and one indigenous or African one was classified as a Spaniard. In a true socioracial system incorporating concrete, constructed racial categories (such as the modern United States), one-eighth black ancestry could classify someone as black (for example). But in a society without such a system, and with plastic socioracial categories, the elision of portions of a person's ancestry was more possible; in fact, if an eighth of one's ancestry could be discounted in theory, in practice it could be as much as a half. Edward Long, an Englishman who wrote about Jamaica in 1774 and compared it to the Spanish colonies, was disgusted by the prevalence of miscegenation and castas in the Spanish Empire, scoffing at how there "it is accounted most creditable to mend the breed by ascending or growing whiter."[64]

Second, neither texts nor paintings claimed to represent a "casta system" or *sistema de castas* (the phrase is a post-colonial invention often misleadingly used by historians); one scholar of the paintings recently noted that they "were rarely, if ever, labeled as casta paintings in the eighteenth century."[65] The paintings were not intended for local consumption, but were commissioned by administrators from Spain as souvenirs—a particular way of packaging the exoticism of the colonies, arguably promoting that exoticism with pride. Their purpose was not so much to illustrate a system of classification, let alone one with clear racial concepts, but to convey the rich variety of human and natural life in New Spain. This emphasis on the environment and on economic productivity, rather than the casta stereotypes that dominated earlier paintings, became increasingly important after 1760, as the Casta Paintings genre evolved through to its disappearance early in the nineteenth century.[66]

Third, most of the casta terms that appear in such texts and paintings were either rarely used or used inconsistently over time and from colony to colony. For example, in early nineteenth-century Guayaquil, the term *zambo*, referring to a person of Afro-indigenous descent, was the most common casta designation of record, having previously been rare;[67] in contrast, it was never used in Yucatan. Others were locally rooted; *calpamulato*, for example, only made sense in eighteenth-century central Mexico, as it originally referred to mulattoes living (and perhaps passing as Nahuas) in the Nahua town of Calpan. Even in areas where certain terms were commonly used, their meaning was plastic. They could be claimed with pride or thrown as insults, depending on the circumstances. In legal proceedings, when detailed physical descriptions were required to ensure protagonists and witnesses were properly identified, terms like "mulatto" required extensive qualification. Inquisition cases from mid-colonial Mexico contain such descriptions as Juan de Borrego, "who is mulatto, although downtown [*en la traza*] he is not, as he is reddish [*bermejo*], of medium height, light-colored [*caricolorado*] and very fat," and Nicolás de la Cruz, whom a witness "took to be black because he is dark [*atezado*] and it is not clear if he is a mulatto."[68] As we shall see below with respect to Yucatan, many of these descriptions do not include casta terms at all; because there were no commonly understood terms of racial reference—that is, because the so-called casta system was not much of a system at all—it made more sense to describe each person individually.

That the plasticity of casta terms made them not only of limited utility, but perhaps even absurd, was not lost on colonial Mexicans—as suggested by a parody of casta and calidad in an unpublished 1754 Mexico City satire called the "Ordenanzas del Baratillo de México." The *baratillo* was an illegal but tolerated thieves market off the Plaza Mayor, by definition a place unregulated by *ordenanzas* or decrees. The manuscript caricatured Spanish attitudes (it included two Spaniards trying to look between their own legs for reassurance that they lacked the dark spot that marked them as mulattoes), invented silly casta categories, and generally lampooned the supposed socioracial ranking of Mexican society.[69]

The rapid pace of miscegenation and the continued proliferation and plasticity of casta terms served to undermine the development of a more coherent system of rank and socioracial classification, but by the late eighteenth century this also contributed to a heightened anxiety among the Spanish elite over issues of calidad. Spaniards went to increasing lengths, through expensive lawsuits and other legal measures, to promote prejudice against castas and preserve their pride in (and public recognition of) their own casta-free ancestry—even to the point of admitting the existence of a non-Spanish ancestor and petitioning on the grounds of other calidad determinants that such an ancestor be officially forgotten. In 1778 the crown provided Spanish colonists with an issue that served as a battleground over rank and reputation until the end of the colonial period; in that year the crown extended to the American provinces the above-mentioned law known as the Royal Pragmatic, which gave non-casta parents (Spaniards and natives) a veto over their children's marriage choices, if the child was under twenty-five and sought to marry someone of African ancestry. The law failed to stem the tide of mixed marriages, which may not have been its intent anyway. But it did provide parents with a weapon with which to exert greater control over their children, encouraging accusations of calidad "inferiority" as a legal strategy, regardless of the accused's actual ancestry, of the ambiguity of casta terms, and of the hypocrisy sometimes involved.[70] The waters of race and rank, in other words, were only further muddied.

Issues of race and casta in Spanish America are not easy to clarify or summarize. For a while, historians of the subject debated whether race or class was the dominant concept behind the colonial social structure and its classifications.[71] More recently, the debate has shifted as scholars have begun to question the relevance of "race" and "class," or to define them in more specifically local terms, or to see them as interrelated elements among the many overlapping elements that determined that structure. In other words, race and class, or race and casta, were "interpenetrating" (as Irene Silverblatt puts it)[72]—interpenetrating elements of a system that has defied easy definition because it was hardly a system at all. One Casta Painting scholar, Ilona Katzew, concluded that race, as colonial Spaniards conceived it, was at best "a metaphor used to categorize people."[73] I think we might see the entire casta "system" as such a metaphor, one that featured a highly plastic terminology of socioracial categories. Behind the metaphor lay stereotypes and prejudices whose ambiguity and contextual nature prevented them from developing into a coherent ideology of race; there was no systematic attempt to impose commonly understood categories onto people and organize society accordingly.

To turn again to the case of Yucatan, two additional bodies of evidence substantiate my argument that the casta structure was not a true "system"—at least certainly not in this colony. These two bodies of evidence are: Spanish descriptions of black and colored slaves and servants (drawn from licenses to travel with these dependents from Spain to Yucatan, 1615–1779); and the patterns of usage of casta categories in eighteenth-century censuses and parish records (1688–1815).

When the Yucatec merchant Geronimo de Yanguas traveled on business to Spain in 1613, returning to Merida two years later, he took two slaves with him, described as:

A mulatto slave, a *criollo* [i.e., born in Yucatan], sixteen years of age, with a wound mark over the shoulder, on the left muscle, running from above to below, and another on the left hand, from birth, on the thumb; and a black named Lorenzo, twenty-five years of age, full-bearded, with a very large mole in the middle of his forehead.[74]

These two men are given casta labels—mulato and *negro*—but the descriptions of their physical features lack the kind of stereotypes typically found in British descriptions of Africans, for example.

Likewise, when Capt. don Francisco Lara Bonifaz, a wealthy member of Yucatan's Spanish elite, prepared to leave Spain to return to Yucatan in 1640 after a two-year business trip, his paperwork included testimony that he was indeed the Lara Bonifaz named in his license to travel. Witnesses described him, along with his free black servant, as simply named Francisco. The following sketches of the two men, removed from the larger context, do not clearly indicate that one was Spanish, the other African:

The said don Francisco is of medium build, dark [*moreno*], thin-faced, and no more than forty years old, and the said Francisco, a dark-skinned man [moreno], is of small build, large forehead, and unsociable [*esquinado*], and no more than fifty-five years old.[75]

There are no blatant racial markers in this description, and only the placement of the word *moreno* in relation to the men's names indicates that for one it refers to his dark complexion, for the other to his casta category—elaborated elsewhere in Lara's travel documents, but not here, as moreno libre and *negro* libre.

A few years later the province's new governor, don Francisco Núñez Melián, brought two esclavos *negros* with him from Spain; the older one was probably African-born, the younger one born in Venezuela, where both had served as slaves to Núñez Melián when he was governor in that colony. Again, while the surname "Criollo" is an implied casta label, the descriptions contain no obvious or stereotypical racial markers:

The said Juan Criollo will shortly be eighteen years old, more or less, of medium height, and on his right cheek he has a black mole, and the said Francisco Antonio will be forty years old, more or less, tall, with a white-streaked beard.[76]

As the seventeenth century wore on, however, descriptions of black slaves began to feature phenotypical references that more obviously coded men as African. Thus Joseph de Padilla, brought to Campeche from Cádiz in 1699 by his owner, a Guipuzcoan merchant named Juan de Antonio de Padilla, was described by the master as "flat-nosed" or "pug-nosed [*la naris chatta*]."[77] By this time, descriptions had begun to feature new adjectives not applied to the Spanish owners of the slaves and servants being depicted. The most common such adjective was *atezado*, "tanned, swarthy, dark." Thus Joseph de Padilla was called "my dark black slave [*mi sclavo (sic) negro atezado*]" by his owner. In 1710 the incoming governor of Yucatan, don Juan Joseph de Vertiz y Ontañón, brought from Spain a servant named Lázaro de los Reyes, who was "a dark black [*negro atezado*], twenty-three years old, Christian, and free of slavery."[78] The most obvious indicator of slave status or a slave past—branding scars—are also mentioned more often by the early eighteenth century. Thus "a black slave named Agustín de Leira, no more than fourteen years old, of medium height, with branding marks on his right arm and on the middle of his ear," was granted passage to Yucatan with his owner (don Diego de Santesteban) in 1718.[79] Some scars on black men, when not clearly identified as branding marks, were probably ritual scarring acquired in Africa—such as Joseph de Padilla's "right cheek, ploughed, and a scar on his forehead."[80]

This shift in the way in which Spaniards described Africans and mulattoes was a gradual one, signaling a greater awareness of difference although not yet representing the development of coherent racist concepts. A parallel small change took place in the way Spaniards described each other. There is a distinct lack of overt racial references in probanza statements of the sixteenth and early seventeenth centuries, in which Spaniards asserted they were "Spaniards of great valor [*español de mucho balor*]" or descended from a colony's first settlers.[81] Similarly, by the mid-seventeenth century, the limpieza de sangre [purity of blood] documents submitted by those traveling to a colony such as Yucatan were still built around age-old phrases recalling the medieval *reconquista*, not colonial-era race-mixing. For example, when Núñez Melián submitted travel documents in order to sail to Yucatan in 1643 to take up the governorship, he included a twenty-page limpieza de sangre report on one of his six dependents; Juan Manuel Sánchez

de León, from Salamanca, was deemed to be "an old Christian" without "the
stain of Moors, Jews, or penitents of the Holy Office of the Inquisition."[82]
One looks in vain among such reports for language showing that the extensive presence of Africans and their descendants in the colonies had impacted
Spanish concepts of "blood purity."

Eighteenth-century evidence suggests that elite Spaniards had adjusted
their conceptions of what determined status to local circumstances. For example, don Manuel Palomeque's 1790 limpieza de sangre petition, comprising documents notarized in Madrid and Merida, insisted that don Manuel's
ancestry contained "no mix of mulattoes, blacks, Moors, Jews, Gypsies,
nor any of Indians [*sin mezcla alguna de mulatos, o negros, moros, Judios,
Gitanos, ni aun de Yndios*]," but this was hardly a clear set of distinct races,
and the echo of medieval concerns was also found in the general preoccupation in the petition with issues of legitimacy, religion, and honor.[83]

Even near the end of the colonial period, the attitudes of most Spaniards
reflected the complex and fluid reality of ethnicity and class in the colonies.
Not surprisingly, evaluations of ancestry were often formulaic. The assertion that one's ancestors were not "from those people" or "of the lineages
banned from traveling to the Indies" becomes a convention of travel documents.[84] Don Diego de Santesteban testified in 1718 as to the identity of the
two servants traveling with him to Yucatan, where he was a salt-tax collector. One was his black slave, the above-mentioned Agustín de Leira, the
other was Juan de Rementeria, a servant from Madrid, "of medium height,
hair really black and curly, with smallpox pock marks, and who is not, nor
descended from, those people who are prohibited passage to the kingdoms
of the Indies."[85]

Traditionally, "those people" were Moors and Jews, although the description of Rementeria's hair, if it suggests anything at all, comes close to an
African stereotype. Yet there is no evidence that he was considered anything
other than Spanish. Nor, presumably, did Rementeria's ancestry matter a
jot to Santesteban, as long as it did not hinder their ability to acquire the
requisite licenses and otherwise take care of business. Even a new bishop of
the province, gathering his entourage and getting their travel papers in order in 1762, merely mentions in passing that his Spanish dependents had
"purity of blood" and his black servants were "free natives of the Indies"—
without further detail.[86] By 1779, the formulaic claim that those seeking
passage to Yucatan are not among "those prohibited from traveling to
America" is in the travel papers of the cathedral schoolmaster, but the
phrase "limpieza de sangre" is absent, and the priest's three servants are
categorized as "two of them white, and the other black."[87]

Do these Spanish descriptions of black and free-colored dependents use
clearly pejorative adjectives or resort to the shorthand of casta labels? Generally speaking, they do not, although evidence suggests a gradual development from the seventeenth to eighteenth centuries of a set of adjectives and

TABLE 3.1 Comparison of self-descriptions with language used to refer
to Afro-Yucatecans

Afro-Yucatecan	Self-description	Labels used by Spaniards	Year
Francisco de Aguilar	Criollo de la yndias; persona libre; tener la color de mulato	Mulato libre; mulato criollo	1619
Ana de Ortega	Vecina; parda	Mulata; parda; de color parda libre de esclavitud	1658–61
Diego Ramos	De color pardo	Pardo	1671
Isabel Toquero	Natural de Merida (in fact born in Dzonotake; she described her relatives as mestizos and mulatos)	Parda; mulata; de casta mulata	1691–1711
Joseph Zavala	Mulato libre	Mulato; de color pardo	1722–32
Francisco Medina	Vecino (of an hacienda)	Pardo	1791
José Antonio	Esclavo of the lord Governor	*Negro* esclavo; *negro* cochero; negrito	1794
José María Correa	Vecino (of Merida)	Mulato; pardo	1815
José María Espinola	Esclavo	Esclavo moreno	1816

Sources: AGI-*Contratación* 5365, 21, 1: ff. 1–3 (Aguilar); AGI-*Escribanía* 316b, 75: f. 2 (Ramos); AGN-*Inquisición* 443: ff. 491–503 (Ortega); AGN-*Inquisición* 519, 3: ff. 301–98 (Toquero); AGN-*Inquisición* 1164: ff. 211–319 (Zavala); AGEY-*Judicial* 1, 6 (Medina); AGI-*México* 3036, 120: ff. 2r, 6v, 8r, 10v (Antonio); AGEY-*Criminal* 1, 7a (Correa); AGEY-*Varios* 1, 27: f. 1 (Espinola).

physical features assigned to castas. There are strong hints of prejudice and perhaps a glimmer of the racism that would emerge in the early nineteenth century.[88] There are also discrepancies between how Spaniards labeled Afro-Yucatecans, and how they labeled themselves; as Table 3.1 illustrates with just a few examples, free coloreds tended to recognize the labels assigned to them, but they gave greater emphasis to their free status and to their home-town affiliation (the latter very much as a Maya would do). Afro-Yucatecans also preferred "de color pardo" or "de color mulato" over the simple "pardo" and "mulato" labels used by Spaniards.

As important as these distinctions surely were to Afro-Yucatecans, the labels used by Spaniards were attempts to apply vaguely legal categories, not prejudicial epithets, and the discrepancies between self-descriptions and those used by Inquisition and civil officials are subtle. Again, there is no evidence of modern concepts of race or racism, or signs that casta labels were systematically defined or universally understood.

Descriptions from travel licenses are too few to lend themselves to quantitative analysis. Census and parish records, on the other hand, offer thousands of examples of casta label usage. The irony of using census materials here is that the very unreliability of colonial censuses, which normally problematizes their use by historians, is further evidence of the unreliability and plasticity of casta categories. In a series of letters sent between 1791 and 1794, the viceroy in Mexico City and the governor-intendant in Yucatan discussed the "difficulties" of obtaining accurate census data.[89] The preoccupation of these officials was primarily over numbers, especially those of the tribute-paying native population. But the accuracy of each census was also determined by the use of casta categories and such a usage varied from year to year and parish to parish. Furthermore, the problem did not just lie with the role played by the local Spanish priest or other colonial official taking the census; his attitudes, and thus the census data itself, reflected the increasingly ambiguous attitude of Spanish colonial society toward castas and their categorization.

If, between the seventeenth and eighteenth centuries, Spaniards in some ways seemed more conscious of "race" as a determinant of calidad, then in other ways their attitudes became more ambiguous. If Spaniards were indeed moving slowly toward modern racism, then casta definitions represented a countervailing tendency. Not that the two tendencies were incompatible. The increasing ambiguity of distinction between free and enslaved was potentially unnerving to slave owners. On the one hand, Spaniards saw "freeman" as synonymous with "servant"—the term *horro* meant both things—and free-colored servants were deemed to be as much in the employer's "power" as slaves were to their masters.[90] On the other hand, in a colony that was not a slave society and where slaves were a small minority of people of color, free coloreds were not "unappropriated" in the way that they were in Barbados, for example.[91] Casta identity was not fixed at birth, but subject to constant renegotiation.[92] As we shall see in Chapter Five, the social stigma of African descent did not preclude the possibility of social mobility and even recategorization in the colony's race-based social structure. If some free servants were treated like slaves, conversely it was not uncommon for slaves to become free servants—by purchasing their emancipation, having it purchased for them by relatives, or by being granted it by an owner (typically in his or her will).[93] Other social and economic factors allowed individuals to pass from being *negro* to pardo, or from pardo to mestizo or Spanish. Some Spaniards were alarmed that passing was possible, even common, an alarm that fed prejudice and the promotion of stereotypes; ambiguous attitudes toward slavery and blurred

distinctions between casta categories hardly amounted to sentiments in favor of racial equality.

The blurring of the line dividing *negros* from free coloreds, and free coloreds from Spaniards, had begun in the seventeenth century. In the rural
census of 1688, the curate of Nabalam noted that "with respect to the res-
idency of Spaniards, mestizos, and mulattoes, I have only one in my district; I certify that he is held to be a Spaniard because he seems to be one,
not because I judge him to have the ancestry [calidades] on all four sides;
named Pedro de Mena, he lives on a corn farm at his ranch, called Yokd-
zonot."[94] However, it is clear from a different source (the bigamy case of
Isabel Toquero, discussed at length in Chapter Six), that there were mestizo and pardo families living in Nabalam and neighboring villages at this
very time (Isabel, a parda, was born in nearby Dzonotake in 1675 and
married a mestizo in Nabalam in 1691); but the same source reveals that
these non-Maya inhabitants lived among Mayas, were related to them, and
worked in the same occupations, no doubt marking them as "Indians" in
the mind of the Spanish curate.[95] Pedro de Mena "seemed to be" a Spaniard
to one priest, but there were others like Mena who were viewed differently
by other priests.

The comment, mentioned earlier, by the census taker from Dallas, Texas,
in 1900 that racial categories were based not on "blood" but "social position
and manner of life" could have been said of the matrículas of the Yucatec
countryside in 1688 and 1700.[96] Antonio Alcaudete was listed as "reputed to
be a Spaniard [*reputado por español*]" by the priest of Ticul in 1700, as
though the priest was not entirely convinced; all the other non-Maya and
non-colored residents of the village were listed as "white." Perhaps the priest
had doubts because Antonio was married to a native woman, albeit a noblewoman or "india hidalga," and made a living as a "farm laborer and hunter
[*labrador y cazador*]."[97]

As we shall see in Chapter Four, Yucatan's rural inhabitants were divided into various casta categories in 1688 and 1700, but the overlap in
lifestyle and occupation was considerable. During the eighteenth century,
the *negro*–pardo and *negro*–mulatto division became increasingly blurred
as the social status, occupation, and appearance of free blacks became indistinguishable from that of free coloreds. In contrast to the slave colonies
of the British, where an African was assumed, even by law, to be a slave,[98]
the assumption in late colonial Yucatan was that a person of African descent was a mulatto, probably free. The separate category of *negro* was
used through to 1802, but only sporadically; after 1807 it disappeared, as
all Afro-Yucatecans became pardos, and after about 1820 all castas and
people of African descent were placed in the umbrella category of "mestizo."[99]

Three specific patterns can be seen in census and baptism records: (1)
most casta terms were not used in Yucatan at all; (2) the meaning assigned

to the few casta terms that were used was not consistent or uniform from one Spanish priest to another, from one Yucatec town to another, or from one decade to another; and (3) casta categories assigned to specific individuals were not immutable, placing a person in multiple categories or allowing passing from one calidad to another. Each of these, detailed in turn below, are patterns of irregularity, reflecting the plasticity of casta terminology and the ambiguity of the so-called system.

First, only a fraction of the full range of casta terms was used. Beyond the primary trio of "español," "negro," and "indio," the only common casta terms used were "mestizo," "pardo," and "mulato." Three terms that appear rarely are *chino, castizo,* and *moreno.* But I did not find a single written case (in male or female form) of *lobo, cambujo, coyote, albino,* or any of the others that appeared in late colonial central Mexican sources such as the Casta Paintings.

I have only found "chino" used in the male form (never "china"), and only by priests in the mid-colonial period. In the 1700 census of thirty-five parishes, it was used by just three priests, those of Conkal, Oxkutzcab, and Becal (see Tables 3.2 and 3.3). It was the only Afro-Yucatecan category used for Conkal, so that priest effectively used it to mean just that—Afro-Yucatecan. The priests of Becal and Oxkutzcab also used "mulato" but not "pardo," so I suspect they viewed "chino" as a reference to Afro-Mayas. This indeed is how Bishop Gómez de Parada used the term in the 1720s; he categorized the casta population in the colony as "Mestizos, *Negros,* Mulatos, y Chinos."[100] But the bishop was not a Yucatecan (he came to the peninsula from Spain to serve as bishop in 1715). Clearly, the term was not commonly understood and used by locals.

"Castizo" (technically meaning of Spanish-mestizo descent) was also seldom used. For example, in the 1700 census, only one priest listed castizos in his parish—a single couple, Julián Baeza and his wife María de Rojas. In the baptism records for Merida's castas, the term is used once—in 1762, referring to a "castiza" wife of a mulatto—in the run of thousands of baptisms from 1710 to 1797. Obviously if the term was widely or consistently used, there would have been more than one castizo couple in the whole colony in 1700, and more than one castiza in eighteenth-century Merida.

I suspect that two factors underlie why "chino" and "castizo" appear in the records at all. First, the priests who used the terms may have been—like Bishop Gómez de Parada—recent arrivals from Spain or from colonies where the terms were more common. Second, they may have been fall-back terms to use in rare cases where the priest was stymied by one particular person's calidad; for example, there was only one chino in Becal, Alonso Jiménez, "*sin oficio* [without occupation]," and the León brothers, Juan and Luis, both married to mestizas, were the only chinos in Oxkutzcab.

Almost as rare as "castiza" was "morena"; more common was the male equivalent, "moreno." The term loosely meant "black" but a crucial

TABLE 3.2 Population and use of casta categories by parish priests in 53 Yucatec pueblos, 1700

	Español	Blanco	Castizo	Mestizo	Mestizo/ Mulato	Negro	Mulato	Pardo	Chino	Indio
BENEFICIOS BAJOS										
Dzemul				21			8			1,308
Cansahcab				1			2			
Suma	1									
Telchac		19		58		1	2			2,552
Sinanche				27			1			
Dzidzantun	28	13		39			17			1,900
Yobain		3		14						
Dzilam				4						
Conkal				17					10	3,859
Chicxulub				16						
Motul	28			6				23		3,792
Temax		26		29						1,502
Teya				21			5			1,408
Tepakan							5			
Acatzim		6								
Tekal				25						
Tekanto		6		13		1	1			2,373
Cacalchen		33								1,470
Izamal	85	54		76			49			2,257
Kantunil				1						
SIERRA										
Mani	15	17		75		1	34			3,884
Dzam	17			18			10			

(continued)

TABLE 3.2 (*continued*)

	Español	Blanco	Castizo	Mestizo	Mestizo/Mulato	Negro	Mulato	Pardo	Chino	Indio
Tipikal				4						
Oxkutzcab	2	19	2	73			15		2	5,199
Teabo	30			19			2			
Pencuyut	5			2			6			
Chumayel				4						
Tekax	7	82		58	125					4,989
Ticul	1	56		31			1	15		4,080
Muna				40						981
Cactum										
(E) Yuncu				13						
(E) Peba				7				1		
(E) Citinkabchen								4		
Abala				8						
CAMINO REAL										
Calkini		41		72				6		3,782
Dzitbalchen				9						
Bolonchen		13		1			3			1,950
Hopelchen				16						
Jonot				7						
Chanchanha		3		7						
Maxcanu	9			1			55			
Halacho		14					12			
Kopena				9						
Opilchen				5			34			

Becal		27	1		1
CAMPECHE					
Uayma	6	1		4	
Tinum		1		5	
Cancumul		4			
Kaua		1		8	
San Diego	2				
Cholul		6	8		
Temozon		4			

Sources: AGI-*México* 1035; Solano (1975: 72–73).
Note: (E) = Estancia.

TABLE 3.3 Use of Afro-Yucatecan casta categories by parish
priests in 35 Yucatec pueblos, 1700

Category		Number of towns and villages	
Negro	3		
Mulato	21	Overlap of *negro* and mulato	2
Pardo	8	Overlap of mulato and pardo	1
Chino	3	Overlap of mulato and chino	2
Mestizo/Mulato	1		

Sources: AGI-*México* 1035; Solano (1975).
Note: See Table 3.2 for full data presentation.

distinction differentiated it from *negro*. Whereas *negro* meant "black" with
an implication of slavery (not the assumption of slavery that came with the
term "negro" in Anglo-America), "moreno" meant "black" with an implication of freedom. In the 1688 census, for example, one of the few *negros* listed
was Francisco Congo (married and living in Samahil), possibly African-born
and probably an ex-slave. In contrast, there were no implications of an
African or slave past in the use of "moreno" by priests in 1688; such morenos
were free coloreds seen by Spanish priests as darker mulattoes (like Juan
Aguirre of Becal) or even types of mestizos (with whom they were categorized
by some priests).[101] Similarly, in the licenses to travel to Yucatan recorded in
the Casa de Contratación (customs house in Seville), enslaved blacks are always called *negro*, but free black servants are variously termed *negro* and
moreno (that is, both terms applied to each man). This pattern goes back at
least to the late sixteenth century, and stretches through the eighteenth.[102]

The *negro–moreno* distinction was not surprisingly more important to
the morenos themselves than to Spaniards, and thus terminological use was
more consistent among morenos than among Spaniards. Carmen Bernand
has suggested that in late colonial Buenos Aires, those whom Spaniards called
"*negro*" prefered to call themselves "moreno," which was probably also true
in Yucatan.[103] It explains, for example, why black militiamen were called
"morenos" (see Chapter Five); the status accorded to them as soldiers carried the right not to be given the slave-associated *negro* label. Furthermore,
in the baptism records of Merida's Jesús parish, during the period from
1785–91, when almost all babies were labeled pardo or parda, only the
children of black slaves were described as moreno or morena; there were
five moreno boys and six morena girls during these years, each with parents
clearly identified not simply as black but either as black slaves or black ex-
slaves [*libertinos*] (see Table 3.4 and Table G.6 in Appendix G). What is significant is that the term was hardly used in the 1710–85 baptism records (it

TABLE 3.4 Use of Afro-Yucatecan casta categories in baptisms of infants by priests of Merida's Jesús parish, 1710–95

Time Period	Pardo(a) usage [usage p.a.]		Mulato(a) usage [usage p.a.]		Moreno(a) usage	Average annual parish baptisms
1710–13	3	[0.8]	3	[0.8]		87
1714–17	4	[11]				99
1718–27	7	[0.7]	5	[0.5]		102
1728–36						102
1737–40	60	[15]			1	99
1741–47	5	[0.7]				97
1748–55						117
1756–59	107	[26.8]	266	[66.5]		116
1760–69	15	[1.5]	1,193	[119.3]	1	156
1770–74	6	[1.2]	421	[84.2]		110
1775–84	2	[0.2]	3	[0.3]		155
1785–95	855	[77.7]	1	[0.1]	11	119 (est.)

Source: AGAY-*Jesús*, Libros de Bautismos (IV-B-7) Vols. 1–6.

Note: The periodizations are irregular in order to highlight the patterns of usage, with the whole numbers being total usages in each period and bracketed numbers being average p. a. (annual) usage of that term within each period. I have listed the average annual number of baptisms of all kinds in the parish, for each period (the final entry is an estimate (est.) as data is incomplete for 1791–93), to show that there was no correlation between total baptisms and trends in terminological usage. I have not included *negro/a* here because my purpose is to illustrate the trends in the usage of pardo/a and mulato/a. No other Afro-Yucatecan mixed-race terms (zambo, lobo, chino, and so on) were used. I have included the rare instances of moreno/a being used, but the term was tied to *negro/a* usage and was not a mixed-race term (see discussion in the text).

appeared a handful of times), and that when it was used with regularity in 1785–91, its usage was specific and consistent.[104]

The second of the three casta-terminology patterns found in census and baptism records is the shift in how terms were used during the colonial period, in some cases a shift in meaning and in others simply one of popularity or trend. "Mestizo" was as concrete a term as "español" and "indio," in that it was used commonly throughout the colonial period and was widely understood to mean someone of Spanish-native descent—but toward the end of the colonial period it began to expand and take on the meaning once held by "casta" (that is, a mixed-race person of any kind).[105]

Theoretically, "mulato" indicated African-Spanish descent and "pardo" African-native descent. But in practice, usage in Yucatan made them more or less synonymous, to indicate a person of partial African and partial Spanish and / or Maya descent, who was (unless otherwise stated) free; in other words, both terms meant "free colored." The above-mentioned Isabel To-quero, in records spanning 1691 to 1711, was variously labeled as "parda" and "mulata" by officials and witnesses in Yucatan; her free-colored friends and acquaintances in Yucatan described her as "a white mulatta" (she was probably paler than they were), while a mestizo witness called her "a non-white mulatta," a stark illustration of how color was perceived in personal, relativist terms. Spaniards in Veracruz and Mexico City (the latter all Inquisition officials) consistently called Isabel a mulatta (only once modifying the term by describing her as "*cocha* colored"—*cocho*, a term never used in Yucatan, meant beige like cooked quince).[106]

Thus with "pardo" and "mulato" effective synonyms in Yucatan, individual impressions and the eye of the beholder played classificatory roles. But there were also society-wide trends of usage in the colony. In 1688 and 1700, "mulato" predominated over "pardo": In the census of 1688, eight in ten priests used the former, the rest used the latter, and none used both; in the 1700 census, twenty-one parish priests used the former, eight used the latter (with only one using both) (see Tables 3.2 and 3.3).[107]

The pattern is even more striking in eighteenth-century baptism records, which reveal shifts in usage during the eighteenth century that correlate not to the preferences of particular priests or other Spaniards but rather to broader trends (see Table 3.4). From 1710 to 1756, the strong preference was for the term "pardo"—if any term for free coloreds was used at all. Then, in 1756, the bishop instructed the priest of Jesús parish to keep more detailed records, and to note the calidad of babies and their parents. For a few years, both "pardo" and "mulato" were used, with a preference for the latter that was overwhelming through to 1774. For a decade after that, priests again abandon using terms for free coloreds. When in 1785 such terms began to appear again in baptism records, "pardo" was effectively the sole term used to refer to free coloreds. These trends in usage, always years-long, do not correlate with changes in priestly personnel in the parish (indeed, there were always at least three priests keeping these records in any one period); rather they reflect larger trends in the culture of casta-term usage in late colonial Yucatan.

By way of an addendum to the point tabulated in Table 3.4, both the "pardo–mulatto" shifts and the late eighteenth-century rise of "moreno" as an acceptable term for "free black" are reflected in the titles given to the baptism books of Merida's Jesús parish. The book begun in 1733 recorded baptisms of "*Negros* y Pardos," but by 1751, when the next volume started, terminological trends had shifted to "niños, mulatos, *negros* y adultos." In 1762, the parishioners were again called "*Negros* y Pardos," while the books begun in 1772 and 1785 both recorded baptisms of "Pardos y Morenos."[108]

The third of three specific patterns seen in census and baptism records is that of category shifts within a person's lifetime; that is, the category assigned to particular individuals was plastic, particularly within the terminology group of "pardo," "mulato," and "moreno." Isabel Toquero was one example.

Another was Ana Chacón, described as a "mulata esclava" in 1712 and a "parda esclava" in 1716 (both instances were under identical circumstances: the baptism of one of her children).[109] Individuals could also be assigned varying casta labels during the course of a single investigation or document of record. This was due not only to the general inconsistency with which casta terms were used and understood, but also due to the fact that labels of self-description tended to differ from those Spaniards assigned to Afro-Yucatecans—as mentioned early in this chapter with respect to Francisco de Aguilar, and as discussed above with respect both to the cases in Table 3.1 and to *negro* and "moreno."

I suspect that further research into the shifts in casta terms assigned to specific individuals would produce detailed evidence that shifts were not only common, but sometimes applied to whole families, even communities of families. The paucity of individual names in the 1688 census means we cannot track down the hundreds of non-Mayas listed in the 1700 census (see Table 3.2) to see how their categories changed in just a dozen years. But a comparison of specific villages reveals stark shifts in category usage. For example, Temax's nineteen Spaniards, mestizos, and free coloreds of 1688 had become twenty-six "blancos" and twenty-nine mestizos in 1700. Motul's priest in 1688 stated that "there are no *negros*, nor mulattoes" in the town, but the priest of twelve years later listed twenty-three pardos. In the earlier census, there were three mulatto families and five single mulattoes in Tekanto and its subject villages of Kimila; twelve years later, there was a single *negro* and a single mulatto in the whole area. Population movements, epidemics, and jurisdictional changes cannot fully explain these shifts; the primary cause is clearly shifts in casta classifications and usage.

These patterns in casta-term usage do not make for an exciting narrative, nor do they easily add depth to our understanding of the Afro-Yucatecan experience. But their importance is immense to our grasp of the so-called casta system, for without concrete, consistent categories there could be no real system—nor a coherent ideology of social rank that placed "race" at its core. Afro-Yucatecans certainly suffered prejudice and discrimination, and Spaniards were not afraid to resort to ugly stereotypes in their legal battles against each other or against fellow Yucatecans of color. But it would be wrong to interpret these facts—and the existence of black African (but not Maya) slavery in the colony—as evidence of institutionalized or endemic individualized racism in colonial Yucatan.

Why, then, did Francisco de Aguilar endure Spanish prejudice in Seville in ways that he had not experienced in Valladolid? The answer is not that in

1619 Spaniards in Yucatan were less prejudiced than they were in Spain; as we have seen, although the province was in many ways on the periphery of the empire, its Spanish community was too closely tied to the larger Spanish world (Mexico, the Caribbean, Spain) to foster a world view that was fundamentally different from the one at the center. Instead, the answer lies in part in the nature of prejudice throughout the Spanish world.

The answer also partly lies in the differences between Seville and Valladolid. Aguilar was a stranger in the Spanish city, and thus by definition subject to suspicion; his skin color merely determined the *type* of suspicion directed at him. Valladolid, on the other hand, was a town on the periphery of a peripheral colony. Not only in comparison with Seville, but even compared to Merida and Campeche, Valladolid was small and poor; this was true in 1619 and is still the case two centuries later. Economically lacking in vitality, politically and socially conservative, in Aguilar's day the town had less than a hundred Spanish families and even fewer Afro-Yucatecans.[110] In other words, everyone in Valladolid knew who Aguilar was; they knew his patron and employer, they knew his mother, they knew more about him than we will ever know.

In this sense, Aguilar's experience was comparable to that of Sebastián Toral. As the reader will remember from Chapter One, Toral was the black conquistador who traveled from Yucatan to Spain to petition in person for tribute exemption—winning it, along with a royal license to bear arms. But having then sailed to Mexico City (in 1579), he found local officials doubting that he was the man named in his royal license, and he was obliged to go to the viceroy's office to pay for a local license to carry his sword and dagger. Like Aguilar, Toral was an unknown man of color in a Spanish metropolis, and thereby subject to the kind of suspicion and harrassment that he must have been largely spared in Yucatan, where he was a well-known and established member of the local colonial community.[111]

It is a cliché of discourse on race that in a racist society individuals are tolerated as "exceptions" when they are personally known. If this is so, what happens in multiracial communities that are small enough for everyone to be known? This was certainly the case in every village and town in Yucatan, with the possible exceptions of late colonial Merida and Campeche (and even there and then, it was arguably true, as we shall see in Chapter Six). As a result, prejudice against Afro-Yucatecans was always personal, which meant it was usually also about something other than "race."

Consequently, too, the tension between a historian's knowledge of larger social patterns and knowledge of the individual lives that complicate (even undermine) those patterns is exacerbated in the case of Afro-Yucatecans. We have seen this illustrated above, from the macro-patterns of Spanish prejudice and the plasticity of casta terminology, to the personal dilemmas of Francisco de Aguilar and José María Correa. We also see it illustrated in the next chapter, which pursues the larger patterns of Afro-Yucatecan occupations, while seeking to complicate and add depth to them with individual examples.

CHAPTER FOUR

Ways of Work

For a period of a year and a half I was forced to work on the construction of the fortress built in this city, into doing the job of having under my charge three loads of lime in the barrio of San Cristobal, overseeing them loaded, burned, and unloaded twice a week, taking care of the Indians who were under my charge.
  —Diego Ramos, free-colored foreman, 1670[1]

For more than three years I have been a slave of the said lady, and never have I been obstinate; on the contrary, I have persevered and consented to exert myself on the cotton and sugarcane farms, thinking to free myself.
  —José María Espinola to the Governor of Yucatan, 1816[2]

Hipólito Ramírez, 18 to 20 years old, healthy and without defects, [knows] the essentials of shoemaking, cooking, and the masonry trade.
  —slave sale advertisement in Merida newspapers, 1821[3]

THE STORY OF JOAQUÍN CHASARRETTA

In February of 1787 the punishing work began. At Potoktok, just outside Merida, twenty Maya men from the city parish of La Mejorada sweated away for eighty days in the Yucatec heat and dust to clear the ground and stockpile rocks and stones for the bridge that they were to build. They were joined by an Afro-Yucatecan, whose trade was demolition, in particular the skill of "blowing up rocks [*bombear piedras*]."[4] "The *negro* Joseph María" used two pounds of gunpowder in the first blast holes [*barrenos*]. In May, the Maya workers were joined by several dozen additional native laborers, and Joseph María was joined by another free black man, Joaquín Chasarretta.

Despite their appearance in the engineer's record of accounts as specialists in rock demolition and extraction, both black men were paid the same wage as the skilled and semiskilled Maya workers—one and a half *reales* a day. This was a meager wage, roughly half that received by bridge and road workers on the *camino real* being constructed during this period between Mexico City and Veracruz.[5] Nor did a laborer get paid if injury or illness stopped him from working; on May 5 Blas Cob was paid one *real* for the work he did up to "three in the afternoon, when he got sick."[6] During the summer, as the Maya masons cut the stones and the bridge began to take shape, Joseph María disappeared from the list of workers. Joaquín Chasarretta, however, continued to work, "removing rocks [*sacando piedra*]" in a work gang that comprised himself and six Mayas.[7]

Joaquín Chasarretta was a free man in the 1780s, but he may once have been a slave and very likely had enslaved Afro-Yucatecan ancestors. Chasarretta was not a common name in Yucatan; most, if not all, Spaniards by that name in the province were descended from two brothers, Domingo and Manuel Chasarretta, who came from Durango, made good in Merida, and married into the local élite in 1688 and 1696, respectively. They almost certainly purchased Africans, giving them the Chasarretta surname, so Joaquín may have been descended from such slaves.[8]

The sparse particulars of this one experience in the working life of Joaquín Chasarretta cannot stand for the varied labor history of all Afro-Yucatecans, but the case does illustrate three key features of that history. First, the Afro-Yucatecan labor experience is not solely a story of slaves and slavery; as soon as one begins to explore the details of certain occupations and individual workers, as we shall do below, one encounters free coloreds as much as black slaves (including former slaves, and even slave-owning former slaves), with free coloreds increasingly common as the colonial period wore on.

Second, unskilled or semiskilled group workers (such as the plantation slave gangs whose working life is so often misleadingly taken as emblematic of all labor by Africans in the Americas) are seldom found in Yucatan. Such workers in this colony were typically Mayas, recruited from their *cahob* [Maya villages, towns, or urban *barrios*] through the labor obligations of the encomienda or the petty wage incentives of the *repartimiento* (or a complex combination of both). The forced-labor repartimiento that rotated through the rural Maya workforce (sometimes called the *tanda*) also caught free coloreds, but in relatively negligible numbers (for example, labor drafts in the Valladolid district in the 1720s typically comprised 160 Mayas but only 8 mulattoes and mestizos combined).[9] In contrast to Mayas, then, Afro-Yucatecans tended to work as individuals, not in groups, and were semiskilled or often fully skilled.

Third, and most directly germane to the thesis of this book, Afro-Yucatecans functioned as middle-men and middle-women in Spanish-owned enterprises. In such a capacity, Afro-Yucatecans were owned by or worked for Spaniards (or sometimes mestizos or pardos), but supervised other workers, mostly Mayas (but sometimes other laborers of color). They were thus middle-ranking both in terms of the operational structure of economic enterprises, and in concomitant social terms (even, arguably, when the black supervisor was a slave). This pattern was endemic to Spanish America as a whole, so it is not surprising to find it in colonial Yucatan.[10] Referred to by Spaniards variously as *mayordomos* (majordomo) or *criados* [a dependent servant, as opposed to a slave], we might also call these Afro-Yucatecans "supervisors," "overseers," or "foremen"; however, I have chosen primarily to call them "managers," a gender-neutral term that covers the various ways in which these men and women managed business and people. Not all Afro-Yucatecans were managers, of course, but this role was so distinctive to their experience that the discussion below will begin with managers, before turning to Afro-Yucatecans who were independent (although usually still middle-ranking in one way or another).

MANAGERS IN THE MIDDLE: TOWN AND COUNTRY

The very earliest Spaniards to settle in Yucatan brought black slaves with them and these first Afro-Yucatecans worked for their owners at the tasks that the invasion required. As we saw in Chapter One, men like Sebastián Toral fought as black conquistadors, and African slaves like the infamous Marcos became intermediaries between invaders and natives. It is not clear how and when Marcos learned Maya, but he spoke it well enough by the mid-1540s to be labeled a *nahuatlato* [interpreter] in official documentation and to be acting as an agent for the Montejo family in Maya villages, where it was said "he was feared more than the adelantado, his master, by the natives of this land."[11]

As the violence of the invasion subsided in the northwest during the 1540s, the first generation of slaves and black servants were moved into one or more of three types of activities: (1) like Marcos, they were sent out into the countryside as agents of conquistador–encomenderos to collect tribute in the form of goods and Maya workers and servants; (2) or they became domestic servants in the new urban households being constructed primarily in Merida and Campeche; (3) or they began work as urban artisans or skilled workers. These latter two often overlapped, as many commercial enterprises—bakeries, for example—were household-based.[12]

The predominance of domestic service among the possible work experiences of Afro-Yucatecan slaves is reflected in the slave gender balance, which tended to favor women (the female-to-male ratio culled from late colonial slave sales was 1:1, but the ratio based on adult slave baptisms in Merida was 1.2:1).[13] Compared to other categories of slave labor, domestic service tended to offer better working conditions and, for non-slaves or slaves not working for their owners, somewhat better pay (see Table 4.1).[14]

TABLE 4.1 Afro-Yucatecan incomes: Some examples, 1660–1787

Type of work	Monthly income (estimate, in pesos)	Year	Source
Hunting deer and turkey	2	1660s	AGI-*Escribanía* 316b, 75: f. 2
Rotational forced personal service [*tanda*]	1–2	1680s–1730s	AGI-*México* 1020; AGN-*Justicia Eclesiástica* 23; Solís Robleda 2003: 69–78
Demolition and road construction	4	1787	CAIHY-CCA #82, 6
Cook or housemaid	7	1666	Vega Franco 1984: 133[a]
Pardo militiaman on active duty	8	1690s	Jones 1998: 467[b]
Pardo militia officer	12	1690s	Jones 1998: 467[b]
Peddler working for a Spanish merchant	4–12	1690s	ANEY Baeza (UTA roll 1); Hunt 1974: 40
Mulatto healer working Maya villages	4–12	1710s	AGN-*Inquisición* 1164: f. 5r

[a] This example is from Cartagena; my assumption is that wages would have been comparable in Merida and Campeche.
[b] Salaries for the campaign against the Itza Maya kingdom. Infantrymen salaries were 8–11 pesos through to 1765, with officer salaries in the 12–18 range (DCP: f. 5).

There is also evidence that slaves born into domestic service in Spanish households were more likely than other slaves to be treated well, even with affection (as we shall see in Chapter Five, they were also more likely to be freed, especially if their owner was a woman, or if their mother's owner was their father). Such distinctions were relative, of course, and of little comfort to the domestic slave abused by his or her owner.

Before the eighteenth century, domestic service by Afro-Yucatecans was an urban phenomenon, as suggested by the 1700 census of rural towns and villages, showing free-colored farmers and artisans living among Mayas and working for Spaniards, many described as criados—but none specifically described as domestic servants in Spanish households. Furthermore, in the entire census only two Afro-Yucatecans were listed as slaves: two sisters, Lorenza and Ceferina de la Huerta, labeled *esclavas* without a casta designation, and owned by Juana de la Huerta, a "white" widow in Calkiní.[15]

Even late in the colonial period, when Spaniards had established small urban communities in Maya towns such as Calkiní, Izamal, and Tekax (see Map 4.1), their households did not come close to equaling the quantity and scale of elite households in Merida and Campeche; they featured Maya servants, and sometimes free-colored servants, but slaves remained rare commodities.

Merida's and Campeche's Spanish elite maintained casas pobladas that featured slaves who worked as domestic servants and also functioned as status markers (as we saw in Chapters Two and Three). Slave owners tended to leave their homes—whether for business or social engagements in the city or for long journeys to Mexico or Spain—with an entourage that included one or two slaves; these slaves acted as bodyguards, porters, butlers or maidservants, and traveling companions. Black slaves and servants were also available

Map 4.1 Afro-Yucatecans in the late colonial countryside. The map shows places mentioned in the chapter's first half. Most Afro-Yucatecans lived within the dotted area that I have dubbed "the colored crescent."

for hire to Spaniards making journeys within or outside the colony. For elite women, female slaves were deemed necessities—as fundamental an accoutrement of elite status as the "doña" title. Elite women in the city were twice as likely to own black women as they were to own black men, whereas Spanish men owned slaves of both sexes, owning men only marginally more than women. Enslaved women were domestic servants (see Figure 4.1), and sometimes concubines whose children were fathered by the slave owner. Male slaves performed a wide variety of functions. As mentioned above, they were house-guards, bodyguards, and caretakers; porters and traveling companions; stableboys and coachmen (liveried, if the owner was the governor or from one of the wealthier elite families).

The more such slaves and servants one had, the higher one's social, economic, and political standing. Governors of the colony thus maintained extensive entourages, bringing slaves with them and purchasing more upon arrival. Don Martín de Ursúa y Arizmendi kept four black slave musicians whom he either brought from Mexico City when he became acting governor

Figure 4.1 A black slave or domestic servant preparing chocolate in the kitchen of a Spanish household. Source: Detail of José de Páez, *De español y negra, mulato, 6*, ca. 1770–80, oil on copper, 50.2×63.8 cm. Private collection. Reproduced by permission.

of Yucatan in 1694 or whom he acquired shortly after arriving in Merida; this slave wind quartet played recorders, accompanied by brass and percussion sections of Maya musicians, at a 1695 celebration of the baptism of Itza Maya ambassadors in Merida.[16]

Not all slaves in the governor's *señorio* [as it was called; his lordship or gubernatorial household] were fortunate enough to be musicians; Africans who ended up working for the governor or another elite Spaniard in Merida had opportunities denied to most Middle-Passage survivors on Caribbean sugar plantations. There is considerable evidence of family life among slaves and servants in Spanish households, for example, and even signs of literacy. José Antonio, an enslaved black coachman to Governor don Lucas de Gálvez, was only fifteen when he witnessed his owner's assassination in 1792, but he was able to sign his own name to the testimony he gave to investigators the following year (see Figure 4.2).[17] In 1816, José María Espinola, enslaved to a Spanish woman in the small town of Espita, wrote an elegant letter in his own hand to the Governor of Yucatan, requesting assistance in his quest for freedom.[18]

One of the earliest governor's slaves immortalized in the archives is Montejo's invaluable servant Marcos; his role as intermediary between the

Figure 4.2 Signature of José Antonio, 16-year-old black slave coachman of assassinated governor don José de Gálvez, 1793. Underneath José Antonio's name, the notary has written, "Before me, Antonio de Argaiz, royal and public notary." Source: AGN-*Criminal* 301, 1: f. 6v.

Montejo administration and native villagers illustrates a crucial interstitial niche occupied by Afro-Yucatecans throughout the colonial period. Indeed, in all three of the occupational groups discussed above—encomenderos' agents, domestic servants, and artisans or skilled workers—black men and women often functioned as intermediaries or middle managers between Spaniards and Mayas.

Records for the late sixteenth century are sparse, but they suggest that the setting up of slaves as artisans happened shortly after the founding of Campeche and Merida. In other words, Africans tended to manage the first generations of colonial Maya workers, establishing a precedent that lasted through the colonial period. The use of slaves as skilled workers and managers was still reflected in the late seventeenth century in the surnames of pardo artisans in the capital; several dozen of them, for example, were named either Pacheco or Magaña. In most artisan operations, Mayas worked under black or pardo managers. Indeed, urban artisanry was a significant area of economic activity where black managers predominated.

Some of the poorer Spaniards to arrive in Yucatan in the decades after the colony was founded may have been artisans—for example, there were still Spanish goldsmiths and silversmiths in Merida in late colonial times—but even they would have hired or purchased black workers to manage their operations. Gradually, Afro-Yucatecans came to be not just middle managers but owners of these businesses. By 1790 there were free-colored silversmiths in Merida and Campeche; two in each place were also in pardo militia companies. For most of the seventeenth and eighteenth centuries almost all the blacksmiths in Merida and Campeche were black. Ten percent of all pardo militiamen in the colony in 1789 stated "blacksmith" as their occupation; most of them were in Merida (eighty-seven) and Campeche (sixteen).[19] The same was true of barbers: most urban barbers were free-colored men, often attached to the militia. Marcial Socobio was one of Merida's pardo barbers in the last decades of the colonial period, although not the most successful; a former militiaman in Bacalar, Marcial was in trouble with the authorities on and off between 1803 and 1819 for drunken and often violent behavior (on one occasion, he terrorized a shop boy with a sabre, walking off with a cask of aguardiente, allegedly "not the first one he had swiped").[20]

In rural communities there seems to have been more of a demand for mulatto blacksmiths than barbers. In the 1700 *matrícula* of fifty-two Maya parishes, there were already almost a dozen mulatto blacksmiths scattered across the colony (one of whom had come north from Campeche to Dzemul with his wife and two grandsons), more than any other type of artisan. Barbers were at the bottom of the list in 1700; there was only one in the census, a Francisco de León in Izamal, compared to six mestizo barbers in rural towns. Significantly, of these fifty-two communities, Izamal had the largest Spanish population (eighty-five, a notch ahead of Tekax with eighty-two;

six others had between five and thirty Spaniards, and most had none). The difference may have been cultural in root. That is, Maya men used mulatto smiths to make and mend tools, but they cut their hair and shaved at home. Mulatto men in villages, often married to Maya or mestiza wives, followed Maya custom. Spanish men, on the other hand, went to barbers, and Francisco de León was one of them; in this small way, by 1700 Izamal was becoming a microcosm of Merida and Campeche, and Tekax was not far behind, whereas even larger Maya towns like Motul and Oxkutzcab were a different world.[21] This pattern persisted through the eighteenth century. For example, in 1790, the three pardo militiamen whose primary occupation was that of barber all lived in Merida (a fourth, a *peluquero*, or wigmaker and hairdresser, lived in Campeche); in contrast, while most pardo-militia blacksmiths were urban, there were still twenty-eight of them scattered across seven rural towns along the colored crescent (from Hool and Tenabo up to Izamal, where there were eleven free-colored blacksmith-militiamen in 1790).[22]

The first generations of tailors and shoemakers were probably all or mostly Spanish, but during the seventeenth century pardos came to dominate these trades too. A mulatto named Domingo, for example, was a shoemaker first in Merida, where he married, and later in Campeche, where he died in 1687.[23] In the 1700 rural census there was only one Spanish shoemaker, but seven mulatto and nine mestizo ones. The take-over of these trades by Afro-Yucatecans was probably a literal ground-up transition, with the shift beginning in shoemaking, followed by tailoring. By 1700 there were eight mulatto and mestizo tailors in the countryside, and no Spanish ones. By 1790, pardo militiamen in Merida and Campeche were more likely to be shoemakers than in any other trade; there were 111 in the city alone, and another 42 in the port town. Tailoring was also a common militiaman's occupation; there were over fifty pardo-militia *sastres* in the colony in 1790, most of them in Merida and Campeche. As with other trades, the shift to free-colored predominance was driven by the Spanish tendency to train blacks or pardos as apprentices and then use them as managers. The same trades naturally attracted manumitted slaves, as well as the children of black managers, whether they were born as slaves or as free coloreds.[24]

Afro-Yucatecans were also involved in most areas of building and construction (see Table 4.2)—the black demolition experts, Joaquín Chasarretta and Joseph María, working partly alone and partly as managers of Maya day laborers, are examples. Yucatec historian Marta Espejo-Ponce Hunt found that in the first colonial century and a half stonemasons and carpenters were mostly Mayas, and indeed the masons that worked the Potoktok bridge in 1787 were all indigenous.[25] However, Afro-Yucatecans can be found among the workers and managers on most, if not all, major construction projects of the seventeenth century—from Campeche's churches

TABLE 4.2 Afro-Yucatecan occupations: Some examples, 1660–1787

Impersonal dependent
  —Militiaman (free state employee)
  —Coastal lookout (free state employee)
  —Plantation laborer (slave)

Personal dependent (enslaved or free, often in managerial role)
  —Domestic slave/servant
          —Caretaker/guard (men)
          —Coachman/driver (men)
          —Housekeeper/maid (mostly women)
          —Concubine (mostly women)
          —Food purchasing/cook
          —Musician (men)
  —Slave/servant/agent in extra-domestic occupation
          —Hired out to another Spaniard (various occupations)
          —Market vendor (mostly women)
          —Working in/managing any of the businesses listed below
          under "Independent" (principal urban examples: retail and
          artisan operations; colonial official's agent) (principal rural
          examples: estancia and muleteer operations; encomendero's
          agent)

Independent (free, sometimes in managerial role)
  —Corn farmer [*milpero*]/farm laborer [*labrador*]/beekeeper
  —Cattle rancher/estancia owner
  —Horse specialist (trainer, breeder, etc.)/cowboy
  —Peddler [*tratante, trajinante*]
  —Retailer (e.g., baker/café owner/see "Artisan" below)
  —Muleteer/carter (men only)
  —Sailor (men only)
  —Shipyard/construction worker (men only)
      —Shipbuilder/dockworker
      —Demolition
      —Mason/bricklayer/sculptor/painter/making lime/ building
      materials mover
  —Artisan (men only unless otherwise indicated)
      —Blacksmith/ironmonger/silversmith
      —Barber/wigmaker/hairdresser/blood-letter/surgeon
      —Shoemaker/saddlemaker/tanner
      —Candlemaker/soapmaker/ropemaker
      —Tailor
      —Carpenter
      —Spinner/seamstress (women only)/weaver/dyer
      —Healer/witch/love–magic practitioner (men and women)
  —Hunter/fisherman
  —Bullfighter

Sources: All occupations are attested at least once in archival sources; see the discussion in this chapter and Chapter Five (esp. Tables 4.3–4.5 and Table 5.4 in Chapter Five) for specific citations.

to the *camino real* to Merida's citadel of San Benito—and skilled stonework-ers of various kinds appear in the pardo militia lists of 1789–90.[26]

One of the foremen on the San Benito project was a pardo named Diego Ramos. In 1670, Ramos responded to the *residencia* investigation into the controversial governorship of don Rodrigo Flores de Aldana by submitting a complaint claiming he had been forced against his will to work unpaid for eighteen months overseeing Maya workers (as quoted at the beginning of this chapter, with the full complaint presented in Appendix A). The Mayas were from Merida's cah-barrio of San Cristóbal, adjacent to San Benito, which was built on the ruins of a Maya pyramid raised centuries earlier by the ancestors of these same workers. Whether work conditions were worse in the 1660s than in pre-Conquest times is hard to say (San Cristóbal's town council filed its own complaint in 1667),[27] but it is certain that working under pardo overseers was a colonial innovation. The semiskilled task of Ramos and "his" Mayas seems to have been to load limestone onto horse-drawn carts, take it to be burned and turned into lime, and then unload the lime at the construction site. The work could hardly have been pleasant, and even though exaggeration was part of the petitionary genre, the larger body of ev-idence detailing the abuse and rapacity of the Flores administration lends some veracity to Ramos's tale. He wrote that he and his crew toiled away . . .

without a stipend or any payment, not putting aside Sundays, neither observing fies-tas, nor Holy Week, nor Corpus Christi, which [processions] I could not even see, working away tearing my clothes; and not having an opportunity to go looking for other work, with my wife and family suffering because of this job, and not having any time for them, although many times I begged and pleaded for the love of God to be given the chance and right to go and rest and have a life [*buscar mi vida*], because I am poor and old . . . ; but I was told that I would be given two hundred lashes or be thrown in jail until the construction was finished, and that there would be no relief.[28]

Ramos remarked that there were "plenty of [*hartos*] pardos and mesti-zos" who could also do his job, many of them already "in the service of His Majesty."

If there were "plenty" of Afro-Yucatecans working for the colonial gov-ernment in Ramos's day—as artisans or workers, guards or militiamen—there were even more a century later. By the final decades of the colonial period, even though blacksmiths were still mostly Afro-Yucatecan and ma-sons were still mostly Maya, there were blacks and pardos working in virtu-ally every trade and occupation in the colony, both in the "private" and "public" sectors (a distinction that was extremely blurred in colonial Spanish America). This variety is shown in the lists of occupations in Tables 4.2–4.5.

Some of these Afro-Yucatecans acquired their skills in another colony. For example, several enslaved Africans who escaped from English owners in Belize in 1801 were detained by Spanish officials in Bacalar, and then auctioned off in Merida. One was sold as a carpenter, whose new owner pre-sumably sought to make use of his new slave's most notable skill. Another

TABLE 4.3 Making a living in the countryside in 1700: Afro-Yucatecan men's occupations

	La Costa and Beneficios Bajos	Sierra	Sierra: Tekax[a]	Camino Real and Campeche[b]	TOTALS
[Corn farmer [*milpero*] total]	[12]	[12]	[19]	[12]	[55]
Corn farmer	5	11	19	10	45
Corn farmer and beekeeper	1	1			2
Corn farmer and cattle rancher	1				1
Corn farmer, horsebreeder, and hunter[c]	1				1
Corn farmer and hunter[d]				1	1
Corn farmer and baking-stone maker				1	1
Farm laborer [*labrador*]	5				5
Farm laborer and stockinger [*mediero*]	1				1
Farm laborer and corn farmer	2				2
Farm laborer and hunter[e]	2				2
Cattle rancher[f]	7				7
Small farm [*sitio*] owner				2	2
Ranch foreman [*mayoral*]	1			1	2
Rancher, healer, and *mayordomo*[g]	1				1
Cowboy [*vaquero*]				2	2
Horse trainer [*picador*]				1	1
Fishery owner, beekeeper, and corn farmer	1				1
Fisherman	1				1
Blacksmith [*herrero*]	2	3	5	1	11

TABLE 4.3 (*continued*)

	La Costa and Beneficios Bajos	Sierra	Sierra: Tekax[a]	Camino Real and Campeche[b]	TOTALS
Shoemaker [*zapatero*]	2	1	1	2	6
Saddlemaker [*sillero*]			1	1	2
Shoemaker and saddlemaker	1				1
Barber [*barbero*]	1				1
Tailor [*sastre*]			2		2
Tailor and corn farmer	1				1
Tanner [*zurrador*]			1		1
Hunter [*cazador*] and tanner [*curtidor*]		1			1
Peddler [*tratante*]	1		2		3
Muleteer [*arriero*]				2	2
Servant/dependent [*criado*]	1				1
Militia sergeant	1				1
None [*sin oficio*]	1		5	1	7
"Lives on charity [*de limosna*]"		1			1
None recorded	4	8	1	11	24
[TOTALS]	[43]	[27]	[37]	[36]	[143]

Source: 1700 matrícula in AGI-*México* 1035; also see Solano (1975).

Notes: The men I have grouped together as "Afro-Yucatecans" are listed under various casta categories according to the usage favored by the priest of each parish (in other words, free-colored men were "mulatos" in Dzidzantun, "chinos" in Conkal, and "pardos" in Motul due to the vagaries of terminological usage by Spaniards, not because such men were in any categorical way different from village to village; see discussion of casta terms in Chapter Two). There were only three *negros* listed (one each from Telchac, Tekanto, and Mani), included in this table. There is no mention in the matrícula of slave/free status.

[a] This town is listed separately because its priest provided census data on "mestizos y mulatos" in a single category, represented here.

[b] Only three of these entries are from villages in the Campeche district, the ranch foreman and two of the eleven without recorded occupations.

[c] This "chino" from Conkal, Sebastián Pérez, with a Maya wife named Josepha Canche and five children, "makes a living shooting [*tirar*, i.e., hunting], breeding horses [*sangrar caballos*] and farming corn."

[d] This mulatto from Maxcanú, Tomás Bonilla, married with four children, "sustains himself by farming a cornfield, [occasionally] killing a deer and a chicken at night."

[e] Two mulattoes in Izamal listed both as farm laborers and as "occupation, shotgun [*ocupacion, la escopeta*]."

TABLE 4.3 (*continued*)

[f] Includes five unmarried brothers listed as co-owners of "a cattle ranch [*estancia de ganado mayor*]" in Motul.

[g] Juan Ignacio Palomino, a mulatto from Oxkutzcab married to a mestiza, was not only a *curandero* who owned a small cattle ranch [*sitio de ganado*] in Muna, but worked as encomendero's agent [*mayordomo de encomienda*] for don Juan del Castillo.

was valued at 200 pesos "for his age and experience as a storekeeper, although he is lame in one foot," while a third slave was put up for sale at 215 pesos because he was "a healthy 30-year-old and a cook by trade."[29] Black carpenters, storekeepers, or cooks, even if they were slaves, still managed other workers; a black slave was as likely as a free pardo to be trusted with authority and responsibility, and such a slave might even be permanently assigned his own native servant.[30]

Afro-Yucatecans who could work traditionally Maya trades such as masonry or carpentry probably developed these as secondary skills. Hipólito Ramírez, for example, was advertised for sale in 1821 as "knowing the essentials of shoemaking, cooking, and the masonry trade," even though he was only "eighteen-to-twenty-years old."[31] This kind of generalization of skill was characteristic of a small market, which Yucatan still was, even in the final year of colonial rule; there was far greater variety and specialization among artisans and tradesmen in central Mexico.[32] Having generalized skills was a way of being economically diversified; in the early modern world, diversification made good business sense and was the goal of pardos as much as it was of Spaniards. Thus a black leatherworker like Juan Fernández Palomino was also a retailer, with a modest store in late seventeenth-century Merida that sold oil and other basic goods.[33]

The organic process that led Afro-Yucatecans from being slave assistants to skilled managers to business owners seems to have spread to a lesser extent to the urban Maya workers typically managed by men of African descent. In other words, some Mayas were able to run their own shoemaking or smith operations; an early example, illustrating this secondary pattern and dating from the turn of the eighteenth century, is that of a Maya blacksmith in the predominantly native San Cristóbal neighborhood of Merida whose workers were pardo boys.[34] I have yet to find a single instance, however, of a Maya owning a black slave.[35]

The muleteer business was associated with blacks throughout the Spanish American provinces, as African slaves drove mule trains from the earliest days of colonial transportation. Blacks not only drove the mules, but loaded them and took care of them; when a mule train was sold, the slave or slaves who had worked it were usually traded with the animals and their tackle.[36] Similar to some of the artisan operations just discussed, the early Yucatec pattern featured a Spanish muleteer who owned and ran the business

Figure 4.3 Casta Paintings tended to portray stereotypical behavior or
occupations; just as Figure 4.1 portrayed a black woman doing domestic work, this
painting depicts two black men working mules on a sugar estancia and a third
offering food to his native wife. Source: Drawing by Robin Restall from painting
by an unknown artist, 9. *De negro e india sale lobo. Negro 1. India 2. lobo 3*, ca.
1780, oil on canvas, 38 × 52 cm.

and a black slave or servant to do most or all of the physical labor (see Figure 4.3). A larger train was administered by a black *capitán*, with a black or
Maya underling to do the dirty work. The largest trains supported two or
three *negros*, who supervised temporary Maya workers when needed—
when packing large loads onto the mules, for example.

However, by the late seventeenth century Afro-Yucatecans had become
the predominant owners, as well as the middle managers, in muleteer businesses. The wealthiest muleteer in Yucatan in the 1690s was the pardo militia captain, Eugenio de Acosta. Another Afro-Yucatecan muleteer during
this same period was less prosperous, but had worked from being a muleteer's slave to the free owner of his own train, complete with his own black
slave; one of his niches in the transportation business was buying cacao
from Maya farmers and selling it at port to Spanish merchants. All three of
the muleteers listed in the 1700 rural census lived in Maxcanú, which was
the main rural transportation hub of the camino real; they were Lucas de
Aguilar, listed as Spanish, and two mulattoes, Antonio Nuncia and Mateo
Perera (all married with three or more children each).[37]

Outside the city and town Spaniards employed Afro-Yucatecan slaves and servants in two principal ways. One was as an encomendero's agent; the other was as a manager of an estate, or estancia. Such black managers were sometimes confusingly called *estancieros* (not to be mistaken for estancia owners, although Afro-Yucatecans also owned estancias and ranches). Diego Aldana, for example, was the mulatto mayoral of Estancia Hontum (near Cholul, in Campeche district) in 1700. Another example is Diego Cuero, who was the free-colored foreman of Estancia Huntulchac (he might not have made it into the historical record had he not been arrested in 1761 as an alleged spy and participant in the Maya rebellion begun in Cisteil; Cuero was acquitted on all charges).[38]

Haciendas and larger estancias were run by a senior majordomo who was more likely to be a Spaniard or the encomendero owner himself (more common in Yucatan than in richer provinces of New Spain). However, in 1700 the majordomo of the encomiendas held by don Juan del Castillo was a mulatto named Juan Ignacio Palomino, who lived in Oxkutzcab with his mestiza wife, owned a farm with some cattle outside Muna, had three servants, and was also a healer [*curandero*].[39] Typically, then, beneath the owner or his majordomo were black or pardo estancieros managing the various operations of the estate. Beneath the black overseers were Maya cowboys and field workers.

African slaves played important roles in the largely unsuccessful efforts by the first generation of encomenderos to make the production of commodities, such as wheat, sugar, silk, and indigo, commercially viable.[40] These roles were not as plantation workers, but as skilled managers—and nor were all such managers men. For example, toward the end of the sixteenth century, don Juan de Montejo y Castillo experimented with indigo production, using Maya workers from his *encomienda* and an African slave as overseer of the production process. At the time of Montejo's death in 1603, the enterprise was defunct, and the slave—who would have been worth almost as much as one of the two 500-peso cauldrons that had fallen into the hands of one of Montejo's creditors—was up for sale. The slave, a black woman named Luisa, was being held by the same creditor, who was to be remunerated with "the maize and hens from the village of Cholul," which was part of the Montejo encomienda. Another black woman, a "*criolla* named Juana," was also to be sold to pay off debts. A plan to buy more cauldrons and another black slave to manage them was never realized.[41]

Examples from later in the century illustrate how black managers enabled Spaniards to maintain their various business interests. Pedro de Carvajal had prospered in Veracruz before moving his principal household to Merida, where his brother lived. When he died in 1692, he left behind a mulatta slave who managed affairs in Merida, and a black slave, named Pedro, who managed his store and his cattle ranch in Veracruz; a third slave was rented out to a Spaniard in Veracruz. As the colony of Yucatan

developed during the seventeenth century, Spaniards acquired property far-
ther and farther from Merida and Campeche, in the process sending out
Afro-Yucatecan agents to manage cattle ranches and other investments.[42]
The variety and geographical spread of such enterprises steadily increased.
For example, by the late-eighteenth century, Spaniards were equipping
gangs of ten to twenty Maya and Afro-Yucatecan men with machetes, axes,
and saws, and food for two weeks in the forests of southern Campeche.
Managed by free-colored majordomos, these workers logged the dyewood
or logwood that had been worked by British loggers and their black slaves
into the early decades of the century.[43]

It was cattle ranching that proved to be the enduring staple of estates in
Yucatan, along with the production of maize and cotton (both of which
Mayas had been growing long before the Conquest), especially with the ben-
efit of encomienda labor. In the final decades of the seventeenth century don
Zeferino Pacheco grew wealthy from his encomienda at Tihosuco (see Map
4.1) and from various related enterprises, including an estancia outside
Merida that was managed by a free mulatto named Ignacio Pacheco, who
had risen to the rank of sergeant in the pardo militia. Eventually, Sergeant
Pacheco was able to invest in his own small cattle estancia, while continuing
to manage that of his patron (and perhaps former owner). Another Afro-
Yucatecan Pacheco, Mateo Lorenzo, probably a mulatto relative of the encomendero's family, was a trader based in Izamal and responsible for getting
tribute goods moved from the Valladolid area to Merida. Yet another mulatto, a Captain Diego González, oversaw the transportation of exportable
goods to the port at Campeche.[44]

As don Zeferino prospered, he moved his principal household, with its mix
of Maya and Afro-Yucatecan servants, from Valladolid to Merida. One of his
free Afro-Yucatecan employees remained in Valladolid and was charged with
collecting Pacheco's tribute in Tihosuco and passing it into the trade network
just described. Indeed, the other principal Afro-Yucatecan managerial role in
the countryside was as an agent of an encomendero, responsible for collecting
tribute in the cahob or Maya villages within his grant.[45]

As we saw in Chapter Two, the slave-owning elite was dominated by the
colony's governor, encomenderos, the district captains, their lieutenants, and
their female relatives. This privileged group employed Afro-Yucatecan slaves
and servants as agents in the countryside—collecting goods, tribute, and other
payments due, delivering and collecting correspondence, and trading. For example, a black slave named Juan Rosado who had managed an estancia near
Valladolid for a priest, Br. Diego de Burgos, in the 1680s, was purchased by
Alférez Pedro Rodríguez de la Paz in 1690; in the 1690s Rosado acted as his
owner's agent, mostly peddling merchandise, along the northern coast of the
peninsula. Likewise, at the turn of the eighteenth century, Capt. Diego de
Acevedo owned three black slaves and employed a free Afro-Yucatecan, all of
whom worked as mercantile agents for him in Maya villages. Not all the pro-

tagonists in this process were men—as illustrated by the case of Maria Riveros, an enslaved *negra* who was both domestic servant and business agent for her owner, doña Melchora Pacheco Sepulveda Benavides. Doña Melchora's father, brother, and brother-in-law were all encomenderos, but she was a business partner primarily to her brother, don Nicolás Pacheco, and her cousin, the above-mentioned don Zeferino Pacheco. Maria, her slave, managed her trading interests in the countryside; she bought grain, raw cotton, cotton *mantas* [blankets], wax, and honey in Maya villages, selling metal tools, alcohol, and other products in the same cahob.[46]

Spaniards with the rights to various forms of taxation invariably used Afro-Yucatecans to do the dirty work. This was true from the highest-ranking Spaniard down to the lowest who could afford a black slave or free-colored dependent. The precedent established in the 1540s by Montejo and his slave Marcos persisted for centuries. For example, the extensive residencia investigation into the 1660s Flores de Aldana administrations brought to the surface Maya resentment of Afro-Yucatecans like Melchor de Segovia. Probably born in Yucatan around 1600, Melchor was a free mulatto servant boy to a priest, Dr. Francisco Ruíz, who took him to Spain in his early teens; they returned to Yucatan in 1615, when Melchor was described as having "a sparse beard, with a wound mark below the right eye, and a tiny little face."[47]

A half century later, in the early 1660s (when he was in his early sixties), Melchor de Segovia reappears in the historical record as one of the "majordomos and collectors [*cobradores*]" of Governor Flores de Aldana and his associates. Based in the small town of Calkiní, Melchor had "for many years" (at least since 1654) run the regional wax collection operation. He did it "with such authority" that he was able to dispatch a junior collector out to the surrounding villages to collect wax, maintaining "stone houses where he collected the wax for blanching." Melchor's middle position between the Flores de Aldana administration and the Maya villagers is vividly illustrated by the accusation that the mulatto collector "forced the Indians to haul water from the well for him, not letting them carry it to their own houses," dictating decisions to the local magistrates, and imposing "on the said Indians such distress and vexation." The Mayas "had no recourse," added the witness, "for they had none in the encomendero, nor in the minister, nor in the public defender, for fear that the governor would destroy them in some way, as he [Melchor] was placed and named by the aforementioned [Governor Flores de Aldana]."[48]

The job of collector was probably also among the tasks assigned to Agustín de Leira, a black slave brought to Yucatan in 1718 by don Diego de Santesteban, who had acquired the lease on the income from sales and customs duties on salt.[49] Collecting tribute and tax payments outside Merida and Campeche required establishing effective, if not friendly, relations with Maya *cabildo* [town council] officers, especially the *batab* [governor]. It is not clear when such agents began to make their homes in the *cabeceras* or head-towns of the encomienda where they worked. But the practice was widespread by the time of the matrículas of 1688 and 1700, when many of the Afro-Yucatecan men and women listed in the matrícula were agents of encomenderos, of district captains, and of priests, or the relatives and descendents of such agents.[50] Over a century later, at the time of the census series of 1798–1815, what had been handfuls of Afro-Yucatecans in the larger Maya parishes had grown to hundreds in the larger towns and villages and dozens in the smaller ones, especially along the strip that I have called "the colored crescent" (see Map 4.1); some of these were still agents of elite Spaniards, but most were the descendents of the slaves, agents, managers, and militiamen of the seventeenth and eighteenth centuries.[51]

The closing topic of this section is sugar. As sugar was grown in late colonial Yucatan, one might expect that the exception to the middle-manager pattern would be the use of African slaves on sugar plantations. However, this use of black slave labor was limited primarily to the late colonial period, to the Campeche region and to the far north of the peninsula, and never amounted to the kind of large-scale slave-labor use typically associated with sugar production in the colonial Americas. The modest boom in the sugar industry in late eighteenth-century Yucatan may help explain why, according to census data, for the first time in the colony's history the number of *negros* rose to over a thousand (see Table 1.1 in Chapter One); the industry was unique in being both labor intensive and profitable enough to pay for slave acquisition. Yet the numbers of African slaves used was never very high, and I have not found this apparent increase in *negro* numbers clearly reflected in other records, such as sale documents or parish records.

The fact is, large-scale planters, who were the only ones who could afford slaves, still had to rely upon peonage and the forced labor of Mayas drafted under the tanda system. The massive importation of African slaves envisaged by Campeche planters, who, lead by don Juan Ignacio de Cosgaya, petitioned authorities in 1785 for permission to initiate such a trade, never took place. The petition was denied, and although a 1787 appeal won royal permission to import up to a thousand Africans, there is no evidence that the license was filled; in fact, six years later the landowning elite, exploring a solution that drew upon the existing pardo population, proposed that "the vagrants who infest the villages of the province with their wicked customs and from whom the Indians receive frequent abuse" be forced by law to work on sugar plantations.[52] This proposal too never became a reality.

To Campeche's east, around Tekax and the other Maya towns of the Sierra Alta, a sugar boom began dramatically in the 1780s. While before this decade little or no sugarcane had been grown in this the most fertile region of Yucatan, it became the top commercial crop there from the 1790s to the outbreak of the Caste War half a century later. But although some of the

Spanish owners of the haciendas and sugar estates in the Sierra Alta owned African slaves, these blacks and mulattoes were few in number and functioned as domestic servants or overseers, not plantation-style workers. An example from the Espita region (where there was a parallel increase in sugar production in these same decades) is José Maria Espinola, who worked in the 1810s as a laborer and then overseer on a small sugar and cotton farm [*labranzas de algodón y cañaveral*].[53] Hacendados had no need to lay out capital on quantities of expensive slave laborers (Espinola was valued at 250 pesos); both around Espita and in the Sierra Alta, they drew instead upon the local Maya population for their labor needs. Maya laborers either came from the many towns and villages of the region or they lived on the haciendas—the largest of which, Hacienda Tabi, had a resident population of close to two thousand by 1803. Some prominent Mayas (most notably nobles of the Pech family) were themselves independent sugar growers. Independence and the decline and abolition of slavery thus had no negative impact on sugar production in the Sierra Alta, which actually increased in the 1820s.[54]

AFRO-YUCATECAN ARTISANS AND OTHER INDEPENDENTS

Not all men and women of African descent worked as managers of Spanish-owned businesses or of non-Spanish workers; many were business owners themselves in—not surprisingly—the same occupations in which Afro-Yucatecan managers tended to specialize. Indeed, as suggested above, making the transition from managing someone else's mule train to owning one's own was a predictable ambition for a mulatto muleteer. Black and pardo blacksmiths, tailors, and shoemakers—managers of Spanish-owned businesses in early colonial times—became independent artisans in the mid-colonial period; by 1700, if not before, Afro-Yucatecans and mestizos dominated these trades throughout the colony. In the seventeenth and eighteenth centuries, just as an enslaved mule captain might plausibly hope to one day be a free, independent muleteer, so might a negra managing a bakery reasonably aspire not only to buy her freedom, but to run her own bakery.[55]

Likewise, just as the majordomos or estancieros of Spanish estates were often free blacks or mulattoes, so did such men form a part of a larger middling group of people who owned smaller estancias and ranches. This middling group consisted of all those below the Spanish elite and above the *macehualob* or indigenous commoners; they were less privileged or poorer-connected Spaniards, mestizos, Maya noblemen, and Afro-Yucatecans of various kinds—most typically free coloreds but including the occasional black slaves with some savings to invest. Holders of small properties hoped to imitate on a more modest scale the large multifaceted estates of the encomendero class. But without the connections and capital of the elite they were usually forced to settle for petty livestock operations. If they were lucky, they raised cattle; if not, some pigs and goats, perhaps a few horses.[56]

Some examples come from the earliest surviving volume of notarial records from Merida (that of 1689–92). Melchor de Medina, a mulatto who worked in a managerial position of some kind on a Spanish estate outside Merida, bought a small *sitio* or undeveloped parcel of land named Xueuel, fifteen miles from the city. He paid ten pesos to an "indio ladino" named Juan Diego (either a mestizo or probably a descendent of one of the Nahua soldiers who settled in the city in the 1540s).[57] Melchor dug a well, planted some fruit trees, built a hut, and sold the sitio for twenty-three pesos—not a huge sum, but an impressive return on his investment.

The pardo militia sergeant Ignacio Pacheco also made a tidy profit that same year (1690), buying small adjacent pieces of land from the parish priest of Tecoh and from a Maya man from the village, selling them a few months later as a single sitio worth thirty-five pesos. Not all Afro-Yucatecans who bought properties outside the city did so with a view to improving and selling the land at a profit. As land became cheaper the farther one moved from Merida, a pardo such as Antonio Lope was simply looking for an affordable plot to own and work. In 1689 Lope bought a vacant plot from the Maya cabildo [town council] of Temax for twenty-one pesos; he farmed corn on the plot (despite the cabildo's claim that they were justified in alienating the land because it was not farmable), settling in this native community where according to the matrícula of the previous year there were nineteen non-Mayas (five Spaniards, three mestizos, ten mulattoes, and one *negro*).

On a larger scale than Lope's *milpa* [cornfield] was the operation run at Hun Pic Ha by María Háuregui, a mulatta who managed the sitio for Juan Muñóz, a low-ranking Spaniard or mestizo who made his living in Merida as a miller and baker. María Háuregui was not only the sitio's manager, but also an investment partner; having contributed a fertile mare, by 1692 she owned ten of the estancia's twenty-one horses. As he lay dying, Muñóz married Háuregui, and then dictated his will, bequeathing to his brand new wife the sitio whose horses, beehives, and land were valued at almost 150 pesos.[58]

At one end of this middling group there were Afro-Yucatecans who lived like Mayas (the focus of the next section), and on the other side there were those who were like nonelite Spaniards. For in some areas of economic activity, as in other aspects of colonial life, there were no clear dividing lines between Spaniards and Afro-Yucatecans. On the one hand, a Spaniard could be a farm laborer (as was Gaspar de Ayala of Izamal) or a corn farmer (like Lucas Herrera, the only Spaniard in Suma, or Pedro de Mena, the corn farmer judged by the Nabalam curate in 1688 as the closest any man came in his district to being a Spaniard).[59] On the other hand, in discussing the more enterprising and successful free coloreds, for example, one might also be talking about mestizos and nonelite Spaniards. One example is Captain Lázaro del Canto, a mulatto militia officer. We shall hear more about Capt. del Canto in the next chapter, but suffice to mention here that he both maintained a house in Merida and ran a small estancia just outside the city, worth something in the fifty to one hundred peso range, raising enough pigs and chickens to make the farm profitable.[60] Spaniards and better-off mestizos preferred to raise livestock, viewing the keeping of pigs and chickens, like apiculture and corn farming, as "Indian" activities; but poorer Spaniards could not be choosers, and Canto's modest estancia might have been that of a low-ranked Spaniard.

Indeed, Table 4.4. shows how free coloreds, mestizos, and Spaniards worked at making a living in the countryside in 1700 in similar ways. Their working lives were certainly not identical, but nor did men of different castas work in completely different occupations; the variations from one casta category to the next reflected contrasts within occupations or categories of occupation. Of course, the very plasticity of casta categories meant that what a man did, and how profitably he did it, very much contributed to defining his casta status. For example, an artisan could be anyone, but he was most likely to be Afro-Yucatecan. Eighteen percent of all free-colored men in the census were artisans of some kind (defined here as blacksmiths, silversmiths, shoemakers, saddlemakers, tanners, tailors, barbers, soap-makers, painters, carpenters, pot-makers, weavers, and stockingers), as opposed to 15% of mestizos and 6% of Spaniards. Those who were not artisans, and even some of those who were, made a living from agricultural enterprise, especially corn and cattle. But Spaniards were more likely to be owners of estancias; mestizos and Afro-Yucatecans more often owned small farms or managed other people's operations.

The most striking example, in fact, is that of corn farming. In rural Yucatan, men of every kind—from relatively wealthy Spaniards to free coloreds to Mayas—were involved in farming milpas or cornfields. The difference was one of degree: 40% of Afro-Yucatecans and mestizos were *milperos* or corn farmers, but only about 20% of Spaniards. Furthermore, most of these Spaniards were corn farm *owners* rather than dirt-under-the-fingernails milperos—like Salvador López of Tekax, who was "a corn farmer with plenty of Indians [*milpero con bastantes indios*]," or Atanasio de la Cruz, who had "cornfields [and] ten servants [*con milpas; ten criados*]." When a Spaniard did the work himself, it was worthy of note; the priest in Pencuyut remarked that Bernardino Parra, a Spaniard who lived in the village with his wife, mother, and two brothers, "personally farmed corn [*su trato es hacer milpas personalmente*]."[61]

Spaniards were also more diversified in their occupations and economic interests (indeed, there was generally a correlation in the colony between diversification and wealth). Dividing occupations into the total number of individuals in Table 4.4 produces an occupational diversity statistic of 0.29

TABLE 4.4 Making a living in the countryside in 1700: Afro-Yucatecan men's occupations in comparative context

	Afro-Yucatecans	Mestizos	Spaniards[a]
[Corn farmer [*milpero*] total]	[55]	[104]	[33]
Corn farmer	45	98	26[b]
Corn farmer and beekeeper	2		1
Corn farmer and cattle rancher	1		
Corn farmer, horsebreeder, and hunter	1		
Corn farmer and hunter	1		
Corn farmer and baking-stone maker	1		
Corn farmer and *saicán* burner[c]		1	1
Farm laborer [*labrador*]	5	10	13
Farm laborer and stockinger [*mediero*]	1	1	
Farm laborer and corn farmer	2		
Farm laborer and hunter	2	1	
Farm laborer and horse rancher			1
Farm laborer and cattle rancher			2
Cattle [*ganado mayor*] rancher	7	2	9
Sheep/goat [*ganado menor*] rancher		4	5
Goat keeper and corn farmer		1	
Pig farmer and wax-cake maker[d]			1
Ranch [*estancia*] owner			4
Estancia and corn farm owner			1
Small farm [*sitio*] owner	2		3
Encomendero and estancia owner			1
Encomendero			3
Ex-*cacique* [pueblo governor]		1	
Manager [*mayordomo*] of an estancia		1	2
Encomendero's foreman [*mayoral*]			1+1[e]
Ranch foreman [*mayoral*]	2	4	1
Rancher, healer, and mayordomo	1		
Cowboy [*vaquero*]	2	1	
Horse trainer [*picador*]	1		
Butcher (of piglets)[f]		2	2

TABLE 4.4 *(continued)*

	Afro-Yucatecans	Mestizos	Spaniards[a]
Butcher (of cattle and pigs)[f]			6
Beekeeper		3	
Beekeeper and horse rancher		1[g]	1
Beekeeper, horse rancher, and butcher		1[g]	
Tobacco farmer			2
Fishery owner			1
Fishery owner, beekeeper, and corn farmer	1		1
Fisherman	1	6	
Fisherman, lookout [*vigía*], and horse rancher			1
Fisherman and saicán burner[c]			1
Ferryman [*barquero*]		1	
Blacksmith [*herrero*]	11	12	
Silversmith [*platero*]		1	
Shoemaker [*zapatero*]	6	6	1
Saddlemaker (or chairmaker; [*sillero*])	2	1	
Shoemaker and saddlemaker	1	1	
Shoemaker and blacksmith		1	
Barber [*barbero*]	1	6	1
Tailor [*sastre*]	2	4	
Tailor and soap-maker ["*cuece jabón*"]		1	
Tailor and corn farmer	1		
Tanner [*zurrador*]	1		
Hunter [*cazador*] and tanner [*curtidor*]	1		
Hunter [*cazador*, or *la escopeta*]		5	
Hunter and soap-maker [*jabonero*]			1
Hunter and farm laborer		2	1[h]
Hunter [*tirador*], shoemaker, and corn farmer	1		
Painter and woodcutter[i]			1
Carpenter [*maderero*]		2	
Pot-maker ["*hace ollas*"]		1	
Weaver [*tejedor*]			3
Stockinger ["*mediero tejedor de medias*"]			1
Stockinger [*calcetero*] and corn farmer			1

TABLE 4.4 *(continued)*

	Afro-Yucatecans	Mestizos	Spaniards [a]
Merchant [*mercader*]			3
Peddler [*tratante*]	3	10	14 [j]
Peddler and sailor			1
Peddler and farm laborer		1	
Peddler and corn farmer		2	1
Peddler and stockinger			1
Peddler and sergeant		1	
Wax peddler and corn farmer		1+1 [k]	1 [l]
Wax peddler and farm laborer			1 [l]
Shopkeeper, farm laborer, and sergeant [m]			1
Muleteer [*arriero*]	2		1
Militia sergeant	1		
Interim lieutenant, unpaid [*sin sueldo*]			1
Squadron corporal and farm laborer			1
Local Spanish official [n]			1
Lookout		1	
Lookout and saicán burner			1
Servant/dependent [*criado*] [o]	1	1	1
Indentured servant [p]		1	
"By his sweat [*vive solo de su sudor*]"		1	
None [*sin oficio* or *sin ocupacion*]	7	6	8 [q]
"Lives on charity [*de limosna*]"	1	2	1
Vagrant [*vago*]			1
Permanently absent [*huido*]			1
None recorded	24	46	19
[TOTALS]	[143]	[256]	[160]

Sources: 1700 matrícula in AGI-*México* 1035; Solano (1975). See Table 4.3 for notes on individual Afro-Yucatecans.

[a] Includes all men listed in the matrícula as *español* or *blanco*.

[b] Most of the Spanish milperos had servants who presumably did the actual farming (e.g., Salvador López of Tekax was "a corn farmer with plenty of Indians [*milpero con bastantes indios*]"; two other Spanish milperos in Tekax used "hired Indians [*indios alquilados*]"; and Atanasio de la Cruz had "corn plots [and] ten servants [*criados*]" in Chanchanha). But at least one Spanish corn farmer, Bernardino Parra, who lived in Pencuyut with his wife, mother, and two brothers, "personally farmed corn [*su trato es hacer milpas personalmente*]."

[c] All three *saicán* burners in the census were Spaniards who lived near the coast and for whom this was an auxiliary occupation; my best guess is that the word derives from the Maya term

TABLE 4.4 *(continued)*

tsakan [snake cactus] (*Selenicereus donkelaarii*; Bricker, Po'ot Yah, and Dzul de Po'ot 1998: 41), and that the cactus was burned either to smoke fish or, more likely, to send smoke signals at times of coastal alarm (one of the saicán burners, Diego León de Salazar of Yobain, was the lookout at the port of Santa Clara).

ᵈ Diego Carballo, a "blanco" in Oxkutzcab, "whose occupation is to raise sucking pigs and make wax cakes [*su ocupacion es criar lechones y hacer marquetas de cera*]."

ᵉ This "+1" is the only castizo in Oxkutzcab (and in the whole census): Julián Baeza's "position and occupation is to regulate tribute thread, paties, honey, wax, and deerskins [*ejercicio y ocupacion es regular hilo de tributo, paties, miel y cera y cueros de venado*]"; he was married to María de Rojas (casta unspecified) and had two servants.

ᶠ The mestizo butchers "kill piglets [or sucking pigs; *mata lechones*]" in Maní and Becal; two of the Spanish butchers, both from Teabo, did the same. Of the other six Spanish butchers, three were Spaniards from Motul: Diego de Anduézar, who "sustains himself through the slaughter of cattle and pigs [*se sustenta de matar reses y cerdos*]"; and the two adult sons of the widowed María de Mena, both "vagrants who sustain themselves by dealing in cattle and pigs [*vagos que se sustentan con su trata de reses y cerdos*]." The remaining three were Spaniards from Cacalchen, likewise not called *carniceros* but men whose occupation [*ejercicio* or *oficio*] was "to kill cattle and pigs [*matar reses y cerdos*]."

ᵍ Both these two were from Teya, father and son, both called Diego de Lugo: the elder with 240 beehives and 9 horses, also a butcher of cows and pigs, married to a mulatta called Juana Moreno; the younger with 60 hives and 3 horses, married to Lucía Chan, a Maya from Tixculum.

ʰ Antonio Alcaudete, the sole Spaniard in Ticul, was only "reputed to be Spanish [*reputado por español*]"; married to an *india hidalga* (the highest rank of native noblewoman, either Maya or descended from the Nahuas who came in the invasion of 1540), he made his living as a farm laborer and hunter [*labrador y cazador*].

ⁱ Miguel Bautista Miranda, listed as "white" in Temax along with his wife Antonia Chacón, "makes a living from paintings and cutting wood [*se busca la vida en pinturas y cortando madera*]."

ʲ One of these, Diego Felipe Herrera, a "blanco" from Cacalchen, was not labeled a *tratante* as such, but "his occupation is to trade and negotiate with the Indians in cloth from Castille [*su oficio es tratar y contratar con los indios generos de Castilla*]."

ᵏ The Franciscans responsible for Dzibalchen state in the census that, of non-Mayas, "nobody lives here [*no vive nadie*]: neither Spaniard, nor mestizo, nor mulatto. Only Tomás del Río, although he has no home, he is itinerant [*viandante*], single and without family; he deals in wax and has extensive corn plots [*rescata cera y tiene copiosas milpas*]." Statistically, Tomás was most likely to be a mestizo, so I have included him here as a "+1."

ˡ Bartolomé Pérez of Tekax was a "corn farmer, [who also] buys wax, blanches it, and seeks a living [selling it] in the villages [*rescate cera y la blanquea y busca su vida por los pueblos*]"; Ensign Antonio Martín Negrón of Ticul was a farm worker who "has a wax blancher and sells it in cakes [*tiene blanqueadero de cera y enmarquetada la vende*]."

ᵐ Sargento Diego Cabañas, married with six children, farm worker [*labrador*] and patron [*patrón*] of a local confraternity, "sells out of his house various small items, such as wax and tallow candles, chocolate and other honest goods [*vendese en su casa de todas menudencias, como es candelas de cera y cebo, cacao y otras cosas honestas*]."

ⁿ Capt. Juan de Figueroa, living single in Bolonchen with two servants, appears to have had no more than the vague local administrative responsibilities of a military district captain; "his position is to assist the *cacique* [Maya governor] and magistrates in the town hall in its administration [*su ejercicio es asistir en las Casas Reales ocupando al cacique y justicias la administracion de ella*]."

ᵒ These were the servants listed by name, with *criado* as their occupation, but there were many more servants in rural Yucatan in 1700; fifty-one individuals in the census are listed as having a combined total of 254 criados (58 of them were *indios de servicio* of Julio Manrique, a mestizo cattle rancher in Dzam).

TABLE 4.4 (*continued*)

[p] Francisco Góngora was "indentured to the Guerrero family [*esta entregado por escritura a los Guerrero*]" in Ticul; the only Guerreros in the census were the "widow of P. [Padre?] Guerrero" and their four children, listed right after Góngora and, like him, mestizos.

[q] One of these, Nicolás Cetina of Tekax, was "without occupation, with a corn plot [*sin oficio, con una milpa*]."

for Spaniards, with Afro-Yucatecans and mestizos less diversified at 0.22 and 0.16, respectively.

Two final examples are those of barbers and butchers. As mentioned above, there were mulatto, mestizo, and Spanish barbers in the 1700 census, six of the eight being mestizo. The Izamal case is perhaps the most revealing, as there were three barbers in that town, one a Spaniard named Simón de los Reyes, one a mestizo named Francisco Ventura, the third the above-mentioned mulatto Francisco de León. Probably serving separate clientele in different parts of the town, Simón may have run a larger barber shop as he had three servants. But they were all in the same trade, and Simón's surname was no more that of an elite Spaniard than were the surnames of the two Franciscos. In fact, "de los Reyes" was more likely the surname of a mulatto, mestizo, or someone of Nahua descent, than of a Spaniard, suggesting that he or an ancestor had passed from one category to another.

Just as anyone could be a barber—yet a man who shaved Spaniards was classified as a Spaniard—so could anyone be a butcher—yet a man who slaughtered cattle was probably a Spaniard. Of the ten butchers listed in the 1700 census, only the eight Spaniards killed cattle, whereas the two mestizo butchers just killed piglets. It is hard to believe that there were no Afro-Yucatecan butchers, so the 1700 census data should probably be taken as merely indicating general patterns. In this case, the general pattern was a kind of loose casta hierarchy within the butcher profession, although because occupation helped define casta identities, it is possible that an Afro-Yucatecan butcher or two passed as Spaniards once their business moved up to cattle slaughtering.

Likewise, although the 1700 census suggests that mestizos and Spaniards still dominated trading in the countryside in this year, there is evidence from other sources that pardo peddlers were not rare. For example, two pardos mentioned earlier, Antonio Lope and Sergeant Ignacio Pacheco, both owned small pieces of property in Merida and in the countryside (Lope's plot outside Temax and Pacheco's sitio near Tecoh). This pattern of property acquisition reflects the petty but nonetheless profitable trading activities of such men. In fact, as far back as the early seventeenth century (and possibly even earlier) there were mulatto merchants who worked the rural Maya communities peddling Spanish goods.

Such goods had to satisfy three criteria: (1) there had to be a Maya demand for them (a demand created by Spaniards in the late sixteenth century); (2) the Mayas needed to be able to afford them (which largely excluded luxury goods like fine imported clothing); and (3) they had to be products not made in native communities (at least, not those of the same region). The articles that qualified were small in number but reasonably profitable, consisting primarily of metal tools, cane alcohol, and gunpowder (for use in fiestas as well as in hunting firearms). Selling such goods to Mayas (and to the small but growing number of non-Mayas in the cahob), and purchasing Maya-produced goods such as cotton cloth and wax (the main tribute goods in the colony), was done primarily by lower-ranking Spaniards, mestizos, and Afro-Yucatecans (the 1700 census lists most peddlers as Spanish or mestizo, but there were also some mulattoes).[62] Wax and mantas of cotton cloth were primarily export goods, destined to pass through Merida and Campeche for sale in Mexico City. But local merchants and peddlers [*tratantes*] also bought raw cotton and salt in Maya villages, reselling them in other Maya villages. And there must have been a small market in Maya villages for semi-luxurious imports, as the occupation of Diego Felipe Herrera, a Spaniard living in Cacalchen in 1700, was "trading and dealing with the Indians in cloth from Castille."[63]

It was not coincidental that peddlers dealt in many of the same goods that Mayas used to make tribute payments to encomenderos. As mentioned earlier, encomenderos and other Spanish officials used Afro-Yucatecan slaves and servants as their agents in the countryside. Such agents inevitably established personal and economic relations in Maya communities, becoming involved to various degrees in local trade. Sergeant Ignacio Pacheco thus acted as an agent for Tecoh's encomendero, don Nicolás Pacheco, in various ways—acting as a liaison between the Spaniard and the batab of Tecoh, for example, and between the Spaniard and the pardo muleteer, Eugenio de Acosta. As Acosta was a militia captain, one imagines that he and the sergeant were not only professional colleagues but periodically business partners.[64]

A small percentage of Afro-Yucatecan men combined their knowledge of livestock and peddling in order to pursue independent enterprise of a different sort. In 1815 the authorities in Merida broke part of a horse-stealing ring run by mestizos and pardos; prosecutors won convictions of two of the three accused thieves, as well as a ringleader named Isidro Espinosa, who "ordered" stolen horses and then passed them down a chain of resellers. The following year two pardo militiamen were accused of horse-theft; one, Asencio Gomez, had to pay thirty pesos in restitution to the Maya horse owner, Victoriano Mex. Pardos also feature prominently in cattle-theft investigations among the criminal cases of the last colonial decade. The most dramatic one features a pitch battle between a group of Maya hacienda workers and a gang of four cattle-rustlers whom they surprised in the act. Machete wounds put one thief, a pardo named Laureano Suárez, and one

Maya cowboy, Juan Puc, in the hospital. Both recovered, but not before Suárez had given up his accomplices (a mestizo and two pardos from the Merida barrio of Santiago) and been sentenced to ten years (he was released in 1823, having done seven years, two of them laboring on public works).[65]

If militiamen had a reputation for being prone to disorderliness, if not criminality, then sailors were likewise seen as potentially troublesome—especially if they were colored. One dimension of this was the tendency to associate mulatto sailors with piracy, partly because the multiracial, multinational crews common to pirate ships invariably included some men of African descent.[66] This association was particularly relevant to Yucatan because of Campeche's experience of piracy in the seventeenth century (see Table 5.1 in the next chapter).

The buccaneer–author Exquemelin published an account in 1678 that included tales of notorious pirates plaguing Campeche in the mid-seventeenth century—tales that must have circulated among Spaniards in Yucatan. Two of these pirates were Bartolomeo el Portugues, and Rock or Roque el Brasiliano, both probably Afro-Brazilian renegades (although Exquemelin claims Rock was Dutch-born). According to Exquemelin, Bartolomeo terrorized the Yucatec coast for years before being captured at sea by Spanish ships, one of which was forced by a storm to take refuge off Campeche. The port's authorities convinced the ship's captain to hand over Bartolomeo to be hanged in the town plaza, but the pirate escaped and fled to the English logwood camps farther down the coast; there he convinced some Jamaican pirates to sail to Campeche, where they seized the very ship that had originally captured Bartolomeo. The Rock story is similar; captured by Spaniards off the coast of Campeche, "which was his usual place for marauding," Rock avoided being hanged by the town authorities by forging a letter from his followers threatening merciless vengeance on Campeche unless he was freed (by way of compromise, he was sent to Spain, where he later escaped).

The third story of Exquemelin's that relates to Campeche tells of the French buccaneer, François l'Olonnais, who was shipwrecked off the Yucatec coast and most of his men slaughtered by Spaniards (and, no doubt, pardo militiamen). L'Olonnais fled to the Yucatec forest, recovered from his wounds, and then convinced some black slaves outside Campeche to join him, "promising them freedom if they would follow his advice." Thus persuaded, the slaves stole one of their master's boats and sailed it to Tortuga; we hear no more of the Afro-Yucatecan recruits, but presumably some or all participated in l'Olonnais's ongoing piratical campaigns against Spanish targets in the Caribbean.[67]

Regardless of their veracity, these tales contain revealing elements; they illustrate the fact that men of African descent played roles on both sides of the Spanish battle with piracy in the seventeenth century, and they reflect the Spanish suspicion that colored men made ready pirates, and that black slaves could easily be recruited by the enemy. Indeed, when two dozen Afro-Cuban fishermen were found among the pirate force that assaulted Campeche in 1685, they were imprisoned and interrogated on suspicion of being willing participants. It was months before Spanish authorities accepted the persistent claims by Miguel Quexo and his comrades that they were grabbed while fishing for turtles near Havana and forced to sail to Campeche, where they fled to the town's defenders as soon as they could.[68]

The association among Yucatec Spaniards of pirates with escaped slaves and other colored men was also stimulated by tales of one of the era's most notorious pirates, Diego el Mulato. Indeed, the name inspired such fear and loathing (or respect) that it was applied (or claimed) by at least three colored sea bandits, one of whom had been born in Yucatan. The first, Diego el Mulato Martín, a former slave in Havana, terrorized the Gulf of Mexico in the 1630s (Campeche narrowly escaped attack), until desperate Spanish officials offered him a royal commission as a way of redirecting his energies against Spain's enemies; the second, Diego de los Reyes, aka Diego el Mulato Lucifer, rampaged the Yucatec coast in 1642, sacking both Bacalar and Campeche (the latter his home town), inspiring a royal edict in 1643 to order "every possible remedy to be taken to capture the mulatto pirate"; the third, Diego el Mulato Grillo, also a former Havana slave, harried Spanish shipping from his base on Tortuga before being captured and executed in 1673.[69]

Before a colony had even been founded in Yucatan, there were enslaved black, free black, and free-colored sailors on Spanish ships crossing the Atlantic and developing new routes of conquest and trade in the Americas. Mulattas also appear prominently in sources that mention *llovidos* [literally, "raindrops"] or stowaways, some of whom were prostitutes, others concubines, lovers, or even wives without license to be on board. An unknown number of Afro-Yucatecans, therefore, particularly in Campeche but to a lesser extent in Sisal too, would have spent time on ships or at sea—as shipbuilders or dock workers, as sailors or "raindrops." Most were free, but some were slaves whose wages were passed on to their owners. A free black or slave with a skill such as carpentry or caulking could earn two or three times more in the shipyards than he could as a seaman.[70] Campeche's first shipbuilding yard was probably founded in the 1650s by don Antonio Maldonado de Aldana, who used a predictable combination of Maya workers and black slave supervisors to cut logs and build small ships.[71] Other Afro-Yucatecans made livings off the sea in a different way, using small boats to fish, to transport goods to port, or to smuggle. In Yucatan, as in other parts of the Spanish Caribbean basin, the large canoes used for these purposes were called *bongos*.[72]

Mulatta "raindrops" did not, of course, appear in the 1700 census. Another example of a possible Afro-Yucatecan occupation (and another possible Spanish-mulatto occupational overlap) not reflected at all in the 1700 census (and Tables 4.3–4.5) is that of colonial offices—both local civil positions and parish priesthoods. It is unlikely that Afro-Yucatecans who were openly known as pardos or mulattoes would have occupied governmental positions at the provincial level or in Merida; no doubt men with some African ancestry attained such offices, but by the very definition of holding such posts, these men would have been seen (and certainly recorded on paper) as being Spanish. In smaller towns and villages the story was a little different, however. A good example comes from Valladolid in the mid-seventeenth century, where the acting *alcalde ordinario* (of the town council) was Miguel Moreno de Andrade, supposedly the pardo son of a mulatto father and Maya mother. The real alcalde ordinario was don Fernando de Aguilar, who had appointed Andrade as his agent (Aguilar's wife was a Vásquez de Andrade, so there was also a familial connection between the pardo and the elite Spaniard). Andrade might have escaped the attention of historians altogether—like other Afro-Yucatecans who served in similar positions—were it not for the fact that in 1652 he made an official decision that outraged some local Spaniards. From 1600 to 1762 alcaldes ordinarios had the power to reassign encomiendas during interregnum periods between the departure or death of the colony's governor and the arrival of his successor. When Governor García Valdés Osorio died in 1652, Andrade took advantage of this law to reassign the lucrative and much-coveted vacant encomienda of Chemax—to none other than his own patron, don Fernando de Aguilar. Rumor had it that Andrade grew rich from his forced-trade business with Maya villagers of the district, and that a three thousand-peso bribe helped convince Osorio's replacement to confirm Aguilar as encomendero.[73]

As for the priesthood, although I did not find specific evidence of mulatto or pardo priests, it is likely that some men of partial African descent were able to enter the church; in 1675 the head of the Franciscans in Yucatan complained that the bishop had ordained men of "low socioracial status [*infame calidad*],"that is, "mestizos and mulattos."[74] In the 1720s the Archbishop in Santo Domingo lamented to the Council of the Indies that the lack of suitable Spanish candidates was forcing him to ordain mulattoes on the island, but that these "rustic people would not rise above the rank of curate."[75] If Afro-Yucatecan "rustics" did indeed become ordained, they were either able to pass as Spaniards, or they faced a quiet prejudice that prevented them from ascending beyond the parish level—where, somewhat ironically, they would have performed such tasks as compiling the matrículas of 1688 and 1700.

AS RUSTIC AS INDIANS

The section above focuses mostly on those rural Afro-Yucatecans whose working experiences were not far from those of nonelite Spaniards (and indeed it may have been simply degrees of wealth that prompted parish priests to classify one man as a mulatto and the other a Spaniard). But most

Afro-Yucatecans living outside Merida and Campeche were less well-off than the most visible free-colored members of this rural middling group—people like Captain del Canto, Sergeant Pacheco, or the mestizo–mulatta couple of Muñóz and Háuregui with their 150 pesos of property. The economic and social status of most was much like that of Maya villagers.

It would be nice to have detailed evidence of how this group of people evolved over the colonial period. But we do at least have various kinds of late colonial evidence, as well as a clear, mid-colonial snapshot provided by the 1688 and 1700 censuses. This snapshot exposes two trends that developed over the seventeenth and eighteenth centuries: the steady, growing migration of free-colored men into Maya villages; and their gradual absorption into local families and Maya village culture—in some senses disappearing, but in others leaving a permanent trace of their presence. The bishop noted in 1757 on the presence of *gente de color* in Maya villages throughout the colony as though they were just another indigenous category.[76] In other words, free coloreds became just like Mayas, but did not actually become Mayas, at least not yet. By the same token, the colony's Maya villages were all gradually becoming, in a certain sense, Afro-Maya.

The curate of Chikindzonot captured the essence of it a century later, beginning a letter to the governor of the province like this:

The village of Chikindzonot has always consisted of Indians, and some fifty residents of other castas, the majority of which are mulattoes, as rustic and pusillanimous as the same Indians, whose language alone they speak. They are not accustomed to leaving for any other part of the province and they pass a wretched life with the meager gain from a strip of cornfield, which they work with their own hands.[77]

The mulattoes of Chikindzonot in 1794 were like the pardo Antonio Lope in Temax in the 1690s, and like Juan Antonio Nobelo. Nobelo was described in 1688 by the Maya authorities in Tahmuy as a *molato*, but he lived on a cattle ranch [*xtança bakero*] with his native wife, Catalina Canche, one of a few Afro-Yucatecans in an area so indigenous that its census record was recorded in Maya; no doubt his eighteenth-century descendents were, like their maternal ancestor, simply seen as Mayas.[78] Nobelo and Lope were like the scores of free coloreds in villages throughout the colony in 1700. They were overwhelmingly free-colored men who farmed corn; a third to a half of them married Maya women (48% in the 1700 matrícula);[79] all would have spoken Maya (and most, like Chikindzonot's mulattoes, spoke only Maya); most were locally rooted and identified themselves with their village. That is, they generally lived like Mayas.

The above-mentioned example of corn farming symbolizes this pattern. The matrículas of 1688 and 1700 did not record the occupations of individual Mayas (that would have taken thousands of pages), but a survey of Maya testaments from the seventeenth and eighteenth centuries confirms my general impression that the vast majority of Maya men (and many

Maya women) were milperos. For example, 88% of Maya men (and 46% of women) dying in Cacalchen in 1646–56 left either fields or corn farming tools (machetes and digging sticks), or both, to their heirs. By way of comparison, a quarter of the men (and half the women) bequeathed beehives and apicultural tools; in other words, beekeeping was important to Maya village life, but corn farming was ubiquitous. A larger database of wills from Ixil in 1748 and 1765–68 confirms this pattern. Mayas in Ixil sustained themselves through various forms of animal husbandry and tree cultivation, but only three types of property were left by most testators: 84% of men (and almost half the women) left house plots (where they lived and kept bees, trees, and animals); 56% of men (40% of women) left chests (to store clothes and other valuables); and 60% of men (a quarter of women) left farming land (for milpas). A couple of dozen wills from other Maya villages suggest that about three in four Maya men were milperos, which is precisely the mean of the Cacalchen and Ixil percentages.[80]

If we compare that figure to the data from the 1700 census, we find Afro-Yucatecans once again in the middle. Colonial data shows that at least 75% of Mayas were milperos; the 1700 data has 41% of mestizos, 39% of free coloreds, and 21% of Spaniards as milperos. Like Maya farmers, mulatto milperos also hunted, kept bees, and reared pigs, chickens, and the occasional cow—some even declared these secondary occupations in the census. Most mulattoes in the countryside, and especially those who farmed as Mayas did, lived in Maya-style thatched houses. Outside the downtown core of Spanish settlements, this was the norm, as the priest of Izamal noted in referring to a Spanish peddler named Mateo Arcila, who had "no more property than a thatched house, which is what all the houses of the residents are like."[81]

The interstitial position of many Afro-Yucatecans meant that they could be both part of a Maya community and yet also distinct in some ways from its indigenous members. One occupational example is that of curanderos, or healers. The above-mentioned mulatto, Juan Ignacio Palomino, worked as a healer among Mayas in the Oxkutzcab–Muna area, but as a cattle rancher and encomendero's agent he was not dependent on Maya clients and was connected to the local Spanish elite. Also at the turn of the eighteenth century, another mulatto curandero, Joseph Zavala, made a good living healing Mayas in the Tenabo–Sacalaca region (just south of Tekax) until a cure went wrong and a Maya woman inhaled copal smoke. The local Maya authorities denounced Zavala to the Inquisition, and as there was no shortage of Mayas willing to testify against him, the healer was soon convicted of witchcraft.[82]

But for every Joseph Zavala, there were dozens of Afro-Yucatecans working as healers and love–magic practitioners in city, town, and countryside. Some, like Juan Ignacio Palomino, appear to have avoided Inquisition attention; others, like Micaela Montejo, a mulatta with a solid reputation in late seventeenth-century Merida as a love–magician, were frequently investigated but never condemned by Inquisition officials.[83] The role of witchcraft as a cultural meeting ground between Afro-Yucatecans and Mayas is explored further in Chapter Six. Suffice to point out here, therefore, that Afro-Yucatecan men were more often healers, their clients tended to be non-Spaniards, and their practices drew on African and Maya cultural traditions; whereas Afro-Yucatecan women were more likely to practice love–magic or sexual witchcraft, more often in city and town than in the countryside, with clients as likely to be Spaniards as not, and their practices rooted in European, African, and Maya cultures.

The paucity of women listed in the 1688 and 1700 matrículas with their names and occupations reflects the limitations of these censuses; the impression given that women lacked occupations or worked less than men is of course completely wrong, as all nonelite women worked. I have thus highlighted the relatively small amount of data in the 1700 census by presenting it separately (see Table 4.5). Of the eight Afro-Yucatecan women with recorded occupations, one was a corn farmer—Ana Contreras, a mulatta in Oxkutzcab, whose seven children and two servants must have done most, if not all, the milpa labor. Three worked with cotton (two were spinners and one a seamstress), as did most Spanish and mestiza women with occupations recorded in the census. The fifth was a widow with a cattle ranch and seven children. The sixth was Damiana Escalante, a parda from Uayma with three children, who "sustains herself by her sweat and toil [*su sudor y trabajo*]." The remaining two Afro-Yucatecan women were sisters, Lorenza and Ceferina de la Huerta, both slaves (esclavas, with no casta label) owned by Juana de la Huerta, a "white" widow in Calkiní.

What Table 4.5 directly reveals is how widows sustained themselves. Sixty percent of all the women in the table are described as widows, and if we add to that the women who appear to be widows (that is, they have children but are not listed as single, married, or separated), that figure rises to 80%. The most striking pattern is the concentration of women's work in the cottage textile industry; nearly two in three women spinned, sewed, or weaved cotton. The fact that Maya women also primarily labored over cotton in their home villages suggests that most of the hundreds of semi-visible free-colored and mestiza women in the census (appearing only as someone's wife) also toiled in the textile business in some fashion or another. The division of labor by gender in Maya families had men working farms or ranches away from the house, and women tending animals and gardens and working cotton in or near the house.[84] Similarly the gender division among the free-colored and mestizo population in the countryside had men as artisans, farmers, and ranch workers, while women toiled at home in the same ways that Maya women did.

Although few women's working lives are detailed in the 1700 census, there are signs that life for a widow was not always easy, regardless of casta status. Not all widows could be as well-off as Leonor González, with her hundred-head of horses; and Damiana Escalante, the parda widow from

TABLE 4.5 Making a living in the countryside in 1700: Afro-Yucatecan women's occupations in comparative context

	Afro-Yucatecan Women				
	La Costa and Beneficios Bajos	Sierra	Camino Real and Campeche	Mestizas	Spanish Women
Corn farmer ["hacen milpas"]		1		1	
Spinner [hilandera]	1	1		1	
Seamstress [costurera]			1	3	1
Weaver [tejedora]				2	2
Spinner and weaver					1
Spinner and weaver ["makes patíes"]					1
Stockinger [hacer medias] and spinner				1	
Seamstress and quilter [hace colchas][a]					1
Figured seamstress [labrados y costuras]				1	1
Needleworker ["se sustenta con la aguja"]					1
Laundress, spinner, and weaver					1
Laundress and landlady[b]					1
Laundress and shopkeeper [tendera]					1
Spinner and cattle ranch owner					1
Cattle ranch owner	1			1	
Horse ranch owner					1[c]
Ranch [estancia] owner				1	
Butcher of piglets				1	
Seller [vendedora]				1	
Beata					1
"By her sweat and toil [su sudor y trabajo]"			1		
Slave			2		

TABLE 4.5 *(continued)*

| | Afro-Yucatecan Women | | | | |
	La Costa and Beneficios Bajos	Sierra	Camino Real and Campeche	Mestizas	Spanish Women
"Lives on charity [*de limosna*]"				2	1
"Extremely poor [*sumamente pobre*]"				1	
Homeless				1	
[TOTALS]	[	8	]	[17]	[15]

Sources: 1700 matrícula in AGI-*México* 1035; also see Solano (1975).

Note: Many more women are listed in the matrícula, but without recorded occupations; instead, almost all are listed with their marital status (single, widowed, married with husband named, number but not names of children given). It was not possible to generate a "None recorded" figure for women, comparable to that for men, as many men's wives were not given casta designations (and almost none given occupations in the matrícula, as at least two-thirds of the women listed above were widows).

[a] Juana Pérez Justiniano must have run a small seamstress business in Izamal; "separated from her husband [*no hace vida con su marido*]," with three children and four servants, "she makes quilts and other local types of textiles [*hace colchas y otros tejidos de la tierra*]."

[b] Juana Delgado, a Spaniard in Izamal, laundress [*lavandera*], with one servant, "owns a house that is rented out [*posee una casa de alquiler*]."

[c] This Spanish woman was Leonor González, "widow of Sebastián Sansones, of Valladolid, three sons, by way of estate [*por hacienda*] one hundred horses, with its donkeys [*con su borrico*]." Apart from another Spanish couple, who probably worked for the widow, there were no other residents of any kind in Acatzim, so the "pueblo" was probably the estancia, with Maya ranch workers coming from nearby villages such as Teya. No other individual in the matrícula is listed with as many horses (or even head of cattle) as Leonor González.

Uayma, was not the only widow who supported her family "by her sweat and toil." Ana María Carrillo (listed in Table 4.5 as "butcher of piglets"), was a mestiza widow with four children in Becal, who "butchers piglets, and gets by on that [*mata lechones, y con esto pasa*]." Ana García (the table's "homeless" woman) had even less to scrape by on; a mestiza from Merida, but a resident of Teya in 1700, Ana was described by the parish priest as "without home or family, being everyone's [*sin casa, ni familia, siendo de todos*]." This was presumably the priest's way of saying that she was either the village charity case or a prostitute. Either way, her benefactors or clients were Mayas, mestizos, or mulattoes, as no Spaniards lived in Teya in 1700.

If Afro-Yucatecans living in Maya villages tended—perhaps not surprisingly—to live like Maya villagers, how did free Afro-Yucatecans make livings in rural communities where they were the majority population? Did such communities even exist? They did, but they were exceptional. Because African slaves entered the colony in a slow trickle and did not work together in large groups, there were no rural settlements of escaped slaves inside or on the borders of the province. And because the growth of the free-colored population was caused in part by miscenegation between Afro-Yucatecans and others, especially Mayas, free-coloreds tended not to form their own separate communities; rather they became part of the multiracial urban neighborhoods in Campeche and Merida and contributed to the partial Africanization of Maya villages. These developments are detailed in subsequent chapters, so suffice to identify here three Afro-Yucatecan rural communities that were exceptional (they were all late colonial and each formed under distinct, particular circumstances) but conforming to the general pattern examined here—that is, the tendency of Afro-Yucatecans in the countryside to sustain themselves in the same occupations pursued by Mayas.

These rural communities were San Fernando Ake, Kikil, and San Francisco de Paula. They were all in the colony's north (see Map 4.2) and were all late colonial (nowhere before the eighteenth century was there a predominantly Afro-Yucatecan community).[85]

San Fernando Ake was founded in 1796 by the colonial authorities as a settlement for Afro-Haitian soldiers who had fought for Spain in the wars over Sainte Domingue and Santo Domingo. The original 115 settlers were set up in a plaza within the abandoned Maya site of Ake, their community dubbed San Fernando de los Negros and constituted as an official *pueblo* of militiamen. Within a decade, the village had doubled in size as its leaders admitted free-colored migrants. But there was also a gradual process of

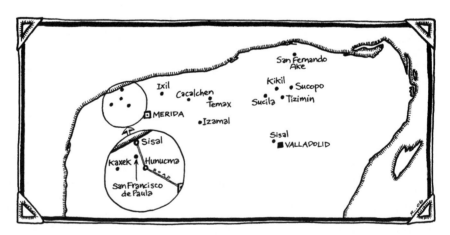

Map 4.2 Northern late colonial Yucatan, showing rural communities with an Afro-Yucatecan majority (San Francisco de Paula, San Fernando Ake, and Kikil) and some of the other settlements mentioned in the chapter's second half.

Mayanization, whose mechanisms were settlement patterns and—most importantly—how they made a living. Inevitably many of the militiamen took Maya wives. They also took up the occupations of their in-laws, most notably cattle ranching, corn farming, hunting, and beekeeping. Black men drifted out of San Fernando, while Mayas drifted in. There were already some Mayas living in the pueblo by 1806; in 1826 a quest for "deserters" revealed that a number of black militiamen had simply settled in the Maya villages adjacent to their cornfields; by 1840 San Fernando was 40% Maya.[86]

Ake was chosen for its location near the vulnerable north coast of the colony, and so there were militia units of Afro-Yucatecans already living in the area. These militiamen, their families, and descendents lived in various pueblos north of Valladolid, most notably Tizimin (which was 27% Afro-Yucatecan by 1813), but only in one parish—that of Kikil—did they become a slim majority by the end of the eighteenth century. Back in 1688, there were only a dozen non-Maya adults in Kikil, and a similar number in its neighboring villages; the area was just a few percent Afro-Yucatecan. In 1757 Bishop Padilla noted that Kikil had over two hundred residents "of all mixes [*de toda mezcla*]."[87] Baptism and burial records show that by the 1790s the communities of Kikil parish were over a fifth Afro-Yucatecan. The census of 1806 categorizes the parish's 2,143 residents as 9% Spanish, 10% mestizo, 47% Maya, and 34% pardo. But a breakdown of communities within the parish reveals a more complex pattern. As the Afro-Yucatecan population expanded in the four villages (Kikil itself and its subject hamlets of Loche, Panabá, and Sucilá), a push–pull factor effectively pushed Mayas out of those villages while at the same time wage labor pulled them into the local haciendas. Thus in 1806 the working population on the haciendas was all Maya, while in the villages Afro-Yucatecans were on average a slim majority; Sucilá was 72% pardo. The census did not record occupations, but it is reasonable to assume that, in addition to militia wages, the pardo families of Kikil sustained themselves with the same agricultural pursuits that supported the black, free-colored, and Maya families of San Fernando Ake and its environs. In other words, as Kikil became more Afro-Yucatecan in demographic terms, its pardo residents became more Maya in occupational terms.[88]

The third late colonial Afro-Yucatecan rural community was San Francisco de Paula. The archaeologists who recently located the ruins of this village (a team headed by Anthony Andrews) have suggested that San Francisco was founded by escaped slaves; I argue against this interpretation in Chapter Five, but otherwise I accept their analysis and base my comments on it entirely. San Francisco does not appear to have been a formal pueblo (it was a *rancho* or hamlet), which means its inhabitants were probably not militiamen, at least not primarily militiamen. More likely it gradually came into being the way that Maya hamlets in colonial Yucatan did—through patterns of long-distance labor. Just as black corn farmers from Ake eventually settled nearer to their fields, so did free-colored workers drift up to work the dyewood groves that ran in a strip below the coastal marshlands. They may have also engaged in contraband trading on the coast, perhaps selling dyewood to European smugglers for imported goods like china and Scottish whiskey (archaeological evidence of which remains). They may have come from Hunucmá, the nearest place with a substantial Afro-Yucatecan population—perhaps an eighth by 1800. By this date, some free-colored log-cutters settled permanently in a spot near the dyewood trees, not far from the Sisal–Hunucmá road, with easy access to well water. Some eight miles southwest of San Francisco was the Maya village of Kaxek (also found by Andrews and his colleagues on a site surrounded by dyewood). In terms of how their inhabitants made a living—dyewood logging supplemented with fishing, corn farming, and modest animal husbandry—Kaxek and San Francisco de Paula were surely the same. Indeed, I expect there were ties of various kinds between the two places, with some Afro-Yucatecans living in Kaxek and some Mayas living in San Francisco.[89]

San Fernando Ake was very likely unique in that no evidence has yet come to light of other settlements of Haitian soldiers in Yucatan; Kikil was unique in that the censuses from the first decade of the nineteenth century show no other parishes where Afro-Yucatecans had begun to outnumber Mayas in the villages. Yet in occupational terms they were not unique at all. And while San Fernando began black and Kikil began Maya, by the early nineteenth century they were both Afro-Maya villages in a Yucatan where there were scores of villages that were more or less Afro-Maya. As for San Francisco, its apparent uniqueness is deceptive. It is significant that I found no reference to it in the colonial archives, that it only came to light as a result of a three-year study of the northeast by Mayanist archaeologists (whose purpose was to locate and survey 249 pre-Conquest Maya sites and 154 post-Conquest sites in the region); by definition, its identity as an informal now-abandoned hamlet meant that it fell below the radar of the colonial authorities and their written records. Thus, by implication, there must have been other hamlets like San Francisco—not many and not large, but small settlements of free coloreds and Mayas that developed and died out as Yucatecans sought to make a meager living out in the countryside.

Afro-Yucatecans lived and worked in a wide variety of occupations and circumstances. Most, however, can be placed in two broad categories: dependents; and independents. With respect to the former, whether African-born black slaves or Yucatec-born free-colored salaried servants, they tended to be treated as individuals in personalized dependent relationships with Spaniards. Although in the late eighteenth century some slaves were placed with militia companies or put to work in groups on sugar plantations, the majority of slaves became subservient members of Spanish households, most likely in an urban setting but sometimes on a Spanish rural estate or hacienda. There they lived and worked not in groups but as individual personal dependents of their owners, possibly with other slaves but more likely with free-colored, mestizo, or Maya servants.

From the onset of conquest and colonization, Spaniards relied in various ways upon the labor of their African slaves and servants, creating a relationship of forced mutual dependency between Spaniards and Africans; the remark of a priest in eighteenth-century Buenos Aires, that "it would not be possible to live here if it were not for the [Africans]"[90] could be said of colonial Yucatan, despite the fact that Yucatan was not a slave society and the colonists were utterly dependent upon Maya labor. Simply put, the difference was one of quality versus quantity; Mayas did most of the work, but Afro-Yucatecan managerial roles were crucial to the functioning of the colony. Most Afro-Yucatecans lived and worked where Spaniards settled, laboring primarily in Merida and Campeche, and later in larger rural pueblos such as Izamal.

In occupational and labor terms, it was primarily Spanish economic demands that determined how and where Afro-Yucatecans worked, but this also placed Afro-Yucatecans in close contact with Mayas and mestizos—with resulting changes in the nature of both the Afro-Yucatecan and Maya population. In the early colonial decades, all blacks and mulattoes in the province were dependents of Spaniards. But the second category of independents soon developed, first in the city and then in the countryside. Just as slaves aspired to be free, so did Afro-Yucatecan managers aspire to run their own economic affairs. The two were not incompatible; in fact, on the contrary, it was common for managers such as estancieros, artisans, muleteers, and encomenderos' agents to develop their own business interests. Free-colored men with fewer opportunities also sought independence in Maya villages, where they tended to marry Maya women and generally live and work like Mayas—while also to a lesser degree turning indigenous villages into Afro-Maya communities. By 1700, the rural occupational experience of Afro-Yucatecans was very much part of "the black middle" pattern. Along with mestizos, free coloreds tended to be between Mayas and Spaniards in terms of what they did and how they were able to do it; for example, mestizo and free-colored men were half as likely as Mayas, but twice as likely as Spaniards, to be corn farmers.

We should not forget, however, that occupational independence did not necessarily mean a total lack of dependence on others—be they Spaniards, other castas, or the Maya community of which some Afro-Yucatecans became members. Not all Afro-Yucatecans had the opportunity to become independent in the first place, let alone to escape the drudgery of subsistence-level manual labor. For every Sergeant Ignacio Pacheco there were many Afro-Yucatecans condemned to a lifetime of loading and unloading mules or washing and cooking for a Spanish household. Joaquín Chasarretta may have sometimes acted as a supervisor of Maya workers, thereby fitting the "manager" pattern, but his wages were no higher than theirs and were barely enough to feed and clothe him, let alone permit the luxuries of savings and enterprise. Most Afro-Yucatecans, then, regardless of how independent they were, contributed to the development of mixed-race nonelite urban communities or to the Afro-Maya communities that Maya villages gradually became (discussed in Chapter Six).

Sergeant Pacheco evokes another occupation that was not only available to men of African descent, but became closely associated with them beginning in the seventeenth century; that of the militia. Service in the militia was a way of work, but it was also the most significant avenue of social mobility that was open to mulattoes in colonial times—and is thus the opening topic of the next chapter.

CHAPTER FIVE

Ways Up and Ways Out

I have come up to this capital with the object of importuning my freedom through the most timely and legal agency of Your Lordship.
　　—José María Espinola, to the Governor of Yucatan, 1816[1]

The virtue of their souls is as white and shining as the color of their persons is black.
　　—José Matías Quintana, on the pardo militias, 1813[2]

May the honorable servicemen of the Division of Pardos of this city [Merida], and that of Campeche, and those who have previously served in them with faithfulness [*puntualidad*], be placed in the class of citizens, with all due rights and privileges.
　　—The bishop of Yucatan, to the king, 1814[3]

I am certain that he is a grandson of a pardo captain who was in the village of Muna, meaning he too is a pardo even though he has served in the white militia, and everyone knows it because they knew his grandfather and his mother, who is well known in Muna to be a parda.
　　—Paula Salazar, trying to stop her daughter from marrying militia officer Francisco Medina, 1818[4]

I have received four dispatches of the fourth of December of last year, in the first of which Your Majesty was pleased to favor Captain Lázaro del Canto with a pension of ten *escudos* a month.
　　—the Governor of Yucatan to the King, 1685[5]

THE STORY OF CAPTAIN LÁZARO DEL CANTO
AND AUGUSTINA BERGARA

In the late seventeenth century, Capt. Lázaro del Canto commanded a militia company in Merida, farmed a small plot of land on the outskirts of the city, and lived in the capital's Jesús María parish, where his daughter was married in 1682. His farm, which may have been worth as much as a hundred pesos, produced a modest income from the pigs and chickens that Canto raised there. He probably kept a horse, maybe two, to ride between his farm and his home in the city, and perhaps to sit upon when his company presented themselves on special occasions in the plaza. The captain's service to the colony, which included a notable campaign of 1685 against the English in the Champotón region, along the southern borders of the peninsula, earned him a royal pension. The Yucatec historian Molina Solís, writing at the turn of the twentieth century, even prefixed del Canto's name with a *don.*[6]

Molina Solís was mistaken, however. Capt. del Canto was never don Lázaro because he was not a Spaniard. The company he commanded was a pardo militia unit, Merida's Jesús María parish was predominantly Afro-Yucatecan, and at his daughter's wedding she is described as a mulatta and her mother as a parda. But del Canto himself is not assigned a racial category in the parish record; his service to the crown effectively earned him the right not to be called a pardo, at least not in writing or to his face, and he was able to pass so well as a Spaniard as to fool the Hispanocentric Molina Solís.

Lázaro may have passed as a Spaniard long after his death, but he would not have been mistaken for one in his lifetime—and nor would his wife, Augustina Bergara. Indeed, back in 1672, a decade before the wedding of her daughter Augustina del Canto, Augustina Bergara drew the attention of the Inquisition in a way that reflected her status as an Afro-Yucatecan. This was a period when the zealous commissary of the Inquisition, Dr. don Antonio de Horta Barroso, was engaged in an energetic campaign against blasphemy, superstition, witchcraft, and other crimes against Catholic orthodoxy—a campaign that aroused many denunciations but few convictions (as we shall see in Chapter Seven). Yucatecans of all kinds, from the capital's Spanish elite to poor corn farmers in the countryside, came under scrutiny during the Horta Barroso years—but Afro-Yucatecan women in Campeche and Merida seemed most often to be cited as having a reputation for witchcraft. It was in this atmosphere that a Spaniard told a priest (who told the commissary) that a woman named Augustina, the wife of "Capitan Lasaro del Canto, mulato," had "suspended an egg" in the passageway at the front of her house, "in the doorway of her hall." Called in to testify directly, the Spaniard claimed he saw "a boy throw a stone at the egg, breaking it, and it was dry inside."[7]

Eggs were commonly used in colonial Yucatan (and to this day) in rituals of curing and purification; for example, the *keex* and *santiguar* curing rituals used, among various other objects and techniques, raw chicken eggs to absorb malevolent winds or spirits. If the egg did its job, the yolk and whites were blackened or dessicated.[8] Like most Yucatec folk practices by the late seventeenth century, this one was not rooted exclusively in European, African, or Maya culture, but reflected the complex cultural interaction that characterized the colonial period. Thus for Augustina to suspend an egg in her doorway—to ward off or cleanse the home of harmful winds—was neither unusual nor something only a person of African descent would do. This was probably why the investigation went nowhere; Augustina was never detained, and as the case lacked further corroboration it languished for nine years, before being dismissed in Mexico City. But the fact remains that Augustina was probably profiled by the Spaniard who denounced her, and the two Spanish priests who wrote down the accusation, because she was Afro-Yucatecan. Her husband achieved success and some social mobility not just despite his free-colored status, but in some ways because of it. Augustina Bergara's brief brush with the Inquisition reminds us that there were limits to such success.

This chapter continues the previous chapter's exploration of Afro-Yucatecan occupations by examining the free-colored or pardo militia (the subject of the first section below). Militia service was not included in Chapter Four partly because it is important enough to the Afro-Yucatecan experience to warrant most of a separate chapter, and partly because I wish to present the topic in a more complex context. That context is mobility—both social and geographical mobility, as well as the limits that colonial society placed on Afro-Yucatecan mobilities. Thus the first section ends by looking at the privileges that pardo service afforded; the second section turns to the types of mobilities that slaves sought, in their quest to become free, either through escape or manumission; and the final section pulls together the threads of the theme of limited mobilities.

A WAY UP: THE PARDO MILITIA

For the first century of colonial rule in Yucatan, indigenous soldiers comprised the majority of those called upon to defend the province with their lives. This was a natural extension of the crucial role played both by Nahua and other Mesoamerican soldiers (brought from central Mexico by the Montejos and other conquistadors who had participated in the Spanish-Mexican war of 1519–21) and by Mayas whose lords, such as the Pech, had allied themselves with the Spanish invaders in the early 1540s. As in central Mexico, Spanish attempts to establish a colony in Yucatan would have continued to fail without the aid of Maya conquistadors. During and after the conquest wars, Mayas were seldom given guns, but they were permitted bow-and-arrow companies—called *indios flecheros*—under their own leaders. These leaders, typically town governors or *batabob*, thereby gained the title of "captain" (which in some *cahob* was passed down from batab to batab). Maya companies played crucial roles in the defense of Campeche against the Dutch, French, and English privateers who repeatedly threatened the town in the seventeenth century. Meanwhile, the late sixteenth and early seventeenth-century campaigns into the southern regions of the peninsula by batab–captains such as don Pablo Paxbolon of Acalan–Tixchel, don Fernando Camal of Oxkutzcab, and don Juan Chan of Chancenote, helped secure the colonial frontier by creating an unstable, sparsely populated buffer zone between Spanish Yucatan and the independent Itza Maya kingdom in the Petén. Then, when Spaniards finally destroyed that kingdom in 1697, Yucatec Maya flecheros also participated in the war, led by batabob such as Capt. don Pascual Itza of Tekax and Capt. don Marcos Poot of Oxkutzcab.[9]

This is not the place to explore this fascinating history in further detail; suffice to make two points of relevance here. First, while many Maya villagers (and the descendents of the Nahua and other Mesoamerican soldiers who settled in Merida and Campeche) continued to man flechero militia units in theory well into the eighteenth century, in practice Spaniards were never comfortable with the fact that their colonies in New Spain relied on armed "Indians" for their defense (especially as natives vastly outnumbered Spaniards and native uprisings were not uncommon). Thus during the course of the seventeenth century, the Spanish authorities sought to replace native militias with units of free-colored soldiers. These were usually called *pardo* militias (in Yucatan as elsewhere in New Spain) but sometimes such *compañías* were labeled as *mulatos*, *mulatos y negros*, or *morenos libres* (*moreno* being a label preferred by the soldiers themselves over *negro* and its slave connotations). A similar fear of arming potentially rebellious, subordinate peoples had prevented the precedent of black conquistadors (like Sebastián Toral) from being the basis for black slave (or even free black) militias; however, the rapid pace of miscegenation meant that by the turn of the seventeenth century there were enough free-colored men, considered less threatening than *negros*, to form exclusive militia units.[10]

Second, the privileges won by cahob and their batabob as a result of successful campaigns and records of military service—from captaincies to tribute relief—comprised a precedent that carried over into the pardo militias. In short, militia service was an avenue of social mobility (a topic to which we shall return shortly).

Whereas Maya militias in the early colonial period had concentrated their activity against other Mayas to the south of the colony, by the mid-seventeenth century the threat to the province had shifted to its coastline. Pardo militia units were therefore placed in the north and northwest of the peninsula, with the initial companies in Campeche and Merida, and subsequent companies placed to defend both the Campeche–Merida *camino real* and the northern coast. This human line of defense was conceived in conjunction with a network of bulwarks (at Campeche and Merida, and later at Bacalar), batteries (at Campeche), and trenches (between Merida and the northern coast).

Yucatec historian Jorge Victoria Ojeda has identified four stages during which this system was planned and built. The first, of 1542–1607, witnessed minimal activity; as yet, the colony was small and poor, the Caribbean was under Spanish control, and the long Yucatec coast largely ignored by European privateers. Certainly, French pirates caused considerable alarm during a series of attacks that began in 1556 (see Table 5.1), but morale was greatly boosted in 1571 when a French crew was captured on Cozumel and marched to Merida to be tried for piracy and heresy (the pirates were al-

TABLE 5.1 Attacks on Campeche, 1556–1685

Date	Attack force	Nature of attack
1556	French pirates	Town threatened
1559	French pirates	Town assaulted and plundered
1561	Three French corsairs	Town sacked
1571	French pirates under Cultot	Pirates raid Sisal and north coast; Campeche in fear; French captured on Cozumel and tried in Merida
1597	English force under William Parker	Town taken and sacked
1624	Dutch force under Pieter Schouten	Sisal sacked and north coast raided, but Campeche spared
1633	Mixed force of 10 ships under Dutchman Cornelis Jol and Diego el Mulato Martín	Town taken and plundered; Jol makes several other minor raids on the town in the 1630s
1642	Pirates under Diego el Mulato Lucifer	Town sacked; Bacalar also sacked (and sacked again by pirates in 1648)
1663	English force of 1,000 under Christopher Myngs and Edward Mansfield	Town taken and sacked
1668	English privateers under Mansfield and Henry Morgan	Town raided and plundered
1672	Mixed Dutch and French force under Laurens de Graaf	Town taken and plundered
1678	English force under Lewis Scott	Town taken, occupied, and for 3 days
1685	Mixed Dutch-led, English, and French force of 1,000 under Laurens de Graaf and de Grammont	Town taken, occupied, and plundered for 6 weeks, then sacked

Sources: AGI-*México* 360 and 363, 3, 6, nos. 1–5; AGN-*Reales Cédulas* (*Originales*) 2, 1, 23: f. 40; López de Cogolludo (1688 [1654]: 596, 601, 658); Exquemelin (1969 [1678]: 83); Jones (1989: 62); Victoria Ojeda (1995: 149–54, 157, 161, 168, 178–80); Landers (1997: 89); Lane (1998: xxi, xxiv, 69–71, 106–16, 166–67).

legedly Lutheran); at least one was sentenced to domestic service as a slave in an encomendero's household in the city. The next threat came from the English, but not until the end of the century. On his rampage through Spanish ports in the Caribbean in 1585–86, Sir Francis Drake bypassed Campeche, which was not seriously threatened until William Parker sacked it in 1597.[11]

There is no evidence of pardo militia units during these early years, and the coastal lookout system set up at this time was apparently manned by Spaniards and Mayas (as detailed below). All Spanish settlers were obliged to maintain a rifle with 25 cartridges and were organized, at least theoretically, into 138 companies of 100 men each. Units of indios flecheros were also incorporated into this system. Beginning in the 1580s, Merida and its entrances were patrolled by twelve Spaniards on horseback—in theory, by night and day, although in practice the patrols were intermittent between alerts.[12]

During the second stage, of 1607–1717, the foundations of the system were laid and a fair amount of infrastructure was built—necessitated both by the growth of the Yucatec economy and the increased Caribbean presence of the Dutch, French, and English. A small fortress was built at Río Lagartos and a series of stone towers was also put up at the southwest corner of the colony, at Champotón, Seiba Playa, and Lerma (see Map 5.1).[13] The Presidio del Carmen was built in stages during the second half of the seventeenth century.[14] Most activity, however, was focused on Campeche and Merida. Campeche's fortifications were begun in 1607, and were still being built when some of the Maya participants in the 1610 Tekax revolt were condemned to labor on the project.[15] Campeche's defenses were periodically expanded (in 1683 to include a wall around the town), although such efforts largely failed to prevent pirate assaults, as Table 5.1 reflects. The modest fortress of San Benito, built in Merida in 1656, was replaced in the late 1660s by a more substantial citadel of the same name. This expensive and controversial project, initiated by Yucatan's most infamous colonial governor, don Rodrigo Flores de Aldana, was built by Maya workers whose dozens of complaints and petitions for redress and back-pay flowed into the colonial courts for years.[16] The complete study of the building of San Benito has yet to be carried out, but among the hundreds of Maya workers there were certainly a number of skilled Afro-Yucatecan laborers, supervisors, and work-gang managers. One of these was a pardo named Diego Ramos, a foreman of the project who supervised a crew of Mayas from San Cristobal; Ramos filed a complaint in 1670 claiming that for the eighteen months that his crew made and transported lime at the construction site, he was not paid a single peso.[17] The Afro-Yucatecans who helped build San Benito were replaced by others to guard it; four colored companies were assigned to the fort in case of attack.[18]

It was also during this century that the militia was expanded to include companies of free Afro-Yucatecans. I have not found sources giving precise

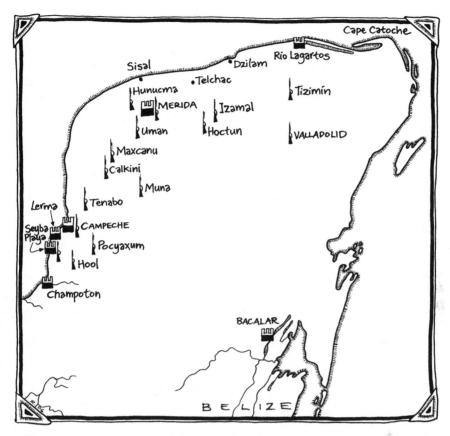

Map 5.1 Afro-Yucatecans and Yucatan's late colonial defenses.

numbers of pardo militiamen comparable to those of the late eighteenth century, but some mestizos and Afro-Yucatecans were included in the sudden mobilizations during the terror alerts of 1607 onward.[19] There was a full mulatto company in Campeche in 1634—although they were outnumbered by eight Maya flechero units—and it was still in place in the 1660s.[20] More Afro-Yucatecan militiamen were hired by 1671, when Governor Escobedo was given approval to plug weak spots in the colony's defenses by continuing fortification projects and adding additional militiamen—both Spaniards, as cavalrymen, and pardos, as footsoldiers.[21] The company of pardos played a central role in the struggle to defend Campeche from the pirate attack of 1685.[22] Merida's militia companies included over two hundred "*negros* y mulatos" by the 1660s; mulattoes were included in the six hundred militiamen who could be theoretically called up to defend the city under Governor Layseca (1677–83). The 712 militiamen assembled in 1704 in a muster in Merida's central plaza for the new governor still consisted of Spaniards, mestizos, *negros*, and mulattoes. The use of pardo and native militias was given the usual justification by colonial officials, that "the forces of the province are insufficient, and within it there is a lack of Spaniards."[23]

The third stage of the development of Yucatan's defenses, 1717–1812, witnessed the consolidation and expansion of the system. By the second half of this period, the whole network of forts and bastions, lookouts and militia companies, was intended to defend the entire peninsula from the Laguna de Términos to Bacalar.[24] By the time Campeche had completed its fortifications (making it the only fully walled city in Spanish America) and built the massive, still-standing Puerta de Tierra in 1732, the era of pirate attacks on the town was over and the Englishmen that Campechanos knew were mostly slave and log traders. But the larger British threat was by no means over. Thus in the second half of the eighteenth century, as the colony's economy continued to grow and be a source of crown revenue, as the British and French consolidated their presence in the Caribbean, and as the Bourbon Reforms turned to military matters, militia numbers in Yucatan gradually increased.

Beginning in the 1720s, British settlers in Belize were a thorn in the side of every Yucatec governor. Concern over the defense of Yucatan was heightened in the 1760s, especially in the wake of the 1762 British seizure of Havana—located very close to the peninsula and a major trading partner with Sisal and Campeche. In 1766 a report and map drawn up for the crown by an engineer (eventually, militia colonel and chief engineer) named don Juan de Dios González described in detail the peninsula's vulnerability to coastal attack. A copy of the report and map was in the hands of the British by 1768;[25] its pessimistic evaluation of the peninsula's defensibility echoed that of the report submitted by Lieut. James Cook to Admiral Burnaby in Jamaica in 1765 (and published in London in 1769).[26]

In 1767, don Cristobal de Zayas, governor since the end of 1765 and comissioner of the González report, formed a new regiment of pardo militia infantry in Merida; their uniforms and equipment are depicted in Figure 5.1. They continued to receive eight pesos a month, the same as all infantrymen and fusiliers, pardo and white (see Table 4.1 in Chapter Four). Another Merida company of *pardos tiradores* [free-colored fusiliers] was also created about this time. Don Antonio Oliver, governor in the 1770s, augmented the batallion of pardos, so that by 1778 there were eight companies of pardos in Merida and eight more in Campeche. Each group of eight formed a division; four of the companies from the Merida division were attached to the city itself, two of Campeche's were in that town, while the remaining ten companies were stationed around the colony (identified in Map 5.1).[27]

Figure 5.1 The heading reads: "Infantry Regiment of Pardo Militias of Merida, Yucatan." The caption reads: "This Regiment was newly formed by order of His Majesty on 10 November of 1767, by Sr. don Cristobal de Zayas Guzmán y Moscoso, Field Marshall of the Royal Armies and Captain General of this Province. The figures show the uniform that they use, being dressed in burlap cloth with cartridge belt and leather boots." Source: AGI-*Uniformes* (*Mapas y Planos*) 101, 1: f. 1. Archivo General de las Indias, Seville.

A document of 1785 depicted a company sergeant (see Figure 5.2), above a half-page report on the state of the free-colored fusilier company in that year. The author was a militia officer named Eugenio Rubio, possibly an Afro-Yucatecan (nine years later he was promoted to the rank of captain in Merida's pardo militia).[28] Most of the report described the uniforms of the officers, riflemen, and drummer. It also explained how the militiamen indirectly paid for their own uniforms and cartridge belts, by having a withholding fee [*masita*] retained from their monthly salary (a peso for senior officers, five reales for sergeants, four reales—a half peso—for everyone else); this "common fund pays for the belting of the officers and troops." Such a system asked to be abused, and sure enough Rubio ended his report with the following comment:

For five years this unit has not received clothes, and has earned a twenty-two thousand-peso credit to supply its troops with hats, twine boots, and cartridge belts crossed at the shoulders because that is more splendid and comfortable; likewise as there is no withholding for minor garments, I judge it to be very necessary that they be given duplicates.[29]

Figure 5.2 The heading reads: "Companies of Pardo Fusiliers of the 1st Division of Merida, Yucatan." Beneath the image is a half-page report on the state of the company, by Eugenio Rubio, July 7, 1785. Source: AGI-*Uniformes* (*Mapas y Planos*) 104, 1: f. 1. Archivo General de las Indias, Seville.

Twenty-two thousand pesos was a considerable sum of money, and indeed the size of the militia by late colonial times put a substantial pressure on the treasury. The 1779 attack by Yucatec military forces on the British settlements in Belize, and the subsequent auction of dozens of black slaves taken from the British, was not just a local and regional strategic success; it was also a much-needed boost to the colony's ability to pay for at least part of its own defense.[30]

Tables 5.2 and 5.3 provide number and distribution details on Yucatan's militia forces toward the end of the century. The grand totals presented in these tables should be taken as approximate numbers; as with all colonial censuses, one cannot be sure that every person was counted and that every district used the same methods and categories. That caveat aside, the tables indicate that the total number of militiamen in the colony increased by 30% between 1778 and 1794. War with the British in 1779–83 created a temporary but pressing demand for black and pardo soldiers, many of whom saw action in defense of the province. However, while so-called *blanco* compa-

TABLE 5.2 Yucatan's militia forces, 1778

District or division	Blanco militia battalions and number of men	Pardo militia companies and number of men	Other companies
Campeche	1 of 676	8 of 85 or 86 each	
Merida	1 of 676	8 of 85 or 86 each	
Bacalar			2 of 63 each, both pardo–blanco mixed units
TOTALS	1,352	1,368	126 (Grand total 2,846)

Source: Vinson (2001a: 235), using AGN-*Indiferente General* 394a.
Note: In 1789–90, the size of pardo companies ranged from 78 to 85 (Campos García 2005: 88, using AGS-*Secretaría de Guerra* 7299, 4 and 6).

nies remained the same, pardo companies were somewhat reduced, with the big increase occurring in mixed companies—this a result of the reforms instituted in 1792 by Viceroy Revillagigedo.[31]

Considering that the viceroy's goal had been to disband all free-colored units, pardo companies in Yucatan survived the reforms well. As mentioned above, of the roughly 3,600 militiamen in 1794, there were militia companies of 85 or so free-colored men in 10 communities running more or less through the districts that bordered the west and northwest coasts of the peninsula (the zone called "the colored crescent" in previous chapters; see Map 4.1 in Chapter Four and Map 5.1 in this chapter). Throughout the final decades of the century, there were thirteen to fourteen hundred Afro-Yucatecan militiamen. One of these soldiers was don Juan de Dios González's own pardo son, Lieutenant Francisco González.[32] As Tables 5.2 and 5.3 show, in most cases the pardo companies were separate but accompanied "white" militias and, in the cities of Campeche and Merida, permanent military forces. For more than a decade after 1794, war with Britain and the crisis that led to Mexican Independence kept militia units active and relatively well manned, with pardo companies still mostly separate from "white" ones. There were even occasional increases to Afro-Yucatecan units. For example, small numbers of *negros auxiliares* were transferred from Havana and Santo Domingo to Yucatan's pardo companies in 1796,[33] and war with England in 1797–1802 prompted a spike in demand for supplies and soldiers, pardo militiamen included.[34]

In the final stage of colonial Yucatan's defensive development, that of 1812–21, all military forces in the Spanish Empire were reorganized under an intendency system, with Yucatan divided into fourteen new military districts. The shift from segregated militias to integrated permanent batallions does not

TABLE 5.3 Yucatan's militia forces, 1794

District and pueblo	Blanco militia companies and number of men	Pardo militia companies and number of men	Detachments and mixed blanco–pardo units
MERIDA (1st division)	1 of 75 grenadiers; 3 of 75 fusiliers each	4 of 87 each	1 of 77 permanent infantrymen; 1 artillery detachment of 7 men from the Campeche company; 1 of 35 dragoons
Camino Real Bajo			
—Hunucmá	1 of 75	1 of 85	
Sierra			
—Muna		1 of 85	
La Costa			
—Izamal	1 of 75	1 of 85	
—Dzidzantun	1 of 75		
—Motul	1 of 75		
—Tixkokob	1 of 75		
Beneficios Altos			1 "batallion of urban militia"
Beneficios Bajos			
—Hoctun		1 squad from the Izamal pardo company	
CAMPECHE (2nd division)	4 of 75 each	2 of 85 each	9 of permanent infantry (8 of 77 fusiliers, 1 of 63 grenadiers); 1 of 63 artillerymen; 1 squad of 12 dragoons from the Merida company
Sahcabchen			
—Seyba Playa	1 of 75	1 of 85	
Bolonchencauich			
—Pocyaxum		1 of 85	
Camino Real Alto			
—Calkini	1 of 75	1 of 85	
—Tenabo	1 of 75	1 of 85	
—Xecelchakan	1 of 75		

TABLE 5.3 *(continued)*

District and pueblo	Blanco militia companies and number of men	Pardo militia companies and number of men	Detachments and mixed blanco–pardo units
Camino Real Bajo			
—Maxcanu	1 of 75	1 of 85	
Bacalar			1 of 100 permanent infantrymen; 2 of 50 permanent militiamen; 1 artillery detachment of 9 men from the Campeche company
TOTALS	1,350	1,198	est. 1,139 (Grand total 3,687)

Source: Created from 1794–95 censuses published in Rubio Mañé (1942, I:207–47).

Note: The data is missing on the companies at Tizimin and Valladolid. I have counted the Beneficios Altos "batallion" as a company of 85, as it seems unlikely that the district would have had a full batallion of 676 men.

appear to have been completed anywhere in New Spain by 1821, let alone in Yucatan; the pardo companies of the Merida and Campeche divisions not only survived into the Independence period, but were praised (as we shall see below) for their stellar service in Mexico against the insurgents of the 1810s. However, the labeling of free-colored companies as "pardo" did not last long; in the summer and autumn of 1822, a series of decrees by Mexican Imperial Governor Melchor Álvarez eliminated the practice of assigning socioracial labels to groups and individuals, all in the interest of "disappearing the odious division of castas." This gave the impression that distinctively Afro-Yucatecan institutions—such as Merida's Jesús parish, free-colored religious brotherhoods, and pardo militia companies—immediately dissolved. In fact, they disappeared in name only. There was no sudden reorganization of Yucatan's military forces—just a change in nomenclature and a slow decline in numbers. One survey of 1823 counted 1,800 fusiliers, another of 1828 recorded 2,022 men at arms in the whole peninsula, both permanent and militia units; the lack of reference to casta categories makes it impossible to trace the decline or integration of "white" and "pardo" soldiers after 1822.[35]

Although the nature of colonial census data means that figures like this must be conjectural, one can reasonably estimate that for the second half of the colonial period 2%–8% of the free-colored population were militiamen. It is thus possible that as many as a fifth of free, adult Afro-Yucatecan men were on the militia books at any one time. Militia involvement was clearly an important part of the Afro-Yucatecan experience. It is therefore worth dwelling on briefly, first, the nature of that experience in terms of occupation and military service; and second, the larger social implications of a militia record.

Militiamen were, by definition, not permanent soldiers, and consequently were drawn from the larger body of free-colored men described in the previous chapter as farmers and artisans of various kinds. An official inspection of Yucatan's pardo militias in 1789–90 recorded the occupations of the militiamen (see Table 5.4). The starkest fact to emerge from this data is the fact that two-thirds (65%) of all pardo soldiers were *labradores* [farmers or farm laborers]. Almost all the rest (31%) were artisans in just one of six occupations (shoemaker, blacksmith, tailor, tanner, carpenter, and *velero* or candlemaker). But a more interesting picture can be seen by dividing urban from rural militiamen, as I have done in the table; this reveals that 91% of militiamen stationed outside Merida and Campeche were farm laborers, but inside the city and port town only 21% worked farms. Over half urban militiamen were either shoemakers or blacksmiths (69% claimed one of the six artisan occupations just listed).

These 1,344 free-colored men earned their living from these occupations, only receiving salaries as militiamen when they were mobilized for action.[36] They were not a separate group, but a subgroup within the Afro-Yucatecan community—one that was in many ways a privileged group that helped to define that community (as we shall see below and in Chapter Six). When militiamen *were* on duty, their experience fell into one of two categories: active military duty; and guard duty (in other words, at any one time a small detachment of militiamen were on duty at all fortifications, at company headquarters, and at major coastal lookout, or *vigía*, posts).

The first of these, military action, was the less common of the two, although during the course of the seventeenth and eighteenth centuries there was more military conflict on the borders of the colony than can be comprehensively summarized here. Some examples must suffice. Afro-Yucatecans participated in most, if not all, the skirmishes and battles that accompanied pirate attacks on Campeche—as pardo militiamen, as black servants to Spaniards, or simply as residents of the town. Some Afro-Yucatecans were taken as items of plunder. One of the pirates that terrorized Campeche in 1642, Diego el Mulato Lucifer (himself a native of Campeche), sacked Bacalar the same year, kidnapping a number of that small town's residents, including a free mulatto named Luís Fernández. The precise number of Afro-Yucatecans in early colonial Bacalar is not known, but they were among the roughly 120 non-Mayas who suffered repeated Maya and pirate attacks on the town between 1638 and 1648, resulting in the abandonment of the site until 1729.[37]

During the three-day pirate occupation of Campeche in 1678, several black and mulatta women were captured and taken, along with almost a hundred Maya men and women (mostly women), to be sold as slaves in Jamaica.[38] Some Spanish-speaking slaves seized in Campeche by Englishmen

TABLE 5.4 Occupations of pardo militiamen, 1789–90

Divisions:	1st (Merida) division		2nd (Campeche) division		
Companies:	4 urban	4 rural	2 urban	6 rural	Totals
Farm laborer	59	297	46	472	874
Shoemaker	111	9	42	4	166
Blacksmith	87	17	16	11	131
Tailor	24	6	19	4	53
Tanner	25	3	1	2	31
Carpenter	3	3	6	10	22
Peddler			13		13
Candle maker	1		9		10
Bricklayer [albañil]			8		8
Saddler	5				5
Silversmith	2		2		4
Barber [barbero]	3				3
Weaver	1	1			2
Carter			2		2
Wig maker [peluquero]			1		1
Mason [cantero]	1				1
Mason [locero]		1			1
Sculptor	1				1
Painter			1		1
Dyer			1		1
Rope maker	1				1
Soap maker	1				1
Muleteer	1				1
Coachman			1		1
Café owner	1				1
Baker				1	1
Bullfighter	1				1
Bookkeeper [partidor]			1		1
Infantryman	1				1
None	2	1	1	1	5
[Totals]	[331]	[338]	[170]	[505]	[1,344]

Sources: AGS-*Secretaría de Guerra* 7299, 4 (Campeche, 1790) and 6 (Merida, 1789); tables in Campos García (2005: 28–29).

Note: The 1st division's urban companies were in Merida itself, the rural ones in Muna, Hunucmá, Umán, and Izamal; the 2nd division's urban companies were in Campeche itself, the rural ones in Seybaplaya, Hool, Pocyaxum, Tenabo, Calkiní, and Maxcanú (see Map 5.1).

in 1678 or, more likely, 1685, ended up in Carolina. In 1686, a group of these Afro-Yucatecan captives approached a native Guale man about escaping their new English masters by canoeing down the coast from Carolina to Spanish Florida; they were probably among the eight black men, two women, and a baby who fled by boat from the English colony to St. Augustine in 1687. The Spanish governor considered the refugees slaves of the crown and put the men to work on the new city defenses while the women were placed as domestics, but they were paid the same wages as free black and native workers (a daily peso for men, half a peso for women) and in 1693 they were all freed by royal edict.[39] Other Afro-Yucatecans sacrificed their lives, as did one unfortunate but subsequently commemorated black slave during the 1685 sacking of Campeche. He was not alone; the pardo company led by Capt. Cristóbal Rabanales lost men in the fighting, and Spanish accounts of the chaotic defense of the town repeatedly mention that the hundreds slain or carried off by the pirates included "Spaniards, blacks, Indians, mulattoes, and slaves."[40] In response to the six-week occupation of the port town by Dutch, English, and French privateers, surviving pardo militiamen, accompanied by a pardo company from Merida under Capt. Lázaro del Canto, went after the only foreigners they could find by chasing English loggers out of the Champotón area.[41]

The pardo companies already established by the 1690s also played a role in the campaign against the Itza Mayas during that decade, from the construction of the road from Yucatan into the Peten (begun in 1695 and effectively initiating open war against unconquered Mayas south of the colony) to the final assault on the Itza capital in 1697. One mixed company of pardos and mestizos was lead by an Afro-Yucatecan, Capt. José Laines. The casta status of another captain, Mateo Hidalgo, is not clear, but he was probably a pardo; his company of forty-nine men consisted of thirty-one pardos from Merida and eighteen pardos or mestizos under an Antonio Franco. The pardo soldiers received eight pesos a month, their officers, twelve. Juan de Vargas was one of the free-colored infantrymen who saw action under Capt. Hidalgo, beginning in 1695. He survived to testify to the experience, especially at Chuntuki (a Cehach Maya town in the Petén, near the Itza border, set up in 1695 as a base for the destruction of the Itza kingdom). There Vargas suffered from a bout of malaria and saw three of his fellow pardo militiamen killed.[42]

In the eighteenth century there was little occasion for pardo militiamen to see action against Mayas. Even during the 1761 Canek Revolt in Cisteil, when pardo militia units were called up, not many actually fought against Maya rebels. At the height of the revolt, the lieutenant of the Sierra captaincy, Pedro Joseph Lizarraga, asked for two hundred pardo militiamen to be sent from Merida to guard Peto and Tekax, which he feared were about to break out in revolt. Lizarraga's fears remained unrealized, however, and it is not even clear how many pardo soldiers went to the Sierra district. The impact of Canek on most pardo militiamen was no more than being told to report to duty and possibly receiving one of the shotguns that were confiscated from Mayas throughout the colony in 1761 and 1762.[43]

Most of the action experienced by pardo militiamen in the eighteenth century was against the British. This was especially true in the second half of the century, as British efforts to establish hegemony in the Caribbean became largely successful and as Anglo-Spanish wars became more frequent and sustained. Although Campeche was spared the sackings it endured in the previous century, there were still regular terror alerts, especially when British fleets approached—Admiral Vernon's in 1739, prompting fears that his mission was to conquer Yucatan and inspiring the governor to call up all militiamen, including a batallion of two hundred pardos from Campeche.[44]

Most hostile encounters between the British and Yucatecans in the late colonial period stemmed from the logging settlements in Belize, which slowly expanded to become a permanent British colony (although remaining an unofficial one until 1862). Belize was never a threat in the way that English and other privateers had been. The combination of British insistence on remaining in the area and British governmental reluctance to make Belize a priority, even within their Central American policy (let alone their Caribbean one), effectively gave Spaniards in Yucatan license to plunder. British settlers occasionally made raids into Yucatan (attacking Chunhuhub and allegedly threatening Tihosuco in 1727),[45] but the Spanish colony was not easily accessible from Belize and neither the settlers nor soldiers eventually posted there ever mounted a major attack on Spanish Yucatan or posed a real threat to it (despite Lieut. Cook's suggestion, in a report published after his 1765 diplomatic-cum-spying journey from Belize to Merida, that the colony was virtually undefended).[46] A detailed plan sent to London in 1779 outlined a projected British assault on Bacalar, and then Merida, but it was never enacted; besides, its goal was not to acquire Yucatan permanently, but to force a major diversion of Spanish forces for its recapture.[47] When, in 1801, the British built a battery on Isla Mujeres, off the northeast tip of the peninsula, Yucatec militiamen were able to expel them and seize their artillery with apparent ease.[48]

In contrast, Yucatec Spaniards made several major and numerous small-scale raids on British settlements through the late eighteenth century, sacking parts of the colony twice in the 1730s and twice again in the 1750s, and forcing the British to abandon Belize temporarily but completely in 1747–49 and 1779–84. The last major attack on Belize was in 1798, although settlers were spared a final sacking when the Spaniards were defeated at St. George's Cay. Spanish raiders were often accompanied by pardo militiamen, and there seem to have always been pardo companies involved in major assaults on Belize.[49]

These attacks were in a way historical revenge for the depredations committed by British privateers against Campeche and lesser coastal sites in early colonial times. Yet such an interpretation is hard to reconcile with the

Afro-Yucatecan experience. Black slaves and free-colored men fought and died in these encounters and slaves became the spoils of war. Pardo militiamen benefited in the sense that survivors enhanced their records of service with the sacrifices of active duty, some winning promotions and pensions as a result. But not all militiamen survived, or avoided injury, and it was not pardo soldiers but the crown and the colony's Spanish elite who benefited from the resale of black slaves stolen from British loggers.[50]

Military action was thus the first category of militia experience. The second category—that of various forms of guard duty—was less life threatening, but also tended to be uneventful. There were pardos on guard duty at all the major fortifications built on or near Yucatan's coast by the middle of the eighteenth century. This sort of work is perhaps best exemplified by the example of the vigía, or coastal lookout. Not only was Yucatan a peninsula, but the Spanish colony there was effectively an island due to its inaccessibility by land from the south. Coastal defense was therefore the most important strategic element of the colony's defense from outside assault. Such defense was only possible if the authorities had warning of an impending attack. Although there may have been vigías posted before 1573, in that year the incoming governor, don Francisco Velázquez Gijón, ordered vigías to be appointed, apparently for the first time. At this stage, there were probably only a few; in the 1580s fray Alonso Ponce described wooden lookout towers at Sisal and Río Lagartos, manned by "a Spaniard," with adjacent thatched-roof houses for the vigía "and a few Indians who served him." In 1657, the governor ordered vigías to be set up at every league between Sisal and Telchac. Although this was overly ambitious, by the late seventeenth century there were apparently fourteen active vigías between Champotón and Cape Catoche, with eight more added by 1766 (see Map 5.1).[51]

Although Ponce described lookouts in the 1580s as Spaniards, assisted by Mayas, at some point in the seventeenth century vigías became non-Spaniards (Afro-Yucatecans included). The shift was probably early in the century, accompanied by the expansion of the captaincy system. Strategically crucial Campeche had been the second captaincy allowed by the governor in Merida (along with a captaincy at Valladolid); subsequent captaincies established in the early to mid-seventeenth century emphasized coastal defense and were obliged to help maintain the vigía system.

For example, the captaincy of Camino Real Bajo was based in Hunucmá and obligated to protect Sisal, on the north coast, where vigías had been stationed since 1573. Hunucmá was a Maya *cabecera* [head-town] that had already begun to develop as a regional center by the mid-seventeenth century, with a very small but steadily growing population of non-Mayas (5% of the thousand people living in the town and its *sujetos*, or subject villages, in 1688 were non-Mayas).[52] Hunucmá and its sujetos were also held in encomienda by the García de Montalvo family until 1674, up to which date the captaincy went to the encomendero or a relative of his; the captain then appointed a lookout, often a militiaman borrowed from the pardo company in the district. After 1674 the captaincy passed through the hands of various Spanish families with interests in the region. In 1690, it was held by don Bernardo Domingo de la Cerda, who had a pardo named Joseph Solís keeping a lonely vigil on the coast near Sisal.[53]

William Dampier, the English navigator, made two voyages to "Campeachy" in the 1670s. By this date the town of Campeche sported stone watchtowers along its seafront fortifications (see Figure 5.3), but lookout posts to the south were less formal. Dampier reported that at Cape Catoche in 1675 the only Spanish colonial presence was a lookout whom he called "a *Spanish Mulatto*" and "the *Mulatto*" (his italics), who was stationed "at a small Hill by the Sea, call'd the Mount . . . not natural, but the work of

Figure 5.3 "The Watchtower," Campeche. Source: Photograph by Reid Samuel Yalom. Reproduced by permission. (See also Yalom 2004: 63.)

Men" (no doubt an old, overgrown Maya pyramid, as the region had been well populated from the Classic period into the early seventeenth century).[54] The ostensible task of the mulatto was to use the pyramid to watch out for pirates, but according to Dampier the lookout spent most of his time guarding bales of salty local earth, bound up in palm leaves, used to make "salt-petre" [gunpowder]. This Afro-Yucatecan vigía told the Englishman that the earth was "to make Powder and that he expected a Bark from *Campeachy* to fetch it away." Dampier encountered other vigías on his journey, but they were not all mulattoes; between Río Lagartos and Sisal the "Watch-Box" lookout towers were manned by "Indians," although these may have been the Maya servants described by Ponce a century earlier, with mulatto managers unseen by Dampier.[55]

The Englishman gives an example of how well the vigía system sometimes worked. "A small Jamaica Privateer once Landed 6 or 7 Men at this Look-out of Sisal," wrote Dampier. Although the vigía (or his Maya assistants) had seen the ship and alerted the local militia, the English captain, for some reason "not suspecting any danger," sent a few of his men to "row along by the shore" in a canoe. "But within half an hour they were attack'd by about forty Spanish Soldiers, who had cut them off from the shore, to whom they surrendered themselves Prisoners. The Spaniards carried them in triumph to the Fort"—meaning the small fortress at Sisal, which was manned by militiamen from the two companies at Hunucmá; one blanco and one pardo (Dampier's phrase "Spanish Soldiers" should not be read as a specific reference to men from the blanco company; they were just as likely to have been pardos). The rest of the story is a rather celebratory account of how one of the English sailors claimed to be the captain (in response to Spanish demands that the captain, who was in fact still on the ship, identify himself), whereupon he was treated to the governor's hospitality in Merida, "frequently Regal'd with Chocolate, &c.," and eventually freed in Campeche, and "ever after call'd *Captain Jack*."[56]

The use of militiamen as lookouts does not appear to have been consistent, and may have tapered off during the eighteenth century.[57] The use of Maya servants or assistants, however, persisted through the colonial period, and their role must have alleviated much of the boredom that otherwise characterized the job. Regular shifts by Maya *atalalleros* [watchtower sentinels] also permitted the Spanish or Afro-Yucatecan vigía to moonlight as a fisherman or *milpero* [corn farmer]. Diego Rodríguez, the lookout at Dzilam in 1700, probably did both; he lived with his family in Dzidzantun, where his brother Pedro was a milpero.[58]

The Dzilam vigía of a century later, Marcos Tiburcio Sansores, was also a corn farmer. However, such activities barely sustained his family, claimed Sansores. In 1811 he petitioned the governor of Yucatan to be relieved as lookout, stating that for eleven years, "I have kept watch continually in fulfillment of my duty, passing the nights in vigil and the days in the watchtower, due to the war that we have maintained with the English." Sansores claimed to be a model lookout, "even risking my life" when the English attacked Dzilam, being the only one to give the alert, thereby handing the Spanish "a complete victory." When not saving Dzilam, Sansores did a little fishing and worked "a few *mecates* of *milpas*" with the same Maya men who assisted him in the watchtower, paying them "immediately what they had justly earned" both in the tower and the cornfield. All told, concluded the vigía, it was "completely impossible to continue in this job" and still sustain his impoverished family. He requested either permanent relief, or at least temporary relief from his lookout duties so that he and his Maya assistants could attend to the 550-mecate cornfield that was already sown.[59]

There is no direct evidence that Rodríguez and Sansores were Afro-Yucatecan. Indeed, Rodríguez is listed in the 1700 census as a mestizo (along with his brother, whose wife was Maya); and officials in Izamal and Merida gave Sansores a "don" as though he were a Spaniard. But Sansores does not claim the title for himself, and even out in Dzilam and with the "don" inflation of late colonial times, it seems unlikely that a fisherman and corn farmer would be a Spaniard with a "don." More likely, he was an Afro-Yucatecan or mestizo passing as a Spaniard by virtue of his vigía post (like the vigía of Santa Clara, who lived in Yobaín and was described by the priest in 1700 as the village's only blanco). Alternatively, as a lookout officer, Sansores may have been attached to a militia company, and at the very end of the colonial period some pardo militia officers were granted a "don." In response to Sansores' request to be relieved, the post of vigía at Dzilam was given to a Felix Domingo, very much the name of a low-ranking non-Maya, probably an Afro-Yucatecan.[60]

Whatever form of suffering endured by free-colored lookouts and militiamen—be it at the hands of Itza Mayas or English pirates, or from malaria or boredom—such men served the colony in ways that surely earned them privileges beyond an eight-peso monthly salary. After all, black conquistadors like Sebastián Toral had earned manumission from slavery and a place among the new colonists as a reward for years of fighting during the invasions of the 1530s and 1540s. Toral worked, lived, and raised a family in early Merida, and was able to raise the funds to cross the Atlantic and return again to New Spain. However, according to his own petition, he continued to serve as an unpaid guard [*portero*], a position commonly assigned to black and free-colored veterans of conquest wars. Furthermore, he was then asked to pay tribute for himself and his family when in the early 1570s the crown imposed tribute burdens on all free black and mulatto residents in the colonies.[61] Toral was able to secure an exemption for him and his descendents, but only after written petitions had failed and he took on the expense and danger of voyaging to Spain to petition the court in person (as detailed at the start of Chapter One).[62]

Toral's experience underscores two related facts about free-colored tribute obligations in Spanish America: first, the law was met with resistance of various kinds, from legal petition campaigns to flight into frontier regions; and second, the collection of tribute from free coloreds was sporadic and often offset by the acquisition of individual or group exemptions—albeit not easily won. In Yucatan, from the 1570s through the seventeenth century, free-colored tribute payers contributed thousands of pesos to the royal treasury of New Spain; as Figure 5.4 shows, from 1581 to 1618 the free Afro-Yucatecans of Merida and its environs contributed a slowly rising lion's share (over a thousand pesos in all), with Campeche and Valladolid each collecting a relatively modest but consistent amount (about 180 pesos in total from each town).

But by the 1630s the pardo militia company in Campeche had won tribute exemption for all its soldiers, probably as a result of their sacrifices in defending the port town from a series of pirate attacks during that decade. By 1644, tribute relief had been extended to the Merida companies, thereby effectively granting all of Yucatan's pardo militiamen exemption from the hated tax. This was no small achievement; most militia units in New Spain did not win tribute relief until the last quarter of the seventeenth century.[63] By the eighteenth century, tribute collection from all free-colored residents in Yucatan, not just militiamen, was sporadic; a report to the viceroy complained that in the 1760s none was levied at all.[64]

Access to an additional privilege, the *fuero militar*, came harder. A *fuero* was a legal immunity from certain kinds of prosecutions, such as criminal courts and debtors proceedings; in all the colonies prior to the 1760s, only

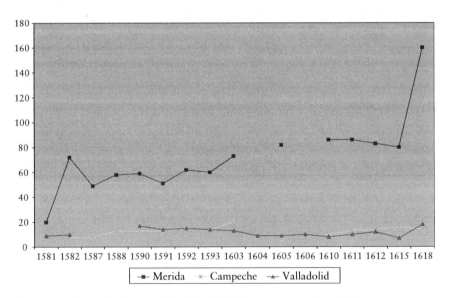

Figure 5.4 Annual tribute paid by free Afro-Yucatecans, 1581–1618.

officers had fuero rights, and the higher ranking the officer the more extensive the fuero. In Yucatan, the Spanish elite prevented free-colored militiamen from getting fuero privileges before the final decades of the seventeenth
century simply by placing a glass ceiling on pardo officer promotions.[65]

Nevertheless, the pardo militia was a unique avenue of social mobility for
free Afro-Yucatecans in the late seventeenth century. Lázaro del Canto was
not the only pardo militia captain who gained considerable status through
military service, coming close to passing as a Spaniard in Merida. Another
free-colored captain, Eugenio de Acosta, achieved an upward mobility perhaps more remarkable than del Canto's. In the final decades of the seventeenth century, Acosta went from being a slave of Capt. Joseph de Acosta to
being a captain in Campeche's pardo militia, a free, independent muleteer
with a train of twenty-eight mules, and himself the owner of a slave. Acosta's
slave was a *negro* named Juan Durán, possibly a relation to a pardo named
Durán who married a niece of Capt. Eugenio's, or else a former slave of this
Durán who became Acosta's nephew-in-law. It was not common, but also not
unheard of, for a wealthy pardo or mulatto to own a slave, so Acosta was not
the only Afro-Yucatecan to own another. The Afro-Yucatecan captain's testament detailed his links to an economic and social network of Campeche pardos, but even in this document his racial status is omitted—save for a slip (or
notarial intention) in a coda to the will, in which he is called "a free pardo."

Another example is that of Capt. Clemente de Acevedo. Like Capt.
Acosta, Capt. Acevedo was a one-time slave whose military career earned
him freedom, a wealth that was considerable relative to his fellow pardos
(both men owned houses in Spanish urban neighborhoods), and a status
that removed the tag of pardo from his name. Indeed it appears to have
been a general rule that the "captain" prefix accorded sufficient status to
delete any race-identifying suffixes.

A final example is that of Capt. Diego González, another militia officer
who accumulated wealth as a merchant and urban landlord in Merida. He
was so successful and his activities so similar to those of a Spaniard, that
Marta Hunt, in her study of seventeenth-century Merida society, confessed
she initially conflated him with a contemporaneous Spanish captain of the
same name; only his will confirmed his separate identity, and labeled him
and his wife as "pardos libres," tags absent from the notarial records of his
business affairs.[66]

González men continued to pursue careers in the free-colored militia into
the nineteenth century, maintaining a tradition of service and status that
was deployed in petitions for preferment. For example, in 1801, two
González cousins, Francisco and Baltazar, competed for the position of
subinspector of Campeche's pardo division. Baltazar, the younger of the
two and only a second lieutenant [*subteniente*], made the most of his record
to date, especially his march to Bacalar in 1790 to prevent a British attack

and his participation in the failed engagements with the British in 1797 and 1798 off the coast of Belize. Francisco, the elder cousin and a full lieutenant, claimed a record of action against the British as far back as the hugely successful Spanish assault on Belize of 1779. He also laid claim to the record of his father, Colonel and Chief Engineer don Juan de Dios González, "who served Your Majesty for more than fifty years with the honor and usefulness of the Royal Duty [*el Servicio Real*]."[67]

Colonel González had been an officer back in the 1760s, and had benefited from the fuero reforms of that decade. From the 1680s to the 1760s, there were still more Spanish officers with fuero rights than pardo ones in Yucatan. But Yucatec militiamen gained as much as other pardo soldiers in New Spain did when a series of reforms in the late 1760s extended fuero privileges to militiamen of all ranks. Under some circumstances, militiamen were covered by the fuero even when not on active duty, and some privileges were also extended to family members. Not surprisingly, the reforms were not popular with regional Spanish officials; fuero privileges were not always recognized, and the whole system came under sporadic attack in the 1780s, followed by a full-scale assault on free-colored military service itself by the viceroy of New Spain in the 1790s.[68]

The tribute exemption and fuero privileges of Afro-Yucatecans remained in place during the period of reforms in the late eighteenth century, but just barely. In 1788, for example, the incoming governor of Yucatan, don Roberto Merino y Ceballos, proposed raising revenue by increasing tribute rates to sixteen reales a year for Mayas and introducing a twenty-four-real head tax on free Afro-Yucatecans. This scheme failed, but had it succeeded, free-colored men would have paid more in tribute than Mayas for the first time in Yucatec history.[69]

Nor did the reforms of the 1790s, initiated by Viceroy Revillagigedo in Mexico City, destroy the pardo militias in Yucatan as they were intended to do. The reforms sought to undermine distinct pardo privileges by integrating white and pardo soldiers into single companies. Ben Vinson, historian of Mexico's free-colored militias, has argued that the resistance to these changes by pardo militiamen in the central regions of Mexico was less to do with racial solidarity and more to do with free-colored privileges; in mixed units, pardo soldiers lost the corporate advantages of exclusive units and competed with white soldiers for preferment.[70] But pardo units that survived the reforms retained their privileges—and this meant most pardo companies in Yucatan. Indeed, for most Afro-Yucatecan militiamen and officers, traditional privileges persisted to the end of the colonial period; when don Ramón Sandoval retired as a pardo captain in 1818, for example, he was granted full emeritus access to fuero privileges—most notably, the use of his uniform and immunity from prosecution in the criminal courts.[71]

One reason why such privileges persisted was the record of service to the loyalist cause by pardos during the insurrections of the 1810s. In response to the first uprising in Mexico, militiamen from Yucatan, including pardos, were sent to Veracruz. Hundreds went in 1811, and more still the following year. Some, such as pardo fusiliers Norberto and Bonifacio Parra, did not return from Mexico until 1818.[72] Many of the veterans were praised and promoted in 1817 and 1818, but mortality rates were high.[73] In 1813, the Yucatec intellectual and politician José Matías Quintana applauded "the fidelity, patriotism, and notorious virtue of the esteemed pardos" who in fighting against the rebels sought "no salary or remuneration other than the honor and pleasure that great souls enjoy in serving their beloved country with fidelity." Although Quintana was a proponent of Spain's 1812 liberal constitution, he denounced its exclusion of people of African descent from citizenship. Significantly, the arguments of Quintana and his allies were based primarily on the pardo record of two centuries of military service, rather than on the larger contribution of Afro-Yucatecans to the colony's development.[74]

The old regime was restored in 1814, but the debate on citizenship was renewed in 1820—as was the idea of dissolving the pardo militia units and folding them into white companies. Once again, as already mentioned, the pardo companies survived; Afro-Yucatecans were still denied the status of citizenship, but could attain its equivalent through the merits of military service. Such a status quo might have persisted for decades, were it not for events outside Yucatan, which in 1821 turned the colony into a province of the independent Mexican Empire. Suddenly, by imperial proclamation, "all inhabitants of New Spain, without any distinction between Europeans, Africans, or Indians, [became] citizens of this kingdom." This meant that Afro-Yucatecans were no longer barred from holding political office; in 1821, the above-mentioned retired pardo militia officer, Ramón Sandoval, was elected *regidor* in Merida.[75]

Many years ago historian Allan Kuethe, studying late colonial New Granada, concluded that free-colored military service did not simply reflect the subordinate position of people of African descent in colonial society; the militia was "in its own right, a catalyst for change," offering "the thousands of pardos who served . . . a promising, welcome avenue for social betterment." A full-length study of Yucatan's pardo militias is long overdue, but it is already clear that Kuethe's sunny summary is widely applicable—to the pardo and free moreno militias of New Orleans, to the Afro-Argentines who defended Buenos Aires, and also to the Afro-Yucatecans who filled the ranks of the peninsula's pardo divisions.[76] Not all pardo militiamen found that service fulfilled its promises—for some it was a road to a routine more restrictive and dull than laboring on a corn farm, or, even worse, an avenue to a premature death. But for many, the pardo militia was quite simply a way up.

WAYS OUT: ESCAPE AND MANUMISSION

In 1800 an African slave named Richard Dobson fled his English owner in Belize and trekked north across the colonial frontier. His escape was coordinated with three other black slaves, all of whom fled their owners' logging settlements south of the Hondo River. Dobson and his friends safely reached the Yucatec town of Bacalar, where they lived for five months as free men. But Bacalar was a small town, even in 1800, and questions about the black men's identities were raised by the local authorities. The escapees had failed to change their names—Dobson had become Ricardo Dopson—or to split up; in fact, they had joined up with two more black escapees who had arrived from Belize almost four months later. All six Afro-Belizeans were detained by officials in Bacalar, and then dispatched to Merida, where they were further questioned. They immediately admitted to being escapees, stating that they had fled abusive, heretical English owners for the salvation and safety of Spanish territory—where they wished to be converted to Catholicism and live "free of slavery," as guaranteed by the law of refuge.[77]

We shall return to Dobson, his friends, and their fate in Spanish hands, at the end of this section—which examines the topics of escape and manumission, for the pursuit of freedom was the first path of mobility that a slave in Yucatan understandably sought. The Capt. del Canto and Dobson cases are contrasting ones in many ways, but both men exhibited a willingness to defy the conventional limitations of African ancestry; both men pursued mobility of some kind or another, despite the limitations placed on such endeavors.

Part of the paradoxical Spanish perception of black slaves both as property with a peso value and as fellow human beings was the Spanish awareness that Africans sought to resist their exploitation and objectification—or, to put it simply, that any slave would prefer to be free. This awareness took several forms: Spanish attempts to separate Africans of the same origin; Spanish fear of slave escape and uprising; and Spanish interest in legislating manumission. With respect to the first of these, slaves did not arrive in Yucatan is sufficient numbers to give Spaniards serious concern that slaves originating in the same part of Africa might be better equipped to organize or plot some act of resistance. There is indirect evidence of a possible concern of this kind. For example, when, in 1760, don Lorenzo Villaelriego purchased four slaves taken from English settlers on the Belize River, he kept them segregrated by sex, with the two men in his house and the two women in the house of an associate.[78] However, such precautions were probably not often necessary. The issue was primarily one of language—Villaelriego's four new slaves spoke English and he presumably did not—and African-born slaves in the Spanish colonies by no means spoke mutually intelligible languages (the 277 black slaves baptized in eighteenth-century Merida with

African places of origin came from 32 different locations in West Africa).[79] Thus to be able to communicate with each other and with the Hispanized blacks and pardos already in the colonies, African natives had their own motives for cooperating with Spanish efforts to teach them the Spanish language.

With respect to the second Spanish concern—fear of escape and revolt— Yucatan was not a colony where Spaniards had reason to be particularly concerned. Of course, enslaved Africans periodically fled their Spanish masters; as a nineteenth-century Brazilian observed, "flight is inherent to slavery."[80] But these overwhelmingly took the form of occasional, individual escapes by male slaves, usually resulting in recapture. In 1793, for example, an escaped slave from Campeche was caught on the road to Bacalar, jailed and questioned in Merida, and his owner informed. In 1801, another escaped slave from Campeche was apprehended, this time in Bacalar itself, and taken under armed guard from there to Merida, and thence to his master. These cases are typical of late colonial escapee patterns in that the slaves were men, they fled to another Spanish settlement (not into the hills or in search of a rural maroon settlement), and they were soon caught—these at least are the patterns found in the written record.[81]

The only large-scale escape of slaves that I have so far found on record is that of the "squad [*quadrilla*]" of twenty black men imported during the conquest years of the 1540s and recaptured around 1550 by veteran conquistador Alonso Rosado. Apparently without much difficulty, Rosado's Spanish-Maya force located the slave escapees in the hills south of Merida and brought them unharmed back to the city.[82] I have found no evidence of similar incidents from later in the colonial period, nor of maroon settlements or *palenques* established near areas of Maya settlement, nor even of the peninsula's slaves escaping Spanish control in order to join Maya communities across the colonial frontier. All this begs the following questions: Why were there no maroon communities in Yucatan? Why were there apparently no mass escapes after the mid-sixteenth century? Why are there no records of female slaves escaping?

In fact, the apparent lack of evidence can be misleading; what needs explaining is more likely the paucity, rather than total absence, of such phenomena as maroon communities and female escapees. Either way, the explanations are rooted in two factors: the nature of slavery in Yucatan; and its geography. The steady trickle of small numbers of Africans into the colony meant that new arrivals became part of a mixed-race, largely free Afro-Yucatecan community with substantial local ties—not a community of slaves who were mostly African-born and to some extent or another alienated from the larger colonial society. The exception would have been the earliest decades of the colonial period—which explains why the only case of mass escape and recapture occurred around 1550. According to the seventeenth-century chronicler, fray Diego López de Cogolludo, the attitude

of Lic. Herrera, the royal judge [*oidor*] in Merida who commissioned Alonso
Rosado to round up the escapees, was somewhat Draconian; Herrera told
Rosado not to be afraid "to use the last resort, gunning them down or killing
them at whatever opportunity presented itself."[83]

The lack of any reference to such instructions in Rosado's own *probanza*
records, the lack of evidence that any slaves were killed during the recapture, and the obvious value of the twenty men to the colonists, suggests
that Cogolludo may have embellished his account. The disconnect between
Yucatec reality and Spanish attitudes (even if the form of a plausible em-
bellishment) is revealing. Slave escapes and revolts were endemic to Spanish colonial life, beginning in the Caribbean at the turn of the sixteenth
century and continuing in Mexico and elsewhere on the mainland. Colonial chroniclers mention slave uprisings, and concomitant Spanish concerns, in most parts of Spanish America; Antonio de Herrera, for example,
writing at the turn of the seventeenth century, describes such revolts in
Honduras, Venezuela, Santa Marta, and other corners of the empire.[84] Yucatan, however, is conspicuously absent from Antonio de Herrera's account, and nor does López de Cogolludo mention subsequent slave escapes
or uprisings in the province. Maroon societies in other circum-Caribbean
regions are increasingly well documented; Yucatan is not included.[85] If
there were maroon communities in the peninsula, they must have been small
or short-lived or too remote to garner Spanish attention. The only report
of Yucatec Maya involvement in *palenque* life is from eighteenth-century
Cuba, not Yucatan.[86]

Yucatan's geography appears to have been a significant factor. The
peninsula's extensive unconquered interior may have offered some sort of
refuge for escapees in early colonial times, and there may have been unrecorded maroon settlements fed by slave refugees from the Spanish and English settlements that eventually surrounded that interior. In general in
Spanish America there were two types of terrain to which slaves escaped: remote regions within a colony, such as unsettled coasts or mountainous
country far from Spaniards; and colonial borders. In both cases, escapees
fared better if there were specific communities in which they might find
refuge. A remote region was a more effective refuge if it contained an existing maroon settlement or band; such settlements did not apparently exist
within colonial Yucatan. With respect to colonial borders, slaves might find
refuge on the other side if the laws were different. This was the case in
northern Mexico (which initially included the American Southwest) after
1829; in the 1830s, 1840s, and 1850s, black slaves regularly fled their masters in the United States to make the arduous journey into Mexico.[87]

This was also true of Yucatan's southern frontiers. For example, there
were maroon communities in Guatemala by the seventeenth century—
Thomas Gage complained in the 1630s that escapees "often come out to the
roadway, and set upon" mule trains and travelers in the highlands—and it

is possible that some slaves made their way from Yucatan to the relative anonymity of highland Guatemala.[88] In 1831, two years after abolition, former masters complained that freedom essentially gave ex-slaves a chance to escape south "into the settlements of Guatemala, from where it will be difficult to extract them."[89] Such a claim, however, probably better reflects Spanish anxieties than it does the realities of slave-escape patterns during the colonial centuries.

A more obvious destination for escapees, beginning in the late seventeenth century, was Belize; it was closer than Guatemala, it could be reached via Bacalar, the English settlements there were heavily populated by other Africans, and English–Spanish hostility was a hurdle to Spanish owners recovering property from across the frontier. But although both the Spanish and British archives contain records of slaves escaping *to* Yucatan from English masters in Belize, I have yet to find a case of a slave escaping *from* Yucatan into Belize.[90] Indeed, the British concern was with their own African slaves fleeing north into Spanish territory. There were several minor slave revolts in Belize in the 1760s, a large one in 1773, and then sporadic small ones through to the last major uprising in 1820. In all cases, British officials complained that slaves escaped either to maroon settlements in the Sibun River area and the adjacent Peten, or north to Bacalar and into Spanish Yucatan. In a typical complaint, the baymen protested in 1773 to the admiral in Jamaica that eleven rebel slaves had fled to Bacalar, where the Spanish commandant refused to give them up.[91]

Similarly, in 1802 the superintendent in Belize, Richard Basset, wrote to Yucatan's Governor Benito Pérez lamenting "the desertion of Negros" during the recent war and requesting their "restoration" to their owners. He also asked Pérez to order the commandant at Bacalar to turn over two black soldiers who had deserted from the 5th West Indian Regiment, promising that he would "pardon their offenses" if the commandant extradited them. The commandant was uncooperative, and Pérez wrote to Basset doubting his sincerity, stating bluntly that the return of escapees to Belize would happen only when the British stopped logging north of the boundary set in the 1783 treaty. Maintaining his diplomatic tone through gritted teeth, Basset seemed to sum up decades of British frustration over Afro-Belizean flight into Yucatan when he remarked to Pérez that "our ideas on the subject appear to be so different."[92]

Significantly, in none of these British complaints is mention made of maroon settlements in Yucatan. This is not surprising; the underlying contrast between Yucatan and Belize was that the Spanish colony was a society with slaves, but the British settlement soon developed into a slave society. Most Belizeans were African-born slaves and they moved seasonally in and out of Belize Town to various logging camps. In contrast, the complex, locally rooted Afro-Yucatecan communities not only failed to produce significant maroonage, but actually attracted Africans from Belize. As George Hyde, a

British merchant in Belize, commented in 1825, "so easy is their retreat to the Spaniards."[93]

It is possible that two Afro-Yucatecan communities founded close to the northern coast of the peninsula in the late eighteenth century were exceptions to the pattern—that they offered refuge to escaped slaves. These were San Fernando Ake (the settlement of black Haitian refugee soldiers created in 1796 by Spanish authorities) and San Francisco de Paula (the black logging village just south of Sisal, described by the archaeologists who recently found and surveyed it as "a small village of escaped slaves").[94] Both places were mentioned in the previous chapter, and are discussed more fully in the next, so I shall limit myself here to tackling the issue of escapees.

In my view, it is highly unlikely that either place was a maroon community. It is possible that San Fernando quietly absorbed a very small number of refugee slaves, in particular escapees from Belize, as British owners could not seek the return of their human property in Yucatan as easily as Spanish owners could. But the archival record makes it very clear that all the founding settlers were Haitian Africans who had fought with the Spaniards in their efforts to take control of the French colony of Sainte Domingue. Furthermore, the community was an officially-sanctioned *pueblo* fully incorporated into the Spanish colony—complete with a Spanish military commissioner. Reports by the commissioners detail how the town doubled in size by admitting free coloreds to settle there, for a fee, as well as some Mayas; they make no mention of escaped slaves. For example, correspondence by José Carreño, commissioner in 1806–09, shows that he was well acquainted with San Fernando's residents. So it seems improbable that more than a handful, if any, slaves escaping Spanish owners in Yucatan settled in the town disguised as free coloreds.[95]

San Francisco de Paula is a less clear case, as most of the available evidence on its history is archaeological (compiled by Anthony Andrews, Fernando Robles Castellanos, and their collaborators). This evidence, combined with passing references in two nineteenth-century sources and folk–historical memory garnered from oral sources in Sisal in 2002, strongly suggests that this was a *rancho* or hamlet (not a formal pueblo) founded around the same time as San Fernando Ake and inhabited through the nineteenth century by Afro-Yucatecans making a living from nearby dyewood trees. However, none of this evidence indicates that San Francisco's inhabitants were escaped slaves. On the contrary, this is unlikely for a number of circumstantial and contextual reasons. First, as detailed above, there is no record of mass escapes or maroon settlements in Yucatan after the mid-sixteenth century. Second, that fact is partly explained by the lack of large-scale slave-based enterprises in the colony (which did therefore not exist anywhere near San Francisco), and, third, by the existence of the Yucatan–Belize border (which was active during the decades when San Francisco was founded). Fourth, by the final decades of the colonial period, free Afro-

Yucatecans greatly outnumbered black slaves, making it demographically most likely that free-colored migrants settled the site. Fifth, Andrews and his team estimate that about eighteen of the structures in the village were houses; a very conservative estimate of three residents per house would put the total population at over fifty, a number that surely would have drawn the attention of the colonial authorities had this been an illegal maroon settlement. Sixth, this is especially the case considering the rancho's location, which was not in remote hills or on the colonial frontier, but just south of the small but important port of Sisal and not far from the road that ran from Sisal to Hunucmá and on to Merida.[96]

If outlaw communities did not exist as a refuge for escaped slaves, nor did the lifestyle of outlaw gangs seem to offer much of an alternative for Africans. One (in)famous pardo pirate, Diego Lucifer de los Reyes el Mulato, terrorized the Yucatec coast in the 1640s, sacking Campeche and Bacalar in 1642 and inspiring a royal edict in 1643 that ordered "every possible remedy to be taken to capture the mulatto pirate." But although Diego Lucifer's gang was multinational and multiracial, there is no sign that he represented a refuge for disaffected black slaves or pardos; indeed one of his kidnapping victims during the assault on Bacalar was a fellow mulatto named Luís Fernández.[97]

The colonial authorities were also concerned with armed robbery by highway gangs, especially on the camino real between Campeche and Merida, and seemed to perceive the threat as an overwhelmingly Afro-Yucatecan problem. However, surviving late colonial records show that free pardos, not black slaves, were seen as the threat, with members of local pardo militias prominently featured among suspects; José Antonio Marcín, an African escapee arrested in 1816 for robbery and other crimes along the camino real, was the exception.[98] Inventories of criminal prosecutions of the 1750s-70s include convictions of free-colored and black men, but not of slaves.[99] Criminal records for the final decade of the colonial period include twenty-three cases of alleged theft, assault, and murder in Merida and the surrounding districts of the colony (analyzed in detail in Chapter Seven). In these cases, thirteen of the accused are Afro-Yucatecan, only two of whom are slaves, both escaped Africans (Marcín being one). This is admittedly a small and late data sample, but it nevertheless does not suggest that slave escapes were a major problem or a significant root of criminal disorder in the late colony.[100]

While Spaniards were aware that slaves might wish to escape, they also knew that escape was almost always futile, and Africans may have perceived this too. Perhaps those who did flee their owners did so simply for escape's sake—to breathe free air even if only for a few days. Slave escape was not only a large-scale activity characterized by famous communities such as San Lorenzo de Los Negros in the Orizaba region.[101] It was also a small-scale phenomenon, one of truancy, or what might be called *daily maroonage*[102]— or perhaps *nightly maroonage*, as it was easier to go out without one's owner's permission at night to meet friends, drink, pursue romance, steal, or simply walk off. José Antonio Marcín's nocturnal flight from his owner in 1816 seems pointless unless we take into account the simple fact of his bondage, regardless of what his living and laboring conditions may have been. Just to walk along the highway without permission was probably motive enough for a man denied the right to do much of anything without permission. Scholars of slavery in the British colonies of North America have observed that many slaves resisted their condition not through outright escape but through local and temporary truancy, maintaining contact with slaves still on the plantation and returning to work before they could be classified—and punished—as official outlaws.[103] Daily and nightly maroonage was the Afro-Yucatecan equivalent to plantation truancy. After his arrest, Marcín did not state that his goal was permanent escape from his master, and despite his obvious motive for lying, he may have been telling the truth; for every rare case of a slave like Marcín, arrested in a Maya village at the dawn following his escape, there must have been dozens of cases of slaves making brief forays into the night and returning undetected—or detected by owners but without running afoul of colonial authorities.

Furthermore, Marcín was probably aware that escaped slaves were seldom punished by the colonial courts beyond being returned to their masters, whose displeasure was often the worse fate faced by those recaptured; the wrath of Marcín's owner was, we must assume, considered by the African to be worth risking. Individual slaves in Spanish America seem to have been less subject to physical abuse and arbitrary corporal punishment than slaves on plantations and in slave societies. Symbolic of this contrast are differences in branding practices, with individual slaves in Spanish America (Yucatan included) rarely branded on the face, even as punishment, in contrast to the experience of plantation slaves.[104] Likewise, the ease with which Marcín escaped, his speedy and accidental capture, and his return unpunished by a Spanish judge to his owner all say much about the attitude of colonial Spanish society toward African slaves. Slave owners seldom went to much trouble to prevent escapes; as we saw in the previous chapter, slaves were often entrusted to act as itinerant agents for their owners, to take mail or goods to other towns, collect goods or debts, close trading deals, or manage businesses in the owner's absence. Although I have found no cases of this in Yucatan, in other Spanish colonies owners were so confident that escaped slaves would be apprehended that slaves were occasionally sold while still on the run. The simple fact was that African slaves, like free blacks and pardos, were attached to the Spanish world, whether they liked it or not. They had nowhere else to go, as Marcín himself seemed to realize; his intended destination, upon escaping his owner's house in Campeche, was the provincial capital of Merida—arguably a leap from the frying pan into the fire.[105]

There is a further reason why slave escapes were not a major problem in Yucatan—manumission, both the pattern of owners actually freeing slaves, and the promise of manumission. I mentioned at the start of this section that Spanish awareness that all slaves preferred freedom to bondage was reflected in manumission laws. The existence of such laws—and their recognition in Yucatan—helps explain the relatively low level of escape and revolt in the colony. The right of slaves to seek their freedom through purchase, including the right to have the price of manumission fixed, and the right to pay in installments, were guaranteed by Spanish law; and although Spanish law was not in general a good guarantee of actual practice, slaves seem to have been able to exercise these rights in the colonies with some regularity.[106] This must have encouraged others to believe that working toward legal manumission was a better choice than escape—a belief that was sometimes justified, and sometimes a cruel illusion.

The legal acquisition of freedom took one of two forms: a slave's freedom was either bought, by a relative or through self-purchase; or freedom was granted by the slave's owner. The following examples all come from the last decade of the seventeenth century. María de Argaiz, owned by don Fernando López de Carvajal, purchased her own freedom and—for a hundred pesos—that of her son, Ventura Baeza. Having bought his own freedom, Tomás Peraza saved up the 225 pesos he needed to buy the freedom of his sister, María de la Rosa, who lived in the cah of Tixkokob as a slave of the town's encomendero. When Luis de Salazar, a black slave, married María de Alejos, the free-colored daughter of the pardo militia captain Juan de Alejos, the young couple immediately began to save money to buy Luis's freedom—which they were soon able to do, from the encomendera doña Catalina de Salazar y Córdova.[107]

The colony's notarial volumes also contain occasional manumission records, or *cartas de libertad* [letters of freedom; sometimes called *cartas de ahorría*]. These documents are outnumbered by about fifteen to one by records of slave sales in Merida's notarial archives. On face value, this would seem to reflect a low level of manumission, but in reality this was high relative to other parts of the Americas. Indeed, the fact that a steady stream of Afro-Yucatecans acquired freedom during the colonial centuries, albeit in quantities never exceeding a small minority of all those enslaved, marked Yucatan as a society with slaves rather than a slave society. As in other Spanish colonies with slaves, such as late colonial Buenos Aires, slaves acquired their freedom without recourse to legal conflict, or they went to court and battled tenaciously to gain concessions, if not manumission, from their owners; even where slaves lost these battles, they found allies and fought hard along the way. As in central Mexico, more women were manumitted than men, and female owners more often freed slaves than did male owners; in other words, the primary context and potential conduit to manumission was domestic service.[108] Such opportunities were far less common in either the English or French slave colonies.[109]

In many cases, freedom papers were granted with little or no explanation, leaving us to imagine contexts such as owners "rewarding" old slaves for years of service. When doña Melchora Pacheco Sepulveda Benavides died in 1691, she freed her black slave, María Riveros, in recognition of her services; doña Melchora offered no further details, but the rest of her long will reveals that María had acted for years as an important and skilled business agent for her owner, buying large quantities of goods both from top Spanish merchants and from Maya villagers. In the same decade, Capt. Don Pedro Carvajal y Montoya left freedom provisions in his will for two slaves: Pedro, who had saved his master's children from pirates during an attack on Veracruz; and Juana, a mulatta who had been his lover, given birth to one of his daughters, and nursed him in illness. A final example, this one from 1809, is that of María Jesús, a slave ordered in her master's will to serve his sister-in-law Micaela Cosgaya y Elizalde for eight years upon his death— but then to be freed and given a thirty-peso house plot and fifty pesos in cash from his estate.[110]

Other cases lack such clues; for example, in 1733, during his final months as Yucatan's bishop, don Juan Ignacio de Castorena gave freedom papers to his mulatto slave, Damián Martínez, without explaining why he chose not to sell or take Damián with him.[111] In 1777 don Antonio de Butrona, a Merideño resident in Campeche, granted Santiago Pacheco his freedom, telling us only that Santiago had been purchased 13 years earlier for 250 pesos from one of the Mugárteguis in Campeche.[112] Antonio de Arcos arrived in Yucatan in 1763 as a free "dark black" servant of the new bishop; a life-long slave in Havana, Antonio had been granted his freedom papers in the city during the British attack, managing to flee by the end of 1762 to Spain and the patronage of a new priestly employer. Another free black servant of a cathedral clergyman in Merida had also been freed in Havana before voyaging to Spain. José Ganga survived the Middle Passage at the age of eight, was sold and baptized in Havana in 1773, and gained his freedom four years later upon the death of his owner, who had stipulated it in his will. Still only twelve years old, Ganga then made his way to Spain. There he became a servant to Br. don Rafael del Castillo y Sucre, who in 1779 brought Ganga to live in Merida, where the priest had been appointed cathedral *maestre escuela* [master of divinity]. In 1780 Castillo y Sucre took over the post of vicar general from Dr. don Juan Agustín de Lousel, who had himself freed a slave at birth two years earlier; the daughter of his black slave, Rosa Lousel, was consequently named María Ignacia Liberata.[113]

On other occasions, one catches mere glimpses of manumission. When doña María Josepha Calderon de Marcos Bermejo sold a twenty-eight-year-old "esclaba ladina" named María Ramos Caldera to her grandmother for the below-market price of one hundred pesos, she stipulated that this was "on the condition that the son or daughter that she has in her belly not be kept in any way subject to servitude, and that the purchaser grant freedom to María Ramos Caldera after her days of constant and faithful service in remuneration for this"—suggesting perhaps, rather vaguely, that her grandmother free María once she had received her hundred-pesos worth of service.[114] Such glimpses can also sometimes be seen in baptism records. For example, in the first week of 1747, a slave in Merida almost died giving birth to a daughter; she was baptized María Eusebia while in labor, and when she survived both she and her baby were freed. But the baptism entry offers no more than an outline of these facts, without the details of the human relationships surrounding the event.[115]

Another incomplete but important piece of evidence on manumission patterns comes from the baptism records of black adults in Merida. These are suggested by breaking down the data to emphasize the balance between enslaved and free black adults, both by gender and by time period (see Table 5.5). The pattern for the early decades of the eighteenth century is as one would expect: Almost all black adults are slaves, with men and women in comparable numbers. Then, beginning in the 1740s, a surprising trend emerges: while slave numbers remain constant, there is a growing number of black adults categorized as free, especially among the men; from the 1740s through the 1770s, there are far more black men than women brought into Merida, and most of them are baptized as free.[116] In the 1780s, the earlier pattern mostly reasserts itself; there are still a number of free black men, but most are now slaves. The figures for the whole century give men a considerable numerical advantage (64%), while there is a notable proportion of free adults (41%); but the breakdown by time periods shows that this is skewed by those middle decades. So why this mid-century leap in free black adults? I believe two factors explain it. The lesser factor is the very slow decline of slavery as an institution in Yucatan, although this is problematic as an explanation because other signs of decline (falling slave numbers, declining prestige of slavery as an elite status marker, and minimal controversy surrounding the subject of abolition) do not kick in until later in the century.

TABLE 5.5 Gender and slave-free balance of black adults baptized in eighteenth-century Merida

| | 1710–39 | | 1740–79 | | 1780–97 | | 1710–97 | | |
	Slave	Free	Slave	Free	Slave	Free	Slave	Free	Totals (%)
Negros	78	9	45	170	47	20	170	199	369 (64)
Negras	91	3	31	25	49	7	171	35	206 (36)
							341	234	575
							(59)	(41)	

Source: AGAY-*Jesús*, Libro de Bautismos Vols. 1–6.
Note: For a breakdown by decades, see Table G.2 in Appendix G.

The predominant factor relates to the source of many of the black adults brought into Yucatan during this period—the British settlements in Belize—and the impact of the law of refuge. The first such law, applicable empire-wide, was issued by a 1693 proclamation of Charles II's. It remained in effect until 1790, but there were variations between colonies and its recognition by local authorities was uneven; its recognition in Yucatan, however, coincided with the influx of slaves from Belize from the late 1750s to the 1780s.[117] The law was technically one of religious sanctuary; it required that black slaves who fled the colonies of Protestant empires, or were captured and taken from those colonies, should both be baptized as Catholic Christians and simultaneously manumitted. Spaniards purchasing such slaves were thus obliged to baptize them in Merida as free men and women, while at the same time being unwilling to grant them full freedom of movement.

The status of these manumitted slaves was thus ambiguous. Many were like Enrique, an adult baptized in 1788 as "a free black of the Señor Colonel don Alonso Peón"—free in name, but attached to his employer and godfather in a way that put Enrique in a middling status between slavery and full freedom. Another was Juan Tomás, born in Cay Kitchen off the coast of Belize and perhaps originally christened John Thomas. He was baptized in Merida in 1788 as a "black servant [*negro moreno criado*]" of don Juan Vicente Mendicuti, who was also his godfather.[118] We will never know how Enrique and Juan Tomás felt about their free status, whether they saw it as a true or false freedom, or whether they could change employers more easily than slaves could. But presumably, for some of these manumitted new arrivals of the 1740s–1770s, the law of refuge was a step toward a life of greater freedom and mobility.

A final glimpse into manumission patterns is found in records of dispute over a slave's status, usually stemming from a promise (or alleged promise) of manumission not honored by an owner (or supposed owner). Two examples suffice. One is that of a black slave named Francisca Antonia. Sold by a Spanish sergeant in Valladolid to the curate of Tixkokob, Lic. don Francisco Martínez de Frías, Francisca worked for many years in the final decades of the seventeenth century as an agent for the curate, buying and selling goods in villages in the Tixkokob area; for this, the curate granted her manumission in his will. However, shortly before he died, he discovered that Francisca had been making a profit for herself on the side; furious, he procured a notary and dictated a revocation of the grant of liberty, ordering the slave to be sold and kept in bondage. Francisca protested, but there is no record of any response. The other example comes from from Espita in 1816, when a colored ("moreno") slave named José María Espinola petitioned the court in Merida with 250 pesos in hand, the sum "for which it is said I was sold." Espinola implied that his late owner had promised him freedom for that price; he had been working hard and saving the money for years, "thinking to free myself." But upon his owner's death, her brother-in-law claimed the slave and refused to recognize Espinola's right to purchase his own freedom. José María's efforts were not in vain; the slave's right to self-purchase was upheld.[119]

Once a slave had acquired a *carta* from his owner—and such a document could be demanded in advance of payment, thereby setting the manumission price—any payments made had to be carried over to the next owner in the event of a sale. For example, this may explain why in 1817 a slave in Havana named Francisco, valued at 360 pesos, was sold to a Spaniard in Sisal, don Tomás Aznar, for only 300 "on condition that [Francisco] serve him for 12 years in the house of the purchaser with the punctuality with which [Francisco] is accustomed, [after which] he will give him his freedom, for which reason he has discounted the excess cost of his full value." The sixty-peso difference may have been the sum that Francisco had been able to pay toward manumission from his Cuban owner. Of course, in theory, Francisco would have then had to pay the remaining sum to Aznar. Either way, the year that Francisco was to be freed was the year that slavery was finally and fully abolished in the new Mexican republic (had he stayed in Havana, of course, he would have lived out his life in a society where slavery remained legal).[120]

The significance of manumission patterns is not just that Spanish law made it possible for slaves to acquire freedom, but that the law was enforced with regularity and not apparently undermined by the slaveholding elite. More than this, the law would have been useless to slaves had Spanish colonial society not afforded them economic opportunities that were limited in many ways but nonetheless sufficient to make purchased manumission feasible. This was the case in other Spanish colonies such as Spanish Louisiana, and it was also the case in Yucatan.[121] In the previous chapter, I made the distinction between dependent and independent Afro-Yucatecan workers, demonstrating at the same time how that distinction was sometimes blurred. The relevance here of slaves working as though they were independent, or engaging in profitable enterprises in their own time, is clear: It permitted them to improve their living conditions and to pay for their own manumission or contribute to that of a relative. The ramifications of such opportunities were larger still, as they lead to two different kinds of mobility—physical and social—the topics of the next section.

But first let us return to Richard Dobson. He told officials in Merida that he reviled the heretical religion of the English in Belize and sought salvation as a "true Christian"—showing that he not only knew about refuge laws, but understood their religious underpinnings. One of Dobson's friends, an Afro-Belizean named Griglo, said that it was commonly known among slaves in Belize that the king of Spain freed slaves who fled to his colonies. The governor's office wrote to Mexico City, requesting clarification on the laws; they had been revoked in 1790, but there was general confusion during the 1790s as to what that meant. In 1795, for example, the Yucatec governor had written to the king asking for policy guidelines on how to handle the steady northward flow of Afro-Belizean refugees, but there was no record of a response. The reply from Mexico City in 1801 was not good news for Dobson. The refuge laws no longer applied, and men such as Dobson were now property of the Spanish crown; he and several of his friends were sent to Cuba "to serve the king" as slaves in the Havana arsenal.[122]

One of Dobson's friends was Julian Rechet, an Afro-Jamaican who insisted he had been a free man in Jamaica (see Table 5.6). Rechet claimed that when he traveled to Belize to join the militia there, the British tried to enslave him; escaping to Yucatan, he ended up enslaved by Spaniards.[123] The fate of Dobson, Griglo, and Rechet offers us a sobering reminder of the limits placed on men and women of African descent seeking ways out—such limits are also an integral part of the next section's discussion.

MOBILITIES

In February of 1778 a free black man named Felis Manuel Bolio, also known as Manuel Bolio and Manuel de Lara, was arrested by the Inquisition under suspicion of having committed the crime of double matrimony. The arrest took place in the city of Cartagena, on the Caribbean coast of what is today Colombia. Interrogated by church officials, Manuel explained how the course of his life had led him into bigamy.[124]

Manuel's life began in Africa, but all we know of his years before he arrived in the Americas is what he told the Inquisitors, confirmed in the record of his first marriage—that he was "a black adult native of Congo [*negro adulto natural de Congo*]." Manuel was probably enslaved in his late teens as a result of the wars in West Central Africa that fed—and were stimulated by—transatlantic slavery. He would have endured the Middle Passage most likely in a British, Dutch, or French ship, and only in the Americas sold into Spanish hands—ending up in Campeche, where he spent the earliest of his Yucatec years.

The details of Manuel's Campeche years are murky, but after that things become clearer. He was owned by a Spaniard named Bolio, who must have had business dealings in Hunucmá, as it was there that the slave was baptized as Felis Manuel Bolio. Spaniards had become heavily involved in cattle ranching in Hunucmá, which by Manuel's day had become about 10% Afro-Yucatecan. There were four Bolio cousins, one of whom was named Manuel, who owned haciendas devoted to cattle and other enterprises all around Merida in the late eighteenth century; don Manuel or one of his cousins probably owned "our" Manuel Bolio.[125]

Manuel was then sold to a prominent Spaniard in Merida named don Julián de Lara, and it is by the name of Manuel de Lara by which witnesses to his life later remembered him.[126] Either in or shortly before 1757, don Julián granted or sold to Manuel his freedom, for he appears as a "black adult," not a slave, in his marriage record of that year. Although an acquaintance of Manuel's from his Merida years later told the Inquisition that Manuel had married in Campeche, marriage records confirm that he was married in Merida—in the Afro-Yucatecan parish of Jesús, where he then settled with his bride (see Table 5.6). As we shall see in Chapter Six, it was not uncommon for Afro-Yucatecan men to marry indigenous women, and indeed Manuel's wife was a Maya, named Josepha Chan.

TABLE 5.6 Patterns of mobility of some Africans who were sometimes resident in the Yucatan, c.1540–1832

Name, Spanish racial category, status	Places of residence in chronological sequence	Time period of recorded mobility [a]
Marcos, *negro* slave, later free	Guinea, Central Mexico, Honduras, Merida	1520–48
Francisco Antonio, *negro* slave	Guinea(?), Venezuela, Spain, Merida	c.1603–44
Melchor de la Torre, free *negro* criollo	Cartagena, Spain, Merida	c.1740–63
Manuel Bolio, *negro* slave, later free	Congo, Campeche, Hunucmá, Merida, Bacalar, Havana, La Guayra, Cartagena	c.1740–78
Juan Josef Sanchez, free *negro*	Jamaica, Havana, Sancti Espiritu Is., Belize, Bacalar, Merida, Sancti Espiritu Is.	c.1780–1802
Julian Rechet, *negro* slave	Jamaica, Belize, Bacalar, Merida, Havana	c.1790–1802
Christopher Hill (aka Cristobal Gil, aka Kingston), *negro* slave	Jamaica, Belize, Merida, Belize, Bacalar, Merida, Havana	1790s–1802
Richard Dobson (aka Ricardo Dopson), *negro* slave	Jamaica, Belize, Bacalar, Merida, Havana	1790s–1802
Francisco Aznar, *negro* slave (freed 1829)	Havana, Sisal, Merida	c.1810–29
Juan Martín, free *moreno*	Santo Domingo, Veracruz, Campeche	1829–32

Sources: AGI-*Justicia* 300, 3: ff. 388–442; AGI-*Contratación* 5425, 1, 1: ff. 1–4; AGI-*Contratación* 5506, 2, 7, 1: f. 13; AGN-*Inquisición* 1131, 2: ff. 80–110; AGN-*Marina* 156, 5: ff. 171–211; AGEY-*Justicia* (Poder Ejecutivo), 2, 20: ff. 4–5; AGN-*Bienes Nacionales* 28, 65.

[a] The initial years are the earliest dates the individuals are recorded as living in the first place listed and the terminal years are the latest dates they are recorded as living in the last place listed; they therefore could have been mobile before and after these time periods. Some of the migrations recorded here were voluntary, others forced by slave traders or colonial authorities.

Josepha Chan had moved into the city from the rural village of Dzithas, leaving behind her parents, Matheo Chan and Martha Dzul, when she was in her early teens—part of a pattern of Maya migration into the city to avoid tribute obligations and find work in domestic service.[127] Josepha found work as a nun's servant, acquiring the nickname "Chepa La Monja" ("because before getting married she had served a nun"). She may have later worked for a member of the Solís family, as she was also known as Josepha Solís. By 1757 she was working for doña Petrona Argaiz, who was married to the same don Julián de Lara for whom Manuel worked. Josepha seems to have spent part of her time selling in the Merida market fish brought by Spanish *tratantes* [petty merchants] from the port of Sisal, and part of her time doing domestic chores. It was thus in the Lara-Argaiz household that Manuel and Josepha met, worked together, presumably fell in love, and married.[128]

We might imagine that for the first three years of their marriage, Manuel and Josepha were happy together, but not happy with their jobs. For during those few years they moved from one household to another, three in total, but always finding work together. They also had a child, but the baby died when just a few months old, and that seems to have been a turning point in the marriage. Restless and disenchanted, in 1759 Manuel left Josepha behind and went south to Bacalar to find work—a journey of a week or two across the colonial border and through unconquered Maya lands on a forest path described by an English traveler in 1765 as "swampy," "serpentine," and "troublesome."[129] Only at the end of this arduous journey did one reenter colonial territory near the grim little port of Bacalar.

It is not clear whether the death of his child or marital problems brought on this move, or whether problems at work led to the separation, which in turn produced the couple's estrangement. Either way, at first Manuel made regular trips back to Merida, returning for as long as three months at a stretch. But as the months turned to years the visits became less frequent and then stopped. Eventually, he moved on to Havana, and then sometime in the 1760s he lived in the Venezuelan port of La Guayra, before reaching Cartagena, where he remarried—committing the sin and crime of "double matrimony"—and settled down among the port city's black community. The community was large; there were more people of African descent in Cartagena than Spaniards or natives, which was not true of any city or town in Yucatan.[130] His second wife was, like Manuel, classified by Spaniards as "black," and when she died, he proposed to another African woman. In the autumn of 1776, he received her consent.

Couples seeking formal union in Spanish America were required to request permission to marry; this was granted, usually within a matter of days, once the priest was satisfied that neither bride nor groom were already married (and, in late colonial times, that the union did not violate laws against interracial marriage).[131] Not surprisingly, the procedure was not always followed with due thoroughness; Manuel was able to marry for the second time, roughly a decade after his first marriage, without being arrested for bigamy, because the priest in Cartagena who performed the ceremony apparently could not be bothered to confirm Manuel's claim that he was a bachelor.

We shall complete the Manuel Bolio story at the end of this chapter; for now, we leave him, happily preparing to marry again in Cartagena, and we return to Yucatan to tie together the threads of the theme of Afro-Yucatecan mobilities. Bolio's tale, thus far, illustrates several types of mobility. First, he was by no means unusual in making the transition from slave status to freedom; not only were most Afro-Yucatecans free, but in the eighteenth century, if not before, there were more free *negros* and negras than enslaved ones. Second, Bolio experienced considerable geographical mobility—from his forced journey across the Atlantic to his voluntary movements across the Caribbean (see Map 1.2 in Chapter One). For free coloreds and manumitted blacks, travel was the equivalent to escape; it underscored the fact that there was no master to stop them moving. Many of the free African men who entered into the Spanish legal record had lived in several towns within and outside Yucatan, giving the impression that African men were exceptionally mobile (see Table 5.6). This may be a false impression, given that it was often their mobility that resulted in such Africans encountering the legal system—as bigamists, for example, or as free men accused in a strange town of being escaped slaves. In contrast, parish records contain the names of hundreds of Africans who were born, married, had children, and died without ever leaving Yucatan or even Campeche or Merida.

Nevertheless, when archival glimpses into the lives of pardos are combined with the scattered evidence on the slave experience, it seems clear that itinerancy was a significant dimension of the African experience in Yucatan. The forms taken by this itinerancy included being forcibly shipped across the Atlantic, being captured as one of the spoils of war (either along the Yucatan–Belize border or off the Yucatec coast), being moved around the Caribbean basin to forts or militia bases, crossing the Atlantic between Spain and Yucatan as a servant to a Spaniard, and migrating to look for work or join relatives or flee a failed marriage.

The written record gives the impression that the vast majority of physical mobility by those of African descent in and out of Yucatan was involuntary. This partly stems from the basic patterns of the slave trade, and partly from the roles played by Afro-Yucatecans as servants and auxiliaries to Spaniards. It also reflects the high cost of long-distance (especially transatlantic) travel in the colonial period, with its lengthy licenses and irregular shipping schedules. It is rare for free Afro-Yucatecans to appear in the customs house records as independent transatlantic travelers.[132] More often they were part of a Spaniard's entourage (see Appendix C). Thus, when a black man named Juan traveled from Yucatan to Spain and back at the turn of the seventeenth century, he did so as the slave of a Spaniard, Joseph

Franquez de Ortega. Likewise, when a free black servant named Francisco crossed from Yucatan to Spain in 1638, returning to the colony two years later, he did so with his master, Capt. don Francisco Lara Bonifaz—all under a series of licenses from officials such as Yucatan's governor and customs officers in Seville. Don Francisco Núñez Melián had the same two black slaves when he was governor of Venezuela and governor of Yucatan, bringing them to Spain when he was between posts in the early 1640s. In 1643 don Juan Joseph de Vertiz y Ontañón paid twenty ducats to cross the Atlantic and another twenty ducats for his black servant.[133]

However, the written record hardly reflects the full spectrum of travel experienced by Afro-Yucatecans. Spanish bureaucracy, with its fees and licenses, was difficult to bypass for elite Spaniards with extensive business interests like Lara Bonifaz or gubernatorial careers like Núñez Melián. But lesser Spaniards, mestizos, and free coloreds were surely able to travel and do business beneath the radar of notarial bureaucracy. We only know of Manuel Bolio's travels because he was denounced as a bigamist; he must have been the tip of an iceberg that consisted of itinerant Afro-Yucatecans whose activities were never noted by colonial officials.

Whether moving involuntarily or by choice, the itinerancy of Africans placed them firmly within the Spanish colonial context, for even Yucatec-born and locally rooted Spaniards maintained connections with the larger colonial world, if not with Spain itself. By contrast, Mayas identified themselves with their lineage and their village community and lacked a strong sense of ethnic or regional consciousness; the indigenous world was a highly localized one, and the free-colored men and women who settled in Maya villages tended to become part of that world. Had Manuel Bolio settled in Josepha Chan's hometown of Dzithas, he might never have left.

The third way in which the Manuel Bolio story illustrates the theme of mobilities lies not in what he did, but in what he did not do (and in his story's end). For Afro-Yucatecans, slavery and subordination were balanced by opportunities for mobility—flight and freedom, manumission and migration, prosperity and pardo militia privileges. But there was often a catch—Capt. del Canto's wife, Augustina, almost suffering an Inquisition investigation; Richard Dobson being enslaved, rather than manumitted, by the king of Spain, because of a change in the law; Manuel Bolio was never quite able to leave behind the long arm of imperial institutions.

To further make this point, I would like to digress into two brief examples. The first is the case of Miguel Duque de Estrada. The Duque de Estrada family were prominent in Campeche business and politics through the second half of the eighteenth century and into the Independence period. Alejandro Duque de Estrada was notary to Campeche's municipal government from 1754 to 1783. His son, Miguel, enjoyed an even more illustrious career, holding various lucrative governmental posts and building a commercial empire stretching from Villahermosa to Merida, beginning in the 1780s. In the first decade of the nineteenth century, don Miguel Duque de Estrada solidified his position among Campeche's colonial elite by initiating *limpieza de sangre* or "purity of blood" proceedings for his family members, including both his parents. He also founded a school for the sons and daughters of the elite—the Escuela Misericordia, also known, in reflection of its founder, as San Miguel de Estrada.

In 1812, when don Miguel was at the height of his wealth and influence, news reached Yucatan of Spain's new liberal constitution. The Yucatec authorities immediately elected new constitutional councils for Merida and Campeche. Duque de Estrada was one of the most obvious candidates for such a post, but don Miguel's position in the new body was denied at the last minute. Why?

Three factors converged during that December of 1812. First, the 1812 constitution had defined citizenship as specifically excluding those of African descent (while including native Americans), thereby excluding the same "noncitizens" from public office. Second, Duque de Estrada had not surprisingly made enemies during the decades of his rise to power and prosperity; these enemies were ready to seize any opportunity to undermine don Miguel. Third, despite the fact that don Miguel and his father had held various governmental positions before, and despite the family's acquisition of limpieza de sangre papers, Duque de Estrada was vulnerable to the accusation that he had "the stain of African origins [*la tacha de originario de África*]."

Duque de Estrada's exclusion from the council fomented a public battle between his allies and his enemies that lasted until the old régime was restored in Spain in 1814. Like the disputes over marriage choice that had periodically popped up in Yucatan since the 1770s (discussed in Chapter Three), codified racial prejudice was used as a weapon in a fight over material spoils. Everybody in Yucatan in the 1810s knew that "African origins" were found all over the province (an 1814 census of Campeche certified 35% of the town's residents as Afro-Yucatecan "noncitizens"). They also knew that such origins did not prevent social and economic mobility (the Duque de Estrada family, as obscure as its African origins were, was a glaring example). Finally, they knew that there were limits to such mobility; where those limits lay was not always clear, making possible the Duque de Estrada affair of 1812–14.

In the end, the door that was closed in don Miguel's face did not matter, as that particular door ceased to exist in 1815. Instead, other doors opened, and like almost all members of Yucatan's elite in the last colonial decade, don Miguel successfully survived the transition to Independence; in 1821, he was elected mayor [*alcalde primero*] of Campeche. But his triumph had not occurred because the Duque de Estrada family embraced their mulatto past and convinced others that it held no shame; neither the Duque de

Estradas nor other Yucatecan Spaniards had decided to remove "the stain" from the notion of African ancestry. Instead, they opted to pretend it never existed—to include Afro-Yucatecans as citizens so that discussions of casta, calidad, and African origins need not occur again.[134]

The second brief digressive point on the limits to Afro-Yucatecan mobility has an ironic connection to the Duque de Estrada affair; it has to do with the colony's schools. During the last hundred years of colonial rule, procreating members of the Spanish élite no longer had to send their sons to Mexico City or Europe to be educated. Although the Franciscans and Jesuits provided schooling in Merida in the seventeenth century, in the following century there were at any one time at least three colleges for *gente decente* boys in the province. Most important were the Colegio de San Pedro and the Seminario de San Ildefonso in Merida, with the smaller (above-mentioned) Colegio de San Miguel de Estrada in Campeche.[135] The graduation records of these colleges have been preserved, and appear to be complete or close to it (see Table 5.7). They include 1,908 entries for the period 1722–1860, of which 2% of the attending boys were of mixed Spanish–Maya ancestry and 0.8% were Maya. The remaining 97.2% were "Spaniards." Not a single student was classified as black, mulatto, or to any degree of partial African descent.[136]

Significantly, the only time Afro-Yucatecans are recorded as resident in the colleges is in reference to their status as workers. For example, in August 1720, two West Africans, recorded as being natives of Ibo and Mina, respectively, were baptized as Pedro and Diego Lorenzo; they were listed as "free blacks," but they must have either fled owners in Belize or been purchased from slave traders shortly before baptism to be resident workers at the Colegio de San Pedro (in Pedro's case, hence his name) and the Colegio

TABLE 5.7 Racial classifications of students graduating from Yucatan's colleges of San Ildefonso, San Pedro, and San Miguel de Estrada, 1722–1860

Classification	Graduates	Time-period
Spaniards	1,854	
"Castizos"	3	
"Mestizos"	35	(1782–1838)
Mayas	16	consisting of 8 "Indios Puros" (1785–1811) and 8 "Indios" (1819–22)
Blacks or mulattoes	none	
TOTAL	1,908	(1722–1860)

Sources: Created from graduation lists in AME; also Arrigunaga y Peón (1975).

de la Compañia de Jesus (probably San Francisco Xavier, the original Jesuit seminary founded in 1618).[137]

In any highly stratified society, the creation and control of elite schools is crucial to the maintenance of class identities and divisions. Although it is true that racial classifications and boundaries were increasingly complex and ambiguous in late colonial times, the Spanish elite nevertheless maintained a consistently prejudicial attitude toward those of demonstrably or admittedly African descent. This attitude is reflected in the fact that not a single Afro-Yucatecan boy was educated in one of the elite colonial schools—despite the ironic fact that the founder of one such school had African ancestors.

Spaniards were willing to tolerate the inclusion of Mayas—but not before the 1780s, and only then in miniscule numbers. Furthermore, these were not poor native boys from the rural Maya villages, but relatively privileged boys like Miguel Pio Gonsales y Pech, who came from one of the dominant mestizo families of Maxcanú and whose mother was doña Juana Pech, an *hidalga*.[138] The perpetuation of class differences within the Maya world meant that upward social mobility into colonial society had always been possible for a small number of native nobles, especially members of the more privileged branches of dynasties such as the Pech and Xiu.

But Spaniards did not recognize a class of African nobility in the colonies. Spaniards with African ancestors could in fact attend elite schools—even found them—but only if such origins were studiously hidden and vigorously denied. Slavery was the great leveler. Slave-owning free pardos like Capt. Lázaro del Canto were far from being black slaves themselves, but there were limits to upward mobility. Not even the likes of del Canto could break open the gates of the Seminario de San Ildefonso. Don Miguel Duque de Estrada might have changed things at the turn of the nineteenth century, by opening the gates of the school he founded to Afro-Yucatecan boys and girls; but I doubt he even contemplated such a move.

Manuel Bolio had married bigamously in Cartagena without problems because the priest had accepted Manuel's claims of bachelorhood. But the priest whom Manuel asked in 1776 to perform the ceremony of what would be his third marriage was not prepared to take Manuel at his word. Because Manuel stated that he had been baptized near Merida, Yucatan, it was to that city that the priest sent a letter. Toward the end of the year it reached the old priest who had been responsible for the sacraments in Jesús parish back in the 1750s. He remembered that in those days there lived in the parish a black servant of don Julián de Lara's, commonly called Manuel de Lara, but baptized Manuel Bolio. The old priest also seemed to remember that Manuel had married an "Indian" servant of don Julián's wife's. The Inquisition was now involved, and a request for formal confirmation of Manuel's first marriage was sent from Cartagena via Mexico City to Merida.

The request from Cartagena was full of small errors, but enough of it was true to show that the Inquisitor was onto something. He stated that "Manuel de Lara (black in color), native of Bacalar, in English territory" had been denounced; that he

was married in Campeche to an Indian woman named Josepha, known commonly as La Monja [the Nun]; she now lives in the city of Merida in the house of doña Josepha Cervera, off the La Mejorada plaza; he [Manuel] remarried in the port of La Guayra with Rosalia de Lara, also colored black, by whom he was widowed, [and now] intends to marry another black woman."[139]

The entry for Manuel and Josepha's marriage was eventually found in the Jesús parish records, copied, and sent to Cartagena in January of 1778. The marriage record was accompanied by a stack of incriminating testimony compiled by Inquisition officials in Merida, including a statement from Josepha herself and corroborating testimony from those who had known the couple in the 1750s.[140]

When these documents reached Cartagena, they sealed Manuel's fate; not only had he committed bigamy in marrying a second time, but he had sought to commit the crime again with a third marriage. His sentence is missing from the records, but bigamists typically had their property seized and were often sentenced to be given two hundred lashes in public before serving five to seven years in the galleys.[141] If the condemned man survived all this, he was to return to his legal wife—which would have sent Manuel back to Merida. But the whipping alone could kill a man. If Manuel survived a whipping or was spared one, as a former slave, he would either have been condemned back into slavery, or treated like one on His Majesty's galleys. His life in the Americas began as a slave on board a ship; it probably ended likewise.

Manuel Bolio's story illustrates the ways in which Africans in the Americas moved between victimhood and agency, between suffering at the hands of European individuals and institutions, and successfully seeking opportunity "in the spirit of finding a better fortune" (in the words of Griglo, one of the Afro-Belizean slaves that fled to Yucatan).[142] Men and women of African descent could also meet with the kinds of triumphs and tragedies that awaited all those who moved within (or in and out of) the Spanish colonial world—an improved working environment, the joy of a new marriage, the death of a child, or condemnation by the Inquisition simply because divorce did not exist.

Capt. del Canto and Manuel Bolio both sought ways up, but Bolio eventually also sought a way out. The aspirations and decisions of these Afro-Yucatecans, the mobility they achieved, and the limitations that Spaniards placed on them, all have implications for identity and community. In short, did Canto and Bolio see themselves as Afro-Yucatecans—not in name (the term is invented by me), but in the sense that they saw themselves as defined in part by membership in a community comprising others of African descent? This is the question tackled in the next chapter.

CHAPTER SIX

Communities

I declare that my parents, and other ancestors listed here, are of the casta of mulattoes and mestizos. —Isabel Toquero, 1708[1]

I decided to make my way to Bacalar in order to become a Christian and be free of slavery. —Richard Dobson, 1800[2]

THE STORY OF ISABEL TOQUERO

At the end of August 1705, a thirty-year-old woman was locked in Cell No. 19 at Inquisition headquarters in Mexico City. She was described by her jailers as "slender in build, the color of cooked quince, with long curly black hair, brown eyes, and an aquiline face."[3] Her name was Isabel Toquero and she had been born in a small Yucatec Maya village. How had she ended up so far from home and a prisoner of the Holy Office?

Isabel was born in 1675 in Dzonotake, on the eastern end of the colony (see Map 6.1). Her parents were pardos, Gaspar Toquero and Isabel Medina, and in Yucatan she was always referred to as a parda. She grew up in the village, learning from her mother how to thread and weave cotton, the occupation of almost all women in Yucatan's rural settlements (whether they were pardas or Mayas). By the age of sixteen, her father had died and her mother married her off (as Isabel later put it) to a local boy, Lucas Tejero. Lucas was eighteen, the mestizo son of Isabel Tapia (who, despite her surname, was consistently described as an *india*). Like Isabel's own father, Lucas's father had been a pardo militia officer. Isabel's father had been a captain, but died working his cornfields. Lucas's father had only been a sergeant, but he enjoyed something of a posthumous, local reputation as a hero of the wars against the English and other pirates; he was, in the words of a pardo ensign, "the Sergeant Tejero who was killed when the enemy invaded the village of Tihosuco." Lucas had not followed his father into militia service; he worked some cornfields between the villages of Dzonotake

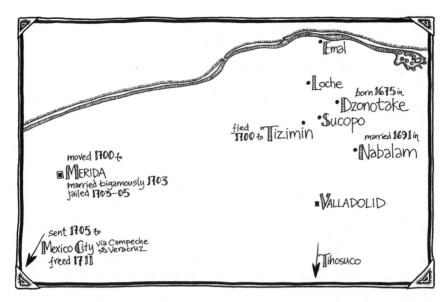

Map 6.1 The world of Isabel Toquero (showing the places mentioned in her life story from birth in 1675 to her transfer to Mexico City by the Inquisition in 1705).

and Sucopo, did some local transporting and peddling of goods, and some weeks took work up at the small port of Emal.[4]

Married in June 1691, in nearby Nabalam, the teenage couple settled in Dzonotake and immediately began having children. In less than a decade, Isabel gave birth four times—to María, Manuel, Juana, and Theodora, all of whom survived. While Lucas labored away from the village, Isabel stayed in Dzonotake; she took care of the children and "sewed clothes, work she knew how to do well." One Spanish curate assigned to the region in the 1690s later said that at first the couple seemed "very much in accord [*muy conformes*]," but after a few years "came discord."[5]

Then, one afternoon in 1700, Isabel's life changed dramatically; Lucas came home unexpectedly and found his wife in the arms of another man, "en fragante delicto" (as another local Spanish priest later put it). Isabel's lover was Joseph, who was married to one of her sisters. One witness later claimed that the two had been together on other occasions, but most witnesses never knew who Joseph was, referring to him as "some guy [*un moso*]." In another version, Lucas caught the two lovers in Joseph's house in Sucopo. Either way, Lucas chased Joseph off; in the most detailed account, Lucas "wishing to kill the perpetrator, forced him to flee, catching only his horse and his hat that he left behind, and [Lucas] then grabbed his wife." One witness claimed Lucas "punished" Isabel; most agreed that he wanted to kill her. Either way, she too escaped that same afternoon and made it to Tizimin, where she took refuge in the convent.[6]

Isabel never returned home. After three months, a local sub-curate, Br. don Nicolás Gregorio Carrión, took her to Merida. In Carrión's version of events, Lucas had been coming around the convent looking for Isabel "to get his hands on her and kill her"; the priest thus took her to the city to protect her from her vengeful husband. In Isabel's version, there was no further contact with her husband; Carrión simply took her to his house in Merida, where she spent a year working for him as a domestic servant. Two more years passed, and Isabel, apparently convinced that she had left her family behind for good, decided to remarry. In May 1703, she celebrated nuptials with Pasqual Campero, a local pardo barber and estancia worker. His father, Francisco Campero, was the manager of an estancia just outside Merida; his mother, Clara Pech, was from an old Maya family in the Merida neighborhood of Santiago. Isabel's second marriage took place in Merida's Afro-Yucatecan parish, witnessed by various free-colored friends of the Campero family. The best man or patron was don Diego de Ancona and his cousin doña María Magaña, who was an encomendera and owned the estancia where Pasqual and his father worked.[7]

Isabel surely hoped her second marriage would turn out better than her first. Unfortunately, married life with Pasqual lasted barely two months—it only took that long for Carrión (the priest who had brought Isabel to the city a few years earlier) to find out she had remarried, and to denounce her to the Inquisition. Within a few weeks, Inquisition officials garnered sufficient evidence to arrest Isabel and place her in the convent of nuns; she soon "scaled the walls" one night and escaped, but before the end of July was back in the convent.[8] If events seemed to move quickly in July 1703, after that the wheels of Inquisitorial justice moved at their characteristically slow pace; it would be five long years before a final judgment was passed.

Isabel spent the next two years as a prisoner in the convent while officials added minor details to a case that had essentially already been made: during the summer of 1703, priests in Yucatan gathered testimony on both of Isabel's marriages, forwarding the case to Mexico City in December; in January its receipt in the viceregal capital was acknowledged; finally, in May, Inquisition officials ordered a fuller investigation; that took place in and around Dzonotake in the summer of 1704; the paperwork was eventually assembled and forwarded to Mexico City at the end of the year, but not until the following spring was Isabel sent down to Campeche, where she spent a month or so in an Inquisition cell awaiting the right papers for her to be put on a ship to Veracruz; arriving in Veracruz in July 1705, she spent several weeks there before an escort arrived to take her to the Inquisition jail in Mexico City.[9]

During the autumn of 1705 Inquisitors in Mexico City repeatedly questioned Isabel, teasing from her further minor details of the story. Interrogators managed to catch her telling half-truths and contradictions. For example, having said two years earlier that a Maya named Diego Chan had told her Lucas was dead, she now claimed it was a mulatto named Juan Primero. She also offered several weak explanations as to why, at the time of her second marriage, she gave her name as Isabel Baeza, and likewise changed her parents names to Baeza and Alcocer, claiming the family was from Valladolid. In short, the name-changing suggested that Isabel knew she was committing bigamy. She also claimed to have one child, not four, then later admitted to having four, saying she had thought it necessary only to mention the eldest. Perhaps Isabel thought Inquisitors would judge her more harshly if they knew how many children she had left back in Dzonotake; or perhaps it was easier to live with the pain of missing them, after five years of separation, if she pretended that the three youngest had never existed.[10]

The *publicación*, or publication of witnesses (effectively a detailed indictment), was made that autumn, but Isabel was then left to sit in her cell for two and a half years awaiting final judgment. The wait and the conditions of her incarceration must have taken their toll on her health; twice in 1706 a physician was called in to attend to her. Then, in July 1708, she was called to confess to her crime once more, the application of torture was deemed unnecessary, and she was condemned to one hundred lashes in public, to exile from New Spain, and to serve three years service in the Hospital for the Poor. The record shows that only the last of these was carried out. Isabel spent a year and a half in the Hospital of Nuestra Señora de las Angusticias before requesting a transfer on the grounds of ill health; she then served the rest of her sentence in the Hospital of Jesús Nazarino. In July 1711, she wrote a petition, in her own hand, requesting release (see Figure 6.1; the petition is reproduced in full in Appendix A).[11]

Two days later Isabel was freed; she was thirty-six years old. There is no record of where she spent the rest of her life. Did she try to return to Dzonotake, to see the legal husband she had fled and the children she had not seen for eleven years? Did she try to see her illegal second husband in Merida, whom she had not seen for eight years? More likely, she stayed in Mexico City. The two lives she had built in Yucatan, and the two communities that had provided the network that had supported those lives, were now far away, both in time and space. She probably had no desire to see Lucas, and Pascual had probably moved on and married legally. Even aside from these issues, the cost of getting back to Yucatan was prohibitive. Instead, Isabel probably forged a third life among the large free-colored population of the viceregal capital.

The Isabel Toquero story prompts a number of questions about community—the focus of this chapter. Was there an Afro-Yucatecan community, or communities? Or were Afro-Yucatecans more often members of multiracial communities defined less by race and more by other factors? Either way, how were such communities constructed and defined? In theory,

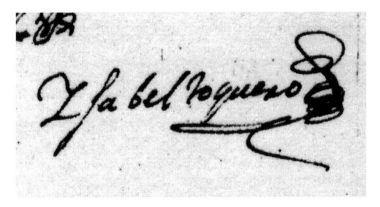

Figure 6.1 Signature of Isabel Toquero, 1711. Toquero was an Afro-Yucatecan convicted of bigamy in 1708. The document is reproduced in full in Appendix A. Source: AGN-*Inquisición* 519, 3: f. 397r.

there are myriad foundations upon which a social group might build a community—by which I mean a body of people consciously bound together by the sense of having something in common (i.e., something those outside the community lack). In practice, I suggest that there were six potential bases of community for Africans and residents of African descent in Yucatan: (1) culture and religion of native African origin; (2) Christian identity; (3) ethnic or racial classification; (4) occupation; (5) kinship and family life; and (6) location.

My approach to these themes in this chapter is as follows. I begin with descriptions of the two major population centers in the peninsula, Merida and Campeche, emphasizing where and how Afro-Yucatecans fit into the urban landscape. I then discuss other locations where the Afro-Yucatecan presence was significant. Finally, I look systematically at the six community bases identified here in order to answer the questions posed above.

AFRO-CAMPECHE

For its first two colonial centuries, San Francisco de Campeche was a small, sleepy port town. It was built right on the waterfront, with its main plaza open to the sea (see Map 6.2). When the sea was calm, the waves that lapped at the town's edge were so small they were barely audible in the plaza; on other occasions, the sea came rushing into the plaza, and flooded the streets, which had consequently been cut deep with high pavements. The downtown streets were narrow and stuffy; when the breeze died down, the smell of fish and other odors wafted in from the bay, and at dusk the mosquitoes were a torment.[12]

Map 6.2 Early colonial Campeche. Map sent to the king by Governor Esquivel in July 1663. The walling in of the center (an area running four blocks in three directions from the plaza, including the Afro-Yucatecan parish but excluding the Maya ones) was not done until later in the century. The Afro-Yucatecan parish church of Jesús can clearly be seen located a block inland from the plaza and cathedral. Source: AGI-*México 1006*; *Mapas y Planos-México 60*, I, 1. Archivo General de las Indias, Seville.

As Yucatan's main gateway to the outside world, Campeche must have seemed less isolated than the rest of the colony; yet for its first two centuries, in a typical year only one or two ships a month came in from Veracruz or Caribbean ports. A ship came from Spain at the rate of less than one a year before 1600, and only two a year in the decades after 1600, while the occasional vessel from the Canary Islands brought wine (but little else).[13] Beginning in the 1580s, Sisal's port rivaled and periodically surpassed Campeche as an entry point for ships that had crossed the Atlantic.[14] Fleets came to Campeche only under exceptional circumstances—such as the dozen ships that took refuge in the bay in September 1599, as a hurricane scattered the annual flota from Spain to Veracruz.[15] Ships had to anchor out in the bay, their arrival prompting a frenzy of activity along the dock as boatmen set off to meet the ship and others prepared for the landing of passengers and sailors, African slaves, and goods imported from other corners of the empire. Occasionally, such ships were hostile, and the frenzy of activity moved in the opposite direction, away from the shore, to the interior hills and up the camino real.

When John Ogilby compiled *America*, his massive volume of descriptions of New World colonies published in 1670, he briefly described Campeche as

a great Town, consisting of about three thousand Houses or more, when first conquer'd by the Spaniards; who found such Monuments of Art and Industry in it, as did clearly argue, that the Place had been once possess'd by some People that were not barbarous. It is now call'd St. Francisco, and was surpriz'd in the Year 1596 by Captain Parker, an *English*-man, who took the Governor himself and some other Persons of Quality with him, together with a Ship richly laden with Gold and Silver, besides other Commodities of good value.[16]

This portrait paints the town as a wealthy Spanish settlement built upon the ruins of some ancient civilization. The Mayas who comprised most of the population of the town and its environs in the colonial period are not directly mentioned (though perhaps given the passing slap of being called "barbarous"); there is no hint of an African presence at all.

Ogilby's omission is not surprising, but it is telling. Africans had become an essential, substantial, but—to Europeans—invisible part of the fabric of a town such as Campeche. As we have seen in previous chapters, enslaved Africans were perceived as property, and thus no more worthy of mention than the horses and carriages of the Spanish elite, or the furniture in their houses. But, like horses and furniture, Africans were needed, they were ubiquitous—and they were taken for granted.

Campeche was founded in 1540, two years before Merida was established and five or six years before Spaniards could be confident that their third invasion of the peninsula had produced a permanent colony. Because African slaves were a part of the invasion company led by the Montejos, they were integral to Campeche's development from the very start. As builders, laborers, and supervisors of local Maya workers, black men would have played central roles in Campeche's evolution in the 1540s and 1550s—as the *villa* grew from little more than a fortified camp on the beach, to a cluster of wooden houses, to a small grid or *traza* of urban blocks spreading out from the central plaza (see Map 6.2). Spanish Campeche was located in the ceremonial center of a group of Maya villages—part of a small kingdom ruled in the 1530s by a priest of the Pech dynasty (Ah Kin Pech, hence "Campeche").[17] This settlement strategy had been attempted disastrously in Chichén Itzá in the early 1530s but successfully in Tiho (upon which Merida was built after 1542). The strategy facilitated access to Maya labor and cut stone (the masonry of the small pyramids, platforms, and temples that characterized Mesoamerican ceremonial centers); it also allowed the invading elite to erect the buildings that symbolized the new power structure (the church, governmental offices, and the homes of the senior conquistador families) on the same sites as those that symbolized the defeated power structure (the precolonial temples and palaces).

At some point, perhaps from its inception, Campeche's planners envisioned the port town extending away from the shore to enclose within its walls all the neighboring Maya villages (likewise the plan in Merida). But this never happened; the walls took centuries to complete and left important Maya settlements such as San Román outside the town's defensive perimeter. The church, meanwhile, was initially built as a tiny masonry building in the middle of the plaza; the larger church that sits today on the north side of the plaza was not started until 1609 and took the whole of the seventeenth century to complete.[18]

The town was founded by thirty conquistadors, each receiving an encomienda of Maya villages in the southwest of the peninsula. But there were no mines or other lucrative sources of income in the region, and the rapid decline of the Maya population that had begun in the 1530s continued into the next century. Even the sugar plantation set up by the elder Francisco de Montejo in the 1530s in Champotón, a little to the south of Campeche, was abandoned in the 1550s because Montejo had temporarily lost access to his encomienda, other Maya workers could not be procured in sufficient numbers, and the plantation was not profitable enough to finance the purchase of African slave laborers.[19]

Campeche's Spaniards therefore soon came to depend less upon their encomiendas and more upon commerce with the outside world—with Santo Domingo, Veracruz, and above all Havana. From the onset, African slaves were a part of this commerce. Half of the founding families of the town received licenses to bring domestic slaves, mostly from Havana, into their new households (Cuba seems to have been a source of African slaves, imported both legally and illegally, throughout the early colonial period). The Havana–Campeche slave trade went both ways. The Montejos and their allies had developed a steady trade in Maya slaves in the 1530s, selling them primarily in Havana. Although such a trade was illegal after 1542, it was continued into the 1550s (and to a lesser extent after that) and is the most common accusation levied against the Montejo faction in the governor's *residencia* records. However, there is evidence that some African slaves were among the hundreds of unfortunate Mayas shipped to Cuba. In 1548, for example, Campeche's Spaniards were allegedly unable to collect sufficient cloth, wax, and cacao from their encomienda Mayas to pay for the imported clothing and foodstuffs sitting on a ship in the bay; they were therefore forced to part with a few of their African slaves.[20]

The small scale of early colonial Campeche—and the close quarters in which Spaniards, Mayas, and Africans lived, worked, and died together—is vividly illustrated by the town's first cemetery. This was located in the central plaza, a site that was recently excavated by archaeologists. The dig revealed not only the foundations of the late sixteenth-century church, but an adjacent burial ground containing the remains of over 180 residents of early colonial Campeche (see Map 6.3). This was certainly the main burial ground for the town from its founding well into the seventeenth century—and probably its only cemetery for the town's first half-century or so. The evidence dug up in the plaza is fascinatingly relevant to Afro-Yucatecan history for several reasons.

First, at least 13 (and perhaps as many as 23) of the more than 150 burials contained Africans, providing vivid material evidence to complement archival proof that black slaves were an integral part of Campeche's history from its very genesis. This material evidence was found in both the teeth and bones of the buried Africans. An analysis of the isotopes in a chemical called *strontium* found in the enamel of some of the men's teeth linked them hydro-geologically to the bedrock of West Africa, where they must therefore have been born and spent at least the first three years of their lives;

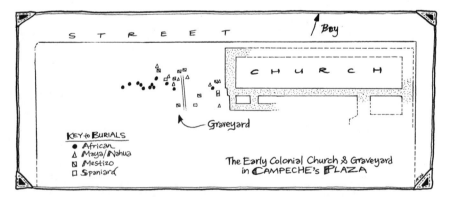

Map 6.3 The church and graveyard of early colonial Campeche, based on archaeological evidence. Source: Map based on drawings by Gustavo Coronel in Coronel Sánchez et al. (2001: 193) and Tiesler Blos and Zabala Aguirre (2001: 206).

more specifically, the strontium data suggest that they were native to the El Mina region. They were therefore slaves, at least when they came to the Spanish colonies (Africans did not migrate voluntarily from El Mina to sixteenth-century New Spain). Not all the Africans buried in the plaza were African-born; an analysis of the teeth of infants buried with African adults suggested that the children were born locally, most in Campeche but at least one elsewhere in the Yucatan peninsula.

Several men and women also had decorative incisions on their incisors, of the kind made by West Africans (see Figure 6.2). These teeth modifications were achieved through a combination of precision chipping and filing; comparable markings have been found on the teeth of buried African slaves in Cuba and other Caribbean sites, all differing clearly from dental decorations made by native Americans.[21] In the Campeche case, we have no way of knowing if such incisions were only made in Africa, or if Africans in early colonial Yucatan continued such practices. But Africans arrived in Yucatan throughout the colonial period with marks on their teeth and skin that reflected the cultures from which they had been taken. For example, Joseph de Padilla, an African-born slave of the Guipuzcoan merchant Juan Antonio de Padilla, was brought to Campeche in 1699 at the age of twenty-two; his description included a reference to "his right cheek, ploughed, and a scar on

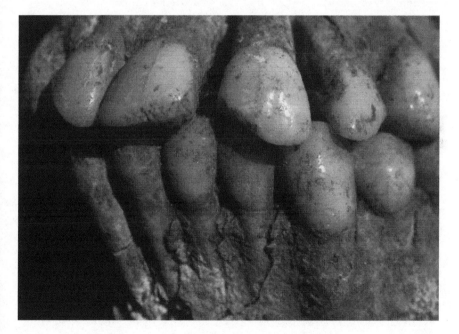

Figure 6.2 Tooth chipping of the upper and lower incisors belonging to an African man buried in Campeche's plaza in the early colonial period. Source: Photograph taken by, and reproduced courtesy of, Vera Tiesler. (See also Tiesler 2002: 278.)

his forehead," the "ploughed [*aradado*]" cheek probably describing parallel lines acquired through ritual scarification—part of coming-of-age rites in parts of West Africa.[22]

Second, the cemetery was used to bury all residents of the city. It was thus a multiethnic site; in addition to the bodies of Spaniards, the graveyard contained Mesoamericans—mostly Mayas, but no doubt some of the Nahuas who fought as allies with the invaders, and their descendents—as well as Africans, and the mulattoes and mestizos that were their early mixed-race offspring (see Map 6.3). It was also an unambiguously Christian site; the bodies were put in the ground stretched out on their backs, laid to rest according to colonial Spanish practice, to the exclusion of offerings or any other material evidence of African or Maya cultural expression.[23] All this reflects the multiethnic nature of the town; the proximate living and working environment of new settlers, native workers, and imported slaves— and the processes of miscegenation and culture change that began with the inception of Spanish colonies; and the tight control that Spanish priests were able to exercise over the burial ground located in the main plaza beside the town's main church.

Thus African slaves, as much as Maya subjects, were to be Christians and buried as such in holy ground; in early Campeche, that meant the plaza's graveyard. But intimacy, interaction, and mutual dependence did not undermine the social hierarchy; Campeche's residents were not equal, and that is reflected in the details of how and where people were buried in the plaza.

As Map 6.3 illustrates with a representative sample of burials, not all graves were equally close to the church. Spaniards tended to be closest to the church walls, although the location of Spanish graves is not dramatically different from that of native and mestizo ones. However, Africans were clearly buried together, apart from other groups and noticeably farther from the church. This spatial manifestation of inequality had a further dimension, one not reflected in the two-dimensional map. The only mass or multiple burial was of Africans; in one case, five Africans were interred in the same grave. All non-Africans were given individual burials.[24]

One final aspect of the archaeological findings in the Campeche plaza is worth mentioning. An analysis of the teeth in the mouths of buried non-Spaniards revealed that Mayas experienced the worst tooth decay (23% decay level), whereas mestizos and Africans had lesser levels (10% for mestizos, 10% for Afro-Yucatecans born in the peninsula, 12% for those born in Africa). Spanish teeth were not tested; but assuming their decay level was the least, this illustrates once again how Afro-Yucatecans were in the middle in multiple ways.[25]

Initially, then, the Spanish parish of Campeche provided the sacraments to both Spaniards and their non-Spanish slaves, servants, and dependents. At first, the church in Campeche's plaza even serviced the Mayas of the surrounding villages, although most Mayas were soon administered in spiritual terms by the small churches that were built in their neighborhoods. The church in the plaza was deemed adequate to Campeche's size in 1599 by the colony's bishop, fray Juan Izquierdo; he wrote to the king that "the town of Campeche, on the shore of the sea, has a church of reasonable size that easily accommodates the people," and that in view of "the ongoing risk" of attacks by "the enemy," seeking "to sack and rob it," it seemed to the bishop that "the town should not take on the costs of either new churches or ornaments."[26]

Nevertheless, six years later the bishop's successor, don Diego Vásquez de Mercado, formally asked Campeche's cabildo for their opinion on the matter; the cabildo submitted that a new church was urgently needed, as the old one was in a state of disrepair and was so small that many parishioners had to stand in the graveyard during mass (and the services during major religious festivals were held instead in the Franciscan convent). In 1609, ground was broken for the new church, located adjacent to the old one (see Map 6.2; the new church is more or less the same structure that is today Campeche's cathedral). But its construction was as protracted as the raising of the fortifications intended to surround the town; both projects dragged on for the entire century, with Campeche's new church finally deemed complete and blessed by Bishop Reyes in 1705. The Franciscan López de Cogolludo wrote in the mid-seventeenth century that "because the [existing] church was so small, there began the building of a much bigger one, and although a large portion of it was done, the work had stopped for many years, for lack of funds dedicated to its construction, as every day there was great poverty in all Yucatan."[27]

Meanwhile, as the town grew, separate churches and a parish were established for black and mulatto residents. The cult of the Black Christ was established in San Román, a Maya village on the edge of Campeche that had received Nahua conquistador-settlers in the 1540s and settlers of African descent during the colonial centuries (when the town's defenses were completed in the late seventeenth century, San Román was left just outside the walls). Another Maya village at the edge of Campeche, founded or renamed Santa Lucía and assigned in encomienda to doña María Gertrudis de Echartea, was according to one source an early colonial neighborhood of Africans and Mayas.

But the main Afro-Yucatecan parish was located within the town center. Like its equivalent in Merida, and likewise called variations on the name "Jesús," the parish was in the middle—between Spaniards and their church on the main plaza, and Mayas and the cah-barrios that orbited the town like satellites. The Jesús church was located a mere block inland from the plaza (it is visible on Map 6.2), initially built as an open chapel in the 1560s and expanded over the ensuing centuries into the large, austere stone structure that stands on the same corner today.[28] In the 1630s, fray Francisco Cárdenas y Valencia noted that in addition to the main church there were now also two small Franciscan churches or *ermitas*, one of which was dubbed Santo

Nombre de Jesús, "and in which the sacraments are administered to the blacks [*morenos*] of this town."[29] The Jesús church was sacked and its records burned in 1685, when pirates looted and torched the whole town, and after that its parish books seem to have been kept in the main church on the plaza. There was also a hospital, called *Misericordia*, for blacks and mulattoes. In 1724, the church of Santa Ana, farther from the plaza than Jesús, became the center of the Afro-Yucatecan parish. During the eighteenth century Afro-Yucatecans were still served by the Jesús church, but the central blocks of Campeche became dominated by elite Spanish homes; by 1830 the church was no longer described as exclusively for blacks and mulattoes.[30]

In the 1780s, Campeche was described thus in Alcedo's famous geographical dictionary:

The city is small, defended by three towers, called La Tuerza, San Roman, and San Francisco; and these are well provided with artillery. It has, besides, a parish church, a convent of the order of San Francisco, another of San Juan de Dios, in which is the hospital bearing the title of Nuestra Señora de los Remedios; and, outside of the city, another temple dedicated to St. Roman; to whom particular devotions are paid, and who is a patron saint. In this temple there is held in reverence an image of our Saviour, with the same title of San Roman, which, according to a wonderful tradition, began, previous to its being placed here, to effect great miracles; accordingly, it is said, that a certain merchant, named Juan Cano, being commissioned to buy it in Nueva España, in the year 1665, brought it to this place, having made the voyage from the port of Vera Cruz to the port of Campeche in twenty-four hours. The devotion and confidence manifested with regard to this effigy in this district is truly surprising. There are also two shrines out of the town, the one Nuestra Señora de Guadalupe, and the other El Santo Nombre de Jesus, which is the parish church of the *Negroes*."[31]

Afro-Campechanos, then, lived and worked all over the town and its environs. They worked as domestic servants, in construction, and in the various urban and rural occupations detailed in Chapter Four; in this respect, their lives were not much different than those of their counterparts in Merida and other corners of the peninsula where Spaniards settled. But there were several aspects of life in Campeche that made it unique in the colony, all related to its location on the coast.

First, there was the heavy labor involved in loading goods on and off ships anchored in the bay, rowing the boats that transported these goods to and from the port, and loading them on and off what passed for docks along the town's seafront. Black slaves and other Afro-Yucatecans did much of this work, although for most of the colonial period Campeche was not a busy port; activity was seasonal, with prevailing winds tending to bring ships from Caribbean ports (and thus from Spain too) only in the summer months, with annual arrivals (before 1770) ranging from none at all to seldom more than a dozen.[32]

However, in the seventeenth century another type of shipping industry labor was added to the Afro-Campechano experience. There was some ship construction going on by 1620, when fray Antonio Vásquez de Espinosa wrote that there was "excellent timber" around Campeche, "for which reason stout ships are built in its harbor."[33] Evidence suggests that in 1650 Campeche's first major shipyard was established by don Antonio Maldonado de Aldana, who was accused by Governor Esquivel in 1666 of illegally exploiting Maya labor to cut dyewood, build ships, and trade the logs in Havana and Veracruz. Part of Maldonado's defense was his assertion that he used his twenty-four black slaves to do the logging and shipbuilding work, with Maya workers merely assisting.[34] In other words, the Africans (as laid out in previous chapters) acted in skilled and supervisory roles, and were elemental to the development of Campeche's shipbuilding industry.

A final dimension to life in the port town for Afro-Yucatecans was its vulnerability to pirate attacks. Although (shown in Chapter Four) escaped black slaves and free-colored men were members of pirate crews, even captains, there were probably fewer black pirates attacking Campeche and the coasts of the peninsula than there were Afro-Yucatecans defending the colony as militiamen (detailed in Chapter Five). Dampier offers vivid descriptions of its seizure by English privateers in 1659 and again in 1678—a few years after Dampier himself visited the town, which he described as making "a fine shew," with its houses of "good Stone" and "a strong Citadel . . . planted with many Guns." Despite this show of defensiveness, according to Dampier, the privateer captain in the 1659 attack, Sir Christopher Mims (or Myngs), took the town after giving its inhabitants three days warning because "he scorned to steal a Victory." The 1678 privateers did adopt a surprise attack, but the people of Campeche seemed to aid them in their strategy; approaching the town at dawn, the privateers were themselves surprised to be welcomed by the locals, who took them to be Campeche's own militiamen returning from a sortie against rebellious Mayas in the countryside.[35]

One suspects that most of the tales of pirate encounters written by the likes of Dampier and Exquemelin in the seventeenth century were apocryphal; but assuming that this one has a kernel of truth, one wonders if Campechanos misidentified the attackers because, from a distance, both the local militia and Mims's pirate company looked like ragged bands of armed men of various colors. If so, behind the story's irony lies the fact that by the late seventeenth century, Campeche's Spanish elite had come to rely on—and take for granted—Afro-Yucatecans not only as a labor source in local households, businesses, and shipping, but also in Spanish efforts to defend the colony from Maya rebels to the south and piratical enemies off the coast.

Campeche's location made it both important and vulnerable from the late sixteenth century to the turn of the eighteenth; in the eighteenth century, its location made it increasingly important to the colony, and thereby more prosperous. The late colonial growth of the black and free-colored population—the increase in the numbers of Afro-Campechanos in various occupations—was tied to the economic development of the port town. This development was in turn a result of the increased trade between the town (or city, as it became in 1777) and other colonial ports, particularly Havana, after 1770. In that year the free trade license was extended to Campeche, with dramatic effects upon shipping activity. In the first half of the century only about a dozen ships had entered Campeche's harbor annually, and in the twelve years prior to 1770 not a single ship had put into the port (at least not according to official records). Yet in 1802 some 960 ships visited Campeche.[36]

As Campeche became part of a commercial and maritime network of Spanish ports in the Gulf of Mexico and the Caribbean, so did the African inhabitants of those ports become to some extent economically and socially linked. The demand for slave labor on late eighteenth-century sugar plantations around Campeche has already been mentioned, but there was also a heightened demand for labor in other industries, in the port, and in the households of the prosperous local elite—a demand which drew into Yucatan *negros* and pardos, the enslaved and the free.

The concentration of Africans in certain barrios of Campeche, the high rate of marriages within those barrios, the rapid growth in free-colored numbers, and the shared experience of working in certain occupations combined to create a sense of community. To what extent that community was

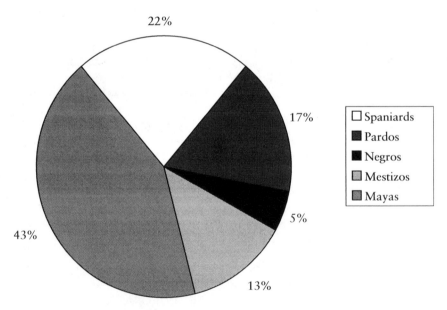

Figure 6.3 Racial distribution of the Campeche district population of 23,479 in 1779. Source: Based on data presented in Patch (1993: 234).

defined by the African ancestry of many of its members is the subject of this chapter's later sections.

As seen in Figure 6.3, by 1779 Spaniards and Afro-Yucatecans each represented close to a quarter of the Campeche district population. In the environs of Campeche in the 1780s, pardos were settling in some Maya communities in similar numbers to Spaniards, although non-Mayas remained very much a minority (see Table B.4 in Appendix B). By the final decade of the colonial period, Afro-Yucatecans were a third of the city population—in reality, more than a third, as many residents categorized as Spanish, mestizo, or "Indian" had some African ancestry. In 1830, Campeche was described as having six native barrios, each with a Maya governor or cacique (Guadalupe, San Francisco, La Ermita, Santa Lucía, Santa Ana, and San Román);[37] the persistence of colonial political structures (in practice, if not in name), and the disappearance in the 1820s of casta labels, disguised the fact that these "Maya" barrios were in some ways Afro-Maya neighborhoods. Indeed, by the end of colonial times Campeche itself had undeniably become an Afro-Yucatecan city.

AFRO-MERIDA

"The city is built on a marvelous site," wrote fray Antonio Vásquez de Espinosa of Merida in 1620, "with bright skies and wholesome air." Founded in 1542 on the Maya site of Tiho, the pyramids, temples, and palaces of the native city were sufficiently impressive to remind the Montejos of the Roman ruins of Merida in Spain. Yucatan's Merida was erected slowly in the heart of Tiho—as the city's Mayas, who remained its majority population, continued to call it throughout the colonial centuries. The main pyramid on the plaza, facing the new cathedral, was not demolished until the mid-seventeenth century (see Figure 6.4). Surrounding the Spanish downtown, or *traza*, were five Maya communities, distinct pueblos with their own Maya municipal governments that were nevertheless part of greater metropolitan Merida (see Map 6.4). This layout gave a somewhat illusory impression of size; as Espinosa put it, Merida "covers the area of a very large city."[38]

The black slaves and free coloreds who settled the new city along with their Spanish masters and employers in the 1540s and 1550s were assigned plots on the edge of the traza—placing them symbolically in a middle position between the Spanish center and the Mayas of the city's outer neighborhoods. Both to the east and west there were two Maya *cah-barrios* (as I have dubbed them, combining the Maya term for municipal community with the Spanish term for an urban neighborhood); the fifth was some distance to the north, making the areas south and north of the center the obvious settlement zones for nonelite Spaniards, mestizos, and people of African descent (see Map 6.4).

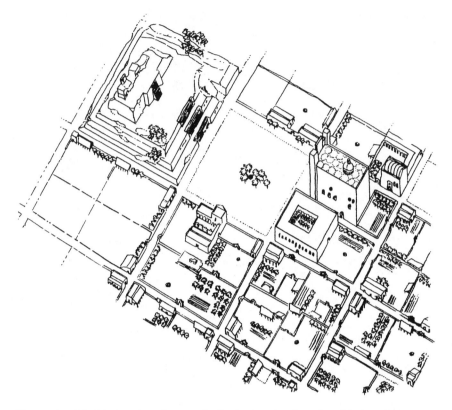

Figure 6.4 Merida in 1610. Source: Author's drawing based on Lindsay (1999: Fig. 3.2).

Thus the original parish and chapel for black slaves and mulattoes in Merida was several blocks north of the main square, on the edge of the original traza. Called Santa Lucía, it was gradually taken over by Spaniards as the settler population grew through the late sixteenth century; the expanded, but still modest, seventeenth-century Santa Lucía church still stands (see Figure 6.5).

The *beneficio curato* for Afro-Yucatecans was a desirable urban curacy in early colonial times, and there was no shortage of applicants for the post when it became vacant in 1607.[39] Espinosa wrote in 1620 that there were three curacies attached to Merida's cathedral, one specifically for "the blacks and mulattoes of the city, both free and slave."[40] A decade later, the Franciscan chronicler fray Francisco de Cárdenas y Valencia provided more detail, similarly describing one curacy as for

the administration of the blacks and mulattoes, slaves and free; the perquisites and emoluments of this benefice are worth two hundred pesos, and it has assigned for its

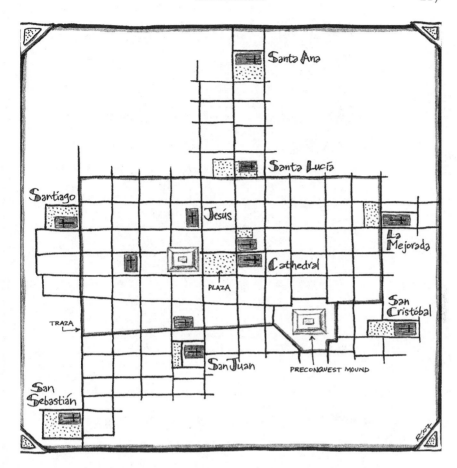

Map 6.4 Colonial Merida. The middle position of Afro-Yucatecans was symbolized in spatial terms by the location of both their first parish (Santa Lucía) and their second one (Jesús) in between the Spanish center and the five satellite Maya neighborhoods or cah-barrios (Santiago, Santa Ana, La Mejorada, San Cristóbal, and San Sebastián). The traza, or central urban grid, excluded Santa Lucía and the Maya parishes but included Jesús. The two large preconquest pyramidal mounds included here were gradually built over by church and state buildings during the seventeenth century.

administration a chapel . . . dedicated to the holy name of Jesus, whose *cofradía* was founded with the authority of the lord bishops; this cofradía is supported with the alms requested on the assigned days, which are for the blacks the same as for the Spaniards, for there are among them many established cofradía members."[41]

By the 1720s some cofradía traditions had developed that Bishop Gómez de Parada deemed worthy of reform; indigenous cofradías should not be

Figure 6.5 Church of Santa Lucía, Merida. This was the original parish church for Afro-Yucatecans in the city, from the 1540s to the 1680s; it continued to serve Afro-Yucatecans even after their parish became centered on the Jesús church, located a few blocks away on what is today Calle 59 and since demolished (see Map 6.4).

forced to provide branches for Jesús processions, the bishop ordered, with the sole exception being the Corpus Christi festivities—and on that occasion the Afro-Yucatecans were to pay the Mayas in full.[42]

Some time in the mid-seventeenth century a new parish church was built for Afro-Yucatecans a few blocks away from the Santa Lucía church, on a block of what is now Calle 59 (see Map 6.4). Both churches appear to have been part of the Afro-Yucatecan parish until 1684, when a new church on the Calle 59 site was consecrated. Named Sacra Familia, Jesús, María y José, by the early eighteenth century it was typically called just Jesús María, although in 1722 Bishop Gómez de Parada described it as "the parish of the Santo Nombre de Jesús, within the walls of this city, where *negros*, mulatos, and chinos of both sexes, and the indias and mestizas that are married to them, are administered." The bishop instructed the parish priests to administer the sacraments in full accordance with church law, implying that corners were not to be cut just because the parishioners were not Spaniards.[43] In 1757, Bishop Padilla commented disapprovingly that the parish of the "Dulcisimo nombre de Jesus," just for "Mulatos, *Negros*, and Chinos," was so poor "it can scarcely support a curate and minister," and "its ornaments were so wretched that I have had to provide it with the broken ones from the Cathedral."[44] After the expulsion of the Jesuits in 1767, the parish may have been moved to the Jesuit church on the same street—although its new name, Dulce Nombre de Jesús, does not predominate in the parish records until the 1790s. Either way, the church on Calle 59 was demolished in the 1970s and the site is now a parking lot.

Meanwhile, Afro-Yucatecans continued living in the Santa Lucía neighborhood throughout the colonial period, initially on their own properties and then in Spanish households as house-plot prices forced nonelites farther from the main square. There were Afro-Yucatecan baptisms and weddings in Santa Lucía at least through the seventeenth century (pardo militia Captain Lázaro del Canto's daughter Augustina was married there in 1682, for example).[45] In 1722, the bishop commented on "the schools that we have founded in the Hermita de Santa Lucía in this city, and in the town of Valladolid, to teach poor Spaniards and other castas."[46]

In theory, Afro-Yucatecans were to live separately from Spaniards and Mayas. But in practice, both when the Afro-Yucatecan parish was centered on Santa Lucía and during its years as the Jesús parish on Calle 59, increasing numbers of Spaniards, mestizos, and Mayas moved into the blocks around these churches, while Afro-Yucatecans could be found all over the city. This process can be illustrated in numerous ways, but I shall mention four.

One is through individual *solar* [house-plot] sales. For example, a pardo named Andrés Pacheco bought a solar from a Maya woman in Santiago, but when she died in 1821 before giving him the papers to the plot, he had to file suit to prove his ownership.[47] The notarial archives contain numerous solar sale records from the 1680s through the nineteenth century, both in Spanish and in Maya; for example, there are at least sixty-one Maya-language records of house-plot sales in Merida barrios between 1725 and 1809, many of them to Afro-Yucatecans (the lack of casta labels in many of them prevents a systematic evaluation).[48] A second way of anecdotally illustrating where in Merida Afro-Yucatecans lived is through references in judicial cases. Three late colonial examples are (1) Marcial Socobio, a pardo barber arrested repeatedly between 1803 and 1817, who stated that he lived with his wife in La Mejorada; (2) three pardo cattle thieves arrested in 1816 who lived in Santiago; and (3) two militiamen brothers in trouble with the law in 1819 who were residents of San Cristóbal.[49]

A third way of illustrating Merida's multiracial development is through late colonial census data. Figure 6.6 shows that one in eight (or 12.7%) residents of the district were Afro-Yucatecan by 1779. In censuses of 1790,

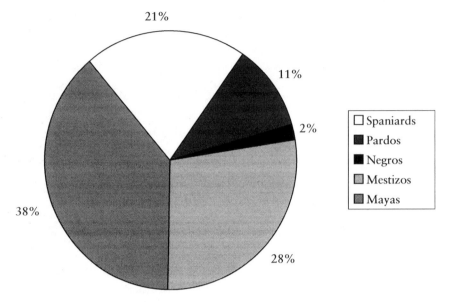

Figure 6.6 Racial distribution of the Merida district population of 15,821 in 1779. Source: Based on data presented in Patch (1993: 234).

1793, and 1794, "mulattoes" were again listed at about 12% of the population, even though the total population was given at a more realistic twenty-eight thousand. All these surveys covered Merida's district (the city and its surrounding villages); the city proper would have been even more Afro-Yucatecan.[50]

The fourth way of examining the city's miscegenative development is through marriage records. These will be discussed briefly at various points in this chapter, but my main treatment of Afro-Yucatecan marriage choices is in the next chapter.

PARDOS IN THE PUEBLOS

There were two other formal Spanish towns in the colony, Valladolid and Bacalar, but neither was large or prosperous enough to hold a substantial black or free-colored population. Cárdenas y Valencia commented in 1639 that the "cofradía of the Santo Nombre de Jesús" in Valladolid was not an exclusively Afro-Yucatecan organization; rather it was for "Indians, blacks, and mulattoes," but dominated by Mayas, due to the small size of the colored population in the city.[51]

The Afro-Yucatecan presence in the first Bacalar (1544–1648) was even smaller; the town had less than a hundred Spaniards (at times, perhaps less than fifty), and their modest means denied them the luxury of black slaves (only one was reported to exist there, in 1571). At any one time there were a handful of mulattoes. One even served as an alcalde near the turn of the seventeenth century—this fact, combined with their low numbers and the poverty of the local Spaniards, suggests that Afro-Yucatecans in Bacalar were simply members of the town's non-Maya community. The second Bacalar (relocated from Chunhuhub and refounded on its original site in 1729) began like the first, but in the second half of the eighteenth century grew steadily. Less plagued by attacks from unconquered Mayas, and benefiting as a gateway to Belize and the Caribbean, Bacalar at the end of the eighteenth century had as many as fifty black slaves and four times that many free-colored inhabitants. But Spaniards and Britons alike tended to depict it as an impoverished, feeble frontier town, and as a provincial gateway its non-Maya population was transient; almost all the black and free-colored residents of Bacalar that have been mentioned in these chapters so far were on the way either to Merida or Belize.[52]

Most free-colored families in Bacalar lived and worked like the free-colored inhabitants of the Maya villages where Afro-Yucatecans increasingly settled in late colonial times. In the eighteenth century many of these "villages" (pueblos) were larger than Bacalar—in economic and demographic terms, they were really small towns. Most ran along the zone that I have called "the colored crescent," which stretched from Campeche, up the camino real to Merida, and across to the Tizimin area; this was also, not coincidentally, where pardo militia units were located (see Maps 1.3, 4.1, and 5.1 in Chapters One, Four, and Five, respectively).[53]

In larger places, like Izamal and Calkiní, there were free-colored blacksmiths and barbers, as there were in the city; in smaller places, like Cacalchen and Sucilá, Afro-Yucatecans married Maya women and worked cornfields. By the census of 1806–13, there were free coloreds in most villages in Yucatan and in every single *cabecera* [parish head town], but the distribution of Afro-Yucatecans followed that of Spaniards and mestizos. For example, in 1806 Maxcanú was 17% Spanish/mestizo and 17% pardo. This was also true of other parishes in the northwest and east. But in Nolo, where there were no Spaniards at all and the parish was only 0.5% mestizo, there were no Afro-Yucatecans. This distribution pattern also persisted within parishes. In 1806, almost all Spaniards in Izamal parish lived in Izamal itself, with just 2.9% of their number in subject Kantunil and none in the other four subject communities; likewise, almost all Afro-Yucatecans lived in Izamal, with 2.5% in Kantunil and none elsewhere.[54]

The point is that Afro-Yucatecans lived and worked in attached subordination to Spaniards, either as slaves or servants or employees, and that as Spaniards began to settle outside the city, these urban patterns became replicated to some extent. Thus in terms of community, in places like Izamal and Tizimín, Afro-Yucatecans were again in a middle position, between a Spanish minority and a Maya majority—but oriented more toward Spaniards and mestizos.

In smaller towns and villages, however, free-colored settlers were more likely to become part of the local Maya community. Because Maya community identity was so highly localized and centered on the village—with a Maya individual being not "Maya" but a member of a specific family in a specific village—it was relatively easy for Afro-Yucatecans to work among and marry into Maya families. Afro-Yucatecans thereby became members of Maya cahob, or municipal communities, at the same time turning those cahob in a certain sense into Afro-Maya communities. We have already seen this pattern emerge, and it will be further pursued in Chapter Seven.

To return momentarily to the 1806–13 census: In the northeast corner of the colony that was the district of Tizimín, the villages of Chancenote parish averaged 14% and Tizimín parish itself was 27% Afro-Yucatecan; the parish of Kikil was over a third colored, but that figure rises to just over a half if one excludes the residents of parish haciendas. At the end of the colonial period, Kikil was one of three villages with predominantly Afro-Yucatecan populations (as discussed in Chapter Four). We now return to examine two of them—San Fernando Ake and San Francisco de Paula—in more detail.

The genesis of San Fernando Ake lies in an agreement made between Spanish officials in Santo Domingo and Afro-Haitian ex-slave rebel leaders early in the war that ravaged Hispaniola in the 1790s. The deal, ratified by a royal edict in February 1793, promised arms, land, and freedom for the rebels in return for their military support. That support could not save Santo Domingo, which the Spanish were forced to abandon in 1795. Spanish adherence to law and due process triumphed over colonial officials' racist distrust of their Haitian allies, at least to an extent. Hundreds of Haitian soldiers and their families were evacuated to Havana, but the Cuban authorities made it clear that they were not welcome there. An immediate diaspora was therefore enforced. Twenty-three families under the leadership of Georges (aka Jorge) Biassou were sent to Florida (where Biassou became head of the black militia and created an alliance with local maroon leader, Prince Witten, whose daughter married Biassou's brother-in-law).[55] The other main leader, Jean François, controlled a group of 707 refugees; most were sent to the island of Trinidad, but a minority, including Jean François himself, crossed the Atlantic to Cádiz, where they stayed only 6 months before recrossing the ocean and settling on the Mosquito coast of Nicaragua. Most of the 500 remaining refugees in Havana also ended up on the Mosquito coast, or in Portobelo on the Panamian coast; 115 of them, led by an ex-slave whom the Spaniards called Marcos, were shipped to Campeche.[56]

The Afro-Haitian families arrived in Campeche in February 1796, were moved up to Merida the same month, and by March had been settled on a remote site in the colony's northeast (see Map 4.2 in Chapter Four). The new black colonists comprised sixty-three soldiers—including Marcos, colonels Juan Pedro and Ambrosio Sasy, and Capt. Juan Casimiro—as well as thirty-five women, six children, and eleven "nursing" infants. Their new home was essentially the abandoned site of an ancient Maya city—its plazas, platforms, crumbling pyramids, and the fertile lands around it. Such ruins were so commonplace in Yucatan that Spanish officials did not apparently see fit to comment on this; nor did they imagine that ancient Ake was being reconstituted by the Afro-Haitians. So what kind of community was San Fernando supposed to be?

It was to be a formal colonial pueblo, complete with a church at the center and houses laid out on a grid. A local priest was to administer the sacraments until the church was built (this was done in 1798). Officials hoped that the cacophony of African and European languages spoken by the settlers would soon be replaced by Spanish; accordingly, the lone Spanish official assigned to live part-time in San Fernando was given the title of "interpreter" (and was to spy on the inhabitants and report on their "conversations"). The militia status of the settlers was downplayed; they were not integrated into the existing militia system (unlike the Afro-Haitians sent to Florida and the Mosquito coast), and were even forbidden from traveling to the nearby northern coast. No doubt had the English attempted to raid that coast, San Fernando's veterans would have been called upon to defend the colony. But such a raid never happened; the northern coast was a windswept strip of salt flats, Maya fishing villages, and smugglers' coves, none of which had ever seriously tempted the English or other interlopers. Thus rather than being a settlement of black militiamen, San Fernando was to be a village of farmers. Marcos and his men were given seed, chickens, and tools, including one hundred axes and the same number of machetes. The land around the village was to be completely cleared so that corn, sugar, and coffee could be grown. The residents were forbidden from moving into the neighboring Maya villages; they were to keep to themselves and sustain themselves.[57]

In other words, San Fernando was not to be a black community. By this I mean that it was not to be an aggregation of domestic servants, slaves, and urban workers of the kind that made up Afro-Campeche or Afro-Merida. Nor was it to be a black militia town. Nor was it to be a hamlet of sugar plantation laborers under the thumb of a Spanish mill owner. It was to be an isolated agricultural settlement modeled on the Maya villages of the colony; separated from them, but essentially like them. The irony of this fact lay not only in the village's location within the ruins of a Maya city abandoned just a century or two earlier, but also in the way in which San Fernando evolved during the early decades of the nineteenth century.[58]

First of all, despite the segregationist attitude of the Spanish authorities, there did not appear to develop an exclusively African identity in San

Fernando. A decade after its founding, the Spanish commissioner for the village, José Carreño, reported that its heads of households comprised fifty-two black men from Santo Domingo, seventeen from England, two Yucatecan mulattoes, two Spaniards, and sixty-nine Africans; among these,

there are *senegales, polares, mandingas, congos, nagoes, males, minaes, arnadaes, ybiés,* some *Balakribies,* some from la Miserable, *mendengos, misambires, gambarraes,* natives [*criollos*] of Santo Domingo, of New York, Charleston, Jamaica, and Rio Tinto."[59]

Carreño's census was not very exact, but it suggests that the variation of origin among Ake's Africans was in the 15%–20% range; as we shall see below, the level of variation was almost as high among Africans in Yucatan's urban communities.

Second, the interaction between Ake's residents and the Mayas of neighboring villages began within a few years and grew steadily. Carreño's job was in part to prevent San Fernando's black founders from moving elsewhere in the colony, so he understandably did not reveal how many had left; but an 1826 report revealed that over the years dozens had settled in Maya villages. The movement went both ways; Carreño admitted that by 1806 four Maya women lived in San Fernando, having already married and had children by their African husbands. Carreño's view of Africans was ripe with the racist stereotypes of the day (they were "ugly," "bad mannered," "cannibals"); he believed that if Ake's black residents were to mix with "Spaniards, mestizos, or mulattoes who might pass as mestizos," or even local "Indians," the village population would develop the docility and discipline needed to produce loyal militiamen. Four Maya women in 1806 may seem negligible, but by 1840 San Fernando was 40% Maya. Perhaps Carreño succeeded in encouraging non-black locals to move to Ake before his term as commissioner ended in 1809; more likely, the Afro-Maya interaction that had intensified in the countryside over the previous century or two gradually took its effect among the ruined pyramids of Ake.[60]

In my previous discussion of the *"rancho de los negros* [black hamlet]" of San Francisco de Paula I drew upon the evidence found by archaeologists Anthony Andrews, Fernando Robles Castellanos, and their team to paint a portait of the settlement as one of free-colored dyewood workers. Here we revisit San Francisco to paint a fuller portrait by adding to Andrews's information, somewhat speculatively, the contextual evidence of pardo settlement and community patterns in the late colony.

San Francisco de Paula is located about four and half miles south of the port of Sisal, a mile or two off the Sisal–Hunucmá road and from a nineteenth-century hacienda named Xtobó. It was adjacent to a small precolonial Maya site named Lolché, abandoned long before San Francisco was settled and perhaps a source of building stones. The site is small (about a quarter of a mile long and a fifth of a mile wide), comprising about

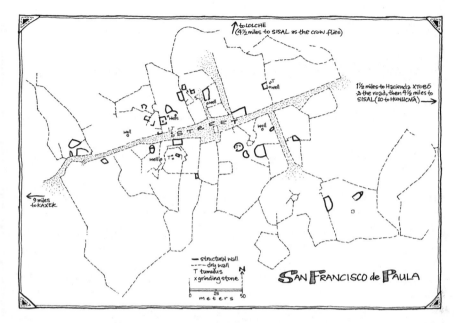

Map 6.5 San Francisco de Paula. Map based on C. Lawton and J. C. Manzanilla in Andrews and Robles Castellanos (2002; 2003: 37, 99).

twenty-eight plots delineated by stone walls (see Map 6.5). Such walls typically marked solar or house-plot boundaries in colonial Maya villages, and indeed in San Francisco about eighteen of these plots contain structural walls from houses; Andrews estimates that another dozen such walls were from secondary structures, such as kitchens and storage sheds. Ceramic evidence suggests that the site was founded in the late eighteenth or early nineteenth century; Andrews found a couple of references to it in nineteenth-century records and one map reference from the same period. Local folk–historical tradition, garnered from oral interviews in Sisal, refers to San Francisco as a "black hamlet" and tells of the population hit hard by an epidemic in the 1920s, when the last inhabitant, a mulatto, left for Sisal, where he died around 1950.

The ceramic and glass items found on the surface by archaeologists included fragments from olive jars (of a style made between 1580 and 1800), imported porcelain, and Scottish whiskey and German beer bottles. Although it is not clear when such goods reached the hamlet, Andrews and Robles Castellanos reasonably speculate that San Francisco's residents acquired them through coastal contraband trade. In the early eighteenth century "Campeachy" logwood or dyewood was legally exchanged in Campeche for African slaves brought by the British, while illegal trade in dyewood had gone on up and down the coast since the late seventeenth century; perhaps the pardos of San Francisco traded dyewood for china and European liquor. Some nine miles from San Francisco lie the ruins of a Maya hamlet named Kaxek, smaller than San Francisco, surrounded by dyewood trees. Although Kaxek was also a late-classic site, its more recent inhabitation was contemporaneous with San Francisco's from roughly the late eighteenth century until the early twentieth; both hamlets were probably sustained primarily by the dyewood industry (which collapsed near the end of the nineteenth century when artificial dyes were developed).[61]

What kind of community was San Francisco de Paula? It is tempting to view it as an example of an independent, isolated Afro-Yucatecan settlement. However, we know too little about the hamlet to make such a leap, especially as there are few signs that such communities existed anywhere in the colony. It is also tempting to imagine San Francisco as a refuge for escaped slaves. But, as I argued in the previous chapter, the larger contextual history of slavery in Yucatan makes this unlikely. I think that San Francisco is best understood in the context of the larger patterns surrounding the growth of the pardo population in the Yucatec countryside. That population expanded partly through migration; San Francisco's founders probably came up from Hunucmá and Merida, at first temporarily to profit from dyewood and contraband trade, but then as permanent settlers.[62] They chose the location for its wells, its proximity to dyewood groves and the coast (and perhaps the cut stones of Lolché), and its distance from the Sisal–Hunucmá road (not right on it, but close enough for convenience; closer to it than Kaxek was, for example).

The rural pardo population in Yucatan also grew through miscegenation between people of African and Maya descent. We saw how San Fernando de los Negros at Ake changed slowly but steadily in two generations from an all-African pueblo to an Afro-Maya one, despite Spanish attempts to supervise and segregate the residents. Likewise, while Kaxek was no doubt mostly Maya and San Francisco was probably mostly Afro-Yucatecan, it is unlikely that they were exclusively so—especially in the case of San Francisco. The two hamlets must have looked alike in terms of material environment; the outlines of the houses and other structures visible in Map 6.5 show that about half of San Francisco's buildings were apsidal or semi-apsidal in shape, as they also were in Kaxek (and as was common in all colonial Maya villages).[63] The two hamlets probably also looked similar in terms of their inhabitants. Like every other place in Yucatan where people of African descent lived, San Francisco was surely, to some extent and in various ways, an Afro-Maya community.

Now that we have viewed Afro-Yucatecan communities from the perspective of specific locations, from Campeche to San Francisco de Paula, we approach the topic from a different angle—the thematic angle of the six above-mentioned community bases, grouped into two sections.

COMMUNITY BASES: CHRISTIANS
OF AFRICAN DESCENT

Slaves bought in Yucatan were primarily destined to be a Spaniard's personal property in a household where the other dependents were free pardos and Maya servants. They thus became part of a complex multiracial hierarchy in which they were often isolated from other Africans, especially those from the same region and language group, and drawn into a Spanish-speaking Christian environment.[64] If Africans were not already Hispanized—baptized and Spanish-speaking—when they reached Yucatan, they were soon thereafter. The likelihood of an African in Yucatan getting married seems also to have been high. For example, a black slave such as José Antonio Marcín, forcibly brought from his African homeland around 1810 when he was eighteen, had by his early twenties become a Christian, Spanish-speaking, married member of Campeche's black community, a resident in the home of his Spanish owner, don Ramón Acosta.[65] As we saw above, Campeche was arguably black enough by the 1810s—indeed, had been for centuries—for an African-born semi-Hispanized young man like Marcín to feel as though he was a member of a community of others who looked similar to him, had similar roots, and were forced into a similar working life. But was this enough to give Marcín a real sense of belonging?

Perhaps not. Marcín felt sufficiently alienated as an African-born slave in his owner's home to flee Campeche one night, only to end up even more alienated as he traveled from one Maya village to another along the camino real to Merida; violence quickly ensued and he ended up in the hospital, accused of various serious crimes (his story is told more fully at the start of the next chapter). Made desperate by the misery of his condition as a slave, Marcín did not apparently turn to Campeche's Afro-Yucatecan community, despite the fact that he was married to a local black woman; was there no support network of others born in Africa, forced across the Atlantic, and sold in Campeche? Nor did Marcín flee to a palenque or maroon settlement; there were none near enough that he could have found them or even known of their existence.

The six potential bases for Afro-Yucatecan community identity listed near the chapter's start were (1) culture and religion of native African origin; (2) Christian identity; (3) ethnic or racial classification; (4) occupation; (5) kinship and family life; and (6) location. Speculations about José Antonio Marcín's sense of belonging and identity lead us to several of these themes, most obviously the first two, which are the subject of this section. When Marcín arrived in Campeche around 1810, would his identity as an African have helped or hindered his settling down in the town? What aspects of African identity were significant, and what do we mean by "African"?

There can be no doubt that African slaves carried within them cultural elements from their native lands and perpetuated them in the Spanish colonies. The African cultural contribution is virtually invisible in some parts of Spanish America today, such as Yucatan, but this does not mean that a good deal of African culture did not survive the Middle Passage and subsequent generations or centuries of slavery and servitude in the Americas. Still, the likely survival and maintenance of African cultural elements was hampered by the fact that slaves were drawn from many regions of a continent that was culturally and linguistically extremely diverse. Consequently, many beliefs and practices that were African in origin survived and developed in the New World in forms that drew upon a mixture of Old World traditions and reflected adaptations to the slave experience. For example, some African religious elements were maintained in quasi-religious forms as part of the continually evolving folk cultures of Africans in the Americas; beliefs and practices of healing, for example, played particularly important roles in Spanish America.

Identifying and classifying the African elements in the cultures created by Africans in the Americas is notoriously difficult, as reflected in the development over recent decades of a debate on the topic. The poles of the debate are "creolization" (emphasizing the New World experience of black slaves) and "African retention" (emphasizing African roots and continuities).[66] Africanist historian Paul Lovejoy has passionately argued that scholars of Africans in the Americas need to adopt a more "African-centric" approach, beginning where the slaves themselves began—in Africa. Lovejoy objects to the image of the melting pot ("many did not melt"), and he questions assumptions that the African origins of American slaves were too diverse "to sustain the continuities of history" and that such slaves "rapidly assimiliated" into new cultures that were more American than African. Historians have too often, he asserts, read "backwards from a present in which African culture has indeed melted into the larger cultural history of the Americas."[67]

I find this position persuasive, and I have sought to approach Afro-Yucatecans from as much of an African-centric perspective as possible. Yet the evidence overwhelmingly suggests that not long after the colony was founded, Africans in Yucatan began to be outnumbered (eventually very much so) by Afro-Yucatecans—that is, people of African descent whose cultural environment and lived experience was mostly or entirely in the colony of Yucatan. Certainly, throughout the colonial period there lived in Campeche and Merida men and women whom we might more accurately label Africans (if not Mandinga or Ibo) than Afro-Yucatecans. But by the late eighteenth century black slaves arriving in Yucatan were as likely to be natives of the British Empire as they were to be African-born. In the end, it is hard to escape the conclusion that Afro-Yucatecan communities were marked more by creolization than African retention.

One reason for this, then, was the demographic imbalance between African-born black slaves and American-born (mostly Yucatan-born) free coloreds; (as discussed in Chapter One) low levels of slave importation and high levels of miscegenation between Africans, Spaniards, Mayas, and castas or the mixed-race populations meant that from the late sixteenth century on, Afro-Yucatecans outnumbered Africans in the colony. This is starkly illustrated by the baptism records of the Afro-Yucatecan parish of Jesús in eighteenth-century Merida. There were an average of just under 120 baptisms a year in the parish, of which an average of about 5% were black adults. That figure ranged from a low of 2% in the 1740s, when the importation of slaves into Yucatan ground virtually to a halt, to almost 10% in the 1760s, when Spaniards found new ways to bring in slaves. Thus, even in years of relatively high numbers of incoming Africans, such adults were greatly outnumbered not only by the existing Afro-Yucatecan population, but even by Afro-Yucatecan births.[68]

Another reason why there was creolization rather than African retention was the diverse African origins of those slaves who were imported into Yucatan (see Table 6.1), a factor underpinned by the fact that Africans did not see themselves as "Africans" (any more than Mayas saw themselves as "Indians," or even "Mayas").[69] Between 1710 and 1789, some 563 adult Africans were baptized in Merida; asked to provide their place of origin, 277 of them (or their new owners or employers) named 32 different places in West and West Central Africa—a 0.12, or 12%, origin variation rate. Most were places, but some were ethnic identifications (like Kanga, usually written as Canca). Two-thirds came from one of four places—Congo, Guinea, Mandinga, and Mina—but those were themselves multiethnic, multilingual locations that were either large and loosely defined (such as Guinea) or often mere departure points for slaves rather than their places of birth (such as Mina).[70] If we look at all 563 black adults, including those declaring non-African origins, the variation drops to 9%; however, this is misleading, as many of the Afro-Belizeans and Afro-Jamaicans would have come to those British colonies from various places in Africa and elsewhere. The true variation rate for all incoming adults was probably closer to 15%.

A survey of the ethnic origins of 196 Africans arriving in Mexico in 1545–56 revealed 16 different places of origin, an 8% origin variation rate; in other words, Yucatan's eighteenth-century incoming slaves were 50% more varied, in terms of their African origins, than Mexico's incoming slaves of the mid-sixteenth century (as well as far fewer in number).[71]

This diversity of new arrivals in Yucatan intensified in the second half of the eighteenth century, when increasing numbers of newly arrived black slaves came not from Africa but from the British Empire. Few African slaves had entered the colony at all during the 1740s, in the wake of the breakdown of the asiento agreement with the British, but from 1756 on, Yu-

TABLE 6.1 Origins of African adults in eighteenth-century Merida

	1710s	1720s	1730s	1740s	1750s	1760s	1770s	1780s
AFRICA								
Anaco						1		
Angola	1		1			1	1	
Arara	5	2	1			1		
Berbara	1							
Burgu [Borgu]						1		
Caboverde	1							
Canca [Kanga]		3	2	1	3	2	4	1
Carabal [Calabar]						4	1	
Caramanti	3				2			3
Congo	5	10	10	1	10	14	3	3
Congo Mangola				1				
Craban	1							
Danguira	1							
Diangla			1					
El Puh							1	
Guavere	1							
Guinea	1	1	1	3	10	16	4	13
Mamona						2		
Manda	1							
Mandinga	6	1	3	2	6	3	4	6
Mangola					1	1		
Mina	5	10	3	1	6	13	3	2
Mingo		1						
Mocó [Moko]				1	1	4	1	
Nanga		1						
Papá [Popo]	1					1		
Samsi						1		
Vazmacontre		1						
Vron					1			
Ybo	1	1	6		6	11		
Yola	1							
Zamba							1	
[Subtotals]	[40]	[28]	[27]	[13]	[45]	[77]	[18]	[29]
BRITISH EMPIRE								
Bermuda					1			
New England				1				
Providence								1
Philadelphia						1		1
Jamaica	3	1	2	5	13	39	4	12

TABLE 6.1 *(continued)*

	1710s	1720s	1730s	1740s	1750s	1760s	1770s	1780s	
Kingston							1		
Belize			(1)		5	20	3		
Cay Kitchen								54	
Mosquito Coast								1	
Grenada						1			
Barbados								1	
England					2	3			
London	1						1	2	
[Subtotals]	[4]	[1]	[3]	[5]	[22]	[63]	[10]	[72]	
CUBA AND EUROPE									
Cuba								1	
Havana		1				1			
The Hague						1			
Holland	1					1			
Lisbon					1				
Portugal						2			
Catalonia							1		
Lujat								1	
France						1			
[Subtotals]	[1]	[1]	[0]	[0]	[0]	[7]	[10]	[2]	
UNKNOWN									
Chanpidona					1				
Frene								1	
Vanico							1		
"No conosida"	2	1			1				
Bosal		6							
[No origin given]	10	28	29	3	1	3		7	
[Subtotals]	[10]	[36]	[30]	[3]	[2]	[4]	[0]	[9]	
[Grand totals]	[55]	[66]	[60]	[21]	[69]	[151]	[29]	[112]	=[563]

Source: Adult baptisms, 1710–89, in AGAY-*Jesús*, Libros de Bautismos Vols. 1–6 (counting all those classified as *negro* (64%) or *negra* (36%), both slave (60%) and free (40%); see Chapter Five and Table G.2 in Appendix G for further details).

Notes: Origin given as "de nación," "natural de," "nacido/ nacida en," or less commonly simply "de." The 1730s Belize entry (given in parentheses) is the daughter of a *negra* slave from Belize; the first 1750s Belize entry is in 1756. The "no conosida" entries are "de tierra no conosida" save for the 1740s one, which is "de padres no conosidos." One of the 1760s no-origin-given entries "has been out in a forest since he was a boy."

Spelling variants: Canca/Cankay / Canga/ Cangáa/ Cancan en Guinea; Carabal/ Carabi/ Carabeo/ Caravari/ Carabari; Caramanti/ Calemanti (i.e., Coromanti); Congo/ Conko/ Conga; Hibo/ Ibo/ Oibo/ Ybo/ Hybo/ Hybo de Guinea; Mocó/ Mocoo/ Mocco/ Mocoa; Papá/ Paapa; el Puh I take to be Fernando Po; Havana is La Vana/ La Havana; Bermuda is Bemudez; Philadelphia is Felidelphe/ Felidelphin; Providence is Provedàns; New England is Ynga la terra noba; England is Yngalaterra;

TABLE 6.1 (*continued*)

London is Londres; The Hague is Hago; Holland is Olanda; Lisbon is Lisboa; Lujàt is presumably Lujat in the Pyrenees; Belize is Balix; Jamaica is Jamaica/Jamayca/Hamayca, and Kingston is Quinzon; Mosquito Coast is la costa de los Mosquitos; Cay Kitchen is Cayo Cosina (or once, Quiquichin); I take Grinat to be Grenada.
I have been unable to determine what or where were Vanico, Frene, and Chanpidona.

catan's Spanish elite solved the problem of supply by regularly raiding logging settlements in Belize. In periods of formal war between Britain and Spain (as in 1779), they lost no time in mounting major assaults on Belize (the fifty-four black slaves from Cayo Cocina, listed in Table 6.1 under the 1780s, were booty auctioned off in Merida in 1779–80). The church stipulated repeatedly that the English and any other Protestants who came from Jamaica "and other islands" (as Bishop Gómez de Parada put it in 1722) and settled in Merida should be baptized; this also applied to the African slaves and free blacks who ended up in the city.[72]

The development of an open Yucatan–Belize frontier—and the resulting fact that about half the black slaves brought into Yucatan in the second half of the eighteenth century came from Belize, Jamaica, and elsewhere in the British Empire—made the colony unique in Spanish America. Yucatan's Mayas lived in a world bound by the peninsula, and the colony's Spaniards looked in part to the Caribbean (especially Havana) but also beyond it to Mexico City and Seville. But late colonial Afro-Yucatecans were connected to a Caribbean world that was as much British as it was Spanish or African.

In terms of community development, this complicates the picture in ways that we cannot access in detail. If only we could know, for example, how Afro-Belizeans in Merida and Campeche overcame language barriers, whether they stuck together as much as they could, or how quickly they assimilated into the local multiracial nonelite communities of the two cities. But the reason why we cannot distinguish these black residents from others is significant; once they were baptized, they became Catholic Christians with Spanish names, symbolizing their incorporation into local society. In other words, Afro-Yucatecans with origins in Belize and Jamaica did not form separate communities; they contributed to the multiplicity of the existing nonelite communities.

"Creolizationists" argue that cultural exchange began on the Middle Passage, with cultural changes beginning with contacts among slaves even before the impact of slave–master contacts.[73] Whether slaves who ended up in Yucatan found few others who spoke their language during their Atlantic crossings, they certainly would have found others from their region of West or West Central Africa to be a minority in Campeche or Merida. And while the dividing lines between the localized identities that black slaves brought with them may have been broken down by the shared experience of enslavement in a Spanish colony, that breaking-down process did not forge a common African identity; at best, it fostered an Afro-Yucatecan one, but even that was not defined exclusively in terms of African descent or origins.

The ethnic labels and places of origin given by adult slaves baptized in Merida were surely specific self-identifications reflecting local identities in West and West Central Africa (and not arbitrary designations by slaves, owners, or priests). But such labels disappear from the written record after baptism; unlike in slave societies (such as Brazil and Louisiana), African-born slaves appearing subsequently in legal records are usually just "black," no longer "Canca" or "of the Mina nation."[74] We should not assume that this meant either that African ethnic identities were covertly maintained, or, if they disappeared, that such a loss reflected Spanish hegemony. Laurent Dubois has shown how ex-slaves in the late colonial French Caribbean created "African citizen" identities, in part because ethnic identities from Africa had become part of slave identities.[75] A similar process occurred in Yucatan, where slaves and ex-slaves replaced local African identities with local Yucatecan ones.

This fact no doubt reflects the realities of creolization in a society with slaves (as opposed to a slave society). But it also reflects a set of considerations that need to be made in studying African diaspora identities: (1) looking at such identities from an Afrocentric perspective is important, but not enough; (2) likewise, finding collective identities among Africans and free coloreds in the colonies only takes us so far; we need to study and grasp individual identities first; and (3) the study of individual identities reveals how people held multiple identities (including multiple ethnic ones), both in parallel and in series, a phenomenon that began in Africa itself (not only on or after the Middle Passage). In other words, identity for Africans in the Americas was a process of transformation and adaptation. Significantly, this process applied to more than the African-born sector of Yucatan's population—as we have seen already, it applied to all castas.[76]

The only element of religion and culture that seems to have survived more or less intact in various parts of the Americas, was actively—even fiercely—maintained for centuries, and was clearly a basis of community for groups of enslaved and free Africans, was Islam.[77] There were a significant number of Muslims brought from Senegal and neighboring regions of Africa to the Americas, particularly in the wake of the 1490–1550 collapse of the Jolof Empire, the 1670s war of the *marabouts*, the mid-eighteenth-century Senegalese civil wars, and the 1804 defeat of various Muslim groups in conflicts in what are now Nigeria and Ghana.[78] As a result, in 1549 almost a third of the slaves in Mexico were Muslims of the Wolof, Tukulor, or Mandingo.[79]

Some Muslims must thus have reached Yucatan; 11% of the adult Africans baptized in eighteenth-century Merida, for example, were of the heavily Islamicized ethnicity of the "Mandinga." But I did not find archival evidence of a distinct Muslim-based community; if one existed, it must have been small and most likely located in Campeche. One can merely speculate, therefore, that those Muslims that did end up in Yucatan were too few in number for Islam to be a major factor in the formation of an Afro-Yucatecan community anywhere in the province. It is also worth adding that the tendency of Muslims to keep apart from "infidel" Africans, a phenomenon well evidenced elsewhere in the Americas,[80] makes it less likely that Yucatan's Muslims would have played much of a role, if any, in the development of Afro-Yucatecan communities, and they may even have hindered the development of any pan-African communities in the colony.

Because polygamy was widespread in Africa for centuries before the Atlantic Slave Trade, and sanctioned in many African cultures by Muslim practice (which limited wives to four in number), it is likely that polygamy was transported to the Americas. However, the sexual imbalance in many slave communities in the Americas, combined with the Christian emphasis on monogamy, ensured that it was rare for an African man in the New World to have more than one wife.[81]

Nor should examples of bigamous unions by Africans be taken as indicators of the persistence of a culture of polygamy. Of 204 cases of bigamy found in Inquisition files from colonial Mexico, only 24% featured bigamists of African descent; as 12 of these Africans were women, which would not have conformed to practice in Africa, that figure really should be 18%. As these cases only include the nonindigenous population, the figure represents a disproportionately *low* bigamy rate among Africans. Furthermore, the patterns of bigamy contained in these cases are not significantly different for Africans and non-Africans, suggesting there was no distinct African culture of multiple marriage in colonial Mexico.[82]

The Mexican bigamy cases do not include Yucatan, but I have located forty Yucatec bigamy cases covering the period 1561–1854. Again, the presence of Africans is disproportionately low—just 5%, or two cases; those of Isabel Toquero and Manuel Bolio (both previously discussed at length). Nor do these cases reveal a different set of patterns.[83] Manuel Bolio was a bigamist black man born in Africa, but there is no evidence that he was a believer in polygamy (he was a "native of Congo" and thus almost certainly not Muslim). Indeed, his eighteenth-century journey into bigamy could have been that of a poor Spaniard or mestizo. Disenchanted with his life as a married domestic servant in Merida, Bolio went to Bacalar without his wife to find work. Marital problems either brought on by his move, or the separation produced the couple's estrangement; either way, Bolio eventually stopped visiting Merida and left the colony completely, ending up under arrest for bigamy by the Inquisition in Cartagena.[84] In other words, bigamy was a part of Hispanic culture, a product largely of the difficulties of procuring a divorce and of the high levels of mobility in the Spanish colonies. Africans appear in the records of bigamy because they were a part of the Hispanic world and its culture, not because they had brought from Africa a different set of marriage practices.

Nevertheless, it is clear that among the underprivileged, the poor Spaniards, people of mixed race, and Africans, there was a significant rate of common-law marriage. Thus, an unknown number of marriages in general—let alone bigamous marriages—escaped the written record, leaving open the possibility that some African men acquired more than one common-law wife. Yet it was not uncommon for Spanish men to maintain regular extramarital relationships—to "keep mistresses"—and thus Africans with multiple partners were doing something that was as typically Spanish as it was African.

While there is no evidence in Yucatan of Islamic or animist African beliefs, practices, or identities (aside from some witchcraft practices; see Chapter Seven), there is plenty of evidence of Afro-Yucatecans participating in the rites of Christianity and professing themselves, before Spanish officials, to be Christian (i.e., Roman Catholic; this is the second potential basis for an Afro-Yucatecan community). This is not surprising; all residents of the Spanish colonies, regardless of origin or status, were required to be baptized, practicing Catholics—and all were subject to the policing of the church.[85]

It is thus hard to determine whether professions of faith were sincere or whether African slaves paid lip service to the religion of their masters—a religion that, like the Spanish language, they were obliged to adopt. Yet Africans in Yucatan also had a motivation to adopt Christianity, at least outwardly, as its rituals and institutions provided them admittance into local society. Furthermore, new arrivals were a minority amidst Afro-Yucatecans who knew no other religion. Finally, if Afro-Yucatecans were "bad" Christians in terms of their sincerity and grasp of orthodox beliefs, they would surely appear in disproportionate numbers in Inquisition records; but they do not, at least not in Yucatan.[86]

Richard Dobson, the Jamaica-born African slave who fled Belize in 1800 only to be captured in Bacalar by Spanish authorities, told his captors that "with three companions he had decided to make his way to Bacalar in order to become a Christian [*con el fin de hacerse christiano*] and be free of slavery."[87] Did Dobson hope to ingratiate himself to his captors by suggesting that, first, the religion of the English was not Christianity, and second, that his soul, being in search of the true faith, deserved freedom? Dobson's situation demanded at least some degree of deception; his companions in flight and capture made near-identical statements of motive.[88] But no doubt Dobson and his friends would have embraced their new religion with more enthusiasm had refuge been granted; I cannot imagine that, dispatched to serve as a slave in Havana's presidio, Dobson became a keen Catholic.

In other words, we cannot ignore the circumstances of personality and individual experience. In most cases, Africans and Afro-Yucatecans surely participated in the social and sacramental rituals of Catholicism with no more or less sincerity and piety than any Spaniard or Maya; in other words, they did so as individuals, with concomitant varieties in perception and comprehension. Just because no evidence can be found that Islam or any other religion native to Africa was the basis of community identity in Yucatan does not mean that religious ideas and practices were not brought to the peninsula from across the Atlantic; some surely were. But it suggests that African religions may have played less important roles in Afro-Yucatecan community formation than did Catholicism. Just as Mayas in their cahob did, Afro-Yucatecans in urban neighborhoods found utility and appeal in many of the social aspects of Catholicism: the religious brotherhood as an economic and political network approved by colonial authorities; the opportunity for community congregation; and the importance placed on marriage and family (institutions destroyed by the transatlantic slave trade and often denied to African slaves in the Americas). Inclusion in the Christian community as "equals" before God did not make slavery or free-colored subordination palatable, but it did allow slaves "to fight the abuses deriving from their marginality" (as Javier Villa-Flores writes of Afro-Mexican slaves) and helped free and enslaved Afro-Yucatecans to contribute to community formation.[89] It is also possible that some of Christianity's doctrines offered spiritual comfort to slaves brought from Africa, for whom the world must have seemed a cruel place indeed.

Two manifestations of Afro-Yucatecan involvement in church rituals are marriage rites and religious brotherhoods. Because marriage is tackled more fully in Chapter Seven, I shall offer a single example here. In 1826, María Luisa López, an African-born slave, was baptized in the Campeche parish of Guadalupe—a significant step in the process of her inclusion in Christian Yucatec society (still in many ways a colonial society, although Independence had come five years earlier). Another step occurred four years later, when Juan Martín, a free *negro* baptized in Santo Domingo and resident in Campeche, petitioned for permission to marry María Luisa. The request lacked controversy—it took only eight days to be granted and most of the paperwork recorded testimony by acquaintances of Martín that he was a bachelor—but its utility to us lies in its routine nature. On the one hand, the subordinate position of this couple within Yucatec society and the circumstances of their tenuous inclusion are terminologically marked throughout the document—*moreno, negra, esclava, natural de Africa, criada*. And while don Benedicto López is frequently mentioned as María's owner, it was not he but other servants of his who were sent to testify that neither María nor Juan Martín were already married. On the other hand, Juan Martín and María Luisa López were also Christian Spanish-speaking colonists entering the series of administrative and social rituals that surrounded matrimony and marked their membership in local society.[90]

The other manifestation of Afro-Yucatecan participation in church activity is that of *cofradías* [religious brotherhoods or confraternities]. The first generation of Spanish settlers in Yucatan founded cofradías in Merida and Campeche; Maya communities followed suit, both in the countryside and in city and town, with Maya cah-barrios such as Santiago founding their own organizations dedicated to the cah's patron saint, to the celebration of religious festivals, and to various economic enterprises. Rural Maya cofradías tended to be funded through cattle ranches, with urban ones maintained primarily through subscriptions from community residents. By the end of the sixteenth century, if not sooner, cofradías were also founded in the urban Afro-Yucatecan parishes in Merida, Campeche, and Valladolid (as mentioned earlier).

These Afro-Yucatecan confraternities maintained themselves through member subscriptions, as neighboring Maya cofradías did, and they processed in the same festivals. Only in Merida and Campeche were there cofradías that were exclusively for men of African descent, and I suspect that a full study of cofradía records (one has yet to be done) will reveal the participation of mestizos and even Mayas (as was the case in Valladolid). The church established cofradías for subject groups, with separate organizations for Mayas and castas, as part of two policies: (1) to segregate subject populations as much as possible; and (2) to promote Christianization. Thus, the existence of cofradías exclusively for blacks and mulattoes did not necessarily reflect the existence of a coherent African, Afro-Yucatecan, or casta identity. Furthermore, blacks and mulattoes also participated in some of the urban cofradías not created exclusively by or for them; Merida's brotherhood to the Soledad de la Madre de Dios, for example, has Spanish, Maya, and Afro-Yucatecan members.[91]

Recent studies of religious brotherhoods in Mexico and Brazil suggest that the role played by black and mulatto cofradías in any given colonial society depended on the degree to which that society was a slave society, or simply one with slaves. Afro-Brazilian brotherhoods were far more important than Afro-Yucatecan ones could have been because, first, religious brotherhoods were more significant for the Portuguese in Brazil than they were for Spaniards, and second, because Brazil was a slave society. Even within Brazil, black brotherhoods developed differently, according to regional slave patterns; in places like Bahía, that received a heavy flow of slaves from Africa, brotherhoods were based on specific origin points in Africa, but where the flow of new arrivals was lighter, brotherhoods were more transnational and homogeneously African.[92]

Mexico City before 1650 was—or came close to being—a slave society, and thus early black cofradías promoted a sense of Afro-Mexican identity, a group-specific religiosity, and occasionally facilitated the organization of rebellion. But eighteenth-century Afro-Mexican brotherhoods were closer to Afro-Yucatecan ones: more of their members were free-colored artisans than slaves; their concern was with integration and participation in colonial society, not revolt; and they often welcomed mestizo and indigenous members, reflecting the multiracial nature of nonelite society.[93] In this sense, Brazilian communities were at various points at one end of the spectrum, early colonial and late colonial Mexico were at different points in the middle, and Yucatan was at the other end.

Afro-Maya villages were off the spectrum completely. In terms of Christian identity, Afro-Yucatecan settlers in Maya villages became members of local Maya-Christian communities; they married Maya women in the village church, participated in religious festivals organized by local cofradía officers, and if they engaged in unorthodox religious behavior at all they simply joined Maya men in doing what locals had done for generations (see Chapter Seven). Nor did they form their own parishes or cofradías; their migration into the countryside was a gradual small-scale process—there was no Spanish support for rural black cofradías (such settlers were not supposed to exist, after all)—Maya communities often accepted settlers of African descent into their families and local organizations. In other words, Afro-Yucatecans in the countryside tended not to perpetuate African religious practices because most arrived in Maya villages as free-colored Christians.

Ira Berlin has remarked that by the early eighteenth century, on plantations in what became the southern United States, "the mass of black people, physically separated and psychologically estranged from the European–American world, had begun to create a new African–American culture"; this Africanization of slave culture was an elemental part of the transition into a slave society. And Berlin and Philip Morgan have noted that in the Chesapeake the shift to a slave society in the late seventeenth century meant that "Jesus disappeared from African–American life" and "the vast majority of eighteenth-century Anglo-American slaves lived and died strangers to Christianity."[94] This was certainly not the case in Yucatan. By contrast, Afro-Yucatecan communities were not separated and estranged from the Spanish world, nor did they experience the influx of larger numbers of slaves from Africa. Afro-Yucatecans certainly contributed to the gradual creation of a new culture, but it was less an African–American culture than a Spanish–American and Catholic–Christian one—albeit a Yucatec variant of which, complete with some African and Maya influences.

COMMUNITY BASES: THE NEXUS OF WORK, FAMILY, AND HOME

Isabel Toquero, whose story opened this chapter, might never have entered the historical record were it not for her bigamy arrest. As much as we might regret the misery endured by Isabel between her detention in Merida in 1703 and her release in Mexico City in 1711, such cases offer invaluable and rare insight into the lives of "ordinary" Yucatecans. Isabel was not African-born, nor even black; but as a free-colored native of the peninsula with African and Maya ancestry, she was broadly speaking a typical Afro-Yucatecan. In which case, the details of her life and those who knew her (see Table 6.2)

TABLE 6.2 Isabel Toquero's personal community of family, friends, and acquaintances

Name	Relation to Isabel	Casta category	Occupation
Isabel Toquero	Self	Parda, mulatta	Textile worker
Capt. Gaspar Toquero	Father	Pardo	Militia officer in Tizimín; corn farmer in Dzonotake
Isabel Medina	Mother	Parda, mestiza	Textile worker
Alonso de Medina	Mother's father	Mestizo	
Ignacio de Medina	Mother's brother	Mestizo	Blacksmith in Merida
Gaspar Toquero	Brother	Pardo	Barber in Tizimín
Juan Toquero	Brother	Pardo	Peddler in Tizimín
Luis Toquero	Brother	Pardo	Ship worker in Campeche
Angela and Pedro	Sister and brother-in-law	Pardos	Pedro, a peddler in Tizimín
Lucas Tejero	1st husband	Mestizo	Corn farmer; Emal port worker; peddler
Sarg. Tejero	1st father-in-law	Pardo	Militia officer
Isabel Tapia	1st mother-in-law	India [Maya]	Textile worker
Sarg. Juan Perera	Witness to 1691 marriage, known her since childhood	Pardo	Tailor in Nabalam and Valladolid militia officer
Alf. Manuel Pérez	Witness to 1691 marriage, known her since childhood	Pardo, mulatto	Militia officer
Gonzalo de Aguilar	Witness to 1691 marriage	Pardo	Laborer in Nabalam and Loche
Joseph	Brother-in-law and alleged lover	Pardo, mulatto	Corn farmer and Peddler in Sucopo
Sarg. Tomás Pérez	Family friend	Pardo	Militia officer in Tizimín
Br. don Nicolás Gregorio Carrión	Gave her refuge in Tizimín; employed her in Merida	Spaniard	Priest
Pasqual Campero	2nd husband	Pardo	Barber; estancia worker
Francisco Campero	2nd father-in-law	Pardo	Estancia manager near Merida
Clara Pech	2nd mother-in-law	India [Maya]	

TABLE 6.2 *(continued)*

Name	Relation to Isabel	Casta category	Occupation
Diego Chan	Acquaintance from Tizimin whom Isabel claimed told her Lucas died in 1703	Indio [Maya]	
Juan Primero	Witness to 1703 marriage; known her two years	Pardo, mulatto, *Negro*	
Sarg. Pascual de Argaiz	Witness to 1703 marriage; known her two years	Pardo	Militia officer in Merida
Juan Mijangos	Witness to 1703 marriage; known her two years	Black slave	Enslaved manservant to Capt. don Diego de Aguaio in Merida
doña María Magaña and don Diego Francisco de Ancona	Padrinos of 1703 marriage	Spaniards	Magaña owned the estancia where the Camperos worked

Source: AGN-*Inquisición* 519, 3: ff. 301–98.
Note: The "casta categories" listed are all those assigned to individuals during the course of the investigation (documents dated 1691–1711).
 See Map 6.1 for the location of the places listed above.

should reflect Afro-Yucatecan social patterns identified in previous pages, and also indicate how her community was defined—as indeed they do.

Beginning with a discussion of the people who made up Isabel Toquero's community, this section tackles the remaining four bases of community proposed at the start of this chapter. These four—(3) ethnic or racial classification; (4) occupation; (5) kinship and family life; and (6) location—were inextricably tied together, forming the nexus of work, family, and home that determined how and where Afro-Yucatecans became part of the community that sustained them.

As Table 6.2 vividly illustrates, five of our six community foundations converged to create the human network that sustained Isabel Toquero. All that was missing was evidence of (1) African cultural elements or consciousness (an absence that conforms to the creolization pattern suggested above). But Isabel was (2) a baptized Catholic Christian who sought a formal church marriage, the second time risking everything when it must have been tempting to take the safer path and live as Pascual Campero's common-law wife; and when she sought refuge from an irate, jealous husband, it was to a church and priest that she fled.

Although Isabel never categorized herself with a casta term, she told Inquisitors that her family were mulattoes and mestizos, a vague multiethnic reference that reflects the various casta categories of her family and friends. The communities to which Isabel belonged were not so much defined by (3) ethnic or racial classification, but the lack of such, or at least lack of a single casta category that exclusively defined those communities. Spaniards played roles in Isabel's life, but at the level of patron or employer or—eventually—jailer; they were not part of her community. However, everyone else was. As a parda of pardo parents, most of her family and friends were free coloreds. But these were variously described as pardo and mulatto, and her first husband was called a *mestizo*, even though his parents were a pardo and a Maya. Indeed, both Isabel's mothers-in-law were Mayas, and both the rural village where she was born and lived for the first twenty-five years of her life (Dzonotake) and the neighborhood in Merida where she sought a second life (Santiago) were predominantly Maya settlements. The two places were not the same—in the 1688 census, Dzonotake is listed as having seventy adult Mayas, and only sixteen "mestisos y mulatos"; Santiago would have had more non-Mayas than that, and was more rapidly becoming multiethnic—but the communities that supported Isabel in both places were nevertheless very similar.[95] Neither was an exclusively Afro-Yucatecan community; both were inclusively nonelite communities, where pardos and mulattoes, mestizos and Mayas, married, lived, and worked together.

This is not to say that African origins were irrelevant to identity or community; on the contrary, they were highly relevant. Isabel Toquero was consistently called a *parda* in Yucatan, because central to her community identity was her link to the pardo militia (both her father and her first father-in-law were pardo militia officers); once in Mexico, that link and that community identity became tenuous, and Spaniards consistently called her a *mulatta*. Isabel's Inquisition interrogators in Mexico City had a fuzzy understanding of Yucatec geography and the casta identity of Isabel's family and friends, as though it was not immediately obvious to them that a parda in Yucatan in 1700 was part of a community that included *negros*, pardos, mulattoes, mestizos, and Mayas.

Such communities were also bound by (4) the occupations that helped to define castas. Various militia officers feature in the list of Isabel's friends and acquaintances, all of them pardos, while most of the men who were close to her farmed corn, as most men did in the countryside. Likewise, most women spun cotton and labored away in the cottage textile industry—including Isabel, her mother, and her first mother-in-law. Militia service was specific to the free-colored casta, and Isabel's connection to the larger community of pardo militia officers helped define who she was. But this was only one part of what defined Isabel's community; aside from anything else, "pardo" was a loosely defined category, and pardo militiamen spent far more time as corn farmers and laborers and petty peddlers [*trajinantes*] than as soldiers. In other words, the occupations of the men and women in Isabel's community were predictable nonelite jobs and activities.

As a free-colored woman in the countryside, Isabel Toquero cannot necessarily represent all Afro-Yucatecans. The experience of a slave in Merida, for example, was different—but not completely different. Slaves and servants in Spanish urban households were both part of a multiracial household and separate from the Spaniards who owned or employed them. Only in exceptional circumstances do we get glimpses of the degree to which domestic servants were privy to the daily lives of elite Spaniards, but these glimpses can be evocative. On occasion, when slaves were given their freedom papers, owners commented with gratitude on the loyal companionship offered by the slave over the years.[96] In criminal or Inquisition investigations, slaves and servants sometimes offered testimony that revealed details apparently not known to the associates or even family members of the Spanish protagonists of the case. One of the legal cases stemming from the 1792 assassination of Governor Gálvez was a conflict between the bishop and the countess widow of Miraflores, doña María Antonia del Castillo y Aguirre; the bishop's nephew was being investigated as a suspect by the countess's alleged lover (the lieutenant governor, don Fernando Gutiérrez de Piñeres), and in 1795 the bishop formally censured the countess for her indiscretions. Witnesses for the bishop claimed that a former African slave of the countess told them that don Fernando had recuperated from an illness in a bedroom in the countess's house, where the countess took care of him alone, personally applying medicine to his body.[97] This slave knew such details in part because she was a member of the household, and by extension a member of the community of elite Spanish households in Merida. But she also knew such details in part because she was "merely" a slave, and thus not a full member of that community; her full membership was with the community of castas in Merida, made up of other slaves, servants, Afro-Yucatecans, and the mixed-race nonelite in the city.

Finally, the network of people surrounding Isabel Toquero both in Dzonotake and its neighboring villages, and in Merida, were defined largely by (5) kinship and family and (6) location. Her parents and her husbands linked her to a supporting community first in the Dzonotake region, then in the Santiago neighborhood of Merida. The men in Isabel's life had broader horizons, but her worlds were geographically small. Furthermore, she perceived these communities as being sufficiently separate for her to marry bigamously in one without her family in the other finding out. Despite being quickly caught, this was probably not an unreasonable expectation. The bigamy records for Yucatan are full of Spaniards, with just a handful of Afro-Yucatecans and

Mayas; while there are probably various reasons for this, one factor is surely the fact that all Spaniards in a small colony like Yucatan were loosely part of a single community, whereas nonelites lived in more localized communities. Significantly, it was someone on the margin of Isabel's communities, the Spanish priest Carrión, who denounced her to the Inquisition.

The details of Isabel's early life in Dzonotake have already provided us with a good sense of how location and kinship combined to create local community identity. For women in the countryside, location was more narrowly defined; Isabel's world was restricted to the area around Dzonotake, Sucopo, and Nabalam (until her dramatic escape to Tizimin and then Merida). Her mother and mother-in-law (both named Isabel as well) worked cloth in the village and likewise would not have traveled far; her sister Angela moved away when she married, but only to Tizimin. The men in her life, on the other hand, worked and lived within a wider radius, extending from Emal on the coast down to Valladolid; two of her brothers lived in Tizimin, the third had moved as far as Campeche (see Map 6.1 and Table 6.2). The brothers in Tizimin would still have been part of Isabel's regional community, bound together by kinship, occupation, and location; their community was a network of the households created by each family member. The brother in Campeche would have been more loosely linked to his community in origin, tied more closely to his local household and to the other non-Spaniards who worked the docks and ships, as he did.

Indeed, one way of viewing how location and kinship helped create community is to see communities as networks of households. Anthony Kaye's exploration of community and identity among slaves in part of antebellum Mississippi emphasizes how labor and kinship defined "neighborhoods"; there was not "a single community" of slaves, but "many neighborhoods." Households were key building blocks of these neighborhoods, which were "the locus of all the bonds that shaped the contours" of slave society.[98] A recent study of the East End of the Caribbean island of St. John, using historical and archaeological sources, argued that black and colored residents forged a community that was based on "strong bonds among households." Households were multifaceted, comprising men and women, the young and the old; members could be free or enslaved, black or mulatto. These multifaceted households connected to each other through ties of kinship and work; the East End was "a community of households."[99] This was true of the Afro-Yucatecan communities, the difference being that because blacks and free coloreds were not isolated, but in a middle position between Spaniards and Mayas, their households were intimately tied to non-Afro-Yucatecan households.

To return to Spanish elite households in the city: Such households were one setting for the forging of community ties, consisting of Spanish family members as well as subordinate household members—the dependents, servants, and slaves whose own families created a kind of micro-household within the larger unit. These took various forms. One vivid example is that of the eighteenth-century Merida household headed by Capt. don Martín de Noguera and his wife, doña Isabel de Avila.

The Noguera–Avila household included various Maya servants and black slaves, including an African who had been baptized Francisco Noguera. In 1732, the captain and his wife purchased a woman from Arara, who was baptized Isabel Noguera (a name that connected her to both her owners; she also appears in the parish records as Isabel de Avila). At some point over the next five years Isabel married Francisco. In 1738 the slave couple conceived a son, who was baptized that December as Francisco Xavier; fourteen months later, they had a daughter (baptized Antonia María de Jesús), another daughter nineteen months after that (Beatriz Josepha), and a third daughter two years later (María Luisa). In the first two cases the godparents were relatives of doña Isabel de Avila (one her mother, the others possibly an aunt and uncle), and the godparents of the other slave girls were also elite Spaniards probably related to Noguera or Avila. This slave family of six were not the only Afro-Yucatecans in the Noguera–Avila household; the Spanish couple had meanwhile purchased in 1736 a slave couple from Congo (whom they baptized as Martín Lorenzo and Rita Benita Ignacia), and at some point acquired another black slave named María Josepha. In 1739 and 1742 this María Josepha gave birth to illegitimate daughters, baptized Juana Francisca de Paula and Thoribia María; the godfather of the first was a Maya named Pasqual Chan, probably the father of the baby and possibly a Maya servant in the same household (the godmother of the second baby was a sister of owner doña Isabel de Avila's).[100]

Thus by 1743, there were at least eleven black and colored slaves in the Noguera–Avila household, five adults and six children, linked to each other through common ownership, work experience, location, love, marriage, and birth—ties that also connected them to the Spanish slave-owning family and possibly to the household's Maya servants.

In fact, the baptism records that are the basis of this reconstruction probably reveal merely the tip of the iceberg of the relationships within the larger household. As Table 6.3 shows, close to a half of slave-owning Spaniards in eighteenth-century Merida kept slaves related to each other as husband and wife or as parent and child. The percentages in the table are gleaned from baptism records alone, so the real incidence of family relations within slave households was probably higher than that; in other words, in most elite Spanish households, there were not just slaves, but slave families.

The culture of slaveholding in Merida and Campeche served to nurture rather than break up families, albeit within an exploitative framework. Specifically, owners tended to buy and sell couples and their children as a unit. For example, Dr. don Juan Salvador González (a priest and member of

TABLE 6.3 Incidence of familial relations among slaves in the same household, Merida, 1710–89 (as recorded in black slave baptisms)

Slave owners	Relationships among slaves	
	Parent–child (%)	Married couple(%)
Spanish men	38	11
Spanish women	48	8

Note: In other words, of the 155 Spanish men who owned slaves in Merida in this century, 59 of them (38%) owned slaves who were related to each other as parent and child; and so on.

one of the colony's old conquistador families) owned a number of black slaves in the 1760s and 1770s, including Juana de Armas, who was married to a free black servant of his named Nicolas Burgos (aka Manuel Burgos); the couple had a baby girl in 1772, María Petrona, and a boy in 1775, Joseph María, both of whom, by the law of the womb, were born as slaves of Dr. González and became part of his Merida household. Not long after, the doctor sold Juana and her children to don Juan Joseph de Castro (a member of a newer elite family, descended from a seventeenth-century Portuguese immigrant and a powerful man in eighteenth-century Campeche); Nicolas, although free, likewise moved into Castro's service; in 1778 Nicolas and Juana had a third child, María Gertrudis, born as Castro's property.[101] Similarly, when Spaniards returned from Belize the following autumn with dozens of slaves captured from the British, they auctioned them off in Merida in family units—mostly couples, but in some cases including children, the largest being a family of four.[102]

Working conditions for slaves and poor Afro-Yucatecans must have often strained family relations, taking parents away from home for long periods and forcing children to work as soon as they were old enough to perform simple tasks. Diego Ramos, a pardo foreman on the San Benito fortress project in 1666–67 claimed that his long hours and lack of holidays—"not putting aside Sundays, neither observing fiestas, nor Holy Week, nor Corpus Christi"—meant that he never had a chance to see his wife and children, while the failure of the governor to pay him meant that his family suffered in poverty.[103]

Yet work did not always separate family members; it also tied them together. Ramos only worked at San Benito for eighteen months; he otherwise supported his family by going out into "the countryside, hunting deer and turkeys in the forest with my shotgun, taking them to be sold in this city." Ramos does not tell us about his family in detail, but he described himself as "a man who sees to and sustains his family," and it is not hard to imagine

him taking his sons hunting—teaching them the family business—as soon
as they were old enough to carry a dead turkey.[104]

The archives are full of passing references by Yucatecans to family, friends,
colleagues, and neighbors, revealing how profoundly and increasingly integrated colonial society was. In 1691, an Inquisition investigation into homosexual activity in a church alleyway opened up a glimpse onto a fairly
open gay network of free-colored, mestizo, and Maya men in mid-colonial
Merida; no doubt the scene extended to Spaniards too.[105] A mulatto estancia foreman named Diego Cuero was caught up in the 1761 Canek revolt and its aftermath; his responses to Spanish interrogators showed him to
be a typical Afro-Yucatecan middle manager, connected through his work
and social life both to Spaniards and Mayas.[106] In 1766, Magdalena Chi, a
resident of the San Román neighborhood of Campeche, complained vocif-
erously to the batab that her teenage daughter had been raped by the encomendero don Diego Rejón, in his city home; when the batab did not
respond quite as Chi had hoped, she took her daughter to be inspected by a
mulatta midwife, Fabiana Gómez, whom she called her *comadre*. One wonders if this was the same Fabiana Gómez who in 1774 was accused of being
a Spanish priest's concubine by Mayas in the Mani area.[107] In 1818, Enrique Chan, a Maya man living on the outskirts of Seyba Playa, named his
neighbors as a Maya nobleman, don Ermenejildo Balam, and Lucas Bera,
the captain of the local militia company; someone walking from Chan's
house into Seyba Playa would have passed the homes of Spaniards, Mayas,
and Afro-Yucatecans of various occupations and casta categories.[108]

These are just a few of the many examples not yet mentioned; dozens of
others have been mentioned or discussed in previous chapters. Together
they support my contention that Isabel Toquero's multiracial community
networks, both in the rural villages of her childhood and in Merida, were
representative of how people of African descent saw themselves and the
people they knew. There still remain to be described a few pieces of this
puzzle; in the next chapter, we look at how Afro-Yucatecans and Mayas came
together—particularly in marriage, and through the practices of love–magic
and folk healing—and how Spaniards so often portrayed African–Maya relations as hostile, rather than harmonious.

CHAPTER SEVEN

Magical Meetings

They [the Mayas] are a very harmless sort of People; kind to any
Strangers; and even to the Spaniards, by whom they are so much kept
under, that they are worse than Slaves; nay, the very *Negroes* will
domineer over them; and they are countenanced to do so by the
Spaniards. —William Dampier, 1699[1]

The mulatto had what is commonly called by the Indians a *sastun*,
which is an idolatry stone, and I took it and turned it over to the señor
curate; and it was at this time that the alcalde of the village of Tenabo
seized him, which gave me great satisfaction, as he could no longer
contaminate some of the Indians by teaching them his ceremonies.
—don Juan Antonio Ek, choirmaster of Tenabo, 1722[2]

THE STORY OF JOSEPH ZAVALA

In the early decades of the eighteenth century, Joseph Zavala earned a reputation as a powerful witch among the Mayas of Tenabo and its neighboring villages. Zavala lived in one of these villages, a hamlet called Xechekan,
and made a good living performing cleansing and curing ceremonies, and
healing sick villagers.

For example, when don Alonso Coyi's grandson became sick, Coyi sent
for Zavala. Coyi was a Maya nobleman and former batab of Becal, now living in Tenabo. He paid Zavala a fee of four pesos and two reales to cure the
boy of what the *curandero* [healer] said was an affliction of *xhunyopolyk*
(as the notary wrote it; *yopol ik* meant "broken wind" or "evil air," what
the Spaniards called *mal aire*). Zavala asked the boy's mother for a new set
of his clothes, which he took off with him to perform "many ceremonies"
to expel "the air of death" (these would have been *santiguar* or cleansing ceremonies). The boy would get better, Zavala assured the grandfather; it was
guaranteed by the amulet, containing a little mirror and some bones that
the healer wore around his neck.

On another occasion, a Tenabo resident, Tomás Ordoñez, came to Zavala with a broken arm; the curandero bought a cockrel and took Ordoñez into a cornfield to perform the curing ritual, which included sacrificing the cockrel and drinking *balché*.[3] If he still felt pain, Zavala told his client, it was because he was not treating his Maya employees [*sus criados los indios*] well. By this comment Zavala probably meant that there were Maya witches who could cause Ordoñez pain as much as Zavala could alleviate it. Indeed, Zavala lived and worked in a world that was primarily Maya. But it was not exclusively so; Ordoñez was a Spaniard, and Zavala himself was Afro-Yucatecan—described variously as a mulatto and *de color pardo* (he referred to himself as a *mulato libre*).[4]

Zavala's Afro-Yucatecan identity played a crucial role in the events that followed a curing ritual that, in January of 1722, went badly wrong. A Maya woman, Juana Uc, had fallen ill on the estancia where she worked; Zavala was called in, but the estanciero sent Zavala, Uc, and some of her family members home to Tenabo. There, in Juana Uc's thatched house, Zavala attended to her by burning copal incense around her bed. The copal burned well—too well, according to the Maya witnesses, who claimed that Uc was overwhelmed by the smoke. She cried out, and her screams brought her neighbors; Zavala was trying to smoke and burn her, they protested. They called the nearest cabildo officer, an alcalde named Diego Be, who locked Zavala in the Tenabo jailroom and sent for the Spanish priest.

Within days, a formal Inquisition investigation was initiated, beginning with denunciations from a stream of local Mayas and Spaniards, all of whom had heard the Uc affair told over and over—and most of whom had hired Zavala in the past to heal them or family members. Some witnesses may have been motivated by customer dissatisfaction; don Alonso Coyi and Magdalena Moo, for example, whose grandson/son seemed at first to respond well to Zavala's cure, but then suddenly worsened and died. Some may have resented Zavala's standing in the villages of the area, a status that rivaled that of local Maya officers—such as Diego Be, the alcalde who arrested him, and don Juan Antonio Ek, the choirmaster who stole Zavala's sastun [ceremonial stone] as soon as the curandero was arrested and gave it to the Spanish curate. Others may simply have wished to distance themselves from a man whom they had once respected and paid, but who now sat in jail, and to ingratiate themselves with the Inquisition (such as Ordoñez and other Spanish witnesses, and don Balthasar Cauich, the batab of Tenabo).

Zavala's story illustrates how witchcraft and magic acted as a meeting ground for Afro-Yucatecans and Mayas. It is important to emphasize that such practices were not marginal or subversive; they do not represent some kind of exotic fringe or medium of African and indigenous resistance. On the contrary, most witchcraft in colonial Yucatan centered on two forms of folk magic—healing and love–magic—both of which were very much mainstream concerns and preoccupations at all levels of colonial society.

The Zavala case also illustrates both the integration of Afro-Yucatecans into Maya communities and, conversely, the antagonistic relations that sometimes developed between Mayas and persons of African descent. As paradoxical as it sounds, both patterns were central to Afro-Maya relations, a dynamic that I have called (in discussing African–native relations in colonial Latin America in general) "the hostility–harmony dialectic." Only through close relations and multiple interactions did both harmony and hostility develop between Mayas and Afro-Yucatecans.[5] Finally, with respect to both intertwined themes of witchcraft and Afro-Maya relations, Zavala's story also reflects the important involvement of Spaniards, and the crucial—and seldom positive—role played by the Spanish colonial authorities.

This chapter offers three categories of evidence to demonstrate the complexity of relations between Mayas and Afro-Yucatecans. The first section examines the role played by Spaniards in exaggerating and fostering antagonism between Mayas and Africans. Also taken into account are the circumstances under which Afro-Maya antagonism did occur—generating one half of the hostility–harmony dialectic. The second section presents striking evidence that Afro-Maya marriages were common, undermining the very notion of Mayas and Afro-Yucatecans as clearly-defined, separate groups. This chapter's third section looks at witchcraft, particularly folk healing and love–magic, as a cultural meeting ground for Mayas, Afro-Yucatecans, and sometimes Spaniards too—but also a potential flashpoint for conflict.

THE SLAVE AND THE POSTMAN: BETWEEN MAYAS
AND SPANIARDS

In the spring of 1816 an African slave by the name of José Antonio Marcín found himself a prisoner of the colonial authorities, recovering from a head wound in the Hospital of San Juan de Dios in Merida. The charges he faced were serious ones—escape, theft, assault, and rape—and although his alleged victims were not Spaniards but Mayas, there was concern among Spanish officials that Marcín had fled his master to become an armed robber on the Campeche–Merida highway. If this were so, an example would have to be made of him, remarked one Merida official.[6]

Marcín had been born in Africa and transported to Spanish America in his teens; by the age of twenty-three or twenty-four he was living as the property of a don Ramón Acosta in Campeche, where he had been baptized and had married. But Acosta abused Marcín "with a great deal of work," as the slave put it. Thus one night Marcín left the house of his master and took off along the road to Merida, precipitating the events that led to his wounding, his arrest, and his imprisonment.[7]

According to the correspondence of the officials assigned to the case, between the communities of Maxcanu and Kopomá a Maya postman driving the weekly mail chest was attacked by Marcín. The bandit slave seized the money the mailman was carrying and then, armed with a small sword, he entered the Maya village of Becal and robbed two more Maya postmen, both express couriers, and raped a local Maya woman.[8]

When, a month after his arrest, Marcín was questioned by the authorities, he not surprisingly told a different tale. En route from Campeche, he had reached Kopomá about dawn, said the slave, where he surprised two sleeping "Indians," who ran off through the bush, apparently believing that Marcín intended to kill them. For his part, Marcín claimed he did not know these were postmen, although he did notice a letter tucked into one man's hat, and nor did he ask them anything or take anything from them. In fact, said Marcín, when he entered the village, the Mayas saw he was carrying nothing with him, and one of them gave him a coin, a half *real*, "to help him out."

When, further down the road, some Mayas approached him to take him back to Kopomá (under orders, it turned out, from the local *juez español*), Marcín resisted arrest because he believed the men had been sent by his master in Campeche (it was at this point that the slave received his head wound). He later denied robbing or raping anyone, and asserted that he had brought a sword from his owner's house solely to protect himself from the highway thieves and murderers about whom he had heard. As for his other alleged Maya victims, he remembered passing two mailmen on the road between Becal and Maxcanu, and he recalled briefly conversing with a Maya woman seated on a rock beside the road.[9]

It is doubtful whether the Spanish authorities believed Marcín's version of events, but in any case he remained under guard in the hospital while local officials were ordered to collect written testimony from the Maya witnesses. As the months passed and spring turned into summer, Marcín's situation must have seemed to him increasingly bleak.[10] Little did he know that the case was meanwhile turning in his favor, for Spanish investigators found Maya witnesses either unwilling to speak of the incidents or ignorant of them.

Only one Maya man, a Clemente Poot, was prepared to make a statement regarding the runaway slave. Poot stated that he had been carrying an express letter [*un extraordinario*] to Merida and was a half-league outside Maxcanu when he encountered Marcín; noticing that the African was carrying a machete or sabre in his hand, Poot became nervous and ran into the bushes. He denied any knowledge of the Maya woman supposedly raped, and as for robbery, admitted only that he had heard it said that Marcín had stolen money from another Maya postman, one from Becal.[11]

The judge assigned to the case in Merida concluded that there was insufficient proof to convict Marcín of theft or rape, and that his only clear crime was that of flight from his master; the other charges could well be, suggested the judge, "pure dissemination and lies." On June 25, 1816, four-

and-a-half months after his arrest, Marcín was absolved and sent back to don Ramón Acosta in Campeche.[12]

The Marcín case is about many things, but one of its prominent themes seems to be African–Maya hostility. If, as late as 1816, a black man could have such an experience in a Maya village, then surely colonial Yucatec history must be marked by antagonism between Africans (and perhaps Afro-Yucatecans) and Mayas. If not, how should the case be read? And what other evidence offsets the impression given above that Africans and Mayas simply did not get on?

First, Marcín's experience suggests mutual distrust between Africans and Mayas. It is clear that people of different casta categories in Yucatan were usually able to converse with each other, frequently had reason to mix with each other in work and social settings, intermarried, and generally contributed to a continuous process of what we might call *interculturation*.[13] Yet could individuals of different castas nevertheless view each other with ignorance and suspicion?

We have seen examples in previous chapters of the attitude toward Mayas of some Afro-Yucatecans in positions of authority: the black slave, Marcos, whose job in the 1540s was to round up Mayas to be servants in Merida; and Melchor de Segovia, who allegedly abused his position as a tribute collector in the Calkiní region in the 1650s and 1660s, inspiring fear and hatred among the local Mayas.[14] But José Antonio Marcín was not an agent of colonial rule, and his attitude and expectations regarding the Mayas are not easily detected. On the one hand, he seems naïve, seemingly unaware of the reactions his appearance provokes from indigenous strangers. Surely he knows not to startle a sleeping man by the roadside at dawn, not to carry his sword in his hand unsheathed, not to strike up conversation with a strange woman in public—especially when all these encounters cross racial barriers. And what are we to make of his claim to have received an unsolicited charitable donation from a Maya man who shortly before had run for his life at the sight of this same African? Yet, paradoxically, Marcín also seems to be aware of the fear that he inspires in Mayas; perhaps the contradictions and naïveté apparent in his statement in fact reflect the slave's skill at dissembling—to borrow a term from the Spanish judge—as a form of defense.

The Maya view of Africans is seemingly easier to detect. There are occasional negative references to Africans in colonial Maya-language documents that suggest prejudicial attitudes may have circulated in the villages. For example, a 1774 petition complaining of various licentious activities by Spanish priests identifies the Maya or mestiza concubines of the priests either by name or community of origin, whereas the one Afro-Yucatecan mistress is tagged, in Maya, "that ugly black devil Rita [*kakas cisin Rita box*]."[15]

The evidence of the Marcín case suggests that the indigenous expectation was that an African stranger would take from them with violence; he would steal, rape, and kill. In one Spanish official's version of the affair, a robbery was provoked by two Maya drivers refusing to take the African with them, leaving him to walk—an incident, whether imaginary or not, in which prejudice appeared to play a role. In Maya eyes, the African had little in material wealth or social status, but he had much in terms of physical strength and sexual menace.

Clemente Poot's admission that he heard rumors about Marcín would seem to support the Spanish judge's conclusion that the spreading of rumors created events that never took place; Maya notions of African behavior provided the fertile ground for those rumors, so that Marcín frightening a Maya postman could become a series of violent robberies by a dangerous *negro* on the loose, and Marcín exchanging a few words with a Maya woman by the roadside could become an African forcing himself upon that woman. Postman Poot admitted that the sight of an African man walking along the highway toward him carrying a weapon was enough to send him running into the bush. In Marcín's own account, two Mayas awoke by the roadside at dawn to see him approaching and assumed that his intention was to kill them; note that this was Marcín's inference based on their running from him, for the Mayas themselves apparently said nothing to this effect. Likewise when a group of Maya men approached Marcín on the road later that same morning, his reaction was to fend them off by force. He waved his sword at them, they threw rocks at his head; each side, distrusting the other and assuming violent intentions, immediately turned the encounter violent.

One context of this mutual distrust was the fact that highway robbery was not uncommon along the camino real; Marcín himself expressed fear of such an attack. Not long after the Marcín case, in 1821, the Spanish authorities arrested, convicted, and in a few cases executed the members of a Campeche gang who had allegedly committed a series of often-violent robberies along the highway and in nearby Maya communities.[16] The accused were all *negro* or pardo militiamen, and most of the victims were Mayas, which is broadly reflective of the ethnic dimensions of the twenty-three criminal cases I have reviewed from the last colonial decade (see Table 7.1). In these the victims are all Spanish, mestizo, or Maya (not a single one is Afro-Yucatecan). All casta categories are represented among the roughly forty people accused of crimes in these cases, but half of the accused are Afro-Yucatecan (two *negro* slaves; the rest free pardos), and 70% of the accused were castas (either Afro-Yucatecan or mestizo).

The pattern suggests a clear bias in a judicial system quick to prosecute cases where free coloreds and mestizos were the alleged criminals, but extremely reluctant to pursue cases where such people were the victims. In fact, the system seemed to serve to protect Spaniards and Mayas from other castas—at least in Merida in the 1810s.[17]

Whether this pattern of prosecution reflected the realities of criminal activity (less likely) or colonial society's view of castas (more likely), it must

TABLE 7.1 Crime and casta in Merida, 1811–21

Case #	Casta of accused	Casta of victims	Type of crime	Convictions
1, 2	Spanish or mestizo*	Maya	Murder	1
1, 4	Maya and pardo*	Spanish	Property theft	1?
1, 6	Spanish	Spanish	Theft	1
1, 7	Mestizo and pardo	Spanish	Horse theft	3
1, 7a	Pardo	Spanish	Abduction	0
1, 8	Spanish*†	Spanish and mestizo	Property theft	1
1, 9	Pardo or mestizo*	Maya	Horse theft	1
1, 10	Pardo and mestizo	Maya	Theft	4
1, 11a	*Negro* slave	Maya	Theft, rape, etc.	0
1, 13	Maya and mestizo	Spanish	Cattle theft	1
2, 1	Maya and pardo*	Spanish	Cattle theft	3
2, 4	Pardo or mestizo*†	Maya	Murder	1
2, 6/6a	Mestizo*	Mestizo*	Murder	1
2, 7	Mestizo	Maya	Theft and assault	0
2, 8	Maya and mestizo	Spanish	Cattle theft	2
2, 8a	Pardo*	?	Theft	2
2, 9	Mestizo?	Spanish	Cattle theft	1
2, 11	Pardo*	Spanish and Maya	Theft and murder	1
2, 13	Pardo*	Spanish	Property theft	?
2, 14	Maya	?	Cattle theft	0
2, 14a	Maya	Maya	Murder	0
3, 2	Pardos*	Maya†	Theft and assault	1
3, 4	*Negro* slave	Spanish and English	Theft and murder	1

Source: AGEY-*Criminal* (Colonial), with the "Case #" being volume and expediente numbers.

Notes: Cases were prosecuted in Merida, with crimes committed in its jurisdiction (i.e., in the city or the surrounding villages). I have not included in this table cases filed in the AGEY under "Criminal" but consisting of nonviolent disputes among the Spanish elite (such as 1, 3, an 1814 libel case between the bishop and a Merida city alcalde) or nonviolent crimes against the state, such as tobacco fraud (1, 1) or bigamy (1, 7b).

* Indicates that one or more of the accused or victims were militiamen.

† Indicates the involvement of women (in 1, 8 a mestiza aunt of one of the accused thieves is accused of being an accessory to the theft but is not prosecuted; 2, 4, mestiza woman witness and possible accessory to murder but never prosecuted).

Note that I have simplified the prosecutorial outcomes—in some cases, for example, convictions are overturned on appeal; in others, an acquitted man ends up doing more time in jail while his case is investigated than a convicted man who has fled.

Militia records contain additional cases from the final decades of the colonial period—e.g., a pardo or mestizo militiaman accused in 1801 of stealing property from a fellow pardo or mestizo militiaman, on the run after charges were filed, archived in AGEY-*Militar* (Colonial) 1, 17—but these by definition feature pardos and would thus have skewed this table.

have partly stemmed from and also fostered Maya (as well as Spanish) prejudicial suspicion of Afro-Yucatecans, who in turn may have resented Mayas and Spaniards for the bias in the system. There may also have been a general awareness that Spanish officials tended to make an example of certain casta criminals, to show they were tough on crime, even though most infractions were committed by Mayas (who were the vast majority of the population, after all). This was what Capt. don Joseph de Marcos Bermejo implied in a 1768 letter to the judge heading the residencia inquiry into the Navarrete governorship. The fact is, asserted Marcos Bermejo, the thieves in Yucatan "are pickpockets, not muggers, and typically they are Indians," and in the few cases when "they are proven to be men of color," the gubernatorial authorities are quick "to throw them in the city jail" and initiate a criminal investigation. Thus in his attempt to defend Governor Navarrete's record, Marcos Bermejo both indicated that Spaniards believed there was a casta crime problem in the colony and dismissed that belief as nonsense.[18]

The cases in Table 7.1 show Afro-Yucatecans interacting with Mayas and Spaniards in numerous ways (reflecting the patterns of community formation discussed in the previous chapter). Yet the prosecution pattern gives the impression that free-colored men—especially pardo militiamen—preyed on late colonial citizens; soldiers are among the accused in eleven of the twenty-three cases. Prosecution patterns both reflect and contributed toward the bad reputation of pardo militiamen. That reputation was also enhanced by a few notorious misfits and troublemakers. The phenomenon went back at least into the mid-eighteenth century. For example, the mulatto militiaman Diego González was convicted in 1766 of leading a shabby, shameful life ["*dessastrada vida*"]—he allegedly disobeyed his captain, threatened to kill his father-in-law, and shacked up with his brother's Maya wife.[19]

Another notorious free-colored troublemaker was Marcial Socobio (his case is included in Table 7.1). Socobio was a literate, pardo barber living with his wife in La Mejorada, one of Merida's old Maya barrios that became a multiracial neighborhood in the eighteenth century. Unfortunately, Marcial had a drinking problem. He was regularly arrested for being drunk and disorderly, and for repeatedly stealing aguardiente from the *tiendas de pulperia* [general stores] in his neighborhood. He was accused of attacking Spaniards on two occasions, and implicated (although not convicted) in the death of a Maya man. His arrest record stretched from 1803 to 1822, when he was captured under accusation of being a highway bandit. Is it being too generous to Marcial to suggest that his problems stemmed from his miserable experience serving with the pardo militia in the fort at Bacalar? He hated the place so much that in 1803 he deserted. When prosecuted fourteen years later for liquor theft, witnesses made much of the "bare sabre," his old militiaman's blade, with which Marcial had terrorized a shop boy.[20]

There is no record of Marcial Socobio's ultimate fate. But his notoriety in Merida extended into the mid-nineteenth century, when he was featured as a bandit in a historical novel by Gerónimo del Castillo Lenard. At the age of ten (in 1814) the novelist had seen his uncle, a priest named Miguel Lenard, assaulted by a pardo; the prime suspect was Marcial Socobio, but he was never prosecuted.[21]

Whether Socobio really was a violent menace to society—or just an unlucky, misunderstood alcoholic—we cannot share the assumption made by early nineteenth-century Spanish Yucatecans that his problems were rooted in his African ancestry. His pardo identity may have influenced his arrest record, but not his behavior. To enlarge the context of the point: Mayas and Afro-Yucatecans did not always treat or respond to each other based on their ethnic or casta identities. For example, the Maya rebels from Sahcabchen plotted in the 1660s, according to loyal Mayas from Hool, to raid Campeche and kidnap the town's black slaves. During the campaign to suppress the Sahcabchen revolt, Mayas from Hool caught Juan Ake coming from Sahcabchen; the cabildo "interrogated him in jail" and found out that Ake had been sent by the batab of Tzuctok, with a message about the plan to steal slaves.[22] But Mayas were not motivated by prejudice against Africans; they simply hoped to do damage to the colony and acquire valuable, fungible property (as Spaniards themselves were to do in Belize the following century). As so often, Afro-Yucatecans were uncomfortably caught in the middle, and when Maya rebels fell on the Spanish estancias close to the frontier, "they consequently caused the deaths of Spaniards and mulattoes" on these properties.[23]

Similarly, Marcín was viewed with suspicion by Mayas along the camino real not simply because he was black, but because he was a stranger, an outsider, carrying a weapon. All Africans were not instinctively feared or distrusted, as there were people of African descent living in Maya villages and marrying Maya women going back two centuries before this.[24]

However, Spanish officials assumed that Mayas responded negatively to Marcín simply because he was an African. By initiating a criminal investigation, Spaniards legitimated the rumors about the runaway slave and they formalized the antagonistic relationship between the African and Maya protagonists. Even if the Spanish judge ultimately deemed the accusations unsupported by evidence, the authorities clearly viewed them with credibility from the onset. This reflects the fact that Spaniards also provided the context that made this case possible. I argued in Chapter Three that Spanish ethnocentrism in the sixteenth to eighteenth centuries should not be equated with modern racism. But by the final decades of the colonial period—and certainly by the time of the Marcín case in 1815—Spaniards were propagating and perpetuating through the judicial system and through colonial culture in general a more coherent set of prejudicial stereotypes. Also circulating among non-Spaniards, these stereotypes arguably were early manifestations of modern racism (recall from the previous chapter the racist sentiments of José Carreño in his 1806 report on the black residents of San Fernando Ake).

In fact, there are signs in the Marcín case record that the evolution of accusations against him resulted less from the Maya reaction to the African, and more from Spanish officials writing down, communicating, and thus spreading over a period of a month increasingly exaggerated accounts of the incident. For example, a week after Marcín's arrest, an *intendente* noted that the slave had assaulted "the Indian driving the [mail] chest"; two weeks after the arrest, the *juez español* in Maxcanú remarks that no mailman or courier had been assaulted, but simply that the African had taken money from the drivers in retaliation for them refusing to give him a ride; four weeks after his arrest, Marcín is told that he is charged with a series of assaults and robberies involving three or four Maya mail carriers.[25] Likewise, at these same points in time Marcín is accused first of hurting a Maya woman, later of hurting or violating her [*estropio a una yndia ó la violentó*], and finally of "forcing her to have carnal relations with him." The fact that in the end no Maya witnesses can be found to support such accusations may reflect not only Maya unwillingness to commit perjury,[26] but also the evolution of rumors outside the Maya community. Clearly Spaniards as well as Mayas played a role in the imaginative development of Marcín's crimes.

A further dimension of this Spanish role in the Marcín case was the Spanish expectation of hostility between Africans and Mayas. One Spanish judge's claim that Maya drivers had refused Marcín a ride is not borne out by the testimony of either Marcín or Clemente Poot, suggesting that this was simply an invented explanation for the incident that seemed plausible to a Spaniard; that is, the Maya reaction to the African was rejection, the African reaction to this was violence. Indeed, a century earlier the province's bishop had asserted that blacks "disdained to be equated with Indians," while around the same time the procurator in Merida reported the Spanish fear that the increasing number of mulattoes in the Sierra region would result in them abusing the local Mayas and provoking a general African–Maya conflict.[27] In the official report on the 1789–91 Merino y Cevallos governorship pardo residents of rural communities are called "vagrants [*bagamundos*]" and "the only people from whom the Indians receive frequent abuse [*frecuentes vejaciones*]."[28]

The Spanish assumption that Africans would harm native people goes back to the Conquest (when Spaniards used armed Africans to subdue Mayas; the reader will recall the story of Sebastián Toral). Around 1550 the veteran conquistador Alonso Rosado was commissioned by Lic. Herrera (at the time senior royal judge in Merida) to hunt down and recapture a "squad" of twenty escaped black slaves; the summary to his 1570 probanza states that these slaves had done "much harm to the natives [*muchos daños a los naturales*]" and López de Cogolludo's mid-seventeenth-century account gives a similar impression. However, the more detailed testimonies contained within the probanza either suggest or clearly state that Rosado's success "prevented" the local Mayas from such harm. Indeed, the very rationale behind the recapture campaign was to protect the indigenous villagers upon whom the colony depended, but Spanish anticipation of African–Maya hostility easily shifted, years later, into an assumption that hostilities actually occurred.[29]

The stereotype of *negro* sexual aggression, seen in the Marcín case, was extended by Spaniards even to homosexual relationships. For example, in 1691, a mulatto named Juan Ramírez was accused of sodomizing a Maya man, Andrés Chan, in an alley behind a church in Merida. Inquisition officials gave credence to another Maya man who claimed to have seen Juan mounting Andrés, and they seemed to accept Andrés's own claim that he was an innocent (even feminized) victim of the mulatto's attempts to "handle and inspect all his private parts." Despite evidence that Andrés was a willing partner, and that Juan was not a predator but part of a social circle of free-colored and Maya homosexuals, Spaniards were quick to categorize Juan as the mulatto sexual aggressor.[30]

This theme of African predators and native victims was not particular to Yucatan; the claim that blacks and mulattoes abused natives was a common refrain throughout New Spain. Alonso de Zorita wrote in his extensive report on the kingdom in the 1560s that abolishing *visitas* or tribute-collecting tours by colonial officials would "do away with harrassment of Indians by servants, blacks, mestizos, mulattoes, and horses that the *visitadors* and their officials bring with them."[31] As in Yucatan, native petitioners in central Mexico employed the theme as a legal strategy to fight competition from Afro-Mexican traders or to prevent blacks from settling in Nahua villages. The use of sexual stereotypes about Africans was common. One late sixteenth-century petition in Nahuatl alleged that blacks were "not married. They go about taking concubines. They take people's spouses away . . ."[32]

Nahua complaints about black men stealing wives has an ironic relevance to Yucatan, where black and colored men married Maya women with a regularity that had a profound impact on Afro-Maya relations and on the nature of Afro-Yucatecan and Maya communities. We have seen earlier how Afro-Maya interaction could foment hostile relations, and the role played by Spanish prejudices and expectations of such hostility. We now turn to look at the primarily harmonious relations reflected in Afro-Maya marriage patterns.

AFRO-MAYA MARRIAGE

Throughout the mid-to-late sixteenth century Spaniards complained of the degree to which Indians interacted with blacks and mulattoes, while the Crown passed a series of laws aimed at keeping the two groups apart and preventing nonnatives from settling in native communities.[33] For example, the viceroy of New Spain in the 1570s, don Martín Enríquez de Almansa, convinced that the colony would eventually be overrun with castas, asked the king to approve a law enslaving the offspring of African men and native women, and to request a papal ban on African-indigenous marriages.[34] The king did neither, of course, but the viceroy's belief that miscegenation between castas and Indians would be the undoing of Mexico is telling. Indeed, central to this discourse was a great deal of finger-pointing.

For example, in a letter to the king in 1572 four Franciscan friars in Yucatan denounced the colonists' use of *negros* and mulattoes to oversee their Maya servants and even to marry Maya women as a way of securing additional servants.[35] Probably in response to this and similar complaints, the crown issued an edict in 1578 that amounted to a mandate for segregation in New Spain; it ordered that "mulattoes, mestizos, and *negros* . . . be prohibited from being in the company of Indians."[36] Four years later the governor of the colony, don Guillén de las Casas, complained to the king that efforts to comply with another royal edict specifically banning Afro-Maya marriages were being undermined by priests continuing to administer such marriages with the bishop's approval.[37] Meanwhile, in a 1567 letter to the king from two Xiu and two Pacab batabob of the Mani region, the Mayas themselves complained that Spanish settlers were taking Maya women and children as servants, "even to serve the blacks and mulattoes."[38]

The language used in these complaints suggests that such documents may tell us more about Spanish—and, to some extent, Maya—prejudicial stereotypes about Africans and less about the demographic and social realities of African–Maya relations. For example, the 1578 royal edict argued that "mulattoes, mestizos, and blacks not only treat [the Indians] badly and use them, but they teach them their bad customs and idleness and also various errors and vices that might corrupt and hinder the desired goal of the salvation of the souls and ordered living of said Indians." The notion that people of mixed-race, especially African in descent, were a threat to civil, social, and spiritual order, was clearly rooted in a perception of such people as being culturally inferior—with ideas of racial inferiority lurking not far beneath the surface. These complaints make it equally clear that the Mayas soon picked up on such ideas—or at the very least were sufficiently aware of Spanish prejudices to make political use of them in a letter to the king.

The late sixteenth-century complaints probably also reflect the fact that in these first colonial decades African–Maya interaction was new enough in the city—and rare enough in the countryside—to be worth complaining about (and worth using as a weapon in the battle between the civil and ecclesiastical administrations in the colony).

However, Afro-Maya unions started occurring in Merida and Campeche in the sixteenth century, and they were common throughout the seventeenth and eighteenth centuries (see Table 7.2). Such marriages in Merida were most likely to occur in the barrios of Jesús María and Santa Lucía, both of which had evolved as Afro-Yucatecan satellites of Spanish Merida (in contrast to the five Maya barrios of Merida, which had evolved from precolonial native communities; see Chapter Six and Map 6.4). Most of Santa Lucía's residents were of African descent throughout the colonial period, whereas Jesús was one of the most racially mixed communities in Yucatan.[39] However, Merida was not a segregated city; mixed couples also married and lived in the five cah-barrios, especially the three that were closest to city center (i.e., Santiago, La Mejorada, and San Cristóbal).

Table 7.2 presents data culled from the marriage records of Merida's Afro-Yucatecan parish for almost the entire colonial period. The column on the far right shows that the total number of black husbands fluctuated and was barely three times larger in the late eighteenth century than it was in the late sixteenth; by contrast, the number of free-colored husbands grew steadily, and was twenty-one times larger in the late eighteenth century than it was two centuries earlier. This pattern loosely corresponds to the general growth patterns of the Afro-Yucatecan population.

The central columns of the table quantify marriage choices. Looking at the colonial period as a whole, black men married Maya/mestiza women and Afro-Yucatecan women in more or less equal numbers (although black men markedly preferred Mayas and mestizas between 1650 and 1750, reversing that preference after 1750). Colored husbands similarly married women from both categories in close-to-equal numbers, but with a general leaning toward Maya/mestiza wives before 1700, and a small pendulum swing after 1700 toward Afro-Yucatecan partners. Arguably, Afro-Yucatecan men were more likely to marry Mayas and mestizas in the early-to-mid colonial period simply because they outnumbered all other women, but by the late eighteenth century the free-colored population in Merida was large enough to provide potential partners of every kind. I suggest, however, that the patterns of shift and contrast in Table 7.2 are ultimately negligible; the existence of many informal unions that went unrecorded in the parish books, and the unreliability and ambiguity of casta classifications, means that we should primarily look for the larger patterns. In this case, that larger pattern is very clear: Black and mulatto men in Merida did not create families within a distinctly Afro-Yucatecan community; their world, down to the most intimate level, was as much Maya as it was African, as much mestizo as it was mulatto.

Not that we must leave things at that. The wives to whom I have referred earlier as Maya were actually identified in parish records as *india*. Indian was generally a more reliable category than pardo (for example), but it was not without its own complexity, especially in the city. We now turn back to baptism records, specifically to those from 1759–74. During that fifteen-year stretch, baptism records identified parents both by name and casta label. This allows us to compare casta label and surname. Most of those classified as "india" and married to black and mulatto men had Maya

TABLE 7.2 Marriage choices by Afro-Yucatecan men in Merida, 1567–1797

	Maya/mestiza wives (100%)	Afro-Yucatecan wives (100%)	Totals (100%)
1567–1601			
Black husbands	30 (54)	26 (46)	56
Colored husbands	22 (56)	17 (44)	39
Both	(55)	(45)	95
1602–51			
Black husbands	76 (54)	65 (46)	141
Colored husbands	50 (64)	28 (36)	78
Both	(58)	(42)	219
1657–1700			
Black husbands	36 (67)	18 (33)	54
Colored husbands	110 (51)	106 (49)	216
Both	(44)	(56)	270
1701–50			
Black husbands	75 (62)	46 (38)	121
Colored husbands	138 (33)	277 (67)	415
Both	(40)	(60)	536
1751–97			
Black husbands	52 (33)	107 (67)	159
Colored husbands	383 (46)	440 (54)	823
Both	(44)	(56)	982
Totals (1567–1797)			
Black husbands	269 (51)	262 (49)	531
Colored husbands	*681 (45)*	*851 (55)*	*1,532*
Both	950 (46)	1,113 (54)	2,063

Sources: AAY, Jesús María, *Libros de Matrimonios*; Fernández Repetto and Negroe Sierra (1995: 28, 31, 32, 35). A version of part of this table also appeared in Restall (2006).

Note: The "black" husbands are those classified as *negro* and moreno; the "colored" husbands are those labeled mulatto and pardo (for reasons explained in Chapter Three, it makes no sense to further separate these categories).

patronyms, as we might expect (see Table 7.3); the Maya patronym system persisted throughout the colonial period (surviving in modified form to this day), and the vast majority of Mayas in Yucatan carried their father's sur-name. But a quarter of these "indias" married to Afro-Yucatecans had Span-ish surnames (not their husband's surname). This does not mean they were not Mayas; the impact of Spanish ways of doing things was more strongly felt in eighteenth-century Merida than earlier and elsewhere in the colony. But it does suggest that such women were more likely to have Spanish,

African, or Nahua ancestry—or some combination of any of these with Maya. One of the surnames I have called Spanish was Conga, probably derived from "Congo" (sometimes used as a surname by Africans in the Spanish colonies). Most notably, the Nahuas (and other Mesoamericans) who accompanied the Spanish invaders and settled in Merida in the 1540s had, or took, Spanish surnames.[40] Two centuries later, despite the steady miscegenation reflected in Tables 7.2 and 7.3, many of the descendents of those Mesoamericans would still have been classified by Spaniards as Indian. This meant that Afro-Yucatecans were part of a community that was not only multiracial, but racially and ethnically highly complex.

The other pattern emphasized in Table 7.3 is the difference in surnames between the Indian wives of black husbands and of mulatto husbands. Black men's wives were more or less equally drawn from the two surname categories, whereas mulatto men were far more likely to have Indian wives with Maya patronyms. Furthermore, while there was some overlap in names, black men largely married women from a different pool, regardless of whether those women had Maya or Spanish surnames. Why this difference?

The question is a problematic one, but I suspect it reflects a subtle distinction between the two *india* groups, one paralleled by a similar distinction between black and mulatto men. Black men, many of whom were slaves or former slaves or the children of slaves, were more closely tied to Spanish owners, employers, and households; they were more likely to live in Spanish households or in the neighborhoods around the Jesús María and Santa Lucía churches, cheek by jowl with blocks of Spanish homes. Women classified as Indian but with Spanish surnames—and thus not only Maya but also mestiza, Nahua, or descended from other Mesoamericans—were also more likely to be attached or affiliated to Spanish Merida through networks of kinship and work.

TABLE 7.3 The surnames of Afro-Yucatecan men's "Indian" wives in mid-eighteenth-century Merida

	Black husbands (%)	Mulatto husbands (%)	Name pool (%)
"Indian" wives with			
Maya patronyms	29 (57)	183 (82)	49 (0.23)
Spanish surnames	22 (43)	41 (18)	37 (0.59)
	51 (100)	224 (100)	

Source: AGAY-*Jesús*, Libros de Bautismos Vols. 3–5.

Note: The 275 couples are all those thus identified who brought babies to be baptized in the Jesús parish, 1759–74. The "black" husbands are those labeled *negro*, both enslaved and free. For further details, including the specific names, see Table G.4 in Appendix G.

Free-colored men, on the other hand, like women with Maya surnames, were more likely to be independent or semi-independent, and reside in one of the indigenous neighborhoods, like Santiago and San Cristóbal that ringed the Spanish downtown. In those neighborhoods, the same Maya families had been intermarrying since before the Spanish Conquest, a fact reflected in the relatively small pool of patronym groups into which Afro-Yucatecan men married (see the far right column in Table 7.3; for example, an eighth of all women with Maya patronyms who married mulattoes during these fifteen years were called "Chan").

We have already seen examples of how Afro-Yucatecans and Mayas met, so one example, introduced in Chapter Five, should suffice. This is the case of the Congo-born free African named Manuel Bolio, who in 1757 married a Maya woman named Josepha Chan (alias Chepa la Monja, because she had been a nun's maid) in Merida's Jesús parish (see the couple in Figure 7.1). Both were domestic servants and were able to find work to-

Figure 7.1 An Afro-Mesoamerican family. Source: José de Páez, *De negro e india, lobo, 5,* ca. 1770–80, oil on copper, 50.2 × 63.8 cm. Private collection. Reproduced by permission.

gether, moving through three Spanish households during three years of married life. However, Manuel then went alone to work in Bacalar for a few months; the months turned into years and his visits back to Merida became less and less frequent. Eventually, he moved on to Cartagena, where, twenty years after his marriage to Josepha in Yucatan, he was arrested by the Inquisition for his bigamous marriage to a negra woman.[41]

As we have seen previously, not all Afro-Yucatecan men who married Maya women were black, or former slaves, but nor too were they domestic servants or poor workers. For example, membership in the pardo militia—even at the officer level—did not mean that a man was more closely oriented to Afro-Yucatecans and somehow less affiliated with local Mayas and mestizos. As examined in Chapter Five, militia officers enjoyed status, privileges, and even social mobility, but they were high-ranking within the multiracial Afro-Yucatecan community, not separate from it. Domingo Aldana, for example, was a captain in one of Merida's pardo militia companies. His wife, Michaela del Castillo, was classified as "india" in their son's baptism record of 1758, but like many of the women in Table 7.3, she may have been of Maya, Nahua, other Mesoamerican, or mestizo ancestry.[42]

Although I have not worked through comparable marriage records for Campeche, I have tabulated marriage choices of non-Spaniards for a thirteen-year, mid-colonial sample period (see Table 7.4). This shows that a third of Afro-Yucatecan men entered Afro-Maya and Afro-mestiza unions; this is less than Merida's 46% for almost the whole colonial period, but as Merida's pattern fluctuated over the years, I suspect Campeche's full-period figure would be higher.

On the other hand, the Campeche figures for the end of the seventeenth century are comparable to the Afro-Maya marriage patterns for rural Yucatan in 1700 (see Table 7.5). As the free-colored population grew during the seventeenth century and spread from Merida and Campeche out into

TABLE 7.4 Marriage choices by non-Spaniards in Campeche, 1688–1700

Afro-Yucatecan couples		Afro-Maya couples	
Negro and negra	5	*Negro* and india	2
Negro and parda	2	Pardo and india	8
Pardo and parda	34	Pardo and mestiza	8
Moreno and negra	1	Moreno and mestiza	1
Moreno and morena	1	Indio and parda	1
Moreno and mulatta	1	Mestizo and parda	1
Afro-Yucatecan endogamy	44 (67%)	Afro-Maya marriage	21 (32%)

Source: Archivo Histórico de la Diócesis de Campeche (AHDC), Caja 90, Libro 650 (marriages of non-Spaniards), fs. 2–23.

Note: There was one pardo–española marriage, so the total number of cases is 66.

TABLE 7.5 Marriage choices in the Yucatec countryside, 1700

	Negra	Free-colored women	Mulattas or Mestizas[b]	Mestizas	Maya women	White and Spanish women[c]
Negro					1	
Free-colored men[a]		24		5	17	
Mulattos or mestizos[b]			17		17	
Mestizos	1			119	50	1
White and Spanish men[c]				3	2	82

Sources: 1700 matrícula in AGI-*México* 1035; also see Solano (1975).

Note: I have excluded marriage choices by Maya men, listing only marriage choices by non-Maya men detailed in the census (which excludes about a fifth for which the man's wife is not identified).

[a] Listed as mulattos, pardos, or chinos.

[b] These are the entries from Tekax, where the two categories were listed as one.

[c] Listed variously as *blancos* or *Españoles*; includes one *castizo* marriage.

the countryside, so did marriages between Mayas and Afro-Yucatecans become more common. Such unions took place at all levels of Maya society. For example, Captain don Nicolás de Chavarría had acquired the titles of don and captain by virtue of heading a company of Maya archers [*indios flecheros*] in the 1670s or 1680s and probably by serving as batab of Motul (Spaniards accorded him the status of "*cacique*" or hereditary noble lord in Motul). Despite this, his name suggests some non-Maya ancestry (Nahua, mestizo, or pardo); either way, by the 1690s he moved in the orbit of that middling group of elite non-Spaniards, in which pardo militia captains and Maya noblemen were prominent. In 1668, don Nicolás had married Ana María Rodríguez; her father was another Maya nobleman with a captaincy and a Spanish surname, Captain don Francisco Rodríguez, and her mother was a parda named Josefa de Acevedo. One of the official witnesses to the marriage was a pardo militia captain, Clemente de Acevedo, who was also the groom's neighbor in Merida.[43]

Table 7.5 presents the marriage choices made by 339 non-Maya men living in towns and villages in the Yucatec countryside in 1700—specifically the 52 rural communities included in the matrícula of that year. What is significant here is the degree to which mixed-race men married Maya women. Whereas those men identified as "white" or "Spanish" married women identified the same way (94%, although I suspect there was a high level of "passing" in this category, especially by mestizos and mestizas), the rate of endogamy was only 52% among free-colored men and 70% among mestizos. Put another way, 38% of men of African descent were married to Maya women

(48% to either mestizas or Mayas), and 30% of mestizos had Maya wives. Among the mestizos and mulattoes of Tekax (who were listed in a single joint category in the census), half had chosen to marry Maya women.

This pattern of mixed marriages obviously perpetuated the resultant pattern of miscegenation, but it also meant that the Maya population (a majority of some three-quarters in the whole colony, and closer to 90% in the countryside) effectively absorbed the mestizo and free-colored minority. For example, Nicolás Sanabria was classified as a mestizo in Tinum, but he had once served as governor of the village (almost always a post reserved for a Maya elder), was married to a Maya woman, Augustina Ucam, and their four sons were all "married to Indian women of the same village." In the eighteenth century the Sanabria name would continue to indicate a seventeenth-century link to a Spaniard, but the Sanabrias in Tinum would be overwhelmingly Maya, both biologically and culturally.

The obscuring of a non-Maya heritage would have been all the more rapid in the case of mulattoes, as a distant African ancestor was less likely to be celebrated or remembered than a Spanish one. For example, Andrés Ruiz was a mulatto tailor and corn farmer in Izamal in 1700. Ruiz and his Maya wife, Pasquala Chan, had five sons and five grandsons; among the sons, two were married to mulattas, one to a Maya woman, making two of the five grandchildren three-quarters (and possibly seven-eighths) Maya in descent. Biology aside, the Ruizes of Izamal, like the Sanabrias of Tinum, were culturally native; the Ruiz sons lived as corn farmers and hunters, and they almost certainly spoke only Maya and lived in thatched-roof houses.[44]

The steady marrying of Afro-Yucatecans into Maya families in the countryside continued into the nineteenth century. To avoid statistic fatigue, the example of one late colonial Maya village should be enough. In late colonial Tekanto, the Afro-Yucatecan population was very small (in 1802, pardos were 1.5% of the parish). Therefore, only 2% of all marriages in the village during the eighteenth century were Afro-Maya unions. However, during these decades, a quarter of all pardo marriages were with Maya women. Their grandchildren, if not their children, were counted as Mayas. In other words, even in a small Maya community, where the Afro-Yucatecan population seemed tiny as late as 1802, there were generations of Afro-Maya marriages gradually turning a population that appeared to be overwhelmingly indigenous into an Afro-Maya one.[45]

LOVE–MAGIC AND OTHER MEETINGS

María de Casanova was born in Merida exactly a century after its founding. A Spaniard of modest background, she grew up in the city and by the age of thirty was married to a Francisco de los Reyes. In March and September of 1672, Casanova went to see the commissary of the Inquisition, Dr. Antonio de Horta Barroso, and made a pair of denunciations against María Maldonado (wife of Alférez Joseph Martín de Herrera) and her brother Manuel Maldonado. Until the previous year, Casanova had lived in María Maldonado's house as a companion who helped her around the house [*en compania en cassa*]. In other words, Casanova was not a servant, as a Maya or mulatta woman might be, but nor was she quite the social equal of the Maldonados.

María de Casanova's first denunciation laid out the framework of her accusation against Maldonado, while also seeking to establish Casanova's own innocence in the matter. Maldonado allegedly "made use of spells and magic, to cast a spell on a certain man." Casanova was told by Maldonado to find and bring to the house a woman named Catalina Álvarez (now dead two years), "who understood spells and witchcraft [*hechissos, y encantasiones*]." Maldonado consulted with Álvarez behind closed doors, as she did with Michaela Montejo, a free mulatta who lived in San Cristóbal and was also an expert on witchcraft; Montejo came twice to the house and she and Maldonado locked themselves in a room so that Casanova could not hear what was happening, although she knew it was all about a spell "to make a man really love her." Maldonado also consulted a third woman, a mulatta whose name she could not recall ("Ana" was later written in the margin), who brought some enchanted flowers [*unas flores encantadas*]. The fourth woman that Maldonado hired was a free *negra* named Ursula, a former slave of doña Isabel de Sepúlveda, who "knew something about witchcraft." Ursula brought a jug of water and some flowers, and told Maldonado to leave them in the man's doorway, and he would consequently love her. She also made similar use of various Maya women, whom Casanova did not know.

Finally, Casanova's sister told her that Sergeant Manuel Maldonado (María's brother) had sought out a Maya woman to put a spell on a woman "whom he was seeing." Casanova may have borne resentment against Maldonado, as a former employer, but she also revealed a more immediate motivation for denouncing her: Casanova claimed that on an earlier occasion she was on her way to denounce Maldonado to the Inquisition when she ran into Maldonado's sister, Isabel, in the street; Isabel threatened to "bear witness" against Casanova should she tell what she knew about her sister; that night, the threat worked, but in the long run it was counter-productive, helping to convince Casanova to seek out the Holy Office "to absolve herself," lest she be implicated as an accessory by the Maldonados.[46]

Casanova's second denunciation, made six months later, was more detailed. In it, she described the love–magic potion that María Maldonado made with the help of one of the four witches she had hired (Casanova did not specify which one). The recipe and ingredients were pubic hair ("plucked from the shameful parts"), fingernail clippings, a tiny piece of material from her skirt, all burned together and the ashes mixed in with a tablet of chocolate, ground, washed, mixed with water, and whipped up in the manner that chocolate was made, with the drink given to a man whose deeper affections Maldonado hoped to win. Having stated earlier that the spells were discussed and cast behind locked doors, Casanova now asserted that she saw all this herself, as she lived in the house as a close friend [*comadre*] in whom Maldonado had "complete confidence." Furthermore, Casanova claimed that Maldonado often soaked tree bark in water to make balché, a drink "much used by the Indians to get drunk and commit idolatries," which she gave to "her beau [*su Galan*]" to seduce him more quickly.[47]

Casanova also offered a little more information about Sergeant Manuel Maldonado's procurement of love–magic services. She claimed to have heard the sergeant discussing with Juana Pacheco her work as a witch [*bruja*] in partnership with Lucas de Arguello, a free black; Arguello had admitted to the sergeant, he said, that "they flew about together as witches."[48]

The Inquisition moved slowly on Casanova's denunciations; the first was not ratified for two years, the second not for two more years (in February 1676). In April that year the commissary sent his report, with a copy of all the interviews, to the senior tribunal of the Inquisition in Mexico City. He commented that María Maldonado had an absentee husband and that it seemed clear that she resorted to "spells and illicit means to retain her lovers." Yet the case's content and evidence did not appear to cause the commissary great concern. Some of the accused were already known to the Inquisition (there were existing files on the free black Lucas de Arguello, the late Catalina Álvarez, and the "ill-reputed" free mulatta Michaela Montejo). Others were insufficiently implicated. María Maldonado was not to be indicted because it had been "years" since her accuser had lived in her house (an ironic judgment in view of the slow pace of the Inquisition's investigation). Nor was her brother Manuel to be further investigated, as he was "not poorly viewed" and his accuser (Casanova's sister) was not a credible witness.[49]

The Casanova–Maldonado case is deceptively straightforward. A lonely wife indulges in a little love–magic and is denounced to the Inquisition by her disapproving friend; the Inquisition investigates slowly, turning up love–magic practitioners already known to the Holy Office, and shies away from prosecuting the Spanish siblings from an old elite family who had allegedly hired the witches. Yet the case also prompts a number of complex questions, whose answers reveal much about love–magic as a cultural contact point or meeting place—and thereby much about the multiracial nature of colonial Yucatec society. For example, to what extent did Spaniards, Mayas, and Afro-Yucatecans share a common culture of belief on the efficacy of love–magic? Was Merida as full of love–magic witches as the case suggests? Was love–magic practice part of a larger popular culture shared by all Merida's residents? What was the role of the Inquisition in this culture and its policing? Did Afro-Yucatecans suffer disproportionate attention from the Inquisition over witchcraft and related matters? Were the 1670s unusual or typical in the history of witchcraft and the history of the Inquisition in colonial Yucatan? What motivated accusers to denounce others for hiring or working as witches? Were these cases primarily about witchcraft, or was the topic merely a medium for the playing out of other social relations?

To answer these questions, we shall step back a moment from love–magic to look at the larger colonial context of how witchcraft (in its broadest definition) acted as a meeting ground for Mayas and Afro-Yucatecans—a context in which both the Casanova–Maldonado and the Joseph Zavala case make sense.

We begin in 1580, when the Inquisition arrested an African slave for eating. The black man, a sexagenarian named Cristóbal Negro, was the property of a Spanish priest in Campeche. The priest's jurisdiction included Xequelchacan, not far from the port town, and Cristóbal found himself regularly in the vicinity of this small Maya village. One day, in the forest outside the village, Cristóbal came across a meal laid out on a rock; the food and drink were fresh and tasted good. He ate it all, remembered the spot, and next time his duties brought him to Xequelchacan he returned to eat his fill again.

The problem was that these meals were not simply the lunches of local Maya farmers momentarily left unguarded. They were offerings made to a Maya deity on a sacred stone in the ruins of what had been an ancient temple. Furthermore, Cristóbal's unwitting intervention in the ritual was observed by several Maya men of the village. At first, one of the Mayas confronted Cristóbal but did not try to stop him. The second and third time, the Mayas hid and watched—no doubt later debating, perhaps heatedly, what could be done to prevent this sacrilege. After the fourth time that Cristóbal had eaten what was intended for a more divine consumer, the elders of Xequelchacan reported the slave to the priest—risking, in the process, their own arrest for idolatry.

There is no record of the Mayas being investigated by the so-called Indian Inquisition—the *Provisorato de Indios*, a separate agency within the Church, less than a decade old in 1580, with jurisdiction over natives only. But the Inquisition proper arrested Cristóbal Negro immediately under suspicion of participation in "idolatrous" practices and engaging in a diabolistic ritual consumption. However, after questioning Cristóbal and seven Maya witnesses, the investigators became convinced that the slave's motive was nothing more than hunger, and the case was promptly closed.[50]

The record of the Inquisition's brief investigation into Cristóbal Negro's idolatrous moments enables us to imagine an early example of a "magical meeting." By this I mean an African–Maya dialogue—in the Cristóbal case literally a conversation, but in the larger sense a cultural exchange, over folk–religious practices. Spaniards condemned such practices as magical in a strongly negative sense (using such categories as witchcraft, idolatry, superstition, magic, heresy, and blasphemy). We can imagine this sixteenth-century example with the assistance of the text of a conversation between Cristóbal and the local Maya *maestro*, Andrés Cuyoc (a Maya maestro was officially a schoolmaster and choirmaster—like don Juan Antonio Ek in the Zavala case—but unofficially he sometimes played an important role in the maintenance of pre-Christian religious practices, especially in the early colonial period). According to the accounts of both men, the maestro happened upon Cristóbal eyeing an offering that had earlier been placed upon a ceremonial stone outside the village. The slave asked the maestro if the bread was good to eat. The maestro said it was; the slave ate it. He then asked about the other items, with the same response and outcome. The exchange seems stilted, strained perhaps, as though each side were sizing the other up, each hoping to avoid open hostility, each aware of the cultural barrier between them—the African wanting the food but hoping to get it peacefully, the Maya wanting to safeguard the offering but preferring to avoid an unpleasant incident.

Although the Inquisition filter through which we must view this encounter may have muted much of its emotional and cultural content, the meeting of Cristóbal Negro and Andrés Cuyoc seems characterized by mutual ignorance accompanied more by bemusement than by hostility. In Merida and Campeche, Afro-Maya marriages were already common, but in the countryside there were as yet few black or free-colored settlers. The Negro–Cuyoc case might therefore be taken as symbolic of the nature of Afro-Maya interaction in the early colonial countryside.

However, much changed during the seventeenth century. Afro-Yucatecans moved gradually but steadily into Maya communities, and Spanish priests began to discover evidence of black and mulatto involvement in the folk–religious practices against which the church continued to battle into the eighteenth century. In 1650, in the village of Tizppitah, a Spanish priest found a stone idol and a copal figurine in the house of pardo militia captain Alonso del Puerto. In 1674—near the start of the Horta Barroso régime—the Inquisition put three mulattoes on trial for idolatry.[51]

Evidence of this kind of collaboration increased in the eighteenth century; although the church seemed sporadically to make headway against the Maya folk practices that it condemned as idolatrous, the growth of the non-Maya rural population and increased links between urban and rural communities served to stimulate folk culture. Inquisition officials in Mexico City were shocked to learn of an idolatry case involving Maya community officials and local mulattoes in Hunucmá parish—as late as 1785 and in a parish so close to Merida. The "idolaters" had performed a traditional New Year's ceremony, complete with animal sacrifices, with an old mulatto named Apolonio Casanova in the role of senior Maya priest. The Mexican inquisitors commented condescendingly that only in Yucatan would "this kind of vice" be "generally practiced."[52]

Thus the existence of Joseph Zavala, as a mulatto curandero or witch-healer operating in Maya villages in the 1710s and 1720s, was not unusual. For years, he lived and worked without open conflict in the villages of the Tenabo area, as did other Afro-Yucatecan healers and love–magic practitioners in other parts of the colony. So why did Mayas turn against him in 1722? The answer lies in four factors: (1) the fact that Zavala's influential position in the area generated covert jealousies that were brought into the open by his arrest; (2) the fairweather nature of public belief in any healer or doctor (denouncing Zavala to the Inquisition was the equivalent of a malpractice suit); (3) the hostility–harmony dynamic that generally characterized Afro-Maya relations; and (4) the divisive role played by Spaniards. Zavala had been a member of the local community; Maya identity was more rooted in community (in what the Mayas termed the *cah*) than in ethnicity. But unlike the Mayas who in 1580 watched Cristóbal Negro eat their offerings four times before turning to a Spanish official to stop him, the elders of Tenabo moved against Zavala as soon as his powers seemed to evaporate. Then, in giving testimony against him to Inquisition officials, these Mayas remembered that he was "a mulatto."

Zavala's methods and materials are also indicative of the way in which Spanish, African, and Maya practices met through witchcraft. In the countryside, the Maya influences were not surprisingly strongest (see Table 7.6). One ancient Maya practice used by native and free-colored healers was the burning of copal incense, both as a cure and a diagnostic tool (that is, a method of divining what ailed the patient and when he or she was likely to die). Mayas used copal; a mestiza named María Rincón was tried in Merida in 1675 for using copal in healing rituals; Joseph Zavala was condemned for using it in his ill-fated attempt to cure Juana Uc in Tenabo.[53]

Zavala also kept a sastun, a Maya stone altar or witch's stone, used for divination, as well as balché. This alcoholic tree-bark beverage served both as an offering placed on an altar and as a beverage consumed by the sick or by all participants in cleansing and curing rituals. Balché usage was very common in Maya villages, and even among Mayas in urban neighborhoods, and the church waged a sporadic, uphill, and ultimately unsuccessful battle against the drink and its ritual use. It was thus commonly employed by Afro-Yucatecan healers too; the three above-mentioned mulattoes tried by the Inquisition in 1674 made, consumed, and offered balché.[54]

Zavala's identification of evil air or winds (such as the *xhunyopolik*) as a cause of illness marked him as an Ah Macik, a kind of shaman or Maya witch able to expel evil winds; for the Inquisitors who tried him, this was idolatrous and suggested that Zavala had made a pact with the devil. A final Maya witch's tool also used by Afro-Yucatecan curers was hallucinogens. This was one of the few methods not apparently used by Zavala, but others used them—ranging from a mulatta named Magdalena, who was arrested in 1614 for using peyote in divination rituals, to Petrona Trujeque, a

TABLE 7.6 The materials of magic: Objects used by Afro-Yucatecan curers and love–magic professionals

	How used in: Curing or preventative medicine	Or in: Love–magic
Amulet	Curer wears it around his/her neck; grants curing power and protection from harm	Wearer has power to seduce
Copal	Curer burns it to divine or cure sickness	
Sastun	Witch's stone used for divination and to make offerings	
Chants	Chant, incantation, or oration spoken or sung by the curer	Love prayers taught to and used by the person hiring the love–magic professional
Balché	Alcoholic tree-bark beverage used as an offering, as a cure, or a ritual drink	Given to seductee
Hallucinogens	Such as peyote, used in divining and curing rituals, sometimes in balché	
Egg	Suspended in a doorway to ward off harmful spirits or winds	
Other food	Spell placed on food (e.g., cucumber) to poison someone	Enchanted food or drink (usually chocolate) given to seductee
Flowers		Usually enchanted roses, to be given to the seductee, or placed under the bed, or ground up and mixed into a chocolate drink
Herbs		Mixed, often as powder, into chocolate or rubbed on the body (e.g., of a wayward husband)
Water		Water from a special flask or vase, used by the professional to enchant flowers or chocolate
Hair and sweat		Seducer places head or pubic hair, and/or sweat from armpits or soles of the feet, in chocolate drink to give to seductee

Source: AGN-Inquisición 39, 4; 3680, 3; 626: ff. 163, 186, 188, 208v, 423; 627, 6; 919, 26.

mulatta tried in 1748 for being a *curandera adivinadora* and using hallucinogenic drinks in divination and curing.[55]

Inquisitors were also particularly interested in Zavala's amulet. Amulets were little bags of leather or cloth, or tiny chests of copper (like Zavala's). They were known as *bolsas de mandinga* in Brazil, where they were the most common witchcraft object in the colonial period. They seem to be both European and African in origin, and perhaps native American too; the differences lay in what the amulet contained. Throughout Spanish America and Brazil, amulets or bolsas typically contained pieces of stone and strips of cloth or ribbon; ideally, chips of altar stone, cloth used to wipe drops of wine from the communion chalice, and ribbon taken from a statue of Jesus or a saint.[56] Zavala's amulet contained pieces of shark [*xooc*] bone, and a red ribbon—that he was accused of revering as though they were saint relics. Amulets strengthened the healing powers of a curer, and protected him or her from snakes, wild cats, human enemies, and so on.

As Table 7.6 shows, some of the tools of a curer's trade were also used by love–magic or sexual witchcraft practitioners. For example, in love–magic, the amulet gave the wearer power over anyone whom they wished to seduce. Balché was used in both healing and love–magic, but more often chocolate was the enchanted beverage of choice; elemental to love–magic culture was the principle that the seductee should be unaware that spells were being deployed, hence the common use of ordinary things like flowers and cups of chocolate (also see Table F.2 in Appendix F). The exception was cases of cheating husbands, who were given herbs or enchanted chocolate to keep them from straying; wives sometimes wanted their husbands to know that magical forces were at work.

Chants or incantations were also used in both healing and love–magic rituals. Usually European in origin, love prayers tended to be adapted from prayers to saints and often accompanied by Christian rituals such as making the sign of the cross or etching it in the dirt. One mulatta's love–magic rituals involved a prayer [*orasion*] to San Antonio; a Spanish woman in Merida paid for this, and then denounced the mulatta (whose name she did not know) because it failed to work. Some of the phrases used did not exactly conform to Catholic orthodoxy, so not surprisingly witches were sometimes denounced for saying "wrong-sounding things [*cossas disonantes*]" (as one denouncer put it).[57]

In Campeche in 1626 a pair of love–magic witches, one Maya (Catalina Puc) and one mulatta (Antonia), used spoken riddles to cast spells. The procurer, a Spaniard named Catalina Antonia de Rojas, one day called in Catalina Puc, who was a servant in her house, for a chat. "Madre," said Rojas (according to her own testimony), "do you know how I can stop a certain man from visiting a certain woman and coming to see me instead?" Puc asked for the names of the man and woman, and over the next few days performed various rituals. One centered on the uttering of riddles, using words, "that she [Rojas] does not understand." On another occasion Puc placed an article of clothing on a table and walked around it, "with other ceremonies and words." Puc also brought in a friend of hers, the mulatta Antonia, when Rojas asked the Maya witch, "Who also knows so much?"[58]

Catalina Puc was a well-known love–magic professional in Campeche; in another case, the following year, a slave named Isabel Morena asked Puc to help her get a lover back. "You must bring him back to me," pleaded Isabel, "as you well know how to do."[59] The same love–magic professionals pop up again and again in the Inquisition records from Merida and Campeche, especially in the 1620s–1630s and 1670s, and they tend to be free mulattas (two-thirds of Afro-Yucatecan accused of love–magic were free mulattas; see Appendix F). Michaela Montejo, for example, one of the witches named in the Casanova–Maldonado case mentioned earlier, is repeatedly denounced or simply mentioned in passing in Merida cases of 1672–76; one gets the impression that when an Inquisitor asked anyone in the city to name a love–magic practitioner, Montejo was usually the first person to come to mind (in none of these cases, however, was she tried).[60]

The extant record of Inquisition investigations—both in general in Yucatan and specifically with respect to Afro-Yucatecans—gives the impression that the seventeenth century was the heyday of such activities. This appears not to be a question of document survival, but a reflection of the larger history of the witch craze in the Atlantic world and its manifestation in Yucatan. The preoccupation with witchcraft and the devil that swept parts of Europe in the late sixteenth and early seventeenth centuries had spread to the Spanish American colonies by the 1590s; it lasted throughout the seventeenth century, peaking variously according to local circumstances, but fading rapidly in the early eighteenth century in every colony.[61]

The phenomenon can be detected in Yucatan as early as the 1570s (with the formal establishment of the Holy Office in New Spain, without jurisdiction over native peoples), but did not translate into sustained Inquisitorial activity until the 1620s. The two periods when the Holy Office was most active in the colony were the 1620s–30s and the 1670s (see Figure 7.2). Yucatec historian Pedro Miranda Ojeda has argued persuasively that the level of Inquisition activity in any year was largely dependent upon the attitude of the commissary. The commissary in Merida was the most senior representative of the Inquisition in Yucatan, and the colony's sole commissary until *comisarías foráneas* [literally "foreign," but meaning "secondary"] were established in Tabasco in 1628, Valladolid in 1635, and Campeche and Champotón in 1645. The late seventeenth-century concentration of cases coincided with the 1671–81 commissary term of Dr. don Antonio de Horta Barroso, the most zealous such official in the history of the Inquisition in Yucatan. After Horta Barroso's death in 1681, Inquisition activity was sporadic (virtually nonexistent under some commissaries), secondary commissary offices were discontinued, and Holy Office commissaries became bureaucrats "dedicated to using Inquisitorial office as a social and political display cabinet."[62]

Therefore, the increase in the number of Inquisition investigations directed at Afro-Yucatecans in the seventeenth century was not rooted in any major shift in attitudes toward people of African descent. Rather the impetus for this activity came from outside the colony, with Yucatan affected by a broader Atlantic world pattern. Afro-Yucatecans were certainly impacted by the active Inquisition of the seventeenth century, as well as by the less vigorous Holy Office of the eighteenth. But this impact was not disproportionate in demographic terms—for example, there were twenty-three love–magic cases initiated against Spaniards between 1616 and 1696, but only thirteen against *negros*, pardos, and mulattoes during the same period (partially illustrated in Figure 7.2).[63] Furthermore, these figures do not include investigations and prosecutions of Maya witches, who did not fall under Inquisition jurisdiction, but do appear in the records of the Provisorato (the so-called Indian Inquisition) and in Merida's cathedral archives through to the nineteenth century.[64] It is tempting to imagine that Inquisitors readily believed that people of African descent were more likely than Spaniards to believe superstitions, to have engaged in acts of witchcraft, and to have uttered blasphemies. But the archival record does not clearly support such an assumption. With Spaniards and Afro-Yucatecans at compara-

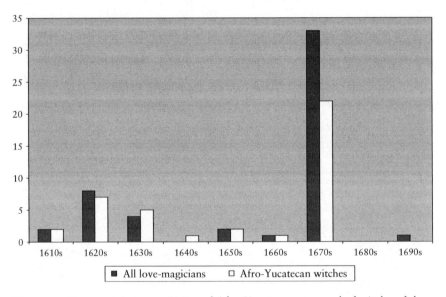

Figure 7.2 Love–magic accusations and Afro-Yucatecans accused of witchcraft by the Inquisition; Merida and Campeche, seventeenth century.

ble numbers in the seventeenth century, it would appear to be Spaniards who are disproportionately investigated by the Holy Office.[65]

Historians of witchcraft had tended to view the practice of magic as subversive in some way, with female practitioners resisting gender-based oppression and black or native American practitioners resisting race-based oppression. In the conventional view, witchcraft was "antithetical to the social order."[66] But was this really the case in colonial Yucatan (and, by extension, elsewhere in the Spanish Empire)? For this to be so, witchcraft would have to have been seen by Spaniards in the colony as a primitive set of beliefs and practices that one might expect to find among *negros* and *indios*, but not Spaniards. Yet in Yucatan Spaniards not only appear in witchcraft investigations as accuser and accused, but they were more often the targets of such investigations than were Afro-Yucatecans and Mayas. Furthermore, Inquisition investigators themselves do not appear in the record as culturally distant or distinct from those they were investigating. On the contrary, Inquisition cases strongly suggest that everyone in the colony shared a common culture of magic, if not in terms of details, then certainly in terms of acknowledging that magic was "real." Not until the late eighteenth century would Enlightenment ideas reconfigure magic and superstition as irrational acts rather than improper ones.[67]

To say that Afro-Yucatecans, Mayas, and Spaniards—including Inquisition officials—shared a common culture of magic is not to claim that they all believed the same thing. As scholars of witchcraft have long noted, faith (or lack thereof) in witchcraft has often been seen, even by practitioners, as separate from an appreciation of its efficacy. In other words, one can claim not to "believe in" witchcraft, but still to assert that "it works"—in part because others believe in it.[68] Nevertheless, putting issues of belief aside, witchcraft practices—especially folk healing and love–magic—were not marginal but mainstream aspects of colonial Yucatec culture. This culture was a product of the colonial encounter, and was created and shared by Afro-Yucatecans as much as Mayas, mestizos, and Spaniards.[69]

In the countryside, as Mayas were the overwhelming majority, they tended to be the customer base for Afro-Yucatecan witches (like Joseph Zavala). But in Merida and Campeche, Spaniards with the means to pay love–magic professionals were the primary (but by no means sole) customer base. Table F.2 (in Appendix F) presents a sample of love–magic cases, showing how the typical case featured Spanish women both as procurers and denouncers, and Maya and mulatta women as love–magic professionals. In other words, love–magic culture was as multiracial as the city was; it was central to city life.

Women hiring professionals were not the only Spaniards participating in love–magic culture. When Spanish priests punished witches, or even just asked questions about them, they validated many of their practices. The free mulatta Michaela Montejo was able to make a living as a love–magic practitioner in Merida in the 1660s and 1670s because her profession was by necessity a public secret. As a scholar of South African witchcraft notes, "gossip is the medium within which [witchcraft] lives."[70] This was certainly true in colonial Yucatan, and when Inquisitors repeatedly interviewed someone like Michaela Montejo they contributed both to the public and secret or illicit nature of her practice.

Indeed this was true throughout the colonial period—from the smattering of late sixteenth-century cases through to the Zavala case in the 1720s. It was also true of a Spanish priest's reaction to the actions of Tomasa Camejo, a mulatta in Panabá (on the northeast coast), who fell ill after walking half-dressed through a cornfield one evening. Concluding that her actions had upset the *balam*, or cornfield deity, Tomasa went to the village shaman or witch for help. The witch, Bernardo Tsahe, took Tomasa, her son, and three other villagers into the field, where they made the balam an offering of tortillas, refried beans, and balché. As luck would have it, the parish priest heard of the ceremony, interrupted it, and arrested the participants, giving them "ninety-nine lashes over three successive days."[71] This incident took place in 1816, illustrating the persistence of folk practices in the countryside, as well as the integral roles played by Afro-Yucatecans. The priest did not understand who or what the balam was (had the shared culture of magic already become a thing of the past?), but his punitive violence nevertheless lent credibility to the beliefs of the free-colored and Maya villagers; to the Spaniard, their beliefs and actions were wrong, perhaps nonsensical, but not to be dismissed as trivial or inconsequential.

We left Joseph Zavala, the mulatto curandero, imprisoned while his former customers and neighbors denounced him to the Inquisition. What, then, was his fate? The Inquisition condemned him in 1723 for idolatry, divination, magic, and superstition, sentencing him to eight years labor in an *obraje* [textile mill]. In 1726 he escaped, but the following year was caught in Chilapa and sold to a Cuernavaca sugar mill for a five-year term; after three years he escaped again and was caught in Iguala, where he remained in jail for almost two years. His repeated attempts to escape, and the resulting damage he caused to the jail, earned him twenty-five lashes in 1732. His petition to be released on the grounds that he had served his eight-year sentence was denied, and he was sentenced to a further four years of "reclusion" in the Hospital of San Pedro in Mexico City. There the case ends.[72]

Zavala's cruel fate is a reminder that the Spanish role in Afro-Maya relations could be devastating. He might have placated the people of Tenabo and continued to work as a healer in the region had it not been for the intrusion of Inquisition priests, stirring up antagonism against the mulatto shaman and ruining his life. When Spaniards were not afraid of African–Maya hostilities they feared a threat to the colonial order from African–Maya collaboration—in, for example, a potent combining of mulatto "witchcraft" and Maya "idolatry." In the end, Spanish concern over Afro-Maya relations, unfounded and misdirected as it was, had less to do with how Mayas and Afro-Yucatecans got on and more to do with the suspicion with which Spaniards viewed non-Spaniards.

Certainly there was often conflict and prejudicial attitudes between Mayas and Africans, especially early in the colonial period and in the countryside where non-Mayas were initially rare. But even later, and in multiracial, nonelite urban neighborhoods, there could be tension and strife between people of different castas; the harmony–hostility dialectic always underlay Afro-Maya relations, to some extent or another.

Yet despite this fact, and despite Spanish interference, most of the time Mayas and Afro-Yucatecans worked and lived together, married and had children together, practiced the rituals of healing and love–magic together, and in general forged complex Afro-Maya communities. Zavala's life story from 1722 on is more dramatic and tragic, and illustrates the hostility that sometimes existed between Afro-Yucatecans and Mayas; but his life before 1722 better symbolizes the harmony that more often characterized Afro-Maya interaction.

Conclusion

The Afro-Yucatecan Middle

One afternoon in 1690, Juan Patricio was tortured in Merida. An African slave owned by the *contador*, don Pedro Enriquez Noboa, the young Juan Patricio had been arrested for beating a Spanish priest with a wooden stick. The beating was severe enough that the priest, Br. don Ignacio de Esquivel, the curate of Hunucmá, had suffered a broken arm and multiple bruises. Because Juan Patricio had fled, and then once captured given inconsistent responses to questions, he was interrogated under *tormento*.

Juan Patricio admitted that he was motivated in part by revenge, as Esquivel had struck him a few days earlier. But he also insisted that he was acting under instructions from his owner. The slave's statements, and those by other protagonists and witnesses, gradually revealed that the real conflict of the case was between the priest, Esquivel, and the slave's owner, Enriquez Noboa—and the cause of the hostility was a Maya girl. The girl lived in Tahmek, part of the Enriquez Noboa encomienda; but the priest decided to take her from Tahmek and deposit her in his mother's Merida household as a domestic servant. This infuriated Enriquez Noboa, who offered to free Juan Patricio if he prevented the priest from taking the Maya girl from the village. As it became clear, after Juan Patricio's capture, that Enriquez Noboa was the true author of the two assaults, the priest and his mother filed criminal complaints against both slave and owner; Enriquez Noboa was excommunicated, and then forgiven by the bishop; and so the dispute dragged on.

What at first appeared to be a case of an escaped slave on the loose (with the pardo militia called in to help, and a reward of fifty pesos or relief from tribute for capturing Juan Patricio), turned out to be a classic colonial example of Spanish conflict over Maya resources—with an Afro-Yucatecan caught in the middle.[1] This book began with a slave who became free by helping to found the colony of Yucatan (Sebastián Toral), so perhaps it is fitting that it end with a slave (Juan Patricio) who risked life and limb in the hope of being freed. Most Afro-Yucatecans were born free, but there would have been no Afro-Yucatan without the transatlantic slave trade.

That trade "remains a puzzle for historians, for the more it is studied, the harder it is to fully explain," as John Thornton has put it.[2] Thornton is thinking mostly in terms of scale; that is, how could so many Africans and Europeans involve themselves in a trade that victimized so many over so many centuries? The immensity of this "moral disaster" may not seem so relevant to Yucatan, which received something like 0.1% of the total number of Africans sold in the Americas as slaves. Yet the size of the Afro-Yucatec population was comparable to the number of Spaniards in the colony throughout its history, rendering the moral question as germane at the local level as it was at the larger one. In fact, issues of racial identity and the morality of the slave trade were always local ones that Spaniards sought to explain away in larger, nonlocal terms. Furthermore, the relatively small scale of slavery in Yucatan hardly obviates the need to explain the existence of the trade in the colony; on the contrary, if there were no silver mines or sugar plantations to provide an economic rationale for African slaves, why were they in Yucatan at all?

The answer is that there *was* an economic rationale to the trade in Yucatan, but (like so many economic patterns), one that cannot be separated from social and political dynamics. For example, black slaves were used as a source of specialized labor—be it skilled tasks, or dirty work (as in Juan Patricio's case). But this was in part because within the social structure of labor in the colony, Mayas were the mass laborers, accessed in rotating groups from native communities in a way that did not motivate Spanish employers to train specialists among them. To be sure, there were skilled Maya workers, but far fewer, as a percentage of the total, than among Afro-Yucatecans. The dynamic of the late colonial Yucatan–Belize frontier was another example of how slavery in the colony was not just about its economics and politics; raids on British settlements for African slaves were economically motivated at the individual level, but politically motivated at the larger level. Yet another example is the role played by the governor of the province in buying up some or most of the Africans sold at auction in Merida, to be sold later on at a profit on the private market. As governor, he was one of the few colonists who had access to the capital that permitted him to make an investment of thousands of pesos. Yet such a large-scale, public purchase, followed by the public baptism and naming of the slaves, also underscored the governor's social status at the top of colonial Yucatan's small social pyramid. This leads me to my final example. Spaniards conceived of African slaves as property, as investments from whom (or which) they hoped to benefit and profit. Yet the cost of slaves and the limited profitability of the work they did strongly suggests that owned Africans were viewed as luxury goods to be consumed through display, as prestigious commodities that projected the status of their owners.

The history of Afro-Yucatan only begins with slavery; within a generation of the Spanish Conquest, free black and colored colonists outnumbered African slaves in the province. The previous chapters charted this development, most notably through the histories of Afro-Yucatecan occupations, the pardo militia, community formation, marriage, and involvement in the religious cultures of the church and folk healing and magic.

The book's chapters have been arranged thematically, but with some regard for chronological considerations. The intended impression of that chronology is one of relative simplicity in the late sixteenth century—with Africans, Mayas, and Spaniards all relatively distinct from one another—giving way to increasing social complexity during the seventeenth and eighteenth centuries. What, then, of this book's thesis of "the black middle" ("the Afro-Yucatecan middle" would be a more accurate, but less catchy, book title)? How does the thesis hold up under the pressure of that social complexity?

The concept of a middle social group or time period is hardly original to historical literature, nor am I the first to suggest that Africans in Spanish America existed in such a space.[3] The "black middle" thesis has not explained every aspect of the Afro-Yucatecan experience or accommodated every person of African descent in the peninsula's colonial history. Indeed, the thesis had struck me as useful and relevant while researching this book, but I was prepared, at any point during its writing, to abandon the thesis should an alternative one emerge from the source material, one that seemed better to contain Afro-Yucatecan societies within a simple conceptual framework. However, the late political scientist Samuel Huntington has commented that to be useful paradigms need to be "simplified pictures of reality," and he refers to Thomas Kuhn's observation that an acceptable thesis, theory, or paradigm "need not, and in fact never does, explain all the facts with which it can be confronted."[4] In the end, then, I believe the very simplicity and ready applicability of the "black middle" thesis has not only provided an appropriate framework upon which to reconstruct the complex and varied Afro-Yucatecan experience, but also offers a portable paradigm for those interested in comparing this colony to others in the Americas.

A related thesis on the nature of slavery in the Americas—one that has been mentioned a number of times throughout this study and that I will now summarize and relate to the "black middle" paradigm—is that of the dual model of societies with slaves versus slave societies. Until recently, this was a model discussed mainly by scholars of slavery in the British colonies and the United States. Drawing upon Frank Tannenbaum's classic definition of a slave society ("Nothing escaped, nothing, and no one. Everywhere in this New World of ours a slave system made a slave society, with all of the *mores* of a slave society"), and on Moses Finley's categorization of slavery in the ancient world, Ira Berlin argued that the model applied variously to North America, depending on region and time period. For example, in the century after 1660 the Chesapeake was transformed from a society with slaves to a slave society.

Berlin is thus by necessity very clear in defining the two types of society. In slave societies, slavery "stood at the center of economic production, and the master–slave relationship provided the model for all social relations"; slaveholders were exclusively "the ruling class," marginalizing other classes and other forms of labor, acquiring slaves in numbers that made them the majority of laborers (if not of the whole population). As Rodolphe Desdunes remarked of the Louisiana where he was born in the 1840s, in such a society, "slavery was the pivot around which everything revolved." In societies with slaves, however, "slaves were marginal to the central productive processes," being just one among various types of workers, with master–slave relations not "the exemplar" but a subset of the larger relationship between the elite and the subordinate. Slave holdings were relatively small, "the line between slave and free could be remarkably fluid, with manumission often possible and sometimes encouraged." Thus in a society with slaves it would be impossible for slaves to live out their lives without ever seeing free people of color (as was possible in a slave society such a nineteenth-century Louisiana).[5]

This model is worth dwelling on for a moment for two reasons. One is that Berlin's argument that regions of North America shifted between models raises this question: Did colonial Yucatan likewise make a transition from one type of society to another? The other reason is that Herman Bennett recently contested Eugene Genovese's conclusion that "continental Spanish slavery did not create a slave society." Bennett made one of the thesis statements of his study of "Africans in Colonial Mexico" his assertion that "New Spain constituted a vibrant slave society in which the institution and its resulting mores informed patterns in the society at large." In short, Bennett claimed that Berlin's definition of a slave society was applicable to New Spain.[6]

Bennett makes a compelling case for the place and time that is the focus of his study—Mexico City between 1570 and 1640. The city was too different in too many ways from the eighteenth-century Chesapeake or the southern United States to be the same kind of slave society, but the sheer number of African slaves and the central roles they played in Spanish urban community suggest that, at the very least, early Mexico City was a variation on the slave society defined by Berlin.

However, the same case cannot be made for all of New Spain (nor does Bennett attempt to do so, despite his sleight of hand in the previous quote). Most of New Spain, including Yucatan, was not "a vibrant slave society" but unambiguously a society with slaves.[7] This was true of Yucatan for all its three centuries of African slavery. Although the Spanish communities in Merida and Campeche may have teetered in the late sixteenth century upon the brink of a shift into slave societies, they never made the transition into plantation-style slave-based export agriculture; nor did the colony generate sufficient wealth to support the level of slave importation reached in Mexico City and the concomitant development of the master–slave relationship as the social exemplar.

Slaveholders in Yucatan were the ruling elite, but not because they owned slaves; rather, they owned slaves because they were the elite. Slave owning was but one among a series of status determinatives. Individual slave holdings were small, and manumission was achieved with some regularity, both through the granting of freedom papers and through purchase. This was one factor that contributed to the lack of maroon communities within the colony (unlike early Mexico City or the North American plantation societies). Indeed, whereas the existence of maroon communities, endemic levels of escape, and the routine torture, abuse, and judicial punishment of slaves helped define slave societies, so did the relative lack of such phenomena—with manumission as a more prominent occurrence—help define societies with slaves. Female slaves tended to be manumitted slightly more than male slaves; this was also true elsewhere in New Spain and might be taken as a further factor defining a society with slaves.

The line dividing slaves from free coloreds was a dotted one, in that the two filled many of the same occupations and tended to be perceived similarly by Spaniards and Mayas. On the one hand this helped slaves to enjoy some of the opportunities afforded to free coloreds—such as marriage, raising children, joining religious brotherhoods, earning and saving money, and investing in property or business. This inclusion of slaves in Christian society was also reflected in naming patterns (in contrast to naming patterns in Anglo-American slave societies). On the other hand, the dotted line between slave and free also contributed to the maintenance of a ceiling to Afro-Yucatecan social mobility. Finally, not only were black slaves never the majority within the laboring class, being always greatly outnumbered by Mayas, but by the end of the sixteenth century slaves were outnumbered by free coloreds; for the next two centuries, the free-colored reproductive rate consistently outpaced that of the importation rate of black slaves.

Thus the steady growth through the seventeenth and eighteenth centuries of a mixed-race and mostly free Afro-Yucatecan population prevented Yucatan from becoming a slave society. It also consolidated the Afro-Yucatecan position in the middle of colonial society. This middle position meant men and women of African descent could never become full and indistinguishable members of the colony's Spanish community. They might achieve a status that in some ways allowed them to live better, and more respected, than poor Spaniards and mestizos (as pardo militia officers, for example); or they might successfully pass as Spaniards (whether by virtue of being the closest thing to a Spaniard in a remote Maya village in 1688, or as a powerful late colonial merchant like don Miguel Duque de Estrada). But Afro-Yucatecans could never embrace, or even acknowledge, the "stain of African origins" and still be fully accepted as an equal by Spaniards.

The pace of miscegenation was impressive, but Afro-Yucatecans had children with Mayas and mestizas far more than with Spaniards, and one of the by-products of miscegenation was Spaniards fighting in the eighteenth-century law courts over who had mulatto ancestors. Yucatan may have been a society with slaves, but those slaves were all black or mulatto, most of them black and African-born. The importation of black slaves did not let up until the nineteenth century, and for all the talk of freedom that accompanied the Independence movement of the 1810s, slavery was not abolished until 1829. Yet the persistence of the black middle was both a symptom of, and a contributing factor toward, the fact that the colony never developed into a slave society.

One important result—perhaps also a further defining factor—of Yucatan not being a slave society was the intimate context and personal, individual nature of relations and interactions that Afro-Yucatecans experienced with Spaniards and Mayas. In the preceding chapters I have tried to balance large-scale patterns gleaned from bodies of sources (like censuses and parish records) with rich case studies (such as the stories of Sebastián Toral, Manuel Bolio, Isabel Toquero, and—even briefly—Juan Patricio) partly in order to create a more engaging portrait of Afro-Yucatecan life. But such case studies are also important because they symbolize the fact that Afro-Yucatecans were not nameless cargo or anonymous laborers like so many of the Africans who suffered the Middle Passage and plantation slavery. They were individual, fully identified, members of Yucatecan society.[8]

The history of Afro-Yucatecans is as rich and varied as that of Spaniards and Mayas in the peninsula, no less so because—as I have tried to show—the experiences of all three groups are intimately intertwined and the dividing lines between them more and more blurred the closer one looks. This book is only a beginning to the study of Afro-Yucatan. As I acknowledged at the start, there have been a number of articles and books on the topic, mostly by historians in Yucatan, and these have been immensely helpful to me; but all are brief and focused on specific aspects of the subject, and, even combined with this book, barely scratch the surface of the source materials that are available.

If Afro-Yucatan is so well evidenced and so worthy of study, where are Afro-Yucatecans today and why is the peninsula so widely perceived as overwhelmingly, if not entirely, Spanish and Maya?

First, why Afro-Yucatecan invisibility (to echo the word I used in the Introduction)? I propose six interrelated reasons. The most obvious is (1) the legacy of slavery and the prejudice that accompanied the institution and outlived its abolition in the Mexican republic in 1829 (a legacy parallel to the one that underpinned what Ralph Ellison described in the 1950s as a refusal to see blacks in the United States). The point is relevant to many other regions of Latin America (it has been made recently with respect to Argentina, Costa Rica, and Guatemala, for example).[9] But it is particularly germane to the history of Mexican nationalism, whose heroic narrative developed as a Spanish-indigenous dialogue that excluded African elements (again there is a parallel to the early United States, whose history has often de-emphasized slavery because it "wrecks the simple heroic narrative of the Founding").[10] Yucatan did not generate a counternarrative that included Africans, partly because there is no less prejudice against blacks in the peninsula than there is elsewhere in Mexico, and partly due to other factors.

These other factors have all been discussed in this book, and are interrelated in various ways. They are (2) the rapid pace of miscegenation in colonial Yucatan—especially the high degree of marriage and sexual interaction between Afro-Yucatecans and others; (3) the gradual decline of the slave trade leading up to abolition in 1829, an abolition that did not generate conflict or lasting controversy; (4) the terminological changes that in the early nineteenth century served to disguise Afro-Yucatecans within the category of "mestizo," one that came to include Mayas too and then to be a referent *only* to Mayas (furthering eclipsing the Afro-Yucatecan past).[11]

A further factor is (5) a historiographical one, rooted in one of Afro-Yucatecans' middle positions: As Yucatan has become the subject of academic study over the past century and a half, scholars have not "seen" people of African descent the way that they have seen Spaniards and Mayas in part because the sources on Afro-Yucatecans are more scattered than those of the colony's other inhabitants. This was largely because blacks and free coloreds were never given their own "republic" or equivalent corporate identity; the pardo militia and urban cofradías were corporations of sorts, but they were not self-governing like Spanish and Maya repúblicas, nor did they have their own notaries charged with generating multiple genres of notarial documents. (A possible corollary to this point is the fact that colonial Yucatan is understudied relative to, for example, central Mexico).

Finally, (6) there is the factor of the postcolonial migration of free-colored workers into Yucatan from other parts of the Mexican republic and from the Caribbean; there was a small but steady flow of black workers into the peninsula from Cuba, for example, during the Porfiriato.[12] Thus the fact that many present-day Afro-Yucatecans are migrants or descended from postcolonial migrants has underpinned the local myth that *all* blacks in the peninsula arrived in this manner. When quizzed about residents of African descent in Campeche in the 1990s, locals were more likely to explain their presence in terms of migration from Veracruz than the colonial slave trade.[13]

The apparent disappearance in the nineteenth century of blacks descended from colonial-era Afro-Yucatecans tended to be explained in terms of a violent extinction—Mayas killed them in the Caste War, for example. Like the myth of black disappearance in nineteenth-century Buenos Aires (supposedly due to disease or war),[14] this explanation conveniently sweeps under the rug any suggestion that today's Yucatecans of Spanish and Maya descent are also of African descent. Yet in biological terms, African ancestry is extensively woven into the fabric of the peninsula's modern population; it is likely that most people living today with deep family roots in Yucatan have African ancestors. Recent genetic studies of the Mexican population concluded that Merida's inhabitants were 43% European, 51% native American, and 6% West African—in terms of their genetic make-up. The town of El Carmen, in the south of what is today Campeche state, was found to be 28% European, 43% native American, and 28% West African. That 6% in Merida and 28% in El Carmen—and other percentages as yet undiscovered for elsewhere in the peninsula—is spread out over a large proportion of the population.[15] Migration patterns over the last two centuries, such as the pattern of immigration from Cuba just mentioned, would complicate any attempts to tie these figures closely to the colonial past. But they surely reflect the colonial centuries of African slave importation, Afro-Yucatecan family formation, and steady miscegenation between Yucatecans of all origins.

The sheer demographic presence of Afro-Yucatecans and their consistent interaction with Spaniards, Mayas, and mestizos all through the centuries of colonial rule make these simple intertwining facts undeniable: Beginning in the mid-sixteenth century, Africans played as much of a role in Yucatan's history as the Spaniards and Mayas who have received almost all the attention in the peninsula's historical memory; not only are Hispanic Yucatecans also Afro-Yucatecans, but more startling is this book's implication that the Mayas of Yucatan must now be viewed as Afro-Mayas; finally, Yucatan's history can no longer be written without including Afro-Yucatecans—indeed, without acknowledging their place in the middle.

Selection of Documents Written or Dictated
by Afro-Yucatecans

1. Petition by Francisco de Aguilar, Yucatec-born mulatto, Seville, 1619
2. Complaint by Diego Ramos, pardo construction foreman, Merida, 1670
3. Petition by Isabel Toquero, parda from Dzonotake, Mexico City, 1711
4. Petition by Francisco Medina, free pardo, Izamal, 1791
5. Petition by José Maria Espinola, slave, Espita, 1816

DOCUMENT 1

Petition by Francisco de Aguilar, free Yucatec-born mulatto, for license to return home to Yucatan, made in Seville, 1619 (AGI-*Contratación* 5365, 21, 1: f. 2r). The petition was dictated to a notary. My main treatment of Francisco de Aguilar is in Chapter Three.

[f. 2r]
Fran^{co} de aguilar criollo de las yndias natural de la villa de Balla
dolid que es en la provinsia de canpeche estante a el prs^{te} en esta
cuidad digo que a mi der° conbiene aberiguar ad perpetuan rey
memorian como yo nasi en la dicha villa y en la dicha provinsia y de
como soy hijo de ynes chica yndia y de como soy *su p^e no conos^{do}* ~~negro~~
  per sonas libres
no sujetas a servidunbre ni cautiberio alguno y como
yo soi libre y no cautibo y como soy criollo y como persona libre soy
avido y tenido y reputado y lo fueron los dichos mis padres y
sienpre yo estado en servisio del doctor don pedro sanches de
aguilar presvitero dean que fue en la dicha villa y provinsia
como persona libre y no sujeta a cautiberio y ahora el dicho
dean bino de la dicha provinsia a esta cuidad de españa y me

trajo en su servisio y lo estoi a el pres^te y por q̃ por tener la color
de mulato las justisias me garan molestias y me pren
deran por entender q̃ soi cautibo siendo p^a libre en lo qual
resiviri notorio agravio

Francisco de Aguilar, creole of the Indies, native of the town of Valladolid, which is in the province of Campeche [Yucatan], being presently in
this city; I say that by right I consent to the ascertaining, ad perpetuam rei
memoriam, that I was born in the said town and in the said province, and
that I am the son of Inés Chica, Indian, and that I am [written in a
      different hand: *his father unknown*] ~~black~~ [crossed out],
free people, not subject to servitude or any captivity, and that
I am free and not captive, and that I am a creole and as a free person I
had, and am known to have had, and those were my said parents; and
I have always been in the service of Dr. don Pedro Sánchez de
Aguilar, priest, who was dean of the said town and province,
as a free person and not subject to captivity; and now the said
dean has come from the said province to this city of Spain and brought
me in his service, where I am presently; and because I have the coloring
of a mulatto, the officials molest me and arrest me,
believing that I am a captive [slave], [despite] being a free person, from
which I have received well-known abuse.

[The record continues, ff. 2r–4v, with a request for witnesses, followed by
statements by the dean and two other witnesses corroborating Francisco de
Aguilar's statement.]

DOCUMENT 2

Statement of complaint to the judge [*juez de residencia*] investigating the
Flores de Aldana governorship, by Diego Ramos, a pardo foreman on the
construction site of the fortress of San Benito, Merida, 1670 (AGI-*Escribanía* 316b, 75: f. 2). Statement dictated to a notary and signed by Ramos.
Him and his complaint are discussed in Chapter Four.

[f. 2r] [top and top left, various stamps, including that of "Carlos II: Años
de 1670 y 1671"]
3 de Jullio

Diego Ramos de color pardo ves^o. destta çiu^d. [. . .]
mejor a mi Justicia conbenga y aya lugar en [. . .]
resco antte V ss.^a y pongo demanda en forma al
señor m^s're de Campo don Rodrigo flores de alda

na Gou.^{or} y capp.^{an} gen.^{l} que fue desttas Provs.^{as} por
averme obligado siendo como soy un hombre y
como y vistto y susttentto a mi muger y famili
a, de mi sudor y ttravajo aqui asistiesse conttin
uamente tpõ. de año y medio en la obra de
de [sic] la fabrica de la cuidadela que hiso en esta
ciu^{d}. en la ocupaz^{on}. de ttener a mi cargo tres horn[adas]
de cal en el varrio de ss^{n}. xpttoval viendolos car
gar quemar y descargar dos veses a la semana
tteniendo cuydado de los Yndios que eran a mi [car]
go de los pue.^{os} ser cum vesinos destta çiu^{d}. q.^{e} traya[. . .]
los trosos de palos p.^{a} quemar y los cavallos que a
rreaban d̶h̶a cal sin esttipendio ni paga algu
na no rreserbando los dias de Domingo y fiesta
de guardar ni semana santta ni corpus christi
que no esttubiese viendolos travajar Romp[. . .]
doseme la rropa, y no ttheniendo lugar [. . .]
travajar para buscar otra, y pereciend[. . .]
[f. 2v]
mi muger y mi familia p^{r} d̶h̶a ocupaz^{on}. y no p[. . .]
der ni tener lugar p^{a}. ello, y aunque le fue muchas ve
ses arrogar y pedir por amor de Dios me diese lugar
de poder ir a descansar y buscar mi vida p^{r} ser pobre
y viejo y que harttos pardos y mestisos auia que podian
tambien ayudar a asistir en d̶h̶a obra pues era del
servis.^{o} de su mag.^{d} me Respondia q.^{e} me avia de dar *200* azo
ttes o q.^{e} me pondria en la carsel hasta que acabase d̶h̶a
fabrica y q.^{e} no avia de asistir aunque no quisiese con q.^{e}
lo asia de miedo y temor y asi sea de servir V ss.^{a} a q.^{e} d̶h̶o ss^{or}.
don Rodrigo me de y pague a dos pessos cada mes de mi asis
tencia de año y medio que es lo que yo gano cada mes en el cam
po con la cassa de mi escopetta de venados y gallos del mon
tte trayendolo a vender a esta ciu^{d}. y p^{a} la justtificaz^{on} de mi
demanda offresco ynformaz^{on} de lo conttenido en estte mi
escritto =
A V Ss.^{a} Pido y supp.^{co} admitta la d̶h̶a mi demanda y avido
mi Relaz.^{on} por berdadera se sirva de condenar y conden[. . .]
al d̶h̶o ss^{or}. m^{s}re de campo Dn R.^{o} flores a que luego me deyo
que mi servis.^{o} personal de tpõ de año y medio q.^{e} por su
orden y contra mi voluntad me obligo asistir en tres jorna[das]
de cal q.^{e} continuamente estaba viendo cargar quema[r]
y descargar a rrason de a dos p.^{s} cada mes p^{r} ser justicia q.^{e}
pido y costas y juro a esta crus † y esta mi ynformass.^{on} no es
de malicia si no sierta y en lo ness^{o} x^{a} =

=Diego Ramos [small rubric; statement written and
signed in his own hand]

[f. 2r] 3rd of July [1670]
I, Diego Ramos, pardo in color, resident of this city, in
my just interests, agree to make an appearance
before Your Lordship and place on record my complaint against
the Sr. Field Marshal don Rodrigo Flores de Aldana,
former governor and captain general of these provinces, for
having forced me—being as I am a man who
sees to and sustains my wife and family—
[to give] my sweat and toil here, to attend continually
for a period of a year and a half to the work of
the construction of the fortress that was done in this
city; [he forced me] into the job of having under my charge three loads
of lime in the barrio of San Cristobal, overseeing them loaded,
burned, and unloaded twice a week,
taking care of the Indians who were under my charge
(of the pueblos but like residents of this city), carrying
the pieces of poles to burn and [working] the horses who were
harnessed to the said [loads of] lime; without a stipend or any payment,
not putting aside Sundays, neither observing fiestas,
nor Holy Week, nor Corpus Christi,
which [processions] I could not even see, working away tearing
my clothes; and not having an opportunity to go
looking for other work, with
[f. 2v] my wife and family suffering because of this job, and not
having any time for them, although many times
I begged and pleaded for the love of God to be given the chance
and right to go and rest and have a life, because I am poor
and old, and there are plenty of pardos and mestizos who could
also help and attend to this said work, who are in the
service of His Majesty; but I was told that I would be given two hundred lashes
or be thrown in jail until the construction was finished,
and that there was no relief even though it could only have been
done in fright and fear; and thus may it serve Your Lordship that the
said Sr. don Rodrigo give and pay me two pesos for every month of my
attendance during the year and a half, which is what I earn each month in
the countryside, hunting deer and turkeys in the forest with my shotgun,
taking them to be sold in this city; and for the just resolution of my
complaint, I offer the information contained in this my
written statement.
To Your Lordship, I implore and request that my complaint be admitted
and my account be seen as true and serve to condemn

the said Sr. Field Marshal don Rodrigo Flores; that he immediately give
me—for my personal service of a period of a year and a half, that by his
order and against my will I was forced to attend to three loads
of lime that continually were overseen being loaded, burned,
and unloaded—the just sum of two pesos for each month, as what I ask
is right; and fees; and I swear at this cross, †, and this is my statement; it
is not made in malice, but is sure and necessary,

Diego Ramos

DOCUMENT 3

Petition to Inquisition officials by Isabel Toquero, parda/mulatta from
Dzonotake, arrested under accusation of bigamy in Merida in 1703 and
subsequently tried and convicted in Mexico City. The petition, requesting
her release, was written by Isabel Toquero herself, Mexico City, 1711
(AGN-*Inquisición* 519, 3: f. 397). Her release was granted two days later (f.
398). My main treatment of Toquero is in Chapter Six.

[f. 397r] [top left and right corners:]
R^{do} en el S^{to} oficio de la Inq^{on} Al Secretario q^e
de la cuidad de mexico en   haze oficio de ^{el} S$_r$
18 dias del mes de Julio   fiscal [rubric]
de 1711 ã^s estando en
Audiencia los SS Inq^{res}
[rubric]

Señores,
Ysabel toquero poniendome a los pies
de Vu^s Señ.^{s} que por aber ya cumplido
el termino, de los tres años, que é esta=
do sirbiendo en los Hospitales del Am=
or de Dios, y Jesus de Nasareno por
horden de V^e Se.^{s}; Y abiendo echo
el año pasado Recuerdo a V. S. salio
de que poreste se cumplia el termi
no; y por aber enaqueste tiempo
pasado tantas enfermedades y en
ellas aber asistido con puntuali
dad a mis hobligaciones de asis
tir con todo cariño a los enfermes
pido a V. Señorias se bean en lo que
a V. S. les pareciere de mi soltura
confiando en la piedad y Grandesa

de V. S.ˢ [word deleted] [rubric]
      Ysabel toquero [rubric]

Received in the Holy Office of the Inquisition   To the secretary who
in the city of Mexico on   acts as the Sr.
the 18th of July   Fiscal.
of 1711, the Lord Inquisitors being in session.

Lords,
I place myself, Isabel Toquero, at the feet
of Your Lords, having now completed
the sentence of the three years that I have
served in the hospitals of Amor de
Dios and Jesus the Nazarene, by
order of Your Lords; and having made
a petition last year to Your Lords to leave,
as a result of which the sentence has been
completed; and for having during that time
endured so many illnesses and in the
meantime having conscientiously assisted
in my obligations to attend
with utmost care to the sick;
I ask Your Lordships that you examine that which
is presented to Your Lords regarding my release,
trusting in the mercy and magnanimity
of Your Lords.
        Isabel Toquero

DOCUMENT 4

Petition by Francisco Medina, free pardo, Izamal, 1791 (AGEY-*Justicia* 1,
6: f. 3r). The petition was written by Medina in his own hand. The dispute
over the Medina–Tolosa engagement is discussed in Chapter Three.

[f. 3r]
Sõr Juez Subdelegᵈᵒ
Franᶜᵒ Medina vecino de la Hazienda Poxcheina
y recid.ᵗᵉ en este Pueb.ᵒ con la salva del respeto devido ante
Vmd. paresco, y digo: que haviendo zelebrado esponsales
con Manuela Toloza de esta vecindad, y vaxo de este trato
contrahe devito a mi honor en esta virtud pase a practicar
las correspond.ˢ dilig.ˢ para efectuar con ella, el matrim.ᵒ
que solicito, y haviendo sido la primera pedirla consen

tim.^{to} a M^a. de Luz Herrera madre de mi pretendida
he hallado en esta fuerte opocicion, p.^r la desigualdad que
entre ella y yo tenemos de calidad, y en esta atencion pa
se, a pedir al Sõr. Opõ. que ciendo asequible, me declara
se libre, de esta oblig.^{on} de q.^e resultaron las dilig.^s que con el Ju
ram^{to} neses.^o presento, p.^a q.^e a su vista, se sirva para mandar
comparescan en su Tribun^l madre e hija, y en Just.^a deter
mina lo que tenga por conv.^{te} que a todo esto y lizo, y llano, y
en estos trños
A Vmd. pido y sup.^{co} se sirba mandar hacer como pido que
es Just.^a Juro en frmã y lo nes^o EE.^a Fran^{co} Medina [rubric]

Lord Justice Subdelegate
I, Francisco Medina, resident of the Hacienda Poxcheina and living in this
town, with the greeting of due respect, appear before Your Honor, and
state: that having celebrated betrothal with Manuela Tolosa of this neighborhood, and under this agreement contracted honorably by me and by
virtue of which, I went and carried out the relevant proceedings in order to
bring about the marriage with her that I am soliciting; and having foremost
asked for the consent of doña María de Luz Herrera, mother of my betrothed, I encountered in her strong opposition, due to the inequality of status [*calidad*] between her and me; and in view of this I went and asked the
Lord Bishop if it was possible for me to be declared free of this obligation,
from which resulted the proceedings which, with the necessary oath, I present for your consideration, so that you might order mother and daughter to
appear in your court, and in justice determine that which you hold to be
right, and all of it plain and clear, and to that end.
To Your Honor I ask and request that it be ordered to be done as I ask, as is
right; I swear in the required manner, etc., Francisco Medina.

DOCUMENT 5

Petition to the Governor of Yucatan by José Maria Espinola, slave of doña
Rosalia Gonzalez, requesting manumission, Espita, 1816 (AGEY-*Varios* 1,
27: f. 1). The petition was dictated to a notary and signed by Espinola. He
is discussed in Chapters Four and Five.

[f. 1r] [in left margin:]
Exped.^{te} promo-
tido p^r el moreno esclavo José
Maria Espinola,
solicitando liber-

tarse exhibiendo
la cantidad p^r q^e
fue vendido

Sõr. Cap^n General
Josse M.ª Espinola Esclavo de D.ª Rosalia Gons^s
vezina del Pueblo de Espita de la comprehencion
de Tisimin, ante V. S. como mas hayas lugar, hago
presente: Haver suvido a esta Capital con el obgeto
de impetrar mi libertad por el conducto mas opor-
tuno y legal de V. S. en los terminos q^e esplicaré.

Ygnoro quien huviese sido mi Madre, y como
fui esclavo del finado cavallero Rex^r Alguazil m͂yor
d^n Manuel Ant^o Espinola, y solo se q^e su m͂rzd me llebó
a cristianan: Dudo igualmente la cantidad en qe fui
vendido a ~~dh~~a d^a Rosalia; pero como solicito libertarme
ya sea exiviendo yo la cantidad de doscientos y cinq^{ta}
pesos en q^e tengo noticia fui pasado a poder de aque
-lla señora, õ ya a satisfazer p^r plasos q^e tambien
puede ser asequible.

Como los bienes de la citada se hallan entre-
dichados p^r litiz con sus coerederos, no se p^r ahora
si quedare como siempre p^r esclavo de la srã viuda
õ si hize a dar a otro poder y desde ahora empieso a
experimentar rigores (hablo con el devido resp.^{to}) de D^n
Jose Rosado q^e pretende Dnõ en mi, unicamente p^r q^e
quando el embargo de su hermana politica d^a Rosa^{a}l.
se persono p^r suplica y a nombre de esta señora y
de su cuenta a habonar la cantidad de 250 p^s en
q^e se dize fui vendido.

Haze mas de tres años q^e soy esclavo de la
citada sin q^e jamas me huviese obstigado, antes
[f. 1v]
bien me ha persistido y consiente q^e me exercite
en labranzas de Algodon y Cañaberal a pensando p^a
libertarme; y es fuente Capital Señor Cap^n Gral
q^e su cuñado d^n Jose Rosado pretenda estorbar la
lizensia de mi Ama, quando solamente espero ver
la definitiba de su pleito apelado, y aver poder hize
a dar p^a exibir sin alterasion de cantidad las de
~~dh~~os 250 p^s p^r todo lo qual.

A la justif.^{on} de V. S. sup^{co} sinseramente q^e en . . . q^e
de su imparcial just.^{a} distributia se sirba acceder
a mi solicitud para quando llegue el caso y entretan

-to, q^e el referido d.ⁿ Josse Rosado me deje librem.^{te}
exercitar en mis agencias, mia gracia con just.^a
imploro y espero desfrutar del bondoso corazon
de V. S. jurando no ser de malicia y lo merez.º J.ª
  Jose maria espinola
  [signed in his own hand, with rubric]

Proceedings brought
forward by the moreno
slave José
Maria Espinola,
petitioning to free
himself, producing
the amount for which
he was sold

  Lord Captain General
José Maria Espinola, slave of doña Rosalia Gonzalez,
resident of the village of Espita in the jurisdiction
of Tizimin, before Your Lordship, as you may permit, I present
myself, having come up to this capital with the object
of importuning my freedom through the most timely and legal
agency of Your Lordship in the terms that I will explain.
  I do not know who my mother was, or how
I became a slave of the late gentleman Regidor and Alguacil Mayor
don Manuel Antonio Espinola, and I know only that His Mercy led me
to Christianity. I am equally uncertain of the amount for which I was
sold to doña Rosalia; but by way of petitioning to free myself
I am now producing the amount of 250
pesos, for which [sum] I have knowledge that I passed into the hands of
that lady, or it can also be available paid in installments.
  As the property of the said lady has been tied up
in litigation with her coheirs, I do not know if for now
I shall continue as always to be a slave of the lady widow,
or if I am to be placed in the hands of another and from now begin to
experience the severity (I speak with all due respect) of don
José Rosado, who claims ownership of me, simply because
when he impounded [the property] of his sister-in-law, doña Rosalia,
he appeared in person to petition in the name of this lady and
on her behalf to vouch for the sum of 250 pesos for
which it is said I was sold.
  For more than three years I have been a slave of the
said lady, and never have I been obstinate, on the
[f. 1v] contrary I have persevered and consented to exert myself

on the cotton and sugarcane farms, thinking to
free myself; and the main source [of the problem], Lord Captain General,
is that her brother-in-law, don José Rosado, seeks to obstruct the
authority of my mistress, when I only wish to see
the conclusion to his appellee lawsuit, and to have the authorization
to give and produce, without altering the amount, the
said 250 pesos, all of it.

      I sincerely appeal to Your Lordship's sense of fairness, that
your impartially dispensed justice works to accede
to my request so that when the case arrives and in the meantime,
the said don José Rosado leave me at liberty
to toil at my own activities; in my favor, with justice,
I implore and hope to benefit from the good-natured heart
of Your Lordship, swearing that I am not in malice and merit justice.

                       José Maria Espinola

Afro-Yucatecans and the Population
of Colonial Yucatan
(1781–1815)

TABLE B.1 Population by casta and percentage in fifty-one Yucatec parishes, 1798–1815

Parish year		Total population	% of Spaniards	% of both	% of Mestizos	% of Mayas	% of Pardos[a]
CAMPECHE							
Pich	1815	2,196[b]	8.7[c]		81.6	9.7	
CAMINO REAL BAJO							
Halacho	1802	2,735		6.7		86.7	6.6
	1806	3,387		2.1		88.4	9.5
Hunucmá	1806	7,039		13.4		73.5	13.2
	1813	11,083	1.8	10.2		80.3	7.8
	1815	8,019	2.1		10.7	78.6	8.6
Kopomá	1802	4,203		13.1		78.3	8.6
	1806	5,088		10.1		83.4	6.5
	1813	5,878	0.3		14.3	69.6	15.9
Maxcanú	1806	5,665		17.4		65.9	16.7
Uman	1802	5,967	0.1		13.3	77.3	9.3
MERIDA							
San Cristobal Tiho	1806	5,705	6.6[d]			92.7	0.8
SIERRA BAJA							
Abala	1806	3,839		3.2		88.0	8.9
Acanceh	1806	2,361		2.6		90.3	7.0
Mama[e]	1802	5,712	2.6		31.0	63.4	3.0
Muna	1806	6,662		17.4		79.5	3.1
Teabo	1806	6,411		18.1[f]		66.7	15.2
	1806	5,909		14.5		84.9	0.6[g]
Tecoh	1802	4,108	1.1		7.4	88.6	2.9
	1806	6,352	1.5		7.7	85.7	5.1[h]
	1807	7,012	1.9		7.3	83.9	6.9

(continued)

TABLE B.1 (*continued*)

Parish year		Total population	% of Spaniards	% of both	% of Mestizos	% of Mayas	% of Pardos[a]
SIERRA ALTA							
Mani	c.1802	4,401		18.0		78.5	3.5
	1806	6,692		22.6		72.7	4.8
	1813	8,180	9.1		16.9	69.9	4.1
Oxkutzcab	1800	13,558		22.2		73.0	4.8
	1806	16,928		22.5		75.1	2.5
	1808	17,559		22.9		74.0	1.5
Tekax	1806	23,478		26.1		72.7	1.2
Ticul[i]	1806	16,249		26.4		68.5	5.2
	1813	19,185	17.2		5.8	69.7	7.3
LA COSTA							
Cacalchen	1806	1,518		27.9		69.5	2.6
Cansahcab	1813	3,389	1.7		22.4	72.9	3.9
Conkal	1802	5,215	1.1		9.2	89.4	0.3
Izamal	1802	5,041	12.9		30.4	47.2	9.5
	1806	4,426	30.9		1.7	58.9	8.9
Mococha	1802	1,916	2.8		8.0	87.4	1.8
	1806	3,804	4.5		10.7	83.4	1.4
Motul	1802	3,713[j]	11.2		8.5	76.5	3.7
	1803	3,919		17.9		78.6	3.5
	1806	7,515		17.1		79.6	3.3
	1807	7,789		17.3		79.3	3.4
	1808	8,009		17.3		79.4	3.4
	1810	8,407		17.0		79.6	3.5

	Year						
Nolo	1813	8,033	16.0		5.8	71.5	6.7
	1806	3,586	0.0		0.5	99.5	0.0
Tekanto	1802	3,337		15.6		82.9	1.5
	1806	3,417		11.4		84.7	3.9k
	1810	5,055		9.7		88.5	1.8
	1813	3,662	17.7		3.1	77.0	1.6
	1815	4,056		14.9		84.2	1.0
Telchac	1802	2,498	6.2		11.6	80.1	5.8
	1806	3,757		18.7		77.2	4.1l
Temax	1802	5,508	9.4		22.8	62.6	5.1
	1806	8,331		23.4		74.0	2.6m
Teya	1806	2,060		6.6		90.2	3.3
	1807	1,479		3.7		88.2	8.1
	1808	1,712		3.3		89.3	7.4
Tixkokob	1806	4,149		19.6		74.7	5.7n
BENEFICIOS BAJOS							
Hocabá	1806	4,920		13.4		73.4	13.3
Tixcacaltuyu	1802	4,929	2.0		4.1	88.4	5.5
	1805	7,373o		4.5		90.6	4.6
	1806	7,171		5.0		90.2	4.8
	1813	7,762	1.4		3.7	89.1	5.9
Yaxcabá	1798	4,056		10.8		85.1	4.1
	1802	6,729		11.7		85.2	3.1
	1806	7,619		12.2		84.9	2.9
	1807	7,901		12.0		84.7	3.3
	1808	8,354		11.3		85.5	3.2
	1809	8,299		12.1		84.6	3.3
	1815	9,178		10.0		87.3	2.8

(continued)

TABLE B.1 (*continued*)

Parish year	Total population	% of Spaniards	% of both	% of Mestizos	% of Mayas	% of Pardos[a]
BENEFICIOS ALTOS						
Chikindzonot						
1802	3,334	0.1		2.8	93.3	3.8
1806	3,111		2.0		95.0	4.1
Chunhuhub						
1802	1,798	8.6	4.3	3.2	87.5	0.6
1806	2,252				94.8	0.9
Ichmul						
1802	9,145	1.7		3.8	92.3	2.6
1804	10,462		7.3		89.3	3.4
1806	10,910		7.8		87.8	4.4
Peto						
1802	3,808	6.3	19.8		71.0	7.4/0.3[p]
1806	5,173		12.4	8.8	73.4	6.8
Tahdziu						
1802	2,191		9.7		86.6	9.6
1806	3,520				88.4	1.9
Tihosuco[q]						
1802	6,879	0.6		9.0	88.5	1.9
1806	7,356		8.4		90.4	1.3
1813	8,238	1.3		9.4	88.5	0.9
VALLADOLID						
Chemax						
1802	2,743	0.5		0.7	97.7	1.1
1808	4,047		0.5		96.2	3.2
Chichimila						
1806	2,319		0.3		99.4	2.6
Sisal						
1806	2,713		0.0		99.3	0.7
Tikuch						
1802	654	0.0		2.9	97.1	0.0
1805	1,049		1.1		98.9	0.0
1806	469		3.4		96.6	0.0
Tixcacalcupul[r]						
1806	1,635	0.9		3.6	95.1	0.4

	Year	Population					
Uayma	1808	1,820		7.1		92.2	0.7
	1805	4,348		8.8		86.0	5.2[s]
	1807	4,866		8.0		83.8	8.2
Valladolid	1806	13,165		62.7		34.5	2.8
TIZIMIN							
Calotmul	1802	1,871	7.8		13.9	73.8	4.7
	1806	2,608		16.9		75.7	7.4
Chancenote	1806	2,861		9.9		74.3	15.7
	1813	3,439	3.6		12.2	72.5	11.6
Espita	1802	4,144	5.1		9.2	80.1	5.5
	1806	5,096		14.9		79.6	5.5
	1813	3,008	5.1		12.7	77.6	4.6
Kikil[t]	1806	2,143	8.5		9.8	47.4	34.4
Nabalam	1806	1,057		14.3		79.0	6.7
	1807	1,064		13.2		83.4	3.5
	1808	960		14.9		79.5	5.6
	1813	2,238	1.6		9.6	82.3	6.5
Tizimin	1813	3,301		7.0	12.2	53.9	26.9[u]

Sources: Original census records in AME; I created this data from the published transcription in Dumond and Dumond (1982: 3–304).

Notes: I have arranged the parishes alphabetically within each ecclesiastical district, and listed the districts from west to east. Although these parishes contained most of the colony's population, not all the colony's parishes are included; the list comprises about three quarters of the parishes in the region that is the modern state of Yucatan (with the exception of Pich and Chunhuhub, which are in modern Campeche and Quintana Roo, respectively).

Most of the parishes include subject communities (*sujeto* in Spanish, *cab* in Maya), haciendas, and *ranchos*, as well as the head community (*cabecera* in Spanish, *cah* in Maya) after which the parish was named. However, the census does not always clearly state whether the entries included such subsidiaries, which would explain in part some of the more dramatic population changes; one example is Mococha, which appears to double in size in four years—although the 1802 census claims to include "the whole district of the parish," the 1806 data specifically names and records the population for the subject communities of Baca and Tixkumchel, which together are as big as Mococha proper.

[a] The census essentially categorizes all Africans in Yucatan as *pardos* or *mulattoes*; in only a few instances is the category named as including *negros*; in a few instances *negros* are given a separate category, but it is empty in every case except for that of Peto (see note p). After 1820, and in some cases before that, pardos are combined with mestizos to create a single category, *vecinos* (with indios as a separate category).

TABLE B.1 (continued)

[b] Only in Pich proper does this include Spaniards and mestizos; in its subject communities of Bolonchen Cauich, Cauich, and Tixmucuy the category contains solely mestizos. The census also includes four haciendas and five *ranchos*, populated exclusively by Mayas.

[c] This column represents Spaniards and mestizos combined, following the way the census was sometimes recorded.

[d] As there is no listing for mestizos, it is not clear if this figure includes that category too. Santiago Tiho was one of Merida's Maya suburbs—a *cah-barrio* (my term: see Restall 1997: 29–37). Unfortunately, the surviving census does not include data either from the other cah-barrios or from the predominantly Spanish and pardo parishes of Merida.

[e] Likewise, the 1806 Mama census includes more Mayas than the 1802 census, apparently by counting more haciendas in the parish jurisdiction; as a result, the African population remains proportionately the same, but the Spanish and mestizo sector shrinks relative to the Maya one.

[f] This figure favors this category a little at the expense of "Mayas" due to the unusual inclusion of *indios hidalgos*, the cream of the Maya nobility, with Spaniards and mestizos.

[g] The census includes Teabo itself, Pencuyut, Chumayel, Xaya, and an unspecified number of haciendas; all the parish's pardos lived in Pencuyut (16; 0.3% of the parish population, 1.4% of the Pencuyut population) and Chumayel (20; 0.3% of the parish population, 2.3% of the Chumayel population).

[h] The pardo population of this parish was divided between Tecoh proper (27% in 1806, 44% in 1807), Telchaquillo (13% in 1806, 12% in 1807), and a number of haciendas (60% in 1806, 44% in 1807); i.e., the figures represent either an influx of pardos from haciendas into Tecoh proper in 1807, or a reclassification of their official place of residence between 1806 and 1807.

[i] There was also a census for 1802, but it included only children and unmarried adults; of the total thereof of 3,160, 7.2% were Spaniards, 19.9% mestizos, 64.9% Mayas, and 8.1% pardos. All the Ticul data includes figures for the subject communities of Nohcacab and Pustunich, as well as a number of haciendas. In 1806 the parish pardo population of 845 resided mostly in Ticul itself (81%), with 17% in Nohcacab, 2% in the haciendas, and less than 1% in Pustunich.

[j] This is the number of adults only; the census lists 2,441 children, making a total population of 6,154, but the racial category of the children is not given. The population figure given for 1803 likewise only counts adults (defined as those who have complied with the relevant church precepts).

[k] Of the 133 pardos represented by this percentage, only 35% lived in Tekanto proper; most lived in the subject community of Kimbila (58%), with one pardo in Citilcum, none in Tixkochoh, and 6% in the parish's haciendas.

[l] Of the 154 pardos represented by this percentage, only 18% lived in Telchac proper; the rest lived in the subject communities of Sinanche (19%) and Dzemul (53%), and in the parish's haciendas (10%).

[m] Of the 216 pardos represented by this percentage, 47% lived in Temax proper; the rest lived in the subject communities of Tekal (45%), Dzoncauich (4%), and Buczoz (3%) (there were no pardos in the parish's haciendas).

[n] Of the 238 pardos this figure represents, 71% lived in Tixkokob itself, 27% in its subsidiary of Ekmul, none in Euan, and 2% in the haciendas.

[o] This apparent dramatic population increase might be explained by the fact that the 1802 census is based on confession rolls and thus includes adults only, whereas the other censuses are based on "the number of residents." The parish comprised Tixcacaltuyu itself and its subsidiary of Tacchebilchen; the censuses of 1805 and 1806 give separate figures for the two communities, showing that most pardos in the parish lived in Tacchebilchen (76% in 1805, 77% in 1806).

[p] These figures represent separate entries for "mulatos y mulatas" (282 individuals) and "negros" (10), the only instance in the AME censuses of a *negros* entry. All the figures for this year appear to be adults only; children are listed partially by race but mostly according to their state of preparedness for Catholic sacraments.

^q The few pardos in this parish lived in Tihosuco itself, none in the subject *cahob* [Maya communities] of Tela, Tepich, and Xcabil.

^r The few pardos in this parish lived in Tixcacalcupul itself, none in the cah of Tekom or the parish's six haciendas and six ranchos.

^s Of the 224 pardos this figure represents, only 5% lived in Uayma itself; 43% lived in the subject community of Piste, 24% in Cuncunul, 11% in Kaua, 7% in Tinum, 5% in the parish hacienda, and 5% in its rancho. By 1807 there had been a shift from Piste to Uayma proper—with 23% of parish pardos in Piste and 14% in its head town—but the pardo population remained proportionately the same elsewhere in the parish.

^t In Kikil proper and its subject communities of Loche, Panaba, and Sucila, pardos equaled or outnumbered other categories (Sucila was 72% African), whereas the haciendas of the parish were entirely indigenous in population (two-thirds of parish Mayas lived on its haciendas); thus with the haciendas factored out, Kikil parish was 50% African in 1806.

^u Although this figure includes the population of the subject communities of the parish, Sucopo and Dzonot Ake, the census does not give them separate entries; however, the baptism and burial records (see Table B.2) show that pardos lived in all three communities.

TABLE B.2 Afro-Yucatecans baptized and buried, by percentage, in fifty-two Yucatec parishes, 1797–1813

Parish	Year	Total baptisms	Afro-Yucatecan baptisms as a percentage of total baptisms	Total burials	Afro-Yucatecan burials as a percentage of total burials
SAHCABCHEN					
Chicbul	1797	30	0.0	16	6.3
CAMPECHE					
Pich	1797	108	15.7	56	17.7
	1798	86	3.5	77	5.2
	1799	74	21.6	62	6.5
	1802	67	19.4	203	9.9
	1805–06 [a]	116	17.2	138	18.8
CAMINO REAL BAJO					
Halachó	1799	323	5.9	113	1.8
	1800	272	3.7	158	6.3
Hunucmá	1797	463	8.4	211	5.2
Kopomá	1797	361	11.6	153	11.8
Maxcanú	1797	279	14.3	67	25.4
Uman	1797	432	8.8	142	14.1
MERIDA					
San Cristobal Tiho	1802 [b]	387	1.3	115	0.0
SIERRA BAJA					
Abala	1797	206	9.2	89	6.7
Acanceh	1797	239	6.3	27	7.4
	1798	251	6.0	65	6.2
	1799	267	5.6	67	1.5
Mama	1797	309	2.6	93	2.2
	1798	324	3.1	90	5.6
Muna	1797	380	14.2	116	10.3
Sacalum	1797	228	5.3	51	2.0
Teabo	1797	324	0.0	76	0.0
	1805	178	0.0	425	0.5
	1806	336	0.3	125	0.0
	1807	312	1.0	142	0.7
Tecoh	1797	286	9.1	86	10.5
	1798	299	4.7	94	2.1

TABLE B.2 (*continued*)

Parish	Year	Total baptisms	Afro-Yucatecan baptisms as a percentage of total baptisms	Total burials	Afro-Yucatecan burials as a percentage of total burials
SIERRA ALTA					
Mani	1798	224	8.5	131	4.6
Oxkutzcab	1798	913	2.2	190	0.5
	1799	880	2.3	141	1.4
Tekax	1797	518	1.5	114	0.0
Ticul	1797	898	5.2	156	12.2
	1806	857	5.4	329	3.0
LA COSTA					
Cacalchen	1797	89	18.0	62	6.5
	1800	122	9.8	34	8.8
	1801	138	4.4	41	4.9
	1806	148	4.7	41	9.8
	1808	144	15.3	46	6.5
Cansahcab	1797	97	4.1	26	15.4
Conkal	1797	413	1.7	75	5.3
	1798	411	0.0	55	0.0
Izamal	1813	494	8.5	172	11.1
Mococha	1797	205	2.0	75	2.7
Motul	1797	345	3.8	111	4.5
	1798	379	3.4	103	5.8
	1799	375	3.7	124	4.0
Nolo	1798	189	0.0	36	0.0
	1799	201	1.0	24	0.0
Tekanto	1797	156	14.1	20	10.0
	1805–06[c]	161	0.6	80	1.3
	1808	192	0.0	71	4.2
	1809–10	208	1.0	48	2.1
	1814–15	238	0.4	57	1.8
Telchac	1797	196	3.6	27	0.0
	1804	202	2.5	84	0.0
Temax	1797	300	3.0	102	7.8
Teya[d]	1797	88	5.9	27	3.7
	1806–07	197	4.6	40	7.5
	1807–08	199	6.0	45	17.8
	1813	113	6.2	23	0.0
Tixkokob	1797	217	3.7	71	5.6

(*continued*)

TABLE B.2 (*continued*)

Parish	Year	Total baptisms	Afro-Yucatecan baptisms as a percentage of total baptisms	Total burials	Afro-Yucatecan burials as a percentage of total burials
BENEFICIOS BAJOS					
Hocabá	1797	246	6.9	38	23.7
	1799	266	10.9	46	6.5
	1800	262	9.5	117	16.2
	1801	213	11.3	108	9.3
Hoctun	1784–1804ᶜ	6,268	7.2	977	7.7
Homun	1797	193	7.3	86	9.3
	1798	195	7.2	37	0.0
	1799	208	6.7	45	8.9
	1800	222	7.7	122	9.8
	1801	185	7.7	90	0.0
Tixcacaltuyu	1808	349	4.6	228	8.3
	1813ᶠ	365	4.4	205	3.9
Yaxcabá	1797	294	3.1	93	6.5
	1799	348	2.6	82	3.7
	1807	510	3.7	165	1.8
	1813	395	3.8	227	2.6
BENEFICIOS ALTOS					
Chikindzonot	1797	120	3.3	24	4.1
	1805	156	3.2	70	2.8
Chunhuhub	1797	135	0.0	50	0.0
Ichmul	1797	478	2.7	142	0.0
	1798	570	2.3	141	0.7
	1800	607	3.3	195	3.1
	1804	560	4.3	187	1.6
	1813	708	2.1ᵍ	332	2.1
Tihosuco	1797	359	1.1	110	1.8
	1798	353	0.9	82	0.0
	1799	385	0.8	100	0.0
	1802	441	0.5	403	0.5
	1813ʰ	467	0.0	159	0.0
VALLADOLID					
Chemax	1797	171	2.3	49	0.0
	1804	252	1.2	71	2.8
	1805	226	1.8	47	6.4
	1806	295	1.0	71	0.0
	1807	259	1.9	50	2.0

TABLE B.2 *(continued)*

Parish	Year	Total baptisms	Afro-Yucatecan baptisms as a percentage of total baptisms	Total burials	Afro-Yucatecan burials as a percentage of total burials
Chichimila	1797	166	0.0	109	0.0
	1798	186	0.0	25	0.0
	1800	287	0.0	52	0.0
Tikuch	1798	50	0.0	11	0.0
	1799	52	0.0	11	0.0
	1800	52	0.0	4	0.0
Tixcacalcupul	1797	77	0.0	19	0.0
	1807	18	0.0	101	1.0
Uayma	1797	172	2.3	35	5.7
	1804	233	3.4	31	6.5
	1805	237	3.8	49	8.2
	1806	269	5.6	87	2.3
Valladolid	1797	370	4.6	147	5.4
TIZIMIN					
Calotmul	1797	110	5.5	30	0.0
	1798	148	7.4	43	4.7
	1800	145	4.8	75	5.3
	1801	149	4.7	40	5.0
Chancenote	1797	109	15.6	41	34.2
	1798	136	16.2	32	9.3
Espita	1798	187	10.7	28	17.9
	1804	236	6.4	108	9.3
	1806	257	5.5	96	4.2
	1813	265	4.2	221	3.2
Kikil	1797	85	18.8	49	24.5
	1798	116	22.4	72	20.8
Tizimin	1813	177	8.5	75	14.7
Xcan	1798	175	0.0	47	0.0

Sources: Original census records in AME; I created this data from the published transcription in Dumond and Dumond (1982: 3–304).

Notes: The note to Table B.1 on which parishes are included and how they are listed applies here too, although the list of parishes is slightly different (and the two lying outside Yucatan state are Chicbul and Pich, both in today's Campeche state). The totals listed include three racial categories: Spaniards and mestizos; Afro-Yucatecans (*negros* and mulattoes or pardos); and Mayas ("yndios"), the last of which contains the vast majority of all entries; in the 1808 entries Spaniards and mestizos are listed separately and the only Africans are mulattoes. Most entries in the original documents are also broken down by sex and by month.

[a] Census covers July 1805 through July 1806.
[b] Data covers only half the year, from April 1 to September 30.

TABLE B.2 *(continued)*

^c Census covers June 1, 1805, to May 24, 1806; similarly, the other non-calendar-year entries for Tekanto cover May 21, 1809, to June 5, 1810, and May 29, 1814, to May 8, 1815.
^d The non-calendar year entries cover May 19, 1806, to September 27, 1807, and 1807 (probably September 28) to June 6, 1808. The 1813 census includes separate entries for the subsidiary community of Tepakam but in the earlier censuses Tepakam's inclusion is evidenced only by the phrase "this parish and its visita (i.e., jurisdiction)."
^e The Hoctun entry appears this way, without any temporal subdivisions, in the original census.
^f The figures for this year combine data from Tixcacal (tuyu) and its subsidiary, Tacchebilchen; it was actually in the latter where most of the parish's pardos were baptized (17 of 18) and buried (5 of 8) that year.
^g This figure breaks down to 2.0% for Ichmul proper, 0.1% for the subject community of Tiholop, and none for the other subject communities of Celul, Saban, Uaymax, and Tinum (for burials the figure is 2.1% for Tiholop proper and none for its subject communities). This distribution is paralleled in the census data (see Chapter Two).
^h This entry includes separate figures for the subsidiary communities of Tela and Tepich.

TABLE B.3 Casta distribution of recipients of baptism, marriage, and burial in the parishes of Campeche *extramuros*, 1781–87

Rite and casta category	Cabecera San Francisco and Santa Lucía (%)	Lerma and Sambula (%)	Hampolol (%)	San Diego and Cholul (%)
BAPTISM				
Spaniards	0.0	3.8	14.4	4.4
Pardos	0.0	5.5	13.5	0.0
Mayas	100.0	90.7	72.1	95.6
MARRIAGE				
Spaniards	3.7	7.4	13.8	7.9
Pardos	4.3	5.9	12.6	5.3
Mayas	92.0	86.7	75.6	86.8
BURIAL				
Spaniards	0.0	4.9	12.7	7.4
Pardos	0.0	4.9	11.5	6.4
Mayas	100.0	90.2	75.8	86.2

Source: Created from data in Patch (1993: 235).

Afro-Yucatecans Traveling Under License from Spain to Yucatan
(1579–1779)

TABLE C.1

Holder of license to cross the Atlantic	Afro-Yucatecans included in the license	Date of travel	Source
Sebastián Toral	Himself, free *negro/moreno*, returning	1579	[C] 5227, 2, 25; and [I] 1969, 22, 1
Melchor Pacheco	Baltasar Hernández, his mulatto servant; both returning	1599	[C] 5260a, 1, 34
Joseph Franquez de Ortega	Juan, his black slave; both returning	1602	[C] 5272, 2, 71
Geronimo de Yanguas	His two slaves: a 16-year-old mulatto creole [*criollo*], and Lorenzo, a 25-year-old black; returning to Yucatan after 2 years	1615	[I] 2075, 83, 1
Dr. Francisco Ruiz	Melchor de Segovia, his 15-year-old mulatto servant; both returning	1615	[C] 5348, 67, 1
Juan de Contreras Duran	His free mulatto servant; returning to Yucatan after 2 years	1618	[I] 2076, 76, 1
Francisco de Aguilar	Himself, a free mulatto criollo, returning	1619	[C] 5365, 21, 1
Br. don Manuel Núñez de Matos, cathedral schoolmaster, Merida	Juan, his black slave; and Domingo, his mulatto servant [*criado*]; all returning	1623	[C] 5387, 16, 1
Capt. Alonso Carrio de Valdés, encomendero	Anton, his black slave; both returning	1634	[I] 2077, 250
Capt. don Francisco Lara Bonifaz, encomendero	Francisco, his 55-year-old free black servant; all returning to Yucatan after 2 years	1640	[C] 5420, 70; and [C] 5422, 29

Don Francisco Núñez Melián, governor of Yucatan (1643–44)	Francisco Antonio and Juan Criollo, his black slaves, 40 and 18 years old, respectively	1643	[C] 5425, 1, 1
Juan Antonio de Padilla	Joseph de Padilla, his 22-year-old dark black slave	1699	[C] 5459, 214, 1
Don Juan Joseph Vertiz y Ontañón, governor of Yucatan (1717–23)	Lázaro de los Reyes, his 23-year-old, free dark black servant	1710	[C] 5465, 2, 77
Don Diego de Santesteban y Zuluaga, lessor of the income from the sales and customs taxes on Yucatec salt	Agustín de Leira, his 14-year-old black slave	1718	[C] 5470, 1, 23
Don fray Antonio Alcalde, Dominican, bishop of Yucatan (1761–72)	His free black servants: Melchor de la Torre, native of Cartagena de Indias; and Antonio de Arcos, native of Havana	1763	[C] 5506, 2, 7
Dr. don Rafael del Castillo y Sucre, cathedral schoolmaster, Merida	José Ganga, his 14-year-old dark black servant; freed in Havana in 1773	1779	[C] 5524, 4, 29

Sources: All AGI; [C] is *Contratación*, [I] is *Indiferente*. Some of the license holders can also be found in the AGI index under *Pasajeros*.

Note: Also see Table 1.1 in Chapter One and Table 5.6 in Chapter Five for further detail on Sebastián Toral (1579), Juan (1602), Francisco Antonio (1643), and Agustín de Leira (1718), as well as the relevant discussions in Chapters One, Two, and Five.

Sales and Values of Slaves in Yucatan

TABLE D.1 Merchandise, property, and slaves sold in Yucatan, 1660–64 (according to sales tax records)

Type of merchandise or property	Number of entries	Peso value of 2% or 4% sales taxes [*alcabala*]
UNSPECIFIED MERCHANDISE		
Merchandise [*mercadurias*]	90	2,294
Petty merchandise [*menudencias*]	47	272
Merchandise from Castile	1	800
Goods [*vienes*]	42	1,306
Cloth goods [*géneros*]	2	22
[Subtotal]	[181]	[4,694]
SPECIFIED MERCHANDISE AND PROPERTY		
Wine	16	154
Wine and vinager	1	206
Wine and other merchandise	1	32
Wine and other petty merchandise	2	65
Wine and *galludero* thread from Spain	1	354
Wine from Havana	1	50
Wine and tobacco from Havana	1	45
Wine and flour	1	12
Wine, cacao, and tallow	1	35
Wine, cacao, and sugar	1	15
Wine from Cartagena	1	40
	(Wine 27)	(1,008)
Cacao	8	118
Cacao and tobacco	1	37
Cacao from Tabasco	2	56
Cacao from Portobelo	1	120
Cacao from Cartagena	1	59
Cacao from Maracaibo	2	60
Cacao from Guayaquil	1	12
	(Cacao 16)	(462)
Flour	9	122
Flour and oil	1	17
Flour, cacao, and other merchandise	2	40
Flour, soap, and other merchandise	1	36
Flour, cacao, and soap foam	1	11
Lead, hats, tobacco, and other goods	1	6
Lead and other goods	1	45
Sugar	3	26
Sugar and tobacco from Havana	2	17
Salt or pepper	2	12
Beef	70	395
Lime (700 *fanegas*)	1	14
Incense	1	2

(continued)

TABLE D.1 *(continued)*

Type of merchandise or property	Number of entries	Peso value of 2% or 4% sales taxes [*alcabala*]
Candlewax	2	16
Dyewood, dyes, and related goods	3	158
Ships and boats	5	147
Mules	2	74
[Subtotal]	[150]	[2,578]
LANDED PROPERTY AND ENCOMIENDA TRIBUTE		
Houses sold or mortgaged	31	612
House plots and a half-plot	41	148
House and plot variants	5	78
Estancia, half-estancia, or rural plot [*sitio*]	24	304
Encomienda tribute from Maya villages	47	328
[Subtotal]	[148]	[1,470]
SLAVES		
Esclavos	11	84
Negros and two *negrittos*	32	280
Mulattoes & two *mulatillos*	13	108
Mulatto and other auctioned goods	1	27
Esclava	3	42
Negras and a *negritta*	14	134
Flour, vinegar, and a *negra*	1	31
Mulatta	1	10
[Subtotal]	[76]	[716]
[Grand total]	[555]	[9,458]

Source: AGI-*Contaduría* 917A, 1: ff. 15–17, 21–26; 2: ff. 24–40.

Notes: The time covered here is 41 months from August 1660 to January 1664. Note that the period covered by each tax was inconsistent; while some taxes were for single sales (such as house plots), and the records imply that most shop sales were for a one-year period, others covered periods from several months to three years.

Merchandise, both unspecified and specified, is sometimes described simply as sold, and sometimes as sold in shops or in taverns in Merida or Campeche. The "goods" category includes the tax on the liquidation of a few large estates.

The purpose of the table is to show how significant the local slave trade was in the local economy, over a sample period: slave sales were 14% of all sale entries on the tax books; the peso revenue from slave sales was 8% of the total sales tax revenue.

This particular source is not ideal for calculating slave values (the application of the 4% was not completely consistent, taxes on multiple items were often grouped together, and during this 1660–64 period the gender balance among slaves sold was far off the norm, with the value of women thus higher than the norm); nevertheless, my estimates are for 56 men, an average of 211 pesos each; for 18 women, 258 pesos (both together average out to 222 pesos).

TABLE D.2 Slave sales in Yucatan, 1667–1672 (as listed in sales tax records)

Slave	Seller	Buyer	Price/Alcabala
Mulata	Joseph de Argaiz	Doña Mariana Pantoja	400/16
Esclavo	Pedro Morillo	Capt. Juan Gutiérrez de Cosgaya	200/8
Esclavo	Pedro Duarte	Juan Francisco Lunbies	275/11
Esclavo	Alf. Santiago Bolio	Pedro de Balenzuela	150/6
Juan, *negro*	Cristóbal Lorenzo Bravo	Capt. Juan de Castro	200/8
Juana, mulata	Capt. Gaspar Guerra and Alf. Alonso Infante	Lic. don Nicolas de Ruias	200/8
Geronimo, esclavo	Juan Mayor	Capt. Mateo Pérez de Garay	100/4
Serafina, esclava	Capt. Juan Gutiérrez de Cosgaya	Capt. Mateo Pérez de Garay	200/8
3 esclavos	Executor for doña Francisca Dorantes	Not given	465/18, 5
2 negrillos pequeños	Don Nicolas Pacheco	Don Iñigo de Mendoza	300/12
Mulata	Don Nicolas Pacheco	Doña María de Pereda y Pantoja	300/12
Mulata	Don Ignacio de Solis	Diego Pérez	300/12
Negro	Juan Mayor	Pedro de Paçio	250/10
Negra	Capt. Andrés Dorantes Solís for Marta González	Br. Alonso Lorenzo de Mansanilla	150/6
Negro	Antonio Maldonado de Aldana	Andrés Rojo de Reylona	415/16, 5
Negro	Doña Juana de la Paz	Doña Juana Dorantes Solís	100/4
Negro	Don Pedro de Lara	Sebastián de Yrrasabal	300/12
Negro	Don Pedro de Lara	Joseph de Arçe	250/10
Antonio Pinto, *negro*	The late Francisco de Lara	Antonio González	300/12
Esclavo	Executors for don Diego de Granda Valdés	Melchor de la Rosa/manumission	250/10
Negra	Br. Nicolas Carrión for don Gaspar Pacheco	Manuel Lozano	200/8
Mulato	Doña Isabel del Castillo	Diego González	200/8
Francisca Sánchez, esclava	Doña Juana Román	Manumission	300/12
Negra	Don Diego de Aranda Aguayo	Not given	100/4

(continued)

TABLE D.2 (continued)

Slave	Seller		Buyer	Price/Alcabala
Negra	Don Diego de Aranda Aguayo		Not given	412/16, 4
Mulato	Luis Díaz		Lorenzo de Idiarte	200/8
Bartolo, mulato	Doña Juana de Bobadilla		Don Pedro Díaz del Valle	300/12
Negra	Doña María de los Angeles		Nicolas de Soto	200/8
Esclavo	Nicolas de Soto		Doña María de los Angeles	300/12
Mulatillo	Doña Ana de Valdés		Dr. don Juan de Escalante	160/6, 4
Mulato	Don Juan de Villareal		Capt. don Carlos Bocardo	200/8
Negro	Doña María Sánchez		Juan González	300/12
Moreno	Doña Ana Valdés		Don Pedro Díaz del Valle	350/14
Mulato	Doña Ana Valdés		The Bishop	500/20
Negro	Doña Thomasa and doña Thomasa		Not given	350/14
Mulata	Francisco Meléndez Morán		Not given	300/12
2 esclavos	Doña Francisca Dorantes Solís		Not given	500/20
Moreno	Francisco Díaz Santiago		Not given	200/8
Mulata	Francisco Díaz Santiago		Juan de la Peña	350/14
Moreno	Bernardo de Monfil		Not given	200/8
2 esclavos	Juan Mayor		Don Bartolome del Balcazar & Thomas González	855/32
Mulata	Lic. Juan de Alamilla for Gregorio Ruiz del Barco		Capt. Gaspar Guerra	380/14
Esclava	Don Bernardino de Balcazar		Catalina Ortíz	350/14
Esclava	Juan Valdés and his wife Mariana Alfaro		Hospital of San Juan de Dios	159/6, 3
Esclava	Juan Gutiérrez de Cosgaya		Alf. Cristóbal Lorenzo Bravo	200/8
Esclava	Juan de Castilla		Cristóbal Santiago	200/8
Negra	Santiago Bolio		Doña Mariana de Perea	[1,200/48]*
Negra	Don Francisco Xavier del Valle		Dr. don Juan de Escalante	250/10

Mulata and mulato	Lic. Pedro de Arguez	Don Bernardino Xavier de Magaña	600/24
Negra	Dr. don Nicolas de Salazar	Doña Mariana Pereda y Pantoja	300/12
Esclava	Magdalena Guerra	Not given	[906/36, 2]*
Mulatillo	Diego González Perea	Lazara Crespo	240/6, 9
Mulato	Pedro de Pestana	Not given (don Francisco Xavier?)	200/8
Esclavo	Don Francisco Xavier	Pedro de Pestana	200/8
Negra	Doña Francisca de Carranza	Luis Díaz	150/6

Source: AGI-*Contaduría* 917a, 5: ff. 15–37bis (1667–69), through to the sale to the Bishop); 917a, 6: ff. 10–18; 917b, 7: ff. 37–45, 52–64 (1670–72).

Notes: These are all the sales, listed chronologically, from October 28, 1667, through August 4, 1672. The 4% alcabala sales tax is given in pesos and tomines.

*The sales of the slaves in these cases were not separated from the larger sales: in the Bolio entry, of Campeche merchandise that he sold in his Merida store; in the Guerra entry, of the auctioned-off property of her late mother, Beatriz de Escobeda.

Pace of sales: for 1667–69, 37 sales (including 2 manumissions) over 26 months, averaging one every three weeks; for 1670–72, 24 sales over 32 months, averaging one every six weeks; for the full 4 years and 9 months, 61 sales at an average pace of one every four weeks.

Identity of slaves: 30 men, 24 women, and 7 in "esclavos" groups; 20 blacks, 17 mulattoes, 3 morenos, and 21 simply described as "slaves."

Average sale prices: for the 30 men, 240 pesos; for the 24 women, 238 pesos; for 1667–69, 239 pesos (231 not counting the anomalous sale to the Bishop); for 1670–72, 249 pesos; for the whole period 1667–72, 243 pesos (including men, women, and the nongendered "esclavos" category).

TABLE D.3 Some examples of peso values given to African slaves in
Yucatan, 1678–1829

Sex/official category	Age; health	Birthplace or origin	Peso value	Year of valuation
Negro	Old; blind		0	1760
Negro	"Unusable"	Via Belize	0[a]	1780
Negro	"Useless"	Via Belize	40[a]	1780
Negra			90[b]	1766
Mulato	Boy		100[b]	1691
Negra	Old; poor health		100	1760[c]
Negra	Very old; poor health		100	1760[c]
Negra	28	"Ladina"	100[b]	1767
Negras	4 adults, 1 girl	Via Belize	100[d]	1779
Negro	Boy	Via Belize	100	1780
Negro	Boy	Via Belize	100	1780
Mulata	3	Yucatan	100	1818
Negro	Adult	Via Belize	120	1780
Negro	Married adult	Via Belize	140[e]	1780
Negro	25	"Africa"	150	1689
Negra	50	Yucatan?	150	1689
Parda	53	Yucatan	150	c.1715
Parda	20	Yucatan	150	c.1715
Negro	Adult		150	1760
Negro	Adult		150	1760
Negra	Young adult		150	1766
Negros	4 adult men, 1 woman	Via Belize	170[f]	1779
Negra	Married adult	Via Belize	180	1780
Negro	25; "defective"[g]	Jamaica	180	1801
Negra	Adult	Via Belize	190	1780
Negra	40	Santo Domingo	200	c.1715
Negras	4 adults	Via Belize	200[h]	1779
Negro	Adult	Via Belize	200	1780
Negro	Adult	Via Belize	200	1792
Negro	Adult	Via Belize	200	1792
Negro	20; good	"Guinea"	200	1801
Negro	20; "robust"	"Guinea"	200	1801
Negro	15; half "lame"	Jamaica	200	1801
Negro	9	"Africa"	200	1818
Negro	30; "healthy"	Jamaica	215	1801
Negra	Young		225	1692
Negra	21		240	1740
Negro			250	1764
Negro			250	1764
Mulata	Adult		250	1765

TABLE D.3 *(continued)*

Sex/official category	Age; health	Birthplace or origin	Peso value	Year of valuation
Negra	12	Congo	250	1766
Negro	Married adult	via Belize	250	1780
Mulato	32; good	Jamaica	250	1801
Negra	Adult; "without defects"		250	1829
Negro	Adult		260	1829
Negra	Adult		290	1817
Negra	Adult		300	1829
Mulato	12	Yucatan	300	1732
Negra	8–13	"Guinea"	325	1805
Negro	8–13	"Guinea"	325	1805
Negro	18–20	"Guinea"	325	1805
Negra	Adult		356	1818
Negro	Adult		360	1817[i]
Mulato	Adult	Yucatan	400	1678[j]
Negras	3 adults		400	1829[k]
Negros	Family: 2 adults, 2 children	Via Belize	450[l]	1780
Negro	18–20; good[m]		600	1821
Average value of men			208	
Average value of women			204	
Average value			206	

Sources: ANEY, Baeza (UTA roll 1) and Hunt (1974: 94–95, 532) (for 1678, 1689, and 1732 entries); ANEY, Baeza (UTA roll 1): n.f. (1692 entry); Negroe Sierra (1991: 18) (c.1715); ANEY, Montero (UTA roll 5): nf (1740); AGI-*México* 3050 (1760); AGEY, Zavala (UTA roll 15): ff. 123–24, 223–24, 243–44, 363–65, 475–76 (1764–67 entries); AGEY, Argaiz (UTA roll 20): f. 175 (other 1764 entry); López Rivas (1975: 119–22, partial transcription of ANEY, Argaiz/Hivarren [UTA roll 21]) (1779–80 entries); Rúz Menendez (1970: 22–25, transcription of AHAY-*Asuntos Terminados* 1792) (1792 entries); AGN-*Marina* 156, 5: fs.188v–89 (1801); AGN-*Alcabalas* 427, 10: f.186 (1805); AGEY-*Justicia* (Poder Ejecutivo) 2, 20 (1817 and 1829); CCA-*caja* X, 1818, 009 (1818); Baqueiro Anduze (1983: 38) (1821); Ruz Menéndez (1970: 17) (1829).

Notes: Averages calculated using 64 representative examples (32 men, 32 women), not including slaves valued at under 100 or over 400 pesos. The average value of my complete database of 168 slaves valued at 100–400 pesos (1672–1829; too cumbersome to include here) is likewise 206.

[a] A slave named "Deiman" (Daman), "seized with another useless one in a ranch on the Sibun River [*apresado junto con otro inutil en un rancho del rio Sibun*]" sold "for 40 pesos because he is useless and the other one completely unusable, left in the hospital because he does not merit evaluation [*en cuarenta pesos por estar inutil y el otro totalmente inservible, quedo en el hospital por no merecer aprecio*]."

TABLE D.3 (*continued*)

^b These low prices are because an owner was willing to make it relatively easy for his former slave to buy her son's freedom (1691 case), or the price was stipulated in the will of an owner as a condition of all future resales (1766 case), or it derived from the condition that the child being carried by the pregnant slave could never be enslaved (1767 case).

^c When the following year these women became ill they were reevaluated as having no peso value.

^d Four adult negras and the daughter of one, a "negrita" named Isabel, sold for 500 pesos together.

^e A booty slave from the 1779 attack on Belize, named "Jam" and sold with his wife Lucía, apparently for the single price of 140 pesos.

^f Five slaves sold together for 850 pesos, four *negros* and a negra.

^g "Defective in one finger of the left hand and another [i.e., a toe] of the right foot," which partially offset the man's skill as "a shoreside carpenter [*carpintero de rivera*]".

^h Four women sold for 200 pesos each.

ⁱ Revalued at 300 pesos when freed under abolition in 1829.

^j This high price at this early date reflects the fact that the slave in question had become highly skilled at managing the Huayalceh *estancia*.

^k Three women valued at this price when freed under abolition.

^l A booty family from the 1779 attack on Belize sold together for the single price of 450 pesos, consisting of "Aupín" and Francis, and their children Bob and Tibi, the latter in puberty ["*en edad de pechos*"] and baptized as María Manuela.

^m "Healthy and without defects." The high sale price might partially be explained by the claim that the man knew "the essentials of shoemaking, cooking, and masonry," yet this is still a suspiciously inflated sum, suggesting the involvement of other factors not included in the record.

Spanish Slave Owners in Merida (1710–89)
(as recorded in black slave baptisms)

TABLE E.1 Slave owners, by sex, number, and sex of slave owned, by duodecades

| Male slave owners | Number and sex of black slaves owned, by twenty-year periods | | | | | | | | Totals |
| | 1710–29 | | 1730–49 | | 1750–69 | | 1770–89 | | |
	M	F	M	F	M	F	M	F	
Aguirre, • d Joseph de					1	1°			2
Aguirre, Con d Santiago de			2	1°					4
Alanis, d Joseph Ambrosio de	1								1
Álvarez, C d Joseph de							1		1
Andrade, d Laureano de			1						1
Anguas, • C R d Francisco de					2		3		5
Aranda y Aguayo, Ch/Arc Dr d Joseph de		2°							2
Araos, d Joseph					1				1
Arias, d Bernardo de			1						1
Ayala, C d Diego de					1	1°			2
Baez, d Francisco					1				1
Barra, TG Juan Fernando de					1				1
Besama, • d Mathias			3	2*°					5
Brito, B d Juan Tomás							1	1°	2
Buendia, Con d Juan de	1								1
Caballero, Alberto		1							1
Caballero, Bac d Juan Tomás	1								1
Cabrera, Pedro		1							1
Calderón, d Francisco Antonio							2	2	4
Calderón y Helguera, • C d Pedro			5	3*°					8
Calderón y Helguera, • C/Conde d Santiago					1		1		2
Camara, d Juan Antonio de la	1								1

	1	2	3	4	5	6	7	8	Total
Campo, C d Joseph Antonio del	1								1
Campo,• C/R d Juan del	2	4°	1	2°			4	4°	9
Cano,• AM d Joseph			1			3°	1	4°	14
Capote, d Juan									1
Cardenas,• C Def d Cayetano					3	2		1	5
Castillo, AM d Juan Francisco del			1		1				3
Castillo y Arrúe,• AM d Juan del	2		1						2
Castillo y Helguera, C d Antonio del	1	1°							2
Castillo y Solís,• MC d Juan del	1	1°	1	3°					6
Castorena y Urzúa, O d Juan Ignacio				1					1
Castro, SM d Juan Joseph de	3	1							4
Castro, d Juan Joseph de								2°	2
Castro, d Laureano de			1				1		1
Castro y Castillo,• C d Domingo de				2					3
Chacon, B d Fernando			1				1		2
Chacon, d Pedro			1						1
Chacon, d Rodrigo	6	13*°	1	3*°	1	1*°		3°	24
Cicero, C d Francisco			2		2	1*°	1		4
Constante, d Tomás			1		1		1		2
Contrera Rendón, d Tiburcio de	2	2°	2	4°					10
Cortayre, Gov d Antonio de	1								1
Cueva Caldera, Arc d Juan de la	2								2
Devia, Miguel					1		1		1
Díaz,• C d Juan									1
Domínguez de la Camara, d Andrés			1						1
Echasarreta, Cura B d Luis de			1				4	2*°	6
Echauri, Con d Juan Agustín de	1	1°		1					3
Escobar y Llamas, P d Juan de	1								2
Espinola y Vira(?), d Mathias	1								1
Estrella, C Joseph de				1					1

(continued)

Male slave owners	Number and sex of black slaves owned, by twenty-year periods								Totals
	1710–29		1730–49		1750–69		1770–89		
	M	F	M	F	M	F	M	F	
Fernández de Estrella, d Joseph		2							2
Fernández de Heredia, Gov d Alonso					2	1			3
Fernández, d Domingo		1							1
Fernández, d Manuel					1	1°			2
Fernández, Pedro	1								1
Figueroa, d Luis de			1						1
Figueroa, Prior fray Antonio							1	1°	2
Figueroa Laso de la Vega, Gov d A'o de	2								2
García, C d Tomás				1					1
García de la Piedra, C d Pedro				1					1
Gómez de Parada, O d Juan	2	2							4
González, Dr d Juan Salvador							1	4°	5
González, Melchor	1								1
González de la Madriz,• C d Joseph	1	3°							4
Helguera y Castillo,• R d Antonio de la	1								1
Herrera,• d Cristobal de	1		1						2
Herrera, Diego de	1								1
Irigoyen,• d Geronimo		2°		1					3
Lanz(?), d Damian							2	1*°	3
Lanz, Tes/Con d Diego				2	1				3
Lira, d Andrés de					1				1
Lizarraga,• C d Pedro de		1							1

López, d Pedro					1	1
Lousel, VG Dr d Juan Agustín de		1			1	2
Maldonado, B d Pedro		1				1
Maldonado, TG Lic d Sebastian			3	2*°		5
Marcano, d Baltasar			1			1
Marcos Bermejo, • C d Joseph de		2				2
Martínez, C Juan	3°					3
Martínez, C d Pedro		1				1
Méndez, • d Francisco	3					3
Mendicuti, Can Dr				1		1
Mendoza, Miguel			1			1
Meneses, B d Cura Feliciano				2°	1	3
Meneses, d Juan Esteban				3*°	1	4
Meneses Bravo, Gov d Alonso de	11			3		14
Meneses Bravo, Gov d Fernando de	4					4
Milanes, d Juan Antonio				1	1	2
Miranda, T Diego de				1		1
Mugartegui, A d Juan Bautista		1°		1		2
Mugartegui, • A/C d Juan de		4°		2		6
Navarrete, Gov d Melchor			6	4*°		10
Noguera, • C d Martín de		8*°	3			11
Novelo, d Manuel			1			1
Olamendi, d Pedro				2°		2
Ontiveros, Matías de		2				2
Padilla, O Dr d fray Ignacio de			3			3
Pantiga, d Joseph Alonso				3°	1	4
Paz, d Antonio de la				2°	1	3
Peña, Con d Juan Esteban				2*°	1	3
Peón, Cor d Alonso Manuel		1°	1		1	3
Pérez, d Crisanto		1°			1	2

(continued)

TABLE E.1 (continued)

| | Number and sex of black slaves owned, by twenty-year periods | | | | | | | | |
| | 1710–29 | | 1730–49 | | 1750–69 | | 1770–89 | | Totals |
Male slave owners	M	F	M	F	M	F	M	F	
Pérez, C d Francisco	1	1							2
Pérez, d Manuel				1					1
Pérez, B Tomás	2	1*°							3
Pimentel, Can Dr d Agustín					1		1		2
Pino, A/T d Joseph del			1	1°		1			3
Pino Capote, d Joseph Jacinto del						2	1		3
Pinto, B d Juan				2°					2
Pinzon, A Pedro	1								1
Pordio, • C d Joseph Domingo					1	1	3	5°	10
Priego, d Juan Alberto de		2°		2°					4
Priego, d Pedro Mathias de				2°					2
Puerto, Can P D d Sancho del	2	3°*							5
Quijano y Cetina, • C d Juan Esteban			1	1°	8	8*°	21	17*°	56
Raquina, d Francisco					2				2
Rejon y Pérez, d Manuel					1				1
Rendón, • A d Nicolas				1					1
Reyes, • d Enrique de los								1	1
Rivas, d Juan de			1	3°					4
Rivas Betancourt, Gov d Roberto de							4	4*°	8
Rivas Calavera, d Diego de	2	2	1	1°					6
Rodríguez, • d Juan							2	1	3
Rodríguez de Trujillo, Tes d Clemente							4	1*°	5
Roela, • C d Miguel de	1	2	1	2°					6

Ruíz, • d Antonio							1		1
Sabala, d Joseph			1	2					3
Salcedo, Gov d Manuel			2	2					4
Sánchez Moro, Juan	1								1
Sanpedro, d Isidro de							2	4°	6
Sarabia, SM d Joseph de	1								1
Seballos, d Manuel de	1								1
Silva, B d Joseph de			1	1°					2
Solís, • Cast d Antonio				1					1
Sosa y Pino, d Joseph de					1				1
Tenorio, d Fernando Martin de	1	1°		2°					4
Tinoch, Manuel			1	1°					2
Torre, d Raphael de la			1	1					2
Umaran, C d Francisco de					1				1
Urgoitia, B d Marcos de	1								1
Urriola, d Juan					1				1
Valdés, B d Bernardo							1		1
Valle, C d Juan Joseph de la							1	2	3
Vásquez, • C d Andrés	1	2°		2°					5
Vásquez, • d Bernardo				1					1
Vásquez, C d Ignacio				1					1
Ventura, d Joseph		2							2
Vertis, Gov d Juan Joseph de	3								3
Villaelriego, • C d Lorenzo									3
Zavalegui y Ursúa, • C d Miguel de	1	1							2
Zayas Guzmán, Gov d Cristóbal de					3	1°			4
Zuazua, • AM d Juan de					1	1°			2
Zubiaur, C d Manuel					2	2*°			4
[55/46/41/41 owners per duodecade]	[74]	[67]	[44]	[70]	[65]	[37]	[77]	[70]	[504]

(continued)

TABLE E.1 (continued)

Female slave owners	Number and sex of black slaves owned, by twenty-year periods								Totals
	1710–29		1730–49		1750–69		1770–89		
	M	F	M	F	M	F	M	F	
Aguirre, d María Antonia								1	1
Aguirre, d María Francisca								2	2
Albertos, d Isabel				1					1
Alpuche, d Petrona		2	4	5°	1				12
Alvarado, d Josepha								2°	2
Amesquita, d María de		2°							2
Arestegui, d Gregoria de						2			2
Armenta, d Juana						1			1
Ávila Carranza, d Isabel María de			3	8*°					11
Ayora, d Beatriz						1			1
Bermejo, Condesa d María Ildefonsa							4	5°	9
Buendia y Enriques, d María Josepha de		1		1					2
Buitron, d Catarina		1							1
Caballero, d Isabel			2	3*°	1	4°			10
Caballero, d María			1						1
Caballero, d María Isabel				1					1
Cabrera, d Micaela			1	2					3
Calderón, d Francisca								1	1
Camara, d Manuela de la								1	1
Camara, d María Teresa de la						1			1
Campo, d María del		2°							2
Carvajal, d Juana de	1								1

Castillo, d Antonia del			1		1
Castillo, d Ignacia del	2°	1	2		5
Chacon, d María Josepha	2°	1		2°	5
Dávila (Ávila?), d Micaela de				1	1
Díaz, d Francisca	1°		1		2
Díaz, d Phelipa			1		1
Echeverría, d María de				1	1
García, d Catalina	2°				2
García, Luisa	1				1
Garrastegui, d Sepherina	2°	1			3
González, Francisca Xaviera	1				1
Lira, d Ignacia de	1°	1			2
Machin, d Ana			1	1°	2
Machin, d María	2°				2
Madera, d Antonia de	1				1
Martín Negroe, d Josepha		3°	1		4
Martínez, d Ana			1		1
Mejía, d Isabel				1	1
Montiel, d Beatriz	1°	1			2
Moreno, d Phelipa	2	1°			3
Muñoz de Aleaga, d Josepha	2°				2
Pacheco, Gertrudes	2°				2
Panplona, d Juana	1°	1			2
Peña, d María del Carmen de la				1	1
Pérez, M Isidora	1°	1			2
Pérez, d María Manuela	1°	1			2
Piedra, d Juana de la			1		1
Pinelo, d Petrona	1°	1			2
Quijano, d María Josepha				1	1

(continued)

TABLE E.1 (*continued*)

Female slave owners	Number and sex of black slaves owned, by twenty-year periods								Totals
	1710–29		1730–49		1750–69		1770–89		
	M	F	M	F	M	F	M	F	
Rodríguez de la Gala, d Lucía								1	1
Rosado, d Theodora						2°			2
Ruíz, d Josepha Estefana							1	1	2
Salazar, d Petrona de			1	1°					2
Salgado, d Inés		3							3
Sánchez de Cepeda y Lira, d Josepha		1							1
Sansores, d Antonia							1		1
Solís, d María Ildefonsa		1	2	2*°					5
Solís, d Tomasa de						1			1
Tonero, d Ignacia							1	1°	2
Urriola, d María de					1	1°			2
Valle, d Juana del	1	1°							2
Vásquez, d Manuela					1				1
Villaelriego, d María Ignacia					1	2*°			3
Zavalegui, d María								1	1
Zubiaur, d María					2	4*°			6
[18/19/20/19 owners per duodecade]	[6]	[25]	[20]	[36]	[10]	[29]	[10]	[23]	[159]

Source: AGAY-*Jesús*, Libros de Bautismos Vols. 1–6.

Abbreviations: [A] Alférez (2nd Lieutenant or Ensign); [Arc] Arcediano (Archdean); [B] Bachiller (Bachelor degree holder); [Bac] Bacionero (aka Bacinero or Racionero, alms collector, Merida Cathedral); [C] Capitán; [Can] Canonigo (Merida Cathedral Canon); [Cast] Castellano (Warden, San Benito fort, Merida); [Ch] Chantre (Merida Cathedral Precentor); [Con] Contador (Accountant); [Cor] Coronel (Colonel); [d] don/doña; [D] Doctor; [Def] Defensor (Defender of the Indians); [Gov] Governador; [Lic] Licenciado (degree-holding lawyer); [M] Madre (Mother, religious); [MC] Maestre de Campo (Field Marshal); [O] Obispo (Bishop of Yucatan); [P] Provisor; [R] Regidor (of the Merida cabildo); [SM] Sargento Mayor; [T] Teniente (1st Lieutenant); [TG] Teniente General (Lieutenant General); [Tes] Tesorero (Treasurer); (VG) Vicario General (Vicar General of Yucatan).

Notes: All titles are given in the original parish record entry (with the exception of VG, which is therefore given in parentheses).

• Marks those men who served at some point on the Merida cabildo (as regidor, alcalde, procurador, alguacil mayor, or escribano público), according to the cabildo records tabulated in Martínez Ortega (1993: 249–64).

° Indicates parent–child relations among the slaves of the same owner; * indicates husband-wife relations.

Note that slaves who have more than one child appear multiple times in the baptism books; these slave parents are only counted once within each twenty-year period. The only instances where a slave is listed twice within the same decade is due to joint ownership; for example: a mother and daughter owned by don Tiburcio de Contreras Rendon and his wife doña María Josepha Chacon (1731); a mother and son owned by Capt. don Miguel de la Ruela and his wife doña Petrona de Salazar (1731); and the 8 slaves owned by Capt. don Martín de Noguera and doña Isabel de Ávila (1732–40).

TABLE E.2 Average slave-owning numbers in Merida, 1710–89 (as recorded in black slave baptisms)

Slave owners	Average number of slaves owned by each owner, by sex of slave, in duodecades									
	1710–29		1730–49		1750–69		1770–89		[1710–89]	
	M	F	M	F	M	F	M	F	M	F
Spanish men	1.35	1.22	0.96	1.52	1.59	0.90	1.78	1.71	[1.42]	[1.34]
Spanish women	0.33	1.39	1.05	1.90	0.50	1.45	0.53	1.10	[0.60]	[1.46]

Source: AGAY-*Jesús*, Libros de Bautismos, Vols. 1–6.

Note: 155 Spanish men owned 260 male and 244 female slaves; 67 Spanish women owned 46 male and 113 female slaves. The total gender balance among the slaves was therefore 357 women to 306 men.

TABLE E.3 Incidence of titles among slave owners in Merida, 1710–89 (as recorded in black slave baptisms)

	Number	Percentage
TITLE (155 MEN)		
Don	137	88
Clergy	22	14
TITLE (133 MEN, NON-CLERGY)		
Captain	40	30
Other military titles	17	13
Government (province)	17	13
(governor)	(10)	(8)
(treasurer and accountant)	(6)	(5)
(defensor)	(1)	(1)
Government (city cabildo)	34	26
TITLE (67 WOMEN)		
Doñas	63	94

Source: AGAY-*Jesús*, Libros de Bautismos, Vols. 1–6.

Notes: The percentages do not add to 100 because of the overlap between "don" and other titles.

"Government (city)" refers to Merida cabildo positions (regidor, alcalde, procurador, alguacil mayor, or escribano público); the figure was created by cross referencing the 133 non-clerical slave owners in the baptism records with cabildo listings for the century (in Martínez Ortega 1993: 249–64).

A shorter version of this table appears as Table 2.7 in Chapter Two.

TABLE E.4 Christian naming patterns among slave owners, Merida, 1710–89 (as recorded in black slave baptisms)

Most popular men's names		Most popular women's names	
Juan	17+19=36	María	7+12=19
Joseph	15+5=20	Josepha	5+1=6
Pedro	11+1=12	Juana	5
Francisco	7+1=8	Isabel	4
Antonio	8	Antonia	3
Manuel	7	Francisca	2+1=3

Remaining men's names		Remaining women's names	
Agustín	1	Ana	2
Alberto	1	Beatriz	2
Alonso	2+1=3	Catal(r)ina	2
Andrés	4	Felipa	2
Baltasar	1	Gertrudes	1
Bernardo	3	Gregoria	1
Cayetano	1	Ignacia	3
Clemente	1	Inés	1
Crisanto	1	Isidora	1
Cristóbal	2	Lucia	1
Damian	1	Luisa	1
Diego	5	Manuela	2
Domingo	2	Micaela	2
Enrique	1	Petrona	3
Feliciano	1	Sepherina	1
Fernando	2+1=3	Teodora	1
Gerónimo	1	Tomasa	1
Ignacio	2		
Isidro	1		
Laureano	2		
Lorenzo	1		
Luís	2		
Marcos	1		
Martín	1		
Mathias	3		
Melchor	2		
Miguel	5		
Nicolás	1		
Raphael	1		
Roberto	1		
Rodrigo	1		
Sancho	1		
Santiago	2		
Sebastián	1		

(*continued*)

TABLE E.4 *(continued)*

Remaining men's names		Remaining women's names	
Tiburcio	1		
Tomás	3		
[42 names]	[155]	[23 names]	[67]
How many Juans?	23%	How many Marías?	28%
How many Josephs?	13%	How many Josephas?	9%
Variation 1	27%	Variation 1	34%
Variation 2	40%	Variation 2	52%

Source: AGAY-*Jesús*, Libros de Bautismos Vols. 1–6.

Notes: Variation 1 is the variation rate of first names only; Variation 2 takes second names into account as well. A zero variation rate means everyone has the same name; 100% variation means no two persons have the same name. The entry 7 + 12 = 19 means 7 women simply named María, and 12 named María plus a second name. The percentages of Juans and Marías (under "How many . . . ?") are based on first names only.

For the presentation of this data in a comparative context, see Table 2.4 in Chapter Two.

Afro-Yucatecans Accused of Witchcraft and Love–Magic

TABLE F.1 Afro-Yucatecans accused of witchcraft by the Inquisition, 1566–1785

Year	The accused	Alleged offense	Accused's location	Methods of the offense; investigation outcome[a]	Source (all AGN-*Inquisición*)
1566	Maria de Lugo, mulatta?	Witchcraft	Mexico and Merida?		39, 1: ff. 1-103
1570	Barbola de Zamora free mulatta, widow	Witchcraft	Merida	Indicted, tried, and sentenced to public punishment	39, 4: f. 54
1580	Cristóbal, *negro* slave	Witchcraft	Near Calkini	Indicted, not tried	125, 69: ff. 254-63
1598	*Negro* slave	Blasphemy	Merida		176, 12: ff. 1-3
1612	Ana de Sossa, mulatta	Witchcraft	Campeche		297, 5: ff. 1-13
1626	Isabel, negra	Blasphemy	Campeche		360, 1: ff. 243-44
1626	Catalina Puc (Maya) and Antonia (mulatta), hired by Catalina Antonia de Rojas (Spanish)	Love–magic	Campeche	Spoken spells (in Maya?); denunciation only	360: ff. 275-76
1626	Isabel de Montejo, mulatta	Witchcraft	Valladolid and Campeche?		360, 2: f. 558
1627	Catalina Rodríguez and unnamed Maya woman	Love–magic	Merida	Self-denunciation	360, 90
1627	Catalina Puc	Love–magic	Campeche	Denunciation only	360, 92
1631	Maria Mo, mulatta	Witchcraft	Campeche		374, 10: ff. 132-45
1634	Francisca de Llanos, mulatta	Witchcraft (healing)	Merida	Brought in by the prior of the San Juan de Dios hospital to cure a sick woman; used enchanted *xuchil* flowers and water and a burned handkerchief; not tried	380, 3: ff. 359-64

1639	Juana Delgado, mulatta	Love–magic	Campeche	Knows how to use roses and other flowers to cast spells to attract men	388: ff. 412-16v
1639	María de Salas, mulatta	Love–magic	Campeche		388: f. 417v
1639	Ana Gonzalez, "la Isleña"	Love–magic	Campeche	Knows spells [oraçiones] to enchant a man in Spanish; two spells included in denunciation; also mentions an unnamed "India" who can make enchanted chocolate with water used to wash body parts	388: ff. 419-20r
1642	Felipa, negra	Witchcraft	Merida		413, 8: ff. 369-93
1650	Capt. Alonso del Puerto, mulatto militiaman	Idolatry	Tixppitah	Denunciation only	908
1658	Agustina de la Cerda, mulatta	Love–magic	Campeche		443: f. 495
1658	Ana de Ortega, mulatta / parda	Love–magic	Campeche	Clients taught to pluck pubic and armpit hair, then steal a handkerchief from the target, sew a button on it, and rip off the button when the target passed by, preferably while standing in a doorway	443: ff. 491-503
1666	Agustín Díaz, mulatto	Love–magic	Merida	Denunciation only	627: f. 278
1672	Agustina, parda	Love–magic	Merida(?)	Denunciation only	626: f. 300v
1672	Isabel, mulatta	Love–magic	Merida	Denunciation only	626: f. 299

(continued)

TABLE F.I (continued)

Year	The accused	Alleged offense	Accused's location	Methods of the offense; investigation outcome[a]	Source (all AGN-*Inquisición*)
1672	Dominga, mulatta	Love–magic	Merida	Denunciation only	626: f. 359
1672	Michaela Montejo and Ana (mulattas), Catalina Alvarez, Ursula (free negra), and indias, hired by María Maldonado (Spanish); Lucas de Arguello (*negro*), Juana Pacheco, and an india hired(?) by Manuel Maldonado (Spanish)	Love–magic	Merida	Enchanted flowers and spells; only Arguello and Montejo to be further investigated (see next case)	620, 7: ff. 595-614
1672	Lucas de Arguello (*negro*), Michaela Montejo (mulatta), and others	Love–magic	Merida	Denunciations only	621: ff. 244-54
1672	Catalina Rejino, Michaela Montejo, Leonor de Toribio, Cecilia, a woman with the surname Jesús (all free mulattas), an unnamed mulatta	Witchcraft, mostly love–magic	Merida	Denunciations only	626, 7: ff. 188-208
1673	Juan de Argaez, mulatto	Idolatry	Campeche		516, 12: ff. 556-87
1674	Baltasar Martín, Manuel Canche, and Nicolas Lozano	Witchcraft, idolatry	Merida	All indicted; Canche and Lozano tried and acquitted after 8 years in jail	629, 4: ff. 328-430

Date	Name	Offense	Location	Procedure	Reference
1675	Augustina, free mulatta, wife of Capt. Lazaro del Canto	Blasphemy	Merida	Denunciation only	626, 7: ff. 160-82
1675	Maria Nogues, free mulatta	Blasphemy, witchcraft [santiguadora]	Merida	Denunciation only	626, 7: ff. 185-202
1670s	various mulattas and mestizas	Witchcraft (healing, love-magic, putting a curse on a priest)	Merida and Campeche	Denunciations only	626: ff. 185-295, ff. 420-31; 627, 6: 273-98
1722–26	Joseph Zavala, free mulatto	Idolatry, witchcraft	Merida	Indicted, tried, sentenced to prison; escaped; captured and sentenced to slavery	1164: ff. 211-319
1748	Petrona Trujeque, mulatta	Witchcraft (healing, divination)	Merida	Tried	919, 26
1785	Apolonio Casanova and other mulattoes	Idolatry	Hunucma	Tried and convicted; sentencing done in Mexico City	1177, 7: ff. 1-193.

Notes: Inquisitorial investigations followed a tripartite procedure: an indictment or *sumario*, in which informal denunciation(s) led to the collection of evidence and a formal accusation; a trial [*prueba*]; and a sentence [*sentencia*]. The case was dropped if the judges voted at the *voto de sumario* not to bring it to trial.

An abbreviated version of this table is Table 7.7 in Chapter Seven.

TABLE F.2 Love–magic cases from seventeenth-century Campeche and Merida: the denouncers, the accused, and motives for denunciation

Year	Denouncer	Accused of hiring a witch	Accused of being a witch	Motive for denunciation
1626	Catalina Antonia de Rojas (Spaniard)	(The denouncer herself)	Catalina Puc (Maya); Antonia (mulatta)	"To unburden her conscience"; failure of magic to work?
1639	Melchora de los Reyes (Spaniard)	Various (unnamed)	Juana Delgado (mulatta); Maria de Salas (mulatta)	"To unburden her conscience"
1639	Catalina Blanco (Spaniard)	(The denouncer herself)	Ana Gonzalez, "la Isleña"; "an Indian woman"	Ana (now dead) taught love-magic spells to denouncer 18 years ago; Maya woman told her how to make make enchanted chocolate; she now wants to unburden her conscience
1658–59	Augustina de la Cerda (mulatta/parda)	Various	Ana de Ortega, mulatta/parda	"To unburden her conscience"
1672	María de Casanova (Spaniard)	María Maldonado (Spaniard) and her brother, Manuel Maldonado	Michaela Montejo (mulatta); Catalina Alvarez; Ana (mulatta); Ursula (free negra, ex-slave); "some Indian women," "an Indian woman"	"To unburden her conscience"; fear of being implicated as an accessory; resentment against María Maldonado as former employer?
1672	Doña Juana de la Paz, Doña Bartolina de Almeida (Spaniards) María, a black slave of doña Bartolina's	None specified	Catalina Rejino, Michaela Montejo, and Leonor de Toribio (free mulattas) Cecilia, a woman with the surname Jesús	"To unburden her conscience" Asked by the Inquisition

Sources: AGN-Inquisición 360: ff. 275–76 (1626); 388: ff. 412–16v (1639); 388: ff. 419–20r (1639); 443: ff. 491–503 (1658–59); 620, 7: ff. 595–614 (1672); 626, 7: ff. 188–199 (1672).

Note: The denouncer's claim to be acting "not out of hate but to unburden one's conscience [no por odio sino por descargo de su consiensia]" was a standard part of the genre's formula and appears in almost every case.

Afro-Yucatecan Baptism Records, Merida
(1710–97)

TABLE G.1 Total numbers of baptisms, 1710–97

1710s	1720s	1730s	1740s	1750s	1760s	1770s	1780s	1790s
101 (1710)	91 (1720)	66 (1730)	103 (1740)	115 (1750)	162 (1760)	131 (1770)	188 (1780)	99 (1790)
77 (1711)	91 (1721)	122 (1731)	90 (1741)	65+38=103 (1751)	167 (1761)	40 (1771)†	131 (1781)	9 (1791)*
75 (1712)	100 (1722)	102 (1732)	96 (1742)	116 (1752)	148 (1762)	136 (1772)	172 (1782)	19 (1792)*
95 (1713)	97 (1723)	22+101=123 (1733)	114 (1743)	136 (1753)	169 (1763)	120 (1773)	163 (1783)	71 (1793)*
97 (1714)	145 (1724)	106 (1734)	88 (1744)	128 (1754)	148 (1764)	121 (1774)	140 (1784)	146 (1794)
96 (1715)	131 (1725)	84 (1735)	91 (1745)	133 (1755)	173 (1765)	144 (1775)	37+104=141 (1785)	121 (1795)
90 (1716)	115 (1726)	119 (1736)	98 (1746)	129 (1756)	160 (1766)	151 (1776)	115 (1786)	145 (1796)
111 (1717)	63 (1727)	90 (1737)	105 (1747)	141 (1757)	144 (1767)	163 (1777)	96 (1787)	40 (1797)*
95 (1718)	81 (1728)	106 (1738)	109 (1748)	144 (1758)	158 (1768)	127 (1778)	114 (1788)	
88 (1719)	113 (1729)	96 (1739)	97 (1749)	50 (1759)	131 (1769)	172 (1779)	122 (1789)	
[Total 925]	[Total 1,027]	[Total 1,014]	[Total 991]	[Total 1,195]	[Total 1,560]	[Total 1,305]	[Total 1,382]	[Total 650]*
[Av. 92.5]	[Av. 102.7]	[Av. 101.4]	[Av. 99.1]	[Av. 119.5]	[Av. 156]	[Av. 130.5]	[Av. 138.2]	[Av. 81]*
55 (6.0%) black adults	66 (6.4%) black adults	60 (5.9%) black adults	21 (2.1%) black adults	71 (5.9%) black adults	150 (9.6%) black adults	29 (2.2%) black adults	106 (7.1%) black adults	18 (2.7%) black adults

Source: AGAY-Jesús, Libros de Bautismos Vols. 1–6.

Notes: †Records may be incomplete

*Records clearly incomplete

Overall annual range: 40 (1771) to 188 (1780)

Overall decade range: 925 (1710s) to 1,560 (1560s); average 92.5 (1710s) to 156 (1760s)

Overall annual average: 925 (1710s) to 1,560 (1560s); average 92.5 (1710s) to 156 (1760s)

Overall annual average: 118.6 (does not include incomplete years in 1790s)

Black adults: decade range of 2.1% (1740s) to 9.6% (1760s); average 5.3%

TABLE G.2 Gender and free-slave balances of black adults baptized in Merida, 1710–89

	1710s slave+free	1720s slave+free	1730s slave+free	1740s slave+free	1750s slave+free	1760s slave+free	1770s slave+free	1780s slave+free	1710–89 slave+free	Total
Men	42+1=43	17+4=21	19+4=23	0+17=17	19+41=60	26+87=113	0+25=25	42+12=54	165+191	356 (64%)
Women	12+0=12	43+2=45	36+1=37	0+4=4	6+5=11	23+14=37	2+2=4	46+6=52	168+34	202 (36%)
	[55]	[66]	[60]	[21]	[71]	[150]	[29]	[106]	333+225 (60+40%)	558

Notes: Women, 1710s (12): There are no women at all in the first half of the decade; the first black woman, free or enslaved, appears in May 1715.

Women, free, 1720s (2): These two are not directly described as "esclavas," but they are together in the same entry (f. 154r–v) as "negras adultas" and "naturales de Cankay" with the Chacon brothers as *padrinos* (the Chacon brothers appear regularly as slave owners and padrinos to slaves, but never in connection with free blacks).

Women, 1730s (37): Includes a nine-year-old slave girl owned by the bishop; she is not in the category of Yucatan-born infants, but appears to be a recent arrival and purchase in the colony, so I have included her with adults.

Men, 1740s (17): Not a single black man or woman is listed in the 1740s as being a slave, for reasons that are not completely clear. It seems unlikely that no slaves at all were baptized during that decade, although clearly slave imports were down dramatically from previous decades, no female adult slaves were baptized, and there certainly was a trend toward baptizing Africans as free servants (see discussion in Chapter Five). Nevertheless, it is possible that eight of the seventeen men listed above—as *negros adultos* and natives of specific locations (one from Jamaica and seven from West Africa), but otherwise neither as *esclavos* nor as *libre* or *criados*—may have been slaves of the men listed as their padrinos, but I have nevertheless listed them as free.

The 1760s: Decade totals hide the fact that a shift takes place, beginning in 1763; before that, the slave:free ratio is 20:19 for men and 15:2 for women, but then starting in 1763 there are more free than slave, with the slave:free ratios being 6:68 for men and 8:12 for women. As discussed in Chapter Five, this was because the slaves taken from English loggers in Belize periodically benefited from the law of refuge, and therefore had to be officially manumitted and listed as free.

The 1770s: Note how every black man is listed as free. There is only one black adult entry (a free man) between November 1775 and June 1779, and no enslaved adults between February 1773 and the end of the decade. There are actually seven slaves baptized December 28–31, 1779, but they are part of a run of nineteen *parbulo* slaves from Belize baptized over five weeks from December 28, 1779, to February 2, 1780, and so I have counted all of them in the 1780s data in Tables G.1–G.3.

Table 5.5 in Chapter Five presents this data through 1797 and in a slightly different format.

TABLE G.3 Casta parentage of all baptized children, start of October 1759 (Vol. 3: f. 136v) through March 19, 1772 (end of Vol. 4)

	1759	1760	1761	1762	1763	1764	1765	1766	1767	1768	1769	1770	1771	1772
Negros libres	1	1	1	1		1				1	1	1	1	1
Negros esclavos		2	2	1	2	1	3		2	1	1			1
Negro libre and negra esclava													1	
Negro libre and mulata	1	1	1	1	2	2	1	5	1	2	3	5[n]	1	1
Negro libre and india[a]		1	2	4	2	1	3	3	3	1	3	4	2	1
Negro libre and mestiza					3				1	1	2			
Negro libre and ncd									1					
Negro esclavo and mulata				1	1	1					2	1	1	1
Negro esclava and mestiza														
Negro esclavo and india[a]			1					1			1		2	
Negro esclavo and ncd								1						
Negra libre and pnc					1					1				
Negra esclava and pnc		1	2		1			2[c]		1	1	2		1
Mulatos	8	64	72	71	81	82	74	78	56	65	50	63	15	9
Mulato and india[b]	3	20	17	13	14	16	19	19	13	14	13	10	3	2
Mulato and mestiza	4	16	18[d]	6	19	4	9	14	9[k]	12	14	7	5	3
Mulato and castiza				1										
Mulato and española				2[e]							1		1	
Mulato and parda		2	2											
Mulato and ncd				1	1		1	1						
Pardo and mestiza						1		1[j]						
Mulata and pnc	5	11	15	20	26	17	26	18	33	13	11	16	2	4
Mestiza and pnc		1												
India and pnc[l]											1			

Pardos or pardos libres

Pardos or pardos libres	2	1	1	2	5	2	1	2	2	2	1	1
	1	1	3	2	1	3	1	2	2	2	5	
Ncd	120	135	125	156	132	142	141	122	115	108	107	33
Pnc, exp ps of mulatos	4	1	2	2	1	3	1	3	2	2	5	1
Pnc, exp ps of pardos		3	2	1								
Pnc, exp ps of a negro libre[g]	2								1			
Pnc, exp ps of a mulato	5	2	4		5	3	1	3	1	1	2	1
Pnc, exp ps of a pardo		1	2[f]								1	
Pnc, exp ps of a negra						1					1	
Pnc, exp ps of a mulata	4	4	4	2	2	2	3	6	3	4	10	3
Pnc, exp ps of a parda		1									1	
Pnc, exp ps of an india[h]	1											
Pnc, exp ps mulato and india			1									
Pnc, exp ps mulato and mestiza										1		
Pnc, exp ps mulato and ncd									1			
Pnc, exp ps neg libre and india							1					
Pnc, exp ps neg libre and ncd							1					
Pnc, exp ps indios[m]	1[i]								1			
Pnc, exp ps of ncd	3	4	12	4	4	3	1	2	2	2	2	1
	15	14	12	11	12	12	8	12	8	9	21	4
	[135]	[149]	[137]	[167]	[144]	[149]	[154]	[134]	[123]	[117]	[128]	[37]

Notes: [a] India surnames (with *negro* libre *or* esclavo husbands) through 1769: Chac, Cox (5); Curz, >ul (3, 2 "de Tiholop"); Ek (2); Hui, May (2); Panti, Pech, Puc, Uc: Alpuche (2); Argaes, de Lara, Díaz (2); Flores, Lopez (2); Mansanilla, Mojon, Regalado, Sosa, Valdez [Baldes] (n.b. in only one case does the Indian wife have the same surname as the black husband, so name changing is not an explanation of high incidence of Indian wives with Spanish surnames).

India surnames (with *negro* libre *or* esclavo husbands) from 1770: Euan, Panti, Tinaal; Osorio, Solis.

[b] India surnames (with mulatto husbands) through 1769: Ake (4); Baaz (2); Cab (2); Camal (7); Canche (2); Catzim (2); Cen (3); Chable (2); Chan (17); Che, Chi (8); Chuc (4); Coba, Cocom, Couoh (4); Coyi (4); >ib (3); >ul (5); Ek (5); Euan (4); Hiuit/Iuit/Yuit (4); Hool, Huchim, Iuitz, Kantun, Ku (2); Kuyoc (3); May (3); Mex, Mo (3); Mukul, Na/Naa (2); Omun, Pech (6); Pol, Poot (3); Toh/Tooh (3); Uc (2); Uic (2); Uicab (7); Yam: Aguayo, Alvarez, Ayora (2); Bojorques, Camara, Cardenas, Casanoba, Castro, Conga, Cosme (2); Curruela, de la Paz, Duran, Enriquez, Fajardo, Gonzalez (3); Lara (2); Magaña, Mendes (2); Muñoz, Peña (2); Puerto, Solis, Vergara (n.b. first Uc entry, 1761, was recorded as "mestisa" and then Uc and "India" were added in).

TABLE G.3 (continued)

India surnames (with mulatto husbands) from 1770: Bax, Camal (1771, "Yndia Ydalga"); Chan, Chi (2); Mex, Pech (2); Poor, Toh, Yuit: Alvarez, de la Paz, Helguera, Muñoz.

^cIn first entry, mother just described as "negra," but she is Maria Antonia Chacon, who appears in November 1760 as a slave.

^dOne of these is described as "moreno mulato."

^eFirst is mulato de Maxcanu.

^fSecond of these is Sargento Mayor Joseph Lucas Menendez, exp boy is Joseph Cyrilo (Vol.4, f.1).

^gFirst of these is Santiago Castañeda *negro* y Maria Josepha Leyton; the rest are "*negro libre*."

^hAnna de los Reyes Yndia Ydalga.

ⁱMulato padrino.

^jThis anomalous entry is written by don Pedro Nolasco de los Reyes, whereas almost all the other entries for this year are by theniente de cura Br Bartolome Antonio Cabañas, supporting the idea that pardo and mulatto are used according to personal preferences, not universal consensus.

^kRef Marcial Socobio case: one of these is Maria Alexandria born to Cayetano Socobio mulatto and Maria Mota mestiza, padrino Joseph Socobio; also one of the pnc, exp ps of a mulatto entry of 1769 is Domingo a ps of Joseph Socobio mulatto (Vol. 4, f. 157r); and in 1770 Miguel Socobio and Antonia Espinosa, mulattoes, baptize Phelipe de la Luz (f. 175v); same parents baptize Pedro de Jesus in 1778 (Vol. 5, f. 108v).

^lncd but mother's name is Juana Chan.

^mncd, but adoptive parents are Julian Chi and Pasquala Ek (child listed in margin as Petrona Chi).

ⁿThe last of these is a "*negro libertino*."

TABLE G.3 (cont.) Casta parentage of all baptized children, 1770–74
(repeat of end of Vol. 4 and part of Vol. 5)

	1770	1771	1772	1773	1774
Negros libres	1	1		2	
Negros esclavos				1	1
Negro libre and negra esclava		1	1		
Negro libre and mulata[c]	5	1	6	1	2
Negro libre and india[a]	2	1	3		3
Negro libre and mestiza					
Negro libre and ncd					
Negro esclavo and mulata	1	1	2	1	1
Negro esclavo and mestiza			2		1
Negro esclavo and india[a]		2			2
Negro esclavo and ncd					
Negra libre and pnc					
Negra esclava and pnc			1		
Mulatos	63	15	56	50	48
Mulato and india[b]	10	3	10	13	15
Mulato and mestiza	7	5	11	8	6
Mulato and castiza					
Mulato and española		1			
Mulato and parda					
Mulato and ncd					
Pardo and mestiza					
Mulata and pnc	16	2	15	25	21
Mestiza and pnc					
India and pnc					
Pardos or pardos libres	1		3	1	1
Ncd			3	1	6[d]
	107	33	112	103	107
Pnc, exp ps of mulatos	5	1	2	2	1
Pnc, exp ps of pardos					
Pnc, exp ps of a negro libre					
Pnc, exp ps of a mulato	2	1	5	2	5
Pnc, exp ps of a pardo	1				
Pnc, exp ps of a negra	1				
Pnc, exp ps of a mulata	10	1	12	6	5
Pnc, exp ps of a parda					
Pnc, exp ps of an india					
Pnc, exp ps mulato and india					1
Pnc, exp ps mulato and mestiza					
Pnc, exp ps mulato and ncd					
Pnc, exp ps neg libre and india					
Pnc, exp ps neg libre and ncd			1		
Pnc, exp ps indios					
Pnc, exp ps of ncd	2	1	1		
	21	4	21	11	11
	[128]	[37]	[133]	[114]	[118]

(*continued*)

TABLE G.3 (*continued*)

Notes: [a] India surnames (with *negro* libre *or* esclavo husbands) 1770–74: Can, Cox, Euan, Huc, Panti, Tinaal; Uc: Chavarria, Osorio, Solis (3); Trejo.
[b] India surnames (with mulatto husbands) 1770–74: Baaz, Bax, Camal (3; 1771, "Yndia Ydalga"); Canche (2); Cauich, Chan (3); Chi (4); Chuc, Couoh, >ib, >ul (2); Ek (2); Huc (2); Kuyoc, Matu, Mex (2); Pech (9); Pib, Poot (2); Toh, Tzab, Yuit: Alvarez, de la Paz, Conga (derived from Congo?), Helguera, Muñoz (2).
[c] The last of the 1770 entries is a "*negro* libertino"; I include here where it just says "*negro*."
[d] These begin in November 1774 with Br. Thomas de Ynsaurraga, who is less consistent than his predecessors (see Notes to Vols. 3–4).

TABLE G.4. (based on Table G.3) Parentage of children baptized in Jesús parish, Merida, 1760–74
[n.b. does not include exposito children]

Negros esclavos	12
Negro esclavo and mulata	6
Negra esclava and [father unknown]	11
Negros libres	12
Negro libre and negra esclava	1
Negro libre and mulata	28
Mulatos	886
Mulato and parda	2
Pardos or pardos libres	13
Afro-Yucatecan endogamy	971 / 58%
Negro esclavo and india	10
Negro esclavo and mestiza	1
Negro libre and india	33
Negro libre and mestiza	9
Mulato and india	204
Mulato and mestiza	154
Pardo and mestiza	2
Afro-Maya miscegenation	413 / 25%
Mulato and castiza	1
Mulato and española	2
Negro esclavo and ncd	1
Negro libre and [not given]	1
Negra libre and [father unknown]	2
Mulata and [father unknown]	238
Mulato and [not given]	8
Mestiza and [father unknown]	1
India and [father unknown]	1
[Not given]	24
Other	279 / 17%
	[1663 / 100%]

TABLE G.5 Casta of all baptized children, 1785–90 and 1794–95

	1785	1786	1787	1788	1789	1790	1794	1795
Pardo	74	47	38	49	60	49	85	32
Parda	67	61	51	59	57	34	57	29
Moreno		2	1	1	1			
Negro			1					
Exp al parsr mestizo			1					
Niño of an esclava								1
Niño ncd								27
Niña of a mulatto						1		
Niña of a negro libre								1
Negra							1	
Morena			1	1	3	1		
Exp al prsr mestiza				1				
Exp al parsr blanca		1						
Niña ncd						4		29
M (%)	53	45	44	45	50	53	59	50
F (%)	47	55	56	55	50	47	41	50
	[141]	[112]	[92]	[111]	[121]	[93]	[143]	[121]
	[No ads]	[+3 ads]	[+4 ads]	[+3 ads]	[+1 ad]	[+6 ads]	+3 ads]	+2 adults]

Notes: Pardo/a includes children exposito al pareser pardo/a; consistency of system begins to break down in the autumn of 1790, and records are incomplete 1791–93; in May 1795 the ncds begin.

Regarding the use of moreno: used to mean child of a black slave, as the two niños morenos in 1786 and one niña morena of 1787 are all children of slaves (all listed in full date file), the moreno of 1787 is the son of *negros* libertinos (ex-slaves); same for 1788 and 1789 (see full data file).

Abbreviations: pnc=padre(s) no conosido(s); ncd=no casta details given; ps=puertas; exp=exposito/a.

TABLE G.6 Christian names of adult slave men baptized in Merida

	Two sample periods		The full data run
	1710–29	1750–60	1710–89
Joseph	4+2=6*	3+14=17	26+71=97
Juan	9+8=17	2+6=8	13+44=57
Francisco	6+4=10	5+5=10	30+18=48
Antonio	9+2=11	5+2=7	21+6=27
Manuel	0+1=1	2+1	6+9=15
Miguel	3+1=4	4+1=5	9+6=15
Domingo	1	4+3	8+5=13
Pedro	1	1+3	4+9=13
Joaquin		1	5+4=9
Tomás		1	5+3=8
Diego	1+1=2	0+1	5+2=7
Santiago	1+1=2	3+1	4+2=6
Augustin	2	1	4
Luis	2		4
Felipe	2		2+1=3
Andrés		0+1	1+1=2
Buenaventura			1+1=2
Cristobal			2
Gabriel			2
Ignacio		2	2
Nicolás			2
Raphael		1	2
Sebastian	0+1=1	1	1+1=2
Alonso	1		1
Anastacio			1
Bartolome		1	1
Cayetano			1
Cosme			0+1=1
Fernando	1		1
Ildefonso		0+1	0+1=1
Lorenso	0+1=1		0+1=1
Mariano			0+1=1
Martín			0+1=1
Pablo		0+1	0+1=1
Vicente		0+1	0+1=1
Total	65	78	354
Variation 1(%)	26	27	10
Variation 2(%)	49	60	64

Notes: *The first figure is incidence of the Christian name as an only given name, the second is its incidence with a middle name: i.e., of the six men baptized Joseph in 1710–29, four were named just Joseph; two were also given middle names (Joseph Antonio and Joseph Benito).

TABLE G.6 (*continued*)

For 1710–29, the middle-name variants were: two for Antonio (Cayetano and Joseph); three for Francisco (Atanasio, Joseph, and Xavier); two for Joseph (Antonio and Benito); five for Juan (Antonio, Joseph, Leandro, Manuel, and Ventura); one for Miguel (Joseph); one for Diego (Lorenso); one for Lorenso (Geronimo); one for Manuel (de Seballos); one for Santiago (Manuel); one for Sebastian (Antonio).

For 1750–60, the middle-name variants were: two for Antonio (Joseph Nicolas, Maria de la Luz); five for Francisco (de la Cruz, Ignacio, Joseph, Raphael, Xavier); seven for Joseph (Antonio [by far the most common], Francisco, Jacinto Maria, Maria, Maria Juan de Dios, Miguel, and Tomás); three for Juan (Cyro, Joseph, Tomás); one for Miguel (Tomás); one for Andrés (Antonio); one for Diego (Francisco); three for Domingo (Cayetano, Joseph, and Miguel); one for Ildefonso (Juan Nepomuceno); one for Manuel (Isidro); one for Pablo (Joseph Maria); three for Pedro (Francisco, Juan, and Luis); one for Santiago (Antonio); one for Vicente (Crispin).

Variation 1 is the variation rate of first names only; Variation 2 takes second names into account. For the full 1710–89 period, there were 35 first names used by 354 people, a 10% variation rate; during the same period, taking second names into account, there were 226 different names, a 64% variation rate.

For the presentation of this data in comparative context see Table 2.4 and the related discussion in Chapter Two.

TABLE G.7 Christian names of adult slave women baptized in Merida

	Two sample periods		The full data run
	1710–29	1730–49	1710–89
María	4+18=22*	0+26=26	7+115=122
Juana	4+5		5+8=13
Ana	0+1	0+1	3+8=11
Josepha	0+5		0+7=7
Antonia	1+4		1+5=6
Isabel	0+2	2+1	3+3=6
Catalina	2	1	4
Francisca		0+2	2+2=4
Manuela	0+2	0+1	0+4=4
Teresa	0+2		1+2=3
Ignacia	1	0+1	1+1=2
Mariana		1+1	1+1=2
Micaela	0+1	1	1+1=2
Clara			0+1=1
Jacoba			1
Juliana	1		1
Lorenza		0+1	0+1=1
Lucia			0+1=1
Margarita			1
Martina			0+1=1
Mathilde			1
Narcisa			1
Nicolasa	0+1		0+1=1
Paula	0+1		0+1=1
Petrona			1
Rosalia		1	1
Tomasa			1
Total	55	40	200
Variation 1 (%)	25	28	14
Variation 2 (%)	67	75	95

Notes: *The first figure is incidence of the Christian name as an only given name; the second is its incidence with a middle name (see Notes to Table G.7).

For 1710–29, 76% women had middle names, with the middle-name variants being: eleven for María (Ana, Antonia [four examples], Beatriz, de la Candelaria, de los Santos, del Carmen, Francisca, Josepha [the most common, with five examples], Luisa, Margarita, Nicolasa); one for Ana (Petrona); three for Antonia (Gertrudis, Josepha, María); two for Isabel (María, Teresa); four for Josepha (Antonia, de la Rosa, Ignacia, María de la Cruz); three for Juana (Ignacia, Jacinta, María); two for Manuela (Isabel, Isidora); one for Micaela (de los Angeles); one for Nicolasa (Antonia); one for Paula (Xaviera); two for Teresa (de la Cruz, Dionicia).

For 1730–49, 85% women had middle names, with the middle-name variants being: sixteen for María (Antonia [three examples], Antonia de los Dolores Gertrudis, Antonia Francisca Ignacia Xaviera, Beatriz, de los Dolores, Felipa, Francisca, Francisca Xaviera de la

TABLE G.7 (*continued*)

Luz, Gertrudis, Ignacia, Josepha [again, the most common, with six examples], Josepha Cecilia, Micaela, Nicolasa, Raphaela, Salvadora); two for Francisca (Ignacia, Xaviera); one for Ana (María); one for Ignacia (María); one for Isabel (María); one for Lorenza (Josepha); one for Manuela (Josepha); one for Mariana (de la Luz).

Variation 1 is the variation rate of first names only; Variation 2 takes second names into account (see Notes to Table G.7).

Regarding the María factor: the popularity of María meant that not only was it the most common first name, but that it was also commonly used as a second name, so that the percentage of women who had María either as a first or second name was 64% for the whole period (1710–89) (down to 51% in 1710–29 but as high as 73% in 1730–49).

For the presentation of this data in comparative context see Table 2.4 and the related discussion in Chapter Two.

Reference Matter

Notes

PREFACE

1. This would be the fourth African diaspora in Palmer's five-diaspora model, consisting of the forced migration of some 12 million Africans to Europe and the Americas between the fifteenth and nineteenth centuries (Palmer 1998). For two recent and illuminating essays on defining "African diaspora" and its implications for the study of colonial Latin America, see Butler (2001) and Vinson (2006). For a detailed introduction to the Atlantic slave trade, see Klein (1986).

2. Restall (1997), the research for which also produced (1995) and (1998a).

INTRODUCTION

1. Ellison (1972 [1952]: 3).

2. Kundera's (1999) specific reference is not to African slavery in the Americas, but to the late-1940s concentration camp at Terezín, Czechoslovakia.

3. The annals excerpt is taken from the primordial titles of the Pech—the Title of Yaxkukul (folio 5r) and the Title of Chicxulub (pp. 10–11)—translated in Restall 1998a, Chap. 6 (excerpt on p. 119). The phrase *ex boxe* I take to be a Maya copyist's error for *ek boxe* (*ex* means "trousers"); note too that the Chicxulub version erroneously has *ual* instead of *uak*.

4. Quezada (2001). For examples of discussions of Africans in colonial Yucatan, in works whose focus is primarily Spaniards and/or Mayas in the colony, see the specific citations in the book to García Bernal (1972; 1978); Hunt (1974); Thompson (1978); Farriss (1984); Peón Ancona (1985); Patch (1993); Restall (1998a); and Chuchiak (2000). Major works, likewise focused on other Yucatec topics, with little or no reference at all to Afro-Yucatecans, include Jones (1989); Victoria Ojeda (1995); Rugeley (1996; 2001); and García Bernal (2006). Peón Ancona's comment that "some modern historians have shown that among the inhabitants of Yucatan, during the centuries of the colonial regime, there was a large percentage of elements of the black race . . ." (1985: 116) is not accompanied by citations, but he may have had in mind Ruz Menéndez (1970); García Bernal (1972; 1978); and Aguirre Beltrán (1989 [1946]), all of whom provide support for that assertion but without any detail. The only publications devoted entirely to Africans or their descendents in Yucatan are studies by Yucatec historians, such as López Rivas (1975); Negroe Sierra (1991); Redondo (1994); Fernández Repetto and Negroe Sierra (1995); and

Campos García (2005). These micro-studies represent a growing local academic interest in Afro-Yucatec history, but this has neither spread outside Yucatan nor translated within the peninsula into a wide public awareness or acceptance of that history.

5. AGI-*Indiferente General* 1381; Roys, Scholes, and Adams (1940: 24).

6. Espinosa (1942 [1620]: 120–28).

7. RAH, 11–5–1, 8785, no. 9 (manuscript of Prieto's report written in Madrid on March 28, 1757).

8. Cook (1769: 11; original edition in JCBL as A24b).

9. Cook (1769: 22–34); Patch (1993: 234–35); Chapter One of this book. The failure to mention Africans in descriptions of Yucatec towns is characteristic of most such accounts; another example is John Ogilby, whose massive *America* of 1670 briefly described the province and its settlements of Spaniards and natives (no Africans) (1670: 222–23; in JCBL as F671–M765al).

10. See, for example, Restall (1998a: 6–7).

11. The phrase is taken from Fernández-Armesto (1995: 69).

12. Having not seen Africans before the Spanish invasion, Yucatec Maya lacked a term for them; so, as Spaniards had long since done, Mayas used their adjective "black" [*box*], here added to the noun "something black" [*ek*].

13. There is also a diverse literature that characterizes peoples in various historical moments as living in a "middle ground" (White 1991, on Native Americans in the Great Lakes Region) or as a "middle nation" (Muldoon 2002, on medieval Ireland and the Anglo-Irish).

14. Vinson (2006: 9) on Africans and their descendents in colonial Spanish America in general.

15. Wade (1997: 3).

CHAPTER ONE

1. AGI-*México* 2999, 2: f. 187r (". . . que ha mas de cuarenta años entró en esa provins^a y desde entonces nos ha servido con sus harmas en las ocasiones que se han ofrecido, especialmente en ayudar a poner esa provins^a devaxo de ñra ovedencia y despues en cosas tocantes a ñro servicio que se le han mandado por los ñros gobernadores . . .").

2. AHAY-*Asuntos Terminados* 1792 (transcribed in Ruz Menéndez 1970: 22–25; quote on p. 23). ("¿hay quien quiera hacer postura a dos negros ingleses esclavos del Rey que parezca y se la admitirá la que hiciere y se han de rematar dadas las doce de este día?")

3. AGI-*México* 2999, 2: f. 187r.

4. JCBL-Codex Sp 33 is a report on royal expenditures in New Spain for 1697; f. 34r lists the 827-peso pensions of two noblemen of the Moctezuma family. On how some members of the Moctezuma family maintained privileges between the Conquest and the date of these pensions, see Chipman (2005).

5. Juan Garrido, the best-known black conquistador in central Mexico (Gerhard 1978), was a guard in Mexico City; on the occupations of the early black conquerors, see Restall (2000b: 190–92; 2003: 62).

6. AGI-*México* 2999, 2: f. 187v.

7. AGI-*México* 2999, 2: f. 187v; (". . . avia Rescebido agravio, porque hera digno de Rescevir mucha mrd por lo que ansi nos havia servido como lo largamente parescia por ciertos Recuados de que ante nos en el ñro cons° de las yndias fue hecha presentacion . . ."). The Toral evidence is in AGI, in *México* 2999, 2: ff. 187–88r (old foliation 180–81, and also foliated 348–49; the first document on f. 187 is also reproduced in CDH: I, 511–12), in *Contratación* 5227, 2, 25, and in *Indiferente* 1969, 22, 1: f. 404; and in AGN-*General de Parte* 2, 498: f. 97.

8. AGI-*Contratación* 5227, 2, 25: ff. 1–2 (". . . negro . . . de color moreno . . . del edad de sesenta años poco mas o menos y barbicano . . . para pasar y volver a la província de yucatan . . . [con] la flota de la nueva [E]spaña . . ."); he is also in the passenger lists for 1579 as "Sevastian de toral de color moreno" (AGI-*Indiferente General* 1969, 22, 1: f. 404v). The later edict is AGI-*México* 2999, 2: f. 188r (". . . para guarda y defensa de una persona y casa quatro espadas quatro dagas y un arcabuz . . . como la traen los españoles . . .").

9. I am grateful to Robert Schwaller for finding, and photocopying for me, Toral's Mexico City arms license in AGN-*General de Parte* 2, 498: f. 97 (the phrase quoted above is "algunos oficios y otras personas").

10. AGI-*México* 3050: fs. 94–184. I did, however, find the surviving black woman's baptism record, and that of her son, in AGAY, Jesús María, *Libros de Bautismos* Vol. IV: ff. 140r, 142v (this case is discussed in more detail in Chapter Two).

11. On the Spanish conquests in Yucatan, see Clendinnen (1987), Restall (1998a: esp. 3–18), Quezada (2001: 31–42), and Chuchiak (2007); on Spanish conquests in the Americas, see Restall (2003).

12. This is of course a simplification of a diverse and complex pattern; a good summary of it is in Klein (1986: 21–88). For an example of how the pattern becomes complex at the local and specific level, see Nazzari on late colonial São Paulo (1991: 50–52, 90–91). The best single, brief discussion of the Middle Passage is Palmer (2002; also see 1976: 9–19; 1981: 42–58). For an account of the Atlantic crossing by the captain of an English slave ship in the 1790s, see Mouser (2002: 101–11).

13. This typology of African slaves in the Americas into "auxiliary" and "mass" categories is introduced and further explained in Restall and Lane (2009: chaps. 7 and 10).

14. For a clear definition of this distinction, see Berlin (1998: 8–10). The earliest use and definition of "slave society" may be by Tannenbaum, who wrote that "so inclusive was the influence of slavery that it might be better to speak, not of a system of slavery in Brazil, Cuba, or the United States [referring primarily to the nineteenth century], but of the total pattern as a slave society" (1946: 117). This was clearly not the case in colonial Yucatan, as will emerge in the coming chapters; for a summation of this point, see the Conclusion. On how Spaniards extracted Maya labor, see Patch (1993) and Solís Robleda (2003).

15. AGS 60, 4, 16 in Paso y Troncoso (1940, XIII: 257–65, 347–48). The ship, captained by a Salvador Acosta, was one of four bringing slaves from São Tomé off the West African coast to Veracruz, under the asiento contracts held by the Portuguese merchant Pero Gómez Reynal; documents published by Paso y Troncoso (1940, XIII: 257–65, 347–48), and others discussed by Aguirre Beltrán (1989: 39–41), were part of a royal investigation into allegations of fraud that led to Gómez Reynal losing his license.

16. AGI-*Contaduría* 912, 11: ff. 714, 719.

17. Aguirre Beltrán (1989: 59). According to Juan de Villalobos's report on "black slaves in the West Indies" published in 1682, in that year the annual allotment was increased to two thousand, but that was for all of Spanish America (Villalobos 1682).

18. Palmer (1981: 77, 78); evidence of the British traders' license is in BL, Add. MS 25553: 10–11, while the Spanish evidence is in AGI-*Contaduría* 267, 8 (both cited by Palmer).

19. Palmer (1981: 109).

20. AGN-*Marina* 36, 5: fs. 167–212.

21. AGAY, Jesús María, *Libros de Bautismos* Vols. 1–6.

22. AGN-*Alcabalas* 427, 10: fs. 183–88.

23. Veracruz slave sale records for 1733–34 are in AGI-*Indiferente General* 2817, 1, with additional examples in other expedientes in 2817 and 2847. I could not find equivalent records for Campeche; they may not exist, as Campeche was never a full-fledged factoría like Veracruz, but I suspect some such records are in the AGI, either in *Indiferente* or *Contratación*.

24. The cargo of 150 had come from Jamaica on *The Eagle*, a Royal Company ship that legally traded under the monopoly license described below; for this reason, the Spanish merchants claimed that the 100 slaves they shipped to Veracruz and attempted to sell to English agents there still fell under the same license, but Spanish treasury officials (and William Butler, the chief English agent in Veracruz) noted that *La Soledad*, the Spanish frigate, was not working for the English but seeking its own profits (AGI-*Indiferente General* 2817, 7).

25. The encomendero don Juan de Montejo y Castillo only mentioned two slaves in his will of 1603 (transcribed in Rubio Mañé 1941: 45–53), while don Iñigo de Mendoza y Magaña and Pedro de Carvajal, both wealthy merchants who died in Merida in the 1690s, each seem to have owned three slaves for much of their lives (Hunt 1974: 34, 73, and 93–94 on Acevedo). Baptism-based slave-owning data is drawn from AGAY, Jesús María, *Libros de Bautismos* Vols. 1–6; also see Chapter Two and Appendix E for relevant tables and further discussion.

26. See, for example, the cases of Morelos (Martin 1985: 13–14, 38, 121–53); Veracruz (Carroll 1991: 29–39, 61–65); Guatemala (Jones 1994: 109–17; Lutz 1994: 83–99; Herrera 2000); and Peru (Bowser 1974; Lockhart 1994: 193–224).

27. On the important role played by black conquistadors throughout Spanish America, see Restall (2000b; 2003: 54–63); on the late colonial military role of Africans in Yucatan, see Chapter Five.

28. Writing on Peru, Lockhart (1994: 224) put it thus: "Though subordinated to Spaniards, blacks in Peru were not employed en masse and impersonally; except for the mining gangs, they counted as individuals."

29. AGI-*México* 3050, fs. 138–39. The exception to this pattern of indirect crown intervention in the importation and immigration of Africans was the direct involvement of the provincial government in the setting up of pardo militias; see Chapter Four.

30. Herrera (1601, VIII: 10, 23); Aguirre Beltrán (1989: 19–20, 22).

31. Benzoni (1857 [1565]: 142–43). Benzoni's account of his voyages and of the Spanish conquests in the Americas was published throughout Europe in various lan-

guages, but never in Spanish, due no doubt to its unflattering portrait of Spanish activities; there is, however, a manuscript version in Spanish, in a seventeenth-century hand, in JCBL (Codex Ital 10).

32. AGI-*Patronato* 66a, 1, 4, 1 (Alonso Rosado's 1570 *probanza*): ff. 1r, 8v, 14v, 17r, 20v, 23r, 26r, 28v, 31v–32r, 35r, 36v, 38v (largely repetitive testimony on the "black rebels [*negros* alçados]"; e.g., f. 28v: ". . . ebitaron el daño que harian a los naturales de esta provinçia que podia seguir . . ."); f. 8r and the paragraphs immediately preceding those just cited refer to the Spanish rebels or "tyrants" [*tiranos*] from Peru, who landed at Campeche, rode up to Mani, and were twenty leagues outside Merida, allegedly hoping to sieze the province, when Rosado confronted and captured them; deposited in the new Merida city jail, the subsequent fate of the "tyrants" is not mentioned. I am grateful to John Chuchiak for drawing my attention to Rosado's *probanza*. Rosado's recapture of the slaves is also mentioned by López de Cogolludo (1957 [1654], I: 273; and cited in Fernández Repetto and Negroe Sierra 1995: 6).

33. AGI-*Justicia* 300: f. 380v (etc.; see n. 34).

34. AGI-*Justicia* 300. The main Yucatan portion of the residencia is 300, 3: ff. 219–727; the questions on the enslaving of Mayas and on Marcos are answered by most of those who testify, e.g.: ff. 380v, 383r–84v, 388v, 403v, 413, 419v–21r, 425r–26r, 429v–30r, 441v–42. I am grateful to John Chuchiak for drawing my attention to this residencia. The perfect correlation between those granted large house-plots on the plaza (the Montejos and his wife's relatives mentioned above, and the Bracamonte brothers) and those denounced in the residencia investigation by other Spaniards for enslaving Mayas is surely not coincidental; see Rubio Mañé (1941: 16) for precise locations of these elite houses. In her *probanza* of 1554, doña Beatriz de Herrera complained that when her husband died, she lost all her Maya servants, and this was one of the reasons why she needed a royal pension; she makes no mention of Marcos as the past procurer of those servants (AGI-*México* 3048: ff. 18–24). On Montejo's campaign in Honduras of 1537–39, see Chamberlain (1953: 69–142) (which makes only passing mention of "*negro* slaves," offering no clue as to how Montejo acquired Marcos). The Montejo faction was also accused of bringing in Nahuas by force to be domestic servants, treating them as slaves, and cutting off ears when they tried to escape (AGI-*México* 359, 1, 1: ff. 4v–5r).

35. AGI-*México* 2999, 2: f. 193r (". . . para q pudiese llevar, ã ãqlla tierra, tres sclavos [sic], negros, para su serviº libras de diºs . . ."). The granting of licenses to import slaves in the hundreds was common crown practice throughout the colonial period, and may have been borrowed from Portuguese crown practices beginning in the fifteenth century. However, the granting of such licenses can be misleading, at least with respect to less lucrative colonies such as Yucatan, where there is seldom evidence of such grants being filled. Another example comes from neighboring Tabasco (which was attached to Yucatan for part of the colonial period), where the *cabildo* [town council] of Santa María de la Victoria petitioned the crown in 1610 for a license to import three hundred slaves and three hundred Maya families from northern Yucatan to meet labor needs; the licenses were granted in 1618, but there is no record of how many Africans and Mayas were actually brought to the town (AGI-*México* 136).

36. For example, don Juan de Montejo y del Castillo, the younger son of the conquistador Montejo, put up for sale two African women, Juana and Luisa, in the pro-

visions of his will of 1603; Juana was described as a *negra criolla*, meaning she was not African-born and may have been born in Yucatan (will transcribed in Rubio Mañé 1941: 45–53, negras on pp. 48, 50).

37. See Chapter Five for discussion of the specific African origins of slaves in Yucatan. García Bernal (2006: 100–108) argues that Sisal rivaled Campeche as a gateway to transatlantic trade, 1580s–1620s, but she makes no mention of African slaves.

38. Another version of this image, painted by the Dutch artist Petrus Schenk (1661–1711) shows the ships sitting peacefully in Campeche's bay (both versions can be seen in color at www.colonial-mexico.com/Yucatan/campeche.html).

39. Palmer (1976: 7–13); Vila Vilar (1977); Vega Franco (1984: 3); Klein (1986: 29); Aguirre Beltrán (1989: 33–80).

40. Vega Franco (1984); Klein (1986: 37).

41. Palmer (1981: 8–9, 85). The demand for slaves was taken so seriously by the Spanish crown that when in 1703 its colonies were banned from trading with the French, the asiento was honored and the slave trade exempted—although in 1706 alone an alleged thirty-six French ships landed cargo in addition to African slaves in Veracruz and Campeche (Aguirre Beltrán 1989: 74).

42. Villalobos (1682) (JCBL Rare Book B682V714m). It is unlikely that the numbers specified in this license were filled. For other licenses, see the facsimile edition of originals published as *Reales asientos y licencias para la introducción de esclavos negros a la América Española (1676–1789)* (No author 1985).

43. Palmer (1981: 4–6, 9, 15, 78, 89, 104, 108–9). For a 1794 English slave-ship captain's account of the process of arriving in Kingston, selling African slaves, and restocking the ship with provisions, see Mouser (2002: 111–17); the captain mentioned at one point that "several Spaniards came on board to look at the Cargo" (112).

44. AGN-*Reales Cédulas* 54, 30; Aguirre Beltrán (1989: 76); Patch (1993: 95).

45. Hunt (1974: 40, 134). The town of Bacalar was abandoned by non-Mayas in or shortly after 1648 and its Spanish *república* located in the Maya villages of Pacha and then Chunhuhub until 1729 (Jones 1989: 62–63); it must have been in the latter, located roughly half way between Belize City and Merida, that Book maintained a base. The network of English slave merchants extended down through Belize into Guatemala, where John Gillis (aka Juan Guillis) and William Lea (aka Guillermo Lea or Lee) were prominent agents in the 1730s (AGI-*Indiferente General* 2817).

46. ANEY, Montero, 1729–35 (UTA roll 3), f. 284.

47. AGN-*Marina* 156, 5: fs. 181, 187v.

48. AGN-*Civil* 1335; Rubio Mañé (1945: 292–94). Joseph Bates was born in 1745 in London, where he trained as a physician, moving briefly to Jamaica, then Tabasco, where he married doña Maria Catalina de Escobedo, the daughter of a wealthy local Spaniard, arriving in Merida at the age of twenty-one. He prospered as a physician, merchant, and accountant (managing the assets of the Convent of Concepcionistas, for example, indicating that he had early on coverted to Catholicism, probably at the time of his wedding). Among his sons, José Francisco Bates became a notary and was credited with bringing the first printing press to Yucatan in 1813 (which was later used in the cause of the Sanjuanista rebels, earning him a prison sentence); Rubio Mañé (1945: 292); Toribio Medina (1907: 24). Another son, José Lauriano Bates y Escobedo, was baptized in 1777 and graduated from one of Merida's elite seminaries in 1802; AME/Arrigunaga y Peón (1975: *expediente* 817). A third was the above-

mentioned José Guillermo, whose mercantile interests included slave trading. Bates descendents still live in Merida and Campeche to this day (Rocio Bates de Villanueva, personal communication).

49. For example, the Galicia Trading Company was formed in 1734 to provide Campeche with slaves and other goods; in 1765 a Cádiz merchant, don Miguel de Uriarte, was given license to bring four hundred slaves a year to Honduras and Campeche; and don Juan Ignacio de Cosgaya gained a permit in 1787 to import up to a thousand slaves into Campeche, where he owned an hacienda (Aguirre Beltrán 1989: 84, 86, 92); however, there is no direct evidence that such licenses were filled, while baptism records suggest that in the late-eighteenth century slaves came annually to Campeche by the dozen, not in hundreds.

50. Patch (1993: 234–35).

51. AGN-*Inquisición* 1131, 2, fs. 80–110. For more of Bolio's story, see Chapter Six and Restall (2006).

52. Modyford quote from Haas in Cook (1935: 5); on Bacalar, see Jones (1989: 230, 272–73); on the 1660s and 1690s, see Jones (1998) and Caso Barrera (2002); on the Hariza attack, see Villagutierre (1983: 215) and Campbell (2003: 178–79). Cay Kitchen was renamed St. George's Cay in the 1760s. Campbell argues that the cay was originally called *Casina* (after an herbal tea found in the Antilles) but that the British misread this is as *Cosina* (i.e., Cocina); this is certainly possible, although Spaniards seem to have called it *Cayo Cocina* from the seventeenth to nineteenth centuries.

53. My study of this frontier was, at an earlier stage of this book's development, a separate chapter; but in the end I decided it made more sense to publish the study elsewhere (see Restall n.d.), while including the Afro-Yucatecan material in the relevant sections of Chapters One, Five, and Six.

54. BL, Add 17569: f. 6; PRO-CO 30/47/17; 137/77; various in Burdon (1931: 61–126); Cook (1769); Haas in Cook (1935: 13–14); Victoria Ojeda (1995: 194); Hall and Pérez Brignoli (2003: 34–37, 142–43); Restall (n.d.). By the 1750s Belize had become a central part of the defense problem that reports on Yucatan tended to rank as the colony's most pressing issue (e.g., the 1757 *Informe Anonimo* in BL, Add 17569: ff. 64–71).

55. ANEY, Argaiz, 1778–81 (UTA roll 21); Argaiz, 1782–84 (UTA roll 22); López Rivas (1975).

56. AGAY, Jesús María, *Libros de Bautismos* Vol. 5: ff. 144r–236r. Appendix G is a complete set of tables presenting data from these baptism records; also see the discussions in Chapters Two, Four, and Five.

57. Bolland (1997: 55; 2002); Campbell (2003: 182–99); Restall (n.d.).

58. AGMM, *Ultramar, Mexico*, caja 5371.

59. AGMM, *Ultramar, Mexico*, caja 5362, 2, 1; and 5371 (on the 1803–05 plan to attack Belize) and cajas 5366 and 5373 (on Yucatec militiamen fighting in Mexico; also see "Abolition" section in Chapter Two). For a longer discussion of the Yucatan–Belize frontier, see Restall (n.d.).

60. AGN-*Marina* 156, 5: fs. 178–79.

61. Victoria Ojeda (1995: 213).

62. AGAY, Jesús María, *Libros de Bautismos* Vols. 1–6 (1710–97).

63. There were small numbers of blacks and mulattoes in Valladolid in the earliest colonial decades (fray Cristóbal Asension hired one in 1570 to accompany him on his journey to Cozumel; AGI-*Indiferente General* 1381; Roys, Scholes, and Adams 1940:

24), but a century after the colony was founded, Afro-Yucatecans in Valladolid were still so few in number that they did not have their own *cofradía*; the Santo Nombre de Jesús brotherhood, run by Afro-Yucatecans in Merida and Campeche, was in Valladolid dominated by Mayas (BL, Egerton 1791, Cárdenas y Valencia manuscript [1638]: f. 48r). Bishop Padilla reported in 1757 that "Spaniards, mestizos, mulattoes, and other mixed-race people [*gente de mescla*]" were in a single parish togther (BL, Add 17569: f. 13v). By 1779, less than 4% of Afro-Yucatecans lived in Valladolid and its jurisdiction (see Map 1.3/Table 1.4, drawn from data in Patch 1993: 235). Even near the end of the colonial period, in 1806, pardos were only 2.8% of the population of Valladolid parish (which was mostly Spanish/mestizo) and 0.7% of neighboring Sisal parish (which was otherwise entirely Maya); see Appendix B; AME, 205 and 299 (parish records in the Archivo de la Mitra Emeritense, Merida, Yucatan, published in Dumond and Dumond 1982: 3–304; hereafter cited as AME with numbers cited being pages in the Dumond edition).

64. AHAY-*Asuntos Terminados* 1792 (transcribed in Ruz Menéndez 1970: 22–25; quotes on pp. 23, 24).

65. BL, MS 17, 569: 181.

66. Aguirre Beltrán (1989: 197–210). The estimate of four hundred Spaniards in 1570 is probably too low; Cook and Borah (1974: 77) estimate the Spanish population at about two thousand in 1580.

67. Hunt (1974: 92–93); Aguirre Beltrán (1989: 211–19); AGI-*México* 1035.

68. On the 1784 liberalization, see Rodas de Coss (1983: lvii, quoting and citing the Gálvez edict of that year).

69. Rubio Mañé (1942, I: 250); Aguirre Beltrán (1989: 222); Patch (1993: 233–34).

70. AGAY, Jesús María, *Libros de Bautismos* Vols. 1–6; data spans 1710–96, with black adult annual averages ranging from 2.1% (1740s) to 9.6% (1760s).

71. García Bernal (1978: 158). Genny Negroe Sierra likewise comments that "the black population was not numerically and socially significant compared to other sectors of the population [such as] mulatos and pardos" (my translation from her 1991: 19).

72. Aguirre Beltrán (1989: 85).

73. The 5% estimate is derived by dividing Yucatan's possible 15,000 by greater Mexico's possible 300,000 (a rough average of estimates discussed in Palmer 1976: 3; Carroll 1991: 27; and Vincent 2001: 277).

74. Furthermore, Yucatecans of African descent were not mass or plantation slaves with higher mortality rates than European settlers, as was the case elsewhere; thus the point made by Brion Davis (2003: 28), that by 1820 whites outnumbered blacks in the Americas due not to immigration but to survival rates, does not apply to Yucatan (or to most Spanish American colonies).

CHAPTER TWO

1. AGN-*Inquisición*, 69, 5: 324; the whole document is reproduced in translation in Restall (2000a: 27–28).

2. AGI-*Contratación* 5425, 1, 1: f. 4v (my somewhat free translation of: ". . . dijo q^{ue} conoce a el dho Gov^{or} de mucho tiempo a esta parte y a su esmo a fran^{co} antt^{o} y a ju^{o} criollo negros y save que los susodhos son esclavos de el dho Gov^{or} suyos pro-

prios, y los que tuvo de las Yndias quando vino de ellas y los contenidos en la cedula Real de Su Mag^d por q^{ue} este tt^o les conocio en la Prov^a de Beneçuela y otras partes de las Yndias, y en estos Rey^{os} y siempre a visto tratarlos por sus esclavos y en esta opinion y reput^{on} son havidos y tenidos y en ella este tt^o le tiene . . .").

3. AGEY-*Gobernación* (Poder Ejecutivo) 2, 58: f. 1r.

4. Thus a shipment of 199 *cabezas* ["head" or individual Africans], delivered in Caracas by English slave traders in 1735, was valued at 166 piezas, with a combined peso value of 49,725 (AGI-*Indiferente General* 2817, penultimate expediente).

5. CCA-*caja* X, 1818, 009.

6. García Bernal (1978: 25).

7. AGI-*México* 3050: fs. 94–184; quotes are by Quiñones, f. 133. I have found no evidence that Quiñones was himself a slave owner. Canon Mendicuti was able to purchase at least one slave from another source; in 1762 he brought an African from Carabeo to be baptized in the Jesús parish as Miguel María (AGAY-*Jesús*, Libro de Bautismos [IV-B-7] Vol. 4: f. 4r).

8. AGAY-*Jesús*, Libro de Bautismos Vol. 4: ff. 140r, 142v.

9. AGN-*Inquisición*, 69, 5: 324; Restall (2000a: 27–28).

10. See the various AGI-*Contratación* and AGI-*Indiferente* files listed in Appendix C.

11. AGN-*Marina*, 36, 5: fs. 168–69. There are numerous other examples of slaves categorized as cargo or commodities. Trade records from Havana, the point of entry for Africans forced to work on Cuba's sugar plantations, state in 1804, for example, that Spanish authorities in the city calculated that in that year they received 53,483 pesos-worth of flour; 45,386 pesos-worth of wine; 1,150 pesos-worth of vinagre; 5,319 pesos-worth of aguardiente; and 8,923 pesos-worth of Africans [*negros bozales de ambos sexos*]; BL-MS 13, 974: f. 516.

12. Proctor (2003a: 49; 2006: 331–34) on Guanajuato and New Spain. I suggest that this further defines a society with slaves (women slaves worth the same or a tad more than men) versus a slave society (men worth more); see discussion in the Conclusion.

13. AGN-*Marina* 156, 5: fs.188v–89; Baquiero Anduze (1983 [1937]: 38).

14. Palmer (1981: 127); Contreras Sánchez (1990).

15. According to an *asiento* of 1682, which permitted the importation on Dutch ships of 2,000 slaves a year into Spanish America, the Dutch were to be paid 105 pesos for each slave transferred to Spanish agents in the port of Cumaná (Villalobos 1682: 4–6). On the profitability of the trade for English merchants in the early eighteenth century, see Palmer (1981: 145–55).

16. On the other hand, the market price for slaves in Yucatan provided little incentive for Spaniards to bring slaves from Spain to sell in the colony, especially considering the cost of an Atlantic crossing (twenty-two pesos each for master and slave, in one 1643 example; AGI-*Contratación* 5465, 2, 77; Appendix C). Slave raids into Belize, however, were still profitable, to the extent that they may even have helped keep prices down, especially as a very successful raid, like that of 1779, tended to swamp the market.

17. Carroll (1991: 34–36, 64–78). On sugar in late colonial Yucatan, see Nichols (2003).

18. Ruz Menéndez (1970: 17, 19; also cited in Hunt 1974: 599); Baquiero Anduze (1983 [1937]: 38).

19. I found slave-sale tax records for the seventeenth century in AGI-*Contaduría* 914–918 (e.g., 917a, 1: ff. 15–28) and records of slave sales for the late seventeenth and eighteenth centuries scattered all through the colonial volumes of the ANEY (e.g., of some found by me: ANEY, Zavala, 1765–66 [UTA roll 15]: ff. 123–24, 223–24, 243v–44, 363v–65, 475–76r; e.g., of some sent to me by Mark Lentz, with my gratitude: Hivarren / Argaiz, 1792–93 [UTA roll 26]: ff. 285v–87, 327–28r).

20. This mulatta was not don Iñigo's only slave; for example, in 1667 he had purchased a pair of black boys [*negrillos pequeños*] for three hundred pesos from don Nicolas Pacheco (AGI-*Contaduría* 917a, 1: f. 28 bis). Both dowry cases are in ANEY, but I was unable to find them, relying instead on Hunt (1974: 34) and Peón Ancona (1985: 120), who omit specific citations.

21. Merida's mortgage notes are scattered through the colonial volumes of the ANEY; the above examples are also mentioned in Peón Ancona (1985: 119). In his testament of 1603, the encomendero and conquistador's son don Juan de Montejo y Castillo implies that he had mortgaged a slave woman named Luisa to one of his creditors, and that the mortgage was to be redeemed with the maize and chickens that the Mayas of Cholul paid as encomienda tribute (transcription of will in Rubio Mañé 1941: 50). Further research may well uncover pre-1725 mortgage notes from Merida, but I doubt there were many, if any, after 1802.

22. The mortgages are archived in four *Libros de Hipotecas* as AGEC-*Registro Público de la Propriedad* [*Fondo Gobernación*], 2, 1–4. As a formal credit mechanism the mortgage became increasingly important and widespread during the nineteenth century. The total number of mortgages did not increase dramatically (a thousand mortgage contracts were recorded in Merida in the second half of the nineteenth century), but their total annual value did, fueled in part by the henequen boom—from seventy-four thousand pesos in 1850 to almost a million pesos by 1895 (Levy 2003: 43–58). I am grateful to Juliette Levy for her assistance in analyzing the Campeche mortgage contracts.

23. For some brief examples of the personal stories behind slave business in another Spanish American province, that of Nuevo León, see Gómez Danés (1996: 39–43).

24. Indeed, naming properties was as common in colonial New Spain as it was elsewhere in the early modern world; see, for example, Taylor (1979: 66) on names given to colonial Mexican pulque taverns or *pulquerías*.

25. On Mexico, Cope (1994: 60–67), on Veracruz, Carroll (1991: 120–24), on Peru, Van Deusen (1999: 7).

26. AGN-*Inquisición* 1131, 2: ff. 80–110. Other examples of name changes are embedded within the baptism records of AGAY-*Jesús*, Libros de Bautismos Vols. 1–6. The same pattern held true in the English Caribbean, meaning Africans who were slaves in Jamaica or Belize before arriving in Yucatan might live through multiple names; for example, Christopher Hill, slave to "Mr. Gil" (in the Spanish records) in Belize, was known as Christopher Kingston when a slave of Gabriel Kingston in Jamaica and then became Cristóbal Gil in Yucatan, probably becoming renamed again upon subsequent sale (AGN-*Marina* 156, 5: f.185).

27. On Spaniards in Yucatan see García Bernal (1972) and Hunt (1974); on Mayas, see Restall (1997: esp. chap. 4).

28. Quotes by Diouf (1998: 85) and Berlin (2003: 54).

29. Quote by Berlin (2003: 54); also see Cody (1987); Handler and Jacoby (1996: 692–97); Berlin (1998: 95, 149–50); and Morgan (1998: 546, 549–51, 555–58). Morgan (1998: 21, 451–55) comments on how a decreasing minority of slaves in the eighteenth-century Chesapeake appear in written records with African names; by contrast, the Spanish emphasis on the Christian identity of black slaves (an emphasis underpinning Bennett 2003) means that not one African name appears in the Afro-Yucatecan written record. Enslaved Africans in some parts of the Americas maintained covert nicknames or their original African names as markers of identity within the slave community as forms of resistance to bondage (1998: 82–87); slaves in Yucatan may have done the same.

30. ANEY, Argaiz, 1778–81 (UTA roll 21); López Rivas (1975).

31. For example, Julián José Castillo, sold by one Spaniard to another in Merida in 1806, had earlier been Guillermo Stox, and before 1798 was an Afro-Belizean slave named William Stocks; his original African name was not recorded (Peón Ancona 1985: 117; ANEY citation omitted).

32. For discussions of how church inclusion of African slaves in Mexico City impacted community formation and the nature of slavery, see Villa-Flores (2002) and Bennett (2003).

33. Rúz Menéndez (1970: 22–25), which is a transcription of the auction record in what he calls the *Archivo Eclesiástico de Yucatán* (which I believe is now the AHAY), in *Asuntos Terminados* 1792. I was not able to find Plato's and Gaius's baptismal records, as the entries in AGAY-*Jesús* are incomplete for the year 1792— unless the bishop sold the slaves to his brother, don Toribio de Piña Mazo Villazan, who had two black adult slaves of his baptized as Tomás and Luis on May 18, 1794 (AGAY-*Jesús*, Libro de Bautismos Vol. 6: ff. 201v, 202v). In some cases, slaves previously named by British owners retained such names informally or as nicknames, a practice that may have been common. For example, in 1779 the captain and officers of the *goleta* San Miguel seized an English ship anchored off Cozumel; the booty included Toby, an eighteen-year-old slave promptly sold in Campeche to don Clemente Rodríguez Truxillo. Toby was baptized in Merida as Antonio Cristóbal Truxillo, but when don Clemente sold him to Governor Arturo O'Neill fourteen years later he was still "known as Toby [*conosido de nombre Tobi*]" (ANEY, Hivarren/Argaiz, 1792–93 [UTA roll 30]: ff. 285v–87; AGN-*Criminal* 291: f. 185r; all found and sent to me by Mark Lentz).

34. ANEY, Argaiz, 1778–81 (UTA roll 21); López Rivas (1975). Slaves imported into Spanish Florida were branded "RF" (Landers 1999: 158). On branding in Spanish America in the 1660s–70s under the Grillo y Lomelín asiento, see Vega Franco (1984: 147–49).

35. AGI-*Contratación* 5470, 1, 23, 1: f. 13r (". . . braco señales de yierro en el lado drõ en la mediania de la oreja . . .").

36. AGI-*Contratación* 5425, 1, 1: ff. 1–4.

37. For example, don Rodrigo Flores de Aldana, governor in the 1660s, surely invested in African slaves some of the profits from his exploitation of Mayas, and no doubt I or another researcher will eventually find evidence of this in his voluminous *residencia* records (AGI-*Escribanía* 315a–318a); his cousin, don Antonio Maldonado de Aldana, a Campeche-based merchant and one of the wealthiest men in the colony, owned at least 24 African slaves in the 1660s (AGI-*México* 361: ff. 14–17; González Muñóz and Martínez Ortega 1989: 106–9, 129).

38. AGAY-*Jesús*, Libros de Bautismos Vol. 2.

39. This practice is detailed in García Bernal (1978; 1979), Patch (1993), and Solís Robleda (2003); archival information is primarily found in gubernatorial residencia records in AGI-*Escribanía* (the mid-colonial examples I have seen are in 315 through 325).

40. Carrillo y Ancona (1880: 77–88). In other words, governors served for an average of 4.3 years, and bishops an average of 10.6 years (although actual service was shorter in both cases, due to the lag between appointment and arrival in Merida).

41. ANEY Baeza (UTA roll 1); Hunt (1974: 532–33).

42. AGI-*Contratación* 5425, 1, 1: ff. 1–4 (Núñez Melián); 5465, 2, 77 (Vertiz); 5506, 2, 7 (Alcalde); 5387, 16 (Núñez de Matos); 5524, 4, 29 (Castillo). It is probably fair to say that all Spaniards preferred to travel with a black slave or free-colored servant—to act as a porter, bodyguard, and status marker. If a Spaniard could not afford to own or permanently retain such a man, he hired one (for example, when in 1570 the encomendero Juan de Contreras failed to heed the bishop's instructions and provide fray Cristóbal Asensio with "a pair of men or blacks [*un par de Hombres o negros*]" for his journey to Cozumel, fray Cristóbal hired one ["*alquile ... un negro*"] in Valladolid; AGI-*Indiferente General* 1381; Roys, Scholes, and Adams 1940: 24).

43. The convent's history is summarized by Rugeley (2001: 85–86); evidence of black slaves in the convent is in Peón Ancona (1985: 119, citing ANEY).

44. Joseph's baptism record is in AGAY-*Jesús*, Libros de Bautismos Vol. 2: f. 138r. The Pérez clan were well represented among Merida's eighteenth-century slave-owning elite (see Appendix E). The prior of another convent, fray Antonio Figueroa, owned a black woman and her son, the latter born and baptized in Merida in 1783 (Vol. 5: f. 225v).

45. Hunt (1974: 27–30); Patch (1993: 160, 163, 167). Bracamonte (1993: 22) states that there were still 109 active encomiendas when the crown finally dissolved them into its own tribute base in 1785.

46. AGI-*Patronato* 66a, 1, 4, 1: f. 5 ("con sus armas y cavallos y criados y esclabos"). On the casa poblada as a foundational concept of nobility and colonization in the Spanish world, see Sanchíz Ochoa (1976: 67–68; also cited by Fernández Repetto and Negroe Sierra 1995: 5); and Hunt (1974: 30).

47. Victoria Ojeda (1995: 150).

48. This analysis is based on two bodies of documents—the notarial records in ANEY and the parish records in AGAY-*Jesús*—as well as on Hunt (1974: 24–151).

49. Martínez Ortega (1993: 96–115) (also see González Muñoz and Martínez Ortega 1989).

50. AGAY-*Jesús*, Libros de Bautismos Vols. 1–6 (especially Vol. 5: ff. 144r–236r); Hunt (1974: 402); Martínez Ortega (1993: 40, 102, 174); Patch (1993: 192); also see Table 2.4 and Appendix E. It is not clear if don Juan Esteban's mother was doña Isabel Ávila Ancona (Patch 1993: 192) or doña Petrona Cetina (Martínez Ortega 1993: 174), or if the former was his illegitimate birth mother and the latter his adoptive mother (meaning that the *limpieza de sangre* document that enabled him to serve on the cabildo [AGI-*México* 3014] contained a fictive pedigree and adoptive link to the older elite family of Cetina). Don Rodrigo Chacón made the money to buy slaves from

his profits as a bondsman for cabildo officers and an agent for moneylending priests, and through his salt-export partnership with don Juan de Uterra Rendón (Patch 1993: 203); a relative (his father or uncle) was don Antonio Chacón y Azcorra, an encomendero and the maestre de campo who led the assault on the English in the Champotón area in 1685 (and whose Afro-Yucatecan aide was Lázaro del Canto, about whom we shall hear more in Chapter Five; also see Hunt 1974: 511).

51. Hunt (1974: 506–10).

52. In contrast to Mixtec nobles, the wealthiest of whom did own black slaves (Terraciano 2001: 238, 250, 339).

53. AGEY-*Sucesiones Testamentarias* 1, 11. Note that Gómez was a Spaniard because he is identified as a *vecino* with no casta-qualifying label, but he may have been a mestizo or mulatto whose wealth allowed him to pass as a Spaniard (see Chapter Three).

54. Nichols (2003). It is possible that the wealthiest Spaniards in Tekax sought to create Merida-style elite households, complete with an African slave or two, but I have not found evidence for this and Nichols makes no reference to it.

55. The European elite male objection to their wives and daughters doing domestic work is a point made with respect to the English colonies by Morgan (1972: 26–27; also see 1975: chap. 3); also see Eltis (2000: 85).

56. For further comparative context, see Table D.1 in Appendix D. For example, as houses and house plots ranged from the affordable to the palatial, a large sector of colonial society participated in the land and housing economy; in 1660–64, there were twice as many sales entries in this category than for slave sales, with tax revenues likewise being double.

57. This was true in other Spanish colonies too; see Gauderman (2003: 86) on Quito, for example. The data in this paragraph is drawn from AGAY-*Jesús*, Libros de Bautismos Vols. 1–6, and is also tabulated in Table E.2 in Appendix E.

58. Eltis (2000: 85).

59. Freyre (1968 [1946]: 278–475, quotes from 278); Baptist (2001: 1649); Magubane (2004: 14–39); Vaughan (2005: 171–72); Kaye (2007: 79). The theme of gender/sexuality and colonial power is explored variously by scholars of colonial Spanish America, most notably in two categories: Spaniards categorizing Africans as hypermale or hypersexual and feminizing "Indians"; and witchcraft (see Chapter Seven); e.g., Silverblatt (1987), Stern (1995), and Lewis (2003).

60. Various kinds of evidence may eventually surface, such as cases of the kind found for late colonial Guayaquil (Townsend 1997: 60–61, 67n6), in which slave owners sued to have slave sales invalidated because previous owners sold female slaves with venereal diseases.

61. AGAY-*Jesús*, Libros de Bautismos Vol. 6: ff. 102v, 210v. Other examples are merely suggested by baptism records; e.g., perhaps María Eusebia and her newborn daughter were freed after a difficult birth in January, 1747, because their owner was the baby's father (Vol. 4: f. 183v–84r).

62. AGAY-*Jesús*, Libros de Bautismos Vols. 4–5; the details of parentage in 1760–74 are also presented in Tables G.4 and G.5 in Appendix G.

63. Put another way, the church's insistence that couples marry, combined with its preference for racially endogamous marriages, effectively promoted illicit concubinage between Spanish men and Afro-Yucatecan women. Because of the inequities

of gender, race, and class, such relationships also became expressions of the differences in status between the Spanish master and black concubine; for a similar pattern and argument made for colonial Brazil, see Nazzari (1996).

64. This was also true in many other Spanish American colonies; in Chile, for example, where there were more slaves than in Yucatan, due to the profits of the wine industry, but the same trio of factors underpinned slave ownership (Lacoste 2003: 144–46). For a full development of the argument that sexually exploited slaves were commodities that were "fetishized" and consumed, see Baptist (2001).

65. Penningroth (2003: 13).

66. Carroll (2001: 110); for example, likewise comments on the lack of debate, protest, or open celebration surrounding abolition in Veracruz in particular and in Mexico in general.

67. The most obvious example is that of Francisco de Miranda, who went from being a slave owner to an abolitionist revolutionary; Racine (2003: 23, 215, 233–34). For the larger context, see Bernand (2001: 173–96).

68. Clementi (1974: 29).

69. Both quotes in Vincent (2001: 45, 46).

70. Quote not from Article 22 itself but from a summary of it in an opposition newspaper in Mexico; Vincent (2001: 49–50).

71. Ruz Menéndez (1970: 15); Redondo (1994: 153); Vincent (2001: 143, 195–205).

72. Clementi (1974: 201–02).

73. Tutino (2003) argues that slavery was no longer a viable institution in the Bajío by the final decades of the eighteenth century; he also notes the simultaneous and related pattern of category slippage in the region, where thousands of residents classified as mulattoes in 1755 are recorded as Spaniards in the 1792 census. Martin (1996: 44) comments on the parallel decline of slavery in late eighteenth-century Chihuahua. The relative unimportance of slavery in New Spain by the early nineteenth century may be reflected in the fact that recent studies of the Independence period tend not to discuss abolition—see Guardino (2005) on Oaxaca, for example. In contrast, Blanchard (2002; 2004) views Independence in South America through "slave voices."

74. *Periodico Constitucional*, 9 April 1821: p. 4; accessed through the UTA microfilm collection; for the same advertisement in *El Constitucionalista*, see Baquiero Anduze (1983 [1937]: 38).

75. AGAY-*Jesús*, Libro de Bautismos Vol. 6 (also see Appendix G); AME (also see Appendix B). It also becomes less common in the final decades of the colonial period for individuals to be listed with racial designations. For example, Ticul's *Libro de Posito* of 1804 lists the corn deposits by the named heads of households—all "the Spaniards, Indians, Mulattoes, and Blacks of the town"—but these groups are not subsequently identified in the list of names. The ten most prominent Spaniards start the list and are identifiable by their "dons" and other titles, while Mayas are clearly identifiable by their native patronymic surnames; in between are the remaining Spaniards, mestizos, and Afro-Yucatecans, identifiable to their peers, no doubt, but not to us (AGEY-*Ticul* [*Fondo Municipios*] 1, 1).

76. AGN-*Bienes Nacionales* 28, 65.

77. This was also true in Peru; Lockhart (1994: 217).

78. AGEY-*Registros Judiciales*, *Penal* 3, 19.

79. Ruz Menéndez (1970: 12); Baquiero Anduze (1983 [1937]: 40); Vincent (2001: 196); Campos García (2005: 131). The five provisions of the decree: (1) prohibited "the introduction of enslaved men" (meaning people); (2) granted immediate freedom to any "enslaved men . . . clandestinely introduced"; (3) declared that "all the children of enslaved parents [*padres*] are born free"; (4) all slaves have the right to purchase their own freedom; and (5) but "the slaves that flee their masters" shall be caught and returned (my translation from the transcription in Ruz Menéndez 1970: 12).

80. My translation from the transcription in Ruz Menéndez (1970: 13).

81. Vincent (2001: 12, 180, 199). I found no evidence in Merida's baptism records of any Zavalas owning slaves in the eighteenth century (AGAY-*Jesús*, Libro de Bautismos Vols. 1–6). In his description of Zavala as "curly-haired, dark-complexioned," Vincent seems to be implying that he may have had some African ancestry (2001: 180). Zavala was one of the *sanjuanistas* of 1814, serving three years in prison with fellow rebel Francisco Bates (Rugeley 1996: 38, 48). Zavala died in 1836 in Texas, where he briefly served as vice president of the independent Texan nation before resigning over Anglo refusals to grant rights to non-Anglos (Vincent 2001: 199).

82. Political verse in these papers is full of lines such as "[our Constitution] loves only truth / applauds freedom / and strikes at despotism" (*Periodico Constitucional*, March 18, 1821: p. 4; UTA microfilm collection). One is reminded of Thomas Paine asking in 1775, How could Americans "complain so loudly of attempts to enslave them while they hold so many hundreds of thousands in slavery?" (quoted by Berlin 2003: 100).

83. Rugeley (1996: 3–4, 62–63); Reed (2001 [1964]: 18, 60, 201–2).

84. Redondo (1994: 153), quoting but not citing Molina Solís (see Molina Solís 1913).

85. Vincent (2001: 197).

86. Rugeley (1996: 62–63); Quezada (2001: 124–26); also see Tutino (1986: 221). Carvajal remained governor until 1832 (Carrillo y Ancona 1880: 89).

87. According to Vincent (2001: 196), "the federal government never achieved the improved financial situation needed to afford the funds."

88. AGEY-*Justicia* [*Poder Ejecutivo*] 2, 20. Don Tomás Aznar was descended from Yucatan's slave-owning elite, his mother being a Peón, and his father and brother both distinguished army colonels (the same brother's father-in-law having been Governor of Yucatan). Two nephews of don Tomás Aznar, Tomás and Ramón, owned sugar plantations in the late nineteenth century (worked by Maya laborers, not black slaves, as was typical in the colonial period too). Don Tomás was uncle and godfather to Ramón, who co-owned the San Antonio Xuxub plantation; for the fascinating tale of how the American co-owner of Xuxub was murdered by *cruzob* Maya rebels in 1875, see Sullivan (2004) (on the Aznar genealogy, Sullivan, personal communication).

89. The documents are in the personal collection of Rodolfo Ruz Menéndez, who reproduces one in facsimile and transcription, and identifies the owner's husband (1970: 15, 17).

90. AGEY-*Gobernación* [*Poder Ejecutivo*] 2, 58: f.1.

91. AGEY-*Gobernación* [*Poder Ejecutivo*] 2, 58: ff. 3–4.

CHAPTER THREE

1. AGI-*Contratación* 5365, 21, 1: f. 2r (". . . por tener la color de mulato las justisias me garan molestias y me prenderan por entender q soi cautibo siendo pᵃ libre en lo qual resivi notorio agravio."); see Appendix A for Aguilar's full statement.

2. AGEY-*Justicia* 1, 6: f. 3r (". . . haviendo sido la primera pedirla consentim.ᵗᵒ a Mᵃ. de Luz Herrera madre de mi pretendida he hallado en esta fuerte opocicion, p.ʳ la desigualdad que entre ella y yo tenemos de calidad."); see Appendix A for Medina's full petition.

3. Torquemada's explanation of differences in human skin color, in *Monarquía Indiana*, book 13, chap. 13: 567 ("No ai mas raçon, de que queriendo Dios mostrar sus maravillas, en la variedad de colores, como en las Flores del Campo."), quoted by Katzew (2004: 213n72).

4. Alcedo (1812 [1786–89], Vol. III: 356).

5. AGEY-*Gobernación* (Poder Ejecutivo) 2, 58: f. 3.

6. Sánchez de Aguilar was the grandson of one of Yucatan's conquistadors. Born in Valladolid, he rose to become Juez Provisor y Vicario General, the highest-ranking priest in the colony after the bishop, in 1602–3; head of the anti-idolatry commission [*Juez de Comisión de la Idolatría*] in 1607; then dean and procurator of the cathedral in Merida (BL, Egerton 1791, Cárdenas y Valencia MS [1639]: f. 63r). His campaigns against idolatry and confiscations of codices began in 1603, ranged from Ppole (on the Caribbean coast) to Tizimin, culminating in an *auto da fé* there in 1608 (Chuchiak 2000: 106–8, 128; 2001; 2004: 72–75, 79–80). His treatise of 1613–15 describing these campaigns was eventually published (Sánchez de Aguilar 1937). My speculation regarding the Madrid Codex on the ship with Francisco is based on John Chuchiak's brilliant essay connecting the codex to Sánchez de Aguilar (Chuchiak 2004). Some of the archival sources on Sánchez de Aguilar that I have seen (and are also cited by Chuchiak 2004) are in AGI-*México* 294; 299; 359. While Francisco presumably made it back to Valladolid, don Pedro went on to become canon in the lucrative diocese of Potosí (in today's Bolivia; Chuchiak 2004: 84n35 cites his *probanzas* of 1623 and 1643 in AGI-*Charcas* 89, 9, 2).

7. Francisco described Valladolid as being "in the province of Campeche," which I initially took to reflect how much of a country bumpkin he was; however, I subsequently found other references to the colony being called "Campeche," rather than "Yucatan," in the late sixteenth and early seventeenth centuries—always by Spaniards in Spain, and all in AGI documents (García Bernal 2006: 43 makes a similar observation on AGI materials from this period).

8. AGI-*Contratación* 5365, 21, 1: f. 1r, 2r (". . . me da licᵃ para que buelba A la provᵃ de yucatan de a donde vino . . . Balladolid que es en la provinsia de can-peche . . . la color de mulato . . ."). Although Valladolid was one of the three main Spanish settlements in the colony, its peripheral geographical location prevented it from developing the way Merida and Campeche did; there were less than 150 Spaniards there in 1619, and perhaps 100 Afro-Yucatecans (BL, Egerton 1791, Cárdenas y Valencia manuscript [1639]: f. 48r; Hunt 1974: 37).

9. This shift took place throughout the colonies; on Peru, for example, see Lockhart (1994: 198).

10. AGI-*Contratación* 5365, 21, 1: f. 2r ("... como yo soi libre y no cautibo, como soy criollo y como persona libre ...").

11. Tannebaum (1946: 45–64); Zavala (1977: 41–104); Negroe Sierra (1991: 9–12); Himelblau (1994: 68–168). Las Casas's later condemnation of African slavery has been the subject of scholarly debate (Lewis 2003: 196 n84).

12. My translation from the quote in Romero Jaramillo (1997: 51), also quoted by Soulodre-La France (2001: 100 n4).

13. Sweet (1997: 165).

14. Solano (1975: 15, quoting Solórzano's *Política Indiana*, published in Madrid in 1648; "... mas fea y extraordinaria ... que le comparan a la naturaleza del mulo."); Walker (2003: 62).

15. ("... mande que los Indios, gente debil, sean dexados en sus oficios, u que se destinen a la labor de Minas, Edificios, Campo y Pan los mulatos, negros y mestizos ...") (transcribed in Pi-Sunyer 1957: 240).

16. For example, see Lewis (2003: 57–66, 73).

17. See, for example, Brooks (2002: 123–25).

18. The free status of children born of slave fathers and free mothers goes back to thirteenth-century Spanish law and was also enscribed in pre-Conquest Mexica law (Pi-Sunyer 1957: 243).

19. Quoted in Tannebaum (1946: 89).

20. Alcedo (1812 [1786–89], Vol. III: 355–56). The full entry (in the 1812 translation) is: "MULATTO, a cast of people of America, produced by a black mother and a white father, or by a black father and a white mother, but the latter very rarely, although the former very commonly, so that America abounds with Mulattoes: they are thus the offspring of a libidinous intercourse between Europeans and female slaves, which the authority of the one and the sensuality of the other tend to make very general. The colour of the children thus produced participate of both white and black, or are rather of a dingy brown colour. Their hair is less crisp than that of the *Negro* and of a clear chestnut tint. The Mulatto is regularly well made, of fine stature, vigorous, strong, industrious, intrepid, ferocious, but given to pleasure, deceitful, and capable of committing the greatest crimes without compunction.

It is a certain fact, that throughout the vast dominions of the king of Spain in America there are no better soldiers than the Mulattoes, nor more infamous men. When the mother is a slave the offspring is also, by the principle of the law that *partus sequitur ventrem*; but inasmuch as that they are in general the offspring of the master of the mother they are made free, and from their earliest infancy are brought up in all kinds of vice. As the Mulatto, as well as the *Negro*, is at the time of its birth nearly white, not taking its real colour till nearly 10 days after; the difference is distinguished by the private parts, for these in the *Negro* child, together with the extremities of its toes and fingers, are already of a dark colour, which is not the case with the Mulatto. The French, in order to keep down the numbers of this cast in their colonies, established a law that the father of a Mulatto should pay a fine of 2,000 lbs. of sugar, and further, that if he were master of the slave, that he should forfeit her as well as the child, the money arising from the fine to be paid into the funds of the hospital of La Charité.

There have been many Europeans, Spaniards, French, English, and other nations of America, who have married *Negro* women; and the sons of these alone are admitted by law to the offices of the state, and although there is a general prohibition against all

Mulattoes whatever, yet has this been in several cases dispensed with. Notwithstanding the bad qualities of the Mulatto, some of them have been found, who from their extraordinary virtues and qualifications have deserved great marks of approbation and distinction from the viceroys, bishops, and other persons of eminence. Such were Miguel Angel de Goenaga, captain of the militia in the city of Portovelo, whose merits had gained him a universal title to respect at home and in the English, French, and Dutch colonies; also in Puerto Rico another person, named Miguel Enriques, who, although in the humble employment of a shoemaker, had done such services to the king, that he was honoured with a royal medal, and allowed to put to his name the title of Don. These examples we conceive to be sufficient to shew how little influence the colour of a man has over the endowments of his soul."

21. Here I am summarizing the conclusion in Gravatt (2003: 111–12).

22. Gravatt (2003: 50–59). The Laws also abolished the *encomienda* (the granting of tribute and labor from whole native villages to Spanish recipients, called *encomenderos*), although encomenderos' rights had not included holding natives in bondage, and in Yucatan the encomienda continued to flourish well into the eighteenth century.

23. Van Deusen (1999: 17); Gravatt (2003: 55, 63–67). Wade (1997: 25–30) is a deft summary of colonial legal conceptualizations of "indians and blacks." On the debate in the Dutch Reformed Church on slavery in New Amsterdam, see Harris (2003: 17).

24. Wood (2003: 10).

25. As Emily Bartels observes; see Davis (1997: 8). Put another way, Europeans who wrote before 1800 of the superiority of some peoples and inferiority of others did not primarily use large-scale categories (like "white" or "African"), as later race and racist writers did (Wade 1997: 6–12).

26. Davis (1997: 7–8); Berlin (1998: 1). The social construct argument originates in U.S. historiography; see Fields (1982), for example.

27. American Anthropological Association (1998).

28. Quoted by Cole (2004: 75).

29. The four were baptized together on May 21, 1725, described as *vosal* (bozal) without a specified place of origin in Africa; AGAY-*Jesús*, Libros de Bautismos Vol. 1: ff. 182v–83r; also see Table 2.5 in the previous chapter.

30. Solís Robleda (2003: 197; 183–269) is a thorough study of Gómez de Parada's reform efforts.

31. The adjective appears regularly, for example, in the investigation into the Sahcabchén revolt (e.g., 1668 testimony in AGI-*México* 307, 3: ff. 15v–18v). See Taylor (1996: 173), who interprets the adjective as highly pejorative, for its use in eighteenth-century central Mexico.

32. This paragraph is based on my reading of Gómez de Parada's 1722 "Constituciones synodales," a manuscript of which is in CAIHY-CCA #145; see esp. ff. 11r, 54r, 59v, 86v, 113r, 116v, 210, and 226v.

33. Sweet (1997: 152–60).

34. DCP: ff. 25–26; DHY, III: 38–40.

35. Blanco (1816).

36. AGI-*México* 3042: f. 53v.

37. On henequen and labor in Yucatan's "Golden Age" of 1876–1910, see Wells and Joseph (1996), Peniche Rivero (2002), and Levy (2003).

38. Wood (2003: 10).

39. I have not found the original criminal case, only an order from the king to the viceroy in Mexico City requesting the case proceedings be sent to Madrid; the order was filed in AGI-*Filipinas* 331, 9, 1: ff. 188v–89r, either because Herrera fled to Manila or due to a filing error (which might explain why I could not find the case itself).

40. AGI-*México* 2999, 2, 1, f. 21v ("... colgados açotandolos hasta hazerce salir gran cantidad de sangre por sus espaldas y piernas queba ... el suelo y pringando-los con çera como a negros esclavos ...").

41. See Proctor (2003a: 53) on *obraje* or textile mill violence against slaves in Mexico.

42. AGI-*México* 368: ff. 1–599 (torture on f. 435v).

43. AGEY-*Reales Cédulas* 1, 45: f. 12r is the notarial record of Betancourt's interrogation on the rack; at first I was convinced it had to be Castro, the slave, who was tortured, but although the document is not very legible I was forced to admit that it is almost certainly his owner, Betancourt.

44. Wiethoff (2002: 165).

45. Sweet (1997: 145) on mamluk and 'abd slaves in Muslim Iberia.

46. For examples from Suriname, see Linebaugh and Rediker (2000: 347); from the United States, see Morgan (1998: 14, 17, 265–67, 271–78, 311–15), and Wiethoff (2002: 48–53, 86, 121).

47. Morgan (1998: 14, 290–91). Note, however, the distinction that Kaye (2007: 11-12) makes between private acts of punitive brutality and public expressions of leniency (writing about slave owners in antebellum Mississippi).

48. On these regions see Borrego Plá (1973), Bennett (2003), and Bryant (2006).

49. AGEY-*Criminal* 1, 7a.

50. On issues of gender, domestic space, and public space (including the windows that revealed the domestic to the public) in the early modern Iberian world, see Perry (1990), Graham (1992), and Lipsett-Rivera (1994).

51. Seed (1988: esp. chap. 4–6, 9, and 11).

52. On the cah-barrios of Merida, see Restall (1997: 32–36), and Chapter Six (which includes a map of the city).

53. AGEY-*Judicial* 1, 6: ff. 3r ("libre de esta oblig.^{on}") and 4 ("... sobre negarme de no prestar mi consentim^{to} p^a contraher martim^o con mi hija Manuela Tolosa, sin reflexar el predho Medina ser inferior su calidad, a la de mi hija; y siendo repugnante la diferencia ... i mi hija mestisa, siendo falso, pues es de publico, y notorio ser la mencionada mi hija Española ordinaria ..."). This case also receives passing mention in Campos García (2005: 47), who includes mostly sound transcriptions of three of the case documents (pp. 150–52).

54. AGEY-*Judicial* 1, 6: f. 6r.

55. AME; Dumond and Dumond (1982); see Appendix B.

56. AGEY-*Judicial* 1, 7.

57. AGEY-*Judicial* 1, 9.

58. Sweet (1997: 144); Carrera (2003: 10–11); Lewis (2003: 22–26, 180–81); Schoenhals (2003); Martínez (2008). Also see Robert Schwaller's doctoral dissertation, currently in progress (Schwaller N.d.).

59. For a discussion of the rare circumstances under which a *república de negros* existed in Mexico, see Landers (2006: 130).

60. Solano (1975: 11) ("porque pocos españoles de honra hay que casan con indias o con negras").

61. Katzew (2004: 46–48, 213n72), who includes the Torquemada quote (cited at the beginning of this chapter). Feijoo claimed that the black birth spots were under an infant's fingernails and also on a boy's genitals; this theory is also affirmed by Alcedo in his 1774 dictionary (1812 [1786–89] Vol. III: 356).

62. McCaa (1984: 477–78); Gutiérrez (1991: 191).

63. Robert Schwaller's research on the evolution of casta terms in the sixteenth century will do much to clarify this (N.d.); he has already found a 1578 usage of "castiza," referring to an orphaned woman named Magdalena Pérez, who married in Atlisco (central Mexico) that year (AGN-*Inquisición* 84, 3: ff. 5–41). I am grateful to Schwaller for his comments on various versions of this chapter.

64. Solano (1975: 9–17); Katzew (2004: 48–51), who quotes Long.

65. Carrera (2003: 48).

66. Carrera (2003: 44–135); Katzew (2004: 1–4). A related development was the increase in royal support for scientific expeditions in Spanish America (see, for example, Safier 2007).

67. Townsend (1997: 55).

68. Aguirre Beltrán (1989 [1946]: 166–72); Katzew (2004: 44).

69. Katzew (2004: 56–61).

70. By hypocrisy I mean that some families who tried to stop a marriage by accusing a suitor of being a mulatto or pardo, were themselves hiding African ancestry—as was revealed, for example, in a marriage dispute case in Campeche in 1787 (AGN-*Civil* 1913, 1). The origins of the Royal Pragmatic seem to have been an effort by Charles III to control his brother's marriage choice, and perhaps to curb some of the church's power; on the law in New Spain, see Gutiérrez (1991: 315–18), Seed (1988: 200–25), and Katzew (2004: 52–53).

71. Among the many works that could be cited here, see McCaa, Schwartz, and Grubessich (1979), Seed (1982), McCaa (1984), Altman (1991), Cope (1994), Castleman (1998), Carrera (2003), Lewis (2003), and Katzew (2004).

72. Silverblatt (2004: 16).

73. Katzew (2004: 202).

74. AGI-*Indiferente* 2075, 83, 1: f. 5r ("... un mulato esclavo criollo de edad de diez y seis años con una señal de herida sobrel arrodilla del muslo yzquierdo que viene de arriva avaxo, y otra en la mano yzquierda en el naçimiento, del dedo pulgar, y un negro llamado Lor.⁰ de edad de veynte y cinco aõ bien barbado, con un lunar muy grande en medio de la frente ...").

75. AGI-*Contratación* 5422, 29, 1: f. 2v ("... el dho d. Fran.co es mediano de querpo moreno rostro delgado de hasta quarenta años y el dho fran.co moreno es pequeño de querpo frente grande y esquinado de hasta çinq.ta y çinco años ...").

76. AGI-*Contratación* 5425, 1, 1: f. 4r ("... el dho Ju.o Criollo sera de pres.te de hedad de diez y ocho a.s poco mas o menos mediana estatura y thiene en la mexilla del rostro al lado der.o un lunar negro, y el dho Fran.co ant.o sera de hedad de quarenta a.s poco mas o m.s alto de cuerpo y la varva le pinta en blanco ...").

77. AGI-*Contratación* 5459, 214, 1: ff. 1r, 4v.

78. AGI-*Contratación* 5465, 2, 77: f. 1r ("... negro atezado de hedad de veinte y tres a.s Christiano y libre de esclavitud ..."). These cases from the Casa de Contratación are also tabulated in Appendix C. A third use of *negro* atezado in the docu-

mentation listed in Appendix C is in reference to Antonio de Arcos, who was freed in Havana in 1762 (*Contratación* 5506, 2, 7: f. 19r).

79. AGI-*Contratación* 5470, 1, 23, 1: f. 13r (". . . un negro esclavo cuio llamado Agustín de Leira de hasta catorce años de mediana estatura braco señales de yierro en el lado drõ en la mediania de la oreja . . .").

80. AGI-*Contratación* 5459, 214, 1: ff. 1r, 4v (". . . el carrillo drõ aradado y una sicatris en la frentte . . .").

81. E.g., AGI-*México* 3048, various folios.

82. AGI-*Contratación* 5425, 1, 1: f. 4r (". . . un viejo Christiano . . . ni macula de Moros Judios ni penitençiados por El Sancto Oficio de la Ynquisiçion . . .").

83. AGI-*México* 3014: ff. 685–98 (quote on f. 687v).

84. Taken from a 1699 example: ". . . de los linaxes proibidos a pasar a las yndiass . . ." (AGI-*Contratación* 5459, 214, 1: f. 3r).

85. AGI-*Contratación* 5470, 1, 23, 1: f. 15r (". . . mediana estatura pelo proprio negro crespo y hoyoso de viruelas y que no es, ni desciende de aquellas personas a quienes esta prohuivido pasaje a los reynos de las Yn.as . . .").

86. AGI-*Contratación* 5506, 2, 7 (f. 5r: "limpieza de sangre"; f. 17r: "negros libres naturales de las Indias.").

87. AGI-*Contratación* 5524, 4, 29, 1 (f. 1v: "los que tienen prohibicion para pasar a mis Dominios de la America"; f. 1r: "los dos blancos, y el otro Negro.").

88. Both in the general sense of the development of racist ideologies in the Western world, and specifically in Yucatan, where an anti-Maya discourse evolved in mid-century, spurred on by the Caste War (Rugeley 1996: 84–90; Gabbert 2004: 64–73). For evidence of anti-black racism in nineteenth-century Yucatan, see Andrade and Máas Collí (1990: 348–79); Rugeley (2001: 219).

89. DHY, III, 95–118. Farriss (1984: 109) cites similar concerns expressed by Yucatan's bishops.

90. The Afro-Yucatecan conquistador introduced in Chapter One was referred to in a 1578 royal edict as "Sebastian de Toral negro y horro" (AGI-*México* 2999, 2, 1: f. 187r). "Power" reference from 1832 (AGN-*Bienes Nacionales* 28, 65).

91. The ambiguous status of free-colored people living in a slave society was characterized as "unappropriated" by Jerome Handler in his study of "freedmen" in colonial Barbados, borrowing it from a British governor of the island who wrote in 1802 that he could not "bring himself to call free" blacks and coloreds who were not slaves; "I think unappropriated would be a more proper denomination for them, for though not the property of other individuals they do not enjoy the shadow of any civil right" (Handler 1974: xiv). A more recent study of another Caribbean colony, the East End of St. John in the eighteenth and nineteenth centuries, suggested that the black and colored residents of the East End of the island made a transition from a society of slaves and unappropriated free coloreds to a society of "appropriated" people, in which free coloreds and even black slaves enjoyed "recognized ownership rights and considerable freedom of mobility" (Armstrong 2003: 8). Also see Klein (1986: 217–41).

92. To paraphrase a point made in Cope (1994: 5).

93. See Chapter Five; also Hunt (1974: 95).

94. AGI-*Contaduría* 920, 1: f. 320v ("En lo qᵉ toca a veçindad de españoles mestisos y mulattos, solo uno tengo en dho, mi parttido, certifico, qᵉ este se tiene pʳ español qᵉ lo sea, no por qᵉ Jusgo qᵉ tiene de ttodas quatro calidades, llamase Pedro

de Mena, vive en una millpa en rancho suyo, llamado *yok>onot*.") (also partially quoted by Farriss 1984: 109, who inexplicably changes "mulattos" to "pardos").

95. AGN-*Inquisición* 519, 3: ff. 301–98.

96. Quoted by Cole (2004: 75).

97. AGI-*México* 1035; Solano (1975: 60).

98. Tannebaum (1946: 66–67); Olwell (1998: 62–81); Brion Davis (2003: 30).

99. AME; also see Appendix B. Not only in colony-wide censuses, but in other types of documents too it became less common in the final decades of the colonial period for individuals to be listed with casta designations. For example, Ticul's *Libro de Posito* of 1804 lists the corn deposits by the named heads of households—all "the Spaniards, Indians, Mulattoes, and Blacks of the town"—but these groups are not subsequently identified in the list of names. The ten most prominent Spaniards start the list and are identifiable by their "dons" and other titles, while Mayas are clearly identifiable by their native patronyms; in between are the remaining Spaniards, mestizos, and Afro-Yucatecans, identifiable to their peers, no doubt, but not to us (AGEY-Ticul [Fondo Municipios] 1, 1).

100. CAIHY-CCA 145: f. 54r.

101. AGI-*Contaduría* 920, 1 (Congo on f. 209r, Aguirre on f. 307r).

102. AGI-*Contratación*, various, all cited in Appendix C. Also evidenced in the sources on Sebastián Toral (AGI-*México* 2999; AGN-*General de Parte* 2, 489; etc.—see Chapter One for full citations).

103. Bernand (2000: 96).

104. AGAY-*Jesús*, Libros de Bautismos Vols. 1–6; "morena" was used in 1737, and "moreno mulato" (for the child of a mulatto and a mestiza) in 1761. For a discussion of the ideological significance of social categories used in a parish census in Brazil during the age of slavery, see Barickman (2003).

105. Later in the nineteenth century "mestizo" continued to expand to encompass Mayas, dividing the inhabitants of the Mexican states of Yucatan and Campeche into *gente de vestido* [people in contemporary dress, also called *yucateco* and *blanco*] and those who wore traje de mestizo (also called simply "mestizo," although "indio" continued to be used as a pejorative and a reference to the Maya rebels of 1847–1901) (Gabbert 2004: 63–64, 115–17).

106. AGN-*Inquisición* 519, 3: ff. 302r, 303r, 324r, 334v–35r, 341r, 349r. *Cocho* was used in colonial Mexico (but not in Yucatan, based on all the examples I have seen) as an abbreviation of *cocido* ["cooked"]; the original phrase appears in AGI sources from sixteenth-century Andalucia as *de color membrillo cocido* ["of the color of cooked quince"] abbreviated to *de color membrillo cocho* or simply *de color cocho* (Leo Garofalo and Michael Francis, personal communications). When used to refer to someone's skin color, it was only applied to mulattoes, and indicated a pale somewhat-yellowish brown or beige tone; the sources compiled in Stephens (1999: 77) indicate usage solely in central Mexico and Michoacán, to mean mulato pardo (i.e., Afro-mestizo). Examples I have seen (thanks to Jason Frederick, who shared this document with me) include LLIU, Latin American MSS, Mexico, March 11, 1779, sale of a mulatto slave in Puebla, "de color cocho," on f. 1r.

107. AGI-*Contaduría* 920, 1; *México* 1035.

108. AGAY-*Jesús*, Libros de Bautismos Vols. 2–6.

109. AGAY-*Jesús*, Libros de Bautismos Vol. 1: ff. 33v, 76r.

110. In Aguilar's day, Afro-Yucatecans were too few in number to have their own cofradía; they were allowed to participate in Maya ones (BL, Egerton 1791, Cárdenas y Valencia manuscript [1639]: f. 48r). On seventeenth-century Valladolid, see Hunt (1974: 37–39, 246, 269, 366); on the town in the early nineteenth century, see Smith (1997).

111. AGN-*General de Parte* 2, 489: f. 97.

CHAPTER FOUR

1. AGI-*Escribanía* 316b, 75: f. 2r.

2. AGEY-*Varios* 1, 27: f. 1.

3. *Periodico Constitucional*, April 9, 1821: p. 4; accessed through the UTA microfilm collection; for the same advertisement in *El Constitucionalista*, see Baquiero Anduze (1983 [1937]: 38).

4. CAIHY-CCA #82, 6 (record of 1787 construction costs by Juan Antonio Elizalde, manuscript of 1792): quote from f. 3r.

5. For example, the stonemasons and laborers who built the Escamela bridge in 1791–92 daily earned five *reales* and two and a half reales, respectively, although laborers on the Mexico City–Toluca road in 1793–95 periodically had wages cut to two reales or to one and a half reales; Castleman (1998: 68, 107–13).

6. CAIHY-CCA #82, 6: quote from f. 5r. Castleman (1998: 85) estimates that intermittent working produced an average income for a *camino real* road and bridge day laborer of 0.7 reales per day, estimated to be the bare minimum income needed to survive in late eighteenth century Mexico.

7. CAIHY-CCA #82, 6: quote from f. 6v.

8. The Chasarretta marriages are recorded in AGAY, Sagrario, *Libros de Matrimonios* Vol. 4: ff. 65r and 118v. Don Domingo also appears as godfather to an African slave bought by Yucatec Governor Meneses and baptized Antonio in 1711, and a doña Thomasa de Chasarretta is godmother to a *parda* child baptized in 1741 (AGAY, Jesús María, *Libros de Bautismos* Vol. 1: f. 16v; Vol. 2: f. 114v).

9. Solís Robleda (2003: 74–75).

10. For example, see the role played by the black and mulatto slaves of a Spanish woman who owned an *obraje* in seventeenth-century Quito (Gauderman 2003: 73–74); for examples from Santiago de Guatemala, see Herrera (2000: 258–63).

11. AGI-*México* 2999; AGI-*Justicia* 300, 2: f. 420v, 430r, and repeated by subsequent witnesses.

12. Hunt (1974: 41); Herrera (2000: 259) observes that the same was true in Santiago de Guatemala.

13. Sales of 1678–1829, 64 cases (see Table 2.1 in Chapter Two for details and sources); baptisms of 1710–89, 663 cases (see various tables and discussion of these AGAY sources, most obviously in Tables E.1 and E.2 in Appendix E).

14. Note that the purpose of Table 4.1 is to show that domestic service and militia pay offered a small but better income than most other occupations. There is no comparison made between Afro-Yucatecan incomes and the incomes of others, as occupation, not casta category, determined salary: a Maya man also earned one to two pesos for *tanda* labor; a Maya or mestiza domestic servant was paid the same as a mulatta; and *all* militia infantrymen received eight pesos a month.

15. AGI-*México* 1035 (discussed further in this chapter; see Tables 4.2–4.5; also see Solano 1975).

16. Jones (1998: 185). The ambassadors came from the Itza Maya kingdom in the Petén in northern Guatemala; Ursúa organized a conquest campaign that destroyed the kingdom two years later, the definitive study of which is Jones (1998).

17. AGN-*Criminal* 301, 1: ff. 5–6v. I am grateful to Mark Lentz for finding this document and photocopying it for me (also see Lentz n.d.).

18. AGEY-*Varios* 1, 27: f. 1 (transcribed and translated in full in Appendix A).

19. Campos García (2005: 28–29), using AGS-*Secretaría de Guerra* 7299, 4 (Campeche, 1790) and 6 (Merida, 1789); also see Table 5.4 in the next chapter.

20. AGEY-*Criminal* 2, 11 (quote from f. 7v; case also discussed in Chapter Six).

21. AGI-*México* 1035.

22. See note 18.

23. AHDC, *Libro* 1285 (Burials): f. 3v.

24. AGI-*México* 1035 (also see Tables 4.3–4.5); Hunt (1974: 87–90). About a fifth of the tailors in early eighteenth-century San Felipe (Chihuahua) were mulattoes (Martin 1996: 44). Regarding the 1790 shoemakers and tailors, see note 19.

25. Hunt (1974: 88); CAIHY-CCA #82, 6. A major spate of road construction, the largest in Yucatan's colonial history, was taking place when the budget report on the Potoktok Bridge was submitted in 1792; while he was governor from 1791 until his assassination two years later, Lucas de Gálvez rebuilt major portions of roads leaving Merida toward Izamal and Campeche and into the Sierra (Pérez Galaz 1942: 5), projects viewed as so stimulating to commerce that they were continued under Gálvez's successors, Govs. O'Neil and Pérez (Patch 1993: 2067). The crown approved the purchase of over two tons of gunpowder to begin these roadworks in 1788 (when Gálvez arrived as intendant, prior to acquiring the governorship), and it is reasonable to imagine that Joaquín Chasarretta and Joseph María had all the back-breaking, exploitation-wage work they wanted in the 1790s. On the early colonial use of Maya workers to build roads, see Solís Robleda (2003: 89–95).

26. AGI-*Escribanía* various *legajos* between 300 and 330, especially 305a; 315b; 316b; and 318a; *México* 1009; 1035; 1036; AGN-*Caminos y Calzadas* 4, 5–6. For an argument that Afro-Guatemalans played a major role in construction projects in that colony, see Markman (1966). For details on pardo-militia stoneworkers, see Table 5.4 in the next chapter (and previous note 19).

27. AGI-*Escribanía* 315b, 31: ff. 10–13.

28. AGI-*Escribanía* 316b, 75: f. 2. The complaint is presented in full transcription and translation in Appendix A. Also see Solís Robleda (2003: 56–60) on the use of Maya labor in the citadel's construction.

29. AGN-*Marina* 156, 5: ff. 188v–89.

30. For an example of a slave having a native servant in seventeenth-century Quito, see Gauderman (2003: 89).

31. Baquiero Anduze (1983 [1937]: 38).

32. Lockhart (1994: 110–11) makes this point with respect to sixteenth-century Lima being less specialized than, say, Córdoba in Spain; Lima, of course, was more specialized than Merida in Yucatan.

33. Hunt (1974: 89).

34. Hunt (1974: 89). On San Cristóbal as a Maya cah in Merida, see Restall (1997: 32–36).

35. This is perhaps not surprising, as even among Spaniards only the elite owned slaves (see Chapter Two).

36. For Guatemalan and Peruvian examples, see Herrera (2000: 262) and Lockhart (1994: 124, 208), respectively.

37. AGI-*México* 1035 (also see Tables 4.3 and 4.4); Hunt (1974: 88–90).

38. Patch (2002: 170).

39. AGI-*México* 1035 (also see Tables 4.3 and 4.4); Solano (1975: 54, 71).

40. For the geographical reasons for this failure, see Patch (1993: 15–17).

41. See Montejo's will, transcribed in Rubio Mañé (1941: 45–53) (also cited by Hunt 1974: 32–33); Montejo was the eldest son of the conquistador don Francisco de Montejo, the younger, and was owner of the Montejo Palace in Merida from 1585 to 1603.

42. Hunt (1974: 73, 387); Carvajal's will is in ANEY, Baeza (UTA roll 1), dated August 13, 1692. For comparable examples of black slaves on Spanish estates in Morelos, see Martin (1985: 38).

43. This was *Haemotoxylon campecheanum,* called "*eek*" ["black"] by the Mayas, logwood or "Campeachy logwood" by the English, and "*palo de tinte*" by the Spaniards. Dampier (1699: 15–19); Contreras Sánchez (1990); Quezada (2001: 102–3).

44. Hunt (1974: 40–42).

45. Hunt (1974: 45).

46. ANEY Baeza (March 1690; March 1695; April–June 1690 and July 1691) (UTA roll 1); Hunt (1974: 533–35).

47. AGI-*Contratación* 5348, 67, 1: f. 2v ("... poco barbado con una señal de herida bajo el ojo derecho pequeño menudo de rostro ...").

48. AGI-*México* 307, 3: 14v, 16r–v ("... con tantta mano ... tenia cassas de piedra donde recogia la zera para blanquearla ... obligando a los yndios a acarrear el agua de la Noria para ello, sin dexarse la llevar a sus cassas no solo sustentandose con esto ... y es el que da arbitrios a los jueces para dhos trattos, hallandose los dhos yndios en tantas afflicciones y vexaciones sin recurso por no tenerlo en el encom^ro, ni en el Ministro de temor que no les destruya con alguna causa el Gov^or, ni el deffensor g^l por ser Puesto y nombrado por el sussodho .."). Caso Barrera (2002: 61) mentions Melchor de Segovia, but her citation does not include legajo or folio numbers, so I am most grateful to Michel Oudijk, who located the relevant folios and transcribed part of the Melchor passage, enabling me to work with this source months before the photocopies arrived.

49. AGI-*Contratación* 5470, 1, 23.

50. AGI-*Contaduría* 920; *México* 1035; Hunt (1974: 533).

51. See Tables B2 and B3 in Appendix B, created from census documents in AME (and published in Dumond and Dumond 1982).

52. AGI-*México* 3042, quote from f. 53v (the document is the *residencia* or report on the governorship of don José Merino y Cevallos); Aguirre Beltrán (1989: 92); Patch (1993: 142–43, 175–78, 205).

53. AGEY-*Varios* 1, 27: f. 1; also see Appendix A.

54. Patch (1985: 34); Nichols (2003: 167–74). For background on the Pech family, see Restall (2001a). The significance of the availability of Maya workers is illustrated by the reverse situation in central Mexico, where textile mill owners were forced to invest in black slaves, despite the industry's low profit margins (Proctor 2003a: 43).

55. For an example of this from San Felipe (Chihuaua), see Martin (1996: 165).

56. Hunt (1974: 410); ANEY, various (UTA rolls 1–45).

57. Nahua and other Mesoamerican auxiliaries from the third invasion of Yucatan were settled primarily in Merida's Maya neighborhoods or cah-barrios of Santiago and San Cristóbal, where they gradually became absorbed into the local Maya population; AGI-*México* 100, 4, 7 is a 1576 report on these "indios mexicanos." Also see Chuchiak (2007).

58. All four examples in ANEY, Baeza (UTA roll 1) (there are no folio numbers in this volume, but two sitio examples are from June and January 1690, the Lope purchase is from 1689, and Muñóz's will is dated July 5, 1692); also summarized by Hunt (1974: 411–13, 415, 427). The 1688 matrícula is in AGI-*Contaduría* 920, 1 (Temax entry is f. 334; Hunt's summary of the Temax census is a little different from mine); a dozen years later, the mix of nineteen Spaniards, mestizos, and free coloreds had become twenty-six "blancos" and twenty-nine mestizos (AGI-*México* 1035; also see Table 3.2 in the previous chapter).

59. AGI-*Contaduría* 920, 1: f. 320r (the passage is quoted in full in the previous chapter).

60. ANEY, Baeza (UTA roll 1); Hunt (1974: 414).

61. AGI-*México* 1035; Solano (1975: 55, 58).

62. Several male relatives of Isabel Toquero (a parda bigamist discussed at length in Chapter Six) were peddlers in the Tizimin area around the turn of the eigheenth century (AGN-*Inquisición* 519, 3: ff. 301–98; esp. see Table 6.2 in Chapter Six).

63. Hunt (1974: 515–36); AGI-*México* 1035 ("su oficio es tratar y contratar con los indios generos de Castilla"); Solano (1975: 45).

64. ANEY, Baeza (UTA roll 1) (March 14, July 31, and November 5, 1691); Hunt (1974: 530–31).

65. AGEY-*Criminal* 1, 7; 1, 9; and 1, 10. For further discussion of the criminal cases of this period, and the Afro-Yucatecan roles in them, see Chapter Six.

66. Linebaugh and Rediker (2000: 165–66).

67. Exquemelin (1969 [1678]: 78–79, 82–83, 89–118).

68. AGI-*México* 363, 3, 6, nos. 2 and 3.

69. AGI-*México* 360; AGN-*Reales Cedulas (Originales)* 2, 1, 23: f. 40 (earlier quote); Landers (1997: 89); Lane (1998: 71, 123); Campos García (2005: 21). An earlier version of this brief summary of the Diegos el Mulato was in Restall (2000b: 201).

70. Pérez-Mallaína (1998: 38–40, 115, 166–67, 172–74, 213–15); Linebaugh and Rediker (2000: 162–73); Bolster (2002).

71. AGI-*México* 361: ff. 14–17; Hunt (1974: 325–28); González Muñóz and Martínez Ortega (1989: 100, 106–9).

72. For example, *bongos* were used as mortgage property in late colonial Campeche (AGEC-*Registro Público de la Propriedad* 2, 1–4).

73. The affair is recounted by Molina Solís (1904–13), but I have here relied on the summary by Hunt (1974: 269).

74. Farriss (1984: 522n43), from a report in the Franciscan archives in BN (FF 55/1141).

75. Rivas (2003: 254–55).

76. BL Add 17569: ff. 1–37.

77. AGN-*Criminal* 335, 1, 56: f. 39r ("El Pueblo de Chikin>onot, se ha compuesto siempre de Yndios, y unos sinquenta vessinos de otras castas, en la mayor

parte mulatos, tan rusticos, y pussilanimes como los mismos Yndios, cuya lengua hablan unicamente; No acostumbran salir a parte alguna de la Prov.ª y pasar una vida miserable con el escaso lucro de una milpa corta de maiz, qu trabajan pr su propria mano"). I am grateful to Mark Lentz for drawing my attention to this document and photocopying it for me.

78. AGI-*Contaduría* 920, 1: f. 59. Tahmuy and its head town of Yaxcaba appear to be missing from the 1700 census (AGI-*México* 1035), so I could not see how Nobelo was identified in the census of a dozen years later.

79. In the 1700 matrícula (AGI-*México* 1035), 38% of Afro-Yucatecan men had Maya wives (48% had either mestiza or Maya wives); in smaller villages, most had Maya wives. See Chapter Seven for a full presentation of marriage patterns in the matrícula, discussed in the larger context of Afro-Yucatecan marriage patterns in mid-to-late colonial times.

80. Christensen and Restall (2008) on the 1748 Ixil wills; Restall (1995; 1997: 349–63) on the 1765-68 Ixil wills.

81. AGI-*México* 1035; Solano (1975: 47); "... no tiene mas hacienda que una casa de paja, que asi son todas las de los vecinos."

82. AGI-*México* 1035 (Palomino; 1700 census); AGN-*Inquisición* 1164: ff. 211–319 (Zavala; discussed in more detail in Chapter Six).

83. AGN-*Inquisición* 620, various *expedientes*.

84. Restall (1997: 124–30, 178–79).

85. According to census data; see the tables in Appendix B.

86. AGI-*Estado* 24, 53 (duplicated as 25, 74); AGEY-*Militar* 1, 13 and 1, 22; AGEY Poder Ejecutivo-*Gobernación*, p. 104; AGEY Poder Ejecutivo-*Censos y Padrones*, pp. 3, 27; Victoria Ojeda and Canto Alcocer (2001; 2006); Kepecs (1999); Vinson (2001a: 216–19); Restall (2005: 1–4). The history of San Fernando Ake is further discussed in Chapter Six.

87. AGI-*Contaduría* 920, 1: ff. 72–73r; BL Add 17569: f. 11v.

88. See Appendix B; census records in AME; Dumond and Dumond (1982: 3–304; the Kikil data is on 131–35, 393–95).

89. Andrews and Robles Castellanos (2002: 2; 2003: 4, 37, 97–99, 102–3, 111–12).

90. Father Cayetano Cattaneo, writing in 1730; Tannebaum (1946: 10).

CHAPTER FIVE

1. AGEY-*Varios* 1, 27: f. 1 (Espinola's petition is reproduced in full in Appendix A).

2. Campos García (2005: 101) (Quintana's phrase is "tan negros en el color de sus personas, como blancos y tersos en la virtud de sus almas").

3. AGI-*Estado* 41, 45: ff. 1–2 (quote from f. 1r: "... a la solicitud de que los honrados Militares de la Division de Pardos, de esta Ciudad, y la de Campeche, y los que han servido antes en ella con puntualidad, sean colocados en la clase de Cuidadanos con todos sus derechos, y distinciones ...").

4. AHAY-*Asuntos Terminados* 11, 352, quoted by Campos García (2005: 51) (whose transcription is: "como estoy cierta que es nieto de un capitán de pardos que estuvo en el pueblo de Muna, resulta que él es pardo aunque haya servido en la milicia blanca, lo cual saben todos porque conocieron a su abuelo y a su madre cuya entrania [sic] es bien conocida en dicho pueblo de Muna por parda").

5. AGI-*México* 363, 3, 5, 1: f. 1r.

6. AGI-*México* 363, 3, 5, 1; ANEY, Baeza, 1689–92 (UTA roll 1); Hunt (1974: 414, 506); Molina Solís (1904–13, III: 315). The "don" prefix, a peer-designated status marker, was reserved for Spanish nobility; although its importance became diluted during colonial times as its usage expanded, and it was also adopted by Mayas (assigned only to *indios hidalgos*, *batabob*, and former *batabob*; Restall 1997: 46, 91), I have yet to find an instance of its application to someone of African descent, save in the case of late colonial high-ranking pardo militia officers or where an Afro-Yucatecan had "passed" as a Spaniard.

7. AGN-*Inquisición* 626, 7: ff. 160–82 ("el guebo colgado . . . en su corredor a la puerta de su sala . . . un muchacho le tiro con una piedra, y lo deribo, y estaba seco la mitad"); ff. 163v, 171r.

8. On the use of eggs in these rituals by Maya folk healers in Yucatan today, see Love (2004: 1–3, 10–15, 21–28).

9. Chuchiak (2007) on Montejo's Mesoamerican allies; Restall (1998a: esp. Chap. 3) on Paxbolon (also see Scholes and Roys 1948) and Maya conquistadors; AGI-*México* 140 (Chan's 1601 *probanza*); AGI-*Patronato* 56, 4, 2 (1610 *probanza* of Juan de Contreras Durán, details some Maya militia campaigns); AGI-*Patronato* 80, 1, 1 (1617 probanza of Alonso Sánchez de Aguilar likewise mentions such campaigns); AGI-*Escribanía* 317b and *México* 307 (on the 1668 Sahcabchén uprising, including attempts by Spaniards to use Maya militias against refugees and rebels); Caso Barrera (2002: 184–204) on Sahcabchén; Jones (1998: 45–53, 134–44, 253–64) on Yucatec Mayas in the Itza wars.

10. Vinson and Restall (2005: 17–25); also see Vinson (2001a: 7–45; 2001b: 61–68). Note that a small number of black men, both free and enslaved, were assigned to pardo militia companies, but—in Yucatan at least—there was never such a thing as an exclusively *negro* militia company.

11. On Drake's campaign, see Lane (1998: 49–57). The bastion construction begun in Campeche in 1607 might have been started a decade earlier had Drake not spared the town.

12. BL, Egerton 1791, Cárdenas y Valencia MS (1639): ff. 41v–42r, 48v–49r; Victoria Ojeda (1995: 41–48, 155); Hunt (1974: 510). Spaniards in the colony certainly seemed to be well armed. For example, Spaniards crossing from Spain to Yucatan declared various weapons on their travel permits; take the case of Melchor Pacheco, who sailed the Atlantic in 1599 with a black slave named Anton, under a license that included two swords, two *dagas* [daggers], two harquebuses, and a coat of mail (AGI-*Contratación* 5260a, 1, 34, 1: f. 2r).

13. Victoria Ojeda (1995: 48–52).

14. AGI-*México* 1006; 1008; and 1009 (documents dated between 1656 and 1719).

15. Records of the investigation into the revolt are in AGI-*Escribanía* 305a (one document from this *legajo* is published in translation in Restall, Sousa, and Terraciano 2005: Chap. 7).

16. AGI-*Escribanía* 315b contains the lawsuit filed by Maya cabildos on behalf of the stonemasons, carpenters, and other artisans and laborers who built the citadel, including petitions in Maya, dated 1667–70, from dozens of cahob complaining of the governor's failure to pay for materials and labor. These cahob were concentrated in and around Merida, but included villages as far away as Sisal to the north and Oxkutzcab to the south. Additional materials on San Benito's construction and sub-

sequent fall-out are in AGI-*Escribanía* 316b; 318a; and parts of *México* 1009. On Campeche's defenses, see *México* 1006 and 1009 (each legajo is about a thousand folios, covering 1656–1719) and Piña Chan (1977: 39–113).

17. AGI-*Escribanía* 316b, 75: f. 2. The Ramos complaint is included in full in Appendix A. The governor also decreed in 1663 that any "mestizos, *negros*, and mulattoes and others of that calidad" who shirked their duties in the defense of the colony would be fined ten pesos and given "a month of personal service on the construction of the fortifications" of Campeche or Merida (AGI-*México* 1006: f. 341r).

18. García Bernal (1972: 18); Campos García (2005: 87).

19. In 1607, Gov. Luna y Arellano sent 150 men from Merida to Campeche and 50 more to Sisal (according to Molina Solís 1900–10, II: 20–21; cited in Victoria Ojeda 1995: 159); had they all been Spaniards, they would have represented as many as half the adult men in the city (on the possible Spanish population at this time, García Bernal 1978: 152).

20. Campos García (2005: 87) on 1634; AGI-*México* 1006: ff. 73r (on 1662), 339r (on 1663).

21. AGN-*Reales Cedulas* (*Originales*) 76 and 90.

22. AGI-*México* 363, 3, 6, nos. 1–5.

23. AGI-*México* 1006: ff. 72r, 339r; Victoria Ojeda (1995: 177, 188 [the new governor was don Alvaro de Rivaguda Enciso y Luyando], 52 [quote from 1694: "por no ser suficiente la fuerza de la Provincia, y por la falta que hay en ella de españoles"]). AGI-*México* contains long lists of militiamen's names, including pardo militiamen (e.g. ff. 826-30, 846-50).

24. Victoria Ojeda (1995: 53–61), who chose 1717 as a milestone date as it was in that year that major construction was begun on the bastions at Carmen and the trench system north of Merida.

25. BL-MS 17, 569: ff. 38–63 (report); BL-ADD.MS 17, 654 (maps of Yucatan and of Campeche). The maps acquired by the British are copies made in Madrid in 1768 and the report may also be a 1768 copy; royal officials in Spain probably did receive the information (although I am not aware of parallel copies in the Spanish archives). The DCP (a 1766 report to the viceroy, still preserved in Mexico City) suggested that González make his own report (f. 52v).

26. Cook (1769; 1935).

27. AGI-*Uniformes* (*Mapas y Planos*) 101, 1: f.1; AGN-*Indiferente General* 394a; AGS-*Secretaría de Guerra* 7299, 4 and 6; Victoria Ojeda (1995: 201); Campos García (2005: 88-89).

28. Rubio's militia career was as an officer in the city's pardo companies, but such officers were often non-pardos in these late decades, and at the time of his 1794 promotion he is called don Eugenio Rubio (AGS-*Secretaría de Guerra* 7210, 55; I am grateful to Mark Lentz for sharing this document with me).

29. AGI-*Uniformes* (*Mapas y Planos*) 104, 1: f. 1 ("esta masa comun se costea el correaje de ofic.^{s} y tropa"; "Hace cinco años q.^{e} no recive Bestuario este cuerpo, y tiene devengados 22000 p.^{s} conviene probeer esta tropa de sombrero, botin de bramante, y de fornitura cruzada por los ombros por q.^{e} es de mas lucim.^{to} y comodidad: igualm.^{te} como no hay retencion de Masitas p.^{ra} las prendas menores, juzgo muy preciso q.^{e} se les den duplicadas").

30. Discussed in detail in Chapter One (ANEY, Argaiz, 1779–81 [UTA roll 21]; Argaiz, 1782–84 [UTA roll 22]; López Rivas 1975; AGAY-*Jesús, Bautismos* Vol. 5).

On Yucatan's finances and the subsidizing of its defenses in 1786–1823, see Campos García (2004: 23-83).

31. On Revillagigedo's reforms in central Mexico, see Vinson (2001a: 176, 212-15). The use of *blanco* ["white"] as an ethnic or racial term was generally rare in Spanish America, and I have found little use of it in Yucatan other than to denote nonpardo militia units in the eighteenth century. While the officers of blanco companies were probably Spaniards, the rank and file were more likely mestizos.

32. Francisco González's 1801 application for the subinspectorship of Campeche's pardo militia division detailed his military service in the peninsula since graduating as a cadet in 1779, and also cited his father's half-century of service to the crown; AGEY-*Servicios Militares* 1, 8. For evidence of military service as a multigenerational family tradition in eighteenth-century Santo Domingo, see Rivas (2003).

33. AGN-*Reales Cedulas (Originales)* 164, 245/f. 392 (edict of 1796).

34. Campos García (2004: 28–30).

35. Victoria Ojeda (1995: 61–64, 221–22); Campos García (2005: 130).

36. Victoria Ojeda (1995: 129).

37. López de Cogolludo (1688 [1654]: 596, 601; 1957); Jones (1989: 62, 71, 226–27). See this chapter for a brief history of colonial Afro-Bacalar.

38. Victoria Ojeda (1995: 178), citing AGI-*México* 1010.

39. Landers (2005: 58–59).

40. On the commemorated slave: my notes taken in the museum of the Puerta de Tierra, Campeche, 1999. A long series of accounts of the attack and efforts to repel it are in AGI-*México* 363, 3, 6, nos. 1–5.

41. ANEY, Baeza, 1689–92 (UTA roll 1); Hunt (1974: 414, 506).

42. Jones (1998: 144, 162, 229, 259, 260, 267). Pardo militias also participated in the campaigns against rebel and unconquered Mayas in the Sahcabchen region in the 1660s and 1670s (Redondo 1994: 90).

43. AGI-*México* 3050: ff. 22v–23r, 59v; Victoria Ojeda (1995: 198); Patch (2002: 161–62); Campos García (2005: 37).

44. Victoria Ojeda (1995: 196).

45. Victoria Ojeda (1995: 194).

46. Cook (1769). Cook's analysis was mirrored in the anxious Spanish reporting in 1766 of Yucatan's vulnerability and the presence of 141 British vessels at Cayo Cocina (St. George's Cay); DCP: f. 15v; Restall (n.d.).

47. PRO-CO 137/75; Burdon (1931: 127–28); a similar report of 1780 is in PRO-CO 137/77: ff. 95-97.

48. AGMM, *Ultramar, México*, caja 5371; Restall (n.d.).

49. Restall (n.d.); Hall and Pérez Brignoli (2003: 34–37, 142–43).

50. AGI-*México* 3050: fs. 94–184; AGN-*Marina* 156, 5: fs. 178–79; ANEY, Argaiz, 1779–81 [UTA roll 21]; López Rivas 1975. In 1732 the king ordered the governor of Yucatan to release an English ship and its cargo that, along with some African slaves, had been impounded by the provincial authorities (AGN-*Reales Cédulas Originales* 51, 141; Aguirre Beltrán 1989 [1946]: 78).

51. Because Yucatan is so flat and its skies usually clear, lookout towers did not have to be very high for a warning system using flags to be viable; the *vigía* system was in place into the late nineteenth century; Victoria Ojeda (1995: 79–82).

52. AGI-*Contaduría* 920, 1: f. 319.

53. Hunt (1974: 540). By the turn of the eighteenth century it was common for pardo militiamen or other mulattoes to serve as vigías elsewhere in the Spanish colonies; the vigía system created along the Pacific coast of Sonora in the 1730s, for example, was staffed by free-colored militamen (Vinson and Restall 2005: 38).

54. The region, called Chikinchel, included a number of large coastal sites; see Kepecs (1999).

55. Dampier (1699: 11, 13–14).

56. Dampier (1699: 15–16).

57. A 1766 report implied that lookouts were not militiamen, but impoverished minor officials so underpaid that they actually encouraged and fostered coastal smuggling (DCP: f. 23).

58. AGI-*México* 1035; Solano (1975: 37).

59. AGEY-*Varios* 1, 15: f. 1.

60. AGEY-*Varios* 1, 15: f. 2. An example of a pardo captain being referred to with a "don" is Ramón Sandoval in AGEY-*Reales Cédulas* 4, 33. The Santa Clara lookout was Diego León de Salazar (AGI-*México* 1035; Solano 1975: 38).

61. The first royal decision was in 1572, ratified in 1573, with a further cedula issued in 1574 (AGI-*Indiferente* 427, 30: f. 248; CDH, I: 482–83; Vinson 2001a: 133).

62. AGI-*Contratación* 5227, 2, 25: ff. 1–2; *Indiferente General* 1969, 22, 1: f. 404v; *México* 2999, 2: ff. 187–88; CDH, I: 511–12; AGN-*General de Parte* 2, 498: f. 97.

63. Vinson (2001a: 139–40, 143–45); Campos García (2005: 87).

64. DCP: f. 7r.

65. Vinson (2001a: 28, 174–98).

66. Hunt (1974: 506–10).

67. AGEY-*Servicios Militares* 1, 7 (Baltazar) and 8 (Francisco); the folios are not numbered, but the reference to don Juan de Dios González is on the penultimate page of 1, 8 (". . . que sirvio a V. M. mas de cinquenta años con el honor y utilidad del Real Servicio . . ."). For a letter to Governor O'Neill blaming the governor of Bacalar for the 1797 failure, see AGEY-*Militar* 1, 8.

68. Vinson (2001a: 175–97).

69. AGN-*Tributos* 40, 9: ff. 88–5, 149–52; also discussed and cited by Vinson (2001a: 135, 157, 271n106).

70. Vinson (2001a: 214–15).

71. AGEY-*Reales Cédulas* 4, 33; also discussed and cited by Vinson (2001a: 281n37).

72. AGEY-*Militar* 2, 2; Campos García (2005: 92).

73. AGMM, *Ultramar, México*, cajas 5362, 2, 2; and 5373.

74. Campos García (2005: 91–104); Quintana's phrases are "la fidelidad, el patriotismo y la virtud notoria de los apreciables pardos" and "sin otro sueldo ni remuneración que el honor y el placer con que las almas grandes se gozan en servir con fidelidad a su amada patria" (p. 101). In January, 1814, the Bishop weighed in with similar sentiments; AGI-*Estado* 41, 45: ff. 1–2.

75. Campos García (2005: 104–33); ("Todos los habitantes de la Nueva España, sin distinctión alguna de europeos, africanos, ni indios, son ciudadanos de esta monarquía"; p. 123).

76. Kuethe (1971: 117); Hanger (1997: 109–35); Bernand (2000: 121–24) on the pardo militias in late colonial Buenos Aires, and (2001: 153–68) on pardo militia service in Spanish America as a larger phenomenon of social mobility.

77. AGN-*Marina* 156, 5: ff. 172, 182.
78. AGI-*México* 3050: f. 134.
79. AGAY-*Jesús*, Libros de Bautismos Vols. 1–6; also see Chapter Six.
80. Quoted in Lohse (2005: 416-425, 427-430).
81. AGEY-*Reales Cédulas* 1, 45: ff. 1r, 5v; AGN-*Marina* 156, 5: ff. 179–81. Presumably, as in other Spanish colonies, there was an appreciable level of unrecorded short-term flight or absenteeism; Martin (1985: 77, 87, 101) remarks on the high incidence of flight from regional haciendas but only in the early eighteenth century when the sugar industry was depressed and there developed administrative lapses and deterioration.
82. AGI-*Patronato* 66a, 1, 4, 1 (Alonso Rosado's 1570 *probanza*): ff. 1r, 8v, 14v, 17r, 20v, 23r, 26r, 28v, 31v–32r, 35r, 36v, 38v.
83. López de Cogolludo (1957 [1654], I: 273; also cited in Fernández Repetto and Negroe Sierra 1995: 6).
84. Herrera y Tordesillas (1601–15), Dec. VIII: 129, 175. On slave revolts in late colonial North America, see Rucker (2006).
85. On Caribbean and circum-Caribbean maroons, see Borrego Plá (1973); Palmer (1976); Price and Price (1992); Price (1996); Landers (1999: 13, 26, 79–80); Linebaugh and Rediker (2000: 193–98); Boland (2002: 54-58); and McKnight (2003). In another article, Landers (2000) compiled evidence from a variety of archives on circum-Caribbean maroons, finding not a single reference to a Yucatec maroon community.
86. Pérez de la Riva (1996: 57).
87. Brooks (2002: 307–10). A similar pattern emerged on the Franco–Portuguese frontier of northern Amazonia in the eighteenth century (Gomes 2002).
88. Gage (1958 [1648]: 195–96; also cited in Lutz and Restall 2005: 211); Boland (2002: 54-58).
89. AGEY-*Gobernación* (Poder Ejecutivo) 2, 58: f. 1.
90. Examples of Spanish records are AGN-*Marina* 156, 5: ff. 172, 182, and AGI-*México* 3050: f. 134–81 (both discussed in this chapter). There may have been an early colonial maroon settlement on the Isla del Carmen or somewhere else in the Laguna de Términos, which was about as far from Spanish Yucatan as was Belize (Redondo 1994: 132–33). But Afro-Yucatecan refugees found by British loggers in the Laguna would surely have enslaved them, as they would have done to black refugees in Belize.
91. PRO-A 1/239; in Burdon (1931: 124).
92. AGI-*Estado* 35, 46 (Basset quotes from 3: f. 1r; 11: f. 1v). I am grateful to Mark Lentz for copying this item for me.
93. PRO-CO in Burdon (1931: 109, 111, 114, 117–19, 124); Bolland (1997; 2002: 54–58).
94. Andrews and Robles Castellanos (2002: 2; reiterated in 2003: 4, 97, 111).
95. AGI-*Estado* 24, 53 (duplicated as 25, 74); AGEY-*Militar* 1, 13 and 1, 22; AGEY Poder Ejecutivo-*Gobernación*, p. 104; AGEY Poder Ejecutivo-*Censos y Padrones*, pp. 3, 27; Kepecs (1999); Victoria Ojeda and Canto Alcocer (2001; 2006); Vinson (2001a: 216–19); Restall (2005: 1–4).
96. Andrews and Robles Castellanos (2002; 2003).
97. AGI-*México* 360; AGN-*Reales Cedulas* (*Originales*) 2, 1, 23/f. 40 (from where I have taken and translated the quote); López de Cogolludo (1688 [1654]: 596, 601, 658; 1957); Jones (1989: 226–27).

98. AGEY-*Criminal* 1, 11a.

99. AHN-*Consejos de Indias* 20.745, 2: ff. 113–14, 166–67, 172; 20.744, 1: ff. 99–111; 20.746, 1: ff. 76–124.

100. AGEY-*Criminal*, various from 1, 2–3, 4 (see Table 7.1 in Chapter Seven).

101. Also known as Yanga, after its West African founder; Palmer (1976: 124–31); Sánchez de Anda (1998); Vincent (2001: 243–46).

102. The phrase used in Spanish is *cimarronaje cotidiana*; for example, Lienhard (2003).

103. Morgan (1998: 56–57, 151–54); Berlin (2003: 66).

104. I have found no references to branding as punishment in Yucatan, and only royal slaves seem to have been given owner brands (a YR symbol, Y for Yucatan and R for Rey), burned onto the arm or shoulder, not face (ANEY, Argaiz, 1779–81 [UTA roll 21]; López Rivas 1975). On Peru and Guatemala, see Bowser (1974: 83–84) and Herrera (2000: 255–56). The latter found only one instance of severe corporal punishment meted out to a slave in Guatemala; condemned for thievery, the slave was branded on the face and one ear was cut off. Africans were also punished this way in the British colonies (Tannebaum 1946: 96), but I have only found one record of this punishment being carried out in Yucatan, and this was against Mayas, and then solely in the wake of the 1761 Cisteil "revolt" (AGI-*México* 3050, e.g. ff. 72–75, 906–18). Of course, Africans were subject to far greater cruelties than the loss of an ear under circumstances of potential or actual group revolt, most typically during the Middle Passage or on plantations (on Muslim slaves and rebellion, see Diouf 1998: 145–63; on the rare case of a full-scale uprising of urban slaves, see Reis 1993 on the 1835 Bahia revolt; and Palmer 1976 on revolts and slave conspiracies in early Mexico City).

105. AGEY-*Criminal* 1, 11a. For sixteenth-century Peruvian examples, see Lockhart (1994: 212–14). For examples of slaves in Cuba attempting in vain to melt into free society (during the same decade as the Marcín escape in Yucatan), see Klein (1967: 161).

106. Tannebaum 1946: 53–62. On manumission in late colonial Buenos Aires, see Johnson (1979; n.d.); Bernand (2000: 101–2); Mallo (2001).

107. ANEY, Baeza (UTA roll 1) (volume's folio numbers lost to page damage; these documents are dated September 16, 1691; June 15, 1692; and July 21, 1692; all are summarized in Hunt 1974: 531–32).

108. As Proctor (2006: 313–17, 324–27) observes in the Mexican case; also see Owensby (2005). On Buenos Aires, see Johnson (n.d.).

109. In the decade after Spain acquired Louisiana in 1769, slaveholders registered 320 deeds of manumission in the New Orleans courthouse, many times more than in the previous half-century of French rule, whose *Code Noir* strongly discouraged manumission. See Tannebaum (1946: 65–74); Hanger (1997: 26–33); Berlin (2003: 8–9, 42–43, 93–95, 142). Morgan (1998: 11) suggests that the Spanish American experience of some blacks in the seventeenth-century Chesapeake explains their insistence on manumission as a legal right. Gómez Danés (1996: 37–39) found 110 slave sales and 11 letters of freedom in the records from eighteenth-century Nuevo León, a balance comparable to that of Yucatan.

110. ANEY, Baeza, 1689–92 (UTA roll 1); Hunt (1974: 534–35); ANEY cases summarized but uncited in Peón Ancona (1985: 118–19).

111. ANEY, Montero, 1729–35 (UTA roll 3): ff. 332v–33.

112. ANEY, Argaiz, 1777 (UTA roll 20): f. 175.

113. AGI-*Contratación* 5506, 2, 7, 1: f. 19r; 5524, 4, 29, 1: f. 7r; AGAY-*Jesús*, Libros de Bautismos Vol. 5: f. 117r. Lousel was vicar general 1776–80 and Castillo y Sucre held the post 1780–95; after the bishop, vicar general was the highest ranking ecclesiastical official in the colony (Chuchiak 2000: 108).

114. ANEY, Zavala, 1767 (UTA roll 15): f. 475.

115. AGAY-*Jesús*, Libro de Bautismos Vol. 2: ff. 183v–84r.

116. Note that the gender balance of slaves in Yucatan, while subject to fluctuations as shown here, is generally even. With respect to other colonies: studies of slaves in Mexico City through to about 1655 show that about 44% were female (Velázquez Guitérrez 2001: 215).

117. On the history of the law of refuge in Spanish Florida, whose developments were central to the law's promulgation and abrogation, see Landers (1999: 25, 28, 76, 79).

118. AGAY-*Jesús*, Libro de Bautismos Vol. 6: ff. 94v, 102v.

119. ANEY, Baeza, 1689–92 (UTA roll 1); Hunt (1974: 535–36); AGEY-*Varios* 1, 27: f. 1 (Espinola's petition is reproduced in full in Appendix A).

120. AGEY-*Justicia* (Poder Ejecutivo) 2, 20: f. 4v.

121. On Louisiana, Hall (1992: 239–40, 258–60); Hanger (1997: 243–63). Tannebaum (1946: 61) also makes this point with reference to Cuba and, to a lesser extent, Brazil.

122. AGN-*Marina* 156, 5: ff. 172–95. The details of the law of refuge were further debated in 1802 between Yucatan's Governor Pérez and Belize's Superintendent Basset in the dispute over escaped slaves and Afro-Belizean soldiers discussed above; Basset argued, in vain, that since 1790, Spanish officials were obliged to return slaves, not give them refuge (AGI-*Estado* 35, 46).

123. AGN-*Marina* 156, 5: ff. 196–210.

124. AGN-*Inquisición* 1131, 2, ff. 80–110. This case was first discussed in Restall (2001b) and is also the foundation for Restall (2006).

125. On Hunucmá, see Patch (1993: 116, 145–47, 233–35) and Restall (1997: 15). On the prominence of the Bolios in the colony, beginning with Manuel's namesake, the colonel of Yucatan's militias, Maestre de Campo don Manuel Bolio Ojeda y Guzmán, who married his way into the Yucatec aristocracy, see García Bernal (1978: 388, 472); Martínez Ortega (1993: 137–38, 290–91, 301); and Patch (1993: 84, 126, 191, 217–18). The marriage records of the Maestre de Campo don Manuel and of his father, Santiago de Bollio [sic], a Genoese merchant who settled in Yucatan and married almost as well as his son later did, are in AGAY-*Sagrario*, Libros de Matrimonios Vol. 3: f. 59v (Santiago's, 1660), Vol. 5: f. 132r (Manuel's second, 1710). On some legal troubles of don Manuel Bolio's during the 1768 residencia investigation into the Crespo governorship, see AHN-*Consejo de Indias* 20.745, 1: ff. 39–61.

126. The de Lara family were prominent in the colony going back at least to the early seventeenth century, holding encomiendas generations before the Bolios, and owning haciendas around Merida as the Bolios did; see García Bernal (1978: 391–93, 513, 518, 532); Martínez Ortega (1993: 137–38, 291–92); and Patch (1993: 191). The various records of Lara marriages in AGAY-*Sagrario*, Libros de Matrimonios, illustrate well the endogamy of Yucatan's Spanish élite.

127. García Bernal (1976).

128. AGN-*Inquisición* 1131, 2, f. 80–81, 94. "Chepa" is an abbreviation of "Josepha" and "monja" means "nun." As Manuel's possible one-time owner, don Manuel Bolio y Helguera, married a doña Rafaela del Castillo y Solís in 1755 (Martínez Ortega 1993: 302), one might speculate that Josepha and Manuel met through work *before* ending up together in the Lara–Argaïs household. The Argaïs or Argaïz family were another Yucatec Spanish dynasty with an early colonial pedigree, and were prominent in both Merida and Valladolid in the eighteenth century; see Martínez Ortega (1993: 54, 137–38, 198, 250, 292) and González Muñoz (1994: 299).

129. Cook (1769); Restall (n.d.).

130. Borrego Plá (1973: 11–28).

131. Most such requests in the AGN are in the *Bienes Nacionales*; an example from the Yucatec archives is AGEY-*Militar*, 1, 24.

132. Exceptions were the free black Sebastian Toral in the 1570s, and Francisco de Aguilar, a free mulatto, in 1619 (AGI-*Contratación* 5227, 2, 25; 5365, 21).

133. AGI-*Contratación* 5272, 2, 71; 5420, 70; 5422, 29; 5425, 1, 1; 5465, 2, 77. The receipts for each payment of twenty ducats states that "they made twenty-two pesos" (f. 2r).

134. Campos García (2005: 59–85; "stain" quote on p. 75); AGEY-*Reales Cédulas* 3, 14 (1813 letter from José de Limonta in Cádiz to the governor of Yucatan).

135. The Colegio de San Pedro, which was also a seminary, was founded in 1711 by the Jesuits and was absorbed into the Seminario de San Ildefonso in 1751. In 1756 the Jesuits established the Colegio de San José in Campeche, but it was taken over by the Franciscans upon the expulsion of the Jesuits in 1767; Ferrer Muñoz (2001: 267–69).

136. AME; Arrigunaga y Peón (1975), which is an indexed transcription of the records in AME. The category of "Spaniards" includes a few boys with a parent of non-Spanish European origin; for example, exp. 817 records the 1802 graduation of twenty-five-year-old José Lauriano Bates, one of the sons of Joseph Bates (aka don José or Josef Bates), the Englishman who married into the Tabasco élite and settled in Yucatan in the late eighteenth century (and appeared as the province's sole Englishman in New Spain's 1796 census of foreigners; AGN-*Civil* 1335; also see Rubio Mañé 1945).

137. AGAY-Jesús María, *Bautismos* IV-B-7, Vol. 1: ff. 127v and 128r.

138. AME/Arrigunaga y Peón (1975), exp. 971 (1805 graduation). An *hidalgo* or *hidalga* was a Maya noble recognized as such both by Mayas and Spaniards, the latter recognition accompanied by an exemption from tribute payment (Restall 1997: 88–90, 96).

139. AGN-*Inquisición* 1131, 2: f. 93r ("... que ciendo casado en Carmpeche [sic] con una Yndia llamada Jossepha conocida Bulgarmente por la Monxa, viviendo esta en la cuidad de Merida en casa de dᵃ Jossepha Zerbera Plazuela de la Mexorana [sic], se bolvio ã casar en el Puerto de la Guayra con Rosalia de Lara, del mismo color negro, de la qual haviendo inviudado, intenta casarse con otra negra ..."); this whole document is transcribed and translated in Restall (2006).

140. AGN-*Inquisición* 1131, 2, ff. 93, 97–98 (Josepha's statement) and 99–108.

141. As Boyer (2001: 158–59) shows with respect to Mexico.

142. AGN-*Marina* 156, 5: f. 186.

CHAPTER SIX

1. AGN-*Inquisición* 519, 3: f. 381v.
2. AGN-*Marina* 156, 5: f. 182r.
3. AGN-*Inquisición* 519, 3: f. 349r. The phrase "cooked quince" is simply *cocha* in the record; *cocho*, a term discussed more fully in Chapter Three, meant a pale beige color, and was an abbreviation of membrillo cocido or *membrillo cocho*; it was used in Spain and central Mexico but not in Yucatan.
4. AGN-*Inquisición* 519, 3: ff. 304r, 315–20v ("el Sarg.º Tejero al qual mataron q^{do} entro el enemigo en el pueblo de Tozuco"; f. 318v).
5. AGN-*Inquisición* 519, 3: ff. 318, 333 ("coser ropa por saber labrar bien" from Sarg. Perera, f. 333v), 337v ("muy conformes . . . andado discordes").
6. AGN-*Inquisición* 519, 3: ff. 335v–36r, 340r ("queriendo matar al Agresor se le huyo, y que le cojio el caballo y el sombrero que dejo, y que pasando a cojer a su muger"), 341r, 362v.
7. AGN-*Inquisición* 519, 3: ff. 304r ("solicitaba a verla a las manos p^a matarla"), 306v, 309, 353v–54.
8. AGN-*Inquisición* 519, 3: ff. 304r, 302r, 310v ("escalando sus paredes").
9. AGN-*Inquisición* 519, 3: ff. 321v–50.
10. AGN-*Inquisición* 519, 3: ff. 306v, 347–74.
11. AGN-*Inquisición* 519, 3: ff. 378–97. On the technicalities of how Inquisition cases against bigamists in Mexico proceeded, see Boyer (1995: 18–22, 26).
12. In terms of architecture and ambience, colonial Campeche has survived better than colonial Merida; see the vivid descriptions of the port town in Hunt (1974: Chap. 1) and Reed (1964: 16; 2001: 16–17).
13. García Bernal (2006: 65, 69, 84, 87); Antochiw (2007).
14. García Bernal (2006: 100–08, 172).
15. AGS 60, 4, 16; in Paso y Troncoso (1940, XIII: 343).
16. Ogilby (1670: 223; original edition in JCBL as F671–M765al).
17. The 1540 founding of Campeche was the Montejos's third attempt to establish a town on this section of the coast; the previous efforts of 1529 and 1531, towns in name only, were called Salamanca, but by 1540 Spaniards had begun to refer to the region as Canpech or Campeche (soon after adopted by the English as Campeachy) (Redondo 1994: 22, 56; Restall 1998a: 9–13;); indeed, the whole colony of Yucatan was often referred to as Campeche, particularly by Spaniards in Mexico or Spain, a usage that gradually faded in the seventeenth century (impression given by general reading of archival sources in AGN and AGI).
18. Casanova Rosado (1995: 30–34); Antochiw (1994; 2007).
19. Patch (1993: 34); Redondo (1994: 60) (who speculates that the plantation had African workers as well as Maya ones; there may have been a few skilled black supervisors, but the fieldworkers would have been Maya men procured through the encomienda system).
20. AGI-*Justicia* 300, 3: ff. 219–442; Redondo (1994: 49–50, 74); García Bernal (2006: 29–43). The growth in direct trade between Seville–The Canaries and the Campeche–Sisal port complex did not begin until the turn of the century, as recently detailed by García Bernal (2006: 61–169). Anecdotal evidence suggests that slave values were higher in early Campeche than they later became; a *negro* from Havana

sold for 356 pesos in 1592, well over the late colonial average of 206; AGI-*Contaduría* 911, 1: f. 8v.

21. Tiesler Blos and Zabala Aguirre (2001); Tiesler (2002); Tiesler, Ramírez Salomón, and Oliva Árias (2002); Medina and Tejeda (2003); Tiesler (2009). I am grateful to Vera Tiesler for sending me in January 2004 copies of published and unpublished reports on her and her colleagues' findings to date. In January and February 2006, a newspaper report on the results of the strontium analysis circulated widely through an Associated Press release and various online venues, appearing in newspapers in North America and Europe. For a summary of equivalent work on the New York City African Burial Ground, see Rucker (2006: 48–52).

22. AGI-*Contratación* 5459, 214, 1: ff. 1r, 4v; Khapoya (1998: 46) on cicatrization in West Africa.

23. Coronel Sánchez et al. (2001: 188, 190).

24. Medina and Tejeda (2003).

25. Data on teeth lost in life shows Africans, mestizos, and Mayas at comparable levels. Cucina (2007).

26. This is a rather free translation of the letter, transcribed (and orthography modernized) in Rubio Mañé (1938: 32) and in Coronel Sánchez et al. (2001: 189) (". . . a la orilla de la mar está una villa llamada Campeche. Tiene una iglesia razonable con que se puede el pueblo pasar buenamente sin que haga otra de nuevo, y también por el riesgo que corre de los enemigos que ordinariamente vienen sobre ella a saquearla y robarla . . . Y supuesto este peligro que queda dicho me ha parecido que en esta villa no se hagan gastos de iglesias ni ornamentos").

27. Coronel Sánchez et al. (2001: 189), citing AGI-*México* 521 and AGI-*Escribanía* 305a; López de Cogolludo (1957, I: 387) (". . . por ser la iglesia tan corta, se comenzó a fabricar otra muy capaz, y aunque se hizo gran parte de ella, ha muchos años que cesó la obra, por no haber rentas particulares para su fábrica, y cada día ser mayor la pobreza que hay en todo Yucatán").

28. Piña Chan (1977: 118); Alcocer Bernés (1986: 49–57); Casanova Rosado (1995: 42–47). None of these authors provide any evidence of the Jesús church's origins as a 1560s open chapel, although as speculation it is perfectly reasonable.

29. BL, Egerton 1791, Cárdenas y Valencia manuscript (1639): f. 50v (". . . otra es del sancto nombre de Jessus y en esta se administran los sacramentos a los morenos de la dha villa").

30. AGN-*Bienes Nacionales* 20, 25; Redondo (1994: 57, 77, 97, 152, 155); Campos García (2005: 35).

31. Taken from the first English edition of Alcedo (1812, vol. I: 255).

32. Exquemelin (1969 [1678]: 75); García Bernal (1998).

33. Espinosa (1942 [1620]: 122). The increase in trade with Spain that began at the turn of the century may have stimulated the port's incipient shipbuilding industry a decade or two before 1620 (on that trade growth, see García Bernal 2006).

34. AGI-*México* 361: ff. 14–17; Hunt (1974: 325–28); González Muñóz and Martínez Ortega (1989: 100, 106–9).

35. Dampier (1699, Vol. II, Part 2: 45–46).

36. Patch (1993: 204–5).

37. AGEC-*Estadísticas* (*Fondo Gobernación*) 1, 4: f. 1.

38. Espinosa (1942 [1620]: 122). Three recent studies of Merida are Peraza Guzmán (1997), Ligorred Perramon (1998), and Lindsay (1999; also see 2004); they complement each other well, and in combination make a strong case for the need to better conserve and restore the architectural and spatial legacy of Merida–Tiho's past.

39. AGI-*México* 3167: ff. 1-2 contains the applications, including one from Diego Jurado, who had been suspended from the curacy in 1604 for negligence; f. 1v shows that the Jesús *cofradía* already existed by 1604. I thank Mark Lentz for sharing this document with me.

40. Espinosa (1942 [1620]: 127).

41. BL, Egerton 1791, Cárdenas y Valencia manuscript (1639): ff. 27v–28r. Cárdenas y Valencia adds (f. 29) that the chapel was often called San Martín, not because it was dedicated to that saint, but because it had been partially endowed by Hernando and Catalina de Sanctmartín—although he says nothing of their identity or why they chose the Jesús church and parish.

42. Gómez de Parada's *Constituciones synodales* (1722), manuscript in CAIHY-CCA #145.

43. CAIHY-CCA #145: ff. 226v–34r.

44. BL, Add 17569: f. 21r ("apenas mantiene escasamente un cura y un Ministro . . . sus ornamentos estaban tan indecentes que me ha sido precisa proveerla con los desechos de la Cathedral"). A 1766 report simply calls the church and parish "*Jesus*" (DCP: f. 50v).

45. Hunt (1974: 414, 506); Campos García (2005: 35).

46. Gómez de Parada's *Constituciones synodales* (1722), manuscript in CAIHY-CCA #145: f. 13v.

47. AGEY-*Tierras* 1, 21.

48. ANEY, most volumes from notaries Baeza through del Rio (UTA rolls 1-58). For discussion of these documents in Maya cultural contexts, see Restall (1997: 31–35, 194, 211–16, 223, 306).

49. AGEY-*Criminal* 2, 11; 1, 10; 2, 8a. Socobio is discussed briefly in Chapter Four; also see Campos García (2005: 39).

50. 1790 census counted 28,392 people (DHY, III: 114); 1793 counted 28,385, with 52% Maya (Aguirre Beltrán 1989: 228); 1794 census tallied 27,829, with 53% Maya (Rubio Mañé 1942, I: 210–34). It is possible that all these censuses were drawing in slightly different ways from the same original database.

51. BL, Egerton 1791, Cárdenas y Valencia manuscript (1639): f. 48r. On the Afro-Yucatecan population of Valladolid, see Chapter One.

52. BL, Add 17569: ff. 6–7r; Cook (1769); Jones (1989: 71–73, 84, 122, 205); Patch (1993: 234–35).

53. See the discussion and citations in the final section of Chapter One, and the tables in Appendix B.

54. AME, 123. Another example, among many, is that of Ichmul in 1806: 69% of Spaniards/mestizos and 77% of Africans in the parish lived in Ichmul itself; 6% of Spaniards/mestizos and 19% of Africans lived in Uaymax; 16% of Spaniards/mestizos and 4% of Africans lived in Tiholop; 9% of Spaniards/mestizos and no Africans lived in Saban; and people of neither category lived in the other two subject communities and the haciendas and *rancho* of the parish (the 1804 data is almost identical); AME, 111–12.

55. Landers (1999: 209–17).

56. AGI-*Estado* 24, 53, 1–5; and 25, 74 (I thank Mark Lentz for photocopying these for me in Seville); also see Victoria Ojeda and Canto Alcocer (2001: 74—77; 2006), and Campos García (2005: 33).

57. AGI-*Estado* 24, 53, 2: ff. 1v–3r; 4: ff. Governor O'Neill's code of regulations ("Reglamento Provisional") for Ake, of March 1796, is 24, 53, 3; the census of founding inhabitants is 24, 53, 4: ff. 3v–5v; 5: ff. 1–2. A 1796 duplicate of AGI-*Estado* 24, 53 is archived as AGI-*Estado* 25, 74.

58. María Elena Díaz (2000) has argued that the colonial Afro-Cuban village of El Cobre, as a corporate slave community, was a juridical anomaly and an exception, as slaves lacked juridical identity; El Cobre was certainly exceptional in many ways, but it was also part of a larger phenomenon of "exceptions"—groups of Africans (or people of African descent) who were able to incorporate communities in Spanish America in some sense or another, from the slaves of El Cobre to the maroons of Esmeraldas to pardo militias throughout the Spanish colonies. San Fernando Ake is part of this phenomenon, but note my emphasis on the relatively rapid transition of the village from an African to an Afro-Maya community (not paralleled in El Cobre, and not even in Esmeraldas, where the Conquest context created a rather different community development; see Lane 2002).

59. AGEY-*Gobernación* 1, 7; also quoted by Campos García (2005: 34).

60. Carreño's phrase is "españoles, o mestizos; o mulatos de los q^e tuviesen pretensiones a mestizos"; AGI-*Estado* 24, 53, 1–5; 25, 74; AGEY-*Militar* 1, 13 and 1, 22; Poder Ejecutivo, *Milicias*, pp. 2, 25; Poder Ejecutivo-*Gobernación*, 1, 6 and 1, 7 (p. 104); Poder Ejecutivo-Censos y Padrones, pp. 3, 27; Victoria Ojeda and Canto Alcocer (1997; 2001); Kepecs (1999); Vinson (2001a: 216–19); Campos García (2005: 33–34, 38–39); Restall (2005: 1–4).

61. Andrews and Robles Castellanos (2002: 2; 2003: 4, 37, 97–99, 102–3, 111–12). The idea that San Francisco's residents took building stones from Lolché is my speculation and is not suggested by any of the data presented by Andrews and Robles Castellanos.

62. Francisco de Paula and Francisca de Paula are names that appear in the baptism records of free coloreds in Merida in the eighteenth century; perhaps men and women named thus were prominent among the founders of the hamlet, hence their choice of toponym (e.g., AGAY-*Jesús*, Libros de Bautismos Vol. 2: f. 93v).

63. Andrews and Robles Castellanos also surveyed Kaxek and included a map of it similar to the one I adapted for my Map 6.1 (2003: 36, 99).

64. With respect to the arrival and sale of Africans in small numbers, and their role primarily as personal servants, colonial Yucatan is comparable to sixteenth-century Peru (see Lockhart 1994: 199–205) and to eighteenth-century Chihuahua (see Martin 1996: 44, 48, 59, 67), although the total number of slaves in Peru was far greater than in Mexico, especially with respect to provinces such as Yucatan. See Chapters One, Two, and Four for my main treatment of slave demography and labor roles in Yucatan.

65. AGEY-*Criminal* 1, 11a.

66. Mintz and Price (1976); Lovejoy (1997); Palmer (1998); Chamosa (2003: 347–51); Sweet (2003: 1–2); Hall (2005: xv–xvii, 166–72).

67. Lovejoy (2000: 1, 2, 18, 20).

68. AGAY-*Jesús*, Libros de Bautismos Vols. 1–6; also see the tables in Appendix G for further details.

69. On the lack of "African" identity, see Eltis (2000: 224–25); on the lack of "Maya" identity, Restall (2004).

70. For the precise location of many of the places in west and west central Africa listed in Table 6.1, see Boyd-Bowman (1969: 40–41); Thornton (1998: x–xxxvi); Van Deusen (1999: 7); Eltis (2000: 307); Carroll (2001: 160); Goldberg (2001: 279); Sweet (2003: 17, 21, 26); Hall (2005: 128). "Mina" did not always mean the port of Mina or Elmina, but (according to Hall 2005: 47) often referred to people from Little Popo, on the Bight of Benin. For reasons of space and focus (and to give me a chance to explore the possibility of a Yucatan–Belize comparison on the topic), my further study of the African origins of slaves in Yucatan will be published separately (Restall n.d.).

71. Palmer (1976: 21). Hall (2005) objects to the notion of fragmented diversity among Africans in the Americas, arguing for the significant clustering of African ethnicities in the colonies; she makes a strong case for regions that I would classify as slave societies, but societies with slaves, such as Yucatan, present different patterns.

72. Gómez de Parada's *Constituciones synodales* (1722), manuscript in CAIHY-CCA #145: f. 155v (statement on baptism of Protestants).

73. Mintz and Price (1976: 40-45); Chamosa (2003: 351).

74. Hall (2005: 45) shows how in eighteenth-century Louisiana, for example, ethnic designations were *more* common in later records, the opposite of the Yucatan pattern. For a vivid example of how important ethnic African identities were in one slave society, see Reis (1997) on the 1857 strike by Nagô slave porters in Bahia.

75. Dubois (2004: 258–62).

76. The work of James Sweet on Brazil was particularly influential to my thinking here; see (2003) and especially (2006).

77. Diouf (1998: 2, 17, 49–70, 94–97, 104–6, 145–78) has argued that Muslims were especially resistant to Christian conversion in the Americas (as in Africa), and were more likely to permanently and consistently refuse to accept their enslaved status. That any African ever really "accepted" the status of slave seems highly dubious, but Muslims certainly seem to have had particular motivation and opportunity to express their lack of acceptance. For the insistence by Muslims on their identity as free servants of Allah was made possible, in the face of great opposition, by the maintenance of Muslim communities in the American colonies—communities that in turn allowed such Africans to pursue the goals of freedom and a better life in the New World, if not a return to Africa. Such a community brought four different ethnic groups of Africans together in Cartagena in the early seventeenth century, according to a Jesuit priest living in the city (Borja 1993: 249; also cited by Diouf 1998: 20). In the early nineteenth century, Muslim communities in Port of Spain and in various parts of Brazil were cohesive and organized enough to be able to secure the freedom of many of their members prior to abolition; some of those freed even had their way paid back to Africa. In Bahia, Muslims made a set weekly payment into a community manumission fund (Reis 1993: 131–33; Diouf 1998: 104–5, 163–78). There were also similar communities in colonial Cuba, although the Afro-Cuban mutual aid societies that flourished in the nineteenth century were not exclusively organized by or comprised of Muslims, nor were the *candombes*, or African Associations, in nineteenth-century Buenos Aires. Called *cabildos de naciones afrocubanos* in the first half of the century, and later, *sociedades de color*, the purpose of the Cuban organizations was not simply to manage manumis-

sion funds, but also to promote among free and enslaved Afro-Cubans an awareness of their African cultural heritage and a community solidarity—a concept that became radicalized in the final decades of the century (Howard 1998; also see Childs, e.g., 2006). The candombes of Buenos Aires served a similar purpose, according to Chamosa (2003).

78. Diouf (1998: 18–33).

79. Curtin (1969: 98).

80. Diouf (1998: 91–93).

81. Diouf (1998: 90–91).

82. Boyer (1995: Appendix). Only the nonindigenous population is included because, with very few exceptions and beginning in the late sixteenth century, native peoples in Spanish America were removed from the jurisdiction of the Inquisition.

83. AGN-*Inquisición*, various; AGN-*Bienes Nacionales*, various; AGEY-*Criminal*, 7.

84. AGN-*Inquisición* 1131, 2: fs. 80–110.

85. As explored most notably, with respect to early colonial Mexico, by Bennett (2003) and Bristol (2007).

86. The exception to this are the witchcraft cases of the late seventeenth century, especially those relating to love–magic (AGN-*Inquisición*, various); see the discussion of this in Chapter Seven.

87. AGN-*Marina* 156, 5: f. 182r.

88. AGN-*Marina* 156, 5: f. 182v–87.

89. Villa-Flores (2002: 467–68). In contrast, when the Dutch stopped baptizing African slaves in New Amsterdam in the 1650s, they highlighted the racial line between Africans and Europeans and prevented the complex community formation that was taking place in Yucatan; the British adopted a similarly divisive attitude when they turned the city into New York (Harris 2003: 17–18, 27–28).

90. AGN-*Bienes Nacionales* 28, 65: ff. 1-8.

91. BL, Egerton 1791, Cárdenas y Valencia manuscript (1639): f. 30v. As well as establishing cofradías for blacks and mulattoes, the Spanish ecclesiastical authorities also promoted the beatification of free coloreds with reputations for devotional or saintly behavior, such as fray (eventually Saint) Martín de Porres in Lima (Cussen 2005: 439–47). Comparable information about religious life in Merida and Campeche may eventually be found; Fernández Repetto and Negroe Sierra (1989) refer to Campeche's cofradia records, but do not summarize or analyze their actual contents.

92. Kiddy (2005).

93. Von Germeten (2006).

94. Morgan (1998: 420); Berlin (2003: 56, 67, 80).

95. Dzonotake's 1688 census entry is in AGI-*Contaduría* 920, 1: f. 316v.

96. ANEY, Argaiz, 1777 (UTA roll 20): f. 175; AGI-*Contratación* 5506, 2, 7, 1: f. 19r; 5524, 4, 29, 1: f. 7r.

97. Lentz (2005), citing TULAL, Viceregal and Ecclesiastical Mexico Collection, 50, 1: ff. 12v, 13v; also see Lentz (n.d.).

98. Kaye (2007: 1-6).

99. Armstrong (2003: 5, 317).

100. AGAY-*Jesús*, Libros de Bautismos Vol. 1: f. 276v (Isabel's baptism); Vol. 2: ff. 59v (Martin's and Rita's baptisms), 87r (Francisco Xavier's), 93v (Juana Francisca de Paula's), 101r (Antonia María de Jesús's), 119v (Beatriz Josepha's), 128r

(Thoribia María's; I am guessing that her godmother, doña María Candelaria de Avila, was a sister of doña Isabel de Avila's), 143r (María Luisa's). Also see Appendix E.

101. AGAY-*Jesús*, Libros de Bautismos Vol. 5: ff. 7v, 55v, 111r (baptisms of Juana's three children), 171v. On the Castro and González families, see Appendix E and Martínez Ortega (1993: 116, 118).

102. ANEY, Argaiz, 1778–81 (UTA roll 21); Argaiz, 1782–84 (UTA roll 22); López Rivas (1975).

103. AGI-*Escribanía* 316b, 75: f. 2. The full document is presented in Appendix A.

104. AGI-*Escribanía* 316b, 75: f. 2v.

105. AGN-*Inquisición* 498, 16: ff. 160–85. Other *pecado nefando*, or sodomy, cases from Merida and Campeche include *Inquisición* 624, 7; 1187, 2; and 1373, 14.

106. Patch (2002: 161, 170).

107. AGN-*Civil* 283, 3 (Maya-language statement by the batab and cabildo on ff. 369v–70v, reproduced in translation in Restall, Sousa, and Terraciano 2005: 165–67); *Inquisición* 1187, 2: ff. 59–60 (reproduced in transcription and translation in Restall 1997: 330–31, and in translation in Restall, Sousa, and Terraciano 2005: 168–69).

108. CCA-*caja* X, 1818, 007, f. 2v. Seyba Playa was about half Maya and half Spanish, and Afro-Yucatecan by the end of the eighteenth century (Patch 1993: 259).

CHAPTER SEVEN

1. Dampier (1699, Vol. II, part 2: 115–16).

2. AGN-*Inquisición* 1164: f. 214v. Ek's statement was made in Maya in the first person, but only written down in the third person in Spanish; I have adjusted the voice, but not the vocabulary (for example, Ek would not have used the term "Indian"; he almost certainly would have said "macehual"; see Restall 2004).

3. "*Balché* (or *baalche*') is a Maya term meaning "wild animal" and is also the name used for several trees of the genus *Lonchocarpus*; the bark is placed in a honey–water mixture and left to ferment for three days (Anderson 2003: 110; Anderson and Medina Tzuc 2005: 104). On the use of balché by colonial Mayas, see Chuchiak (2003).

4. AGN-*Inquisición* 1164: ff. 211–319 (Coyi and Ordoñez accounts on ff. 212–15 and repeated throughout the expediente; a 1732 statement by Zavala, in his own hand, is on f. 315r). On Maya rituals used today to cleanse people and places of evil winds, see Love (2004: 1, 10–14, 27–28, 47–61).

5. Restall (2005: 4–10).

6. AGEY-*Criminal* 1, 11a: "example" comment on f. 6. As the Campeche–Merida *Camino Real* was a vital link in the chain of communication that connected Yucatan to the outside world, banditry along the route was viewed very dimly by the Spanish authorities.

7. Ibid.: ff. 8, 10.

8. Ibid.: ff. 1–7.

9. Ibid.: ff. 9–10.

10. Although hospital was certainly a better place to be in colonial Yucatan than jail; incarcerated men regularly sought transfer to hospital, where they would be better fed (and might more easily escape). For example, the accounts of the San Lázaro Hospital in Campeche for this same period detail the daily purchase of "bread and chocolate, loin, shark, eggs, beef, pork, three chickens, one more by order of the doctor, avocados, chiles and onions, saffron and cloves, a dry measure [*almud*] of rice, half a measure [*carga*] of corn, sugar, two pitchers of fat, eggs for dinner, two flasks of habanero pepper, bottles of wine, bread and chocolate to be administered to the gravely ill to get through the night, . . ." (AGEC-*Período Yucateco* [*Fondo Gobernación*] 1, 1, entry for Monday, July 31, 1820).

11. AGEY-*Criminal* 1, 11a: ff. 18–19.

12. Ibid.: ff. 19–20.

13. For my prior use of this term, applied to colonial Yucatan, see Restall (1998b).

14. AGI-*Justicia* 300, 3: ff. 403v, 413, 420v, 424, et al.; *México* 307, 3: ff. 14v, 16.

15. AGN-*Inquisición* 1187, 2: fs. 59–61. Also see Restall (1997: 141–47, 330–31).

16. AGEY-*Criminal* 3, 2.

17. It is difficult to prove that the Spanish colonial judicial system gave credibility to and perpetuated racial stereotypes, in part because many of these stereotypes were taken for granted and thus seldom articulated in a way that we would find blatant. Sample cases must suffice; for example, in 1794 an African was arrested for suspicious loitering in Merida because he had been standing on a street corner at night wearing a cape and hat; it turned out that he had been placed there as a guard by his master in an adjacent house, but his effect was to frighten the neighbors and passersby, primarily because of the menacing combination of the hat, cape, and color of his skin, as witnesses made clear (AGN-*Criminal* 316, 2, fs. 83–86). The context to this incident was the 1792 assassination of the intendant-governor don Lúcas de Gálvez. The prolonged murder investigation made Merida's Spanish citizens decidedly jittery and brought out a variety of their prejudices; the same month the caped slave was arrested local authorities had interrogated eighteen citizens of Merida in an effort to discover who had been threatening royal officials involved in the murder investigation, including the caped slave's owner, the assessor don Francisco de Guillén (AGN-*Criminal* 316, 3; I had done some preliminary research into the Gálvez assassination, whose voluminous records are in AGEY, AGN, and AGI— also see Pérez Galaz (1942)—but the topic is now being given full treatment by Mark Lentz of Tulane University in his doctoral dissertation; Lentz n.d.).

18. AHN-*Consejos de Indias* 20.745, 2: f. 172 ("son unos ladrones rateros, y no salteadores; y q.ᵉ de ordinario son Yndios . . . quando se ha verificado en algunos hombres de color . . . las remitan a la Real carcel de esta ciu.ᵈ en donde se les ha seguido la caussa conforme a derecho"). The residencia files of Yucatan's eighteenth-century governors, still archived in Madrid, contain details of the criminal prosecutions of most gubernatorial terms. Free coloreds sometimes feature prominently. For example: four of the eight men convicted in the 1750s for various kinds of theft and being "*mal inclinado*" were free coloreds; and in 1766, four mulattoes and a *negro* were sentenced to six years labor on the Havana fortifications for such crimes as theft, rape, wife-beating, and vagabondage (AHN-*Consejos de Indias* 20.745, 2: ff.

113–14, 166–67; 20.744, 1: ff. 99–111). But it is not clear how comprehensive or representative these cases were, and so I have not tried to quantify them in a way that compares to Table 7.1. Furthermore, the casta identity of convicted men is not always made clear. For example, twenty-three convictions were secured under the Oliver governorship of 1771–75, for crimes ranging from uxoricide and sedition against the Bacalar commandant to the theft of two pesos; one was a *negro libre*, six had Maya patronyms, but the rest were not categorized (AHN-*Consejos de Indias* 20.746, 1: ff. 76–124).

19. AHN-*Consejos de Indias* 20.744, 1: ff. 99–111.

20. AGEY-*Criminal* 2, 11. His 1822 arrest is in AGEY-*Justicia, Penal* 1, 14.

21. Campos García (2005: 39–40).

22. AGI-*México* 307, 5: ff. 17r, 18r (the Hool cabildo made a brief report on the incident, written in Maya by the notary and signed by batab don Bonifacio Cime and other cabildo officers, but only a Spanish summary was included in the inquiry files).

23. AGI-*México* 307, 5: ff. 11v (". . . sucesivam^te executaron otras muertes de españoles y mulatos bajando a las estancias . . . ").

24. For example, the matrícula of 1700 shows that although in Kopomá in that year there were no non-Mayas beyond a couple of mestizo families, there were eighty-five Afro-Yucatecans living in six of the Maya villages on or near the *Camino Real*, including twelve mulatto families (totaling fifty-five people) in Maxcanú; AGI-*México* 1035 (also see Solano 1975). Because mulatto and pardo men in the countryside married Maya women about a third of the time, by 1816 some of the Mayas who encountered Marcín along the highway would themselves have had some African ancestry.

25. AGEY-*Criminal* 1, 11a, fs. 2, 6, 9.

26. It is clear from the evidence of other cases, many including petitions in Maya authored by community *cabildos*, that Mayas were in no way timid about engaging or participating in the colonial legal system; arguably this evidence suggests that had a Maya woman indeed been raped, plenty of witnesses, let alone the community elders in the form of the cabildo, would have been eager to make statements (see Restall 1997; 2000a).

27. Both cited in Patch (1993: 95–96), the latter also in García Bernal (1972: 19).

28. AGI-*México* 3042: f. 53v.

29. AGI-*Patronato* 66a, 1, 4, 1: ff. 1r, 8v, 14v, 17r, 20v, 23r, 26r, 28v, 31v–32r, 35r, 36v, 38v (e.g., f. 28v: ". . . ebitaron el daño que harian a los naturales de esta provinçia que podia seguir . . ."); López de Cogolludo (1957 [1654], I: 273).

30. AGN-*Inquisición* 498, 16: ff. 160–85 ("manosear y registrar todas sus partes"); also discussed by Lewis (2007: 136–40), whose insightful analysis I have more or less followed here.

31. Zorita (1994 [c.1570]: 257).

32. Horn (1997: 79 [quote is Horn's translation], 205).

33. Taylor (1979: 17).

34. CI, I: 300, quoted in Katzew (2004: 40–41).

35. AGI-*México*, 3048: f. 37. The friars were de la Torre, Miranda, Brugett, and Valdemayor.

36. CDH: 513.

37. AHN, *caja* II, 21; DHY, II, 52–53. Bans on interaction and cohabitation between Mayas and non-Mayas (especially *castas* or mixed-race people) were repeat-

edly issued by various colonial authorities; for further references, see Farriss (1984: 441, n.68).

38. AHN, *caja* III; CI: LXXII; translation in Restall (1998a: 165–68 [quote on p.166]).

39. Patch (1993: 95), on Santa Lucía. For examples from the Jesús María parish, see Hunt (1974: 88–97, 386–87, 410–44, 506–12, 529–36). On the rarity of African–Nahua marriages, see Bennett (1993: 66–69, 88–95, 160); Horn (1997).

40. On the Mesoamericans who settled in Merida in the 1540s, see Chuchiak (2007).

41. AGN-*Inquisición* 1131, 2, fs. 80–110.

42. AGAY-*Jesús*, Libros de Bautismos Vol. 3: f. 108v.

43. Hunt (1974: 511).

44. AGI-*México* 1035; Solano (1975: 49, 70).

45. AME: 220; Thompson (1978: 253).

46. AGN-*Inquisición* 620, 7: ff. 595–614 (quotes from f. 598: "se balia de encantos, y hechisos, para echisar, y encantar a çierto hombre ... que entendia de hechissos, y encantasiones ... a un hombre, para que la quisiesse mucho ... tiene opinion de hechisera ... con quien el trataba ... lebantar un testimonio"). This case is also summarized and analyzed in Restall and Bristol (2009); on love-magic in Mexico at this time, see Bristol (2007: 164–72).

47. AGN-*Inquisición* 620, 7: ff. 595–614 (quotes: "... se rapava los pelos de las partes vergonsosas ... toda confiansa ... que usan mucho los indios para embriagarse, y idolatrar").

48. AGN-*Inquisición* 620, 7: ff. 599v–600v ("... volavan juntos como Brujos").

49. AGN-*Inquisición* 620, 7: f. 596r ("... encantos y medios ilicitos para conservar a sus amantes ... de mal fama ... no es mal opinado").

50. AGN-*Inquisición*, 125, 69: 254–63.

51. AGN-*Inquisición* 908 (1650); 629, 5 (1674); Chuchiak (2000: 474–75) summarizes these cases; I probably would not have found these and many other cases were it not for his citations and suggestions.

52. AGN-*Inquisición* 1177, 7: ff. 1–193; Chuchiak (2000: 477–78).

53. Rincón case is AGN-*Inquisición* 626, 10.

54. Chuchiak (2003).

55. AGN-*Inquisición* 919, 26; Chuchiak (2000: 481–82).

56. Sweet (1997: 179–86); Sommer (2003: 422).

57. AGN-*Inquisición* 626, 7: ff. 208 ("orasion"), 186 ("disonantes").

58. AGN-*Inquisición* 360: ff. 275–76 ("... con otras ceremonias y palabras").

59. AGN-*Inquisición* 360, 92.

60. Among the cases that mention Michaela Montejo are AGN-*Inquisición* 620, 7; 621: ff. 244–54; and 626, 7 (e.g., f. 188v).

61. On Guatemala, see Few (2002); on Mexico, see Lewis (2003) and Bristol (2007); on Peru, see Silverblatt (2004: 165–85).

62. In the words of Miranda Ojeda (2001: 67; "... consagrada a utilizar la función inquisitorial como un escaparate social y político ..."). There were also five *comisarías temporales* set up at various times between 1698 and 1807, but this appears to have been a bureaucratic development that did not generate an increase in Inquisition activity in the colony (ibid.: 73–75). Horta Barroso died in 1681 or in the first weeks of 1682; AGI-*México* 363, 1, 1: f. 1.

63. This statistic is calculated from the list of fifty-one cases in Miranda Ojeda (1999: 324–25); there were also two cases against *mestizos* and thirteen against Mayas (who technically were under the jurisdiction of the *Provisorato de Indios*). I located and read Ojeda Miranda's thirteen cases against Afro-Yucatecans, in addition to others listed in Table 7.1, but did not note the total number of Yucatec Inquisition cases in any category or time period and am therefore relying here on Ojeda Miranda's list being comprehensive, at least for seventeenth-century love–magic cases.

64. See, for example, the early nineteenth-century AHAY-*Decretos y órdenes* cases cited by Rugeley (2001: 124–32).

65. The central Mexican evidence likewise fails to show that Afro-Mexicans were heavily targeted as witches by the Inquisition, although they were investigated disproportionately more often in eighteenth-century Mexico than Afro-Yucatecans were in the previous century (see Proctor 2003b: Table 7.1). On relative population sizes, see García Bernal (1978: 155–56) and Aguirre Beltrán (1989: 219).

66. Romberg (2003: 10).

67. To paraphrase Bailey (2006: 402) on magic's "disenchantment" in Europe.

68. Romberg (2003: 3–4), using modern evidence from Puerto Rico and also citing Claude Lévi-Strauss's 1963 essay, "The Sorcerer and His Magic."

69. For a parallel example of how seventeenth-century Venetians, from senior clergy to poor citizens, shared a common culture of everyday beliefs and practices that some Inquisition officials saw as witchcraft, see Ruggiero (2001). For a fascinating discussion "On Believing, and Not Believing, in Witchcraft," in South Africa today, see Ashforth (2005: 111–30).

70. Ashforth (2005: 65).

71. Rugeley (2001: 125).

72. AGN-*Inquisición* 1164: ff. 211–319.

CONCLUSION

1. AGI-*México* 368: ff. 1–599.

2. Thornton (2002: 35).

3. Lockhart (1994 [1968]: 194); Herrera (2000: 249, 259). Morgan (1998: 334–53) is a section titled "Slaves in the Middle" on slaves who acted as intermediaries between masters and other slaves in the Chesapeake and Lowcountry.

4. Both quotes in Huntington (1993: 186).

5. Tannenbaum (1946: 117–18); Berlin (1998: 8–9, 109–42; 2003: 8–10, 55–67); Scott (2005: 15, 27–28) on Louisiana.

6. Bennett (2003: 15); the Genovese quote dates from 1971.

7. Similarly, Sherwin Bryant (2006: 82, 87) has persuasively argued that in the late seventeenth century Popayán shifted into being a slave society; but he pushes the envelope, arguably too far, when he uses his Popayán evidence to claim that all colonial Ecuador (the Kingdom of Quito) "was a quintessential Spanish American slave society . . . quite similar to those of Peru and New Spain."

8. Johnson (n.d.) seeks to make the same point in his study of slaves in late colonial Buenos Aires.

9. Cáceres (2000: 1–2) on Costa Rica; Herrera (2000: 248–49) on Guatemala; Reel (2005) on Argentina (specifically, Buenos Aires).

10. In the words of Henry Wiencek, quoted by Wood (2003: 10).

11. See Gabbert (2004: esp. pp. 60–78, 110–24).

12. Muñoz Mata (2001).

13. Research notes made in Campeche, 1999.

14. Reel (2005).

15. Lisker and Babinsky (1986); Lisker, Ramírez, and Babinsky. (1996); Bonilla et al. (2005: 7).

Glossary

The number in parenthesis ( ) after each term indicates the chapter in which the term is introduced; the Index gives the page numbers for the main treatment of each term.

Asiento (1) — A royal license to trade in African slaves

Cabildo (1) — Town council; every municipality had one, from the largest Spanish city to the smallest Maya village

Cah (4) — Maya town or village (cahob in the plural); a cah-barrio was a Maya municipal community located within or adjacent to the walls of Merida or Campeche (Restall 1997: 13–40)

Casta (2) — Socioracial rank; in Yucatan (and elsewhere in New Spain), usually a reference to those of African or mixed-race descent (i.e., neither Spanish nor indigenous)

Cofradía (5) — Religious brotherhood or confraternity, maintained by parishes, racially segregated into Spanish, Maya, and Afro-Yucatecan organizations

Criollo (2) — Creole; used by Spaniards to refer to a person of African descent born in Spain or the Spanish American colonies; in Yucatan, a local-born Afro-Yucatecan

Encomendero (1) — Yucatec Spanish aristocratic holder of an *encomienda*

Encomienda (2) — A royal grant of the inhabitants of an indigenous community or group of them, licensing the recipient (the encomendero or *encomendera*) to receive labor and tribute

Estancia (1) — A rural estate, typically of livestock, owned by an *estanciero*, although the Afro-Yucatecan managers of estancias were sometimes also called *estancieros*

Factoria (1)   A slave "factory" (i.e., an official, permanent slave-trading office); Campeche was given the right to *factoria* status, but it remained a secondary office

Hacienda (2)   A large, diversified rural estate, owned by a Spanish *hacendado*; sometimes described as comprising various estancias

Manta (4)   Blanket or measure of cotton cloth; important item of tribute and trade in colonial Yucatan

Matrícula (3)   Register; a type of census in which, in theory, every resident is listed by name; I have thus far found two surviving matrículas for Yucatan; those of 1688 (AGI-*Contaduría* 920) and 1700 (AGI-*México* 1035)

Mayordomo (4)   Majordomo, manager, or foreman for an agricultural enterprise, such as an estancia or hacienda; Afro-Yucatecans were often estancia foremen

Mestizo (1)   A person of mixed Spanish–indigenous descent; *mestizaje* refers to race-mixing or miscegenation in general

Milpa (3)   Cornfield; adopted by Spaniards in New Spain, including Yucatan, from Nahuatl (a corn farmer was a *milpero*)

Mulato (1)   Mulatto, a person of mixed Spanish–African descent, assumed to be free unless otherwise indicated

Naboría (1)   Native dependent of a nobleman; used by Spaniards to refer to native servants in the Americas who were attached to Spanish households and free from native community obligations; Spanish term derived from Arawak

Nahuatlato (1)   Interpreter; first used in central Mexico in the 1520s to mean "Nahuatl speaker"; by the time of the first settlement of Yucatan in the 1540s the term referred to someone who spoke both Spanish and a native language

Negro (1)   Literally "black" or "a black man," the term referred to someone born in Africa, or perceived as such, or someone descended entirely from such; it often implied "slave" (as in *un negro de* [owner's name]), necessitating the caveat *libre* if the person was free; italicized in this book so as not to be taken for the English word "negro"

Pardo (1)	Technically, a person of mixed African–indigenous descent, and in some Spanish colonies used strictly in this way, but in Yucatan sometimes also used as a synonym for mulatto or more generally to mean a person of mixed African–Spanish, African–Maya, or African–Spanish–Maya descent
Peso (1)	Most common unit of Spanish currency (literally, "weight"); subdivided into eight *reales*
Repartimiento (4)	Literally "allotment, division," the repartimiento in Spanish America took various forms; in Yucatan its two main types were the allocation of Maya workers to Spanish officials or settlers (also called the *tanda*), and the imposition on Maya cahob of the forced sale or purchase of goods (the Afro-Yucatecan role was as supervisor or intermediary in repartimiento business)
Residencia (1)	Official investigation into a term of office, such as a term as governor of an imperial province like Yucatan; headed by a specially appointed judge, or *juez de residencia*; early residencia records for Yucatan's governors are in the AGI, and later ones are in the AHN
Tanda (4)	See Repartimiento

References

Aguirre Beltrán, Gonzalo. 1989. *La Población Negra de México: Estudio etnohistórico* [1st ed., 1946]. Mexico City: Fondo de Cultura Económica.

Alcedo, Antonio de. 1812. *The Geographical and Historical Dictionary of America and the West Indies*, 5 vols. (1786–89). G. A. Thompson, ed. London: Longman, Hurst, Rees, Orme, and Brown (copies of Spanish and English first editions in JCBL).

Alcocer Bernés, José Manuel. 1986. *Las Iglesias Coloniales del Puerto de Campeche*. Campeche: Universidad del Sudeste.

Altman, Ida. 1991. "Spanish Society in Mexico City After the Conquest," in *Hispanic American Historical Review* 71:3 (August), pp. 413–45.

American Anthropological Association. 1998. "AAA Statement on 'Race,' " in *Anthropology Newsletter* (September), p. 3.

Anderson, E. N. 2003. *Those Who Bring the Flowers: Maya Ethnobotany in Quintana Roo, Mexico*. San Cristóbal de las Casas, Chiapas: ECOSUR.

Anderson, E. N., and Felix Medina Tzuc. 2005. *Animals and the Maya in Southeast Mexico*. Tucson: University of Arizona Press.

Andrade, Manuel J., and Hilaria Máas Collí. 1990. *Cuentos Mayas Yucatecos, Tomo I*. Merida: Universidad Autónoma de Yucatán.

Andrews, Anthony P., and Fernando Robles Castellanos. 2002. "An Archaeological Survey of Northwest Yucatan, Mexico: Final Report of the 2002 Season." Unpublished manuscript.

———. 2003. *Proyecto Costa Maya: Reconocimiento Arqueológico en el Noroeste de Yucatán, México*. Merida: Centro INAH Yucatán and National Geographic Society.

Antochiw, Michel. 1994. *Historia Cartográfica de la Península de Yucatán*. Campeche: Gobierno del Estado de Campeche.

———. 2007. "La Plaza de Armas de Campeche," in Vera Tiesler, ed., *Orígenes de la Campechaneidad. Vida y Muerte en la Cuidad de Campeche Durante los Siglos XVI y XVII*. Mexico City: UNAM.

Armstrong, Douglas V. 2003. *Creole Transformation from Slavery to Freedom: Historical Archaeology of the East End Community, St. John, Virgin Islands*. Gainesville: University Press of Florida.

Arrigunaga y Peón, Joaquin. 1975. *Españoles, Mestizos e Indios Forjadores de la Intelectualidad Yucateca 1722–1860*. Merida: Publicaciones de la Academia Yucateca de Historia "Francisco de Montejo" (copy in CAIHY).

Ashforth, Adam. 2005. *Witchcraft, Violence, and Democracy in South Africa.* Chicago: University of Chicago Press.

Bailey, Michael D. 2006. "The Disenchantment of Magic: Spells, Charms, and Superstition in Early European Witchcraft Literature," in *American Historical Review* 111:2 (April), pp. 383–404.

Baptist, Edward E. 2001. " 'Cuffy,' 'Fancy Maids,' and 'One-Eyed Men': Rape, Commodification, and the Domestic Slave Trade in the United States," in *American Historical Review* 106:5 (December), pp. 1619–50.

Baquiero Anduze, Oswaldo. 1983. *Geográfia Sentimental de Mérida (Las Piedras Que Hablan)* [1937]. Merida: Maldonado Editores.

Barickman, Bert. J. 2003. "Reading the 1835 Parish Censuses from Bahia: Citizenship, Kinship, Slavery, and Household in Early Nineteenth-Century Brazil," in *The Americas* 59:3 (January), pp. 287–323.

Bennett, Herman L. 1993. "Lovers, Family and Friends: The Formation of Afro-Mexico, 1580–1810." PhD dissertation, Duke University.

———. 2003. *Africans in Colonial Mexico: Absolutism, Christianity, and Afro-Creole Consciousness, 1570–1640.* Bloomington: Indiana University Press.

Benzoni, Girolamo. 1857. *History of the New World* [1565]. Rear-Admiral W. H. Smyth, ed. London: Hakluyt Society. (Also see references in notes to *Historia de la Conquista del Nuevo Mundo*, an unpublished seventeenth-century manuscript version in JCBL.)

Berlin, Ira. 1998. *Many Thousands Gone: The First Two Centuries of Slavery in North America.* Cambridge, MA: Belknap Press of Harvard University Press.

———. 2003. *Generations of Captivity: A History of African-American Slaves.* Cambridge, MA: Belknap Press of Harvard University Press.

Bernand, Carmen. 2000. "La Población Negra de Buenos Aires (1777–1862)," in Mónica Quijada, Carmen Bernand, and Arnd Schneider, *Homogeneidad y Nación. Con un Estudio de Caso: Argentina, Siglos XIX y XX.* Madrid: Consejo Superior de Investigaciones Científicas, pp. 93–140.

———. 2001. *Negros Esclavos y Libres en las Cuidades Hispanoamericanos.* Madrid: Fundación Histórica Tavera.

Blanchard, Peter. 2002. "The Language of Liberation: Slave Voices in the Wars of Independence," in *Hispanic American Historical Review* 82:3 (August), pp. 499–523.

———. 2004. "Slave Women and their Struggle for Personal Freedom during the Wars of Independence." Paper presented to the American Historical Association and Conference on Latin American History, Washington, DC.

Blanco, Ciprian. 1816. *Vacuna.* Campeche (Copy in the JCBL).

Bolland, Nigel O. 1997. *Struggles for Freedom: Essays on Slavery, Colonialism and Culture in the Caribbean and Central America.* Belize City: Angelus Press.

———. 2002. "Timber Extraction and the Shaping of Enslaved People's Culture in Belize," in Verene A. Shephard, ed., *Slavery Without Sugar: Diversity in Caribbean Economy and Society Since the 17th Century.* Gainesville: University Press of Florida, pp. 34–62.

Bolster, Jeffrey W. 2002. "Black Sailors Making Selves," in Beverly C. McMillan, ed., *Captive Passage: The Transatlantic Slave Trade and the Making of the Americas.* Washington, DC: Smithsonian Institution, pp. 171–85.

Bonilla, Carolina, Gerardo Gutiérrez, Esteban J. Parra, Christopher Kline, and Mark D. Shriver. 2005. "Admixture Analysis of a Rural Population of the State of Guerrero, Mexico," in *American Journal of Physical Anthropology* 128:4, pp. 861–69.

Borja, Jaime. 1993. "Barbarización y Redes de Indoctrinamiento en los Negros Cartageno XVII y XVIII," in Astrid Ulloa, ed., *Contribución Africana a la Cultura de las Américas*. Bogota: Instituto Colombiano de Antropología Colcutura.

Borrego Plá, María del Carmen. 1973. *Palenques de Negros en Cartagena de Indias a Fines del Siglo XVII*. Seville: Escuela de Estudios Hispano-Americanos.

Bowser, Frederick P. 1974. *The African Slave in Colonial Peru, 1524–1650*. Stanford, CA: Stanford University Press.

Boyd-Bowman, Peter. 1969. "Negro Slaves in Early Colonial Mexico," in *The Americas* 26:2, pp. 134–51.

Boyer, Richard. 1995. *Lives of the Bigamists: Marriage, Family, and Community in Colonial Mexico*. Albuquerque: University of New Mexico Press (Abridged ed., 2001).

Bracamonte y Sosa, Pedro. 1993. *Amos y Sirvientes: Las Haciendas de Yucatán, 1789–1860*. Merida: Universidad Autónoma de Yucatán.

Bricker, Victoria, Eleuterio Po'ot Yah, and Ofelia Dzul de Po'ot. 1998. *A Dictionary of the Maya Language as Spoken in Hocabá, Yucatán*. Salt Lake City: University of Utah Press.

Brion Davis, David. 2003. *Challenging the Boundaries of Slavery*. Cambridge, MA: Harvard University Press.

Bristol, Joan Cameron. 2007. *Christians, Blasphemers, and Witches: Afro-Mexican Ritual Practice in the Seventeenth Century*. Albuquerque: University of New Mexico Press.

Bristol, Joan, and Matthew Restall. 2009. "Potions and Perils: Love-Magic in Seventeenth-Century Afro-Mexico and Afro-Yucatan," in Ben Vinson III and Matthew Restall, eds., *Black Mexico*. Albuquerque: University of New Mexico Press.

Brooks, James F. 2002. *Captives and Cousins: Slavery, Kinship, and Community in the Southwest Borderlands*. Chapel Hill and Williamsburg: University of North Carolina Press and Omohundro Institute of Early American History and Culture.

Bryant, Sherwin K. 2006. "Finding Gold, Forming Slavery: The Creation of a Classic Slave Society, Popayán, 1600–1700," in *The Americas* 63:1 (July), pp. 81–112.

Burdon, Sir John Alder. 1931. *Archives of British Honduras, Volume I, From the Earliest Date to A.D. 1800*. London: Sifton Praed and Company.

Butler, Kim. 2001. "Defining Diaspora, Refining a Discourse," in *Diaspora* 10:2, pp. 189–219.

Cáceres, Rina. 2000. *Negros, Mulatos, Esclavos y Libertos en la Costa Rica del Siglo XVII*. Mexico City: Instituto Panamericano de Geografía e Historia, Pub. No. 518.

Campbell, Mavis C. 2003. "St. George's Cay: Genesis of the British Settlement of Belize—Anglo-Spanish Rivalry," in *The Journal of Caribbean History* 37:2, pp. 171–203.

Campos García, Melchor. 2004. *De Provincia a Estado de la República Mexicana: La Península de Yucatán, 1786–1835*. Merida: CONACYT and Universidad Autónoma de Yucatán.

————. 2005. *Castas, Feligresía y Ciudadanía en Yucatán: Los Afromestizos Bajo el Régimen Constitucional Español, 1750–1822*. Merida: CONACYT and Universidad Autónoma de Yucatán.

Cárdenas y Valencia, fray Francisco. 1639. *Relación Historial Eclesiastica de la Provincia de Yucatán de la Nueva España*. Manuscript copy of 1643 in BL, Egerton 1791.

Carrera, Magali M. 2003. *Imagining Identity in New Spain: Race, Lineage, and the Colonial Body in Portraiture and Casta Paintings*. Austin: University of Texas Press.

Carrillo y Ancona, Crescencio. 1880. *Catecismo de Historia y de Geografía de Yucatán*. Merida: Libreria Catolica.

Carroll, Patrick J. 1991. *Blacks in Colonial Veracruz: Race, Ethnicity, and Colonial Development*. Austin: University of Texas Press (2nd ed., 2001).

Cartas de Indias. 1877. Madrid: Ministerio de Fomento.

Casanova Rosado, Aida Amine. 1995. *Campeche Intramuros*. Campeche: Universidad Autónoma de Campeche.

Caso Barrera, Laura. 2002. *Caminos en la Selva: Migración, Comercio y Resistencia. Mayas Yucatecos e Itzaes, Siglos XVII–XIX*. Mexico City: El Colegio de México and Fondo de Cultura Económica.

Castleman, Bruce A. 1998. "Workers, Work, and Community in Bourbon Mexico: Road Laborers on the Camino Real, 1757–1804." PhD dissertation, University of California, Riverside.

Chamberlain, Robert S. 1953. *The Conquest and Colonization of Honduras, 1502–1550*. Washington, DC: Carnegie Institution of Washington.

Chamosa, Oscar. 2003. " 'To Honor the Ashes of Their Forebears': The Rise and Crisis of African Nations in the Post-Independence State of Buenos Aires, 1820–1860," in *The Americas* 59:3 (January), pp. 347–78.

Childs, Matt D. 2006. " 'The Defects of Being a Black Creole': The Degrees of African Identity in the Cuban *Cabildos de Nación*, 1790–1820," in Jane G. Landers and Barry M. Robinson, eds., *Slaves, Subjects, and Subversives: Blacks in Colonial Latin America*. Albuquerque: University of New Mexico Press, pp. 209–45.

Chipman, Donald E. 2005. *Moctezuma's Children: Aztec Royalty Under Spanish Rule, 1520–1700*. Austin: University of Texas Press.

Christensen, Mark, and Matthew Restall. 2008. "Return to Ixil." Paper presented to the American Society for Ethnohistory, Eugene, OR.

Chuchiak, John F., IV. 2000. "The Indian Inquisition and the Extirpation of Idolatry: The Process of Punishment in the Provisorato de Indios of the Diocese of Yucatan, 1563–1812." PhD dissertation, Tulane University.

————. 2001. "Pre-Conquest Ah Kinob in a Colonial World: The Extirpation of Idolatry and the Survival of the Maya Priesthood in Colonial Yucatán, 1563–1697," in Ueli Hostettler and Matthew Restall, eds., *Maya Survivalism*. Acta Mesoamericana, vol. 12. Markt Schwaben, Germany: Verlag Anton Saurwein, pp. 135–160.

————. 2003. " 'It Is Their Drinking That Hinders Them': Balché and the Use of Ritual Intoxicants Among the Colonial Yucatec Maya, 1550–1780," in *Estudios de Cultura Maya* XXIV, pp. 137–71.

————. 2004. "Papal Bulls, Extirpators, and the Madrid Codex: The Content and Probable Provenience of the Madrid 56 Patch," in Gabrielle Vail and Anthony F. Aveni, eds., *The Madrid Codex: New Approaches to Understanding an Ancient Maya Manuscript*. Boulder: University of Colorado Press, pp. 74–114.

————. 2007. "Forgotten Allies: The Origins and Roles of Native Mesoamericn Auxiliaries and Indios Conquistadores in the Conquest of Yucatan, 1526-1550," in Laura E. Matthew and Michel R. Oudijk, eds., *Indian Conquistadors: Indigenous Allies in the Conquest of Mesoamerica*. University of Oklahoma Press, pp. 175–225.

Clementi, Hebe. 1974. *La Abolición de la Esclavitud en América Latina*. Buenos Aires: Editorial La Pléyade.

Clendinnen, Inga. 1987. *Ambivalent Conquests: Maya and Spaniard in Yucatan, 1517–1570*. Cambridge: Cambridge University Press.

Cody, Cheryll Ann. 1987. "There Was No 'Absalom' on the Ball Plantations: Slave Name Practices in the South Carolina Low Countries, 1720–1865," in *American Historical Review* 9, pp. 563–96.

Cole, Stephanie. 2004. "Finding Race in Turn-of-the-Century Dallas," in Stephanie Cole and Alison M. Parker, eds., *Beyond Black and White: Race, Ethnicity, and Gender in the U.S. South and Southwest*. College Station: Texas A&M University Press, pp. 75–96.

Contreras Sánchez, Alicia. 1990. *Historia de una Tintorea Olvidada: El Proceso de Explotación y Circulación del Palo de Tinte, 1750–1807*. Merida: Universidad Autónoma de Yucatán.

Cook, Lieutenant James. 1769. *Remarks on a Passage from the River Balise, in the Bay of Honduras, to Merida: The Capital of the Province of Jucatan in the Spanish West Indies*. London: C. Parker.

————. 1935. *Remarks on a Passage from the River Balise, in the Bay of Honduras, to Merida: The Capital of the Province of Jucatan in the Spanish West Indies; A Facsimile of the Original with Perspective by Muriel Haas*. New Orleans: Midameres Press.

Cook, Sherburne F., and Woodrow Borah. 1974. *Essays in Population History: Mexico and the Caribbean, Volume II*. Berkeley: University of California Press.

Cope, Douglas R. 1994. *The Limits of Racial Domination: Plebeian Society in Colonial Mexico City, 1660–1720*. Madison: University of Wisconsin Press.

Coronel Sánchez, Gustavo, Gabriel Cortés, Karina Osnaya, Cybele David, Vera Tiesler Blos, and Pilar Zabala Aguirre. 2001. "Practicas Funerarias e Idiosincrasia en la Ciudad Colonial de Campeche," in *Los Investigadores de la Cultura Maya* 9, pp. 183–96.

Cucina, Andrea. 2007. "La Desigualdad social Durante la Colonia: Patologías Orales y Defectos Hipoplásicos en la Antigua Población de Campeche," in Vera Tiesler, ed. *Orígenes de la Campechaneidad: Vida y Muerte en la Ciudad de Campeche Durante los Siglos XVI y XVII*. Mexico City: Universidad Nacional Autónoma de México.

Curtin, Philip. 1969. *The Atlantic Slave Trade: A Census*. Madison: University of Wisconsin Press.

Cussen, Celia L. 2005. "The Search for Idols and Saints in Colonial Peru: Linking Extirpation and Beatification," in *Hispanic American Historical Review* 85:3 (August), pp. 417–48.

Dampier, William. 1699. *Voyages and Descriptions*. Vol. II, Part 2: *Two Voyages to Campeachy*. London: James Knapton (Copy in the JCBL).

Davis, David Brion. 1997. "Constructing Race: A Reflection," in *William and Mary Quarterly* 54:1 (January), pp. 7–18.

Díaz, María Elena. 2000. *The Virgin, the King, and the Royal Slaves of El Cobre: Negotiating Freedom in Colonial Cuba, 1670–1780.* Stanford, CA: Stanford University Press.

Diouf, Sylviane A. 1998. *Servants of Allah: African Muslims Enslaved in the Americas.* New York: New York University Press.

Documentos para la Historia de Yucatán. 1936–38. 3 vols. Merida: n.p.

Dubois, Laurent. 2004. *A Colony of Citizens: Revolution and Slave Emancipation in the French Caribbean, 1787–1804.* Williamsburg and Chapel Hill: Omohundro Institute and University of North Carolina Press.

Dumond, Carol Steichen, and Don E. Dumond, eds. 1982. *Demography and Parish Affairs in Yucatan, 1797–1897: Documents from the Archivo de la Mitra Emeritense Selected by Joaquín de Arrigunaga Peón.* Eugene: University of Oregon Anthropological Papers No. 27.

Ellison, Ralph. 1972 [1952]. *Invisible Man.* New York: Vintage.

Eltis, David. 2000. *The Rise of African Slavery in the Americas.* Cambridge: Cambridge University Press.

Espinosa, Antonio Vásquez de. 1942 [1620]. *Compendium and Description of the West Indies (c. 1620).* Trans. by Charles Upson Clarke. Washington, DC: Smithsonian Institution Press.

Exquemelin, Alexander O. 1969. *The Buccaneers of America* [1678]. Trans. by Alexis Brown. Harmondsworth, UK: Penguin. Reprinted Mineola, NY: Dover, 2000.

Farriss, Nancy M. 1984. *Maya Society Under Colonial Rule: The Collective Enterprise of Survival.* Princeton, NJ: Princeton University Press.

Fernández-Armesto, Felipe. 1995. *Millennium: A History of the Last Thousand Years.* New York: Scribner.

Fernández Repetto, Francisco, and Genny Negroe Sierra. 1989. "Las Relaciones Interétnicas en la Provincia de Yucatán Durante el Período Colonial y su Manifestación en la Cofradía de Campeche," in *Revista de la Universidad Autónoma de Yucatán* 171:4, pp. 7–13.

———. 1995. *Una Población Perdida en la Memoria: Los Negros de Yucatán.* Merida: Universidad Autónoma de Yucatán.

Ferrer Muñoz, Manuel. 2001. "Los Comienzos de la Educación Universitaria en Yucatán," in *Temas Antropológicos* 23:2 (September), pp. 267–86.

Few, Martha. 2002. *Women Who Live Evil Lives: Gender, Religion, and the Politics of Power in Colonial Guatemala.* Austin: University of Texas Press.

Fields, Barbara J. 1982. "Ideology and Race in American History," in J. Morgan Kousser and James MacPherson, eds., *Region, Race, and Reconstruction: Essays in Honor of C. Vann Woodward.* New York: Oxford University Press, pp. 143–77.

Frederick, Jason. 2005. "The Landscape of Discontent: Community and Conflict in Papantla, Veracruz, 1750–1800." PhD dissertation, Pennsylvania State University.

Freyre, Gilberto. 1968. *The Master and the Slaves: A Study in the Development of Brazilian Civilization* [1946]. New York: Knopf.

Gabbert, Wolfgang. 2004. *Becoming Maya: Ethnicity and Social Inequality in Yucatán since 1500.* Tucson: University of Arizona Press.

Gage, Thomas. 1958. *Travels in the New World* [*The English–American, 1648*]. Edited by J. Eric S. Thompson. Norman: University of Oklahoma Press.

García Bernal, Manuela Cristina. 1972. *La Sociedad de Yucatán, 1700–1750*. Seville: Escuela de Estudios Hispano-Americanos de Sevilla.

———. 1976. "Los Servicios Personales en el Yucatán Durante el Siglo XVI," in Papers of the *Simposio Hispanoamericano de Indígenismo Histórico*. Valladolid, Spain: Terceras Jornadas Americanistas de la Universidad de Valladolid.

———. 1978. *Yucatán: Población y Encomienda bajo los Austrias*. Seville: Escuela de Estudios Hispano–Americanos de Sevilla.

———. 1979. "El Gobernador de Yucatán Rodrigo Flores de Aldana." In *Homenaje al Dr. Muro Orejón*. Seville: Escuela de Estudios Hispano–Americanos.

———. 1998. "El Comercio de Campeche con España: Del Aislamiento a la Integración (1700–1770)," in *La economía maritíma del Atlántico: pesca, navegación y comercio*, 3 vols. Zaragoza: Diputación Central de Aragón, Vol. 3, pp. 1465–84.

———. 2006. *Campeche y el Comercio Atlántico Yucateco (1561–1625)*. Mexico City and Campeche: Consejo Nacional de Cultura y Artes, Instituto Nacional de Antropología e Historia, and Gobierno del Estado de Campeche.

Gauderman, Kimberly. 2003. *Women's Lives in Colonial Quito: Gender, Law, and Economy in Spanish America*. Austin: University of Texas Press.

Gerhard, Peter. 1978. "A Black Conquistador in Mexico," in *Hispanic American Historical Review*, 58:3 (August), pp. 451–59.

Goldberg, Marta Beatriz. 2001. "Los Africanos de Buenos Aires, 1750–1880," in Rina Cáceres, ed., *Rutas de la Esclavitud en África y América Latina*. San José: Universidad de Costa Rica, pp. 269–88.

Gomes, Flávio dos Santos. 2002. "A 'Safe Haven': Runaway Slaves, *Mocambos*, and Borders in Colonial Amazonia, Brazil," in *Hispanic American Historical Review* 82:3 (August), pp. 469–98.

Gómez Danés, Pedro. 1996. *Negros y Mulatos en el Nuevo Reino de León, 1600–1795*. Monterrey: Archivo General del Estado del Nuevo León.

González Muñoz, Victoria. 1994. *Cabildos y Grupos de Poder en Yucatán (Siglo XVII)*. Seville: Diputación Provincial de Sevilla.

González Muñoz, Victoria, and Ana Isabel Martínez Ortega. 1989. *Cabildos y Elites Capitulares en Yucatán (Dos Estudios)*. Seville: Escuela de Estudios Hispano–Americanos.

Graham, Sandra Lauderdale. 1992. *House and Street: The Domestic World of Servants and Masters in Nineteenth-Century Rio de Janeiro*. Austin: University of Texas Press.

Gravatt, Patricia. 2003. *L'Église et L'Esclavage*. Paris: L'Harmattan.

Guardino, Peter. 2005. *The Time of Liberty: Popular Political Culture in Oaxaca, 1750–1850*. Durham: Duke University Press.

Gutiérrez, Ramón. 1991. *When Jesus Came, the Corn Mothers Went Away: Marriage, Sexuality, and Power in New Mexico, 1500–1846*. Stanford, CA: Stanford University Press.

Hall, Carolyn, and Héctor Pérez Brignoli. 2003. *Historical Atlas of Central America*. John V. Cotter, cartographer. Norman: University of Oklahoma Press.

Hall, Gwendolyn Midlo. 1992. *Africans in Colonial Louisiana: The Development of Afro-Creole Culture in the Eighteenth Century*. Baton Rouge: Louisiana State University Press.

———. 2005. *Slavery and African Ethnicities in the Americas: Restoring the Links*. Chapel Hill: University of North Carolina Press.

Handler, Jerome. 1974. *The Unappropriated People: Freedmen in the Slave Society of Barbados*. Baltimore, MD: The Johns Hopkins University Press.

Handler, Jerome S., and JoAnn Jacoby. 1996. "Slave Names and Naming in Barbados, 1650–1830," in *William and Mary Quarterly* 53:4, pp. 685–728.

Hanger, Kimberly S. 1997. *Bounded Lives, Bounded Places: Free Black Society in Colonial New Orleans, 1769–1803*. Durham: Duke University Press.

Harris, Leslie M. 2003. *In the Shadow of Slavery: African Americans in New York City, 1626–1863*. Chicago: University of Chicago Press.

Herrera, Robinson. 2000. " 'Por Que No Sabemos Firmar': Black Slaves in Early Guatemala," in *The Americas* 57:2 (October), pp. 247–67.

Herrera y Tordesillas, Antonio. 1601–1615. *Historia General de los Hechos de los Castellanos en las Islas y Tierra Firme del Mar Oceano, 8 decadas*. Madrid: Juan de la Cuesta (Copy in JCBL).

Himelblau, Jack J. 1994. *The Indian in Spanish America: Centuries of Removal, Survival, and Integration: A Critical Anthology, Vol. 1*. Lancaster: Labyrinthos.

Horn, Rebecca. 1997. *Postconquest Coyoacan: Nahua–Spanish Relations in Central Mexico, 1519–1650*. Stanford, CA: Stanford University Press.

Howard, Philip A. 1998. *Changing History: Afro-Cuban Cabildos and Societies of Color in the Nineteenth Century*. Baton Rouge: Louisiana State University Press.

Hunt, Marta Espejo-Ponce. 1974. "Colonial Yucatan: Town and Region in the Seventeenth Century." PhD dissertation, University of California, Los Angeles.

Huntington, Samuel P. 1993. "If Not Civilizations, What? Paradigms of the Post-Cold War World," in *Foreign Affairs* 72:5 (November/December), pp. 186–94.

Johnson, Lyman L. 1979. "Manumission in Colonial Buenos Aires, 1776–1810," in *Hispanic American Historical Review* 59:2 (May), pp. 258–79.

———. n.d. "Saying No and Other Forms of Resistance: Defining Slavery at its Margins." Unpublished article manuscript (2005).

Jones, Grant D. 1989. *Maya Resistance to Spanish Rule: Time and History on a Colonial Frontier*. Albuquerque: University of New Mexico Press.

———. 1998. *The Conquest of the Last Maya Kingdom*. Stanford, CA: Stanford University Press.

Jones, Oakah L., Jr. 1994. *Guatemala in the Spanish Colonial Period*. Norman: University of Oklahoma Press.

Katzew, Ilona. 2004. *Casta Painting: Images of Race in Eighteenth-Century Mexico*. New Haven, CT: Yale University Press.

Kaye, Anthony E. 2007. *Joining Places: Slave Neighborhoods in the Old South*. Chapel Hill: University of North Carolina Press.

Kepecs, Susan. 1999. "The Political Economy of Chikinchel, Yucatan, Mexico: A Diachronic Analysis from the Prehispanic Era through the Age of Spanish Administration." PhD dissertation, University of Wisconsin, Madison.

Khapoya, Vincent B. 1998. *The African Experience*. 2nd ed. Upper Saddle River, NJ: Prentice Hall.

Kiddy, Elizabeth W. 2005. *Blacks of the Rosary: Memory and History in Minas Gerais, Brazil*. University Park: The Pennsylvania State University Press.

Klein, Herbert S. 1967. *Slavery in the Americas: A Comparative Study of Virginia and Cuba*. Chicago: University of Chicago Press.

———. 1986. *African Slavery in Latin America and the Caribbean*. New York: Oxford University Press.

Konetzke, Richard, ed. 1953. *Colección de Documentos para la Historia de la Formación Social de Hispanoamérica, 1493–1810.* Madrid: Consejo Superior de Investigaciones Superiores.

Kuethe, Allan J. 1971. "The Status of the Free Pardo in the Disciplined Militia of New Granada," in *Journal of Negro History* 56:2 (April), pp. 105–17.

Kundera, Milan. 1999. "Such Was Their Wager," in *The New Yorker* (May 10).

Lacoste, Pablo. 2003. "Vitivinicultura en Chile Trasandino: Mendoza, 1561–1776," in *Colonial Latin American Historical Review* 12:2, pp. 113–50.

Landers, Jane. 1997. "Africans in the Spanish Colonies," in *Historical Archaeology* 31:1, pp. 74–92.

———. 1999. *Black Society in Spanish Florida.* Urbana: University of Illinois Press.

———. 2000. "Cimarrón Ethnicity and Cultural Adaptation in the Spanish Domains of the Circum–Caribbean, 1503–1763," in Paul Lovejoy, ed., *Identity in the Shadows of Slavery.* London: Continuum, pp. 30–54.

———. 2005. "Africans and Native Americans on the Spanish Florida Frontier," in Matthew Restall, ed., *Beyond Black and Red: African–Native Relations in Colonial Latin America.* Albuquerque: University of New Mexico Press, pp. 53–80.

———. 2006. "Cimarrón and Citizen: African Ethnicity, Corporate Identity, and the Evolution of Free Black Towns in the Spanish Circum-Caribbean," in Jane G. Landers and Barry M. Robinson, eds., *Slaves, Subjects, and Subversives: Blacks in Colonial Latin America.* Albuquerque: University of New Mexico Press, pp. 111–45.

Lane, Kris E. 1998. *Pillaging the Empire: Piracy in the Americas, 1500–1750.* Armonk, NY: M. E. Sharpe.

———. 2002. *Quito, 1599: City and Colony in Transition.* Albuquerque: University of New Mexico Press.

Lentz, Mark. 2005. " 'El Honor de una Señora Distinguida Injustamente Manchado': Sexual Honor, Social Standing, and the Decline of Religious Authority in Colonial Yucatan." Unpublished article manuscript.

———. n.d. "Murder in Mérida, 1792: Yucatecans Before the Law." PhD dissertation, Tulane University. In progress.

Levy, Juliette. 2003. "Yucatan's Arrested Development: Social Networks and Credit Markets in Mérida, 1850–1899." PhD dissertation, University of California, Los Angeles.

Lewis, Laura A. 2003. *Hall of Mirrors: Power, Witchcraft, and Caste in Colonial Mexico.* Durham: Duke University Press.

———. 2007. "From Sodomy to Superstition: The Active Pathic and Bodily Transgressions in New Spain," in *Ethnohistory* 54:1 (Winter), pp. 129–57.

Lienhard, Martin. 2003. "Hacia una 'Historia Oral' de los Esclavos Negros Insumisos (Caribe y Brasil, ca. 1790–1840)." Paper presented at the First International Interdisciplinary Symposium of the Colonial American Studies Organization, Georgetown University.

Ligorred Perramon, Josep. 1998. *T'Hó, la Mérida Ancestral.* Merida: Ayuntamiento de Mérida, Dirección de Desarrollo Urbano.

Lindsay, Mark Childress. 1999. "Spanish Merida: Overlaying the Maya City." PhD dissertation, University of Florida.

———. 2004. "Urban Planning in 16th Century Yucatan: Regular Grids for Idealized Repúblicas," in *The Latin Americanist* 48:1 (Fall), pp. 45–58.

Linebaugh, Peter, and Marcus Rediker. 2000. *The Many-Headed Hydra: Sailors, Slaves, Commoners, and the Hidden History of the Revolutionary Atlantic.* Boston: Beacon Press.

Lipsett-Rivera, Sonya. 1994. "Configurations within a Pattern of Violence: The Geography of Sexual Danger in Mexico, 1750–1850." Paper presented at the Conference on Latin American History and American Historical Association, Chicago.

Lisker, R., and V. Babinsky. 1986. "Admixture Estimates in Nine Mexican Indian Groups and Five East Coast Localities," in *Rev Invest Clin* 38, pp. 145–49.

Lisker, R., E. Ramírez, and V. Babinsky. 1996. "Genetic Structure of Autochthonous Populations of Meso-America: Mexico," in *Human Biology* 68, pp. 395–404.

Lockhart, James. 1994. *Spanish Peru, 1532–1560: A Social History* [1st ed., 1968]. Madison: University of Wisconsin Press.

Lohse, Russell. 2005. "Africans and Their Descendants in Colonial Costa Rica, 1600-1750." PhD dissertation, University of Texas at Austin.

López de Cogolludo, fray Diego. 1957. *Historia de Yucatán* [1654]. Mexico City: Editorial Academia Literaria. [Earliest edition consulted: *Historia de Yucathan.* Madrid: Juan García Infanzón, 1688 (Copy in JCBL).]

López Rivas, Luís. 1975. "Venta de Negros en Mérida a Fines del Siglo XVIII," in *Revista de la Universidad de Yucatán* 99–100, pp. 118–22.

Love, Bruce. 2004. *Maya Shamanism Today: Connecting with the Cosmos in Rural Yucatán.* Lancaster: Labyrinthos.

Lovejoy, Paul. 1997. "The African Diaspora: Revisionist Interpretations of Ethnicity, Culture and Religion under Slavery," in *Studies in the World History of Slavery, Abolition, and Emancipation* 2:1. Available online at http://www.h-net.msu.edu/~slavery/essays/esy9701love.html.

———. 2000. "Identifying Enslaved Africans in the African Diaspora," in Paul Lovejoy, ed., *Identity in the Shadows of Slavery.* London: Continuum, pp. 1–29.

Lutz, Christopher, and Matthew Restall. 2005. "Wolves and Sheep? Black-Maya Relations in Colonial Guatemala and Yucatan," in Matthew Restall, ed., *Beyond Black and Red: African-Native Relations in Colonial Latin America.* Albuquerque: University of New Mexico Press, pp. 185–221.

Lutz, Christopher H. 1994. *Santiago de Guatemala, 1541–1773: City, Caste, and the Colonial Experience.* Norman: University of Oklahoma Press.

Magubane, Zine. 2004. *Bringing the Empire Home: Race, Class, and Gender in Britain and Colonial South Africa.* Chicago: University of Chicago Press.

Mallo, Silvia C. 2001. "Negros y Mulatos Rioplatenses Viviendo en Libertad," in Rina Cáceres, ed., *Rutas de la Esclavitud en África y América Latina.* San José: Universidad de Costa Rica, pp. 305–21.

Markman, Sidney David. 1966. "The Non-Spanish Labor Force in the Development of the Colonial Architecture of Guatemala," in *Congreso Internacional de Americanistas XXXVI, Sevilla, 1964: Actas y Memorias.* Seville, pp. 189–94.

Martin, Cheryl English. 1985. *Rural Society in Colonial Morelos.* Albuquerque: University of New Mexico Press.

———. 1996. *Governance and Society in Colonial Mexico: Chihuahua in the Eighteenth Century.* Stanford, CA: Stanford University Press.

Martínez, María Elena. 2008. *Genealogical Fictions: Limpieza de Sangre, Religion, and Gender in Colonial Mexico.* Stanford, CA: Stanford University Press.

Martínez Ortega, Ana Isabel. 1993. *Estructura y Configuración Socioeconómica de los Cabildos de Yucatán en el Siglo XVIII.* Seville: Diputación Provincial de Sevilla.

McCaa, Robert. 1984. "Calidad, Class, and Marriage in Colonial Mexico: The Case of Parral, 1788–90," in *Hispanic American Historical Review* 64:3 (August), pp. 477–501.

McCaa, Robert, Stuart Schwartz, and Arturo Grubessich. 1979. "Race and Class in Colonial Latin America: A Critique," in *Comparative Studies in Society and History* 21:3, pp. 421–33.

McKnight, Kathryn Joy. 2003. "Gendered Declarations: Testimonies of Three Captured Maroon Women, Cartagena de Indias, 1634," in *Colonial Latin American Historical Review* 12:4 (Fall), pp. 499–527.

Medina, Cecilia, and Roberto Tejeda. 2003. "El Cementerio Colonial en la Plaza Principal de Campeche. Estratigrafía y Tafonomía," in *Los Investigadores de la Cultura Maya* 11, pp. 134–41.

Mintz, Sidney W., and Richard Price. 1976. *The Birth of African-American Culture: An Anthropological Perspective.* Boston: Beacon Press.

Miranda Ojeda, Pedro. 1999. "Hechicería Amorosa en Yucatán Durante el Siglo XVII," in *Temas Antropológicos* 21:2 (September), pp. 307–27.

———. 2001. "Las Comisarías Inquisitoriales de Yucatán," in *Temas Antropológicos* 23:1 (March), pp. 36–80.

Molina Solís, Juan Francisco. 1904–13. *Historia de Yucatán Durante la Dominación Española.* 3 vols. Merida: Imprenta de la Lotería del Estado de Yucatán.

Montanus, Arnoldus. 1671. *Beschryving van America.* Amsterdam (Copy in JCBL).

Morgan, Edmund S. 1972. "Slavery and Freedom: The American Paradox," in *Journal of American History* 59, pp. 5–29.

———. 1975. *American Slavery, American Freedom: The Ordeal of Colonial Virginia.* New York: Norton.

Morgan, Philip D. 1998. *Slave Counterpoint: Black Culture in the Eighteenth-Century Chesapeake and Low Country.* Chapel Hill and Williamsburg: University of North Carolina Press and Omohundro Institute of Early American History and Culture.

Mouser, Bruce L., ed. 2002. *A Slaving Voyage to Africa and Jamaica: The Log of the Sandown, 1793–1794.* Bloomington: Indiana University Press.

Muldoon, James. 2002. "The English of Ireland Are Not the English of England: Creating a Middle Nation on the Irish Frontier." Paper presented at the Calibrations Conference, Texas A&M University.

Muñoz Mata, Laura. 2001. "De la Raza de Color: Esclavos para Yucatán," in Adriana Naveda Chávez-Hita, ed., *Pardos, Mulatos y Libertos: Sexto Encuentro de Afromexicanistas.* Xalapa: Biblioteca Universidad Veracruzana, pp. 217–29.

Nazzari, Muriel. 1991. *Disappearance of the Dowry: Women, Families, and Social Change in São Paulo, Brazil, 1600–1900.* Stanford, CA: Stanford University Press.

———. 1996. "Concubinage in Colonial Brazil: The Inequities of Race, Class, and Gender," in *Journal of Family History* 21:2 (April), pp. 107–24.

Negroe Sierra, Genny. 1991. "Procedencia y Situación Social de la Población Negra de Yucatán," in *Boletín de la Escuela de Ciencias Antropológicas de la Universidad de Yucatán,* Nos. 106–107, 3–20.

Nichols, Christopher M. 2003. "Solares in Tekax: The Impact of the Sugar Industry on a Nineteenth-Century Yucatecan Town," in *Ethnohistory* 50:1 (Winter), pp. 161–89.

No author. 1985. *Reales Asientos y Licencias para la Introducción de Esclavos Negros a la América Española (1676–1789)*. Windsor: Rolston-Bain.

Ogilby, John. 1670. *America: Being an Accurate Description of the New World*. London: n.p. (Copy in JCBL).

Olwell, Robert. 1998. *Masters, Slaves, and Subjects: The Culture of Power in the South Carolina Low Country, 1740–1790*. Ithaca: Cornell University Press.

Owensby, Brian P. 2005. "How Juan and Leonor Won Their Freedom: Litigation and Liberty in Seventeenth-Century Mexico," in *Hispanic American Historical Review* 85:1 (February), pp. 39–79.

Palmer, Colin A. 1976. *Slaves of the White God: Blacks in Mexico, 1570–1650*. Cambridge, MA: Harvard University Press.

———. 1981. *Human Cargoes: The British Slave Trade to Spanish America, 1700–1739*. Urbana: University of Illinois Press.

———. 1998. "Defining and Studying the Modern African Diaspora," in *Perspectives* 36:6, pp. 1, 22–25.

———. 2002. "The Middle Passage," in Beverly C. McMillan, ed., *Captive Passage: The Transatlantic Slave Trade and the Making of the Americas*. Washington, DC: Smithsonian Institution, pp. 53–75.

Paso y Troncoso, Francisco del. 1939–42. *Epistolario de Nueva España, 1505–1818*. Mexico City: Porrúa.

Patch, Robert W. 1985. "Agrarian Change in Eighteenth-Century Yucatan," in *Hispanic American Historical Review* 65:1 (February), pp. 21–49.

———. 1993. *Maya and Spaniard in Yucatan, 1648–1812*. Stanford, CA: Stanford University Press.

———. 2002. *Maya Revolt and Revolution in the Eighteenth Century*. Armonk, NY: M. E. Sharpe.

Peniche Rivero, Piedad. 2002. "El Dulce Encanto de la Burguesía Henequenera: Resistencia de los Sirvientes de Haciendas y Estructuras Demográficas en la Época Dorada, 1879–1910," in Piedad Peniche Rivero and Felipe Escalante Tío, eds., *Los Aguafiestas: Desafíos a la Hegemonía de la Élite Yucateca, 1867–1910*. Merida: Archivo General del Estado de Yucatán, pp. 17–80.

Penningroth, Dylan C. 2003. *The Claims of Kinfolk: African American Property and Community in the Nineteenth-Century South*. Chapel Hill: University of North Carolina Press.

Peón Ancona, Juan Francisco. 1985. *Chucherías de la Historia de Yucatán*. Merida: Maldonado Editores.

Peraza Guzmán, Marco Tulio. 1997. *El Origen Reparador: El Centro Histórico de la Mérida Moderna*. Merida: Ediciones de la Universidad Autónoma de Yucatán.

Pérez de la Riva, Francisco. 1996. "Cuban *Palenques*," in Richard Price, ed., *Maroon Societies: Rebel Slave Communities in the Americas*. 3rd ed. [1st ed., 1973]. Baltimore, MD: Johns Hopkins University Press.

Pérez Galaz, Juan de D. 1942. *El Asesinato de Dn. Lucas de Gálvez (Un Pasaje de la Historia de Yucatán)*. Campeche: n.p.

Pérez-Mallaína, Pablo E. 1998. *Spain's Men of the Sea: Daily Life on the Indies Fleets in the Sixteenth Century*. Translated by Carla Rahn Phillips. Baltimore, MD: Johns Hopkins University Press.

Perry, Mary Elizabeth. 1990. *Gender and Disorder in Early Modern Seville*. Princeton, NJ: Princeton University Press.

Piña Chan, Román. 1977. *Campeche Durante el Período Colonial*. Mexico City: Instituto Nacional de Antropología e Historia.

Pi-Sunyer, Oriol. 1957. "Historical Background to the Negro in Mexico," in *Journal of Negro History* 42:4 (October), pp. 237–46.

Price, Richard, ed. 1996. *Maroon Societies: Rebel Slave Communities in the Americas* [1st ed., 1973]. Baltimore, MD: Johns Hopkins University Press.

Price, Richard, and Sally Price, eds. 1992. *Stedman's Surinam: Life in an Eighteenth-Century Slave Society*. Baltimore, MD: Johns Hopkins University Press.

Proctor, Frank "Trey," III. 2003a. "Afro-Mexican Slave Labor in the Obrajes de Paños of New Spain, Seventeenth and Eighteenth Centuries," in *The Americas* 60:1 (July), pp. 33–58.

———. 2003b. "Slavery, Identity, and Culture: An Afro-Mexican Counterpoint, 1640–1763." PhD dissertation, Emory University.

———. 2006. "Gender and the Manumission of Slaves in New Spain," in *Hispanic American Historical Review* 86:2 (May), pp. 308–36.

Quezada, Sergio. 2001. *Breve Historia de Yucatán*. Mexico City: Colegio de México and Fondo de Cultura Económica.

Racine, Karen. 2003. *Francisco de Miranda: A Transatlantic Life in the Age of Revolution*. Wilmington, DE: Scholarly Resources.

Redondo, Brígido. 1994. *Negritud en Campeche*. Campeche: Ediciones del Honorable Congreso del Estado.

Reed, Nelson A. 2001. *The Caste War of Yucatán* [1964]. Rev. ed. Stanford, CA: Stanford University Press.

Reel, Monte. 2005. "In Buenos Aires, Researchers Exhume Long-Unclaimed African Roots," in *Washington Post*, May 5, p. A14.

Reis, Joao José. 1993. *Slave Rebellion in Brazil: The Muslim Uprising of 1835 in Bahia*. Baltimore, MD: Johns Hopkins University Press.

———. 1997. " 'The Revolution of the *Ganhadores*': Urban Labour, Ethnicity, and the African Strike of 1857 in Bahia, Brazil," in *Journal of Latin American Studies* 29:2 (May), pp. 355–93.

Restall, Matthew. 1995. *Life and Death in a Maya Community: The Ixil Testaments of the 1760s*. Lancaster, CA: Labyrinthos.

———. 1997. *The Maya World: Yucatec Culture and Society, 1550–1850*. Stanford, CA: Stanford University Press.

———. 1998a. *Maya Conquistador*. Boston: Beacon Press.

———. 1998b. "Interculturation and the Indigenous Testament in Colonial Yucatan," in Susan Kellogg and Matthew Restall, eds., *Dead Giveaways: Indigenous Testaments of Colonial Mesoamerica and the Andes*. Salt Lake City: University of Utah Press, pp. 141–62.

———. 2000a. "The Telling of Tales: A Spanish Priest and his Yucatec Maya Parishioners," in Richard Boyer and Geoffrey Spurling, eds., *Colonial Lives: Documents on Latin American History, 1550–1850*. New York: Oxford University Press, pp. 18–31.

———. 2000b. "Black Conquistadors: Armed Africans in Early Spanish America," in *The Americas* 57:2 (October), pp. 171–206.

——. 2001a. "The People of the Patio: Ethnohistorical Evidence of Yucatec Maya Royal Courts," in Takeshi Inomata and Stephen Houston, eds., *Royal Courts of the Ancient Maya: Volume 2*. Boulder, CO: Westview Press, pp. 335–90.

——. 2001b. "La Falacia de la Libertad: La Experiencia Afro-Yucateca en la Edad de la Esclavitud," in Rina Cáceres, ed., *Rutas de la Esclavitud en África y América Latina*. San José, Costa Rica: Universidad de Costa Rica, pp. 289–304.

——. 2003. *Seven Myths of the Spanish Conquest*. New York: Oxford University Press.

——. 2004. "Maya Ethnogenesis," in *Journal of Latin American Anthropology*, 9:1 (Spring), pp. 64–89.

——, ed. 2005. *Beyond Black and Red: African-Native Relations in Colonial Latin America*. Albuquerque: University of New Mexico Press.

——. 2006. "Manuel's Worlds: Black Yucatan and the Colonial Caribbean," in Jane G. Landers and Barry M. Robinson, eds., *Slaves, Subjects, and Subversives: Blacks in Colonial Latin America*. Albuquerque: University of New Mexico Press, pp. 147–74.

——. n.d. "Yucatan and Belize: The Colonial Frontier as Bridge and Border." Unpublished manuscript.

Restall, Matthew, and Kris Lane. 2009. *Latin America in Colonial Times*. Cambridge: Cambridge University Press.

Restall, Matthew, Lisa Sousa, and Kevin Terraciano, eds. 2005. *Mesoamerican Voices: Native-Language Writings from Colonial Mexico, Oaxaca, Yucatan, and Guatemala*. Cambridge: Cambridge University Press.

Rivas, Christine. 2003. "The Spanish Colonial Military: Santo Domingo 1701–1779," in *The Americas* 60:2 (October), pp. 249–72.

Rodas de Coss, Francisco. 1983. *México en el Siglo XVIII, Tomo I: José de Gálvez Gallardo, 1720–1787*. Madrid: Comisión de Historia, Embajada de México en Madrid.

Romberg, Raquel. 2003. *Witchcraft and Welfare: Spiritual Capital and the Business of Magic in Modern Puerto Rico*. Austin: University of Texas Press.

Romero Jaramillo, Dolcey. 1997. *Esclavitud en la Provincia de Santa Marta, 1791–1851*. Santa Marta, Colombia: Instituto de Cultura y Turismo del Magdalena.

Roys, Ralph L., France V. Scholes, and Eleanor B. Adams. 1940. "Report and Census on the Indians of Cozumel, 1570," in *Contributions to American Anthropology and History* No. 30. Washington, DC: Carnegie Institution, Pub. No. 523, pp. 4–30.

Rubio Mañé, Ignacio J. 1938. *Documentos Para la Historia de Yucatán. La Iglesia en Yucatán, 1560–1610*. Merida.

——. 1941. *La Casa de Montejo en Mérida de Yucatán*. Mexico City: Imprenta Universitaria.

——. 1942. *Archivo de la Historia de Yucatán, Campeche, y Tabasco*. 2 vols. Mexico City.

——. 1945. "Extranjeros en Mérida y Campeche, 1796," in *Memorias de la Academia Mexicana de la Historia* IV:3, pp. 290–98.

Rucker, Walter C. 2006. *The River Flows On: Black Resistance, Culture, and Identity Formation in Early America*. Baton Rouge: Louisiana State University.

Rugeley, Terry. 1996. *Yucatán's Maya Peasantry and the Origins of the Caste War*. Austin: University of Texas Press.

————. 2001. *Of Wonders and Wise Men: Religious and Popular Cultures in Southeast Mexico, 1800–1876*. Austin: University of Texas Press.

Ruggiero, Guido. 2001. "The Strange Death of Margarita Marcellini: Male, Signs, and the Everyday World of Pre-Modern Medicine," in *American Historical Review* 106:4 (October), pp. 1141–58.

Ruz Menéndez, Rodolfo. 1970. "La Emancipación de los Esclavos de Yucatán" [Pamphlet]. Merida: Ediciones de la Universidad de Yucatán. Reprinted in *Por los Viejos Caminos del Mayab . . . Ensayos Históricos y Literarios*. Merida: Ediciones de la Universidad de Yucatán, 1973, pp. 199–220.

Safier, Neil. 2007. *Itinerant Enlightenment: Geography and Cultural Encounter from Paris to Colonial Peru*. Chicago: University of Chicago Press.

Sánchez de Aguilar, Pedro. 1937. *Informe Contra Idolorum Cultores* [1613–15]. Madrid: E. G. Triay e hijos.

Sánchez de Anda, Guillermo. 1998. *Yanga: Un Guerrero Negro*. Mexico City: Circulo.

Sanchíz Ochoa, Pilar. 1976. *Los Hidalgos de Guatemala*. Seville: Escuela de Estudios Hispano–Americanos de Sevilla.

Schoenhals, Martin. 2003. *Intimate Exclusion: Race and Caste Turned Inside Out*. Lantham, MD: University Press of America.

Scholes, France V., and Ralph L. Roys. 1948. *The Maya Chontal Indians of Acalan–Tixchel*. Washington, DC: Carnegie Institution.

Schwaller, Robert. N.d. "Defining Difference in Early New Spain." PhD dissertation, Pennsylvania State University. In progress.

Scott, Rebecca J. 2005. *Degrees of Freedom: Louisiana and Cuba After Slavery*. Cambridge, MA: Belknap Press of Harvard University Press.

Seed, Patricia. 1982. "Social Dimensions of Race: Mexico City, 1753," in *Hispanic American Historical Review* 62:4 (November), pp. 596–606.

————. 1988. *To Love, Honor, and Obey in Colonial Mexico: Conflicts over Marriage Choice, 1574–1821*. Stanford, CA: Stanford University Press.

Silverblatt, Irene. 1987. *Moon, Sun, and Witches: Gender Ideologies and Class in Inca and Colonial Peru*. Princeton, NJ: Princeton University Press.

————. 2004. *Modern Inquisitions: Peru and the Colonial Origins of the Civilized World*. Durham, NC: Duke University Press.

Smith, Stephanie Jo. 1997. "A Reconstruction of Early Nineteenth-Century Valladolid, Mexico." MA thesis, University of Oklahoma.

Solano y Pérez Lila, Francisco de. 1975. *Estudio Socioantropológico de la Población Rural No Indígena de Yucatán, 1700*. Merida: Ediciones de la Universidad de Yucatán.

Solís Robleda, Gabriela. 2003. *Bajo el Signo de la Compulsión: El Trabajo Forzoso Indígena en el Sistema Colonial Yucateco, 1540–1730*. Mexico City: CIESAS/ICY/INAH.

Sommer, Barbara A. 2003. "Cupid on the Amazon: Sexual Witchcraft and Society in Late Colonial Pará, Brazil," in *Colonial Latin American Historical Review* 12:4 (Fall), pp. 415–46.

Soulodre-La France, Renée. 2001. "Socially Not So Dead! Slave Identities in Bourbon Nueva Granada," in *Colonial Latin American Review* 10:1 (June), pp. 87–103.

Stephens, Thomas M. 1999. *Dictionary of Latin American Racial and Ethnic Terminology*. Gainesville: University of Florida Press.

Stern, Steve J. 1995. *The Secret History of Gender: Women, Men and Power in Late Colonial Mexico*. Chapel Hill: University of North Carolina Press.

Sullivan, Paul. 2004. *Xuxub Must Die: The Lost Histories of a Murder on the Yucatan*. Pittsburgh, PA: University of Pittsburgh Press.

Sweet, James H. 1997. "The Iberian Roots of American Racist Thought," in *William and Mary Quarterly* 54:1 (January), pp. 143–66.

———. 2003. *Recreating Africa: Culture, Kinship, and Religion in the African-Portuguese World, 1441–1770*. Chapel Hill: University of North Carolina Press.

———. 2006. "Mistaken Identities? Olaudah Equiano, Domingo Alvares, and the Methodological Challenges of Studying the African Diaspora." Paper presented at The Pennsylvania State University, October.

Tannebaum, Frank. 1946. *Slave and Citizen: The Negro in the Americas*. New York: Vintage.

Tardieu, Jean-Pierre. 1998. *El Negro en el Cusco: Los Caminos de la Alienación en la Segunda Mitad del Siglo XVII*. Lima: Pontificia Universidad Católica del Perú and Banco Central de Reserva del Perú.

Taylor, William B. 1979. *Drinking, Homicide, and Rebellion in Colonial Mexican Villages*. Stanford, CA: Stanford University Press.

———. 1996. *Magistrates of the Sacred: Priests and Parishioners in Eighteenth-Century Mexico*. Stanford, CA: Stanford University Press.

Terraciano, Kevin. 2001. *The Mixtecs of Colonial Oaxaca: Ñudzahui History, Sixteenth Through Eighteenth Centuries*. Stanford, CA: Stanford University Press.

Thompson, Philip C. 1978. "Tekanto in the Eighteenth Century." PhD dissertation, Tulane University [Published as *Tekanto, A Maya Town in Colonial Yucatán*. New Orleans, LA: Middle American Research Institute, Tulane University, Pub. No. 67, 1999].

Thornton, John. 1998. *Africa and Africans in the Making of the Atlantic World, 1400–1800*. 2nd ed. Cambridge: Cambridge University Press.

———. 2002. "Africa: The Source," in Beverly C. McMillan, ed., *Captive Passage: The Transatlantic Slave Trade and the Making of the Americas*. Washington, DC: Smithsonian Institution, pp. 35–51.

Tiesler, Vera. 2002. "New Cases of an African Tooth Decoration from Colonial Campeche, Mexico," in *Homo* 52:3, pp. 277–82.

———, ed. 2009. *Orígenes de la Campechaneidad: Vida y Muerte en la Ciudad de Campeche Durante los Siglos XVI y XVII*. Mexico City: Universidad Nacional Autónoma de México.

Tiesler, Vera, Marco Ramírez Salomón, and Iván Oliva Árias. 2002. "Decoration Techniques in Ancient Mexico—A Study of Dental Surfaces Using Radiography and S.E.M.," in *Oral Health* 92:9, pp. 33–41.

Tiesler Blos, Vera, and Pilar Zabala Aguirre. 2001. "Reflexiones Sobre la Composición Poblacional del Estado de Salud y las Condiciones de Vida Vigentes en la Cuidad de Campeche Durante los Siglos XVI y XVII," in *Los Investigadores de la Cultura Maya* 9, pp. 197–206.

Toribio Medina, José. 1907. "La Imprenta en Guadalajara, en Mérida de Yucatán, en Oaxaca, y en Veracruz," in *Boletin de Instituto Bibliografico Mexicano*, num. 6, pp. 17–32.

Townsend, Camilla. 1997. "Story Without Words: Women and the Creation of a Mestizo People in Guayaquil, 1820–1835," in *Latin American Perspectives* 95 (July), pp. 50–68.

Tutino, John. 1986. *From Insurrection to Revolution in Mexico: Social Bases of Agrarian Violence, 1750–1940*. Princeton, NJ: Princeton University Press.

———. 2003. "Emancipation without Abolition: The Demise of Slavery in the Bajio." Paper presented at the First International Interdisciplinary Symposium of the Colonial American Studies Organization, Georgetown University.

Van Deusen, Nancy E. 1999. "The 'Alienated' Body: Slaves and Castas in the Hospital de San Bartolomé in Lima, 1680–1700," in *The Americas* 56:1 (July), pp. 1–30.

Vaughan, Megan. 2005. *Creating the Creole Island: Slavery in Eighteenth-Century Mauritius*. Durham, NC: Duke University Press.

Vega Franco, Marisa. 1984. *El Trafico de Esclavos con America (Asientos de Grillo y Lomelín, 1663–1674)*. Seville: Escuela de Estudios Hispano–Americanos.

Velázquez Gutiérrez, María Elisa. 2001. "Africanas y Descendientes en la Cuidad de México del Siglo XVII," in Rina Cáceres, ed., *Rutas de la Esclavitud en África y América Latina*. San José: Universidad de Costa Rica, pp. 211–22.

Victoria Ojeda, Jorge. 1995. *Mérida de Yucatán de las Indias: Piratería y Estrategia Defensiva*. Merida: Ayuntamiento de Mérida.

Victoria Ojeda, Jorge, and Jorge Canto Alcocer. 2001. "La Aventura Imperial de España en la Revolución Haitiana. Impulso y Dispersión de los Negros Auxiliares: El Caso de San Fernando Aké, Yucatán," in *Secuencia* (nueva época) 49 (Jan–April), pp. 70–87.

———. 2006. *San Fernando Aké: Microhistoria de una comunidad afroamericana en Yucatán*. Merida: Ediciones de la Universidad Autónoma de Yucatán.

Vila Vilar, Enriqueta. 1977. *Hispanoamérica y el Comercio de Esclavos: Los Asientos Portugueses*. Seville: Escuela de Estudios Hispano–Americanos.

Villa-Flores, Javier. 2002. "'To Lose One's Soul': Blasphemy and Slavery in New Spain, 1596–1669," in *Hispanic American Historical Review* 82:3 (August), pp. 435–68.

Villagutierre Soto-Mayor, Juan de. 1983 [1701]. *History of the Conquest of the Itza*. Frank E. Comparato, ed., Robert D. Wood, trans. Lancaster, CA: Labyrinthos.

Villalobos, don Juan de. 1682. *Manifiesto que a su Magestad (Que Dios Guarde) y Señores de su Real, y Supremo Consejo de las Indias, Haze el Capitan don Juan de Villalobos, Vezino de la Nueva Ciudad de la Veracruz en el Reyno de la Nueva España, Sobre la Introduccion de Esclavos Negros en las Indias Occidentales*. Seville (Copy in JCBL).

Vincent, Theodore G. 2001. *The Legacy of Vicente Guerrero, Mexico's First Black Indian President*. Gainesville: University Press of Florida.

Vinson III, Ben. 2001a. *Bearing Arms for His Majesty: The Free-Colored Militia in Colonial Mexico*. Stanford, CA: Stanford University Press.

———. 2001b. "La Dinámica Social de la Raza: Los Milicianos Pardos de Puebla en el Siglo XVIII," in Adriana Naveda Chávez-Hita, ed., *Pardos, Mulatos y Libertos: Sexto Encuentro de Afromexicanistas*. Xalapa: Biblioteca Universidad Veracruzana, pp. 61–97.

———. 2006. "Introduction: African (Black) Diaspora History, Latin American History," in *The Americas* 63:1 (July), pp. 1–18.

Vinson III, Ben, and Matthew Restall. 2005. "Black Soldiers, Native Soldiers: Meanings of Military Service in the Spanish American Colonies," in Matthew Restall, ed., *Beyond Black and Red: African–Native Relations in Colonial Latin America*. Albuquerque: University of New Mexico Press, pp. 15–52.

Von Germeten, Nicole. 2006. *Black Blood Brothers: Confraternities and Social Mobility for Afro-Mexicans*. Gainesville: University Press of Florida.

Wade, Peter. 1997. *Race and Ethnicity in Latin America*. London: Pluto Press.

Walker, Charles F. 2003. "The Upper Classes and Their Upper Stories: Architecture and the Aftermath of the Lima Earthquake of 1746," in *Hispanic American Historical Review* 83:1 (February), pp. 53–82.

Wells, Allen, and Gilbert M. Joseph. 1996. *Summer of Discontent, Seasons of Upheaval: Elite Politics and Rural Insurgency in Yucatan, 1876–1915*. Stanford, CA: Stanford University Press.

White, Richard. 1991. *The Middle Ground: Indians, Empires, and Republics in the Great Lakes Region, 1650–1815*. Cambridge: Cambridge University Press.

Wiethoff, William E. 2002. *The Insolent Slave*. Columbia: University of South Carolina Press.

Wood, Gordon S. 2003. "Slaves in the Family," in *New York Times Book Review* (December 14), pp. 10–11.

Yalom, Samuel Reid. 2004. *Colonial Noir: Photographs from Mexico*. Stanford, CA: Stanford University Press.

Zavala, Silvio. 1977. *La Filosofía Política en la Conquista de América*. Mexico City: Fondo de Cultura Económica.

Zorita, Alonso de. 1994. *Life and Labor in Ancient Mexico: The Brief and Summary Relation of the Lords of New Spain* [c. 1570], Benjamin Keen, ed. 2nd ed. Norman: University of Oklahoma Press.

Index

Abolition, 33–39 passim, 80, 131, 181, 283–84; main treatment, 67–73
Acalan-Tixchel, 156
Acevedo: Capt. Clemente de, 175, 264; Capt. Diego de, 14, 128
Acosta: don Ramón, 227, 249, 251; Eugenio de, 63, 126, 139, 175
Aguardiente. *See* Alcohol
Aguilar: don Fernando de, 142; Francisco de, 54, 75–77, 99, 109–11, 286–87, 310; Gonzalo de, 239; Lucas de, 126
Aguirre Beltrán, Gonzalo, 29
Ake, San Fernando, 148–50, 182–83, 222–26, 255
Alcalde, don fray Antonio, 53–54
Alcaudete, Antonio, 101
Alcedo, Antonio de, 75, 79, 212, 373n20
Alcohol: as aguardiente, 119, 139, 254; as balché, 248, 270–71; in various forms, 129, 225–26, 254–55, 267–76 passim, 365n11; as wine, 41, 206, 313, 370n64, 399n10
Aldana: Capt. Domingo, 263; Diego, 127; don Antonio Maldonado de, 213
Aldequa, Bernardo, 90
Alpuche, doña Petrona, 14, 60
Amulets, 247, 271–72
Ancona family, 202, 240, 368n50
Andrews, Anthony, 149, 182–83, 224–25
Anguas family, 65–66
Argentina. *See* Buenos Aires
Asensio, fray Cristóbal, 2
Auction of slaves, 11, 20, 23–26, 46–48, 53, 70, 122, 279; in Merida (1779–80), 23, 26, 46–47, 62, 162, 232, 245
Ávila family, 60–61, 244
Ayora family, 41
Aznar y Peón, don Tomás, 72, 189

Bacalar, 119, 191–92, 234; and Belize, 23–25, 38, 122, 178–81, 235; colonial description, 2; defenses, 141, 156–75 passim; foundings and locations, 21–22; militia, 163, 165, 254; population, 31, 166, 220–21
Balché. *See* Alcohol
Baptism, 14, 23–26, 37, 47–59 passim, 66, 70, 101–18 passim, 187, 196, 219, 233, 244–45, 259–63, 304–8. *See also* Campeche; Jesús parishes; Merida
Baptist, Edward, 65
Barbados, 100
Barbers, 119–35 passim, 157, 167, 202, 219, 221, 239, 254; main treatment, 119–20, 138
Bates family, 21, 362n48, 391n136
Becal, 102, 105–6, 137, 147, 247, 250
Belize: 160; main treatments, 21–26, 169, 181–82; slaves fleeing or taken from, 9–36 passim, 47–50, 62, 122, 170, 178, 196, 229–32, 245, 255, 279; Spanish raids and attacks on, 9, 22–24, 162, 176
Bennett, Herman, 281
Benzoni, Girolamo, 16
Bergara, Augustina, 153–55, 195
Berlin, Ira, 81, 238, 280–81
Bermejo and Marcos Bermejo families, 41, 60, 94, 186, 254
Bernand, Carmen, 106
Betancourt, don Sebastián, 86
Bishops of Yucatan, 11, 14, 25, 48–56, 70, 82–108 passim, 142–53 passim, 186, 211–19 passim, 232, 242, 256, 258, 278, 292
Boats, 41, 140–41, 212, 314. *See also* Ships
Bolio, Manuel, 21, 44, 190–99, 234, 262–63, 283; family, 190

Branding of slaves, 23, 26, 48–49, 97
Brazil, 13, 19, 32, 65, 67, 69, 78, 140, 179, 233, 237, 272, 396n77
British. *See* English
Bryant, Sherwin, 402n7
Buenos Aires, 106, 177, 185, 283, 284, 396n77
Burials, 149, 208–11, 304–8

Cacalchen, 63, 103, 139, 144, 298
Cacao, 37–41 passim, 93, 117, 126, 137, 173, 208, 267–72 passim, 313–14, 399n10
Calidad. *See* Casta categories
Calkini, 104, 115–16, 129, 164, 221, 251
Campeche: 11–97 passim, 110–215 passim, 221–85 passim; attacks on, 140–41, 157–60, 206; founding, 12, 206–7; illustrations, 18, 205; and independence, 68–71; main treatment, 204–15; population, 195, 213–15, 263; slaves in, 13–37 passim, 116. *See also* Jesús parishes; Mortgages of slaves
Campero family, 202, 239–40
Canary Islands, 206, 392n20
Canek. *See* Cisteil Revolt
Canto, Capt. Lázaro del, 133, 143, 168, 175, 178, 197–99, 219, 369n50; main treatment, 153–55
Captaincies, 57–59, 156, 170. *See also* Encomiendas; Militias and militiamen
Caracas, 20, 39–40, 49
Cárdenas y Valencia, fray Francisco, 211, 216, 220, 394n41
Carolina, 168
Carreño, José, 182, 224, 255
Carrión, Br. Don Nicolás Gregorio, 202, 239, 243
Cartagena, 19, 20, 21, 40, 48, 86, 190–93, 197–98, 313, 396n77
Carvajal: Capt. don Pedro, 127, 186; don Fernando López de, 185; General don José Segundo, 71–73; Pedro, 127, 186
Casanova, María de, 265–68
Casta categories, 31, 76–77, 86, 236–65 passim, 284; main treatment, 87–109; paintings, 93–96, 102, 117, 126, 262. *See also* Race
Caste War, the, 71, 130, 284, 371n88
Castillo: Br. Don Rafael del, 54, 186; don Juan del, 127; family, 60–61, 242, 263, 367n31
Castizo, 92, 102, 137, 196, 264. *See also* Casta categories

Castro: don Juan Joseph de, 245; family, 60; Francisco de, 86
Catholicism. *See* Church; Religion
Cattle. *See* Livestock
Cayo Cocina, 22–24, 169, 188, 231–32, 386n46
Chacón, don Rodrigo, 14, 60–62; family, 60–61, 109, 137, 369n50
Champotón, 154, 158, 168, 170, 207, 273
Chan: Andrés, 257; Diego, 203, 240; Enrique, 246; family, 262; Josepha, 191–94, 198, 262–63; Pasqual, 244; Pasquala, 265
Chasarretta: family, 113; 379n8; Joaquín, 112–13, 151–52, 380n25
Chavarría: Capt. don Nicolás de, 264; family, 348
Chesapeake, 32, 86, 238, 281
Chihuahua, 370n73, 380n24, 395n64
Chikindzonot, 143, 300, 306
Chino, 102, 106. *See also* Casta categories
Chocolate. *See* Cacao
Chunhuhub, 21–22, 169, 221, 300, 306, 362n45
Church: Afro-Yucatecan clergy, 141–42, 154; buildings, 120, 207–12, 216–19, 223; clergy as slave owners, 52–55; on slavery, 80–83. *See also* Baptism; Bishops of Yucatan; Cofradías; Jesús parishes; Religion
Cisteil Revolt (1761), 127, 168–69, 246, 389n104
Clothing and textiles, 85, 139–47 passim, 161, 201, 208, 239–47 passim, 272–73, 276, 313
Cofradías, 217–18, 220, 284, 363n63; main treatment, 236–38
Cogolludo, fray Diego López de, 179–80, 211, 256
Cook, Lieutenant James, 2, 16, 23, 160, 169
Colored crescent, the, 29, 116, 120, 130, 163, 221
Congo, 10, 52, 56, 106, 190–91, 224–34 passim, 244, 261–62, 319, 348
Conquest of Yucatan, 6–12, 15–17, 27, 155–56
Constitution of 1812, 68, 195
Contreras: Ana, 145; Juan de, 368n42, 384n9
Convent of Nuestra Señora de la Concepción, 55
Copal, 144, 248, 269–71

Corn farming, 78, 101, 121–54 passim, 172–73, 177, 200, 221, 223, 239–48 passim, 265, 399n10
Correa, José María, 87–88, 99, 111
Cosgaya: don Juan Ignacio de, 130, 363n49; Micaela, 186
Costa Rica, 283
Coyi, don Alonso, 247–48
Cozumel, 2, 157, 367n33, 368n42
Creolization debate, 228, 232
Crime, 85–88, 139–40, 183, 202, 249–56, 399n18
Cuba, 78, 180, 209, 231, 284, 365n11. *See also* Havana
Cuero, Diego, 127, 246
Curaçao, 19, 48

Dallas, 82, 101
Dampier, William, 171–72, 213, 247
Desdunes, Rodolphe, 281
Defense of Yucatan, 156–77. *See also* Belize; English; Militias and militiamen; Pirates and privateers
Demography, 12–14, 25–33, 149, 229, 285, 296–308. *See also* Bacalar; Campeche; Colored crescent; Merida
Dobson, Richard, 178, 189–91, 194, 200, 235
Dowries, 41, 43, 64
Dubois, Laurent, 233
Durango, 113
Dyewood. *See* Logwood and loggers
Dzonotake, 101, 200–203, 239–43

Ek, don Juan Antonio, 247–48, 269
El Carmen or Villa del Carmen, 34, 71–72, 158, 285, 388n90
El Cobre (Cuba), 395n58
Ellison, Ralph, 1, 283
Eltis, David, 65
Encomiendas: and encomenderos, 14, 18, 41, 55–64, 113–14, 119–58 passim, 170, 185, 207–8, 278, 314; and encomenderas, 58, 61, 185, 202, 211
English: 81, 154, 160, 168, 173–76, 200, 221; slave owners, 24, 32, 44, 47, 79, 101, 128; slave traders, 13, 20–22, 24–25, 38–39, 67, 229–31, 360n24. *See also* Belize
Enriquez Noboa, don Pedro, 278
Escalante, Damiana, 145
Escaped slaves, 16, 149, 227, 249–57; main treatment, 178–84. *See also* Belize
Espinola, José María, 99, 112, 118, 131, 153, 188–89, 292–95

Espita, 118, 131, 188, 292–94, 301, 307
Esquivel, Br. Don Ignacio de, 278
Estrada: Miguel Duque de, 194–97, 282; sisters, 90
Exquemelin, 140, 213

Families among slaves, 64–66, 243–45, 259–60
Flores de Aldana, don Rodrigo, 122, 129, 158, 287, 367n37
Florida, 23, 168, 222–34, 367n34
Fort of San Benito, 64, 122, 158, 245, 287
Feijoo, Benito Jerónimo, 92
Francisca Antonia, 188
Franciscans, 17, 36, 85, 137, 142, 196, 211, 258. *See also* Cárdenas y Valencia; Cogolludo; Landa
Freyre, Gilberto, 65

Gage, Thomas, 180
Gálvez: don José de, 83; don Lúcas de, 52, 118, 242, 380n25, 399n17
García Bernal, Manuela Cristina, 29
Genovese, Eugene, 281
Gómez: de Parada, Dr. don Juan, 50, 82–83, 102, 217–18, 232; Fabiana, 246
González: Baltazar, 175–76; Diego, 175, 254; Dr. don Juan Salvador, 244–45; Francisco, 163, 175–76; Juan de Dios, 160, 163, 176
Governors of Yucatan: in general, 6, 14, 56–59, 70, 83, 279; specific, 10–34 passim, 46–75 passim, 96–100, 112–29 passim, 142–94 passim, 213, 242–56 passim, 310–11, 380n25
Guatemala, 22, 73, 180–81, 283, 389n104
Guayaquil, 94, 313, 369n60
Guerrero, Vicente, 68–69, 71–72
Gumilla, José, 92

Haiti, 148, 150, 182, 222–23
Hallucinogens, 270–72
Handler, Jermone, 377n91
Háuregui, María, 132, 143
Havana, 19, 20, 43, 141, 160, 163, 186–92 passim, 207–8, 213–14, 222, 235. *See also* Cuba
Healers, 115–34 passim, 144–45, 154–55, 247–49, 270–76
Herrera: Alférez Joseph Martín de, 266; Antonio de, 180; Diego Felipe, 139; doña Beatriz de, 16–17, 361n34; Juan Martín de, 85; Lucas, 132; María de Luz, 89–90

Hidalgo: Capt. Mateo, 168; Miguel, 68
Holpatán tax, 55
Holy Office. *See* Inquisition
Honduras, 10, 13, 16, 17, 22, 180, 191
Honey. *See* Wax and honey
Horses. *See* Livestock
Horta Barroso, Dr. don Antonio, 154, 265–66, 269, 273, 401n62
Huerta family, 115, 145
Huntington, Samuel, 280
Hunucmá, 71–72, 150, 164, 170–72, 190, 224–26, 269, 278, 297
Hunt, Marta Espejo-Ponce, 120, 175

Idolatry, 76, 85, 247, 268–69, 276–77, 372n6
Independence, 67–70, 163–65, 177, 283
Indigo, 127
Inquisition: Index, 80; in Mexico and Spain, 37, 94, 98, 200–202, 234, 241, 269, 290–91; in Yucatan, 144, 154–55, 191, 199–202, 235, 242–76 passim
Interpreters, 10, 114, 223, 406
Ipil, 87–88
Isla Mujeres, 24, 169
Islam, 83, 91, 233–36, 396n77
Iturbide, Agustín de, 68
Itza Mayas, 22, 118, 156, 168, 173, 380n16
Izamal, 63–90 passim, 103, 116–51 passim, 164, 173, 221, 265, 291, 305
Ixil, 144

Jamaica, 18–20, 39, 48–52, 78, 94, 166, 190–91, 229–35, 360n24, 366n26; governor or admiral in, 22, 160, 181; pirates from, 140, 172
Jefferson, Thomas, 85
Jesuits, 80, 92, 196–97, 219
Jesús parishes, 23, 26, 47–70 passim, 106–8, 153–54, 165, 186–229 passim, 258–62. *See also* Campeche; Merida
Jews, 81, 91, 98
José Antonio, 99, 118
Juan Patricio, 86, 278–79, 283

Katzew, Ilona, 95
Kaxek, 150, 226
Kaye, Anthony, 65, 243
Kikil, 148–50, 222, 301, 307
King of Spain, 6–7, 76, 80, 83, 153, 188–90, 376n70
Kopomá, 249–50, 297, 304, 400n24
Kuethe, Allan, 177
Kuhn, Thomas, 280

La Mejorada (Merida-Tiho), 112, 198, 217, 219, 254, 259
Labor roles, 13–17, 30–39 passim, 62–69, 78–86, 101, 206–14, 279–83; main treatment, 112–77
Landa, fray Diego de, 85
Lara: Bonifaz, Capt. don Francisco, 96, 194, 310; family, 69–70, 190–92, 197, 390n126
Las Casas: Bartolomé de, 78, 80; don Guillén de, 17, 51, 258
Leira, Agustín de, 10, 48, 97–98, 129
Lentz, Mark, 399n17
Lima, 78, 380n32. *See also* Peru
Livestock, 2, 26, 41, 44, 57, 63–64, 121–58 passim, 190, 201, 206, 219, 237, 253, 257, 289
Logwood and loggers, 2, 21–24, 39, 128, 150, 170, 182, 213, 225–26. *See also* Belize
Look-outs, 135, 166, 386n51, 387n53; main treatment, 170–73. *See also* Defense of Yucatan
L'Olonnais, François, 140
London, 21, 160, 169, 231, 362n48
Long, Edward, 94
Lope, Antonio, 132, 138, 143
Louisiana, 189, 281. *See also* New Orleans
Lovejoy, Paul, 228
Love-magic, 144–45, 248; main treatment, 265–76

Madrid, 6–7, 15, 23, 72, 98; Codex, 76
Magubane, Zine, 65
Maldonado family, 60, 213, 266–68, 273, 367n37
Mani, 103, 258, 298
Manumission, 69, 79, 84, 173, 178, 194, 281–82, 292; main treatment, 184–90
Marcín, José Antonio, 183–84, 227, 249–57
Marcos: (1540s), 10, 16–17, 114, 118–19, 129, 191, 251; (1790s), 222–23
Maroons. *See* Escaped slaves
Marriage: bigamous, 190–203 passim, 234, 242–43; conflicts over, 87–90, 95, 201; patterns, 66, 191–93, 198, 221–22, 235–36, 257–65
Martín family, 89–90, 191, 236, 394n41
Martínez Ortega, Ana Isabel, 59
Mauritius, 65
Maxcanú, 104, 124, 126, 164, 167, 197, 249–50, 256; population, 221, 297, 304, 400n24

Maya-language sources and literature, 1, 3, 143–44
Maya pyramids, 122, 172, 207, 215–17, 223–24
Mazo, don Toribio del, 25–26
Medina: family, 239; Francisco, 75, 89, 99, 153, 291–92; Melchor de, 132
Mena, Pedro de, 101, 132
Mendicuti family, 9, 56, 188, 365n7
Meneses y Bravo de Sarabia, don Alonso, 50–51
Merida: 2–77 passim, 87–88, 96–290 passim; cabildo, 59, 368n50; colonial descriptions, 26, 215–17; founding, 12, 16, 26, 215; main treatment, 215–20; population, 2, 26, 216–20, 304; slaves in, 14, 25–31, 39, 116, 215
Mexía, Andrés de, 34, 37
Mexico City, 19, 68–71, 80, 95, 110, 113, 117, 139, 232; imprisoned in, 200, 276; Inquisition in, 37, 108, 154, 202, 241, 267–69; slaves in, 38, 40, 51, 86, 117, 237–38, 281–82; viceroy, archbishop, and their offices in, 9, 22, 26, 57, 78, 100, 176, 189–90, 258
Middle Passage, 4–20 passim, 37, 118, 186, 190, 228, 283
Militias and militiamen, 23–24, 57, 115, 120, 149, 239–42, 252–55; main treatment, 153–77
Mina, 10, 51, 209, 230, 233, 396n70
Miranda Ojeda, Pedro, 273
Miscegenation, 27, 33, 283–84. *See also* Casta categories; Demography; Race
Mississippi, 32, 243
Moctezuma family, 7
Molina, doña María Joaquina, 34–37, 43–44, 49
Molina Solís, Juan Francisco, 154
Montejo: Francisco de and family, 10–18, 51, 114–29 passim, 206–8, 215; Isabel de, 336; Micaela, 144–45, 266–76 passim, 338, 340
Moreno, 7, 70, 96–109 passim, 156, 177, 188, 191, 212, 236, 263, 294. *See also* Casta categories
Morgan, Philip, 238
Mortgages of slaves, 11, 41–43, 70
Mosquito coast and natives, 22, 222–23, 231
Motul, 63–64, 103, 109, 120, 264, 298
Mulato, Diego el, 141, 157, 166, 183
Mulatto. *See* Casta categories; Race
Muleteers and mules, 63, 121–39 passim, 151, 167, 175, 314

Music, 51, 117–18, 121
Muslims. *See* Islam

Nabalam, 101, 132, 201, 301, 243
Nahuas, 94, 257; in Yucatan, 77, 132, 138, 155–56, 210–11, 261–63
Nahuatl, 17, 114, 257
Naming patterns, 35, 43–49, 279–82, 350–53
Navarrete, don Melchor de, 50, 52, 60, 254
Negro, Cristóbal, 268–70
Newspapers in Yucatan, 69–71
New Orleans, 177
Nobelo, Juan Antonio, 143
Nogal, Juan de, 13
Noguera family, 60, 244
Núñez Melián, don Francisco, 49, 51, 54, 96–97, 194

Ogilby, John, 206, 358n9
Ontiveros family 87–88
Ortuño de Olano, Juan, 13
Oxkutzcab, 102, 104, 120, 125, 127, 137, 144–45, 156, 298, 305

Pacheco family, 128–52 passim, 186, 219, 267, 310, 366n20
Padilla: Dr. don fray Ignacio de, 52–53, 149, 219, 364n63; Joseph de, 97, 209
Palmer, Colin, 20
Palomeque, don Manuel, 98
Palomino: Juan Fernández, 125; Juan Ignacio, 125, 127, 144
Panabá, 149, 276
Pardo. *See* Casta categories; Race
Parker, William, 157–58, 206
Patch, Robert, 62
Pech family, 1, 4, 12, 131, 155, 197, 202
Peón, Colonel don Alonso, 188
Pérez family, 55, 60–61, 88, 124, 137, 147, 181, 239, 368n44
Peru, 16, 39–40; Africans in, 44, 78, 360n28
Petén. *See* Guatemala; Itza Mayas
Pigs. *See* Livestock
Piña y Mazo, don fray Luis de, 48, 50, 53
Pirates and privateers, 22, 57, 140–41, 155–88 passim, 200, 212–13
Ponce, fray Alonso, 170, 172
Poot family, 156, 250, 252, 256, 348
Popayán, 87, 402n7
Pope Paul III, 80
Portugal and Portuguese slave traders, 7, 18–20, 32, 80

Prieto, don Joachin Fernando, 2
Puc: Catalina, 272–73, 336, 340; Juan, 140

Quezada, Sergio, 1–2
Quijano, don Juan Esteban, 47, 60–62
Quintana, José Matias, 153, 177

Rabanales, Capt. Cristóbal, 168
Race, 31–32, 75–111, 224, 241, 258. *See also* Casta categories
Ramos, Diego, 99, 112, 122, 158, 245, 287–90
Rechet, Julian, 190–91
Rejón, don Diego, 246
Religion, 47–48, 80–83, 154, 178, 188, 210, 228, 232–40, 272. *See also* Baptism; Bishops of Yucatan; Cofradías; Church; Islam
Rementeria, Juan de, 98
Repartimiento, 53, 113
Revillagigedo, Viceroy, 163, 176
Reyes, Lázaro de los, 97
Robles Castellanos, Fernando, 182, 224–25
Rodríguez family, 172–73, 264
Rosado: Alonso, 16, 57, 179–80, 256; Juan, 128
Royal Pragmatic, the, 89–90, 95
Rubio, Eugenio, 161–62
Ruiz family, 265, 310

Sahcabchen, 31, 164, 255, 304
Sales tax, 40–41, 129, 313–17
San Cristóbal (Merida-Tiho), 112, 122, 125, 158, 217, 219, 259, 262, 266, 289; population, 297, 304
San Francisco de Paula, 148–50, 182–83, 224–26
San Lorenzo de los Negros, 183
San Román (Campeche), 207, 211–12, 215, 246
Sanabria family, 265
Sánchez de Aguilar, Dr. don Pedro, 54, 76–77
Sandoval: Alonso de, 80; Capt. don Ramón, 176–77
Sansores, Marcos Tiburcio, 172–73
Santa Lucía (Merida), 211, 215–19, 258–61
Santesteban, don Diego de, 97–98, 129
Santiago (Merida-Tiho), 88, 140, 202, 217–19, 237, 241–42, 259, 262
Santo Domingo, 142, 148, 163, 222, 224
Schools in Yucatan, 55, 195–97, 219

Schwaller, Robert, 376n63
Segovia, Melchor de, 129, 251
Seville, 7, 9, 10, 19, 40, 53, 75–77, 106, 109–10, 194, 232
Sexual relationships, 88, 145, 201, 251–71 passim, 284; forced, 65–66, 246, 250–56, 399n18, 400n26; homosexual, 246, 257; master-slave, 65–67, 86. *See also* Love-magic
Seyba Playa, 246
Shark, 272, 399n10
Ships, 37, 41, 72, 157, 206, 212–14, 243, 314; British or English, 13, 20–24, 367n33, 386n50; Dutch, 20; Portuguese, 20, 32; Spanish, 18, 20, 121, 140–41. *See also* Boats; Spain
Shoemakers, 120–135 passim, 166–67, 374n20
Sisal, 11, 18, 72, 141, 150, 157, 160, 170–92 passim, 206, 224–26
Slave owners, Spanish, 11–25 passim, 34–86 passim, 97, 100, 114, 181–86, 242–45, 279–82; main treatment, 49–67
Slave society vs. society with slaves, 3, 13, 32–33, 80, 280–83
Slave traders, European, 19–20. *See also* English; Portugal and Portuguese
Slave peso values, 34–43, 62–64, 70, 125, 312–20
Smallpox, 84, 98
Smiths, 119–35 passim, 166–67, 221, 239
Socobio, Marcial, 119, 219, 254–55
Solís family, 60–61, 192, 391n128; Joseph, 171
Solórzano Pereira, Juan de, 78, 91
Sosa, Capt. don Juan de, 9, 15, 23, 36, 49
Sotuta, 54
Spain, transatlantic travel to, 7, 14, 54–55, 64, 96–97, 129, 193–94, 206
St. George's Cay. *See* Cayo Cocina
St. John (Caribbean), 243, 377n91
Sugar, 13, 39, 118, 276; in Yucatan, 15, 27, 39, 63, 84–85, 126–31, 150, 207, 214, 223, 295
Sweet, James, 78

Tabasco, 14, 29, 273, 313, 361n35
Tailors, 120–35 passim, 166–67, 239, 265, 380n24
Tannenbaum, Frank, 280, 359n14
Tekanto, 63–64, 103, 109, 299, 305
Tekax, 63, 103, 116–44 passim, 156; population, 265, 298, 305; revolt in, 158, 168

Temax, 109, 132, 137–38, 143, 299, 305, 382n58
Tenabo, 120, 144, 164, 247–48, 270, 276
Texas, 68–69, 101
Thompson, Robert, 21
Thornton, John, 279
Ticul, 101, 103, 298, 378n99
Tihosuco, 31, 128, 169, 200, 300, 306
Tizimin, 149, 202, 221–22, 243, 307
Toquero, Isabel, 99, 101, 107–8, 234, 246, 283; main treatment, 200–4, 238–43, 290–91
Toral, Sebastián, 33, 51, 110, 114, 156, 173, 256, 278, 283, 310; main treatment, 6–12, 15–16
Tortuga, 140
Torture, 85–86, 203, 276, 278, 282
Tribute paid by Afro-Yucatecans, 6–7, 173–75

United States, 180, 283. *See also* Carolina; Chesapeake; Louisiana; Mississippi
Ursúa y Arizmendi, don Martín de, 51, 117

Valladolid, 2, 75–77, 109–10, 128, 142, 174, 188, 220, 237–44 passim, 273; population, 25, 31, 113, 149, 301, 306–7, 372n8
Vargas, Juan de, 168
Vásquez de Espinosa, fray Antonio, 2, 213, 215
Vaughan, Megan, 65
Venezuela, 10, 34, 49, 68, 180, 191–92. *See also* Caracas
Veracruz, 18–20, 37, 39–40, 108, 127, 177, 202, 284

Vertiz y Ontañón, don Juan Joseph de, 51, 54, 97, 194
Victoria Ojeda, Jorge, 156
Villaelriego, Capt. don Lorenzo, 9, 14–15, 36–37, 178
Villa-Flores, Javier, 236
Villamil family, 66
Vinson, Ben, 4, 176
Vitoria, Francisco de, 80

Wade, Peter, 4
Wars between Britain and Spain, 22–24, 160–63, 169–70, 181, 232. *See also* Belize
Washington, George, 85
Wax and honey, 85, 129–39 passim, 208, 314, 398n3
Weaponry, 8–9, 24, 139, 155–62, 245, 250, 254, 264, 384n12
West Africa, 7, 18–19, 67, 179, 190, 208–10, 228–34, 284. *See also* Congo; Mina
Wills, 38, 43, 49, 63–64, 144
Wine. *See* Alcohol
Witchcraft. *See* Healers; Love-magic
Witch craze, 273
Wood, Gordon, 80, 85

Xequelchacan, 268
Xiu family, 197, 258

Yanguas, Geronimo de, 96, 310

Zavala: Joseph, 99, 144, 247–49, 268–77, 339; Lorenzo de, 70–71, 371n81
Zorita, Alonso de, 257